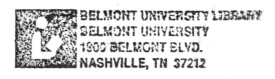

BRITISH WRITERS
Classics

VOLUME I

ISSN 1541-8995

BRITISH WRITERS
Classics

VOLUME I

EDITED BY JAY PARINI

CHARLES SCRIBNER'S SONS®

THOMSON

GALE

New York • Detroit • San Diego • San Francisco • Cleveland • New Haven, Conn. • Waterville, Maine • London • Munich

THOMSON

✳

GALE

™

British Writers Classics, Volume I

Jay Parini, Editor in Chief

© 2003 by Charles Scribner's Sons. Charles Scribner's Sons is an imprint of The Gale Group, Inc., a division of Thomson Learning, Inc.

Charles Scribner's Sons™ and Thomson Learning™ are trademarks used herein under license.

For more information, contact
Charles Scribner's Sons
An imprint of The Gale Group
300 Park Avenue South, 9th Floor
New York, NY 10010
Or you can visit our Internet site at
http://www.gale.com

For permission to use material from this product, submit your request via Web at http://www.gale-edit.com/permissions, or you may download our Permissions Request form and submit your request by fax or mail to:

Permissions Department
The Gale Group, Inc.
27500 Drake Rd.
Farmington Hills, MI 48331-3535
Permissions Hotline:
248 699-8006 or 800 877-4253, ext. 8006
Fax: 248 699-8074 or 800 762-4058

ISBN 0-684-31253-0 (volume 1)
ISSN 1541-8995

Printed in the United States of America
10 9 8 7 6 5 4 3 2 1

Editorial and Production Staff

Project Editor
PAMELA PARKINSON

Assisting Editors
MARK DROUILLARD
NICOLE WATKINS

Copyeditors
SHANE DAVIS
LINDA SANDERS
ELIZABETH WILSON

Proofreaders
SHANE DAVIS
ANNA NESBITT
KATHLEEN ROMIG

Indexer
CYNTHIA CRIPPEN

Production Manager
EVI SEOUD

Composition Specialist
GARY LEACH

Buyer
STACY MELSON

Publisher
FRANK MENCHACA

List of Subjects

Introduction

Ralph Waldo Emerson once remarked in an essay called "Thoughts on Modern Literature" that "all great men have written proudly, nor cared to explain. They knew that the intelligent reader would come at last, and would thank them." This new volume, which we call *British Writers Classics*, is the first in a continuing series of volumes devoted to individual works of British and Commonwealth literature. We describe these works as "classics" because they have been shown to possess enduring value. They are works—of fiction or poetry, drama or nonfiction—that readers want to return to again and again.

One of the justifications for the kind of close reading that readers will find in this volume is this: in the past thirty years, attention in literary studies has increasingly tended toward the theoretical. This has meant that close reading of actual texts has waned, and students and general readers will have difficulty in finding up-to-date readings of important works that are written in simple but intelligent language, meant for a wide audience and not a small circle of scholars trained in a particular theoretical branch of criticism. It is hoped that these essays do, in fact, provide such readings, but that the readings are sophisticated as well, taking into account the latest thinking while not occluding the work.

Classics may be regarded as a further strand of the ongoing series called *British Writers*, where the full careers of authors are discussed at length by critics, putting their work in its appropriate historical and biographical context. Readers of this series noticed, however, that the most important works by authors often received short attention. In surveying, for example, the career of Charles Dickens, it was necessary to dispense with *Great Expectations*, perhaps his most widely read novel, in a few paragraphs. The essay by Peter Scupham in this volume remedies that by offering a full-blown critical treatment, in sophisticated critical terms, looking at the novel from many different angles. Most crucially, it looks at the language of Dickens in considerable detail.

The subjects discussed in this volume are all major works of British literature, from *The Alchemist*, a classic play by Ben Jonson, to *Wuthering Heights*, one of the most broadly known works of British nineteenth century fiction. Along the way readers will encounter lengthy and intelligent critical readings of Tom Stoppard's *Arcadia*, Chaucer's *The Canterbury Tales*, Jane Austen's *Emma*, Swift's *Gulliver's Travels*, Conrad's *The Heart of Darkness*, the "Holy Sonnets" of John Donne, Wilde's *The Importance of Being Earnest*, Kipling's *Kim*, *Man and Superman* by George Bernard Shaw, Eliot's *Middlemarch*, *A Portrait of the Artist as a Young Man* by Joyce, Wordsworth's *The Prelude*, Pope's

"The Rape of the Lock," *The Return of the Native* by Hardy, Sterne's *Tristram Shandy*, and Thomas More's *Utopia*. One can hardly imagine a more diverse or significant range of texts.

The writers of these articles are each, in their own way, writers themselves. In fact some of them, such as Peter Scupham, N. S. Thompson, Claire Harman, and Caitriona O'Reilly, are themselves well known as writers in the British Isles. The other writers are well-published and highly respected scholars and critics; most of them are professors of English at some institution of higher learning in the United States, Britain, or elsewhere (Patrick Vincent teaches at the University of Fribourg in Switzerland). These writers were in each case held to a high standard, as readers of these essays will soon appreciate. Clarity and concision, concreteness and fidelity to the text were always stressed by this editor. The results have been, I think, especially pleasing.

One hopes that these astute critical readings of major texts will enhance the availability of these works to general readers, and that these readers will come to appreciate the huge efforts of imagination and intelligence that went into their creation in the first place.

—JAY PARINI

Contributors

Cates Baldridge. Professor of English at Middlebury College, Middlebury, Vermont. He has published two books, *The Dialogics of Dissent in the English Novel* (1994) and *Graham Greene's Fictions: The Virtues of Extremity* (2000) as well as articles on the Bröntes, Dickens, and other Victorian figures. He is currently at work on a study of the assimilation of romance plots within the realistic novel. HEART OF DARKNESS

James Berg. Assistant professor of English at Iowa State University. Berg specializes in sixteenth- and seventeenth-century English literature and has published articles on Shakespeare and Tudor-Stuart drama. He is currently at work on a book, *Pre-possession: Hospitality, Gift-Giving, and the Literary Experience in Early Modern England.* HOLY SONNETS

John A. Bertolini. Ellis Professor of the Liberal Arts at Middlebury College, Vermont where he teaches film and literature. He has written *The Playwrighting Self of Bernard Shaw,* edited *Shaw and Other Playwrights,* and published articles on Renaissance drama, modern British drama, and Alfred Hitchcock. He is currently working on a study of Terence Rattigan's plays, and a two-volume edition of selected plays by Shaw. MAN AND SUPERMAN

Fred Bilson. Lecturer in English, linguistics, and computer studies. Currently works supporting dyslexic students at the University of Glamorgan, Trefforest, South Wales. Bilson is completing a doctorate on the sound structure of natural languages. ARCADIA

Dan Brayton. Teaches literature at Middlebury College in Vermont. Brayton received his doctorate in English from Cornell in 2001, having specialized in Renaissance drama, utopian literature, and literary and cultural theory. His article, "Angling in the Lake of Darkness: Possession and the Politics of Discovery in King Lear," is forthcoming in English Literary History (ELH). He has published articles on Christopher Marlowe, Robert Greene, and Anne Bradstreet. Brayton is currently working on a book about Shakespeare and early modern geographical discourse. UTOPIA

Sandie Byrne. Fellow in English at Balliol College, Oxford. Her publications include works on eighteenth and nineteenth-century fiction and twentieth-century poetry. EMMA, THE IMPORTANCE OF BEING EARNEST, and WUTHERING HEIGHTS

Alexandra Gillespie. Bradley-Maxwell Junior Research Fellow at Balliol College, Oxford and Lecturer in English at Magdalen College, Oxford. Gillespie works on early Tudor court and city poetry; late sixteenth-century historiography and antiquarianism; and the history of the book in the late medieval period, focusing on the impact of the transition from manuscript to print and the dissolution of the monastic libraries. She has published articles in numerous journals and has a monograph entitled *The Medieval Author in Manuscript and Print: Chaucer, Lydgate, and the History of the Book, 1476–1561* forthcoming from Oxford University Press. She is currently co-editing of a collection of essays, *John Stow (1525–1602) and the Making of the English Past,* for the British Library. THE ALCHEMIST

Claire Harman. Biographer, formerly coordinating editor of the literary periodical, *PN*

Review. Her life of the poet and novelist Sylvia Townsend Warner won the John Llewellyn Rhys Prize in 1990 and she has also edited Warner's *Diaries* (1994) and *Collected Poems* (1982). Her biography of the eighteenth century novelist Fanny Burney appeared in 2000 and she is currently writing a life of Robert Louis Stevenson. THE STRANGE CASE OF DR. JEKYLL AND MR. HYDE

Tom Jones. Lecturer in English at the University of St Andrews. Jones has written on Pope's reading in and relation to Greek philosophers and is currently writing a book on philosophies of language and Pope's poetry. THE RAPE OF THE LOCK

Deanna Kreisel. Assistant professor of English at Mississippi State University. She is the author of an article on George Eliot in "Novel: A Forum on Fiction," and has another forthcoming in "ELH (English Literary History)." She is currently at work on a book entitled "Economic Woman: Political Economy, Medical Discourse, and Problems of Closure in Victorian Prose," which explores the relationship between metaphors of nineteenth-century political economy and medicine and narrative modes of the Victorian novel. MIDDLEMARCH

Scott MacKenzie. Assistant Professor of English at Davidson College. His most recent published article is "Confessions of a Gentrified Sinner: Secrets in Scott and Hogg" in *Studies in Romanticism*. He has also published articles and reviews in several other scholarly journals and is working on a study of prose fiction and its influence on British concepts of nationality, which is entitled "Home Economics: The Configuration of Britain, 1742–1830." TRISTRAM SHANDY

Christopher MacLachlan. Senior Lecturer in the School of English, University of St Andrews, Scotland. Research interests include Scottish and eighteenth-century literature. MacLachlan has published essays on Burns, Hume,

Fielding, John Buchan, and Muriel Spark, and edited Matthew Lewis's Gothic novel *The Monk* for Penguin Classics. *Before Burns*, his anthology of eighteenth-century Scottish verse, was published in April 2002 and he is preparing a new edition of travel writings by Robert Louis Stevenson for Penguin Classics. GULLIVER'S TRAVELS

Philip Mallett. Senior Lecturer in English at the University of St. Andrews, Scotland. He has written widely on English literature, especially on the period 1830–1930, and is the editor of, among other collections of essays, *Kipling Considered*, *The Achievement of Thomas Hardy*, and *Thomas Hardy: Texts and Contexts*. His most recent book is *Rudyard Kiping: A Literary Life*. He is currently writing a study of Hardy and sexuality, and completing an edition of Hardy's *The Return of the Native*. THE RETURN OF THE NATIVE

Caitríona O'Reilly. Catríona O'Reilly was educated in Trinity College, Dublin, where she wrote a doctoral thesis on Emily Dickinson, H. D. and Sylvia Plath. Her collection of poetry *The Nowhere Birds* was published by Bloodaxe Books in 2001 and awarded the Rooney Prize for Irish Literature. A PORTRAIT OF THE ARTIST AS A YOUNG MAN

Peter Scupham. Poet. Has published ten collections, mostly with Oxford University Press. *Night Watch*, his most recent collection, was published by Anvil Press in 1999. His *Collected Poems* is due from Oxford/Carcanet in October 2003. He is a Fellow of the Royal Society of Literature and has received a Cholmondeley award for poetry. GREAT EXPECTATIONS and KIM

N. S. Thompson. Lecturer in English at Christ Church, Oxford. He is the author of *Chaucer, Boccaccio and the Debate of Love* (Oxford, 1996), a comparative study of the *Decameron* and the *Canterbury Tales*, as well as many articles, reviews, and translations of modern Italian poetry and prose. His work was included in *Oxford Poets 2001: An Anthology* (2001). THE CANTERBURY TALES

CONTRIBUTORS

Patrick Vincent. Lecturer in English at the University of Fribourg, Switzerland. Vincent received his Ph.D. from the University of California at Davis. Author of several articles on women's sentimental poetics as well as on Mary Shelley and on William Wordsworth, he is presently completing a monograph entitled *Elegiac Muses: Europe's Romantic Poetess, 1820–1840*, editing a travel account by Helen Maria Williams, and researching a book on British Romantics and Switzerland. THE PRELUDE

Ben Jonson's
The Alchemist

ALEXANDRA GILLESPIE

LONDON AT THE turn of the sixteenth century was a city of incongruities. The population had more than trebled during the Elizabethan period. By 1603, perhaps as many as 180,000 people dwelled in its environs, several times the number in any other English city. It was in London that the nation's rich and powerful assembled their households and courted the monarch; that ambitious gentry sent their sons for education at the Inns of Courts; and that 90% of trade was handled by merchants who were still organized into medieval guilds from which the London Mayor and Aldermen were elected. While old systems of government remained intact, the city itself had changed, long since spilling out of the confines of its medieval walls. The old precincts of Westminster and London had merged into a single, uneven sprawl, and much of the populace lived outside of the jurisdiction of the civic authorities. Many were to be found in London liberties, for instance—former monastic sites that retained the right of sanctuary, such as Blackfriars, where pimps, prostitutes, debtors, and heretics taking advantage of the distance from the law lived cheek-by-jowl with gentry, puritan shopkeepers, artisans, and artists. In greater London, amid

the nation's richest, its poorest and most desperate lived. The immigrants who flooded to the city from smaller towns and the countryside to fill the city's streets and shops or the taverns over the bridge at Southwark only rarely found a better life. Dwellings were overcrowded, and untreated sewage ran in open drains to the Thames. Children had little chance of surviving infancy, and the plague struck with frightening regularity. London was home to thousands whose voice did not accord with that of the authorities who claimed to represent them; to the dispossessed as well as the powerful; to the ailing and the leprous; to the gamblers, pickpockets, and conmen of the city's extensive criminal underworld. Ben Jonson was born into this world in 1572. It was there, in the liberty of Blackfriars where he lived, that he set his comic masterpiece of 1610, *The Alchemist*. The play's prologue marks out the territory for satire:

> Our scene is London, 'cause we would make known
> No country's mirth is better than our own.
> No clime breeds better matter for your whore,
> Bawd, squire, imposter, many persons more,
>   Whose manners, now call'd humours feed the stage,

And which have still been subject for the rage
Or spleen of comic writers.

(Prologue, 5–11)

The growing population and wealth of London had bred theatres as well as subjects for the stage. Prohibitions against public performance, seen as a threat to order, were issued by London's Common Council in the 1550s and 1570s, but there was still money to be made. From the late sixteenth century on, dozens of theatres were built outside the civic authoritiesrsquo; reach. Huge, open arenas such as the Globe were built just south of the Thames at Bankside, and accommodated up to 3,000 men and women from every walk of life. There were also smaller, "private" theatres, such as the establishment built by Richard Burbage at Blackfriars in 1596. It was covered and candlelit, seated five hundred, and charged higher admission to a socially restricted audience. The players who used these performance spaces were organised into separate private companies such as Shakespeare's, Lord Chamberlain's Men. Members were actors (and sometimes writers) and "sharers." Each held a part of the company's property, costumes, and the capital needed to hire performers and playwrights. When he wrote *The Alchemist* in 1610, Jonson was at the height of his most productive period as a part of England's first professional theatrical community. In the first years of the seventeenth century he penned his great comedies: *Volpone* in 1606, *Epicoene* in 1609, and *Bartholomew Fair* in 1614.

In this same period, Jonson's personal life was anything but settled. As a youth he was educated at Westminster School at the expense of an unknown benefactor. Tutored by the famous antiquary William Camden, he read the histories of Sallust, orations of Cicero, and poems of Horace, Virgil, and Ovid. He compiled Latin commonplace-books, was schooled in rhetoric, and even acquired a little Greek. In 1589, however, he was removed from the school and

CHRONOLOGY

1572	Jonson is born in Westminster; clergyman father dies before his birth.
1580s	Studies at Westminster School under William Camden.
1589	Leaves school to take up a bricklaying apprenticeship with stepfather.
1592	Joins English army stationed in the Netherlands.
1594	Marries Anne Lewis in London. Terminates his apprenticeship.
1595/6	Birth of first son, Ben. Begins touring as an actor with Pembroke's Men.
1597	Writes *The Case is Altered*; co-writes *The Isle of Dogs* (now lost). *The Isle* is found to be seditious; Jonson is imprisoned along with players from Pembroke's Men.
1599	Writes *Everyman Out of His Humour*. Imprisoned for killing member of Pembroke's Men in a duel. Death sentence commuted. Converts to Catholicism while in prison.
1603	Queen Elizabeth dies. Accession of James I. Eldest son, Benjamin dies. Writes *Sejanus* and entertainments for the king and queen.
1605	Gunpowder Plot. Collaborates on *Eastward Ho!* for which he is imprisoned for fourth time. Collaborates with Inigo Jones on *Masque of Blackness*.
1608	Writes *The Masque of Beauty*. Another son, Benjamin, is born.
1610	Writes *The Alchemist*, having returned to the Church of England.
1616	Awarded annual royal pension; arranges publication of *Works*; writes *The Golden Age Restored* and *The Devil is an Ass*.
1618	Writes *Pleasure Reconciled to Virtue* while in Scotland.
1621	Writes *The Gypsies Metamorphosed*; performs regularly before James I.
1624	Composes *Neptune's Triumph for the Return of Albion* to celebrate the return

	of Prince Charles from Spain.
1625	James I dies; Charles I accedes to throne.
1628	Questioned by authorities over seditious verses; suffers a stroke; becomes London's City Chronologer.
1634	Writes *A Tale of a Tub*. Last of his masques, *Love's Welcome to Bolsover* is performed.
1637	Dies at Westminster.

apprenticed to his stepfather's trade, bricklaying. The transition from the gentle world of humanist education to that of the city guilds was not successful. Jonson failed to complete his eight-year term and left London for soldiering in the Netherlands. He returned and married in 1594 but separated from his wife after fathering several children. In the late 1590s he sought another outlet for his restless energies, joining the players of Pembroke's Men first as an actor and then as a playwright. It was for Pembroke's Men that he and Thomas Nashe wrote a play called *The Isle of Dogs* in 1597. The play was deemed seditious by the authorities; Nashe escaped to the country but Jonson was imprisoned along with two of the company's players. A year after his release, Jonson was again in jail, judged guilty of the murder of one of Pembroke's players with whom he had been imprisoned a year earlier. He was sentenced to death and saved from the gallows at Tyburn only by his humanist education. His knowledge of Latin enabled him to claim an ancient "benefit of clergy," and his sentence was commuted. Thereafter he bore a "T" for Tyburn branded on his thumb to remind him and those who met him of his crime and narrow escape. If this mark set Jonson permanently apart—neither ordinary criminal nor honest citizen—his conversion to Catholicism prior to his release from jail distanced him from his society further still. Even before the Gunpowder Plot to kill James I, the Protestant state suspected Catholics of divided loyalties and treason on top of their theological heresies. Perhaps shocked by the level of

violence planned by those involved in the 1605 plot, Jonson began to doubt his new faith, and had returned to the Church of England by the time he wrote *The Alchemist*.

From his youth, then, Jonson was a kind of exile, voluntary and involuntary—from his artisan background, his education, his early career, his marriage, the sanctioned religion of his country, and even his chosen faith. In the early seventeenth century, he set an unsteady foot in another social sphere: that of the royal and noble courts. Early modern actors' companies were nominally patronized by a member of the aristocracy. The growth period before 1610 saw them brought into a formal system of licensing operated by the Master of the Revels and under direct royal patronage. Playwrights were well placed to catch the eye of a wealthy aristocrat seeking a new way to seem important. Jonson wrote the first of his famous masques with the court architect Inigo Jones in 1610 and dedicated poems and printed editions of his plays to real and prospective benefactors. In 1616 he received a royal pension, effectively becoming a national laureate. However, the place of the former murderer and bricklayer among the high born was uneasy, as Jonson's enemies were fond of reminding him. The London playwright and court poet was never fully of one realm or the other. But he was also ideally placed to explore the tensions and gaps between the world he knew and the world he saw others invent around him. Jonson's *The Alchemist* is played out in this creative space. It is at once a vivid celebration of the fecund imagination of the Renaissance and a vigorous attack upon the hypocrisy of his age.

THE ALCHEMIST: PATRONAGE AND PRINT, AUTHORITY AND AUDIENCE

Created by a rancorous professional playwright who was also a court poet of growing reputation, recreated in the collaborative space of London's professional theatre for diverse audiences, and preserved in various printed forms, *The Alchemist* is hard to interpret. The play was printed soon after its first performance in a quarto of 1612 and in the folio edition of his *Works* that Jonson edited himself in 1616. The front matter of these editions reveals various efforts by Jonson and others to exert control over the play.

The 1616 title page to *The Alchemist* informs us of its history as a performance: "A Comedy. Acted in the year 1610. By the King's Majesty's Servants." Since 1609, the King's Men had been performing at Richard Burbage's private theatre in Blackfriars, for which Jonson wrote his play. It may have first been performed elsewhere; the Blackfriars theatre was closed by plague from July until October or November of 1610, and there is evidence of a touring performance in Oxford in September. The content of the play mirrors this record of its enactment. The domicile in Blackfriars inhabited by Jonson's characters has also been closed by plague. Its characters are at liberty to "play" in the absence of the master of the house as His King's Majesty's Servants were in the Blackfriars liberty. The play is set in the near future, on 1 November 1610 according to the calculations of Jonson's Anabaptist character Ananias in act 3 (1.129). At the end of the folio edition, there also appears a statement of the "principal comedians" who appeared in the first performance and a statement of the "allowance" of the Master of the Revels. The text is thus bracketed, as it is on stage, as unfinished, available for collaborative appropriation by actors, its liberties curbed by the politics of the Renaissance theatre.

But the preliminaries to these early versions of the play gesture to other stages upon which the meaning of *The Alchemist* is to be played out. Unlike most of his predecessors and contemporaries, including Shakespeare, Jonson insisted on seeing his texts through the press. His name, not the names of the players, appears on the title page to the 1612 edition. The play may elide evidence of its origins in performance, but it announces Jonson's authorship in the perennial and enduring form of print. The production of the 1616 folio edition magnifies

this concern with Jonson's authority. *The Alchemist* is fronted by a quote from Lucretius about the garland worn by a laureate poet. It is embedded among all of Jonson's major texts up to 1616 which are prefaced by an engraving of the writer and declared to be his "Works." Jonson was the first English writer to arrange to have his own texts printed in this format. It had previously been the preserve of great classical authors and posthumously laureated English writers such as Chaucer and Sidney. There is further evidence of Jonson's efforts to authorize his own text. Both the editions of *The Alchemist* are dedicated to Mary Wroth, cousin and mistress of one of Jonson's patrons, the Earl of Pembroke, and niece of Sir Phillip Sidney. The dedicatory epistle redirects the public, theatrical text to a private, courtly context, and translates its comedic meanings from the London stage to the classical school. Indeed, the epistle opens with a translation, a quote from Seneca which suggests that the "devotion" with which Jonson dedicates his text and its dedicatee are its only value. And yet at this moment textual worth resides as much in the rhetorical skill of the learned translator, Jonson, as in the noble lady to whom he makes his offering.

In the early editions of *The Alchemist*, then, Jonson is at work to prescribe a courtly, humanist value for his text, and to proscribe or distance himself from the multiple and unstable interpretations offered by diverse audiences to multiple performances. A second epistle, found only in the quarto edition, makes it clear that the "Reader" should be wary,

> at what hands thou receivest thy commodity; for thou wert never more fair in the way to be cozened (than in this age) in poetry, especially in plays, wherein now the concupiscence of jigs and dances so reigneth, as to run away from Nature and be afraid of her, is the only point of art that tickles the spectator.

This attack on the deceptive, theatrical "commodities" of his day, "jigs and antics" written for spectators and not readers, may be likened to

Jonson's more explicit assault on contemporary plays including Shakespeare's *Titus Andronicus* in the Introduction to *Bartholomew Fair.* Such plays, unlike Jonson's learned productions, did not take their proper place in an Aristotelian comedic tradition. They violated the dramatic decorum. "Decorum" refers to edicts derived from the poetics of Aristotle, Horace, Cicero, and Sidney that a play should exclude the incredible, maintain stable separation of genres and consistent characterization, and conform to the "unities,"—that is, consist in a single sequence of actions in a single place on a single day. According to Jonson, all plays which breach such theatrical decorum "run away from Nature." The humanist poet is determined to distance his text from that of the profit-seeking playwright, and a proper reading of Renaissance theatre from the judgement of spectators who have been "cozened" so that

> they commend writers as they do fencers and wrestlers, who, if they are come in robustiously and put for it with a great deal of violence, are received for the braver fellows, when many times their own rudeness is the cause of their disgrace.

ACT 1: THEATRICALITY AND ANTI-THEATRICALITY

It is with surprise then, that the reader (if not the spectator) encounters the first, robustious lines of *The Alchemist*:

[*Enter*] *Face* [*and*] *Subtle* [*quarrelling violently*] *followed by Dol Common* [*attempting to quiet them*].
FACE: [*Threatening with his sword*] Believe't, I will.
SUBTLE: Thy worst! I fart at thee!
DOL: Ha' you your wits? Why, gentlemen! For love—
FACE: Sirrah, I'll strip you—
SUBTLE: What to do? Lick figs Out at my—
FACE: Rogue, rogue, out of all your sleights!
                                              (1.1.1–4)

This is the most explosive opening of Renaissance theatre. The three central characters, Subtle, Face, and Dol, appear in the midst of a furious row—the play does not so much begin as erupt upon the stage. In one sense, Jonson meets his own demands: the informed comic writer knows that his play should commence in the middle of the action, which will be brilliantly worked out over the five acts of the play. On the other hand, the opening to *The Alchemist* reminds us that Jonson is a peddler of that which he professes to abhor—the schemes, spectacles, and myriad significations of the Renaissance stage. Face's bald and immoveable imperative, "believe it, I will," is violently disrupted by Subtle, who finishes Face's statement (proving it unfinished) and then transforms it into a "fart." Further scatological references follow. The "figs" Face should lick are feces or piles, but also a literary trope. They gesture away from the likely classical sources for Jonson's plot: Plautus's *Mostellaria*, where a servant like Face is left in charge of his empty house by his master; and Lucian's *Alexander*, in which gullible visitors flock to a fake oracle, just as Subtle, Face, and Dol's "gulls" flock to their fraudulent performances of alchemy and magic. The figs gesture toward base vernacular fictions: Rabelais's fabliau *Pantagruel*, in which a story about rebels forced to remove figs from the posterior of a mule is told. The author of *The Alchemist* turns out to be entirely complicit in the jigs and blurred genres of the Renaissance stage. His complicity is figured in the creative force of his bickering characters. Their insults accord with the principles of theatrical decorum. Traditionally, comic language, while it violates everyday good manners, is nevertheless in keeping with the station of the speaker and the genus of the subject enhanced or disparaged. The rogues' degenerate and degenerating utterances are appropriate to the seamy, criminal world they inhabit. When a fart is substituted for Face's words, *both* are shown to be noise and air, signifying nothing.

From the moment they appear on stage, then, Face, Subtle, and Dol are part of the reflexive, antitheatrical impulse that gives Jonson's comedies much of their taut energy. They signify, respectively, a pimp, a conman, and a prostitute—inhabitants of the squalid London described in the Prologue. But they are textual as well as mimetic inventions. Jonson assembles characters from types found in "coney-catcher" pamphlets of the period. These printed news stories about criminals were sold in the thousands to Londoners in the early seventeenth century. And Face, Subtle, and Dol are satirists themselves, as well as inventions of Jonson's satiric wit. In act I, they too generate a script from learned and lewd sources. Dol succeeds in quelling her co-conspirators' row just in time for the arrival of the first of their victims, Dapper, a lawyer's clerk. Like all the dupes of *The Alchemist*, Dapper is willing to hand over his money and his dignity if the tricksters will promise him fulfillment of his most melodramatic desires. He comes wanting a "fly," a familiar spirit, to help him win at gambling. He is announced to Subtle by Face as no "Climo'the-Cloughs or Claribels," but a gentleman who courts his beloved with Ovid in hand (1.2.46). Face's literary references promote Dapper's romantic sense of self. They also prompt Subtle to write a new script drawn from precisely the kind of texts to which Face alludes: "The Ballad of Adam Bell" and Spenser's *Faerie Queene*. The tricksters persuade the clerk that he is "o'the only best complexion / The Queen of Fairy loves." The queen, they say, is his aunt,

> a lone woman
> And very rich, and if she take a fancy,
> She will do strange things. See her, at any hand.
> 'Slid, she may hap to leave you all she has!
>
> (1.2.105–106, 155–158)

Subtle and Face draw on multiple sources simultaneously: popular ballads and romances; reports of Jacobeans duped by con-artists posing as kings and queens of fairy; and the plays of Jonson's rivals, such as Fletcher's *The Scornful Lady* or Shakespeare's *Midsummer Night's Dream*, in which young wastrels redeemed by wealthy widows and tradesmen wooed by fairy queens were favored devices.

Abel Drugger, a tobacconist and the second dupe of act 1, likewise writes himself into the conspirators' literary game:

SUBTLE: Your business Abel?
DRUGGER: This, an't please your worship,
    I am a young beginner, and am building
    Of a new shop, and't like your worship, just
    At corner of a street. [*Shows a ground plan*] Here's the plot on't.
    And I would know by art, sir, of your worship
    Which way I should make my door, by necromancy.

> (1.3.6–11)

The "plot" for Drugger's shop is also Jonson's figure for the tobacconist's "beginning" or aspirations. This resembles the plots of Thomas Deloney's *Gentle Craft* (1598) or Thomas Dekker's play, *The Shoemaker's Holiday* (1599), romanticized accounts of a historical figure who rose by mercantile enterprise to become a wealthy Lord Mayor. As Face and Subtle plot to outwit Drugger they borrow from these literary traditions, promising him his fortune; the rich widow, Dame Pliant, who lives next door; and that "this summer / He will be of the clothing of his company / And next spring called to the scarlet," the garb of London Mayors and Aldermen (1.3.35–37).

If Face, Subtle, and Dol are simultaneously satirized by and made to represent the work of the Renaissance writer, the elevated role assigned to Subtle by Drugger—the repeated "sir" and "your worship"—signals their further collusion in Jonson's self-reflexive theatrical spectacle. Face, Subtle, and Dol write the scripts for *The Alchemist*'s many fraudulent performances, but they are also characters—the consummate, shape-shifting performers of those scripts. They change guise only slightly less often than they change their names. In Renaissance theory, indebted to classical authorities such as Theophrastus, character was understood as a kind of writing, as the word itself implies. The word "character" was used to refer to a face or outward appearance rather than a personal interior. Face's name is suggestive of the Renaissance theory of characterization. He does indeed have many faces, each one proving impenetrable to those who encounter him on stage. He is Captain Face, a servant who has usurped the control of his master's house and whose real name, Jeremy, we learn only in act 5. He is a pimp for Dol and an assistant to the coney-catching Subtle. He will serve as a priest of fairy when Dapper's meets Dol dressed as a fairy queen. He will be a pander to Sir Epicure Mammon, who also desires Dol after she appears to him disguised a learned gentlewoman, "My Lord What's' Hum's sister" (2.4.6). And when Subtle, who, Dapper is assured, is a "doctor," assumes the mantle of the alchemist, Face will be "his fire-drake / His Zephyrus, he that puffs his coals"—his "Lungs," which is Mammon's name for him throughout (1.2.9; 2.2.97; 2.1.26–27). Dol is "Royal Dol" to Subtle and "Claridiana," heroine of the popular Spanish *Mirror of Knighthood* (1.1.174–175). These epithets herald the romantic guises she will assume—as Mammon's vision of "Bradamante," the woman knight from Ariosto's *Orlando Furioso,* as well as Dapper's fairy queen (2.3.225). Dol's names also suggest, however, that character itself is disguise, a trick, an allusion or illusion. Even her own name, Dol Common, fails to serve as a straightforward mark of identity. Like the names Face or Subtle, it simply initiates a series of readings. Dol Common is a grammatical type, a logically distributed subject, property held in common, a garden-variety whore. In the conspirators' quarters—"*novo orbe,*" "this dark labyrinth," a "citadel," a "mere chancel," "this cave of coz'nage," "this house ... run mad" (2.1.2; 2.3.308; 4.6.9; 5.3.2; 5.5.115; 4.1.13)—names cease to be a stable index to identity and become an index to the instability inherent in the very

idea of dramatic character. The characters cannot be all that they claim, or appear, to be. They are actors. They implicate the real author and actors of the play in their deceptions. Even Jeremy's baptismal name is intended for a performer in a theater at Blackfriars.

In this way, the intricate comic plots scripted and acted by the rogues of *The Alchemist* extend logically to encompass theater itself in Jonson's satire. For in the theater, the King's Men and the playwright conspire to "cozen" a willing audience into parting with its money by dramatic "sleights." The play's initial Argument has already announced this analogy. Like members of a Renaissance theater company, Subtle, Face and Dol "contract / Each for a share, and all begin to act" (7–8). Even before they are absorbed into the play's celebration of the dramatic arts, the static humanist values of the epistles are compromised by this Argument. *The Alchemist* embodies the instability it condemns—in contemporary literature and in the subterfuge of the immoral inhabitants of a house in Blackfriars. The trope of alchemy is witness to this distrust of theatricality. It is first applied by Subtle to his ungrateful partner Face:

> Thou vermin, have I not ta'en thee out of dung,
>
> ...
>
> Raised thee from brooms and dust and watering
>   pots?
> *Sublimed* thee and *exalted* thee and *fixed* thee
> I'the *third region,* called our *state of grace?*
> Wrought thee to *spirit,* to *quintessence,* with pains
> Would twice have won me the *philosopher's
>   work?*
>
> (1.1.64–71)

The italicized words are technical terms applied by the alchemist to the preparation of an elixir or philosopher's stone from crude materials. "Dung" and "dust" are the servant Face once was; the "*philosopher's work*" has been to elevate and fix him in his new role. Like the stone or elixir produced in this way, Face will enable Subtle to turn base matter—the gulls—into gold.

Moreover, if both playwright and player are represented in Subtle's counterfeit magus, then dramatists are also alchemists, making gold from the base metal of their audiences in their magic houses—Renaissance theaters.

ACT 2: ALCHEMY AND RENAISSANCE ECONOMIES OF DESIRE

The trope of alchemy is most memorably figured by the gull introduced in act 2: Sir Epicure Mammon. Jonson's epistle to the reader describes his disdain for art which "run[s] away from Nature"—which upsets the natural connection between appearances and reality. Mammon is therefore set up for contempt from the first. His name suggests he is a hedonist, sensualist, and materialist, and when Subtle announces him, his ambitions resemble those of the indecorous playwright. With the philosopher's stone Subtle has promised him,

> he will make
> Nature ashamed of her long sleep, when art
> Whose but a stepdame, shall do more than she,
> In her best love to mankind, ever could.
>
> (1.4.25–28)

In act 2, Jonson deploys his characters—Subtle and Face, Mammon, and Mammon's skeptical companion, Surly—to reveal something of the "nature" of alchemy. Over the course of the act, they describe the practices and meanings with which alchemy was associated in the Renaissance and make considerable use of the learned, textual tradition that preceded it. But in *The Alchemist*, alchemy's only natural basis is greed: it is not knowledge newly possessed by Renaissance man. It is the perfect figure for his impulse to penetrate the mysteries of the world and refashion it to conform to his "runaway" desire.

The possibility of transforming base metals into gold was taken entirely seriously by the authorities in the Renaissance, and famous alchemists such as John Dee, Della Porta, and Cornelius Agrippa were highly esteemed for their learning. In 1566–1567, Elizabeth I employed Cornelius Lannoy to perform alchemical transmutations and imprisoned him when he failed to produce results. But official interest had long been matched by official disapproval and widespread skepticism. Chaucer's late fourteenth-century *Canon Yeoman's Tale*, a source for Jonson's own play, is a bitter satire upon alchemy. A 1403 statute made multiplication of gold and silver a felony. In a 1584 pamphlet on witchcraft by Reginald Scot, flattery and extortion are described as the most important alchemical principles. According to more credulous alchemical tracts such as those printed in the mid-seventeenth century in Elias Ashmole's *Britain's Alchemical Theatre*, he who possessed the stone had to be "a pious, holy, and religious man / One free from mortal sin, a very virgin," as Surly argues in act 2 (2.98–99). Once he had it, such a man would be God-like: able to release the spirit naturally occurring in matter; to intensify its power through distillation; to make a stone or elixir impervious to the depredations of time or decay; and thus to remake the universe in its own, prelapsarian image—transmuting base metals into gold, curing illness, reversing the aging process, turning all to good. But to Chaucer, Scot, and Jonson, the alchemist was simply a charlatan and profiteer, turning all to greed.

In *The Alchemist* the best explanations of the Renaissance science of alchemy come in response to this sort of skepticism, usually from Surly. Surly states firmly that he "would not willingly be gulled. Your stone / Cannot transmute me" (2.1.78–79). Mammon tells Subtle to "pound him to dust," and Subtle responds by defining dust, and all the world, as gold *in potentia*:

> A humid exhalation which we call
> *Materia liquida*, or the unctuous water,
> [And] a certain crass and viscous
> Portion of earth . . . concorporate,
> Do make the elementary matter of gold—

Which is not yet *propria materia*,
But common to all metals and all stones.

(2.3.142–149)

The sources for this and similar speeches by Subtle and Mammon are learned: Aristotle's *Meteorology*, Paracelcus' *Concerning the Generation of Things*, and the *Speculum Alchemiae*. As in act 1, however, specialized texts and languages prove untrustworthy. Surly responds to Mammon and Subtle's catalogues of learned terms with a list of his own. He does not seek to explain or even to enumerate but merely to heap up words. His piles resemble the conspirators' loot; they ultimately reveal the real stuff of alchemy to be the waste and excrement of excess consumption:

Your *sun*, your *moon*, your *firmament*,
your *adrop*,
Your *lato, azoch, zernich, chibrit, heautarit*,
And then your *red man*, and your *white woman*,
With all your broths, your *menstrues*, and *materials*,
Of piss and egg-shells, women's terms, man's
blood,
Hair o' the head, burnt clouts, chalk, merds, and
clay.

(2.3.190–195)

Mammon, who believes Subtle's flummery, is exposed to ridicule along with any reader who attempts to decode the alchemical terminology of the play. Subtle's dense language is no more meaningful than Surly's. It is designed to mystify, not to inform. But Surly exposes another, equally important aspect of Jonson's satire in *The Alchemist*. Alchemy is a metaphor for an illusion of self-fulfillment. It describes the human desire to make meaning out of words and things and to impose that meaning upon an inchoate universe.

Mammon is the main device by which Jonson demonstrates this particular human folly. Just before his arrival, Subtle says

Methinks I see him ent'ring ordinaries,
Dispensing for the pox, and plaguy-houses,

Reaching his dose; walking Moorfields for lepers;
And offering citizens' wives pomander-bracelets
As his preservative, made of the elixir;
Searching the spital to make old bawds young;
And the highways for beggars to make rich
I see no end of his labours.

(1.4.18–25)

Mammon himself sees "no end" of anything. His ambition extends beyond the limits of the known world. He transforms the cozeners' house into a *"novo orbe* [new world]" as he approaches it:

Here's the rich Peru,
And there within, sir, are the golden mines,
Great Solomon's Ophir! He was sailing to't
Three years. But we have reached it in ten
months.

(2.1.2–5)

His desire is timeless as well as boundless. It reaches backwards to the biblical age described in 1 Kings 10.22, when Solomon was able to make gold and deliver it to Jerusalem every "three years." It reaches inexorably forward. Mammon will extend the life of "an old man of fourscore," restoring him to "the fifth age" (2.1.53, 56). He will "fright the plague / Out o'the kingdom in three months" and "serve th'whole city with preservative, / Weekly" (2.1.69–70, 74–75). As Subtle puts it "he'll turn the age to gold" (1.4.29). The "Golden Age Restored" is a familiar trope of the Renaissance, and the title of one of Jonson's own masques. It is the optimism of an age which believed in the possibility of a fully realized, ennobled humanity: in the recovery and perfection of the great period of classical learning; in the new science of Copernicus, Galileo, and Bacon; in the imperialism of Ralegh and Columbus; in the burgeoning wealth of capitalist economies.

Renaissance thinkers sought universal explanations for things. When Surly refuses to let Mammon "transmute" him, Mammon replies,

MAMMON: Will you believe antiquity? Records?
     I'll show you a book where Moses
       and his sister
     And Solomon have written of the art,
     Ay, and a treatise penned by Adam
SURLY: How!
MAMMON: O'the philosopher's stone, and in
     High Dutch.

            (2.2.80–84)

High Dutch or German was the dialect that Renaissance thinkers believed was the world's originary language. It was therefore the language in which Adam must have written. According to Mammon, the existence of a tract on alchemy in High Dutch proves the antiquity of the tract, of alchemy, and the language, and thus the authorship, of Adam. The hermetically sealed argument makes alchemy a key to decoding human language; it is, similarly, a key to all mythology. Mammon regards the Bible as an alchemical sourcebook; Jason's fleece is none other than "a book of alchemy," and Pythagoras's thigh, Pandora's box, Medea's charms, Cadmus's dragon's teeth, and Jove's shower are also "abstract riddles of our stone" (2.1.90, 104).

Jonson's *Alchemist* matches Renaissance man's desire to invent unifying theses about the world with his impulse to possess it. Mammon intends to recreate the universe to accord with his immeasurable appetites. The *fiat lux* of his genesis is not "be" but "the happy word 'be rich'" (2.1.7). He is so pleased with this biblical allusion that he repeats it a second time, "I speak it first, 'be rich'" (2.1.24), and a third, "Again, I say to thee aloud, 'Be rich'" (2.2.6). His desire is pleonastic and pleonectic. He tells Surly he means to have "wives and concubines / Equal with Solomon" and that he will "encounter fifty a night" (1.2.35–36, 39). He will have airbeds and cut glass mirrors in which he can watch himself walk naked between his *succubae*. He will have perfume, gossamer, roses, and ostrich tail fans waved by "court and town stallions" turned eunuchs (1.2.66). In Indian shells and dishes of gold and agate, he will have

The tongues of carps, dormice, and camels' heels
Boiled i'the spirit of sol and dissolved pearl
     …
The beards of barbels served instead of salads
Oiled mushrooms, and the swelling unctuous
  paps
Of a fat pregnant sow, newly cut off.

         (2.2.75–76, 82–84)

The flesh of the fat pregnant sow literalizes the insistent orientation of Mammon's desire towards consumption and sex. Mammon's aspirations are self-fulfilling, expressed and realized within his own language of excess. The "glasses / Cut in more subtle angles to disperse / and multiply the figures as I walk" become a metaphor for this process: Mammon sees himself naked in the mirrors and proliferating fantasies with which he surrounds himself (2.2.45–47). Sexual imagery is a persistent reminder that Mammon's extravagant claims to all-pervasive knowledge and power will end in naught, or at best in the stripping back of his language to reveal the base human impulses beneath. Even the London landscape marked out for Mammon and his healing elixir by Subtle can be read as a territory of explicitly sexualized desire. Mammon will cure the "pox," make "old bawds young," give plague-resisting bracelets to "citizens' widows," who might favor him with their attention.

The sensual tendencies of Mammon's discourse therefore alert us to its emptiness and his gullibility. It indicates that desire is precisely what makes Mammon susceptible to his humiliation. In scene 3, Dol appears and Mammon immediately desires knowledge of her and of how one might "do t'have conference with her" (2.3.243). "Conference" means both verbal and sexual intercourse here. For the reminder of the play Mammon will attempt to use his verbosity to realise his sexual fantasies directly. Dol is dressed up as a "lord's sister" and a "most rare scholar / . . . mad from studying" (2.3.221, 237–238). Face tells Mammon she is under the protection of Subtle, who would forbid any liaison.

Secrecy adds excitement to Mammon's prospective conquest and enhances his sense of his value. The notional worth of the lady and the play's controlling trope of alchemy converge. In act 4, Mammon prepares himself to address her,

> Now Epicure,
> Heighten thyself. Talk to her all in gold.
> Rain her as many showers as Jove did drops
> Unto his Danae.
>
> (4.1.24–27)

The image of Jove appearing as a flood of gold in Danae's lap has already featured in the play. It is one of the stories encompassed by Mammon's interpretation of all myth as alchemy, a symbol for Renaissance man's longing for universal knowledge. But the gold that simultaneously figures Mammon's sexual, pecuniary, linguistic, and intellectual desire is a debased currency. Subtle tells Mammon that the consummation of his relationship with Dol will "retard / The work a month at least." Face orchestrates an explosion off-stage and Mammon is made to believe that he is

> MAMMON: Cast from all my hopes—
> FACE: Nay, certainties, sir.
> MAMMON: By my own base affections.
>
> (4.5.50–51, 75–76)

On one hand this explosion is a ruse, prolonging the rogues' elaborate deceit. On the other hand, Subtle and Face are right. Mammon's encounter with Dol ironically manifests the impotence of Renaissance man. She is far from a "rare scholar"; she is "Common" property, a prostitute. Mammon has been fooled into revealing that his never-ending aspirations are nothing more than "base affection." Opulent promise becomes sordid reality as Surly predicted it would in act 2:

> Heart, this is a bawdy-house! I'll be burnt else.
> ...
> Give me your honest trick yet at primero
> Or gleek, and take your *lutum sapientis*,

Your *menstruum simplex*. I'll have gold before you
And with less danger of the quicksilver
Or the hot sulphur.

> (2.3.226, 284–288)

The gambler Surley, offering his skills at the card games "gleek" and "primero," reduces alchemical terms to sexual ones. Latin words for paste and solvent are transformed into vulgar quicksilver and sulphur, substances commonly used to treat venereal disease. Mammon's final humiliation in act 5 involves a similar appropriation of language. Already stripped of his dignity, Mammon is stripped of his rich vocabulary and syntax as well, at the same moment that he is divested of his lost goods by Face's master, Lovewit:

> LOVEWIT: What should they ha'been sir? Turned into gold all?
> MAMMON: No.
> I cannot tell. It may be they should.
> What then?
>
> (5.5.73–74)

The simple imperative of the start of act 2, "Be rich"—signifying the offer made by alchemy and the optimism of the Renaissance—becomes, equally simply, negation and uncertainty.

ACT 3: COMMERCE, POLITICS, AND PURITANISM

The intersection of sexual and pecuniary motives that underpins the *The Alchemist*'s satire upon Sir Epicure Mammon was a convention of Jonson's period. The women of *The Alchemist*, Dol and Dame Pliant, the widow promised to Drugger at the end of act 2, are sexually available. Dol is a whore and, as Subtle points out, Pliant is neither virgin nor married, but a widow, a transferable asset and "*bona roba*," a fashionable, easy woman (2.6.39). Such women are used by men, but their free exchange suggests they possess a certain chaotic power. They are uncontrollable within a social world governed by the laws of patrilineal inheritance and patriarchal authority. They bear a conventional, gender-specific relation to anxiety about commodification, market exchange, and power. From the first, Jonson's *Alchemist* exhibits this anxiety. It is set in a world where traditional social hierarchies and bonds of affection have been replaced by economies of purchase and exchange. The marketplace is no longer a bounded entity; it is everywhere and nowhere, without location or fixity. It accommodates all things and in the process, reduces those things to commodities. The three plotters speak the language of modern business. Face has drawn "customers" to Subtle's "trades," given him "credit" and a "house to practise in" (1.1.45, 40, 43, 47). Dol reminds the quarrelling partners of their business obligations, denouncing Subtle for claiming the largest part of the cash:

> You must be chief? As if you only had
> The powder to project with? And the work
> Were not begun out of equality?
> The venture tripartite? All things in common?
> Without priority?

> (1.1.132–136)

Dols' deployment of the terms—the powders and projections— of alchemy is a reminder that the image accommodates everyday commercialism. Modern capitalism is a kind of all-pervasive alchemy, by which things are converted into revenue. However, Dol's description of the fraudulent practices of the conspirators has further significance. She dignifies the quarrel by the language of radical political thought. The house is in the liberty of Blackfriars and liberated from its master's authority. It is free state, with "all things in common." Dol fears it will be rent by Subtle and Face's "civil war." She begs the men to "have yet some care of me, o'your republic" (1.1.82, 110). The connection between political liberty and corrupt female sexuality is explicit. Dol, for all her claim to equality, is common property, easily conflated, even in her own discourse, with a "republic," free from

authority and available for any transgression. Jonson's intention is to satirize the desire for freedom itself, which is corrupted by self-interest in a capitalist economy in which all desire is commodified and so debased. This aspect of the play's satire is a controlling force in the representation of the conspirators' remaining gulls: the boy Kastril, brother to Dame Pliant, and the Anabaptists Ananias and Tribulation. The characters are introduced or mentioned in scenes 5 and 6 of act 2. But it is in act 3 that their stories and the unstable political economies of Renaissance England hold sway.

The Anabaptists who arrive at the house in Blackfriars are members of an extremist puritan sect implicated the socio-political concerns of *The Alchemist*. In 1610, puritan tradesmen, many of whom dwelled in Blackfriars, formed a successful London community. Their rigorous work ethic helped them amass wealth and goods at a tremendous rate. Despite doctrines of asceticism, the Anabaptist faith accommodated this commercialism. Adherents believed in an elect, a group of men and women predestined for heaven. Their worldly success was believed to be God-given, and their financial rewards on earth thought to prophesy their spiritual reward in heaven. They considered themselves, in this sense, above the moral and legal codes of the rest of society. Tribulation describes them as "we of the separation" who "know no magistrate" (3.1.2, 3.2.150). Millenarianists, they also believed that the corruption and decay of contemporary society was a sign of the approaching apocalypse and preached that widespread social and political reform should be part of an effort to attain spiritual perfection. Unable to achieve their goals within society, the more radical sectarians, including "holy brethren / of Amsterdam, the exiled saints" to whom Ananias and Tribulation are linked, wanted a puritan republic (2.4.29–30). Such a free state was achieved by radical activists in sixteenth-century Münster and closely resembled the "republic" of Jonson's *Alchemist*. The sectarians held property in common and had equal rights.

Some radical puritans even espoused alchemy because such occultist theories of spiritual perfectibility matched their own beliefs. Alchemist and Anabaptist alike dreamed of a better life based on the miraculous transformation of corrupt matter. Gold was the stuff by which the these dreams were to be made real:

> When as the work is done, the stone is made,
> This heat of [Subtle's] may turn into a zeal
> And stand up for the beauteous discipline
> Against the menstrous cloth and rag of Rome.
>
> (3.2.30–33)

But in *The Alchemist*, alchemy is a sham, and gold a symbol for human cupidity. Between Ananias and Tribulation's Anabaptist fanaticism and the material nature of their aspirations, their desire for spiritual perfection, and their desire for gold, there is a plenty of room for Jonson's satire. The Anabaptists intend the stone for political bribery, not for social improvement as Tribulation intimates, "*aurum potabile* being / The only med'cine for the civil magistrate / T'incline him to a feeling of the cause" (3.2.41–43). Subtle makes a similar point when he mocks the brethren's concept of "friend," one of their terms for a fellow Anabaptist. Such "friends" are made by bribery and corruption:

> Some great man in state he have the gout,
> Why, you but send three drops of your elixir,
> You help him straight. There you have a made a
>   *friend*.
> Another has the palsy or the dropsy,
>   ...
> He's young again. There you have made a *friend*.
> A lady that is past the feat of body
>   ...
> There you have made a *friend*,
> And all her *friends*.
>
> (3.2.27–37, emphasis added)

The Anabaptist characters' intentions are further debased by their methods for acquiring base metal to take to the alchemist. Theirs are good commercial but dubious moral practices. They purchase "goods" from the desperately poor—orphans and widows—to bribe the rich (2.5.47). Moreover, while some sectarians were interested in the occult, including the venal Tribulation, Ananias alerts us to the hypocrisy of the Anabaptists' association with the idolatrous, animistic, even Satanic practices of Subtle:

> He bears
> The visible mark of the beast in his forehead.
> And for his stone, it is a work of darkness,
> And with philosophy blinds the eyes of man.
>
> (3.1.7–10)

Subtle's work will indeed blind his puritan gulls, and it will be by way of a performance that they would consider Satanic. Jonson's bitter satire against puritan fanatics was partly inspired by their own invective against the stage, which, like alchemy, was associated with devilish ornament, superstition, and idolatry. In *The Alchemist*, this hatred is one ironic meaning for Ananias' attack upon the Spanish dress of a visiting "Don," who is in fact Surly in disguise. His trousers

>   are profane,
> Lewd, superstitious, and idolatrous breeches.
>
> (4.7.48–49)

Face points out to Drugger that they are actually a "Spanish suit" but Ananias can no more penetrate this disguise than Face's own. He remains assured that as "Spaniards hate the brethren, and hath spies / Upon their actions . . . this was one" (4.7.65, 73–74). Ananias incorporates the Spanish Don into a unifying, puritan theory which proves no less prone to error or self-interest than Mammon's. For all they are "of the separation," the Anabaptists are unable to escape social reality—a world controlled by material desire. They thus write themselves into the conspirators' plots and Jonson's satire as other gulls have before them. They will be duped, Subtle says,

Now,
In a new tune, new gesture, but old language!

(2.4.26–27)

The final irony is that the Anabaptist haters of theater are implicated in a theatrical as well as alchemical performance. Jonson gives his sectarian neighbors at Blackfriars new gestures, the old language of greed, and a place on the stage they so despised.

The other comic creations of act 3 are Kastril and his sister. Like Dapper, Drugger, and the Anabaptists, Kastril is trapped by the language of contemporary literature and theater. With the burlesqued accent and style of a rustic and illiterate—"that's my suster. I'll go thump her" (5.5.45)—he is the country bumpkin of an estates' satire or London morality play, hazarding the city. He aspires to be another character, a roaring or "angry boy," a noisy, late-Elizabethan fellow given to raising public disturbances who was a stock figure in popular comedies and ballads (see Persons of Play, 11). Kastril has come to town because he wishes to see his sister well married to fortify his family's fortune and defend honor against social derision. But above all, he has come because he wants to learn how

To carry a business, manage a quarrel fairly,
Upon fit terms.

…

I have heard some speech
Of the angry boys, and seen 'em take tobacco,
… and I can take it too.

(3.4.18–23)

But Kastril is not merely another example of how the gulls' fantasies facilitate the tricksters' schemes. The plot resonates in the context of *The Alchemist*'s anxiety about market economies and their effect on society. The angry boy wishes to "advance the house of the Kastrils" whose status is determined not by standing or merit, but by money (4.4.88). He tells Subtle he is "the best o'the Kastrils. I'd be sorry else / By fifteen hundred a year" (3.4.14–15). He is afraid that gambling "will spend a man." Identity is a risky commercial transaction. Face exposes the risk even as he tries to persuade Kastril to take it, using Dapper as evidence:

Spend you? It will repair you when you are spent.

…

Here's a young gentleman
Is born to nothing, forty marks a year,
Which I count nothing. He's to be initiated
And have a fly o'the Doctor. He will win you
By irresistible luck, within this fortnight,
Enough to buy a barony.

(3.4.51–60)

Only the commercial has any value in the world described by Face—everything which exists outside of it is "nothing." However, in the absence of any morally verifiable measure of worth, anything within Face's world is also nothing. A barony that can be purchased has no place in a traditional social order. Social ranking—one's estate as a gentleman, priest, or peasant—was traditionally determined by the bonds established through loyal service to a nobleman, king, or God. The estates are not settled in this estates' satire. Like the play's characters, they are freely moving signifiers without moral worth, available for cash, changeable for gold. Dame Pliant, Kastril's sister, is the play's perfect empty, commercial signifier. At the hands of the cozeners, her brother, and the playwright, she is a transferable promissory note, first for Drugger, then Surly, Face, Subtle, and finally Lovewit, whom she marries in act 5. At the end of *The Alchemist* she becomes the "pliant" basis for the play's only enduring contract or alliance. Jonson's play becomes a satire of a market-driven, labile society in which no contract or alliance can be considered reliable or selfless.

ACT 4: CANTING AND THE CONTEST OF LANGUAGE

The action of *The Alchemist* up to act 4 has been governed by desire—of the rogues for goods, of the dupes for gold or women, and of all the characters for a kind of literary or social self-fulfillment. The characters on Jonson's stage wish to be just that: characters. They want the freedom to take on the new political, commercial, sexual, and historical roles they have imagined for themselves. As the play reaches its climax, they are each given their opportunity with hilarious results. At the end of act 3, Dapper returns to meet his aunt, the Fairy Queen. He is dressed up in a whore's underclothes which he is told are the queen's "petticoat of Fortune" and her "smock" put "about his eyes, to show that he is fortunate" (proverbially, Fortune's favoured child was indeed swaddled in her smock). He is then told to "throw away all worldly pelf," pinched by the queen's "elves," gagged with some gingerbread, and put in the toilet, where the "fumigation's somewhat strong" (3.5.7, 10, 15, 17, 31, 81). Dapper is left there for the whole of act 4, taking whatever sadomasochistic pleasure he can from this perverted Spenserian dream. Meanwhile, Kastril is shown some impressive instruments for quarrelling. Surly, who refused to be gulled, has returned to the stage in Spanish dress to gull the rogues into revealing their house as a brothel. Subtle and Face decide to use Dame Pliant as a whore for the Spaniard in place of Dol. Dol herself is busy playing the learned lady seduced by the loquacious Mammon, whose amorous endeavors are said to be the cause of the alchemical explosion in scene 5. By that time, Plaint has been told she will marry a Spanish knight, Drugger has been assured he will have the widow, and Subtle and Face have persuaded Kastril to let them kiss her to ensure by the "subtlety of her lip which must be tasted / Often to make a judgment" that she is ripe for a good match (4.2.40–41). Each has begun to plot to have her for himself. Surly, given Pliant as a whore, persuades her she is being prostituted and feels that as he has done the honorable thing he should have her hand in marriage himself. But in scene 7 the other characters turn on him. The roaring boy

has his day at last. Convinced Surly is a liar and seducer, Kastril chases him from the house:

KASTRIL: Did I not quarrel bravely?
FACE: Yes, indeed, sir.
                                                        (4.7.59)

The greater part of the play's development, then, occurs in act 4. It is a theatrical riot, full of guises and disguises, entries and exits, plots, counterplots, and plots to counter the counterplots. Every scene brings another knock on the stage door, and every knock brings another twist to conspirators' and the playwright's plan. Act 4 of *The Alchemist* is also the linguistic equivalent of a riot. Before the dense alchemical jargon of the play crescendos in scene 5, Subtle speaks the language of another science—a "grammar" and "logic" of quarrelling designed to bewilder Kastril:

SUBTLE: You must render causes, child!
        Your first and second intentions, know
            your canons,
        And your divisions, moods, degrees, and
            differences,
        Your predicaments, substance and
            accident,
        Series extern and intern, with their
   causes
        Efficient, material, formal, final,
        And ha'your elements perfect —
KASTRIL: What is this!
        The angry tongue he talks in?
                                                        (4.2.21–29)

Dol concludes her encounter with Mammon by taking on the role allocated to her by Face in act 2—a learned lady driven mad by reading too many puritan pamphlets. Her language is an incomprehensible babble of phrases drawn from Hugh Broughton's puritan gloss on the Old Testament, *A Concent of Scripture*, printed in 1590. It fills no communicative function. She talks through and over the other characters:

DOL: *And so we may arrive by Talmud skill*

15

> *And profane Greek to raise the*
> *building up*
> *Of Helen's house against the*
> *Ismaelite,*
> *King of Thogarma and his Habergeons.*
> FACE: How did you put her into't?
> MAMMON: Alas, I talk'd
> Of a fifth monarchy I would erect
> With the philosophers stone, by
>   chance, and she
> Falls on the other four straight.
> FACE: Out of Broughton!
>
> (4.5.25–8)

But Dol's ranting is no more meaningless than Mammon's ridiculous love-making, which, given its object, has no communicative function either:

> MAMMON: There is a strange nobility i'your eye,
>   This lip, that chin! Methinks you do
>   resemble
>   One of the Austriac princes.
> FACE: [*Aside*]   Very like!
>   Her father was an Irish
>   costermonger.
>
> (4.1.54–57)

Meanwhile, Surly exposes the play's normative approach to language by pretending to speak only Spanish. The rogues desire to be misunderstood. Surly pretends to misunderstand and thus speaks a duplicitous language of his own:

> SURLY: *Señores, beso las manos a vuestas mercedes*
>   [Sirs, I kiss your honor's hands].
> SUBTLE: Would you had stooped a little, and kissed
>   our *anos.*
>
>   …
>
>   Do you mark? You shall
>   Be cozened, Diego.
> FACE: Cozened, do you see?
>   My worthy Donzel, cozened.
> SURLY: *Entendio* [I understand].
> SUBTLE: Do you intend it? So do we, dear Don.
>   (4.3.21–22, 38–41)

However, even Surly is ultimately driven off the stage by Ananias' ranting, which sounds biblical but is not, and by Kastril's cries of "otter and a shad, a whit / A very Tim," which he believes to be good insults but which he apparently just made up (4.7.45–46).

Contesting languages have been important throughout *The Alchemist.* One of the concerns of the play is the unstable or failed connection between words and intended meanings. It is manifest in the multiple names for Face, Subtle, and Dol; in the catalogues of unrealizable desires compiled by Mammon; and in the characters' borrowing from the semantic domains of commerce and politics. This consciousness of the unverifiable character of the spoken vernacular seems to be the corollary of Jonson's classicism. According to his preliminary epistles, he wishes to control the literary meaning of his play by containing it within humanist categories: noble audience, classical antecedents, dramatic unity, and satiric purpose. But the text cannot be so contained. In thinking about how the *The Alchemist* plays itself out, we have considered the contrast between the enduring printed word, and the immediate social transaction of the stage. There, the failure of an author to make his text mean what he wants it to mean is exposed to the gaze and the laughter of an audience. However, the fact that Jonson has written a play which examines the tendency of language to contradict and parody itself endlessly suggests that he is interested in a problem greater than the stage upon which it is set. All language is ultimately destined or available for social purposes. Even quiet study of a literary classic may result in the disruption and interrogation of its meanings. The figure for Jonson's anxiety about this is cant. "Cant" is a Renaissance word for language spoken by vagabonds, pimps, and con-men. It refers specifically to the part-Romany, part-slang dialect of the underworld. In the "coney-catcher" pamphlets of this period, it is described and used to represent the shifty dealings of gamblers, prostitutes, thieves, and con-artists. Face, Subtle, and Dol speak cant when they shout insults at one another in the first lines of

The Alchemist; when they swear upon on "'slid" and "'slight" (God's eyelid and God's light); and when they describe their criminal activities and their consequences, for instance when Dol refers to "ear-rent," the ear-clippings at the pillory and "Don Provost" the hangman (1.1.160–161, 169–170). But if cant is language implicated in the illicit and the illegal, then theirs is not the only cant of the play. In *The Alchemist,* characters are canting when they speak the language of love, of alchemy, of rhetoric, grammar, and logic, of Renaissance discovery and expansion, of early modern commerce, religion, and politics. When spoken by the gulls, words are believed to be true but are not. The same words in mouths of the criminals do not intend sense at all. What is crucial about cant as it is defined by Jonson is the blurring of legitimate and illegitimate languages. Cant reveals that all words are available for precisely the opposite ends than those for which they were intended. The words of act 4 of *The Alchemist* are just as capable of functioning as meaningless, disruptive noise as the fart of act 1—Subtle's response to the very first words of the play.

Alchemy, which has served as a figure for the theater, for Renaissance desire and learning, for prostitution, rank commercialism, and political freedom, is finally also a metaphor for language. The promise of language, like that of alchemy, is that something of tremendous value can be made out of something base: gold out of lead, poetry out of noise. The climax of *The Alchemist* is therefore the explosion of scene 5 of act 4. It isolates and emphasizes the continual, riotous collapse of linguistic signification in the play. It puts an end to the generative promise of language just as it puts an end to the promise of alchemy. It is anticipated by the skeptic Surly, whose accumulation of alchemical terms in act 2 also ends with a bang:

> Hair o'the head, burnt clout, chalk, merds, and
>   clay
> Powder of bones, scalings of iron, glass,

And worlds of other strange *ingredients*
Would burst a man to name?

> (2.3.195–198)

It would "burst a man," that is, to find any meaningful resolution to *The Alchemist*'s cant. At this and other moments Surly resembles the skeptics and moralists who appear in other Jacobean and early Jonsonian dramas, attempting to inject some common sense into proceedings. Surly is honest; he cannot be duped by Subtle, Face, and Dol's deceptive theater, and when he speaks untruth it is only to expose the dishonesty of others. He marks out his deceptive discourse clearly—all his lies are in Spanish. His failure to trick the tricksters therefore creates a problem for interpretation of *The Alchemist.* Is he able to recognize but not defeat trickery because, as a gambler, he is complicit in double-dealing? He is willing to concede

> That alchemy is a pretty kind of game,
> Somewhat like tricks o'the card, to cheat a man
> With charming.

> (2.3.180–182)

Or does Surly represent a more complex attitude to morality in *The Alchemist*? The key to understanding Surly's failure to achieve his moral purpose in the play may be that it occurs while he is in costume. Even when honest, and when seeking to reveal dishonesty, he is assuming a role. He must use the same methods as the dishonest and self-deceiving characters around him. Surly's defeat therefore signals *The Alchemist*'s want of any fixed position from which to judge some aspect of the play to be moral. If all language is a kind of cant, accommodating the likelihood of its inversion, then only those self-conscious of the limit to their power as the authors or speakers are likely to achieve their purpose. In this sense, the classical pose struck by Jonson in the preliminary matter to the editions is self-consciously ironic. Even the stability of the Latin epigram of the title page, a text fixed in relation to its own past, proves an illusion. Lucretius offers laurels to a playwright, Jonson, for a play in which he interrogates the virtue of playing. The stable forms of print are likewise confounded by the prospect of the "cozened" readers described in the epistle, who are victims of the sort of early seventeenth-century commodity swindles mentioned *The Alchemist* (see 3.4.97–98, for example). They have has been tricked into buying something of little or no value to them. Printers'—and authors'—are written in words, which have been shown to have no fixed value. They therefore supply another meaning for alchemical gold. Indeed, books prompt the first use of the play's prevailing image:

> A book, but barely reckoning [Subtle's]
>   impostures
> Shall prove a true *philosopher's stone* to printers.
>
> (1.1.101–102)

ACT 5: SATIRE AND DECORUM

The question of how the meaning of *The Alchemist* is to be resolved brings us to the play's ending, and Face's epilogue to the audience:

> Gentlemen,
> My part a little fell in this last scene,
> Yet 'twas decorum.
>
> (5.5.157–159)

Face is concerned that he has not behaved as would be expected. Dramatic decorum required consistent characterization, an aspect of which was the register of a character's language. By the time he reaches his epilogue, however, Face has been transformed from an absolute rogue into a willing servant whose scheming is legitimized by Lovewit, now restored to his rightful place as master of the house. Face thinks his part "fell" a little while he was becoming the servant Jeremy. This comment on decorum at the play's resolution alerts us to another possible breach of Renaissance decorum. In a classically framed comedy such as *The Alchemist*, the ending should be satisfying in all its points: the unities intact, the plot coherently worked out, and justice and order restored so that the play has not "run away from Nature" like so many of the plays of Jonson's rivals.

Jonson has met the first two of his requirements by the end of act 5. The play has never shifted from the unified moment or place of its unfolding. Indeed, control of time and space is a theme of the play. The plague which sets the action in motion positions the text in seventeenth century history at the same time that it constrains the plotters' performances. They believe Face's master will stay away as long as there has "died one a week within the liberty" and the comic timing and ending depends upon his early return (4.7.116). Plague also confines the text in space. It localized it in London and in a closed-up house in the liberty of Blackfriars which was full of theaters closed up by the pestilence in 1610. Having confined his characters to a few hours and a single room, Jonson is able to subject their performances to the same problems that confront the dramatist. They must handle the exits and entrances of each character in order to sustain the development of separate plots. The timing of initial visits is anticipated and controlled, but each unexpected guest and need for improvisation brings them closer to their downfall. Lovewit's final discovery of their intrigue is a masterstroke of comic timing and staging. Dapper, confined to a nearby privy throughout act 4, has chewed his way through his gingerbread gag and feels he has spent enough time off-stage. His complaint is loud enough to be heard by master and audience alike:

> For God's sake, when will her Grace be at leisure?
>
> (5.3.65)

Lovewit's response is straightforward:

> Come, sir. No more o' your tricks, good Jeremy.
> The truth, the shortest way.
>
> (5.3.73–74)

Lovewit retakes dramatic control—of the space of the house; the "truth" of the plot; the identity of the characters including "good Jeremy"; even of time. His will be "the shortest way" to the play's perfectly unified ending.

The major issues as well as formal strands of the play are drawn together in act 5. The resolution of the plot is also witness to a final interrogation of the play's intersecting themes of desire—sexual and sensual, material, social and political, but above all pecuniary. The economies of *The Alchemist* turn the end of all desire to naught. The conspirators are divested of their loot by Lovewit but it proves a debased currency anyway—as tawdry as the fantasies of the gulls: the jewel of the waiting-maid who wishes to usurp her mistress, fish-wives' rings, whistles, tavern cups, French petticoats, bolts of lawn, girdles and hangers (5.4.110–120). Amidst this pile of human detritus even the cash won from Mammon seems valueless. It is the stuff of excess consumption, and its emptiness, as Face tells his former partners,

> Determines the indenture tripartite
> 'Twixt Subtle, Dol, and Face. All I can do
> Is to help you over the wall o' the back side
> Or lend you a sheet to save your velvet gown,
> Dol.
>
> (5.4.131–134)

There is nothing left to do but to conceal Dol's form—Jonson's misogynist symbol for lubricious desire throughout the play.

The play's overarching interest in language and the language of theater especially also finds final expression in act 5. The cozeners' many dramatic roles become an angry list in the mouths of the gulls outside Lovewit's house. When Lovewit demands of them "Whom do you seek?" they respond,

MAMMON:	The chemical cozener.
SURLY:	And the Captain Pander.
KASTRIL:	The nun my suster.
MAMMON:	Madam Rabbi.

| ANANIAS: | Scorpions and caterpillars. |

> (5.5.18–21)

Subtle, Face, and Dol's new roles reflect their new status in the eyes of those they have duped. However, the terms used are still in contest, the assignations still interchangeable, the language still cant. Ananias' Old Testament "scorpions and caterpillars" literalize the affinity between the conspirators' schemes and the plague. But they are nevertheless a ridiculously heightened description of some petty criminals. The allusion threatens to corrupt the sacred text from which it is drawn. The connection between the Blackfriars house and the stage is also maintained. The neighbors who gather outside are like a somewhat hostile audience, milling about after the performance. When Lovewit asks them if there has "been such resort" to his house, they review the "ladies and gentlewomen," "citizens' wives," "knights," "Tobacco-men," "gallants," "sailors' wives," "oyster-women," and "lords" they have seen, leading Lovewit to wonder that his servant has not put out "banners" for drawing a crowd to a freak show (5.1.2–7).

However, if Jonson's unified play is to conform wholly to the rules of decorum it must also conform to the rules of satire. Formally, satire is a genre in which vices, follies, abuses, and shortcomings are held up to censure by means of ridicule or irony, usually with an intent to bring about improvement. True satirists are moralists: the ideas and behaviours they consider mistaken or foolish are subject to a final judgement. Lovewit's return supplies the opportunity for this judgement. But as his charactonym suggests, he would rather participate in the verbal games at his house than condemn them. Lovewit simply writes himself into the scripts of *The Alchemist*. He forgives Face in exchange for the dupes' goods and the part of Spanish suitor to the rich widow Pliant, whom he quickly marries. Kastril is reconciled to the match when Lovewit assumes a new part to meet the angry boy:

LOVEWIT: Come, will you quarrel? I will feeze you,
   sirrah.
   Why do you not buckle to your tools?
KASTRIL: God's light!
   This is a fine old boy as e'er I saw.

         (5.5.131–133)

The rogues' alliance is simply replaced by another social contract motivated by self interest, lust, and greed and realized through duplicity. Moreover, the court case which might resolve matters by the arraignment of the criminals, and which is a crucial part of the ending of other Jonson comedies, including *Volpone, Epicene,* and *Bartholomew Fair,* is conspicuous by its absence in *The Alchemist.* Lovewit tells Mammon he cannot have the "goods / That lie i'the cellar":

MAMMON: Not mine own stuff?
LOVEWIT: Sir, I can take no knowledge
   That they are yours but by public
    means.
   If you can bring certificate that you
    were gulled of 'em,
   Or any formal writ out of a court
   That you did cozen yourself, I will not
    hold them.
MAMMON: I'll rather lose them.

        (5.5.63, 66–71)

In the absence of formal judgement, Jonson's satire proposes no improvement. The outlook at the end of the play is bleak:

LOVEWIT: What a great loss in hope have you
    sustained!
MAMMON: Not I. The commonwealth has.
FACE: Ay, he would ha'built
   The city new, and made a ditch about it
   Of silver.

        (5.5.75–78)

Face's mocking tone recalls Subtle's vision of Mammon healing London's sick in act 2. Here, his ambition to transform the territory of his desire is again satirized. However, if places such as Spittle and Moorfields are unchanged at the end of Mammon's dealing with Face, Subtle, and Dol, the play offers no alternative scheme for their betterment. The London of the Prologue is unreconstructed; the loss is the commonwealth's. By act 5 of the play, both alchemy and satire have failed to achieve their professed moral purpose. How, then, are we to judge the satire that is *The Alchemist?*

The answer is perhaps not how, but when. Face tells us in his Epilogue that he is

Got off from Subtle, Surly, Mammon, Dol,
Hot Ananias, Dapper, Drugger, all
With whom I traded, yet I put myself
On you, that are my country, and this pelf,
Which I have got, if you do 'quit me, rests
To feast you often and invite new guests.

        (5.5.160–165)

It is impossible to tell if we have actually been invited to leave the play at this moment. He who addresses us is both a character and an actor. As Face, he seems pathologically unable to stop assuming guises. He is still a businessman; now he is also a defendant before court and country, seeking acquittal. But at this moment he is also an actor. He trades with his audience as he has traded with "all," measuring the "pelf" received for this performance, hoping for more from the next. The distinction between actor and character blurs. An actor who "falls" out of character and addresses the audience is still playing a role. When we applaud, then, whom do we condone? The character who has conned his way thought the play and out of trouble? Or the author and performer who have presented us with this display of immorality? Then answer is neither, and both. Until we are "clean got off" from Face, we are, as audience or readers, implicated in Jonson's distrust of theatricality and language, denied a fixed position from which to judge the play. It remains to do what Lovewit does: to be a guest, feast on the language—take simple pleasure in the riotous joy of *The Alchemist,* one of the great achievements of Renaissance theater.

Select Bibliography

MODERN EDITIONS

Helen Ostavich, editor. *Four Comedies*. London and New York: Longman, 1997. (I refer to this edition when quoting from *The Alchemist*.)

Alvin B. Kernan, editor. *The Yale Ben Jonson*. New Haven and London: Yale University Press, 1974.

F. H. Mares, editor. *The Alchemist*. Manchester and New York: Manchester University Press, 1967.

SECONDARY SOURCES

Arnold, Judd. "Lovewit's Triumph and Jonsonian Morality: A Reading of the Alchemist." *Criticism* 11 (1969), 151–66.

Barish, Jonas. *The Antitheatrical Prejudice*. Berkeley: University of California Press, 1981.

Barton, Anne. *Ben Jonson: Dramatist*. Cambridge: Cambridge University Press, 1984.

Burt, R. *Licensed by Authority: Ben Jonson and the Discourses of Censorship*. Ithaca and London: Cornell University Press, 1993.

Butler, M. "Jonson's Folio and the Politics of Patronage." *Criticism* 34 (1993), 377–390.

Cave, R. *Ben Jonson*. Basingstoke: Macmillan, 1991.

Cave. R., E. Safer, and B. Woolland, editors. *Ben Jonson and Theatre: Performance, Practice and Theory*. London: Routledge, 1999.

Craig, D. H., editor. *Ben Jonson: The Critical Heritage: 1599–1798*. London: Routledge, 1990.

Dessen, Alan C. "*The Alchemist:* Jonson's 'Estates' Play." *Renaissance Drama* 7 (1964), 35–54.

Donaldson, Ian. *Jonson's Magic Houses*. Oxford: Clarendon Press, 1997.

Duncan, Edgar Hill, "Jonson's *Alchemist* and the Literature of Alchemy." *Publications of the Modern Language Association of America* 61 (1946), 699–710.

Fish, S. "Authors-Readers: Jonson's Communities of the Same." *Representations* 7 (1984), 26–58.

Gibbons, Brian. *Jacobean City Comedy*. 2nd edn. London: Methuen, 1980.

Greene, Thomas. "Ben Jonson and the Centred Self." *Studies in English Literature 1500–1900* 10 (1970), 325–348.

Harp, Richard and Stanley Stewart. *The Cambridge Companion to Ben Jonson*. Cambridge: Cambridge University Press, 2000.

Haynes, J. *The Social Relations of Jonson's Theatre*. Cambridge: Cambridge University Press, 1992.

Holdsworth, R., ed. *Every Man in His Humour and The Alchemist*, Casebooks. Basingstoke; Macmillan, 1979.

Hoy, Cyrus. "The Pretended Piety of Jonson's *Alchemist*." *Renaissance Papers* (1957), 15–19.

Levin, Harry. "Two Magician Comedies: *The Tempest* and *The Alchemist*." *Shakespeare Survey* 22 (1969), 47–58.

Loewenstein, J. "The Script in the Marketplace." *Representations* 12 (1985), 101–14.

Loxley, James. *The Complete Critical Guide to Ben Jonson*. London and New York: Routledge, 2002.

Miller, S. "Consuming Mothers/Consuming Merchants: The Carnivalesque Economy of Jacobean City Comedy." *Modern Language Studies* 26 (1996), 73–97.

Partridge, E. B. *The Broken Compass: A Study of the Major Comedies of Ben Jonson*. London: Chatto and Windus, 1958.

Riggs, David. *Ben Jonson: A Life*. Cambridge, MA: Harvard University Press, 1989.

Stallybrass, P. and A. White. *The Politics and Poetics of Transgression*. London: Menthuen, 1986.

Summers, J. and T. Pebworth, eds. *Classic and Cavalier: Essays on Jonson and the Sons of Ben*. Pittsburgh: University of Pittsburgh Press, 1982.

Sweeney, John Gordon III. *Jonson and the Psychology of Public Theater*. Princeton: Princeton University Press, 1985.

Watson, Robert N. *Ben Jonson's Parodic Strategy: Literary Imperialism in the Comedies*. Cambridge, MA: Harvard University Press, 1987.

Wayne, D. "Drama and Society in the Age of Jonson: An Alternative View." *Renaissance Drama*, n.s., 13 (1982), 103–129.

Womack, Peter. *Ben Jonson*. Oxford: Blackwell, 1986.

Tom Stoppard's
Arcadia

FRED BILSON

STOPPARD DOES NOT mine his own experience of life for material. One example may illustrate why. Stoppard has recounted that he has "nothing that came from my father, nothing he owned or touched," but on one occasion he met a Czech lady who had on her hand a small scar left when his father, Dr. Eugen Sträussler, had stitched a wound for her. This was, in Ira Nadel's words, "the only tangible sign of [his father's] existence" (*Double Act: A Life of Tom Stoppard,* p. 6). That the scar should survive, and that Stoppard should meet the woman who carried it, are both as unlikely as that he should escape both the Holocaust in Europe and the Japanese occupation of Singapore. This is an incident that cannot be transmuted into literature: it can only be told simply and directly. Stoppard at first wished to be a reporter, a witness who makes sure the truth is told. It was the fact that he was assigned as a play and film critic that turned his attention to drama.

Stoppard is generally ready to discuss and analyze his views, his life, and his plays. This does not make analysis easier. Nadel says he "unintentionally misleads, setting false traps for his biographer and offering explanations that don't quite match either with the record or with other statements of his" (p. xiii). For instance, A. S. Byatt reported that Stoppard had told her that he "pinched" the idea of *Arcadia* from her novel *Possession* (1990), according to Nadel (pp. 429–430 and footnote 10, p. 578). It is hard to assess this story without knowing how seriously Stoppard made his remark, or how seriously Byatt took it, but it will be considered below.

As a writer, Stoppard is haunted by multiple identity, as though he continued to be both Tomik and Tom; partly for this reason, what he puts into his plays sometimes comes as a surprise to him. Paul Delaney has a careful working out of this element of double identity in Stoppard's work ("Exit Tomas Sträussler, Enter Sir Tom Stoppard," in *The Cambridge Companion to Tom Stoppard,* 2001, p. 20).

ARCADIA: THE CONTEXT WITHIN STOPPARD'S WORK

In many ways, Stoppard's first major play, *Rosencrantz and Guildenstern Are Dead* (first performed 1966), shaped his reputation. Some critics, while acknowledging the verbal wit and dexterity in the play, found it lacking in human emotion, and Stoppard has had the reputation of being all head and no heart throughout his career.

The play is absurdist in the tradition of Samuel Beckett's *Waiting for Godot;* the debt to Beckett is a critical commonplace, acknowledged by Stoppard. The play had a strong structure that was external in origin, because it used conventions derived from the interscene tradition (in which actors at rehearsal improvise what their characters will be doing between their scenes) and because it transformed and adapted material drawn from Beckett and Shakespeare.

Arcadia (first produced and published 1993) similarly has traces of the absurdist tradition and transforms material ultimately derived from Shakespeare, as well as containing pastiche of Oscar Wilde's *The Importance of Being Earnest.* It follows Stoppard's *Hapgood* (first produced 1988, published 1994) in treating scientific ideas as a source of dramatic material; in *Hapgood* the interest is in wave and particle theory. Additionally, in a seminal and indispensable article on Stoppard, Hersh Zeifman sees *Arcadia* cohering with *The Real Thing* (1996) and *The Invention of Love* (1997) as representing a new development in Stoppard's work. No longer afraid of showing his genuine emotion, he has become a genuine writer on love ("The Comedy of Eros: Stoppard in Love," in *The Cambridge Companion to Tom Stoppard,* p. 185).

At the time of writing *Arcadia*, Stoppard was working on the script of the film *Shakespeare in Love.* Though centering on *Romeo and Juliet,* the script also refers to *Twelfth Night.*

CRITICAL RECEPTION

Arcadia opened on 13 April 1993 at the Lyttelton Theatre, London, part of the National Theatre complex, with a brilliant cast. Emma Fielding, one of the most gifted ingenue actors of her generation, created Thomasina. Other

CHRONOLOGY

1937	Born Tomás (Tomik) Sträussler in Zlín, Southern Moravia, Czechoslovakia, the second son of Dr. Eugen and Mrs. Martha Sträussler. His father is a distinguished physician employed by Bata, the shoe manufacturing company.
1939	The Nazis invade Czechoslovakia.
1939	Using a plan prepared months in advance, Bata evacuates the Sträusslers, along with other doctors and their families, to various foreign branches. The Sträusslers chose to go to Singapore, Southeast Asia.
1942	With a Japanese invasion imminent, Mrs. Sträussler and her sons are evacuated to India; Dr. Sträussler is killed when the ship taking him to Australia is bombed.
1943–1945	Tom and his older brother, Peter, attend a boarding school in Darjeeling, India, and are educated through the medium of English.
1945	Mrs. Sträussler marries Major Kenneth Stoppard.
1946	Family moves to Yorkshire. Ken Stoppard adopts Peter and Tom Sträussler and they take his surname.
1946–1954	Tom Stoppard at private schools in England.
1954	Stoppard leaves school and becomes a journalist in Bristol. Writes a great deal of original work and is a theater and film critic
1966	*Rosenkrantz and Guildenstern Are Dead* has an amateur production at the Edinburgh Fringe and attracts the attention of Kenneth Tynan, literary manager of the National Theatre.
1967	*Rosenkrantz and Guildenstern Are Dead* is produced at the National Theatre in England.
1967–	Productive and varied career writing plays (stage and TV), film scripts, and adaptations of plays from Austrian, Czech, Spanish, and Hungarian theater.

1976	Begins sustained campaign for Soviet dissidents and for Charter 77, the freedom movement in Czechoslovakia. Becomes friend of playwright Vaclav Havel, whose work he will translate.
1989	Following the Velvet Revolution, Havel becomes president of Czechoslovakia.
1992	Stoppard writes screenplay for *Shakespeare in Love* and play *Arcadia*.
1993	Slovakia secedes from the Czechoslovak Republic: the Czech Republic takes on its present form.
1993	*Arcadia* opens in London.
1994	Stoppard learns from a relative that he had not one Jewish grandparent but four, and that all his grandparents, and three of his aunts, had died in the Holocaust.
1996	Martha Stoppard dies; his stepfather, Ken, asks Stoppard to stop using his surname, because Tom is becoming "tribalized."
1997	Death of Ken Stoppard. Tom Stoppard is knighted and becomes Sir Tom Stoppard.
2001	New trilogy, *The Coast of Utopia*, on life of nineteenth-century Russian revolutionaries, opens in London.

strong performances came from Felicity Kendal (Hannah), Bill Nighy (Bernard), Rufus Sewell (Septimus), and Sam West (Valentine).

Warmly praised for both its script and its staging, the play won the *Evening Standard* award for best new play of the year and was a commercial and artistic success. It also played in New York at Lincoln Center. Nadel reports this as an unhappy production; he gives the impression of a cast daunted by the Englishness and the English accents of the play and overawed by Stoppard himself, where the British cast always found him approachable. The play did not do well (*Double Act,* pp. 472–474).

Possibly as a result of this, the American public has tended to focus on the scientific ideas

within the play. Unusually, the play was reviewed in *Scientific American,* where Tim Beardsley found that its "verbal virtuosity . . . rests on a respectful, even sympathetic, examination of the way modern science looks at the world." It was this review as much as anything that initiated an interest in the play well beyond the range of the normal theater audience among readers whose principal interest was in the science and mathematics that were part of the subject matter of the play.

But there were qualifications to the enthusiasm. One of the most balanced reviews was by Lloyd Rose in the *Washington Post* ("Stoppard's Coolly Clever 'Arcadia,' 20 December 1996, p. D1). He wrote: "Stoppard's wit and erudition are as impressive as ever. . . . And his optimism is invigorating: He seems to regard curiosity as one of the virtues. But his facility undermines him here. He does too much too well, and the result is that he does nothing wonderfully." Rose found that "[f]or all its surface brilliance, *Arcadia* lacks passion and urgency." He compared it unfavorably with *Hapgood* and its representation of "the physicist Kenner's ecstatic, semi-mystical speech on quantum theory," as well as *Rosencrantz and Guildenstern Are Dead,* where the characters found themselves in an "existential predicament: Who were they anyway, and why was this terrible thing happening to them?"

Something of this apparent lack of passion and urgency appears in two illustrations in *The Cambridge Companion to Tom Stoppard.* A still from *The Real Thing* (p. 209) is dramatically engaging. Harry (Roger Rees) holds an object like a sword pointed at Annie (Felicity Kendal) as though about to behead her. Is this menace or coincidence? A second look shows that the object is, in fact, a cricket bat, and the composition is in fact more puzzling than it was at first sight: the image engages. A still from *Arcadia* (p. 226) shows Bernard Nightingale (Bill Nighy, standing) rehearsing his paper to the Byron Society. Chloë (Harriet Harrison), Hannah

(Felicity Kendal), and Valentine (Sam West) lounge. There is no tension in the composition.

All the same, *Arcadia* has now become a cult classic and is regularly performed by both amateur and professional companies. There are several Web sites devoted both to productions of the play and to the math and science. *Arcadia* regularly features in educational projects designed to promote cross-disciplinary approaches.

STRUCTURE AND NARRATIVE

The action alternates scenes set in the early nineteenth century, in 1809 and 1812, with scenes set in the present; all are located in a large room on the garden front of Sidley Park, a fictitious stately home in Derbyshire. The nineteenth-century scenes center around the daughter of the house, Thomasina Coverly, and her tutor, Septimus Hodge. Thomasina is thirteen years and ten months old when *Arcadia* begins (*Arcadia,* p. 17); Shakespeare's Juliet is thirteen years and eleven months old (*Romeo and Juliet,* act 1, scene 3). Gradually Thomasina falls in love with Septimus. The business of the 1809 scenes focuses on a challenge to a duel that Ezra Chater, a minor poet staying at the house, issues to Septimus, because he has enjoyed "carnal embrace" with Mrs. Chater. The documents built up by this challenge are preserved to the present. Thomasina's mother, Lady Croom, prevents the duel, by expelling the Chaters from the house together with Lord Byron, a guest. She is jealous: wanting Byron herself, she finds him leaving Charity Chater's bedroom.

When he thought he was likely to die in the duel, Septimus had written two letters: one to Thomasina and one, declaring his physical passion, to Lady Croom. Lady Croom reads both and returns them to Septimus, who burns them in front of her, together with an unopened letter addressed to him from Byron; this also goes on the pyre because Lady Croom objects to it. His

gesture wins him access to her bed. These latter three documents therefore do not survive to the present.

The modern scenes introduce three characters from a later generation of the Coverly family. Valentine Coverly, in his late twenties, is a mathematician researching chaos theory; his sister, Chloë, is eighteen, and his brother, Gus, is fifteen. Gus does not speak; he is an elective mute who hates noise but is very much in touch with the earlier Coverly family. He was able to locate the position of the old boathouse when scientific methods failed.

Visiting the house are two researchers. Hannah Jarvis is researching the history of the garden, which was re-planned in the contemporary taste of 1809. Bernard Nightingale has found a copy of Ezra Chater's poem *The Couch of Eros,* which had been in Byron's library.

Valentine, Hannah, and Bernard are all engaged in interpreting the documents left over from the past. Bernard has the book and the letters it contains. Valentine is using the "game books" for his data; these record the birds and animals killed by people hunting on the estate. Hannah is using the garden books kept by Lady Croom and the plan books of Culpability Noakes (whose name is reminiscent of the famous eighteenth-century landscape gardener Capability Brown); he was redesigning the garden in 1809.

The major action in these scenes is Bernard's attempt to prove his "gut feeling" that the letters in the book prove that Byron killed Chater in a duel. While warning him of the risks he is taking, Hannah and Valentine feed him the evidence he needs. Bernard sweeps aside alternative explanations. He presents a paper to the Byron Society and accompanies it with press releases that are taken up by the Sunday papers. Later we see his humiliation. Hannah finds a reference in Lady Croom's garden book that proves Bernard Nightingale had been totally wrong.

The audience is privileged over the researchers in that they have actually witnessed the events of 1809–1812, rather than having to reconstruct them from fragmentary data. For example, Hannah is interested in the Hermit of Sidley Park. There is a legend that a hermit actually lived in the hermitage in the re-planned garden. Bernard finds her the documentary evidence for this. She believes she has found his likeness in one of Culpability Noakes's plan books for the new garden "drawn in by a later hand, of course" (p. 33). We know, however, that it was Thomasina who drew a hermit into the plan book before the garden was finished. "I have made him like the Baptist in the wilderness," she says. Septimus responds, "How picturesque" (p. 18).

THOMASINA'S DEATH

Much of the reading of *Arcadia* depends on a remark made by Hannah near the end of the play suggesting that Thomasina had died, burned to death, on the eve of her seventeenth birthday in June 1812 (p. 101). Practically everyone who sees or reads this play appears to take this at face value. We might be a little more cautious after all we have learned from Bernard's brush with the "Byron letters." This is not to suggest that the story is untrue, simply to point out that it is not established as carefully as the identity of Septimus and the hermit.

There are difficulties with the story of Thomasina's death, starting with social history. A young lady of her social status did not go to bed on her own with a candle, even if she needed a candle at, say, 9:30 P.M. in June. When she got to her bedroom (which was unlikely to be an attic under the dormer, by the way), her maid would be waiting to put away her clothes and brush her hair, especially if she was to "come out" (begin keeping adult company and adult hours) the next day. The second difficulty is Valentine's reaction. He is surprised when Hannah connects Thomasina with "the girl who died

in the fire." "There's a memorial to her in the Park," says Hannah. An "irritated" Valentine responds: "I know—it's my home" (pp. 101–102).

Obsessed as he has been with Thomasina, why is he surprised at Hannah's announcement? That monument in the park cannot be inscribed, otherwise Valentine would know the story already. It must be tied to Thomasina by some local legend or some document that is not produced.

The end of the play itself is open and unresolved. All possibilities remain available. Septimus lights Thomasina's candle. "Be careful with the flame," he says, ambiguously, knowing that she loves him. Thomasina says: "I will wait for you to come." Septimus tells her he will not, and "she puts the candlestick . . . on the table, responding, "Then I will not go. Once more, for my birthday" (p. 129). By "once more," she means "Let us dance again." They waltz. The play ends here.

Of course, Stoppard knows his Wittgenstein. Death is not an event in life; we do not live through it. Thomasina's death does not belong in 1812. If it happens, it marks the beginning of the posthumous retelling of her life.

The original encounter between Stoppard and A. S. Byatt referred to above came partly because her novel *Possession* has a double articulation of time, with modern scholars, Roland Michell and Maud Bailey, reconstructing a set of incidents in the life of a (fictitious) Victorian writer called Ash and his mistress Christabel la Motte. Stoppard, however, had used this double articulation device earlier in his 1973 *Artist Descending a Staircase* (see Nadel, *Double Act*, p. 237).

Possession also ends with a tragic resolution, except that this is a double resolution. Christabel writes Ash a letter telling him she has given birth to his child. But since the scholars discover she never sent the letter, the historical "fact" is that Ash never knew he had a daughter. However, a later postscript tells us that Ash did meet his daughter and told her to pass on the news to Christabel. The child forgot to do so, and so the "real" truth was never known.

Nadel draws the parallel with *Arcadia.* The fact that Christabel's letter was never sent represents a piece of "tragic news [that] satisfies the scholars' need for an ending, providing a conclusion for the novel" (pp. 429–430).

The detective story has always been a favored form of Stoppard's. Hannah's revelation parallels the set speech where the detective offers a resolution of the mystery: conventionally the revelation must not be counterintuitive and there must be circumstantial evidence for it. Hannah's story "explains" why Septimus lived on at the Park as a hermit, trying either to prove or disprove Thomasina's conjecture. It "explains" why Thomasina did not become famous. It is also one possible explanation for the two clues on the modern estate—an irregularity in the roofline of the house and a memorial in the park. But it is always subject to Byatt's qualification—there might be another piece of evidence that does not fit.

The story enables readings that give closure. From Thomasina's "Oh, phooey to death" (p. 18) through her talk of Dido on the funeral pyre (p. 47), the irony of death by fire for someone preoccupied with heat loss (p. 115) right up to the final waltz, we now read or re-read Thomasina's story as tragic. It is the comfortable feminine tragedy to which audiences react with both sorrow and satisfaction, familiar from the death of Violetta in *La Traviata* or of Mimi in *La Bohème*, where some young woman is offered up on the altar. It satisfies the very many antifeminist readings of *Arcadia*, because it wipes out Thomasina, who represents a challenge to her society, where the masculine is hegemonic.

Despite her originality and genius, Thomasina cannot study at a university, take a degree, follow a profession, vote, hold any public office or even, except on very peculiar terms, own property. Hannah in the present, though more privileged, is still discriminated against as a woman. Entry to university teaching and promotion within university hierarchies is more difficult for her than for Bernard Nightingale. She instead becomes an author, writing on a publisher's commission books devoted to academic topics—Lady Caroline Lamb, the eighteenth-century garden. This fact enables the initial condescension Bernard feels for her and her work, which parallels the condescension that Septimus feels for Thomasina. In both cases, the original condescension gives way before closer contact with these minds that are in fact better. In this reading, Stoppard challenges male presumptions.

Not always effectively, be it said. It is noticeable how often critics—who see nothing unusual in the idea of the younger Thomasina wanting the older Septimus, or the younger Chloë wanting the older Bernard—find something odd in the younger Gus wanting the older Hannah. It makes a good test of implicit sexism in readings of the play.

THE SET

The garden room is a bare, anomalous room, with "no more pretension than a school-room, which is indeed the main use of this room [in 1809–1812]" (p. 1). Later in the present it is a workroom and a corridor from the garden to the house. "The upstage wall is mainly tall, shapely, uncurtained windows, one or more of which work as doors" (p. 1). One door goes to the garden, one into the house. "Nothing much need be said or seen of the exterior beyond" (p. 1). As in the absurdist tradition from which Stoppard has drawn since his earliest successful play, *Rosencrantz and Guildenstern Are Dead*, the set is simply a nowhere place where people can be. It is free of troublesome indications of period; props are simply left on a central table and used as needed. At one point, Septimus in 1809 leaves a carafe of wine and a glass behind; later Hannah in the present pours herself a drink using the same carafe and glass. In a house of this sort, there is no reason why she should not use glassware previously used by Septimus (p. 125). When the characters from the present change into Regency clothes for a dance, they can merge visually into the earlier period and intercut speeches and actions with the earlier characters. The staging of the end of the play regularly has Hannah and Gus dance (like Thomasina and Septimus) to music from 1812, while the windows are lit up by a fireworks display from the present.

Offstage sounds are used for a variety of effects. First, they mark off one period from another, and most are assigned to 1809–1812. An offstage pistol shot marks the end of scene 4, set in 1809 (p. 69), and a reprise of the same shot marks the return to 1809 at the start of scene 6 (p. 88). Noakes's steam engine represents the intrusion of the almost industrialized work in the redesigned garden. The piano represents passion. The present is initially noise free. Gus, who is closest to the earlier world, hates noise, because it prevents him from listening. For the others, the quietness represents the fact that messages from the past do not reach them clearly.

The National Theatre set used in the first London production, and adapted for the New York production at Lincoln Center, can be seen in the illustration referred to above (*Cambridge Companion to Tom Stoppard*, p. 226). John Fleming's authoritative work on Stoppard gives further details of these stagings of the play (*Stoppard's Theater: Finding Order amid Chaos*, p. 196). The front curtain was based on a theme from Nicolas Poussin and depicted a vision of Eden with Eve offering the apple.

A production at Zurich, however, represented the setting as much shabbier and used a skrim. Lit from in front, a skrim is opaque; lit from behind it is translucent and gives an effect of dissolve. The skrim showed an idealized landscape in the Poussin/Lorraine tradition and dominated the wall. In dissolve it showed the garden, where characters might be seen; if they then entered the room, the skrim would become opaque again. Fleming reports Stoppard as finding this "a very brilliant notion," though it was against his original intentions (p. 291).

Another difference at Zurich was in the portrayal of Gus. "He didn't say anything, but it didn't seem important," Fleming reports Stoppard as saying. "[T]here's nothing spooky about it. He files. A lot of the time he just hangs out. And I liked it" (p. 292). It is an important illumination that Gus "files:" he puts information away and knows where to find it.

CLASSICAL THEATER

The description of the London/New York set is reminiscent of the traditions of Greek and Roman theater. An upstage wall (the "scene" in classical terms), representing doors and windows, puts the action "outside" (outside the palace in Aeschylus' *Agamemnon*, outside the city walls in Sophocles' *Antigone*, and curiously outside both the house and the garden in *Arcadia*). There are two entrances: one goes "in" (into the palace, the city, the house, respectively) and one goes "out" (to the country, the scene of the battle, the garden).

One of the conventions of the classical theater is that most action takes place offstage: in *Arcadia*, very little of the action takes place onstage, except action that establishes the documents (the challenges, Charity Chater's note, Bernard's lecture). The expulsion of Brice and the Chaters takes place offstage and is relayed to Septimus by Jellaby, who is therefore a "messenger," a character whose function is to report action. Because he has witnessed the events, by convention his report is veridical: we accept it as true. It is precisely because Hannah is not a witness to Thomasina's death that a problem can arise in interpreting her story.

A second convention of the classical theater is one that generally limits the number of actors on stage to two or at most three. One actor (the protagonist) is always present as one character only; the other actors take appropriate other roles. A similar convention is particularly noticeable in the 1809–1812 scenes in *Arcadia.* Except briefly in scene 7, when his entry is preceded by an irruption of Thomasina and Augustus (p. 102), Septimus is always present. Generally he appears in a two-hander with Thomasina, but in scene 6, where Thomasina does not appear, there are broadly two two-handers, one at the start with Jellaby (pp. 88–90) and one with Lady Croom (pp. 91–96). There is also a strong drive toward the creation of two-handers (Hannah and Valentine, Hannah and Bernard) in the scenes set in the present.

INTRODUCING BERNARD

The opening of scene 2, which introduces the present, is curiously absurdist (pp. 19–20). We discover Hannah Jarvis, whose only function is to establish by her clothes that we are now in the present. Otherwise her presence is unmotivated. She then makes an unmotivated exit, without having done anything except compare Noakes's plan book with the view outside (which we cannot see). Felicity Kendal, the original Hannah, is one of those actresses who always gets a storm of applause for getting in from the dressing room ("Thank God, it's not the understudy"), and it may be that Stoppard wished to isolate this demonstration from any action; her immediate exit would then underline Hannah's isolation from both the audience and from 1809.

Enter Chloë and Bernard. Chloë immediately exits to the garden in search of Hannah, saying "Hang on." The text then reads, including two stage directions:

> *Bernard hangs on. The second door opens and Valentine looks in.*
> VALENTINE: Sod.
> *Valentine goes out again, closing the door.*
>
> (p. 20)

It is only after this that Bernard finds himself in a series of two-handers, first with Chloë, then with Valentine, and finally with Hannah. During the conversation with Valentine, it becomes clear that Bernard has more idea than Valentine does about what is going on in the house, which is open to the public on this occasion. Anybody who has ever started work in a new office will understand Bernard's feelings about all this, and empathize with his sense of dislocation.

THE SHAKESPEARIAN ELEMENT

Stoppard quotes directly from *Anthony and Cleopatra* at the start of scene 3 (p. 46), where Septimus has given Thomasina a piece of Latin to translate unprepared. It is not, as Jim Hunter suggests (*A Faber Critical Guide: Tom Stoppard*, p. 255) "a passage from the Roman Historian Plutarch." That passage, which is in Greek, not Latin, is adequately represented by Sir Thomas North's translation of 1579 that Shakespeare used as his source. (See, for example, Michael Neill, ed., *The Tragedy of Anthony and Cleopatra*, Oxford: Clarendon Press, 1994, p. 332.). It does not match what Thomasina has at all. This is a translation into Latin of Enobarbus' description of Cleopatra at her first meeting with Anthony: "The barge she sat in . . . ." One of Septimus' messages to Thomasina here is, "You think you know this. You know about love from the outside, but it presents problems. You have to be able to translate in order to understand." Further, as Paul Edwards observes, Thomasina's difficulty with it shows how much meaning has been lost, how much noise the process of translating English to Latin and back has generated. Meaning is not always preserved through transformation. (See "Science in *Hapgood* and *Arcadia*," in *The Cambridge Companion to Tom Stoppard*, p. 179.)

This unseen is a peculiar document, illustrating Stoppard's interest in the problems of reproducing in a new language a text of genuine literary merit. The Latin text cannot be reached directly by considering what Thomasina says, because she is construing it; she takes sets of words that can be separated in the original text but which belong together logically (nouns plus adjectives, verbs plus objects) and reads them together. The original has been rendered into Latin hexameters as used by Virgil in the *Aeneid.* The words used must follow strict patterns based on the occurrence of short and long vowels within the words. Some of the phrases used fit the pattern: *Velis purpureis* (or, better, *Purpureis velis*), meaning "with purple sails," would make a good first half of a line, and *sedio regina sedebat,* meaning "the queen was sitting on a throne," would make a good second half of a line. But almost anyone translating this text would produce something very like these two half lines. Even if we came across an original that matched these details, we could not be completely sure it was the one Thomasina was looking at.

The text is full of items that reflect the problems of translation, beginning with things that ought to work but do not and have to be abandoned. For example, *insessa* does not mean "seated in," it means "besieged." *Musica* does not mean "the sound made by instruments," it means "the abstract art of music." Secondly, some of the words (*imperabat* and *descriptionem*) cannot fit into the line because of their syllable pattern.

More centrally, Shakespeare and Virgil differ in their use of metaphor. Shakespeare regularly introduces a metaphorical word or phrase and moves on. Virgil almost never does this, preferring always to mark off such a figure with a word that converts it into a simile (*sicut, velut* which mean "like"). Shakespeare says Cleopatra's barge "burned"; his listeners know at once it did not really burn, but it was as though it was burning in some way—it was bright or dazzling, perhaps. So how to represent the metaphor in Virgil's terms? Preserve it, and make something non-Virgilian? Or abandon it and make something less than Shakespearean?

Thomasina's reading rejects the metaphorical. She reads "the queen was seated in fire" and,

because she knows her Latin poetry, she assumes at once that the phrase is literal and that this is a description of Queen Dido's suicide after her betrayal by Aeneas, when she burns herself alive on a funeral pyre. What has been lost is a feature impossible in Latin. Because of the tricky political context, Enobarbus avoids using Cleopatra's name—it is only spoken once in the scene. As a result, since he always refers to her simply as "she," Cleopatra becomes the archetypal woman. Later in the scene he says, "Age cannot weary her nor custom stale / Her infinite variety": love is preserved and renewed through the iterations within a relationship. Further, woman is magical in her sexual passion, "the holy priests / Bless her when she is riggish," and her sexuality has an element of the girl in it: "I saw her once / Hop forty paces through the public street."

There are two interesting lines about the reception of poetry in this scene. First, Septimus says, "Put more poetry into it," as though either poetry was harder to do than prose ("Put more effort into it") or as though poetry was an extra ingredient you add to a basic prose mixture ("Put more cinnamon into it"). Both are, in effect, philistine responses (p. 47). Secondly, when Septimus, offering to translate, simply recites Shakespeare's original lines, Thomasina accuses him of cheating, partly because he is avoiding the effort of translation but principally because he has been making a mystery where there is none (p. 51).

At the end of Shakespeare's play, Cleopatra has lured Anthony back to Egypt, and both lovers are destroyed in the events that follow. What will follow if Thomasina lures Septimus?

At the time of writing *Arcadia,* Stoppard was working on the script of *Shakespeare in Love,* which includes the triumph of *Romeo and Juliet* (whose original working title in the film was *Romeo and Ethel, the Pirate's Daughter*). Queen Elizabeth I intervenes to save the cast from the consequences of allowing the part of Juliet to be taken by a girl, Shakespeare's lover, Viola, but the queen is powerless to set aside the social rule that Viola must go with her husband to Virginia. In his loss, Shakespeare begins work (unhistorically) on *Twelfth Night*, starting at act 1, scene 2, where Viola's ship is wrecked on the coast of some virgin country and only she survives.

Much of the action of the 1809 scenes is reminiscent of Shakespeare's *Twelfth Night*. Clearly the business with the duel and the expulsion of Byron, Brice, and the Chaters in *Arcadia* owes much to *Twelfth Night* and is a transformation of items within that text. *Arcadia* also reinterprets Viola/Cesario's response to Olivia's threatened denial of Orsino. "I would not understand it," Viola says. "Why, what would you?" Olivia asks, and Viola replies, "Make me a willow cabin at your gates / And call upon my soul [that is, yourself] within the house" (*Twelfth Night*, act 1, scene 5). Thomasina will not accept Septimus' denial of her love, but it is Septimus, if we are to believe Hannah's account of the hermit, who will end up in the cabin.

One of the closest parallels is between Malvolio's misreading of the letter he finds and Bernard Nightingale's misreading of the texts within *The Couch of Eros*. Malvolio convinces himself that the letter he finds is from Olivia, because he wishes it to be, and that if he follows through the instructions it contains he will have greatness thrust upon him (*Twelfth Night*, act 2, scene 5). Nightingale convinces himself that the challenge is to Byron because he wishes it to be. It will give the world an explanation of why Byron left England in 1809, it will establish two reviews of Chater's poems in the *Piccadilly Review* as being by Byron, and above all it will bring Bernard fame.

When in *Twelfth Night* Malvolio had been taken away to be tormented by Maria and the Clown, thinking it was part of a test of his love for Olivia, he had quoted the proverb "Nightingales answer daws": the wise must respond to the chattering of fools. A great comic scene in *Arcadia* occurs when Bernard Nightingale rehearses his paper before an audience of daws in the shape of Hannah, Chloë, and Valentine (p. 70ff.).

Parallel to *Twelfth Night* too are the sister-brother bonds (strong for Valentine-Chloë-Gus, weaker perhaps for Lady Croom–Captain Brice), the use of matched dressing to equate characters (Viola/Cesario with Sebastian, Gus with Augustus), and the assumption of false names (Cesario by Viola, Roderigo by Sebastian, and Peacock by Nightingale).

A NOTE ON NAMES

Like Shakespeare, Stoppard is happy to label his characters with indicative names. Shakespeare has semantically obvious names—Toby Belch the drunkard, Malvolio the malevolent steward. Stoppard uses the name Nightingale, with its echoes of Malvolio's proverb, and Valentine in *Twelfth Night* (despite his name) is the unsuccessful suitor to Olivia, who precedes Viola/Cesario.

"Nightingale" gives a good internal joke (p. 23). Nightingale has assumed the surname Peacock to conceal from Hannah the fact that he is the Nightingale who savaged her book in a review. Half-forgetting this, he says to Valentine, "I'm Bernard Nigh— I've come to see Miss Jarvis." The actor who played the part originally was Bill Nighy: it sounded as though he was about to commit the gaffe that haunts actors, referring to someone on stage, possibly themselves, by their real-world name rather than their dramatic name.

Hannah is a palindrome, apt for someone who can move from present to past and then back from past to present. Gus and Thomasina are fractal, to use a term to be discussed later. Gus is an unusual abbreviation, being the middle syllable of the full name Augustus, rather than the first syllable as is more usual for abbreviated names, and "Gus" can expand to left and right to become "Augustus," as Gus becomes Augustus when he dresses in period costume at the end of the play. Fractal displays also imply not just that we can see the part in the whole, we can also see the whole in the part. (Not only is "a" in "Thomas," "Thomas" is also "in" "a.") Finally, Septimus means "seventh son," a traditionally lucky or magically gifted character, and Hodge was a twentieth-century Cambridge mathematician who worked on the geometry of irregular solids.

ARCADIA: THE TRADITION OF THE NAME

Arcadia was a remote area of Greece of cut-off mountain valleys, and in classical poetry it had the reputation as a place where innocent shepherds and their lovers led lives of a pastoral simplicity in a golden age. There was a dark side to this pastoral idyll, the haunting presence of Death. Poussin's painting *The Arcadian Shepherds* (Louvre, Paris, dated 1638) represents three young shepherd boys and a female companion examining with some puzzlement a tomb on which they can make out a Latin inscription: ET IN ARCADIA EGO ("and / even in Arcadia I . . ."). This has to be a claim by the dead shepherd, "Here I am in Arcadia" if it is to be an epitaph at all, and that is the comfortable translation Lady Croom selects (p. 16).

Later Septimus cites the alternative translation, where Death is the "I," in talking of the shooting of the game birds:

SEPTIMUS: A calendar of slaughter. Even in Arcadia, there am I!
THOMASINA: Oh, phooey to Death!

It is at that point that Thomasina draws the figure of the hermit into Noakes's sketch (p. 18). Unwittingly she enters Septimus into one of the documents that will be read by the future, just as the dead birds go into one of the other documents, the game book: she has changed and falsified the evidence.

Arcadia is a garden, even an Eden. One of the themes of the play is the bitter regret felt by Lady Croom in 1809, and by Hannah in the present, that the estate is being ruined by successive redesigning of the grounds.

THE APPLE

The apple that Gus presents to Hannah (p. 45), in a reversal of the Eden story, becomes the apple whose leaf Thomasina draws and that Septimus feeds to his tortoise. Together, the apple and the tortoise reach across time.

In Eden, the apple represents the temptation to seek the knowledge of good and evil, but it is also reminiscent of Newton: the falling of an apple from a tree illustrates gravitational attraction. Newtonian physics is a temptation, discussed by Valentine and Chloë, in which Valentine also mentions Eve's apple. Broadly the temptation is to believe the universe is deterministic rather than chaotic.

VALENTINE: . . . you could predict everything to come—I mean, you'd need a computer as big as the universe but the formula would exist.
CHLOË: But it doesn't work, does it?
VALENTINE: No . . . the math is different.

Chloë believes "the only thing going wrong is people fancying people who aren't supposed to be in that part of the plan." As in other readings of Eden, the sexual drive is the principle of chaos (p. 97).

ALTERNATIVE HISTORY

Looking back at the past we see only a single line of history, and we feel that those who lived through this history have only one possible script to follow. We do not, however, feel that we are bound to a script that will be read two hundred years into our future. The debate on whether we have free will or are subject to determinism is central to *Arcadia* and is mirrored in the consideration of Newtonian science (highly deterministic) and chaos theory (deterministic but with local windows of spontaneity).

Thomasina invents, almost casually, an entire modern literary subgenre, the alternative history, which is based on the premise that a single divergence in the past from the history line we have today would produce a totally changed present.

> THOMASINA: If Queen Elizabeth [the First] had been a Ptolemy, history would have been quite different—we would be admiring the pyramids of Egypt and the Great Sphinx of Verona.
> SEPTIMUS: God save us.

She does not simply say that history would have been different if Queen Elizabeth had been a Ptolemy; others had already made similar points. Blaise Pascal, the French mathematician (1623–1662), had said: "Cleopatra's nose: if it had been shorter, the whole face of the earth would have changed." As in alternative history, Thomasina also begins to work out how everyday experience would be different as a result—art, especially, would be changed.

Such works usually produce Septimus' reaction in the reader. Anything else would be worse than what we have now. They comfort and confirm; they reconcile us to determinism (p. 50).

One of the most famous among English alternative histories is Kingsley Amis' *The Alteration* (1976) where the English Reformation has failed and a repressive Catholicism dominates Europe. Interestingly, Cowley, in our world a suburb of Oxford, is the capital of England and is called Coverley.

THE SCIENTIFIC COMPONENT

Probably no other recent play has created as much public interest in hard science as *Arcadia*, and this fact must be part of our reading of it. Stoppard uses math models covering iteration, catastrophe theory, and its associated discipline deterministic chaos theory. There is also consideration of entropy, and the heat death of the universe, as predicted by the second law of thermodynamics. In 1959 in his Rede Lecture *The Two Cultures and the Scientific Revolution*, C. P. Snow, who was both a scientist and a novelist, argued for an extension of scientific education and had proposed the second law of thermodynamics as an example of a scientific principle that every educated person should understand. This in turn led to a fierce attack on him by Dr. F. R. Leavis, who defended humanist, literary values. Nadel reports that Trevor Nunn, the producer (a pupil of Leavis), picked up the reference to this debate in *Arcadia* (*Double Act,* p. 440). Stoppard's achievement was to make literary use of these models derived from science. In this respect, John Fleming's analysis should be consulted (see chapter 10: "*Arcadia,*" in *Stoppard's Theater,* pp. 191–207). Stoppard does more than simply include explicatory speeches in the play: elements of the dramatic structure mirror the scientific ideas under discussion.

THOMASINA'S SCIENCE

ENTROPY.

Thomasina takes a bowl of rice pudding (warm, say, and white) and puts into it a spoonful of jam (strawberry, say, cold and red). She has in front of her an ordered system: the rice pudding here, the jam there, separate and differentiated. She then stirs the ordered system with her spoon, creating a pink streak. Both the rice pudding and the jam contribute to the streak. First they contribute data. The rice pudding tells the streak about being white, and the jam tells it about being red, so the streak is able to build up its own data set about how to be pink. Secondly they contribute energy, from their varying conditions of heat and cohesion (pp. 4–5).

What Thomasina realizes, and Septimus confirms, is that she cannot stir the pink back so that the jam data and energy and the rice pudding data and energy can be separated and recovered. This means that, since we cannot reverse the process, we cannot reverse time. Secondly she realizes that in the end everything in the bowl will be pink; the original order, the separation, will have been destroyed and there can be no further exchanges of data or energy. This is a local entropy. Heat, for her, is the most convincing feature that demonstrates this; heat leaks out into the environment, it equalizes itself out. It cannot be returned to an original ordered, differentiated state. Valentine makes the same point: your cup of tea is getting cold, he reminds Hannah. Why does it never get hot by itself? (p. 104). Mr. Noakes's Newcomen engine must give back less energy than the energy needed to run it, says Thomasina's diagram (pp. 113–115). She deduces the second law of thermodynamics.

There is an important sense in which the scenes set in the present represent a greater degree of entropy than those of 1809–1812. This point is discussed below.

ITERATION, CATASTROPHE, CHAOS

ITERATION.

Suppose you want to make a list of all the even numbers. You take three integer numbers, A, B, and Seed (integers are whole numbers, with no fractions attached). Set $A = 0$ and $B = 0$, and choose any value you like for Seed. It is called Seed because it starts the iteration going. You can pick your Seed randomly if you wish. You then use an algorithm, a set of rules for proceeding, like this:

1. If $A = 0$ and $B = 0$ then let $A = $ Seed and $B = $ (Seed + 1).
2. If $A > 0$ then add $2A$ to the list of even numbers and let $A = (A-1)$.
3. Add $2B$ to the list of even numbers and let $B = (B + 1)$.
4. Repeat the above from 1.

Once you've done the initial set, the algorithm generates the values it needs for A and B in the next iteration: this is "feedback." When A reaches 0 again, it stops generating new values, but B can go on forever. Notice that rule 1 only operates the first time the algorithm runs, and this is a regular feature of iterations. Also, once A reaches 0, you cannot deduce the initial seed value. In effect, once again, you cannot reverse time. If you run the iteration again and chose the same seed, you get the same output; the algorithm generates even numbers in the same order as it did on the first run.

Thomasina uses an iteration to plot coordinates on a graph. As more and more coordinates are penciled in, patterns begin to emerge representing natural objects—leaves, for example. The Coverly Set shows how such natural objects have an underlying order, rather like the order Benoit Mandelbrot had found in fractals. "How long is the coast of Britain?" Mandelbrot had asked; the answer is that as we look at the coastline in increasingly smaller scales we perceive a repetition of similar, irregular ("fractal") patterns, every part becoming a new whole with its hierarchy of parts beneath it (Nadel, *Double Act*, p. 579, note 36).

Speeches are iterated in the play. Lady Croom twice asks Thomasina how old she is "today" (pp. 17, 112). Valentine iterates to Chloë a remark Septimus makes to Thomasina (pp. 7, 97). Situations are iterated too, such as Bernard's situation in respect of Hannah; Chloë and Lady Croom iterates Septimus' situation in respect of Mrs. Chater, Thomasina, and his Lady Croom. It also inverts it. Because of his different sexuality, Bernard succeeds only with the youngest, and is discovered by Lady Croom in an iteration of the fear that had probably haunted Septimus.

CHAOS.

Valentine wants to write an iterated program that models the number of grouse found on the estate year by year as deduced from the game books that record the number of grouse shot. This population figure is a determined chaos; it looks random, but actually it is governed by extremely complex formulas, like the pattern water makes on the surface of a stream. The formulas will give him the algorithm.

Some of the formulas can take last year's figures and predict part of this year's: How many grouse survive? How many chicks would those survivors produce? Some co-vary with other systems. How many foxes are there? Does the number of foxes vary with the number of grouse? We may find that the more grouse, the more food for foxes, and so the more fox cubs: this is "positive feedback," and unchecked positive feedback destroys systems. What normally happens is that more fox cubs mean more grouse being eaten by foxes. Eventually, as a direct result, there is less food for foxes, and so fewer fox cubs: this is the "negative feedback" that keeps systems stable. Valentine will either find a formula for this covariance of grouse and foxes or he will build a separate program to model the fox population and input data from that into the grouse program.

When the program is finished, he will input a pseudo-random Seed (a real fraction between 0 and 1, like 0.3574). This will model the fact that the system seems to be random. As the program runs, the new value output to seed the next iteration will settle down and the run will produce either a single value repeated year by year, or a short loop. The first pattern might go, for example: 1901, 348 grouse; 1902, 348 grouse; 1903, 348 grouse; 1904, 348 grouse. The second pattern might go 1901, 348 grouse; 1902, 572 grouse; 1903, 298 grouse; 1904, 348 grouse. If the output of the program matches the figures in the game books, Valentine has found the right formula.

But he is frustrated by noise—unstructured input that he cannot model. For example, one of the ways grouse are removed from the moors is when local people come in and steal them, a crime called poaching. Suppose a new game-

keeper is better or worse than the previous gamekeeper at stopping poachers? Suppose Lord Croom rounds up all the poachers and transports them to Australia? Such events will affect the grouse population, but Valentine cannot know about them, so the effects they produce are simply noise. "Very hard to spot the tune. Like a piano in the next room, it's playing your song, but . . . it's out of whack."

HANNAH: What do you do?
VALENTINE: You start guessing what the tune might be . . . putting in notes which are missing or not quite the right notes—and bit by bit . . . the lost algorithm.

(pp. 60–61)

Valentine also realizes that Thomasina had been doing the reverse to what he is doing. She starts with the algorithm and iterates it to produce her leaves; he has his game books and must produce his algorithm.

Chaos theory also includes two further features that figure in *Arcadia*. The "butterfly effect" suggests that small variations at the beginning of a run can produce a large effect later on. Nowadays this is often stated as "A butterfly landing on a leaf produces a storm a thousand miles away." Ray Bradbury popularized this concept in a his 1952 short story "A Sound of Thunder," in *R Is for Rocket*. Thomasina's drawing of the hermit in the game book is a butterfly.

Secondly, it suggests local effect is centrally important and that there will be windows of order even within deterministic chaos. Stoppard wishes to show a universe with an order that is not governed by the remorseless determinism of Newtonian physics but by the organic order that emerges from chaos.

One of the behaviors possible in a chaotic system is a bifurcation—the same pattern begins to be repeated several times simultaneously. A lake, for example, may have several distinct whirlpool patterns. In the scenes set in the present, Thomasina's relationship with Septimus is iterated separately for Valentine, Chloë, and Gus, the men with Hannah, the woman with Bernard.

CATASTROPHE.

An important underlying concept in chaos theory is the catastrophe theory of René Thom. Popularized in an influential article by E. C. Zeeman ("Catastrophe Theory," *Scientific American* 234, April 1976), catastrophe theory deals with events that represent not "disasters" but "turn-overs" (the Greek word has both meanings). Zeeman looked at such behavior as that of a dog in a scrap with another dog. It has two and only two modes of action, fight and flight, and it will characteristically switch suddenly from one to the other. Each switch is a "catastrophe." Such systems are always the result of two variables interacting—in this case aggression (which motivates "fight") and submission (which motivates "flight"). As the values of these variables change, the behavior changes. The system "bifurcates"—it has two distinct subsystems. Catastrophes often give rise to chaos in case they switch more and more rapidly (a dripping faucet represents a catastrophe, switching from gathering water for the drip to releasing it; turn the faucet on and you have a characteristic chaos—running water).

Stoppard had extended catastrophe theory into the moral sphere in his play *Professional Foul* (first TV production 1977, published in *The Television Plays 1965–1984*). Here he used it to model Professor Anderson's change of mind that results in his deciding to help his former pupil defy the Czech police state. The situation in *Arcadia* is referred to below.

THE HEAD AND THE HEART

If this intellectual content were all, it would be a great deal: the theater is not overstocked with plays whose pleasure depends in part on generating this kind of excitement. But *Arcadia* is more: it is a play in the continental tradition of Arthur Schnitzler or Ferenc Molnar that looks at the way in which our existential situation depends on the fact that we face an individual death (our own personal entropy), for which we cannot prepare. We must live as hard as we can and engage in two quests. The first is the pursuit of intellectual understanding—otherwise "we're going out the way we came in," as Hannah says, half quoting the *Rubaiyat of Omar Khayyam* (p. 100). In our pursuit of intellectual understanding we may be frustrated or mistaken: in the end, as Septimus says, "We die on the march. But there is nothing outside the march so nothing can be lost to it. The missing plays of Sophocles will turn up piece by piece or be written again" (pp. 50–51).

The second quest is the pursuit of love, without hypocrisy, seeing ourselves as sexual beings even if we are calculating and exploitative (Lady Croom exploits Septimus, Septimus exploits Mrs. Chater, Bernard exploits Chloë). In our pursuit of love we may not get what we want (Thomasina does not get Septimus, Bernard does not get Hannah) or we may find out that what we get is not what we want (as Chloë does not get what she wants from Bernard). The phrase "bittersweet" is regularly used in discussions of this tradition: for an example of the feeling, compare Rodgers and Hammerstein's *Carousel*, which is based on a work by Molnar.

WOMEN IN LOVE

Stoppard creates four strong female roles, two in the 1809–1812 scenes and two in the present, and offers interesting parallels and contrasts in their relationships. In terms of entropy Thomasina ("an uncomplicated girl" according to a stage direction, p. 19) is a young system; she pours out data and she takes in data—her thinking is fast and profound. She is young in terms of energy—she enjoys her food, asking Jellaby what is for dinner; "Oh, goody" is her response

(p. 6). Stoppard sketches in the girlishness in her language without intruding it. She runs onto the stage in pursuit of her brother, and she wants to learn to waltz. Her curiosity about "carnal embrace" is intellectual, not prurient, and she points up its contradictions with wit: "Mrs. Chater [gave me] a note for you. She said it was of scant importance, and therefore I should carry it to you with the utmost safety, urgency and diligence. Does carnal embrace addle the brain?" "Invariably," Septimus answers (pp. 18–19).

This is the thirteen-year-old Thomasina; the slightly older girl is subtly different. Septimus recognizes the change in his role; he says to Augustus of his work with Thomasina, not entirely humorously, "I do not rule here, my lord. I inspire by reverence for learning and the exaltation of knowledge whereby man might approach God" (p. 106).

Lady Croom is given some magnificent lines representing a pastiche of Lady Bracknell from Oscar Wilde's *Importance of Being Earnest.* Of Byron's reported urge to travel abroad, which she deplores, she says, "The whole of Europe is in a Napoleonic fit, all the best ruins will be closed, the roads entirely occupied with the movements of armies . . . and the fashion for godless republicanism not yet arrived at its natural reversion" (p. 54).

The characterization of Lady Croom is an example of Stoppard's use of catastrophe in dramatic construction. One drive tells her that respectability demands she expel the Chaters and Byron from the house; the other drive feels the need for sexual adventure, especially with Byron. After discovering Byron emerging from Mrs. Chater's room, she turns into "expel" mode, only to turn back to "retain" mode when faced with Septimus' subtle flattery.

The drives continue through time. By 1812 she has moved on, now wanting the Polish pianist Zelinsky. Septimus' consequent heartache is sketched in very lightly. Now it is Thomasina who wants to marry Byron and thinks he has been encouraging her, as Septimus has not.

In 1809–1812 Sidley Park is relevant in English social life; the family enjoys wealth and prestige. Lady Croom may not like what Noakes is doing in the park, but energy is going into the project. She is as energetic in her pursuit of her lovers as Thomasina is of Septimus. Also there is a sense that Thomasina and Septimus are devoting themselves to learning for its own sake. Chater is a terrible poet but will later be a competent biologist, part of the movement that explores and classifies the natural life of the whole world. Byron's visit may end in farce, but he recognizes Sidley Park as worth visiting, as Hannah will recognize it as worth researching. Even in the presence of Jellaby there is a sense of a domestic order working in the background.

In the scenes in the present, we have the sense of things running down. The house has no function in society any more, except as a place to visit. Hannah, Bernard, and Gus all live in the past of the house; Valentine looks elsewhere. Lord Croom is a mass of tedious eccentricities, hating typewritten letters and Japanese cars—hating modern life, in fact. In a faint echo of the earlier Lady Croom's libido, the modern Lady Croom lends Bernard her bicycle as a form of safe sex (p. 67). Mercifully, neither of these Crooms appears.

Hannah is direct in her view of Chloë. "[S]he's old enough to vote on her back," she says (p. 98)—like Thomasina, in fact. Why do we reject this as a view of Thomasina but accept it as a view of Chloë? Why does it seem so likely that Bernard should exploit Thomasina, where Septimus had not exploited Thomasina? The answer must be that the house is no longer Arcadia.

But when Hannah tries to comfort Chloë after Bernard rejects her, Chloë in turn rejects Hannah's overtures (p. 128). She has her youthful naiveties: "You've been deeply wounded in the past, haven't you, Hannah?" she asks "earnestly" (p. 75). It is a young person's view. Passing through endless iterations of encountering the predatory Bernards and the vague Valentines, Hannah has reached entropy.

"Believe me it gets less important," she tells Chloë (p. 45). To Hannah, love is no longer a demand for the exchange of energy or data. It is a pink rice pudding.

Select Bibliography

EDITION

Arcadia. London: Faber and Faber, 1993. Reprinted in *Plays 5*, 1999.

OTHER WORKS BY STOPPARD

Rosencrantz and Guildenstern Are Dead. London: Faber, 1967.

Stoppard The Television Plays London 1965–1984. London: 1993. Reprinted as *Plays 3*, 1998.

SECONDARY WORKS

Fleming, John. *Stoppard's Theatre: Finding Order amid Chaos.* Austin: University of Texas Press, 2001. (Extremely perceptive. The author has regular access to the Stoppard archive at Texas.)

Hodgson, Terry, ed. *The Plays of Tom Stoppard for Stage, Radio, TV and Film.* Cambridge: Icon, 2001.

Kelly, Katherine, ed. *The Cambridge Companion to Tom Stoppard.* Cambridge: Cambridge University Press, 2001. (An essential collection of critical essays.)

Nadel, Ira. *Double Act: A Life of Tom Stoppard.* London: Methuen, 2002. (Unauthorized biography but full and detailed. Nadel is a professor of English at the University of British Columbia, and his book contains good background.)

Geoffrey Chaucer's
The Canterbury Tales

N. S. THOMPSON

WRITTEN IN THE last quarter of the fourteenth century, the *Canterbury Tales* re-creates in dramatic form the narratives told by a group of pilgrims as they journey from London to the popular shrine of St. Thomas à Beckett in Canterbury, some fifty miles southeast of the capital in Kent. Medieval pilgrimage was a reminder of the Christian pathway to God but was also undertaken specifically to pray at a saint's shrine as an act of penance or for intercession with regard to health or other matters. In England, the two most popular shrines were Our Lady of Walsingham in East Anglia and St. Thomas à Beckett at Canterbury, both renowned for their effect on health. At Canterbury, small pewter ampullae (flasks) were sold as souvenirs with the Latin motto *Optimus egrorum medicus fit Thomas bonorum* (For good people [who are sick] St. Thomas is the best of physicians). Nevertheless, the popularity of pilgrimages soon led to criticism that they were little more than social outings, although the great pilgrimages to Jerusalem or to the shrine of St. James of Compostella in northern Spain were both costly and dangerous.

The convivial reality of pilgrimages seen against their devotional intent was obviously a ripe target for both preacher and satirist. With vivid irony Chaucer creates not only a company of pilgrims who are—with notable exceptions—mainly irreligious individuals, but who also represent the new social and economic conditions of the late middle ages. But Chaucer cleverly adds a perspective on this contemporary aspect of the tale and teller but combining them with those having a historical dimension.

Western Europe in the fourteenth century was undergoing radical dislocation in the accelerated breakup of the feudal system brought about by the growth of towns and the burgeoning markets of the mercantile economy, aided by developments in banking and credit. The move to urban life was also given drastic impetus by the devastating plague known as the Black Death in 1348 (with recurring episodes), which offered survivors the possibility of leaving traditional rural situations to seek new urban opportunities created by increased demand for labor and services.

Furthermore, there was a renewed call for the Church to become more responsive to its believers and return to its apostolic status as spiritual leader and guide. Despite earlier attempts at grassroots renewal, such as the founding of the

Franciscan friars (1209) and the Dominicans (1216), the Church was still a powerful landowning corporation, its wealth and political importance second to none. In the fourteenth century, there was renewed pressure for disendowment and the creation of a "poor Church." Fearing the possible success of such pressures, and with fierce rivalry among the college of cardinals, Philip the Fair, the King of France, transferred the Papacy to Avignon in 1309, where it was ruled by a succession of French popes until 1378, when a rival Italian pope was elected in the traditional papal seat of Rome. This state of affairs, known as the Great Schism, lasted until 1417. In England during this time, the followers of the reforming theologian John Wycliffe c. 1330–1384, known as the Lollards, were campaigning for an end to papal power, the eventual disendowment of the Church, a new emphasis on the Bible as sole mediator between man and God, and even creating an English Bible for general use. Very influential in Chaucer's day, the Lollard movement was firmly quashed early in the fifteenth century, its aims and ideals only taken up again in the Protestant Reformation.

Finally, during Chaucer's lifetime and beyond, England was locked in a protracted struggle with France, known as the Hundred Years' War (1337–1453), a series of campaigns in which the English were gradually driven from the Angevin territories inherited from the Norman Conquest. Chaucer himself took part at the siege of Rheims in 1359 and was with John of Gaunt's expeditionary forces in 1369 and 1370.

Chaucer was therefore writing during a time of significant change, in an age where the old ideals of the medieval world were disappearing, yet could still be recalled as touchstones in an era of uncertainty. The reading of the *Canterbury Tales* that follows will put fresh emphasis on aspects of "old" and "new" in the work, looking at the contrast between worlds past and present and the rift between public and private worlds created under changing conditions.

CHRONOLOGY

1340?	Geoffrey Chaucer born in London, son of John Chaucer, a prosperous wine merchant, and his wife Agnes.
1357	Geoffrey appears as a page in the household records of Elizabeth, Countess of Ulster, wife of Lionel, the second son of Edward III, and later Duke of Clarence.
1360	In the service of Prince Lionel in France he is captured at the siege of Rheims and ransomed. Continues in royal service for the next fifteen years, receiving regular payments and gifts.
1365	Marriage to Philippa, also in the service of Elizabeth, and thought to be sister to Katherine Swynford, who was mistress and subsequently third wife of John of Gaunt, Duke of Lancaster.
1366	Death of father; his mother remarries. February–May: on a diplomatic mission to Navarre (Spain).
1367	Receives an annuity of 20 marks as esquire of the royal household. Birth of son, Thomas. Translating from and perhaps composing poetry in French.
1368–1369	Death of Blanche, Duchess of Lancaster. He later composes *The Book of the Duchess*. Campaigning with John of Gaunt's expeditionary force in France.
1372	Appointed Esquire of the King's Chamber. Diplomatic trip to Genoa and Florence.
1374	Appointed controller of customs of hides, skins, and wool in the port of London. Lives rent-free in apartments over the city gates at Aldgate.
1380–1381	Birth of son Lewis. *The Parliament of Fowls* written.
1385	Member of the commission of the peace in Kent, where he is probably resident. Completes *Troilus and Criseyde* about this time, together with *Boece*, his translation of *The Consolation of Philosophy* by Boethius.

1386	Gives up lease on Aldgate apartment. Member of Parliament for Kent for one session. Resigns from customs post.
1387	Death of Philippa. Begins *Canterbury Tales* around this time and continues working on it up to his death.
1389	Appointed clerk of the king's works, overseeing building and maintenance of royal estates and residences.
1391	Resigns from post as clerk of king's works. Appointed deputy forester of royal estate in Somerset, but no evidence he moved there. He continued to receive extra gifts and grants from the crown in addition to his usual payments.
1392	Composes *The Equatorie of Planets,* an astronomical work.
1394	Receives royal annuity of £20.
1397	Receives a tun (barrel) of wine a year as royal grant.
1399	Takes lease on house in grounds of Westminster Abbey.
1400	Dies on 25 October (a traditional date), buried in Westminster Abbey. Tomb later moved to form first occupant of Poet's Corner.

THE TEXT

The tales in the standard *Riverside* edition (1987) are grouped into ten fragments following one of the earliest known manuscripts of the work, the Ellesmere Manuscript (now in the Huntingdon Library, San Marino, California), comprising those of: (I) Knight, Miller, Reeve, Cook; (II) Man of Law; (III) Wife of Bath, Friar, Summoner; (IV) Clerk, Merchant; (V) Squire, Franklin; (VI) Physician, Pardoner; (VII) Shipman, Prioress, *Sir Thopas, Melibee,* Monk, Nun's Priest; (VIII) Second Nun, Canon's Yeoman; (IX) Manciple; (X) Parson. Although internal links from narrative to narrative suggest this order, its arrangement is not definitive as there are discrepancies in the match of tale to teller and in geographical references. With other

evidence, it is taken that the work was unfinished at the time of Chaucer's death and was assembled for manuscript publication by other hands. Nevertheless, the general opinion remains that there is enough of the work for it to be considered a complete and coherent whole, even if critics have often debated the idea of its unity.

SOURCES

What is most striking about the *Canterbury Tales* is the variety of narratives that Chaucer has gathered together in the work. They cover most, if not all, of the types of medieval fiction, including the sermon and moral treatise, as well as the more familiar beast fable and popular tales of everyday life, known as fabliaux. In some cases it is possible to pinpoint exactly the source of learned material Chaucer used, whereas the more popular tales have many different analogues, rather than exact sources. The reader is directed to the two-volume edition of *Sources and Analogues of the Canterbury Tales,* edited by Robert M. Correale and Mary Hamel (2002, 2003), as well as the endnotes in *Riverside,* for details. A third group of "literary" narratives have a source or analogue in the work of known literary authors, mainly from Italy. The works of Dante, Boccaccio, and Petrarch represent the emergence of authors of serious literature from the anonymous works of lyric and popular narrative arising from oral tradition, and again from authors of courtly love romances such as Chrétien de Troyes in France or Gottfried von Strassburg in Germany. Chaucer was well acquainted with the work of these Italian authors, as his many references show.

For the *Canterbury Tales* as a whole, the only model offering the same mixture of serious and comic, and same variety of narratives set in a frame, is Giovanni Boccaccio's *Decameron* (c. 1350), a collection of one hundred short tales in prose (novelle). Even if there is no direct reference to it in Chaucer's work, and several of the six narratives they share are transposed to different locations or elaborated or reshaped by Chaucer in some way, Boccaccio's work is the only one that provides a new setting for both serious and comic fiction among a company of narrators who are directed by one of their number, who discuss and criticize the variety of narratives according to whether they are *utile* (useful) or *diletto* (pleasant, amusing) and whether they are told in a serious fashion to instruct or simply to amuse. It should be mentioned that Boccaccio also portrays his contemporary world with a satiric thrust.

GENERAL PROLOGUE

After a celebrated blazon to the renewal of spring (*GP* 1–18), the pilgrimage frame is established in a series of twenty-one introductory sketches of the total of thirty pilgrims assembled in the Tabard Inn, Southwark. Although they conform to the medieval rhetorical tradition of description seen in books of Vices and Virtues, and in works such as the thirteenth-century French dream vision of the *Romance of the Rose* (c. 1235–1275), the pilgrims are more individual than anonymous generic representatives, although there has long been a debate as to how far they should be seen as stock medieval "types" or as modern "individuals." The solution is to see them as both, perhaps, in the way that Dante has historical and mythical figures to represent particular virtues or vices in the *Divine Comedy* (1320), rather than the usual allegorical personifications such as Sloth or Gluttony. Chaucer's pilgrims are sometimes very real individuals with names (Prioress, Friar), sometimes shadowy figures (Knight, Merchant, Nun's Priest) but whose virtues or vices, according to medieval Christian definition, are plain to see.

Chaucer was also perhaps following attempts to portray the shortcomings of the various classes and occupations in the form of an estates satire as found in John Gower's *Mirour de l'Omme* ("Mirror of Mankind," late 1370s), his later *Vox Clamantis* ("Voice of One Crying," 1380s) and the opening to William Langland's *Piers Plowman* (1380s). It was understood that the three estates (social classes)—consisting of the "men who pray" (clergy), "men who fight" (knights), and "men who work" (peasants)—were an interlocking unity, the clergy looking after mankind's spiritual welfare, the knights protecting mankind's social world, and the peasantry providing for mankind's sustenance. In contrast to this standard feudal model of society, Chaucer's pilgrims represent the mercantile and artisanal middle classes newly sprung up, together with characters such as the Summoner and Pardoner, who represent the wider extent and abuse of ecclesiastical power and influence.

Most importantly, these new middle classes reflect the introduction of a monetary economy into feudalism's exchange of goods and services. No matter how exploitative the feudal system was in practice, it was used as a model of life by writers of the time to explain how things had gone wrong in their own age: money allowed for private gain and self-interest over society's common good and bred corruption in both individual and institution.

Three figures stand out as moral touchstones in the *General Prologue*: knight, priest, and peasant. If the Knight is a "verray, parfit gentil knight" (a true, perfect, noble knight, *GP* 72) who loves "chivalrie, / Trouthe and honour, fredom and curtesie" (chivalry, truth and honor, generosity and refined manners, *GP* 45–46), he is an anachronism in the mercantile world, a warrior crusading long after the Crusades had finished (Jerusalem fell in 1244) and the use of mercenaries had become common across Europe. The trouble with Chaucer's virtuous Christian warrior is that there is no campaign worthy of him. The list of his campaigns extends all along the eastern and southern margins of Christendom (from Lithuania and Russia down through Turkey, round North Africa to southern Spain) in a chronology of over forty years that is impossible for one man to have accomplished. It is possible that Chaucer's knowledge of some dates was notional, but the whole adds up to a generic portrait rather than a recognizable individual. The rusty stains on his surcoat may be emblematic of his long and hard travel, but they also suggest a certain tarnishing and decline as both Crusades and knight errantry had long vanished. Nevertheless, his ideals were still valued.

The "povre persoun of a toun" (poor parish priest, *GP* 478) exhibits selfless working for the good of his community and represents a more effective promoter of Christendom's true ideals than the knight. His diligence in teaching, his willingness to live on a small income, to travel far and wide to look after his parishioners are praised: "This noble ensample to his sheep he yaf, / That first first he wroghte, and afterward he taughte (He gave a noble example to his flock, acting first as a model, then only teaching afterwards, *GP* 496–497), reinforced by the lines "Cristes loore and his apostles twelve / He taughte; but first he folwed it hymselve" (He taught the law of Christ and his twelve apostles, but first he followed it himself, *GP* 527–528). Noting that he has never been tempted to farm out his benefice to seek paid employment as a chantry priest or chaplain to a guild in London, Chaucer places his parish priest in the very center of the community as leader and guide, which has given rise to speculation about his possible Lollard sympathies.

Third, representing the peasantry is the priest's brother, a ploughman who exhibits the same sentiments for good and for the good of the community:

> God loved he best with al his hoole herte
> At alle tymes, thogh him gamed or smerte,
> And thanne his neighebor right as hymselve
> He wolde thresshe, and therto dyke and delve,
> For Christes sake, for every povre wight
> Withouten hire, if it lay in his myght.
>
> (He loved God best with his whole heart at all times, whether it pained him or pleased him, and

he would thresh for his neighbor as readily as for himself, and make ditches and dig for any poor person, for the sake of Christ and not for wages, if it lay in his power.)

(*GP* 533–538)

The rest of the company can be seen and judged against these three exemplary figures. In contrast, most of the other clerical and lay characters (with the clear exception of the Second Nun) have a private world that either competes with public office, or in some way represents their personal gain (usually monetary). The Monk (*GP* 165–207), who holds after the "newe world," would rather hunt and go about on business outside the monastery, having a great appetite for worldly things, while the Prioress (*GP* 118–162) has her "conscience" and "tender heart" focused on her pet dogs, (whom she feeds extravagantly on exotic tidbits), rather than on the care of souls. The Summoner, a server of summonses for an ecclesiastical court, which dealt with infractions of heresy, tithes, and sexual behavior, is portrayed graphically with a skin disorder and a great appetite for wine and food that aroused the senses. He minimizes the threat of excommunication that the court could exercise, emphasizing instead the amount a person could be fined. He knows all the secrets of his parish and is in a position to take bribes and other gifts. The Pardoner, named as his traveling companion, is of equally unsavory appearance, well known for selling false relics of saints (pigs' bones) and other artifacts, such as a portion of "Oure Lady veyl" (that is in fact a pillowcase). His greatest abuse is to usurp the office of preacher and then offer his "pardons" for money, when he was only strictly allowed to sell indulgences: "He moste preche and wel affile his tonge / To wynne silver, as he ful wel koude" (He had to preach and sharpen his tongue to gain silver, as he well knew how to do, *GP* 712–713). Chaucer's usual satiric technique here is to present the particular failing as if it were a positive feature, only to undercut it with some qualifying comment, as with those who openly desire private financial gain.

Friar: He was an esy man to yeve penaunce,
          Ther as he wiste to have good pitaunce.

(He was lenient when hearing confessions, especially when he expected to receive a gift.)

(GP 223–224)

Physician: And yet he was but esy of dispence;
          He kepte that he wan in pestilence.
          For gold in physik is a cordial,
          Therefore he lovede gold in special.

(And yet he was careful with his money, keeping what he gained during times of plague. For gold in medicine is a cure for the heart, therefore he loved gold in particular.)

(GP 441–444)

Miller:
Wel koude he stelen corn and tollen thries;
And yet he hadde a thombe of gold, pardee.

(He knew very well how to steal corn and charge three times over; indeed, he had a thumb of gold [mark of a miller from testing grain, but also a reference to their traditional dishonesty].)

(GP 562–563)

Reeve:
He koude bettre than his lord purchace.
Ful riche he was astored pryvely.
His lord wel koude he plesen
   subtilly,
To yeve and lene hym his owene good,
And have a thank, and yet a cote and hood.

(He knew how to buy property better than his lord. He secretly provided himself with riches. He knew cunningly how to please his lord by giving and lending the lord his very own income, then receiving his thanks and a coat and hood as well a gift.)

(GP 608–612)

Shipman:
Ful many a draughte of wyn had he ydrawe
Fro Burdeux-ward, whil that the chapman sleep.
Of nyce conscience took he no keep.

If that he faught and hadde the hyer hond,
By water he sente hem hoom in every lond.

(Many a shipment of wine had he hauled from Bordeaux while merchants were asleep [he stole wine in France and shipped it to England]. He had no fine scruples. Wherever he was, if he fought and had the upper hand, he sent them home by water [that is, they met a watery grave].)

(GP 396–400)

With the professional classes their secret life is only hinted at more mysteriously:

Man of Law:
Nowher so bisy a man as he ther nas,
And yet he semed bisier than he was.

(There was nowhere a man so busy as he, and yet he gave the impression of being busier than he was.)

(GP 321–322)

Merchant:
This worthy man ful wel his wit
   bisette:
Ther wiste no wight that he was in dette
So estatly was he of his governaunce

(This reputable man used his wits very ably: so dignified was he in his behavior that no man knew that he was in debt.)

(GP 279–381)

Of the rest, the Clerk and the Franklin are given more neutral portraits—the one ascetic, the other genial—while the Wife of Bath is presented as a bold, boisterous woman, having had five husbands (apart from other adventures), whose wandering on pilgrimages is equaled by her wandering in sexual dalliance. Of the three priests mentioned accompanying the Second Nun nothing more is said, but a Nun's Priest is introduced with a tale in Fragment VII. A collective portrait is given of five townsmen (Haberdasher, Carpenter, Weaver, Dyer, Tapestry Maker), all members of the same parish guild, all prosperous and potential candidates for public office, with wives who would enjoy being called "madame" (my lady), but none tell a tale.

Harry Bailey, the Host, owner of the Tabard Inn where the pilgrims meet, is a large, impressive man, fit to be a "marchal in an halle" (master of ceremonies), who suggests that the company ride together with a storytelling competition for amusement under his guidance. His call is for "Tales of best sentence and moost solaas" (tales of the best worthy matter and most pleasure, *GP* 799), but whether the "and" is a conjunction here, meaning that the narratives have to convey both sobriety and pleasure at the same time, or implies two separate categories, is left unclear.

Introducing the various pilgrims, Chaucer the pilgrim appears comically deferential when he imparts views that the pilgrims hold of themselves, but satiric when providing information he could not possibly have learned in their company, such as the underhand dealings of the Miller and the Reeve, the Merchant's debts, and the Shipman's theft and violence. Rather than a wide-eyed observer, Chaucer presents himself as truthful witness, anticipating the scurrilous material he is about to relate and begging his audience's forgiveness in advance by saying that he must tell the stories he has heard as truthfully as possible (*GP* 725–742). By implication he views fiction as a truthful thing, as something that occupies its own space and has its own laws, a strikingly new departure for literature.

FRAGMENT I: KNIGHT, MILLER, REEVE, COOK

In this opening fragment Chaucer sets out his greatest contrast on the themes of time and order, the *Knight's Tale* showing the emptiness of the pagan world (ancient Greece) where the "gentilesse" (noble feeling) and "pite" (compassion) of the Athenian ruler Theseus are of little avail in a universe of capricious gods. This is followed by a downward progression into tales of contemporary sexual shenanigins in

the university towns of Oxford (*Miller's Tale*) and Cambridge (*Reeve's Tale*) and, finally, the capital city of London (*Cook's Tale*). If the gods are cruel and disordered in the pagan world, in the Christian one it is humanity that lacks all direction, blithely unaware of the order, purpose, and meaning of Christ's promise of salvation.

Ostensibly a chivalric romance, the *Knight's Tale* is about the love of two young Theban knights, Palamon and Arcite, for Emily, the sister-in-law of Theseus, duke of Athens, who has taken them prisoner after capturing their city. It shows how the disordering force of love makes the two captive cousins renounce their bonds of family, friendship, and chivalry and reduces them to quarreling beasts. When they argue as to which loves Emily the more, Arcite declares:

Love is a gretter lawe, by my pan,
Than may be yeve to any erthely man;
And therfore positif lawe and swich decree
Is broken al day for love in ech degree.

(Love is a greater law, according to my thinking [literally, skull], than may be given to any earthly man, therefore man's legislation and decrees are broken for love daily by all classes.)

(I.1165–1168)

When the two finally escape and arrange a duel, Theseus finds them ankle-deep in blood and ridicules the attempt to settle their differences by force, especially when the object of affections is unaware of her two suitors, who were only able to spy on her from imprisonment in a tower. Showing pity after his wife, Hippolyta, pleads for their lives, he arranges a tournament to decide which one will be given Emily's hand. A vast amphitheater is built with shrines to the gods. Arcite prays to Mars that he be granted victory, Palamon prays to Venus that he shall win Emily, and Emily prays to Diana that she remain a virgin. With the god's intervention, Arcite is granted his request, but Saturn commands Pluto (god of the underworld) to upset Arcite's horse, and the knight is thrown and crushed to death. After such an elaborate spectacle to decide a husband for Emily, Theseus is left to offer her to Palamon, with a long speech about the fair chain of love and the stability of the Aristotelian "Firste Moevere" (God), ending on the fact that it is wisdom to make a virtue of necessity and that it is best to die when young and in possession of an honorable name—none of which adequately sums up or resolves the events related. Indeed, the reader is most likely to agree with the speech of Egeus, Theseus's father:

> This world nys but a thurghfare ful of wo,
> And we been pilgrymes, passynge to and fro.
> Deeth is an ende of every worldly soore.
>
> (This world is nothing but a pathway full of sorrow, and we are pilgrims passing to and fro. Death is the end of all the world's woes.)
>
> (I.2847–2849)

In general this tale mocks the niceties of courtly love, presenting a bleak vision of a universe without redemption, despite the agency of the "gentil duc" (noble duke) with his "herte pitous" (compassionate nature). If Theseus seeks to right wrongs in as virtuous a manner as he knows how, he is still helpless in the face of meaningless death in the chaotic world he inhabits.

If the private world of love in the *Knight's Tale* is set against larger forces of disorder in the pagan gods, the *Miller's Tale* shows a reverse image in the capricious actions of humanity. John, a rich carpenter, has taken a young wife, Alison, but is extremely jealous of her. In addition to two servants, the couple have a young student named Nicholas lodging with them, who violently protests his love to Alison in the formulaic language of courtly love, while gripping her fondly around the buttocks:

> " . . . For deerne love of thee, lemman, I spille."
> And heeld hire harde by the haunchebones,
> And seyde, "Lemman, love me al atones,
> Or I wol dyen, also God me save!"

> And she sproong as a colt dooth in the trave,
> And with hir heed she wryed faste awey,
> And seyde, "I wol nat kisse thee, by my fey!
> Why, lat be!" quod she. "Lat be, Nicholas,
> Or I wol crie 'out, harrow' and 'alas'!
> Do wey youre handes, for youre curteisye!"

> ("I am dying because of the secret love I have for you, sweetheart," and he held her tightly below the buttocks and said, "Sweetheart, love me at once or I will die, God save me!" And she sprang back as a colt in the frame and twisted her head rapidly away and said, "Upon my faith, I will not kiss you. Let me go! Let me go, Nicholas, or I will cry out for help! Get your hands away, out of courtesy!")
>
> (I.3278–3287)

In the space of another six lines Nicholas succeeds in obtaining the promise he desires, and the two set about devising and executing the elaborate plan of fixing three barrels to the roof in which Nicholas, Alison, and John will spend the night in anticipation of the coming biblical flood that Nicholas declares he has had secret knowledge of in a vision. When the gullible carpenter falls asleep, the amorous couple sport in bed until interrupted by Alison's other suitor, the fastidious and effeminate town clerk, Absolon. When this rival succeeds in branding Nicholas's bottom with hot iron, the latter screams for water, and John thinks the flood has arrived. When he cuts his barrel loose from the rafters, it crashes to the ground, and he breaks a leg. The play of "pryvetee" in this private house undergirds the secret goings-on of love between Nicholas and Alison, the private knowledge Nicholas purports to have of God's workings, the warning that mankind should not spy on "Goddes pryvetee," and the private way the three main protagonists seek only to save themselves. It is finally the secretive revenge of Absolon that makes the whole affair public.

If this narrative is purposely set in juxtaposition with the *Knight's Tale*, it does not offer an alternative view of love so much as a further perspective on the disorder caused by human love set against Christian love. It is a stark reminder of the secretive ways of the town, where everyone is about their private business (compare the *Shipman's Tale*). Even Absolon is aware that the most effective lure is money in wooing a townswoman: "And, for she was of town, he profred meede" (And because she lived in town he offered money, I.3380).

In the country, matters are somewhat different. The *Reeve's Tale* sets two students after the wife and daughter of a miller because the Reeve sees the *Miller's Tale* as a slight on carpenters, in which craft he was trained in youth. In order to have time to steal flour from the two students, Symkyn the miller sets their horse free, only to have the two sleep with his wife and daughter when they have to stay the night after finally finding their mount. This ribald little tale that appears in many medieval versions, including the *Decameron* (Day IX, 6), is here given a greater weight by Chaucer than a simple fabliau. It is set against the pretensions of a parish priest whose illegitimate daughter the miller has married, the priest being very keen to see the couple's daughter married well so that he may make her a legacy of his possessions:

> This person of the toun, for she was feir,
> In purpos was to maken hire his heir,
> Both of his catel and his mesuage,
> And straunge he made it of hir mariage.
> His purpos was for to bistowe hire hye
> Into som worthy blood of auncetrye;
> For hooly chirches good moot been despended
> On hooly chirches blood, that is descended.
> Therfore he wolde his hooly blood honoure,
> Though that he hooly chirche sholde devoure.

(Because she was fair, this town parson intended to make her the heir to his property, his house and contents, and made difficulties about her marriage. He wanted to place her highly into some worthy lineage, because the goods of the Holy Church must be spent on the Church's own blood descendents. Therefore he desired to honor his holy blood [his offspring] at the cost of eating up [the good of] the Holy Church.)

(I.3977–3986)

The dense word play in this passage shows the priest's total inversion of the church's values: it is the blood of the Church (Christ's sacrifice) that is its good, whereas the priest wishes to bestow the material goods he has appropriated on his own bloodline, neither of which the "church," (that is, a priest), was supposed to possess at all. The Church's material wealth is seen to corrupt it even at a local level.

The final portrayal of corruption in the fragment is in the Cook's unfinished tale, which barely manages to set the scene of a young apprentice who has learned more about debauchery than about his craft of victualler. When his master throws him out, he goes to live with a friend whose wife is a prostitute. There are no more than fifty-eight lines, and perhaps Chaucer needed no more than set the scene for the picture of the modern world to be complete: the corruption of town and gown, where private gain and satisfaction have superceded the communal values of the old world of the countryside.

FRAGMENT II: THE SERGEANT OR MAN OF LAW

The *Man of Law's Prologue* is famous for its sketch of "Chaucer," whose works he proceeds to enumerate and comment on. Whether or not this lawyer knows he is addressing Chaucer among the pilgrims is impossible to say. Other literary problems associated with the passage are discussed in the *Riverside* notes, but the humor and irony are obvious. A further anomaly is the complaint against poverty (II.99–121) taken from *De miseria condicionis humane* ("On the Poverty of Mankind," c. 1190s) by Pope Innocent III, to which is added a passage in praise of wealthy merchants (II:122–132), where the original actually condemns wealth.

The tale is a condensed version of a narrative from Nicholas Trivet's Anglo-Norman *Chronicle* (c. 1334) about Constantia, daughter of the sixth-century Byzantine emperor, but the story is a well-known one of an exiled princess wrongly accused and appears in several Middle English versions, including Gower's *Confessio amantis* (Book 2, 587–1598) as well as the *Decameron* (Day V, 2). In Chaucer's version, the tale is told as an exemplum of Christian constancy, where the heroine is full of virtue and the pathos of the narration make it almost a saint's legend. Constance, daughter of the Roman emperor, is married to the king of Syria, who converts to Christianity; but his mother kills him and his fellow converts, putting Constance to sea in a rudderless boat. When she finally lands on the shores of Northumbria, Constance again finds herself in difficulties when she marries Alla, the king, and again falls foul of a jealous mother-in-law who by a trick has her put to sea once more with her newborn son. This time Constance is found at sea by the Roman senator returning from exacting vengeance on the Syrians and, unrecognized, becomes a handmaiden to the senator's wife. In time, Alla comes to Rome on a pilgrimage as penance for inadvertently allowing his mother to banish his wife and son, and the family is united. The happy ending is short-lived, as Alla dies after a year and Constance returns to Rome, where she lives in "vertu and hooly almus-deede" (virtue and charitable deeds, II.1156), while the pope crowns her son the next emperor.

Despite the extreme pathos in its narration, this tale is a stern reminder from the beginnings of European Christianity of faith in its workings and the providential hand of God operating in a true believer's life. If nothing else, it offers a corrective to the misdemeanors so fulsomely portrayed in the previous fragment.

FRAGMENT III: WIFE OF BATH, FRIAR, SUMMONER

The Wife's self-revealing prologue is over twice the length of her tale and catalogs the adventures of her adult life through five marriages. She makes a "text" out of her personal story and cites "experience" over "authority" to justify her endeavor, but she also twists many biblical passages to her own end, proving herself to be a subtle rhetorician as well as forceful personality, a woman with a good store of learning put to use in defense of her life. In many ways, the Wife is all that medieval antifeminism declared of women: garrulous, materialistic, disobedient, and a slave to her appetites (as a "daughter of Eve"), as she herself admits:

> For certes, I am al Venerien
> In feelynge, and mine herte is Marcien.
> Venus me yaf my lust, my likerousnesse,
> And Mars yaf me my sturdy hardynesse.

> (For certainly I am under the planet Venus in feeling, and my heart is ruled by Mars. Venus gave me my desires and lecherousness and Mars gave me my sturdy boldness.)

> (III.609–612)

This stereotypical portrait has to be qualified by the fact that she stands up for herself as a woman and argues against the "auctoritees" (authoritative texts) that would support ecclesiastical dominance of women. But in creating a space for herself in the medieval world dominated publicly by men, she paradoxically embodies and celebrates the abuse of freedom traditionally associated with men's access to money, property, sex, and travel. She has been able to do this by making a business out of marriage, first to three older men from whom she inherited wealth, then enjoying two younger men on whom she lavished her arts of love and argument in order to subdue them to her will. With her fourth husband she was unsuccessful, but the accord that she achieves with her fifth husband, Jankyn, the clerk half her age who owns a book of antifeminist tracts ("the book of wikked wives"), is something she fondly reminisces over (III.811–825), even if we learn it was a hard-won thing. The most telling point of all this enterprising nature is that she sees her body as a commodity in a market:

And therfore every man this tale I telle,
Wynne whoso may, for al is for to selle;
With empty hand men may none haukes lure.

(And therefore I say this to every man, every one
should try for gain as everything is for sale; a hawk
cannot be lured with an empty hand.)

(III.413–415)

It is this fundamental corruption of her nature
that vitiates the Wife's vitality and freedom and
(as she is in the cloth trade) makes her symbolic
of the new mercantile state of mind rather than
any stereotype of gender.

For all the Wife's "hard sell" attitude to life
and self, her tale reveals a more human center,
indeed a more moral view of marriage than she
has learned perhaps herself. In Arthurian times,
a knight convicted of rape has his sentence commuted on the intercession of the queen and
ladies of court. In the space of twelve months,
he has to discover "What thyng is it that wommen moost desiren" (What it is that women
most desire, III.905). After hearing many bald
and humorous possibilities, nearing the end of
his time, the knight finds an ugly old hag who
reveals the answer that saves his life: "Wommen
desiren to have sovereynetee / As wel over hir
housbond as hir love, / And for to been in maist-
rie hym above" (Women desire sovereignty over
their husbands as well as their love, and to have
mastery over them, III.1038–1040). In return,
she demands marriage, but on the wedding night
the knight is unable to fulfill his obligations,
which elicits her speech on "gentillesse"
(III.1109–1212) that reminds him of true moral
virtue. When he acquiesces to her demand for
mastery, she miraculously changes into the
beautiful young woman he desires. It has left
many readers thinking that the Wife's tale
reflects some wishful thinking on her part that
she might equally regain youth and beauty, even
though she declares herself to be happy with the
way she is, content with the "bran" she now has
to sell (III.478).

The Wife's prologue and tale have been held
to initiate a "marriage debate," continued in the
next fragment by the Clerk and Merchant, but
the tales immediately following reflect the
traditional rivalry between a Friar and a Summoner, revealing the abuses for which each was
known. The Friar relates the adventures of a
Summoner who meets a devil when out riding,
both of them intent on "wynninge" (gain) and
"purchas" (profit). The summoner's method is
to threaten both innocent and guilty with the
ecclesiastical court, especially those guilty of
sleeping with a prostitute he is in league with,
sharing the bribe he takes to bury the matter.
When the summoner tries to extract money from
one innocent old widow, she curses him and
asks the devil to take him, which this particular
devil does, fetching him away to hell for his own
"wynnyng," saying that the summoner who
wanted to learn from him "shalt knowen of oure
privetee / Moore than a maister of dyvynytee"
(shall know more of our secret doings than a
master of divinity, III.1637–1638).

Incensed by this outward attack on his calling, the Summoner retaliates in his prologue
with an anecdote about friars in hell, then with
an extremely realistic portrait of a smooth-
talking friar out to gain a large donation for his
convent from an ailing man. Appearing to relent
under the friar's persuasion, the bedridden man
says that if the friar would feel under the sheets
he will find something "hyd in pryvetee"
(hidden in private, III.2143). As soon as the friar
complies, the man breaks wind into the friar's
grasping hand. A parody of a logical problem
("question") in the schools follows about how
such a donation may be divided up between the
members of a convent.

Where the Miller and the Reeve use their narrative space to score points, the former against
the Knight's tale, the latter against the Miller in
person, the Summoner and the Friar first have
an altercation before the Wife begins her tale,
then continue in like mode after it, subverting
the narration away from a competition about
narrative to one based on personal and professional rivalry. Summoners and friars were in
competition for any money the public wished to

donate to causes out of guilt or charity, much to the annoyance of parish priests, who were thus marginalized. With the narration fully locked into the frame story, individual tales reflecting tellers or answering other tales, the narratives now begin to connect in theme as well.

FRAGMENT IV: CLERK, MERCHANT

The *Clerk's Tale* is based on the last novella of the *Decameron* (Day X, 10), but Chaucer gives the source as Petrarch, who made a Latin version of it appended to a letter. The reality of the narrative as history is underlined by the inclusion of Petrarch's geographical description of the Italian Piedmont, where the story is located. Walter, the marquis of Saluzzo, is persuaded by his subjects to marry to ensure continuity of governance, but he insists on taking a simple peasant girl, Griselda, from whom he extracts a vow of utter obedience (IV.351–371). Griselda's natural virtue calms any misgivings the people may have, and in time she bears Walter a daughter and later a son, both of whom Walter takes from her on the pretext that the people are against Griselda and her offspring because of her low birth. Griselda is led to believe that they are killed, when in fact they are brought up safely elsewhere. Finally Walter announces that he is returning Griselda to her father's house (the burial-service echo increased by the fact that he causes her to be stripped naked) and will take a new young wife. At the ceremony, the new "wife" is revealed as Griselda's daughter, and it appears that everything has simply been a test of her obedience and faithfulness. In a flood of thankful tears, Griselda assumes her rightful place with her two children.

According to the Clerk, the narrative is not related as an exemplary tale for wives to follow but as an allegory to show that "every wight, in his degree, / Sholde be constant in adversitee / As was Grisilde" (every person, of whatever station in life, should be as constant in adversity as Griselda was, III.1145–1147) and live in "vertu-

ous suffraunce" no matter how dire the scourges of adversity. But the Clerk is mindful that the Wife has said that "it is an impossible / That any clerk wol speke good of wyves" (it is impossible for any cleric to speak well of married women, III.688–689). He teases the company by saying that even if it were an exemplary tale for women to follow, it would be very difficult to find one as virtuous as Griselda. Therefore he merrily praises the Wife "and al hire secte" (those like her) and says quite clearly that women should stand up to men. Despite this, Harry Bailly still wishes this was a tale his wife might hear and emulate, thus continuing the series of misreadings of tales beginning with the Reeve taking offense at the Miller's tale (I.3855–3866).

The *Merchant's Prologue* opens with a heartfelt admission that suggests that he too has taken the Clerk's tale to be literally about marriage:

"Wepyng and waylyng, care and oother sorwe
I knowe ynogh, on even and a-morwe,"
Quod the Marchant, "and so doon other mo
That wedded been . . .

. . .

There is a long and large difference
Bitwix Grisildis grete pacience
And of my wyf the passing crueltee."

("I know enough of weeping and wailing, cares and other sorrows, both night and day," said the Merchant, "and so do many others who are married. . . . There is a great difference between Griselda's great patience and my wife's extreme cruelty.")

(IV.1213–1216, 1223–1225)

But his tale of a rich old merchant of Pavia who takes a young wife simply to have legitimate and—so he thinks—sin-free sex after years of lechery, qualifies his words and the reader's sympathy. The tale about a blind husband and a pear tree was a popular one, with a version found in the *Decameron* (Day VII, 9; see also Day II, 10) and other folk versions. After satisfying his lusts on his young wife, May, the aged merchant

January becomes blind. This gives May the opportunity of a dalliance with one of January's servants, Damian, who slips into January's secret garden and blatantly makes love to May in a pear tree at the moment that January suddenly regains his sight. The couple manages to persuade the old man that he was "seeing things," his sight still momentarily impaired, but the reader thinks perhaps that January, knowing there is little else he can do, simply prefers to close his eyes to the truth. This sad and loveless tale is interspersed with reflections by both the Merchant and his characters on the nature of marriage taken from the Bible, St. Jerome's well-known attack on marriage in *Adversus Jovinianum* ("Against Jovinian") and the work of the fourteenth-century French poet Eustache Deschamps in his *Miroir de Mariage* ("Mirror of Marriage").

FRAGMENT V: SQUIRE, FRANKLIN

The Squire's long fragment of a magic ring that allows Canacee, daughter of Ghengis Khan ("Cambyuskan"), to listen and speak to a falcon that pours out to her its distraught tale of courtly love is so prolix critics have thought it an example of how not to tell a tale. That it reflects its youthful, possibly idealistic narrator is a possibility, but the narrative still remains mysteriously placed in the tales, an exotic Oriental frame that contains the standard expressions of love and "gentilesse" (for example, V.483–494) and appears to be cut short by the Franklin.

A genial character, in whose house it snows meat and drink (*GP* 345), the Franklin picks up the topic of "gentillesse," and there follows a brief altercation on the subject with the Host, who does not care a straw for the Franklin's thoughts on the matter but cordially invites him to speak his tale, which introduces a new twist to the debate on marriage. Rather than center on who has dominance in marital relations, this tale sees an equal partnership put to the test, requiring a sequence of virtue to resolve the difficulty.

The story of an impossible task of love is a common one, and again there is a version in the *Decameron* (Day X, 5), with a more philosophical question on the narrative also given in Boccaccio's earlier epic romance the *Filocolo* (c. 1336). In the *Franklin's Tale* the secret world of courtly love is prefaced by the Franklin's comments on the nature of marriage, where he says that "an humble, wys accord" (V.791) comes from mutual patience and sharing of power in the relationship (V.790–798). Into a Breton lay, a genre that normally deals with Arthurian matter and Celtic magic, Chaucer places a very realistic, if hypothetical, problem: an idyllic marriage threatened by the private obsessions of courtly love. When Dorigen, married to the knight Arveragus, who is absent for a time in England, finds herself courted by the persistent squire Aurelius, she sets him to an impossible task to perform in the hope that he will desist in his attentions. If he can make the rocks off the Brittany coast disappear, she will be his. If a rash promise and seemingly impossible task, this choice touchingly reveals Dorigen's anxiety about her husband's safe return across the Channel. To her great distress, Aurelius succeeds in fulfilling this task with the aid of a magician (who is equally learned about tides), and she is forced to reveal her predicament to her newly returned husband. After some anguished deliberation, Arveragus sorrowfully declares that she must keep her promise and fulfill her vow as "trouthe is the hyeste thyng that man may kepe" (truth is the most noble thing by which man may abide, V.1479). When Aurelius sees Dorigen's demeanor and learns of Arveragus's decision, he is moved to reciprocate and generously releases Dorigen from her vow. In turn, the magician releases Aurelius from the thousand pounds he had promised to pay. Thus each man reciprocates in a "gentil dede" (noble action), and the Franklin ends his narrative by asking the company which of the three men it thinks has been the most generous. In Boccaccio's *Filocolo*, this *demande d'amour* (question of love) is fully debated in all its philosophical nicety, but the question concludes the matter in the *Canterbury Tales.* This narrative is also held to resolve the marriage debate, showing a marriage based on mutual respect, even if paradoxically it opens up the couple to adultery; Dorigen's personal integrity in keeping her vow is seen as paramount, but it leads to a chain reaction of generous reciprocity and the return of marital stability.

FRAGMENT VI: PHYSICIAN, PARDONER

The *Physician's Tale* begins without a prologue or endlink to the previous narration. Although this story of a corrupt Roman judge and a father's drastic solution to preserving his daughter's chastity is ultimately found in Livy's *Annals* (I.3.44–58), Chaucer's source is the thirteenth-century French work *The Romance of the Rose* (5589–5658), with a version in Gower's *Confessio Amantis* (Book 7, 5131–5306). In the *Romance,* the story is related by the allegorical figure of Reason as an instance of the corruption of judges ("But now they sell their decisions, and turn the elements of the legal process upside down," 5579–5580). In the *Tales,* the lack of correspondence between Physician and tale has long been noted, together with dissatisfaction at the story's literary competence. Related in its pathos to the *Man of Law's Tale* and the *Clerk's Tale,* the story recounts the stratagem of the judge Appius to possess the virtuous Virginia, daughter to Virginius, by having a collaborator named Claudius accuse Virginius of having stolen Virginia from him as a slave girl many years before. When Appius allows the plea, Virginius decapitates his daughter and takes the head to court in defiance. Rather than censure him for his hasty action, the crowd turns on Appius, who kills himself in prison, and Claudius only escapes with exile upon the intercession of Virginius. If there is any connection with the preceding tale, it is in Reason's speech on Justice in the *Romance* (5551–5554): "But if men loved, they would never harm each other; and since Transgression

would leave, what end would Justice serve?" In the Franklin's story, mutual respect and sympathy eliminate transgression, whereas here overweening desire brings about further sin.

As the subject of the next tale, sin is shown to bring about its own retribution in a beautifully exemplary narrative that has its origins in stories of the Buddha but finds its way into the early Italian collection of stories known as the *Novellino* (c. 1300), where the action is witnessed by Christ and his disciples during the course of a day. In Chaucer's version, three young "riotoures" (profligates) during a time of plague in Flanders set out to find Death and kill him. They find a mysterious old man who tells them they will find what they seek at the edge of a field. When they discover a cache of gold, two stay to guard it and, in order to have a greater share, plot to kill the third, who goes off to town for bread and wine. When he arrives back, the two kill him, then drink the wine that he in turn has poisoned so that he might take all. This simple but effective tale is given a local habitation, lively characterization, and is rendered all the more chilling as an extempore sermon by the Pardoner on *Radix malorum est cupiditas* ("Greed is the root of all evil," I Timothy 6:10). The company is thus treated to a full-scale performance by the Pardoner when he extracts money from the simple folk who would buy his indulgencies (temporary remissions of sins). At the end of his story, he is so carried away as to try to sell his false relics to the company, only to be rudely told by the Host what he can do with them.

FRAGMENT VII: SHIPMAN, PRIORESS, *TALE OF SIR THOPAS, TALE OF MELIBEE,* MONK, NUN'S PRIEST

By far the largest group of stories in the collection, Fragment VII has been called the "literature group" in that it represents a selection of different medieval genres that are allowed to speak for themselves without any overt resonance or association from their narrators.

As such, it might take its genesis from the Pardoner's performance and allows the company and present-day reader to see how narratives compete and interact generically, as it were. It also shows the connectedness of the tales and suggests what Chaucer was perhaps working toward had he been able to finish the collection in detail.

The *Shipman's Tale* is a realistically told story on the motif of what is euphemistically known as "the lover's gift regained." Overtly it is the simple story of a Parisian merchant and his wife, but its conclusion establishes a brutal connection between money and sex within a marriage that is shocking in its frankness and at the same time amusing in its insouciance. A monk borrows a sum of money off a merchant and offers it to the merchant's wife in return for sexual favors. When the amount is due, the monk says he has already repaid the money to the merchant's wife. In this version, the wife boldly declares that she in turn has spent the money, but that the husband may reclaim the sum while paying off the "marriage debt" (conjugal sex; see St. Paul, I Corinthians 7:3–4). The merchant appears well satisfied with the arrangement, and this curiously nonjudgmental tale concludes with a plea from the Shipman for similar credit. This turning of the marriage debt into a real debt to be paid off by a form of marital prostitution is, of course, a damning indictment of mercantile values, and the privacy and secrecy of this world is alluded to throughout the tale. It is because the transgression never comes to light in public that no overt moral can be made and condemns the protagonists all the more for their selfish desires.

The Prioress follows with a miracle of the Virgin set in Asia, where a "litel clergeoun" (schoolboy) is murdered by a company of Jews, who hide the body in a privy. When his distressed mother looks for him, the corpse sings out the boy's favorite hymn to Mary "O Alma Redemptoris," which he learned from an older boy. Once found, the body is laid on a bier, and again the corpse sings the hymn until the local abbot removes a seed placed by the Virgin in the boy's mouth. Notable for the stark contrast between its sentimental view of the child and the violence of its anti-Semitism, the tale reflects perhaps the dangerous provincialism of the Prioress's narrow outlook, but it has a "sobre" effect on the company.

Central to this literary fragment are the next two tales from the pilgrim Chaucer, following another thumbnail sketch of him when hailed by Harry Bailly to speak next:

> This were a popet in an arm t'enbrace
> For any womman, smal and fair of face.
> He semeth elvyssh by his contenaunce
> For unto no wight doth he dallianunce.
>
> (This is a little doll for any woman who is slender and fair of face to cradle in her arm. He seems bewitched and not sociable to anyone.)
>
> (VII.701–704)

No matter how distracted he may look and whatever innuendo is to be inferred by reference only to attractive women, Chaucer the pilgrim readily assents, but with two of the most unexpected performances in the whole collection. Firstly, in *Sir Thopas*, he gives the company a "rym lerned longe agoon," a parody of knight errantry in Flanders—a country noted for its towns and industry—told in the style of a minstrel's tail-rhyme romance. The poem abounds in comic misapplications and proceeds nowhere until the disgruntled Host calls a halt and refers to it in very undignified terms indeed. Chaucer then obliges with "a litel thyng in prose," a "moral tale vertuous" (virtuous moral tale), that is a translation via the French of Albertanus of Brescia's *Liber consolationis et consilii* ("Book of Consolation and Advice," 1246), a collection of proverbs and *sententiae* drawn up for a son. Translated and edited by Renaud de Louens as the *Livre de Melibée et de Dame Prudence* (c. 1336) it acquires the frame of a thinly veiled allegory about a man, Melibeus, who takes advice from his wife, Dame Prudence, when under attack from his enemies. This strange choice of subject from the author of the *Canterbury Tales* is perhaps more understandable when one considers Chaucer's professional life as diplomat, civil servant, man about court and even for a time member of Parliament. But more pertinent to the collection as a whole is its debate on the role of women in marriage (VII.1049–1110) and the way Melibee listens favorably to his wife's advice (VII.1113), to say nothing of his concluding emphasis on Christian forgiveness and penance (VII.1885).

It could be said that *Sir Thopas* and *Melibee* form the undeclared center of the collection in that one tale is all frivolous "solaas" while the other is all barely disguised "sentence." At the core of this literary fragment, they show in essence the unvarnished polarities of Harry Bailly's call for tales and suggest by implication that each should be tempered by the other to achieve an audience. It has to be said that, despite the pilgrims' critical reactions to what they hear, they allow *Melibee* to continue to its end, and all the evidence of the previous manuscript tradition shows that the work was a popular one to include.

The *Monk's Tale* which follows painfully demonstrates the consequences of not taking the implied advice about mixing "earnest" with a little "game." Taking his cue from Boccaccio's prose collection *De casibus virorum illustrium* ("On the Falls of Famous Men"), named in the subtitle, Chaucer shows the Monk attempting to repudiate his bon vivant image with a serious mien and group of unrelieved tragedies. Defining tragedy in the medieval fashion as the workings of Fortune that first raises individuals up and then casts them down (VII.1991–1998), the Monk proceeds to illustrate the point with tedious repetition through seventeen examples (mythical, biblical, historical) until the Knight firmly begs an end, "for litel hevynesse / Is right ynough to mucche folk" (a small amount of gloomy matter is enough for most people, VII.2769–2770). The Host follows with his own comments about tales and audience: "Whereas a

man may have noon audience, / Noght helpeth it to tellen his sentence" (If a man has no audience, he cannot convey any meaning, VII.2801–2802). Harry Bailly allows the Monk another chance, but when the Monk refuses, he invites the Nun's Priest to speak.

In contrast, the *Nun's Priest's Tale,* overtly a simple beast fable of a fox, a cock, and a hen, is so richly and subtly endowed with meaning, picking up on many of the previous tales and themes, that its climactic place in the fragment seems acutely designed as a showcase of narration for the whole collection. The narrative has a rich ancestry in the Reynard the Fox cycles of twelfth- and thirteenth-century France, with a close outline of the story seen in Marie de France's *Fables* (60: The Cock and the Fox), a twelfth-century English imitation of Aesop written in Anglo-Norman French verse. The plain narrative occupies only one-fifth of the material, which includes a realistic farmyard setting and a host of mock-epic analogies and scholarly allusions, such as the anguish of the hens likened to that of the senators' wives watching when Nero burned Rome, taken from Boethius's *Consolation of Philosophy* (Book 1, metrum 6). Thus what emerges is a beautifully aggrandized mock-heroic epic rather than barnyard fable, with Chauntecleer a prince among cocks, a learned and well-read creature married to an equally knowledgeable hen, Dame Pertelote, with an additional harem of extra hens for his pleasure. One night he dreams of an infernal red beast and asks Pertelote for her advice. The sum of her medical learning is that he take a laxative, but the dream also brings in the medieval debate about predestination and free will: Does the dream mean that the event will happen? Later, when Chauntecleer finally does meet "daun Russell" the fox, he forgets all previous discussions and is flattered into closing his eyes and showing off his singing, thus allowing the fox to take him by the throat and run off with its prize, followed by the hue and cry of the farm's household. Despite his plight, Chauntecleer is quick enough to suggest to the fox that he address his pursuers in defiance as they near the safety of the wood; when the fox obliges, Chauntecleer is able to fly to the safety of the nearest tree. The Nun's Priest supplies three morals to the fable: Chauntecleer admits that one should not listen to flattery; the fox that one should hold one's tongue; and the Nun's Priest repeats their words, adding that one should not be careless and negligent (VII.3431–3437) with a further invitation to the audience to discover more in the tale themselves (VII.3438ff.). At its simplest, portraying marriage in its beautifully controlled conversations, the *Nun's Priest's Tale* looks back to the many tales dealing with relations between the sexes. But at its most sophisticated, this tale of a cock and a hen illustrates the workings of redemption through free will: the tragic dream of a fox that warns Chauntecleer of his fall and damnation is proven true but redeemed by the cock in quick-witted fashion. More generally, the many mock-tragic elements look back in comic fashion to the *Monk's Tale*, the many passages of female counsel recall *Melibee*, the miracle of his escape recalls the *Prioress's Tale*, and his sexual proclivities the *Shipman's Tale*. After the coherence of this long connected fragment, the remaining tales appear somewhat disconnected to the whole, but the Parson clearly rounds off the collection.

FRAGMENT VIII: SECOND NUN, CANON'S YEOMAN

The two tales here represent opposing views of clerical culture. The Second Nun relates a saint's life of St. Cecilia, concentrating on the conversion of her husband and his friend (and others in turn) and the attempt at burning her to death before her ultimate martyrdom. Although it has a source in the famous *Golden Legend* by Jacobus de Voragine (especially for the interpretation of her name in the prologue), recent research has shown that the tale also has a source in an anonymous liturgical version which in turn, like the *Golden Legend*, can be traced back

to the original *Passio S. Ceciliae*, a fifth- or sixth-century account of the saint's life. Given Chaucer's penchant for creating tales of pathos (*Man of Law, Clerk, Physician, Prioress*), one might expect the same from this pious woman who, in her prologue, invokes the Virgin in a version of St. Bernard's prayer from Dante's *Paradiso* (XXXIII.1–39). But this saint is a fierce and fearless exponent of her faith, exemplifying the early Church's muscular Christianity.

The arrival of two newcomers to the company, a Canon and his Yeoman, returns the narration to more contemporary clerical abuse in the vein of the Friar's and Summoner's tales. When the Yeoman reveals that his employer is an alchemist, the Canon rides off as quickly as he came, leaving the Yeoman to reveal what he knows of chemistry and alchemy in the first part of his tale and, in the second, the story of an alchemist canon who swindles a gullible priest into purchasing a bogus recipe for transmuting mercury into silver. As no source has been found for these two parts, it is assumed that Chaucer is writing from his personal knowledge, whether literary or experience.

Taken together, the failure to transform a base metal into silver in the *Canon Yeoman's Tale* harks back to the failure to convert Cecilia to pagan practices in the *Second Nun's Tale*, and the failure to burn her exemplifies her essential purity, where mercury simply evaporates in heat. It is significant that the real Canon the company meets lives, as the Yeoman says, "In the suburbes of a toun":

> Lurkynge in hernes and in lanes blynde,
> Whereas thise robbours and thise theves by kynde
> Holden hir pryvee fereful residence.
>
> (Lurking in hideouts and blind alleyways where robbers and thieves naturally take up their fearful private residence.)
>
> (VIII.658–660)

The fictional Canon in the Yeoman's tale also works privately and secretly for gain in the chamber where he cheats the priest.

FRAGMENT IX: MANCIPLE

The *Manciple's Tale* is a much-elaborated version of Ovid, *Metamorphoses* (2.531–632), which Chaucer may have read in other medieval versions such as the *Ovide moralisé*, a French adaptation with Christian morals attached. In this version, Phoebus Apollo learns from his pet crow that he has been cuckolded. After killing his wife in anger, Apollo repents in shame at what he has done and blames the crow, turning its white plumage black and its beautiful song to crowing. The Manciple's unsurprising moral is to beware of rash speech and action, but it leads to the surprising conclusion that many have taken to be a farewell to the fictions of the *Tales,* given the concluding stance of the Parson (see next section):

> be noon auctor newe
> Of tidynges, wheither they be false or trewe,
> Whereso thou come, amonges hye or lowe,
> Kepe wel thy tonge and thenk upon the crowe.
>
> (Do not be the author of new tidings, whether false or true; wherever you go, among people of high or low degree, remember the crow and hold your tongue.)
>
> (IX.359–362)

FRAGMENT X: PARSON

Although given as a separate fragment, the *Parson's Tale* opens with a reference to the Manciple. Despite Harry Bailly's plea to the Parson, "breke thou nat oure pley" (do not stop our game, that is, the storytelling), the Parson is clear about what he thinks of fiction, saying that he will "enden in som vertuous sentence" (end with some virtuous matter) and not relate any "fable." He reminds the company of the spiritual valency of the journey of life, and it seems clear that Chaucer meant the Parson to conclude the *Tales* as the company approaches Canterbury, rather than relate further tales on the return, as Harry Bailly states in the *General Prologue* (790–795).

What the Parson relates is a translation of two short treatises on how to prepare for the "glorious pilgrimage," namely penance before God. The first is on the nature of penance, deriving ultimately from a chapter of Raymund of Pennaforte's *Summa de paenitentia* ("On Penitence," 1225–1227, revised c. 1235), and the second is on the Seven Deadly Sins and their remedies, taken from William Peraldus's *Summa de vitiis et virtutibus* ("On the Vices and Virtues," c. 1249), one of the most popular medieval sources on the topic, but again very probably with mediating versions. What is significant about Chaucer's final shaping of this material is that it takes the original texts away from the technical exposition designed for a clerical audience to a more popular conception of penitential manual of the kind that was increasingly being used by the laity throughout the fourteenth century and beyond. It is significant, therefore, that the Parson is keen to examine man's moral rather than spiritual life in this concluding "tale" and discuss how individuals may both guard against and make up for their sins. It therefore looks back to the vices portrayed in most of the preceding tales and silently offers advice on how to remedy those vices depicted in the fictions. As such, it is an integral part of the collection rather than a perfunctory nod toward the hereafter and should not be omitted from any consideration of the *Canterbury Tales* as a whole. In a work held together by contrast, this last perspective on life for the medieval reader is the most crucial of all.

CONCLUSION

The European Middle Ages possessed a total vision of the world as ruled by God and man's life in it under the dispensation of Christ's incarnation. From the compendia of knowledge that adorned the great cathedrals in visual art to the compendia of theological treatises, encyclopaedias, and summas, to works such as the *Divine Comedy,* the comedy and tragedy of that vision was depicted in full public view with its rewards and punishments. In the *Canterbury Tales,* Chaucer puts a finishing touch on that fast-disappearing synthesis, showing how the private world of gain was encroaching on and breaking up the vision of public good. His realistic vision of humanity shaking loose from the Church makes him one of the first modern authors, while his final pointing the reader back to God shows him firm in his faith in the ineffable. If the influence of the *Tales* has not been as marked on English literature as might be expected, given its enduring popularity, there are specific historical reasons caused by linguistic change and aesthetic taste.

Judging from the number of extant manuscripts of the complete *Tales* (fifty five) and the many mentions of Chaucer and his work from fourteenth- and fifteenth-century writers, the *Canterbury Tales* was a much read and highly esteemed work, spawning later additions and inferior continuations of the unfinished tales. Its popularity must still have been considerable when William Caxton established England's first printing house and published two editions of the *Tales* (1478, 1484). As Caxton noted, however, with changes in the language it was becoming a less accessible work, although it continued to enjoy influential editions (William Thynne, 1532; Thomas Tyrwhitt, 1775) and draw writers to it, if not the general reader. John Dryden published modernized versions of two tales in his *Fables* (1700), and Alexander Pope did the same in two miscellanies at the same time.

When a romanticized view of medievalism became popular in the nineteenth century, it led to the foundation of a Chaucer Society in 1865 and more publications, culminating in W. W. Skeats's six-volume Oxford edition (1894). But given Chaucer's sometimes down-to-earth material, access to the work in school and home was restricted, and the *Tales* as a whole continued to be an antiquarian taste. For the late pre-Raphaelite market, William Morris produced a Kelmscott edition with illustrations by Edward Burne-Jones (1896).

In the twentieth century, translations in verse and prose and the first adaptations into other media appeared, most being attempts at popularizing, such as Neville Coghill's adaptions for BBC radio in 1946, a London musical in the late 1960s, and others since, including recent animations. During World War II, Michael Powell and Emeric Pressburger interestingly prefaced their patriotic war film *A Canterbury Tale* (1944) with an opening sequence of the Canterbury pilgrims, the Squire's hawk flying into the air becoming a fighter plane to bring the time into the present. In 1972, the Italian director Pier Paolo Pasolini made a controversial film version *(I Racconti di Canterbury)* to complement his adaptation of the *Decameron* (1971). Most recently, to celebrate Chaucer's six-hundred-year anniversary in 2000, BBC Radio Three commissioned tales told by modern characters set in a motorway service station when a group of people are forced to abandon their journeys in a snowstorm and pass the time telling tales.

Despite all this activity, no subsequent work has captured the intelligence, complexity, and humor of the original, whose stark contrasts and profound perspectives make it at times hauntingly Gothic, at others utterly modern, in its analysis of what corrupts and redeems mankind.

Select Bibliography

STANDARD EDITION

The Riverside Chaucer. 3d ed. Larry D. Benson, general editor. Oxford: Houghton Mifflin, 1987.

IN OTHER COLLECTED WORKS

The Complete Poetry and Prose of Geoffrey Chaucer. Edited by John H. Fisher. New York: Holt, Rinehart and Winston, 1977.

The Variorum Edition of the Works of Geoffrey Chaucer. Paul G. Ruggiers, general editor. Norman: University of Oklahoma Press, 1979– .

OTHER INDIVIDUAL EDITIONS

The Canterbury Tales by Geoffrey Chaucer. Edited from the Hengwrt Manuscript by N. F. Blake. London: Arnold, 1980.

TRANSLATIONS

The Canterbury Tales. Translated by Nevill Coghill. Harmondsworth, U.K.: Penguin, 1951; London: Allan Lane, 1977.

The Canterbury Tales. Edited and translated by A. Ken Hieatt and Constance B. Hieatt. New York: Golden Press, 1964. Dual text.

The Canterbury Tales. Translated by David Wright. Oxford: Oxford World's Classic, 1998. Verse.

CONCORDANCE

Benson, L. D. *A Glossarial Concordance to the Riverside Chaucer.* New York: Garland, 1993.

BIBLIOGRAPHIES

Allen, Mark, and John H. Fisher. *The Essential Chaucer: An Annotated Bibliography of Major Modern Studies.* London: Mansell, and Boston: G. K. Hall, 1987.

Baird-Lange, Lorraine Y. *A Bibliography of Chaucer 1964–1973.* Boston: G. K. Hall, 1977.

Baird-Lange, Lorraine Y., and H. Schnuttgen. *A Bibliography of Chaucer, 1974–1985.* Cambridge: Archon, 1988.

Chaucer Bibliographies. Toronto: University of Toronto Press, 1983– .

Crawford, William R. *Bibliography of Chaucer 1954–1963.* Seattle: University of Washington Press, 1967.

Griffith, Dudley David. *Bibliography of Chaucer 1908–1953.* Seattle: University of Washington Press, 1955.

Leyerle, John, and Anne Quick. *Chaucer: A Bibliographic Introduction.* Toronto: University of Toronto Press, 1986.

LANGUAGE

Burnley, David. *A Guide to Chaucer's Language.* Norman: University of Oklahoma Press, 1983.

Cannon, Christopher. *The Making of Chaucer's English.* Cambridge: Cambridge University Press, 1998.

Davis, Norman, et al. *A Chaucer Glossary.* Oxford: Clarendon Press, 1979.

Elliot, Ralph W. V. *Chaucer's English.* London: Deutsch, 1974.

Kökeritz, Helge. *A Guide to Chaucer's Pronunciation.* Toronto: University of Toronto Press, 1978.

Smith, J., ed. *The English of Chaucer and His Contemporaries.* Aberdeen, Scotland: Aberdeen University Press, 1988.

SOURCES AND BACKGROUND

Benson, Larry D., and Theodore M. Andersson. *The Literary Context of Chaucer's Fabliaux.* Indianapolis: Bobbs-Merrill, 1971.

Boitani, Piero, ed. *Chaucer and the Italian Trecento.* Cambridge: Cambridge University Press, 1983.

Correale, Robert M., and Mary Hamel, eds. *Sources and Analogues of the Canterbury Tales.* 2 vols. Cambridge: D. S. Brewer, 2002, 2003.

Crow, Martin M., and Clair C. Olson. *Chaucer Life Records.* Austin: University of Texas Press, 1966.

Hanawalt, Barbara A., ed. *Chaucer's England.* Minneapolis: University of Minnesota Press, 1992.

Havely, N. R., ed. *Chaucer's Boccaccio: Sources of Troilus and the Knight's and Franklin's Tales* Woodbridge, U.K.: D. S. Brewer, and Tottowa, N.J.: Rowman & Littlefield, 1980.

Jeffrey, David Lyle, ed. *Chaucer and Scriptural Tradition.* Ottawa: University of Ottawa Press, 1984.

Koff, Leonard M., and Brenda D. Schildgen, eds. *The "Decameron" and the "Canterbury Tales": New Essays on an Old Question.* London: Fairleigh Dickenson University Press, 2000.

Miller, Robert P. *Chaucer: Sources and Backgrounds.* Oxford: Oxford University Press, 1977.

Muscatine, Charles. *Chaucer and the French Tradition.* Berkeley: University of California Press, 1957.

North, J. D. *Chaucer's Universe.* Oxford: Clarendon Press, and New York: Oxford University Press, 1988.

Pearsall, Derek. *The Life of Geoffrey Chaucer.* Oxford: Blackwell, 1992.

Taylor, Karla. *Chaucer Reads the Divine Comedy.* Stanford, Calif.: Stanford University Press, 1989.

Thompson, N. S. *Chaucer, Boccaccio, and the Debate of Love.* Oxford: Oxford University Press, 1996.

Wimsatt, James I. *Chaucer and His French Contemporaries.* Toronto: University of Toronto Press, 1991.

GENERAL GUIDES

Aers, David. *Chaucer.* Atlantic Highlands, N.J.: Humanities Press International, and Brighton, Sussex, U.K.: Harvester Press, 1986.

Allen, Valerie, and Ares Axiotis, eds. *Chaucer.* London: St. Martin's Press, 1997.

Boitani, Piero, and Jill Mann, eds. *The Cambridge Chaucer Companion.* Cambridge: Cambridge University Press, 1986.

Bowden, Muriel. *A Reader's Guide to Geoffrey Chaucer.* New York: Farrar, Straus, 1964.

Brewer, Derek, ed. *Chaucer: The Critical Heritage.* 2 vols. London: Routledge and K. Paul, 1978..

————. *Geoffrey Chaucer: The Writer and His Background.* Woodbridge, Suffolk, U.K., and Rochester, N.Y.: D. S. Brewer, 1990.

Burrow, J. A., ed. *Geoffrey Chaucer: A Critical Anthology.* Harmondsworth, U.K.: Penguin, 1969.

Gardner, John. *The Poetry of Chaucer.* Carbondale: Southern Illinois University Press, 1977.

Hussey, S. S. *Chaucer: An Introduction.* London: Methuen, 1981.

Kane, George. *Chaucer.* Oxford: Oxford University Press, 1984.

Kean, P. M. *Chaucer and the Making of English Poetry.* 2 vols. London: Routledge and K. Paul, 1972.

Mann, Jill. *Geoffrey Chaucer.* London: Humanities Press International, 1991.

Rowland, Beryl. *A Companion to Chaucer Studies.* Oxford: Oxford University Press,1968.

Schoeck, Richard J., and Jerome Taylor. *Chaucer Criticism.* 2 vols. Notre Dame, Ind.: University of Notre Dame Press, 1960.

CRITICAL STUDIES

Allen, Judson B., and Theresa A. Moritz. *A Distinction of Stories.* Columbus: Ohio State University Press, 1981.

Cooper, Helen. *The Canterbury Tales.* Oxford: Clarendon Press, and New York: Oxford University Press, 1990.

Crane, Susan. *Gender and Romance in Chaucer's "Canterbury Tales."* Princeton, N.J.: Princeton University Press, 1994.

David, Alfred. *The Strumpet Muse: Art and Morals in Chaucer's Poetry.* Bloomington: Indiana University Press, 1976.

Elbow, Peter. *Oppositions in Chaucer.* Middletown, Conn.: Wesleyan University Press, 1975.

Ferster, Judith. *Chaucer on Interpretation.* Cambridge: Cambridge University Press, 1985.

Hansen, Elaine Tuttle. *Chaucer and the Fictions of Gender.* Berkeley: University of California Press, 1992.

Howard, Donald R. *The Idea of the "Canterbury Tales."* Berkeley: University of California Press, 1976.

Knapp, Peggy. *Chaucer and the Social Contest.* New York: Routledge, 1990.

Lumiansky, R. M. *Of Sondry Folk: The Dramatic Principle in the "Canterbury Tales."* Austin: University of Texas Press, 1980.

Mann, Jill. *Chaucer and Medieval Estates Satire.* Cambridge: Cambridge University Press, 1973.

Patterson, Lee. *Chaucer and the Subject of History.* Madison: University of Wisconsin Press, 1991.

Pearsall, Derek. *The Canterbury Tales.* London: G. Allen and Unwin, 1985.

Phillips, Helen. *An Introduction to the "Canterbury Tales": Fiction, Writing, Context.* New York: St. Martin's Press, 1999.

Richardson, Janette. *Blameth Nat Me.* The Hague: Mouton, 1970.

Strohm, Paul. *Social Chaucer.* Cambridge, Mass.: Harvard University Press, 1989.

PERIODICALS

Chaucer Review. University Park, Pa.: Pennsylvania State University Press, 1966– .

Studies in the Age of Chaucer. Columbus, Ohio: Ohio State University Press, 1979– .

Jane Austen's
Emma

SANDIE BYRNE

EMMA WAS THE FOURTH of Jane Austen's novels to be published, following *Sense and Sensibility, Pride and Prejudice,* and *Mansfield Park,* though it was written after *Lady Susan* and *Northanger Abbey,* which was not published until after the author's death. During the writing of the novel, Austen was living with her mother, her sister, and a friend in the cottage owned by her brother Edward, who, having been adopted by the wealthy Knight family, had gone to live with them at Godmersham Park in 1783 and had inherited a considerable estate. Chawton cottage was not a large or grand house, but it was commodious enough, and though located in a small country village, was close enough to a busy coach road to prevent the women from feeling too isolated. Jane Austen had celebrated their installation in their new home, as well as the birth of a nephew, in some verses that she sent to the child's father, her sailor brother, Francis, on 26 July 1809:

> Our Chawton home—how much we find
> Already in it, to our mind,
> And how convinced, that when complete,
> It will all other Houses beat,

> That ever have been made or mended,
> With rooms concise or rooms distended.
>
> (*Letters,* ed. Le Faye, p. 176)

Jane Austen began *Emma* in January 1814 and had finished by 29 March 1815. Q. D. Leavis, in "A Critical Theory of Jane Austen's Writings" *Scrutiny* (10 [1941]: 61–90, 114–142), developed the idea, suggested by earlier critics, that Austen's unfinished novel, *The Watsons* (whose heroine is Emma Watson), was a sketch for *Emma,* but this view is countered by B. C. Southam in the appendix to his *Jane Austen's Literary Manuscripts* (pp. 136–148). During the period of Emma's composition, Austen's niece, Anna Austen, was also trying to write a novel. It is almost impossible not to read the aunt's advice as describing the technique she was employing in the creation of *Emma:* "3 or 4 Families in a Country Village is the very thing to work on" (9–18 September 1814, *Letters,* ed. Le Faye, p. 275).

Austen had the encouragement of seeing the relatively small first edition of *Mansfield Park* sell out between its publication in May and the beginning of November 1814, but in spite of this modest success, the publisher, Egerton, did not print a second edition. Acting as his sister's agent, Henry Austen opened negotiations with the London publisher John Murray, who offered £450 for the copyright of *Emma* —but asked for the copyrights of *Sense and Sensibility* and *Mansfield Park* to be included in the deal. This offer was declined, and *Emma* was published on a profit-sharing basis. Austen was later to note that the first profits of *Emma* amounted to £39.

The Prince Regent (later George IV) was a fan, and kept a set of Austen's works in each of his houses. Austen did not reciprocate his admiration, as an earlier letter to her friend Martha Lloyd makes clear (16 February 1813; *Letters,* ed. Le Faye, p. 208). During one of her rare visits to London, during an illness of Henry's, the Prince Regent's librarian, James Stanier Clarke, sought out Austen and conveyed the information that she had royal assent to the dedication of her next work to his employer. This was tantamount to a royal command; to decline would have been a serious lapse of etiquette. Thus *Emma* is dedicated correctly, if perhaps stiltedly, to HRH. Perhaps hoping that she would model a hero on him, Clarke suggested that Austen write a story about a clergyman, and following his appointment as chaplain to the Prince Regent's son-in-law, and later that a story based on the history of the House of Coburg would be well received. Austen declined politely, but unequivocally. In her correspondence with Clarke, she enumerates what she describes as the limitations of her artistic techniques and expresses her anxieties about *Emma.* On 11 December 1815 she wrote:

> My greatest anxiety at present is that this 4th work shd not disgrace what was good in the others. But on this point I will do myself the justice to declare to declare that, whatever may be my wishes for its' [*sic*] success, I am strongly haunted by the idea that to those Readers who have preferred P&P. it will appear inferior in Wit, & to those who have preferred MP. inferior in good Sense.
>
> (*Letters,* ed. Le Faye, p. 306)

CHRONOLOGY

1775	Jane Austen born on 16 December, seventh of eight children of Rev. George Austen and Cassandra Leigh, at Steventon, Hampshire.
1783	Jane and her sister Cassandra are sent to Mrs. Cawley's school, where Jane contracts a putrid fever.
1784	Jane and Cassandra go to Abbey School, Reading, run by Mrs. Latournelle.
1785	Jane and Cassandra at home, where their education continues.
1787	Jane begins to write, including sketches for family theatricals.
1790	*Love and Freindship* [*sic*]
1791	Marriage of Edward Knight to Elizabeth Bridges. *The History of England*
1792	Marriage of James Austen to Anne Matthew. *Evelyn, Catherine*
1794	Execution by guillotine of the Comte de Feuillide, husband of Austen's cousin Elizabeth Hancock. *Lady Susan* begun
1795	Death of Anne [Matthew] Austen. Cassandra becomes engaged to Thomas Fowle
1796	*Elinor and Marianne* (later *Sense and Sensibility*), *Susan* (later *Northanger Abbey*) and *First Impressions* (later *Pride and Prejudice*) begun.
1797	Death of Thomas Fowle in the West Indies, marriage of James Austen to Mary Lloyd, Edward Knight inherits the estates of Thomas Knight, Henry Austen marries Elizabeth de Feuillide.
1800/ 1801(?)	Jane meets and becomes attached to a young man at Sidmouth. He dies soon after.
1801	The Austen family moves to Bath.
1802	Jane is engaged for one evening; she accepts Harrison Bigg-Wither's proposal but changes her mind the next morning.

1803	Crosby and Sons pays £10 for the manuscript of *Northanger Abbey*.
1804	Jane Visits Lyme Regis, begins *The Watsons*.
1805	Rev. George Austen dies; Mrs. Austen, Cassandra, and Jane move to Southampton.
1807	Charles Austen marries Frances "Fanny" Palmer.
1809	Edward Knight gives Mrs. Austen and her daughters a cottage on his estate at Chawton; Crosby returns the manuscript of *Northanger Abbey*.
1811	Publication of *Sense and Sensibility*.
1812	*Mansfield Park* begun.
1813	Publication of *Pride and Prejudice*.
1814	Publication of *Mansfield Park*.
1815	Jane visits Henry Austen in London, where she meets James Clarke, librarian to the Prince Regent.
1816	Publication of *Emma*, dedicated to the Prince Regent. Walter Scott favorably reviews Austen's work in *The Quarterly Review*.
1817	Completion of *Persuasion*. Ill, Jane moves to Winchester to be close to doctor. 18 July she dies, probably of Addison's disease.
1818	Publication of *Northanger Abbey* and *Persuasion*.

Emma was published in three volumes on 29 December 1815, though the colophon gives the date as 1816. Austen's name did not appear on the title page, which attributes the novel to "the author of 'Pride and Prejudice' &c. &c," but her identity was beginning to be known. Although 1,250 of the 2,000 copies of the first edition had sold within a year, a second edition did not appear until 1833. Since Austen's novels went into the public domain, versions have proliferated and a number of reliable and annotated editions are available in both paper and hardback formats. The definitive editions are those of R.W. Chapman, published by Clarendon Press. Based on collations of the early editions and supplemented with notes and illustrations, the editions are in five volumes, of which *Emma* is the fourth. Chapman's edition of *Emma* was published in large paper format in 1923 and in smaller format in 1926; since then it has been reprinted many times. Quotations from *Emma* below are taken from the 1966 reprint of the third (1933) edition, in which Mary Lascelles made some minor alterations and additions to Chapman's edition. Chapman noted that the text of the first edition was well printed and required very little correction. Useful paperback editions with notes have been published by W. W. Norton, Oxford World Classics, and Penguin, among others.

Unusually for one of Jane Austen's heroines, Emma's is not the Cinderella story. Far from being ragged, dispossessed, and in need of rescue by a fairy godmother and a Prince Charming, Emma is attractive, popular, and wealthy. Indeed, we receive an impression of a young woman so blessed with good fortune that perhaps she is a little complacent, even smug. We wonder whether, instead of putting her on a pedestal, the hero will knock her off the one she imagines she is on. Austen suggested that Emma would be a heroine whom no one but she would like, and that there should be much to dislike about her: she is snobbish; managing; meddling; intellectually lazy; patronizing; and given to thinking too well of herself. She becomes so carried away by the high spirits of a young man with whom she is flirting that she cruelly insults a vulnerable older woman. Yet modern readers, on the whole, do like her, much more than they like the pious, prim, all-too-perfect heroine of *Mansfield Park*, Fanny Price. Emma is perhaps not, as Mr. Knightley remarks, faultless in spite of her faults, but faultless because of them. Emma is a refreshing change from the idealized models of virtue to be found in the novels of Austen's predecessors, a realist character to whom we can relate as to a real person.

As a kind of anti-Cinderella, Emma must undergo a courtship ordeal in order to attain Mr. Knightley, Donwell Abbey, and all they represent. She must shed several layers of prejudice and narrow-mindedness in order to cure her self-delusions and see clearly. She must see through the illusion that her life is not perfect and complete, and acknowledge that she lacks an equal, or superior, partner. Later she must see through the illusion that Frank Churchill is her true partner, and acknowledge him as a symbolic brother, and see through the illusion that Mr. Knightley is a symbolic brother, and acknowledge him as her true partner, and superior. Then she must deserve Mr. Knightley, or at least make a moral improvement sufficient to warrant her being rewarded beyond her deserts. Mr. Knightley will not bestow wealth upon her, nor rescue her from obscurity and ill-usage, but he does offer her a more fulfilled and better life. Like most of Austen's heroines, Emma is removed from proper parental guidance and care in order that she should be more vulnerable, and less wise in her choices. In Emma's case, her mother is dead, her father is weak-minded, and her governess (never a stronger influence than Emma's own will) has married.

The social, as opposed to the geographical, setting of *Emma*—that is, the social position of its principal characters—is the middle class, a diverse and populous stratum of society that reached from the lower ranks of the aristocracy to the upper ranks of the working people; from the gentry or squirearchy, whose income derived from the land and whose estates could have been in the family since the Conquest or before, through the higher professions (the church, the law, the navy and army) to the lower professions (apothecaries, solicitors, clerks, teachers). This was the class into which Jane Austen was born and from which her readership would largely have been drawn. It was the most socially mobile class of the time, its members able to move from the professions to the gentry by purchasing or marrying into an estate, but also liable to downward descent. New money, earned in trade, was less prestigious than old money, but a mercantile origin could be obscured by the purchase of a country house and/or estate and

the investment in the Funds, which would provide a genteel (unearned) income.

Emma may at first seem to depict a rigidly ordered society; Highbury society is arranged in concentric circles, and to hear Emma speak of, for example, Robert Martin and his family, one would think that the worlds never meet. The circles do overlap, however, and the distinctions are more fluid than they might seem. The Woodhouses' visiting circle is technically composed of their family, Mr. Knightley, the Westons, Mr. Elton, and the Bateses—the upper ranks of Highbury society—but Emma accepts an invitation from the Coles, though Mr. Cole has only recently ceased to be in trade; she invites Mrs. Goddard, who runs a school, to Hartfield, and rubs shoulders with the Coxes (the father is a lawyer) and others. Emma takes as her best friend Harriet Smith, a parlor-boarder of Mrs. Goddard's who is known to be illegitimate and unclaimed, and turns out to be the daughter of a tradesman. The woman whom Mr. Knightley and Mrs. Weston believe Emma should befriend, Jane Fairfax, is the daughter of a man who, like Frederick Wentworth in *Persuasion,* had his fortune to make from a military profession, but died before he could make it, and Jane seems destined to descend to the level of her aunt and grandmother, Mrs. and Miss Bates.

Highbury contains many examples of the mobility of the age: the Bateses are downwardly mobile because they have lost the income of the father and husband who was in orders, but retain the status of gentlewomen because women kept the social status of their father until they married, and then took that of their husband. Mr. John Knightley, as younger son, will not inherit the estate of Donwell Abbey, and is in a sense downwardly mobile, but he is clearly making his way in the world, both in his profession and in his marriage; his wife is the elder daughter of the wealthy Mr. Woodhouse. Mr. Weston descended socially, from a military profession and a wealthy wife (whose family, the Churchills, disowned her) to relative poverty and trade, but by the time period of the novel he has recovered and, having sold his business, is well enough off to afford both a small estate and a wife. Mrs. Elton is determinedly upwardly mobile. Coming from Bristol, a large trading port, with an income perhaps derived from the flourishing trade in exotic goods (including slaves), she marries into the respectable position of vicar's wife, and is careful to advertise her collateral background (her sister has achieved a good marriage), harping on her brother-in-law's estate (which we suspect to be newly purchased). Mr. Knightley, like many landowners, may be in somewhat straitened circumstances and need to supplement the estate's income (deriving from rents and the sale of surplus produce) by investments and even mercantile and speculative enterprises. Thus Emma, product of the upper mercantile classes, is financially, as well as socially and personally, an eligible marriage prospect. Even minor characters illustrate this process: Mr. Perry has set up his carriage, making his rounds of Highbury and its surrounding houses much easier, and representing a contemporary controversy about the status of apothecaries.

Oliver MacDonagh very concisely puts the case for *Emma*'s providing invaluable glimpses of social history:

> When Harriet Smith tells Emma that Miss Nash would be surprised to learn that Robert Martin had proposed marriage to her, " 'for Miss Nash thinks her own sister very well married, and it is only a linen-draper,' " and Emma replies, " 'One should be sorry to see greater pride or refinement in the teacher of a school' " (pp. 55–56), at least three scales of early nineteenth-century social evaluation are delicately indicated and interwoven in thirty words.
>
> (*Jane Austen: Real and Imagined Worlds*, pp. 144–145)

Geographically, the fictional town of Highbury is in Surrey, a county to the south-west of London, in gently rolling and fertile countryside. We are told that Highbury is nine miles from Richmond and sixteen from London. The model for Hartfield, the Woodhouses' home, is said to be a real eighteenth-century house in Surrey, Polesden Lacey. Hartfield is a modern house of the kind built by those who had made their fortunes and were now settling on the profits; large by our standards, and luxurious, but not comparable to Mr. Knightley's Donwell Abbey, which, together with its estates, we infer has been in his family for generations, perhaps since the dissolution of the monasteries and the sale or redistribution of their wealth under Henry VIII in the sixteenth century. Just as Mr. Knightley represents the ideal of a gentleman, and an English gentleman, so Donwell Abbey represents the ideal home of an English gentleman; it is in some senses an ideal of England. Emma does not aspire to be mistress of Donwell Abbey; her own home is more than adequate, and she is its unquestioned mistress. Neither does she aspire to the income of its estate, since hers is the wealthier of the families.

Nonetheless, in marrying Emma, Mr. Knightley is conferring on her something besides his peerless self. Donwell Abbey and its owner represent the settled Tory squirearchy; an old name and old money; the antithesis of the all that the industrial revolution and nascent capitalism were hastening toward: stability, worth, order, old values; they represent England. The usually diplomatic and courteous Mr. Knightley reveals his proprietorial feelings for the place when he repels Mrs. Elton's attempt to elect herself Lady Patroness of the strawberry party. He throws few parties, perhaps because he cannot afford to entertain on a large scale, but, we might feel, more because to throw open Donwell Abbey to the masses (even the circumscribed society of Highbury) would threaten this haven and sanctuary of privacy and peace. Emma admires the abbey and seems to acknowledge the symbolic value of the place, and in acknowledging her present connection to the house and family, to be anticipating the closer alliance she will have in future. She notes that solid values and pride in continuity have preserved the estate from the depredations of fashionable landscapers (known as "improvers"):

> She felt all the honest pride and complacency which her alliance with the present and future proprietor could fairly warrant, as she viewed the respectable size and style of the building, its suitable, becoming, characteristic situation, ...meadows washed by a stream, of which the Abbey, with all the old neglect of prospect, had scarcely a sight—and its abundance of timber in rows and avenues, which neither fashion nor extravagance had rooted up.
>
> (p. 358)

Like its owner, Donwell Abbey "was just what it ought to be, and looked what it was," and Emma feels "an increasing respect for it, as the residence of a family of such true gentility, untainted in blood and understanding" (p. 358). Exploring the grounds, Emma reflects that the view is "sweet to the eye and the mind. English verdure, English culture, English comfort, seen under a sun bright, without being oppressive" (p. 360). The abbey has "appendages of prosperity and beauty"; it will provide for both body and soul.

Though the male characters, apart from Mr. Woodhouse, are capable of travelling and following outdoor pursuits, the novel's settings are largely interiors, and its occupations those of female society. Even Emma, the healthiest and most active of heroines, finds the half-mile walk to her friend Mrs. Weston's house unpleasant without a companion. When characters are forced beyond their familiar settings and exposed to the most minor trials of untamed nature (snow following a party unusually late in the winter; the gentle slopes of a local beauty spot; the heat of a June day), they seem to have little resistance or stamina, and become irritable and confused; their manners fail, and disorder sets in. Mrs. Elton fondly envisages herself as the crowning ornament of a fashionable picturesque scene with her fake rusticity of bonnet, basket, and donkey, but quickly tires of the

effort; though stronger and more fitted to outside work, Mr. Knightley, aesthetically aligned to the Augustan neoclassicism of an earlier generation, insists that rustic simplicity is better enjoyed with the creature comforts of shade and servants.

Emma is well named. Though the epistolary novel *Lady Susan* is named for its villainess, and the working titles of *Sense and Sensibility* and *Northanger Abbey* were, respectively, *Elinor and Marianne* and *Catherine*, *Emma* is the only one of the six major published works to be named for its heroine. This seems appropriate, since Emma Woodhouse is not only the central protagonist and heroine, but also very much the consciousness of the novel. The narrative voice is not Emma's; this is a third-person narrative with an omniscient perspective; but the narrative focuses almost exclusively on Emma's experience and frequently adopts her speaking style, retaining just enough distance to allow for the characteristic Austen irony. Emma's voice is vigorous, youthful, and above all confident. As John Wiltshire points out, when the narrative voice tells us that "'Harriet was to sit again the next day; and Mr. Elton, just as he ought, entreated for the permission of attending and reading to them again' (*Emma*, p. 47), though this is formally information given out by the narrator, the phrase 'just as he ought' construes his motives according to Emma's point of view" ("*Mansfield Park, Emma, Persuasion*," pp. 66–67). This enables Austen to direct the reader toward Emma's interpretation of events as the "real" and accurate one, as though we were being informed by the (reliable) narrator of "fact," when we are actually seeing through Emma's deluded eyes. "Mrs Weston is said to talk to Mr Elton of Miss Smith 'not in the least suspecting she was addressing a lover'; Frank Churchill, pressed to visit the Bateses, is said to consent only 'with the hope of Hartfield to reward him' (*Emma*, p. 235). In each of these cases, Emma's view of motives is allowed to tease the reader, to appear as if it is the book's" ("*Mansfield Park, Emma, Persuasion*," p. 67). Wiltshire calls this "a tunnelling of vision," which he finds most effective in the first two volumes, replaced by a looser style in the third. The trickery is enhanced by observations that Emma, secure in her perspicacity, makes to herself about other characters' beliefs, as when "Emma divined what every body present must be thinking. She was his [Frank Churchill's] object, and every body must perceive it" (p. 220). Emma seems to assume that the reader is included in "every body."

The narrative voice is protean, slipping from its own style of detached ironic good humor into not only Emma's sometimes maddening complacency, but also Miss Bates's garrulity, Mr. Knightley's measured good sense, and Mrs. Elton's vulgarity.

The stream of Mrs. Elton's remarks continues to flow even when the company is employed in picking strawberries, and no one is much attending to her. The narrative voice is effaced and omits the usual indicators of speech. The progress of Mrs. Elton's thoughts, with their interruptions, disconnections, and abbreviations, in a voice that is recognizably hers, is represented through a technique similar to that used by modernist writers such as Virginia Woolf and James Joyce to represent characters' interior monologues.

> Mrs. Elton, in all her apparatus of happiness, her large bonnet and her basket, was very ready to lead the way in gathering, accepting, or talking—strawberries, and only strawberries, could now be thought of or spoken of.—"The best fruit in England—every body's favourite—always wholesome.—These the finest beds and finest sorts.—Delightful to gather for one's self—the only way of really enjoying them.—Morning decidedly the best time—never tired—every sort good—hautboy infinitely superior—no comparison—the others hardly eatable—hautboy very scarce—Chili preferred—white wood finest flavour of all—price of strawberries in London—abundance about Bristol—Maple Grove—cultivation—beds when to be renewed—gardeners thinking exactly different—no general rule—gardeners never to be put out of their way—delicious fruit—only too rich to be eaten much of—inferior to cherries—currants more refreshing—only objection to gathering strawberries the stooping—glaring sun—tired to death—could bear it no longer—must go and sit in the shade."

> (pp. 358–359)

Mrs. Elton's appearance and her conversation, both overdecorated with material objects—reticules, bonnets, donkeys, baskets, pearls, trimmings, lace veils—expose her mercantile origins and materialist mind. Having married into the lower spheres of the gentry from a rung below, Mrs. Elton tries to scale linguistic as well as social heights. Her lexicon, however, betrays her want of gentility. Emma pounces on the references to Mrs Elton's "*Caro sposo*" and "Mr. E" as glaring evidence of vulgarity, and is incensed by her inappropriate reference to Mr. Knightley as "Knightley." The affected use of foreign terms—particularly if, as we suspect, Mrs. Elton is far from being fluent in the language, is pretentious and socially damning.

Glibness or overreadiness of speech is often a sign of a less than perfect character in Austen's novels, and fluent literacy, a sign of effeminacy. Emma's initial attraction to Frank Churchill does not survive his flow of small talk and witticisms, or his ready pen. Although she is flattered by his attentions, and indulges in fantasies about their union, Frank seems unable to awaken a sexual response in Emma. Her feelings soon devolve into nonsexual sisterly affection, and her mature, sexual response awaits the less articulate, and therefore more masculine, Mr. Knightley, who strides through Highbury in his gaiters, flushes red with exertion, and does not write loquacious letters. (Frank is active, but sometimes in a girlish way, as, for example, a too-nimble dancer and a great payer of morning visits.) Mr. Elton's prosy compliments sound pre-prepared, and his impertinent protestations of love may result from an over-indulgence in Mr. Weston's good wine, but they sound rehearsed. Mr. Knightley, of course, is a model of restraint. He says: "'I cannot make speeches, Emma,'" but reinforces the point most beautifully. "If I loved you less, I might be able to talk about it more" (p. 430). Later, "It was in plain, unaffected, gentleman-like English, such as Mr. Knightley used even to the woman he was in love with" that he considers how he can make his formal proposal (p. 448).

One of the many great things about Austen's novels is the representativeness of their opening paragraphs, each of which introduces us to the self-contained world of the respective novel. Each introduction sets out many of the novels' motifs. In the case of *Emma,* an important opposition is set up between what seems to be and what is; between assumptions and actuality. The recurrence of qualifications, particularly the word "but," is significant. Emma "seemed" to unite some of the best blessings of existence; she is happy and indulged, yet her mother is dead; her mother's place is taken by a governess, yet Miss Taylor falls a little short of a mother; Miss Taylor is like a mother to both sisters, but particularly attached to Emma; Miss Taylor holds the authority of governess, but her mild temper hardly allows her to exercise it; Emma esteems Miss Taylor's judgment, but is directed by her own; Emma has disadvantages that threaten to alloy her enjoyments, but as yet the danger is unperceived; sorrow comes, but it is a gentle sorrow; Emma is happy in having promoted the match, but it was a black morning's work; the change is unbearable, but the distance between the families is only half a mile, though Emma is aware that the difference will be great. We end with a picture very different from the spoiled princess of the first line: "with all her advantages, natural and domestic, she was now in great danger of suffering from intellectual solitude" (p. 7). The word "danger" appears three times, and the word "evil" is applied to the disparity in ages and dispositions between Emma and her father. Though "evil" is not used with any connotations of true wickedness, the point is clear; Emma is vulnerable; she could be lonely and bored.

Nonetheless, our initial impression of Emma is of a girl who thinks a little too well of herself and much too well of her penetration. Mr. Knightley rapidly punctures Emma's vision of herself as seeress/matchmaker. *He* is the story's seer; he generally knows, though he is too discreet to tell, the truth. While Mr. Woodhouse supports Emma's assertion that she made the Westons' match herself, by begging her not to foretell anything else, Mr. Knightley forestalls further congratulation, self- or otherwise, for Emma's supposed success in making or predicting the match, by making the attempt seem indelicate and inappropriate, and a mere lucky guess something less shameful to confess.

> "I do not understand what you mean by 'success,'" said Mr. Knightley. "Success supposes endeavour. Your time has been properly and delicately spent, if you have been endeavouring for the last four years to bring about this marriage. A worthy employment for a young lady's mind! But if, which I rather imagine, your making the match, as you call it, means only your planning it .... where is your merit?—what are you proud of?—you made a lucky guess; and *that* is all that can be said."
>
> (pp. 12–13)

Emma is not cowed; she replies with spirit, but she does modify her claim, to "a something between the do-nothing and the do-all."

Emma is a comedy of errors as well as of manners. It presents the reader with a set of events whose significance we are left to interpret or misinterpret, enacted by a set of characters a few of whom see the truth but most of whom are deceived, and some of whom some tell the truth, and some practice deception. The comedy comes partly from the conflict between manners (codes governing behavior) and desires (how people really want to behave), but also, together with the poignancy, from the characters' (and readers') errors of interpretation.

The behavior of the middle-class country-town society of Highbury is highly codified. Its inhabitants modify their words, deeds, and appearance to suit their company, the surroundings, the social situation, and the subject of conversation. Though they profess to admire openness and naturalness of behavior—"being" over "seeming"—they practice good manners—"seeming" over "being." Before entering the Westons' Christmas Eve party, Mr. Elton and Mr. John Knightley must adjust their countenances (facial expressions); Mr. Elton must "compose his joyous looks," and smile less; John Knightley must "disperse his ill-humour" and smile more (p. 117). Although she finds the subject of Jane Fairfax irritating, and listening to Miss Bates's reading of Jane's letters tedious, Emma is constrained by good manners to appear delighted to hear that Jane has written, and to offer compliments about the handwriting. She must even meet Mrs. Elton, whom she detests, with an appearance of civility.

In spite of these constraints, Austen manages to convey much that her characters could not say through their body language, especially glances. Emma and Frank Churchill exchange through "smiles of intelligence" (p. 220) all they cannot say about their suspicions when they glance at Jane Fairfax. Emma's suspicions are incorrect, of course; she is still deceived. Not so Mr. Knightley, who suspects "something of a private liking, of private understanding even, between Frank Churchill and Jane" because "he had seen a look, more than a single look, at Miss Fairfax, which, from the admirer of Miss Woodhouse, seemed somewhat out of place" (pp. 343–344). Where speech and actions are most constrained and codified, sometimes characters reveal their feelings through the involuntary signals of the body. Blushes, smiles, and frowns are always significant, but these signs are not immune from interpretation; and even if they are unnoticed by other characters, they are available for the edification of the reader. We notice Jane's blushes of consciousness and guilt, her headaches and low spirits; and even Mr. Knightley, a model of transparency and probity, is "too tired" to play with his brother's children when he thinks Emma loves someone else. The usually robust Emma, manifesting symptoms of a virus or mild depression—a "sensation of listlessness, weariness, stupidity, this disinclination to sit down and employ myself, this feeling of everything's being dull and insipid about the house!"—attributes them to Frank's departure from Highbury: "I must be in love" (p. 262). Jane Fairfax, truly in love, suffers more, with "headache" and "langour" (p. 263).

Highbury society may feel that there is little more to know about and little to tell one another. Games, like gossip, provide novelty. Like the intricate patterns of dancing, games represent the social nexus in microcosm, imposing rules on the players and, unlike hard fact, providing matter for reiteration and speculation. Highbury (i.e., Miss Bates, Mrs. Goddard, Mrs. Perry, Harriet Smith) is exercised by puzzles both real—whether Frank Churchill will visit his father, whom Mr. Elton will marry—and artificial—charades, acrostics, and word games. The two come together in courtship. Courtship provides the impetus and the retardation of the plot, and courtship ritual and play could embody several kinds of deception; indeed, for the modest or shy, it almost required deception. Somewhere between the acceptable deceit of the suitor who makes advances ambiguous enough to protect against loss of face, and the unacceptable deceit of false or hidden courtship, is the complex code of flirting. Emma is a far more flirtatious heroine than Catherine, Elinor, Lizzie, Fanny, or Anne, which adds to her charm.

Helping Harriet to compile her album of riddles enables Emma to help Mr. Elton to practice an acceptable deceit; his contribution will have an encoded meaning that the recipient may choose to understand or not. The first riddle he offers would give a hint of his interest.

My first doth affliction denote   ["woe"]
Which my second is destin'd to feel.   ["man"]
And my whole is the best antidote
That affliction to soften and heal.   ["woman"]

(*Emma*, p. 70)

The second is more explicit:

My first displays the wealth and pomp of kings,
Lords of the earth! their luxury and ease.
   ["court"]
Another view of man, my second brings,
Behold him there, the monarch of the seas!
   ["ship"]
But ah! united, what reverse we have!
Man's boasted power and freedom, all are flown;
Lord of the earth and sea, he bends a slave,
   ["courtship"]
And woman, lovely woman, reigns alone.
Thy ready wit the word will soon supply,
May its approval beam in that soft eye!

                 (*Emma*, p. 71)

Emma is not puzzled; she divines the answers immediately, but she is deceived, assuming that Harriet, not she, is the object of Mr. Elton's courtship. Failing to see Emma's failure to see, Mr. Elton, Malvolio-like, adopts what he thinks is his assigned role. The more attributes of the role (suitor) he employs—sighs, studied compliments, gallantry—the less we believe in him as the real thing (lover). The more Mrs. Elton *caro sposo*'s him and talks of his persistence in courtship, the less we believe in this as a love match. Mrs. Elton also unwittingly provides a puzzle that gives a clue to her character when she uses a poem of John Gay's to half-encode and half-parade her possession of a secret she believes Emma does not understand. Gay's "The Hare and Many Friends" from *Fifty-One Fables in Verse* (1727) tells the story of a hare pursued by hounds begging her supposed friends to save her from hunters, but each animal gives some trivial excuse.

She next the stately bull implor'd;
And thus reply'd the mighty lord.
"Since ev'ry beast alive can tell
That I sincerely wish you well,
I may, without offence, pretend
To take the freedom of a friend;
Love calls me hence; a fav'rite cow
Expects me near yon barley mow:
And when a lady's in the case,
You know, all other things give place.

To leave you thus might seem unkind;
But see, the goat is just behind."

                 (*Emma*, p. 454).

Whether Mrs. Elton is envisaging Frank Churchill as the bull and Jane Fairfax as the cow, we are left to wonder, but either way the bull is being hypocritically deceptive, putting his carnal desires before his duty as a friend, and using the courtly love code as an excuse. This would have been considered a somewhat indelicate note to introduce into the conversation, and Mrs. Elton introduces it because she probably doesn't know or doesn't remember the poem well.

Mr. Woodhouse similarly remembers only the first stanza of his contribution to Harriet's collection.

David Garrick, "A Riddle," The New Foundling Hospital for Wit, Fourth Part, 1771.

Kitty, a fair, but frozen maid,
Kindled a flame I still deplore;
The hood-wink'd boy I call'd in aid,
Much of his near approach afraid,
   So fatal to my suit before.
At length, propitious to my pray'r,
The little urchin came;
At once he sought the midway air,
And soon he clear'd, with dextrous care,
The bitter relicks of my flame.
To Kitty, Fanny now succeeds,
She kindles slow, but lasting fires:
With care my appetite she feeds;
Each day some willing victim bleeds,
To satisfy my strange desires.
Say, by what title, or what name,
Must I this youth address? [chimney sweep's boy]
Cupid and he are not the same,
Tho' both can raise, or quench a flame—
   I'll kiss you, if you guess.

                 (*Emma*, p. 454)

As self-centered as a toddler, Mr. Woodhouse realizes his days of courtship codes and games are gone, and he can come up with nothing better to contribute than an old verse by David Garrick. The poem retains some mysteries for modern readers, however. Emma says that she and Harriet copied Garrick's riddle from *The Elegant Extracts* (p. 79). These were anthologies of improving and educational extracts collected by the Christian philosopher and proponent of liberal education Vicesimus Knox (1752–1821). The *Elegant Extracts from the Most Eminent British Poets* follows the formula satirized in *Northanger Abbey* through six volumes. The first, "Devotional and Moral" poetry, includes selections from the work of poets who would have been known to Emma: Alexander Pope, Matthew Prior, Robert Blair, and Joseph Addison, as well as from some of Jane Austen's favorite writers, such as James Thomson and William Cowper, but the *Extracts* do not include "Kitty a Fair but Frozen Maid." The conventional solution to the riddle is also unsatisfactory, and there have been suggestions that it has a double, and scurrilous, meaning.

Unlike Mr. Woodhouse, Frank Churchill is by no means retired from courtship, and he energetically deceives everyone except Mr. Knightley. He uses the playful untruthfulness of games for real deceptions, making alphabet blocks a "vehicle for gallantry and trick" (p. 348) by pressing the acrostics "Dixon" and "blunder" on Jane Fairfax. As Mr. Knightley reflects, it was "a child's play, chosen to conceal a deeper game" (p. 348). Conversely, he treats life as a game, heedless of consequences, such as the pain he inflicts on Jane and Emma (though Austen family tradition suggests that the last alphabet block message, which Jane ignores, is "pardon"). From him comes the impetus that leads to Mr. Weston's pun on Emma's name and, ultimately, to Emma's cruelty to Miss Bates when, following Frank's lead, she overplays the game and transgresses against the rules of human relations.

Mr. Knightley tacitly removes himself from the courtship ordeal in his avuncular behavior toward Emma and, at the ball, by taking his place "among the standers-by, where he ought not to be [again, this is Emma's view]... classing himself with the husbands, and fathers, and whist-players" rather than with those who take part in the courtship ritual (p. 325). Notably, he does not contribute to Harriet's collection of riddles, nor to the Box Hill entertainments.

If Emma thinks herself a Sybil, Miss Bates is a Cassandra. In relating her anecdote of the mending of her mother's spectacles, she indirectly tells that of Frank's attempt to get rid of her in order to be alone with Jane. Frank has encouraged Miss Bates to go to find Emma, expecting her to detain the visitors with the anecdote, which she does, at length. Perspicacious readers will be envisaging an interesting scene from which they are excluded, while they suffer, with Emma and Mrs. Weston, the monotonous rambling trivialities of Miss Bates. They are less fortunate than Emma when she is excluded from Mr. Weston's relation of his son's fascinating letter by Mr. Elton's incessant claims on her attention, and the necessity of returning a civil reply to his inane inquiries about her comfort; Mr. Weston is happy to repeat himself for her benefit, but we never see Jane and Frank alone together.

As Mary Lascelles shows, Miss Bates is always among the first to be informed (of the Dixons' voyage; of Mr. Elton's marriage; of Frank and Jane's engagement) but she rarely gets to announce the news: Frank's blunder reveals that Mr. Perry is buying a new carriage (Miss Bates takes responsibility, but the reader gets an important clue), Mr. Knightley announces to Emma Mr. Elton's marriage, and Mrs. Weston discloses the news of Frank and Jane's engagement. (See Lascelles, *Jane Austen and Her Art*, pp. 93–95.) When Miss Bates gives away clues, it is usually unconsciously. The greatest talker of the novel is doomed to be unintelligible. If we listen carefully, we find in the stream of her garrulity snippets of important facts, but perhaps we don't listen as carefully as we should. Like Emma, mildly amused and condescending, we let the flow wash over us. This makes Emma's humiliation of Miss Bates at Box Hill, and Miss Bates's resolve to hold her tongue, all the more poignant.

The Box Hill scene is doubly important in bringing together several strands of the narrative's codifications—social, moral, linguistic—and in making Mr. Knightley the agent of their partial decoding. ("Partial" because some mysteries must be kept from Emma for the plot to play out.) This is only one of a series of epiphanies that Emma undergoes: she realizes with painful clarity that slighting Miss Bates was not simply a private amusement but an insensitive and wounding act; she has already learned that she entirely misread Mr. Elton's behavior; she finds that she failed to penetrate Frank and Jane's deception; she learns that she was wrong about which courtship ordeal Harriet has been involved in; finally, she acknowledges that she loves Mr. Knightley. She is beginning to distinguish supposition and speculation from actuality, and to learn the acceptable limits of playfulness.

Puzzles and playfulness enter into even in the most solemn scenes in the novel, however, as when Emma blushingly undertakes to call Mr. Knightley "George," "in the building in which N takes M for better, for worse" (p. 463). This could be a phonetic representation of the first sounds of Knightley and Emma, but we should remember that Austen was a minister's daughter. The "Form of Solemnization of Matrimony" in the Anglican Book of Common Prayer put *n* wherever the name of the bride or groom was to be inserted, since *n* stands for *nomen* (Latin for "name"). *M,* which is double *n,* stood for *nomina* (names). Later editions put *n* to indicate the groom's name and *m* to indicate the bride's. Perhaps this, like the famous "Bad Tuesday" was an in-joke for the Austen family, or perhaps Austen relished the double signification of the heroine whom no one but herself was to like in this most overdetermined of courtship/detective stories.

Emma contains one of Austen's very few errors of chronology. During the strawberry-picking party at Donwell Abbey, Emma observes the apple trees in blossom, which of course would happen in spring, not high summer.

The novel is structured around a series of set pieces; the big social events suitable for the season and its weather: a Christmas party, excursions to beauty spots, a ball, strawberry-picking; and the usual social round of visits, dinners, and walks.

Ellen Moody's detailed examination of the chronologies of Austen's novels reveals that many unpleasant or momentous events happen on a Tuesday. The Coles' party at which Emma makes such a fool of herself happens on a Tuesday—15 February. Emma tells Frank the piano is a gift from Mr. Dixon, is herself mortified by the piano-playing of Jane (who suffers far more from knowing what is being said about her and has the preening triumphant offers of Mrs. Cole to let Jane use the piano any time, echoing Lady Catherine de Bourgh's patronizing offer to Elizabeth Bennet in *Pride and Prejudice*). The day the pianoforte arrives for Jane is therefore Valentine's Day. Frank leaves Highbury on a Shrove Tuesday, having said good-bye to Jane Fairfax and tried to confess to Emma, who has misunderstood him and believes that he is in love with her. In 1814 Shrove Tuesday was on 22 February. Emma's nadir, the day after Harriet has confessed that she loves Mr. Knightley and that she believes her feelings are reciprocated, is Tuesday, 5 July. On the next day, Wednesday, 6 July, the weather improves, Mr. Knightley explains himself to Emma, and asks her to marry him. (See http://mason.gmu.edu/~emoody/tuesdays.html and Ellen Moody, "A Calendar for *Sense and Sensibility*," *Philological Quarterly* (Iowa City) 78, no. 3 (Summer 1999): 301–334.)

IMPORTANCE AND INFLUENCE

Austen collected the opinions of some of the first readers of *Emma*. Most seemed to have liked it, many, though not all, more than *Pride and Prejudice* or *Mansfield Park*. Some disliked *Emma*; others though there was too much of Mrs. Elton or Miss Bates, or found Harriet silly, but everyone loved Mr. Knightley. Austen's brother, then Captain Austen, liked it "extremely...though there might be more Wit in P & P—& an higher Morality in M P—yet altogether on account of it's [*sic*] peculiar air of Nature throughout, he preferred it to either"; her sister, Cassandra, liked it "better than P. & P.—but not so well as M.P.—"; their mother "thought it more entertaining than M.P.—but not so interesting as P. & P.—No characters in it equal to Ly Catherine & Mr Collins" (Chapman, ed., *Minor Works*, pp. 436–439).

One advantage of Austen's change of publisher from Egerton to Murray was that Murray was an influential figure in literary circles, and founder of the *Quarterly Review,* which his reader, William Gifford, edited. Gifford's favorable report on *Emma* prompted Murray to ask Sir Walter Scott to review the novel for the *Quarterly Review* (dated October 1815, issued March 1816). Scott not only reviewed Emma most favorably, but he also produced a 5,000-word piece commending *Pride and Prejudice* and *Sense and Sensibility* as well as *Emma,* and arguing that these works exemplify the best kind of narrative fiction, the kind that justifies the elevation of the novel genre from the status of frivolous entertainment to the status of art. Locating Austen firmly in the tradition of realist narrative fiction rather than in the earlier kinds of novel that owe more to the romance tradition, such as gothic novels and novels of sentiment, Scott writes that such works "proclaim a knowledge of the human heart, with the power and resolution to bring that knowledge to the service of honour and virtue." They "belong to a class of fictions which has arisen almost in our own times, and which draws the characters and incidents introduced more immediately from the current of ordinary life than was permitted by the former rules of the novel." He feels that he bestows "no mean

compliment" on *Emma*'s author when he says that "keeping close to common incidents, and to such characters as occupy the ordinary walks of life, she has produced sketches of such spirit and originality that we never miss the excitation which depends upon a narrative of uncommon events, arising from the consideration of minds, manners, and sentiments, greatly above our own." He compares this kind of realism to the Flemish school of painting: "The subjects are not often elegant, and certainly never grand; but they are finished up to nature, and with a precision which delights the reader" (*Quarterly Review* 14 [March 1816]: 188–201; repr. B. C. Southam, ed., *Jane Austen: The Critical Heritage,* vol. 1, pp. 58–69).

Austen's response to the article was to say that she had nothing to complain of except that its author (the piece was unsigned) had ignored *Mansfield Park*. (1 April 1816, *Letters,* ed. Le Faye, p. 313).

In a similar vein, the *British Critic* of July 1816 praised Austen's verisimilitude and moderation because it did not "dabble in religion," since "of fanatical novels and fanatical authoresses we are already sick" (pp. 96–98; repr. Southam, ed., *Critical Heritage,* p. 71). The reviewer found *Emma* "amusing, inoffensive and well principled," and admired the interest that Austen had contrived to bring to the circumscribed setting and few characters. The *Gentleman's Magazine* (September 1816) was more temperate in its praise, and even patronizing. It finds that "a good novel is now and then an agreeable relaxation from severer studies" and that though *Emma* does not have "the highly-drawn characters in superior life which are so interesting in *Pride and Prejudice*; it delineates with great accuracy the habits and manners of a middle class of gentry; and of the inhabitants of a country village at one degree of rank and gentility beneath them." It approves that "the language is chaste and correct," and sums up: "If *Emma* be not allowed to rank in the very highest class of modern Novels, it certainly may claim at least a distinguished degree of eminence in that species of composition. It is amusing, if not instructive; and has no tendency to deteriorate the heart" (pp. 248–249; repr. Southam, ed., *Critical Heritage,* p. 72).

Reviewers of the first editions of the novels and of the reprints of the 1830s continue to praise Austen for her production of lifelike miniatures, and *Emma* was frequently cited as the apex of Jane Austen's art. That the novels were something more was often overlooked, with some notable exceptions. Perhaps the most perspicacious of the nineteenth-century responses to Austen's work was written by the Shakespeare scholar Richard Simpson, in the *North British Review* of 1870. As David Lodge notes, Simpson shows how Austen's so-called miniatures of Regency society

mediate a complex and challenging vision of experience, and he does so in terms which remarkably anticipate the conclusions of the most sophisticated and modern criticism. That Jane Austen had an essentially critical and ironic vision, defined initially by parodic contrast with literary stereotypes; that her fiction was not thrown off by a kind of effortless knack, but "worked up by incessant labour into its perfect form … that she was a subtle and unsentimental moralist, particularly concerned with the processes of self-discovery and the attainment of maturity through personal relations"—all these points made by Simpson, reappear in such modern critics as Dr. and Mrs. Leavis, Marvin Mudrick, and Lionel Trilling.

(Lodge, ed., *Jane Austen,* pp. 17–18).

Not every reader has admired *Emma,* of course. The novelist Anthony Trollope annotated the end pages of his copy with some censorious comments on the novel in general and its heroine in particular. He found the story a period piece, timid, and "very tedious," but it showed "wonderful knowledge of female character, and is severe on the little foibles of women with a severity which no man would dare to use." Emma, he felt was treated "mercilessly", in every passage:

She is in fault for some folly, some vanity, some ignorance,—or indeed for some meanness.

Her conduct to her friend Harriett [*sic*],—her assumed experience and real ignorance of human nature—are terribly true; but nowadays we dare not make our heroines so little. Her weaknesses are all plain to us, but of her strength we are only told; and even at the last we hardly know why Mr. Knightley loves her. (1865; repr. Lodge, ed., *Jane Austen,* p 51).

Charlotte Brontë, whose own work, with its elements of Romantic symbolism and the elevation of the individual, is the polar opposite of Austen's, deplored *Emma*'s want of warmth or enthusiasm:

Anything energetic, poignant, heart-felt is utterly out of place in commending these works: all such demonstration the authoress would have met with a well-bred sneer, would have calmly scorned as outré and extravagant … The passions are perfectly unknown to her; she rejects even a speaking acquaintance with that stormy sisterhood. Even to the feelings she vouchsafes no more than an occasional graceful but distant recognition … Her business is not half so much with the human heart as with the human eyes, mouth, hands, and feet. What sees keenly, speaks aptly, moves flexibly, it suits her to study; but what throbs fast and full, though hidden, what the blood rushes through, what is the unseen seat of life and the sentient target of death—this Miss Austen ignores.

(letter to W. S. Williams, 12 April 1850; repr. Southam, *Critical Heritage,* pp. 127–128)

After the publication of the enlarged memoir in 1870, much writing about Austen was biographical, and contributed to the growing myth of the genteel, refined, modest, retired woman in a quiet provincial town. It wasn't until the first decades of the next century that Austen's work received the tribute of full-length scholarly analysis.

Emma vies with *Pride and Prejudice* as readers' favorite Austen novel. Its wit, pace, comedy, and the tearingly high spirits in which it leaves us make it an exceptionally pleasurable read. The complexity of its construction and the deftness with which clues to its mysteries are both given and withheld make rereading it an even greater pleasure.

A. C. Bradley in 1911 and Reginald Farrer in 1917 set a high standard for twentieth-century Jane Austen studies, placing the novels in the context of eighteenth-century literary antecedents and eighteenth- and nineteenth-century culture, and contributing to our understanding of their structure rather than to the myth of genteel Jane. As fellow novelists, E. M. Forster and Virginia Woolf were acutely aware of Austen's skill in handling characterization and narrative structure, though Woolf's suggestion (in *The Common Reader,* 1925) that Jane Austen was one of the hardest of authors to catch in the art of being great perhaps added to the myth of the stories having been spontaneously thrown off practically without art.

R. W. Chapman's great scholarly endeavor of the 1920s and 1930s provided definitive editions of the novels and accessible collections of Austen's letters, and made possible the flood of papers, articles, monographs, collections of essays, and other material that has constituted the Austen industry ever since. Q. D. Leavis, D. W. Harding, and Mary Lascelles, in her *Jane Austen and Her Art* (1939), were among those responsible for finally freeing Austen's work from the myth. Harding's essay "Regulated Hatred," which appeared in F. R. Leavis's Cambridge periodical *Scrutiny* in 1940, established Austen as a satiric writer with a clear-sighted sense of the follies and vices of those around her: "This eruption of rage and hatred into the relationships of everyday social life is something that the urbane admirer of Jane Austen finds distasteful; it is not the satire of one who writes securely for the entertainment of her civilised acquaintances. And it has the effect, for the attentive reader, of changing the flavour of the more ordinary satire amongst which it is embedded" (repr. Lodge, *Jane Austen,* p. 71).

This produces caricature in works such as *Pride and Prejudice,* but more subtle characterizations in *Emma,* where

a much more complete humility is combined with the earlier unblinking attention to people as they are. The underlying argument has a different trend. She continues to see that the heroine has derived from the people and conditions around her, but she now keeps clearly in mind the far bolder conclusion that even a heroine is likely to have assimilated many of the more unpleasant possibilities of the human being in society. And it is not that society has spoilt an originally perfect girl who now has to recover her pristine good sense, as it was with Catherine Morland [in *Northanger Abbey*], but that the heroine has not yet achieved anything like perfection and is actually going to learn a number of serious lessons from some of the people she lives with.

(repr. Lodge, *Jane Austen,* p. 73)

Collections such as David Lodge's *Casebook* are extremely useful in juxtaposing some of the polarized readings and opinions that *Emma* provokes. Two of these are Marvin Mudrick's "Irony as Form: Emma" (pp. 104–130) and Edgar F. Shannon Jr.'s "*Emma*: Character and Construction" (pp. 130–147). Mudrick finds that *Emma* is "a throwing off of chains," a comic chain of misunderstanding described with "a freedom and assurance unparalleled in Jane Austen's earlier work" (p. 104). Yet he sees Emma as in many ways deeply unpleasant, and using her father's dependence on her to mask her horror of marriage and preference for her own sex. "The only character in the story who sees Emma at all clearly is Frank Churchill. He is as egotistic and calculating as she, but he beats her at her own game because he is far less self-deluded" (p. 120). Frank "has no scruples, for he needs none: charm and wealth excuse everything. One wonders whether Emma—even under the vigilance of Mr. Knightley—will not be polished into the same engaging ruthlessness after several years of marriage" (p. 122).

Shannon sees Austen as primarily a moral writer "striving to establish criteria of sound judgement and right conduct in human life" (p. 131). He finds the character of Emma endowed with good qualities that provide a firm basis for her redemption: her happy disposition, lack of personal vanity, devotion to her father and sister, and charity toward the poor. Although she sometimes behaves badly, she always has a pang of conscience. She may not be perfect in the execution; she is human; but she knows right from wrong. Shannon cites Austen's use of phrases such as "true contrition" and "the penitence so truly, so justly hers" as evidence of Emma's moral development. Austen reminds us of "human fallibility and the need for modesty, unselfishness and compassion. She requires charity and forebearance toward the less gifted and fortunate than we .... She demonstrates that we cannot escape the consequences of our acts, that love is not a game. Such truths she inculcates objectively through Emma's progress from self-deception to perception and humility" (p. 146).

Although Austen's satire is not didactic in the manner of Pope or Jonathan Swift, this tendency to see the novels as lessons in morality has been pervasive in the twentieth century. Critics from Bradley to Bradbury have found Austen's "moral universe" reactionary, Tory, Established (i.e. Anglican) Church and anti-revolutionary. But as Graham Hough points out, we should also remember that *Emma* is primarily a comedy. The story ends conventionally with a marriage, seemingly rewarding virtue with happiness, but "happiness of a very uninflated kind. There is nothing passionate, exalted or transcendental about this eminently satisfactory marriage" (repr. Lodge, *Jane Austen*, p. 73). The description of the wedding is filtered through the eyes of the pretentious and vulgar Mrs. Elton, who sees it in terms of the material trappings with which she would have arrayed it, but which are excluded by the better and more austere taste of the bride and groom. "She thought it all extremely shabby, and very inferior to her own. 'Very little white satin, very few lace veils; a most pitiful business! Selina would stare when she heard of it' " (*Emma,* p. 484). Hough comments:

> To the last it is dependent on trivialities, surrounded by absurd accidents and foolish com-

ments. This dense atmosphere of the contingent, the small-scale and the ludicrous surrounds all the serious issues in *Emma* and forms an essential part of its nature. To distil the pure moral elixir gives no idea of this.

(repr. Lodge, *Jane Austen,* p. 85)

Just as Miss Bates does not function primarily as social irritant, "a try-your-strength machine for Emma to measure herself against," but exists for her own sake, so "the same is true of the whole closely particularised texture of Highbury life; the mere contingent facts interest, amuse and delight" (repr. Lodge, *Jane Austen,* p. 85).

The two hundredth anniversary of Austen's birth was the occasion of a number of publications on her work, including an important collection of essays edited by John Halperin, *Jane Austen: Bicentenary Essays* (1975). Austen's work ceased to be treated as an isolated outcrop without ancestors or descendents, and instead was examined as the product of specific time and place. Analyses of the novels in their cultural context include Julia Prewitt Brown, *Jane Austen's Novels: Social Change and Literary Form* (1979); Marilyn Butler, *Jane Austen and the War of Ideas* (1975); Alistair Duckworth, *The Improvement of the Estate* (1971); Warren Roberts, *Jane Austen and the French Revolution* (1979); Roger Sales, *Jane Austen and Representations of Regency England* (1994); and Maaja Stewart, *Domestic Realities and Imperial Fictions: Jane Austen's Novels in Eighteenth-Century Contexts* (1993). A thought-provoking politicized reading of Austen's work is provided by Claudia Johnson, in her *Jane Austen: Women, Politics, and the Novel* (1989).

Other important areas of context to have been explored in depth are religion, education, marriage, and the rights of women in Austen's time. Feminist theory has also produced powerful readings of Austen's work, including *Emma.* Nina Auerbach, *Communities of Women* (1978); Rachel Brownstein, *Becoming a Heroine* (1982); Sandra Gilbert and Susan Gubar, *The Mad-*

woman in the Attic (1979); Ellen Moers, *Literary Women* (1976); Mary Poovey, *The Proper Lady and the Woman Writer* (1984); Elaine Showalter, *A Literature of Their Own* (1977); Patricia Meyer Spacks, *The Female Imagination* (1975); and Jane Spencer, *The Rise of the Woman Novelist* (1986) all contain sections on Austen. Margaret Kirkham's *Jane Austen, Feminism and Fiction* (1983) argues that Austen's works make

a feminist case, while full-length feminist readings of Austen's work include Mary Evans, *Jane Austen and the State* (1987), Leroy W. Smith, *Jane Austen and the Drama of Woman* (1983) and Alison Sulloway, *Jane Austen and the Province of Womanhood* (1989).

Many indispensable essays from all phases of the study of Austen's work appear in the collections listed in the bibliography below.

Selected Bibliography

EDITIONS

The Novels of Jane Austen. Edited by R. W. Chapman. 6 vols. Oxford: Clarendon Press, 1923. Revised edition 1965–1969.

LETTERS, FAMILY REMINISCENCES, AND PAPERS

Austen, Caroline. *My Aunt Jane Austen.* London: Spottiswoode Ballantyne, 1952.

———. *Reminiscences of Caroline Austen.* Winchester: Jane Austen Society, 1986.

Austen, Henry. "Biographical Notice of the Author." Preface to *Northanger Abbey* and *Persuasion* (1818), revised for 1833 edition.

Austen-Leigh, J. E. *A Memoir of Jane Austen.* London, 1870. Reprinted, edited by R.W. Chapman. London: Oxford University Press, 1926.

Austen-Leigh, Mary Augusta. *James Edward Austen-Leigh: A Memoir by His Daughter.* 1911 [privately printed].

———. *Personal Aspects of Jane Austen.* London: John Murray, 1920.

Austen-Leigh, Richard A. *Austen Papers 1704–1856.* Colchester: Spottiswoode Ballantyne, 1942.

Austen-Leigh, William A. and Richard A. Austen-Leigh. *Jane Austen: Her Life and Letters: A Family Record.* London: 1913.

Hill, Constance. *Jane Austen: her Homes and Her Friends.* London: J. Lane, 1902.

Hubback, J. H., and Edith Hubback. *Jane Austen's Sailor Brothers.* London: J. Lane, 1906.

Jane Austen's Letters. Edited by Deidre Le Faye. 3d ed. Oxford: Oxford University Press, 1995.

Letters of Jane Austen. Edited by Edward, Lord Brabourne. 2 vols. London: R. Bentley & Son, 1884.

SECONDARY WORKS

Austen-Leigh, William, and R. A. Austen-Leigh. *Jane Austen, a Family Record.* Revised and enlarged by Deidre Le Faye. London: British Library, 1989.

Cecil, Lord David. *A Portrait of Jane Austen.* London: Constable, 1978.

Chapman, R. W. *Jane Austen: Facts and Problems.* Oxford: Clarendon Press, 1948.

Craik, W. A. *Jane Austen and Her Time.* London: Nelson, 1969.

Fergus, Jan. *Jane Austen: A Literary Life.* London: Macmillan, 1991.

Halperin, John. *The Life of Jane Austen.* Baltimore: Johns Hopkins University Press, 1984.

Hodge, Jane Aiken. *The Double Life of Jane Austen.* London: Hodder and Stoughton, 1972.

Honan, Park. *Jane Austen: Her Life.* London: Weidenfeld and Nicolson, 1988.

Jenkins, Elizabeth. *Jane Austen: A Biography.* London: Gollancz, 1938.

Lane, Maggie. *Jane Austen's Family Through Five Generations.* London: R. Hale, 1984.

Laski, Marghanita. *Jane Austen and her World.* London: Thames and Hudson, 1969.

Tucker, George Holbert. *A Goodly Heritage: A History of Jane Austen's Family.* Manchester: Carcanet New Press, 1983.

————. *Jane Austen the Woman: Some Biographical Insights.* London: Robert Hale, 1994.

BIBLIOGRAPHIES

Gilson, David. *A Bibliography of Jane Austen.* Oxford: Clarendon Press, 1982.

Roth, Barry. *An Annotated Bibliography of Jane Austen Studies 1973–1983.* Charlottesville: University of Virginia Press, 1985.

Roth, Barry, and Joel Weinsheimer. *An Annotated Bibliography of Jane Austen Studies 1952–1972.* Charlottesville: University of Virginia Press, 1973.

Southam, B. C. *Jane Austen's Literary Manuscripts.* Oxford: Oxford University Press, 1964.

CRITICISM

Babb, Howard S. *Jane Austen's Novels: The Fabric of Dialogue.* Columbus: Ohio State University Press, 1962.

Bradbrook, Frank. *Jane Austen and Her Predecessors.* Cambridge: Cambridge University Press, 1966.

Brown, Julia Prewitt. *Jane Austen's Novels: Social Change and Literary Form.* Cambridge, Mass.: Harvard University Press, 1978.

Brown, Lloyd W. *Bits of Ivory: Narrative Techniques in Jane Austen's Fiction.* Baton Rouge: Louisiana State University Press, 1973.

Burrows, John F. *Computation into Criticism: A Study of Jane Austen's Novels and an Experiment in Method.* Oxford: Clarendon Press, 1987.

Bush, Douglas. *Jane Austen.* London: Macmillan, 1975.

Butler, Marilyn. *Jane Austen and the War of Ideas.* Oxford: Clarendon Press, 1975.

Collins, Irene. *Jane Austen and the Clergy.* London: Hambledon Press, 1994.

Copeland, Edward, and Juliet McMaster, eds. *The Cambridge Companion to Jane Austen.* Cambridge: Cambridge University Press, 1997.

Devlin, D. D. *Jane Austen and Education.* London: Macmillan, 1975.

Duckworth, A. M. *The Improvement of the Estate: A Study of Jane Austen's Novels.* Baltimore: Johns Hopkins University Press, 1971.

Dussinger, John. *In the Pride of the Moment: Encounters in Jane Austen's World.* Columbus: Ohio State University Press, 1990.

Farrer, Reginald. "Jane Austen, *ob.* July 18 1817." *Quarterly Review* 228 (October 1917): 1–30.

Fergus, Jan. *Jane Austen and the Didactic Novel*: Northanger Abbey, Sense and Sensibility, and Pride and Prejudice. London: Macmillan, 1983.

Forster, E. M. "Jane Austen." In his *Abinger Harvest.* London: E. Arnold, 1936.

Gard, Roger. *Jane Austen's Novels: The Art of Clarity.* New Haven: Yale University Press, 1992.

Gillie, Christopher. *A Preface to Jane Austen.* Rev. ed. London: Longman, 1985.

Grey, David J. *The Jane Austen Companion.* New York: Macmillan, 1986.

Halperin, John, ed. *Jane Austen: Bicentenary Essays.* Cambridge: Cambridge University Press, 1975.

Handler, Richard, and Daniel Segal. *Jane Austen and the Fiction of Culture: An Essay on the Narration of Social Realities.* Tucson: University of Arizona Press, 1990.

Hardy, Barbara. *A Reading of Jane Austen.* London: Peter Owen, 1975.

Hardy, John. *Jane Austen's Heroines: Intimacy in Human Relationships.* London: Routledge and Kegan Paul, 1984.

Harris, Jocelyn. *Jane Austen's Art of Memory.* Cambridge: Cambridge University Press, 1989.

Horovitz, Barbara. *Jane Austen and the Question of Women's Education.* New York: Lang, 1991.

Johnson, Claudia. *Jane Austen: Women, Politics and the Novel.* Chicago: University of Chicago Press, 1988.

Kaplan, Deborah. *Jane Austen Among Women.* Baltimore: Johns Hopkins University Press, 1992.

Kirkham, Margaret. *Jane Austen: Feminism and Fiction.* Brighton: Harvester Press, 1983.

Koppel, Gene. *The Religious Dimension of Jane Austen's Novels.* Ann Arbor: University of Michigan Research Press, 1988.

Lascelles, Mary. *Jane Austen and Her Art.* Oxford: Clarendon Press, 1939. Repr. London: Oxford University Press, 1968.

Leavis, Q. D. *A Critical Theory of Jane Austen's Writing.* Cambridge: Cambridge University Press, 1963.

Litz, A. Walton. *Jane Austen, A Study in her Literary Development.* London: Chatto and Windus, 1953; 2d ed., 1965.

MacDonagh, Oliver. *Jane Austen: Real and Imagined Worlds.* New Haven: Yale University Press, 1991.

McMaster, Juliet. *Jane Austen on Love.* Victoria, B.C.: University of Victoria Press, 1978.

———. *Jane Austen the Novelist: Essays Past and Present.* London: Macmillan, 1996.

———, ed. *Jane Austen's Achievement: Papers Delivered at the Jane Austen Bicentennial Conference at the University of Alberta.* London: Macmillan, 1976.

McMaster, Juliet, and Bruce Stovel, eds. *Jane Austen's Business: Her World and Her Profession.* London: Macmillan, 1996.

Mansell, Darrel. *The Novels of Jane Austen: An Interpretation.* London: Macmillan, 1973.

Moler, Kenneth L. *Jane Austen's Art of Allusion.* Lincoln: University of Nebraska Press, 1968.

Monaghan, David. *Jane Austen: Structure and Social Vision.* London: Macmillan, 1980.

————, ed. *Jane Austen in a Social Context.* London: Macmillan, 1981.

Mooneyham, Laura G. *Romance, Language and Education in Jane Austen's Novels.* London: Macmillan, 1988.

Morgan, Susan. *In the Meantime: Character and Perception in Jane Austen's Novels.* Chicago: University of Chicago Press, 1980.

Mudrick, Marvin. *Jane Austen: Irony as Defense and Discovery.* Princeton N.J.: Princeton University Press, 1952.

Nardin, Jane. *Those Elegant Decorums: The Concept of Propriety in Jane Austen's Novels.* Albany: State University of New York Press, 1973.

Odmark, John. *An Understanding of Jane Austen's Novels: Character, Value and Ironic Perspective.* Oxford: Blackwell, 1981.

Page, Norman. *The Language of Jane Austen.* Oxford: Blackwell. 1972.

Phillipps, Kenneth C. *Jane Austen's English.* London: André Deutsch, 1970.

Pinion, F. B. *A Jane Austen Companion: A Critical Survey and Reference Book.* London: Macmillan, 1973.

Roberts, Warren. *Jane Austen and the French Revolution.* New York: St. Martin's Press, 1979.

Rose, Peter L. de, and S. W. McGuire. *A Concordance to the Works of Jane Austen.* 3 vols. New York: Garland, 1982.

Sales, Roger. *Jane Austen and Representations of Regency England.* London: Routledge, 1994.

Sulloway, Alison G. *Jane Austen and the Province of Womanhood.* Philadelphia: University of Pennsylvania Press, 1989.

Smith, Leroy W. *Jane Austen and the Drama of Woman.* New York: St. Martin's Press, 1983.

Southam, B. C., ed. *Critical Essays on Jane Austen.* London: Routledge and Kegan Paul, 1968.

————. *Jane Austen: The Critical Heritage.* 2 vols. London: Routledge and Kegan Paul, 1968–1987.

Stafford, Walter, Earl of Iddesleigh. "A Chat About Jane Austen's Novels." *Nineteenth Century* 47 (1900): 811–820.

Tanner, Tony. *Jane Austen.* Cambridge, Mass.: Harvard University Press, 1986.

Tave, Stuart M. *Some Words of Jane Austen.* Chicago: University of Chicago Press, 1973.

Todd, Janet, ed. *Jane Austen: New Perspectives.* New York: Holmes & Meier, 1983.

Wallace, Tara Ghosal. *Jane Austen and Narrative Authority.* New York: St. Martin's Press, 1995.

Watt, Ian, ed. *Jane Austen: A Collection of Critical Essays.* London: Prentice-Hall, 1963.

Weinsheimer, Joel, ed. *Jane Austen Today.* Athens: University of Georgia Press, 1975.

Wiessenfarth, Joseph. *The Errand of Form: An Assay of Jane Austen's Art.* Rev. ed. New York: Fordham University Press, 1967. First published 1953.

Williams, Michael. *Jane Austen: Six Novels and the Methods.* London: Macmillan, 1986.

Wiltshire, John. *Jane Austen and the Body: "The Picture of Health."* Cambridge: Cambridge University Press, 1992.

Wright, Andrew. *Jane Austen's Novels: A Study in Structure.* London: Chatto and Windus, 1953.

SECONDARY WORKS ON *EMMA*

Booth, Wayne C. "Control of Distance in Jane Austen's *Emma.*" In his *The Rhetoric of Fiction.* Chicago: University of Chicago Press, 1961.

Bradbrook, Frank W. *Jane Austen: Emma.* London: Edward Arnold, 1961.

Bradley, A. C. "Jane Austen: A Lecture." *Essays and Studies by Members of the English Association* 2 (1911): 7–36.

Burrows, J. F. *Jane Austen's Emma.* Sydney: Sydney University Press, 1969.

Kettle, Arnold. "*Emma.*" In his *Introduction to the English Novel.* Vol. 1. 2d ed. London: Hutchinson, 1967.

Lodge, David, ed. *Jane Austen: Emma.* Casebook Series. London: Macmillan, 1968. Reprinted 1972.

Monaghan, David, ed. *Jane Austen: Emma.* New Casebooks Series. London: Palgrave Macmillan, 1982.

Parrish, Stephen M., ed. Emma: *An Authoritative Text, Backgrounds, Reviews, and Criticism.* Norton Critical Edition. New York: Norton, 1972.

Trilling, Lionel. "Emma." *Encounter* 3, no. 3 (September 1954): 9–19. Reprinted in his *The Opposing Self: Nine Essays in Criticism.* London: Secker and Warburg, 1955.

WORKS CONTAINING MATERIAL ON AUSTEN'S WORK

Armstrong, Nancy. *Desire and Domestic Fiction: A Political History of the Novel.* London: Oxford University Press, 1987.

Auerbach, Nina. *Communities of Women: An Idea in Fiction.* Cambridge, Mass: Harvard University Press, 1978.

Brownstein, Rachel. *Becoming a Heroine: Reading About Women in Novels.* New York and London: Viking, 1982.

Ghent, Dorothy van. *The English Novel: Form and Function.* New York: Holt, Rinehart and Winston, 1953.

Gilbert, Sandra M., and Susan Gubar. *The Madwoman in the Attic: The Woman Writer and the Nineteenth-Century Literary Imagination.* New Haven: Yale University Press, 1979.

Johnson, Claudia. *Equivocal Beings: Politics, Gender and Sentimentality in the 1790s: Wollstonecraft, Radcliffe, Burney, Austen.* Chicago: University of Chicago Press, 1995.

Moers, Ellen. *Literary Women.* New York: Doubleday, 1976.

Poovey, Mary. *The Proper Lady and the Woman Writer: Ideology as Style in the Works of Mary Wollstonecraft, Mary Shelley and Jane Austen.* Chicago: University of Chicago Press, 1984.

Williams, Raymond. *The Country and the City.* London: Chatto and Windus, 1973.

Showalter, Elaine. *A Literature of Their Own: British Woman Novelists from Brontë to Lessing.* Princeton, N.J.: Princeton University Press, 1977.

Spacks, Patricia Meyer. *The Female Imagination: A Literary and Psychological Investigation of Women's Writing.* New York: Knopf, 1975.

Spencer, Jane. *The Rise of the Woman Novelist: From Aphra Behn to Jane Austen.* Oxford: Blackwell, 1986.

Stewart, Maaja. *Domestic Realities and Imperial Fictions: Jane Austen's Novels in Eighteenth-Century Contexts.* Athens: University of Georgia Press, 1993.

Charles Dickens's
Great Expectations

PETER SCUPHAM

ICKENS WAS SPURRED to write *Great Expectations* by the failure of Charles Lever's novel *A Day's Ride: A Life's Romance*, which was being serialized in Dickens's periodical *All the Year Round*, to engage its readers. On 1 December 1860, the first installment of *Great Expectations* appeared, sales of *All the Year Round* began to pick up again, and the novel was published in its three volumes in August 1861. Dickens was forty-eight and about to enter his last decade; the storm and stress habitual to him were aging him prematurely. Out of the buffeting he had given life, and that life had given him, came one of his finest novels, dark in tone, its autobiographical elements strong, but transposed and concealed. It is also a response to the disasters then besieging him, as well as to the pressures of his past. Two years previously he had separated from his wife in a public, messy and self-justifying rejection. His relationship with Ellen Ternan was unadmitted; he had quarreled with some of his closest friends, particularly Mark Lemon and William Makepeace Thackeray; his children were disappointing him; there were deaths and estrangements—life was proving more obdurate in resisting his desires than his fictions were. In *Great Expectations* Dickens comes to terms with

limitation and boundary. The dream surrenders its place to the possible.

In 1856 Dickens had brought his life full circle by purchasing Gad's Hill Place in Kent, the old house his father had once told him could be his own if the boy worked hard and became successful. Peter Ackroyd says of this house, "From the roof it is possible to glimpse the river Thames and the dark shape of London, to see Rochester and the valley of the Medway and, to the north, to view the flat and desolate marshes" (p. 780). The scenery was there at his command, the suggestive landscapes of his own childhood and youth. *Great Expectations* reshapes Dickens's own experience in many ways. It is a study in surrogate fatherhood, exploring again the impact of the exasperating, attractive John Dickens on his son Charles's life. It is a study in the failure of love to live up to its apparent promises, as Dickens recasts his early feelings for the teasing Maria Beadnell, the failure of his marriage to Catherine Hogarth, his socially inadmissible relationship with Ellen Ternan. It is a study in dispossession, a revisiting of that childhood in which Dickens felt himself so signally rejected by his parents. Put to work at the age of twelve in Warren's Blacking factory while his father was imprisoned in the Marshalsea, the debtors' prison, it would have been easy to sink through the levels of the laboring poor to further degradation. It is a study in money, its use and misuse, its ability to disguise its origins, to appear and disappear. Dickens was always a hard businessman, conscious of the need for a substantial financial bulwark between himself and indigence. He was also, despite the improvident and shameless cadgers in his own family, notably generous. *Great Expectations* is a study in social mobility. Dickens had worked with unremitting energy to turn the clerk's son into a kind of gentleman—a dandified gentleman who had given his heart to journalism and the theater. Ten years before, he had recast his past in *David Copperfield.* Now he reread that novel so as to ensure the freshness of this revisiting.

Although *Great Expectations* first appeared in 1860, when the Victorian age was well under way, the novel is set in an earlier period. The accepted dating has the chief character, Pip, born about 1800, and his age is about seven when the story opens. England at this period was poised between the robust and largely agricultural society of the eighteenth century and the thrusting, urban, and entrepreneurial society of the nineteenth. Pip grows up during the long French wars that culminated in Napoleon's defeat at Waterloo in 1815 and during the industrial revolution's creation of a manufacturing base in northern England, but these are not Dickens's concern. Travel is by coach, for not until the 1830s and 1840s was a national rail network established, and there is an eighteenth-century leisureliness to the pace of life lived by Joe and the tradesmen of Rochester. The population, though, was rapidly rising during Pip's youth, and London, the great trading center, was hugely increasing its unregulated size, drawing surplus labor in from a countryside that had no need for their work. In *Great Expectations* Dickens presents an apparently unchangeable rural life. When he turns his attention to London, we move between pictures of the leisured class Pip

CHRONOLOGY

1812	7 February: Charles John Huffam Dickens born in Portsmouth. Son of John Dickens, a clerk handling naval payroll accounts, and Elizabeth Barrow.
1817–1822	His father is transferred to Chatham, Kent. Chatham, Rochester, the River Medway, and the estuarial Kent landscape become the great good places of Charles's imagination.
1822–1824	John Dickens is transferred back to London. The family struggles to remain solvent, but lives above its means. While his sister Fanny trains at the Royal Academy of Music, twelve-year-old Charles starts work in February 1824 at Warren's Blacking factory. Later that month John Dickens is imprisoned for debt in the Marshalsea. This period will always be remembered as one of degradation and betrayal.
1824–1827	John Dickens, on his release, sends Charles to a local school, 1827 Wellington House Academy. His mother wishes him to continue at Warren's, an attitude that builds up a permanent sense of alienation from, and resentment of, his mother.
1827–1833	Works first as a solicitor's clerk, then learns shorthand and becomes a reporter in the ecclesiastical courts. In 1830 begins a protracted and unrequited love affair with Maria Beadnell that lasts for about three years.
1834–1836	Becomes a reporter on the *Morning Chronicle.* Publishes his essays as *Sketches by Boz* in 1836. In April of that year he marries Catherine Hogarth—they will eventually have ten children; of his seven sons only Harry (Henry Fielding) makes a success of life. 1836 also sees the start of the monthly publication of *Pickwick Papers.* His importance as a writer is established.
1837	In May, Mary Hogarth, his wife's sister, dies suddenly, at age seventeen. It is

	one of the huge emotional catastrophes of his life.
1842	Asks Georgina Hogarth, Mary's sister, to join the Dickens family. She will stay as friend, confidante, and housekeeper until he dies, and then act as a Keeper of the Flame. Visits America. Publishes *American Notes*.
1843	Publishes *Martin Chuzzlewit*, which continues his quarrel with what he sees as American hypocrisy and materialism, and the first of his Christmas books, *A Christmas Carol*. This continues the association of Dickens with Christmas conviviality and benevolence that started with *Pickwick Papers*.
1848	Fanny, his sister, dies of tuberculosis, followed in 1849 by her crippled son, Henry.
1849–1850	Serial publication of *David Copperfield*, the novel in which he revisits his own childhood, and which he rereads before starting *Great Expectations*.
1850	Edits, publishes, and half-owns the weekly *Household Words*, which runs until 1859. It is then supplanted by *All the Year Round*, which he edits until his death.
1851	Death of John Dickens. Charles is deeply affected, despite his father's feckless improvidence.
1855	Receives a letter from Maria Beadnell, now Mrs. Winter. His rush of sentiment turns to disillusion when they meet.
1856	Buys Gad's Hill Place, in Kent, within view of the country of his childhood. He will move there in 1860, and it will be his home until he dies.
1858	After years of increasing alienation, separates from his wife, Catherine. There is never a reconciliation on his part, though she remains faithful to her love for him. The secret relationship begun the year before with the young actress, Ellen Ternan, deepens. Begins his paid public readings.
1860–1861	*Great Expectations*, his penultimate completed novel, is published in weekly episodes. It will be followed by *Our Mutual Friend* in 1864 and the unfinished *Edwin Drood* in 1870.
1865	Involved in a serious railway accident at Staplehurst, Kent. Assists in rescue work and comforts the dying. The physical and emotional cost is permanent.
1867–1868	Undertakes a reading tour in America, against medical advice.
1870	Suffers a stroke on 8 June and dies at Gad's Hill the following day.

aspires to belong to—those living on inherited, unearned, or invisibly earned incomes—and pictures of those at the bottom of the social pile, the slum dwellers, Newgate fodder. The brief lives of the poor end in disease and early death, or in suffering the exactions of a ferocious penal code that sentences men, women and children to execution by hanging or to transportation to the colonies for a host of minor offenses. Despite the carefully drawn period details, Humphry House, in *The Dickens World* (1941), points out that the prevailing mood of *Great Expectations* "belongs not to the imaginary date of its plot, but to the time in which it was written" (p. 159). The novel's deep demonstration of the power of money to mold its possessors, its explorations of class consciousness and the finishing schools of respectability—these belong to a later period than the pre-Victorian one.

The single most useful aid to further study of *Great Expectations* is the Norton Critical Edition, edited by Edgar Rosenberg (1999). All page numbers in this article refer to this edition, which, with its supplementary background and critical material, is exhaustive without being exhausting. Rosenberg's commentary is wonderfully perceptive and wonderfully funny.

A READING

Great Expectations is a bildungsroman, a novel of character formation. Pip's narrative takes us through his childhood as an orphan on the lonely Kent marshland, where he is brought up by his harsh sister, "Mrs. Joe," and her soft-hearted husband Joe, the village blacksmith. He offers a guilty kindness to Magwitch, an escaped convict; is introduced to the jilted Miss Havisham's reclusive lost domain, Satis House, and to her adopted daughter Estella. Halfway through his apprenticeship to Joe, he is informed he has "great expectations" by a London lawyer, Mr. Jaggers, who announces himself as the boy's future guardian. Pip leaves his home, sure that Miss Havisham is his benefactress, and spends his minority, with Mr. Jaggers as paymaster, in acquiring a veneer of worldly accomplishment. He develops a disdain for Joe and his earlier associates, and nurses a hopeless passion for Estella, who has been educated as an ice maiden by her surrogate mother, and who eventually gives herself in marriage to the sadistic Bentley Drummle. Humanity is in short supply at this time, though the decent kindnesses of Pip's friend Herbert Pocket, a relative of Miss Havisham's, and of Wemmick, Mr. Jaggers's clerk, act as a counterbalance to Pip's youthful dabblings in the shallows of social life. A darker thread to Pip's life is woven in by the plots and subterfuges of Dolge Orlick, Joe's hireling in the years at the forge, and of Compeyson, Miss Havisham's former lover and Magwitch's dominating criminal accomplice. When Pip is a man of twenty-three, Magwitch returns from transportation to Australia, and announces himself as Pip's true benefactor. The final third of the book charts the growth of a chastened wisdom in Pip, as his feeling for Magwitch moves through loathing to what must be called love. Pip's release from his great expectations comes with Magwitch's capture, his death before sentence of execution on him can be carried out, and the forfeiture of his possessions to the crown. Pip reestablishes his affection with Joe and works in Cairo with Herbert Pocket, for whom he has bought a partnership in a small trading company. Whether Pip marries a widowed Estella, or finally parts from an Estella remarried to a Shropshire doctor, depends on which of Dickens's two possible endings the reader prefers.

OPENINGS: THE PUNISHMENT OF CHRISTMAS

Dickens, the evangelist for festivity, whose social life seems a nonstop performance of conjuring and charades, parlor and party games, created in the first six chapters of *Great Expectations* a Christmas book with a difference, to stand in that long line which began with the publication of *A Christmas Carol* in 1843. This new Christmas book is dark and disturbing. Family reunions take place between an orphan and his family hidden in the grave; festivity is a grotesque and self-satisfied guzzle for the respectable or a gnawing and gulping of scraps by the outcast. The Christian message of love finds expression only when offered from a man who is half child to a brutalized convict, and lights are conspicuous not for illuminating the darkness but for intensifying it, as the torches carried by a hunting party of soldiers are tossed into the black water where a moored prison ship rides. The opening chapters drive headlong through the glooms of a landscape suggestive of lost and buried life. They carry a burden suggested by two repeated words: guilt and terror.

Pip, whose long retrospect will be a sinuous and painful uncovering of his own buried, discarded, or false selves, is first seen as the child of vacancy. It is Christmas Eve, and Pip is in the churchyard. The family gravestones are protean, turning themselves backward and forward into imagined people, those "five little stone lozenges" (p. 9) which suggest to the six- or seven-year-old Pip "that they had all been born on their backs with their hands in their trousers-pockets, and had never taken them out in this state of existence" (p. 9). The vacancy left by the unknown dead is emphasized by the receding vacancies of the estuarial Kent landscape. The "bleak place overgrown with nettles" that is the churchyard moves seamlessly out to a "dark flat wilderness" of marsh, to a "low leaden line" of river, to a "dark savage lair" of sea, and then homes back again on a "small bundle of shivers growing afraid of it all," who is Pip. In a book deeply concerned with identity, we are given at the outset a stripped and naked life to build on.

Then this naked life is given a terror. Pip encounters the convict Magwitch, an accidental meeting that will shape the course of Pip's journey to self-knowledge. Magwitch rises like a dead man—indeed, a dead father, for that is the role he will eventually play—from among the graves. In a parodic version of Christmas feasting, he licks his lips over Pip's chubby cheeks and threatens him with the culinary skills of an imaginary companion, who will ensure "your heart and your liver shall be tore out, roasted, and ate" (p. 11) unless a file to remove his leg irons and food are brought to him on Christmas Day. As Pip watches him limp off, "he looked in my young eyes as if he were eluding the hands of the dead people, stretching up cautiously out their graves, to get a twist upon his ankle, and pull him in" (p. 12). The compelling power of the opening of the novel closes with two suggestive images, the only verticals in this scene of horizontals, burials, and phantasmagoria. There is a black and unlit beacon, like a cask on a pole; there is a gibbet with chains that once held a pirate—and in Pip's imagination the convict appears to be transposed into that pirate "going back to hook himself up again" (p. 12). It is as if Magwitch is seen as he will be seen: as redeemed and redeemer, crucified through love.

The eldritch and otherworldly terrors into which Dickens plunges us are now domesticated. Pip's sister, Mrs. Joe, exercises strict quasi-paternal authority over Pip and her husband, Joe, regarding these two as interchangeable and incorrigible children. Her furious redness of skin, as if she "washed herself with a nutmeg-grater instead of soap" (p. 13), and her black hair and eyes suggest a domestic devil, as Joe's "curls of flaxen hair" and eyes of "undecided blue" (p. 12) suggest an unformed innocence. As they are now defined, so they will remain, as immutable as the characters in a puppet show. Christmas Eve, punctuated by the reverberations of "great guns" (p. 17) announcing another escape, reduces Pip, who has slipped bread and butter down his trouser leg for Magwitch, to conscious terror and guilt, a conscious terror transposed to image that night when he dreams of drifting down the river to the Hulks, the prison ships, hearing "a ghostly pirate calling out to me through a speaking-trumpet, as I passed the gibbet-station, that I had better come ashore and be hanged there at once, and not put it off" (p. 18). When Pip wakes on Christmas Day, the damp on his windowpane looks "as if some goblin had been crying there all night," and as he sets off with file and food, he is crowded by creatures and objects who seem to direct a universal judgment at him: the signpost that shows "like a phantom directing me to the hulks"; the ox, white-collared like a clergyman, who seems to move his head "in an accusatory manner" (p. 19). Pip finds his convict, after a brief encounter with Magwitch's enemy and fellow escapee, Compeyson, and Magwitch gorges Pip's Christmas offering like a dog, with "strong, sharp, sudden bites" (p. 21). The ritual of eating then is repeated in the forge's kitchen by a Christmas dinner in which the local tradesmen scoff their pickled pork, roast fowls, plum pudding and mince pie, echoing the signpost and the ox with further moral injunctions and improving comments designed for Pip's benefit. The stiff puppetry of the tradesmen is emphasized by Dickens's telling visual shorthand. Mr. Wopsle is a Roman nose and a shining forehead; Uncle Pumblechook, a fishlike mouth, dull eyes, and a vertical hairstyle; Mr. Hubble, a smell of sawdust and a pair of wide-set legs. Such trademark Dickensian images, perfectly suited to a child's perception of importance, could almost be comic drawings printed on cards that can be fitted together to make convincing composites. Pip's fat cheeks, so noted by Magwitch, are appraised again as Wopsle and Pumblechook extemporize a dinner-table sermon on pork, with Pip transmogrified into a "four-footed Squeaker" (p. 27), a young porker fattened for slaughter.

The set-piece Christmas dinner swings back into narrative as the soldiers arrive, "ringing down their loaded muskets on the door-step" (p. 29) and demanding the repair of broken handcuffs. Christmas Day is galvanized into brutal and swift-moving action, and Pip realizes "what terrible good sauce for a dinner my fugitive friend on the marshes was" (p. 31). The scene—as the forge's fire is lit, the sparks rise and the metal is beaten—makes a mimic pandemonium, and respectability takes a devilish delight in the chase. The search for the convicts, conducted through an inky darkness punctuated by "great blotches of fire upon the track" dropped from the blazing pitch of the soldiers' torches, continues to reek of devildom, and only Joe redeems the time with his closing message to Magwitch before the torches go out and the two convicts, recaptured as Magwitch, an avenging fury, grapples with Compeyson—as he will grapple with him again under the paddles of the Hamburg steamer—are again immured in their Hulk: "We don't know what you have done, but we wouldn't have you starved to death for it, poor miserable fellow-creatur.—Would us, Pip?" (p. 36). And so the inversion of Christmas is concluded, its promises parodied, its message of reconciliation recast as a message of punishment, and an unholy pleasure taken in its infliction.

THE SPECTER AT THE FEAST AND THE ICE MAIDEN

The book's opening chapters are dynamic, filled with the abrasive ministrations of Mrs. Joe and the violent presence of Magwitch. Dickens sets against such energy the frozen, timeless world of Satis House, where Miss Havisham and her adopted daughter, Estella, will bear an equal share with Magwitch in shaping Pip's future. To this world of excised hearts and watchful eyes

the seven-year-old Pip is brought to play, to be beggared at cards, to be hurt, chastened, filled with self-contempt. Our first impression of Miss Havisham emphasizes the whiteness—white shoes, white veil, white hair: "Some bright jewels sparkled on her neck and on her hands, and some other jewels lay sparkling on the table" (p. 50). That chill dazzle will finally spring into an eldritch living light at her death, when she will run at Pip "with a whirl of fire blazing all about her, and soaring at least as many feet above her head as she was high" (p. 299). For a moment she sits there in glacial state—and in the next paragraph, she decays and crumbles. The white fades into yellow; the only brightness left is "the brightness of her sunken eyes" (p. 50), and the images that swim into Pip's recall are of a fairground waxworks and a dressed skeleton exhumed from an old vault. We are drawn emotionally into the world of depth images from the märchen, the Germanic fairy tales. Miss Havisham is allied to Coleridge's spectre woman in *The Rime of the Ancient Mariner*:

> Her skin was white as leprosy,
> The Night-mare LIFE-IN-DEATH was she,
> Who thicks man's blood with cold.
>
> (ll. 192–194)

She is allied, too, with Hel, Loki's child in Norse mythology, who is half woman and half corpse—such images have the force of our unconscious life powering them. This being so, we can believe unresistingly in her power to manipulate, falsify, and control the lives of all who come into her orbit. In the developing characters of both Magwitch and Miss Havisham we are presented with a transition from archetypal images associated with terror and fear to figures of a recognizable humanity—though the archetypal qualities are never lost. What passes for life at Satis House takes place in rooms where all timepieces are stopped at twenty to nine, where picked-up objects are always replaced in their original position, where daylight never enters. Of course the arresting of decay and the reversal of entropy are impossible, except in fiction, where mice and beetles cannot quite get through a wedding cake in some thirty years, for according to Dickens's chronological notes, Miss Havisham is about twenty-six when jilted, thirty-nine or forty years old when Pip first visits Satis House, and fifty-six at the time of her death (pp. 484–485). Hardly a reader, faced with Pip's first description of Miss Havisham, would not add some twenty or thirty years to make such an apparition tolerably credible. Time has gone to live somewhere else; here its ghost is condemned to an endless circularity. It is appropriate that on returning to the forge after his first visit, Pip can describe his experience only in terms of an alternative theater of the impossible, where Miss Havisham sits in a "black velver coach," and Estella hands her cake and wine on a gold plate, while four dogs "fought for veal cutlets out of a silver basket" (p. 57). The only interruptions the world makes into the slow decay of Satis House—Enough House—come from the ritual visits of the legacy-cadging Pocket relations, "toadies and humbugs," as the young Pip correctly identifies them, and the enigmatic London lawyer, Mr. Jaggers (p. 66).

We gradually learn to see Miss Havisham as the victim of vicious human behaviors, a bride forsaken by her bridegroom, Compeyson, the fortune-hunting manipulator and crooked gentleman whose machinations have also destroyed Magwitch. The decaying casks in the yard are a constant reminder that she is the ruined heiress to a rich brewer, tricked and wrecked by her stepbrother Arthur and his accomplice Compeyson. Arthur's comeuppance, as related by Magwitch, is to die of delirium tremens, "the horrors," pursued by Miss Havisham's spectral double, who, with blood-spotted breast and raging eyes, attempts to entrap him in a shroud. One would not put it past her. Miss Havisham has money enough to institutionalize herself by becoming a self-immured, will-shaking nun, and enmity enough to see love and money as the best weapons to hand. Her extended sisterhood of women in

white outside the world of *Great Expectations* has been mapped by Harry Stone in his essay "The Genesis of a Novel: Great Expectations" (reprinted in the Norton edition, pp. 556–563). There we can find the Berners Street White Woman, first recalled in print by Dickens in his essay "Where We Stopped Growing," published in *Household Words* in 1853, and Miss Mildew, an old lady in a dramatic sketch performed by the comedian Charles Mathews at the Adelphi Theatre in 1831. Dressed in her bridal clothes, she calls yearly at the "Expectation Office," looking for her lost husband. Dickens also knew of Martha Joachim, whose suitor blew his brains out while sitting beside her in 1825, and who died, a white-dressed recluse, in 1850. Stone winds together such images, relating them to Dickens's marriage and to a minor ghost story interpolated into a story he and Wilkie Collins wrote for *Household Words* in 1857, "The Lazy Tour of Two Idle Apprentices." As for Wilkie Collins, his *The Woman in White* had been running in *All the Year Round* just before the serial publication of *Great Expectations*.

And Estella? Estella is a weapon, an instrument to destroy men as Miss Havisham perceives herself to have been destroyed: "Break their hearts, my pride and hope, break their hearts and have no mercy!" (p. 77). Though she will never know it, she is the daughter of Magwitch and Mr. Jaggers's housekeeper, Molly. She is brought up to break hearts as icebreakers break ice and stone breakers break stone; the only warmth Pip ever perceives in her is when he fights a visiting relation of Miss Havisham's, young Herbert Pocket, and floors him. Then Estella appears "with a bright flush upon her face, as though something had happened to delight her" (p. 75), and invites Pip to kiss her. This creepy episode foreshadows the kind of indifferent masochism with which she later contracts herself in marriage to the callous Bentley Drummle, that heavyset young gentleman who "even took up a book as if its writer had done him an injury" (p. 158). Her position in the novel is to remain poised endlessly between image and personality, as arrested in her own indifference to change as Miss Havisham herself. As Pip moves from his childhood into youth, his desire seems the desire of the moth for a star; he is tormented and self-tormented by Estella's very existence, a torment intensified by Miss Havisham's plots for future meetings between them as both acquire their worldly gloss, apparently become citizens of equivalent worlds.

The repetitive phrases change now, the force of Miss Havisham's personality constantly expressed with a vigor neither Pip nor Estella can ever match: "Love her, love her, love her! If she favours you, love her. If she wounds you, love her. If she tears your heart to pieces—and as it gets older and stronger, it will tear deeper—love her, love her, love her!" (p. 184). The anguished hope Pip suffers because he believes that Estella is somehow part of Miss Havisham's plan to fulfill his great expectations is intensified by Estella's removal from Satis House to Richmond, where she is introduced into London society. Just before Pip's house of cards falls about him with the return of Magwitch, he returns with Estella to Satis House and witnesses the first signs of change in Miss Havisham when Estella proclaims herself unable to return the old woman's love: "All that you have given me, is at your command to have again. Beyond that, I have nothing. And if you ask me to give you what you never gave me, my gratitude and duty cannot do impossibilities" (p. 230). The scene prepares us for Miss Havisham's change of heart, a tricky maneuver since we have had every sign of a permanent atrophy in that organ.

Estella gives herself to Drummle and Pip moves toward his final visit to an inhabited Satis House, arranged to confirm Miss Havisham's surprising and secret financial assistance to Herbert Pocket in acquiring his partnership. In a scene of high drama, or melodrama, Miss Havisham pleads for forgiveness, her final repetition being "'What have I done! What have I done!' She wrung her hands, and crushed her white hair, and returned to this cry, over and over again. 'What have I done!'" (p. 297). The recantation made, Pip leaves Satis House and for the second time in his life has a sudden vision of Miss Havisham hanging from a door beam. On his alarmed return to her room, he sees her engulfed by flame as she sits huddled in her fireside chair. Later, laid out on the table where the wedding feast was laid, swathed in cotton wool that mimics her bridal dress, her last words to Pip are another repetition: "Take the pencil and write under my name, 'I forgive her'" (p. 301). The reader is carried by the intensity of the scene into a conviction of its plausibility.

Indeed, the pictorial strength of Dickens's writing frequently carries the reader along by a series of emotive kangaroo bounds from image to image; the converse of the conversational unfoldings of, say, his predecessor Jane Austen. Miss Havisham has made her emblematic transition from wicked witch to good fairy, and her human transition from a settled misanthropy to the first stirrings of understanding and generosity. She has started time running again in its customary direction, but can hardly be expected to survive such a series of shocks to her system.

CITY CITS AND COUNTRY BUMPKINS

The power made explicit in the creation of Magwitch, Miss Havisham, and to a lesser extent Estella, is power of the highest imaginative order. The other characters who accompany Pip in the various stages of his quest, with the possible exception of Dolge Orlick, are more recognizably fabrications of mortal flesh and blood. In the long literary debate between town and country, urban sophistication and rural contentment, *Great Expectations* has its place. There is no sentimentality in Dickens's picture of country life, but particular opportunities for the reader to share in what Peter Ackroyd in his *Dickens* (1990) calls Dickens's "anarchic, liberating and sometimes harsh laughter" (p. 269). At the forge Mrs. Joe's energetic brutality of temperament is understandable, her time spent in organizing a slow husband and a recalcitrant younger brother, in "talking to mere Mooncalfs, with Uncle Pumblechook waiting, and the mare catching cold at the door, and the boy grimed with crock and dirt from the hair of his head to the sole of his foot!" (p. 45). We can laugh, but with a sharply indrawn breath, at her furious scrubbings and scarifyings, the way Pip claims "to be better acquainted than any living authority, with the ridgy effect of a wedding-ring, passing unsympathetically over the human countenance" (p. 45). Uncle Pumblechook is pomposity writ large, the corn chandler and seedsman of Rochester, then a small market town. His role as the intermediary through whom Pip is introduced to his supposed benefactress, Miss Havisham, provides his life with a meaning that swells his sense of his own importance, and as Pip's fortunes decline, Pumblechook's attitude changes: "Young man, I am sorry to see you brought low. But what else could be expected! What else could be expected!" (p. 351).

The comedy implicit in Dickens's re-creation of the world of these petty tradesmen is vivid and shot through with a hard and frequently retributive streak. Pumblechook's house is broken into by roughs led by Orlick, and Joe describes how "they tied him up to his bedpust, and they giv' him a dozen, and they stuffed his mouth full of flowering annuals to prewent his crying out" (p. 346). Trabb's boy, the undertaker's urchin son, makes his own barbed comment on Pip's uppity metamorphosis into a gentleman as he "smirked extravagantly by, wriggling his elbows and body, and drawling to his attendants, 'Don't know yah, don't know yah, pon my soul don't know yah!'" (p. 188). The undertaker himself creates a comic-ghastly set piece as stage manager of Mrs. Joe's funeral, "it being a point of Undertaking ceremony that six bearers must be stifled and blinded under a horrible black velvet housing with a white border, the whole looked like a blind monster with twelve human legs" (pp. 213–214). Dickens had a hatred of the macabre rituals associated

with death and burial, and was inclined to disgrace himself by sudden exits or suppressed laughter on such occasions. A warmer theatrical set piece is the description of Mr. Wopsle, the parish clerk, in his amateur stage persona as Mr. Waldengarver, playing Hamlet: "When he asked what should such fellows as he do crawling between earth and heaven, he was encouraged with loud cries of 'Hear, hear!'" (p. 194). At times we could be in an early version of Garrison Keiller's Lake Woebegone.

In this self-satisfied carnival of the grotesque, Joe is an anchor point of fundamental decency, a decency always in danger of toppling into sentimental caricature. By Dickensian sleight-of-hand, Joe survives the eternal comedy of his verbal mannerisms and malapropisms: the "apoplectic fit" that becomes "purple leptic fit" (p. 41), the "codicil" that becomes "coddleshell" (p. 345). His goodness and childlike sensibility keep a hold on the reader's serious affection. At the forge he is perfectly fitted to life; when he visits Pip in London, he is absolutely wrong, and knows it: "You and me is not two figures to be together in London; nor yet anywheres else but what is private, and beknown, and understood among friends" (p. 173). After the death of Magwitch, Pip succumbs to fever, and after a long illness wakes to find Joe has been his nurse: "And as my extreme weakness prevented me from getting up and going to him, I lay there, penitently whispering, 'O God bless him! O God bless this gentle Christian man!'" (p. 344). On Pip's recovery, Joe slips away, and Pip now has only one object in mind—to go back to the forge and ask Biddy, Joe's helpmeet after Mrs. Joe's death, to marry him.

Biddy? Biddy is Pip's first effective teacher, and an orphan distantly related to Mr. Wopsle. She is also the unsung heroine of *Great Expectations*. When the boy Pip first notices her, her "hair always wanted brushing, her hands always wanted washing, and her shoes always wanted mending and pulling up at heel" (p. 39). Biddy is consistently undervalued or patronized by Pip in his apprentice days: "She was not beautiful—she was common, and could not be like Estella—but she was pleasant and wholesome and sweet-tempered" (p. 100). Her steady, affectionate common sense is instrumental in Pip's slow maturation, but his complacent assumption that she will still be available as a suitable partner for his new "humbled and repentant" (p. 350) self is quickly shaken by finding he has arrived back at the forge on her wedding day to Joe. We are left to wonder whether the new little Pip who is soon to make a third at the forge will be content with the fetters of decent and unambitious love, or will find his own restless equivalents for Mr. Jaggers and Magwitch, Estella and Miss Havisham. Biddy and Joe might be thought to represent those true values which can blossom only in untainted country air; they are certainly instruments in transforming guilt into reconciliation and shallow sophistication into a sense of true human worth and dignity. But Herbert Pocket, bobbing delightfully about in the social shallows of metropolitan life, is also a good man, and Wemmick, that divided creature, purchases his goodness at a higher cost than Biddy or Joe will ever have to pay. As Joe anchored Pip's childhood the forge by his integrity of character and dependable generosity of spirit, so Herbert Pocket and Wemmick keep the idea of goodness alive for Pip in the restless and rootless world of London.

LITTLE BRITAIN LOGIC AND WALWORTH SENTIMENT

The link between Satis House, the Hulks, and London is made in the figure of Mr. Jaggers, the criminal lawyer who acts in various capacities for Miss Havisham, Magwitch, and Pip. He is a swarthy figure apparently composed of an implacable forensic logic, a stabbing and bitten forefinger, a smell of scented soap, and a metaphorical suit of armor that is proof against all assaults of the emotions. Mr. Jaggers and Miss Havisham form contrasting power centers; each

exercises a magnetic attraction by forcing the tide of personality into one constricting, intense channel. Mr. Jaggers is for sale; the sum a client can raise opens or closes the doors of life and death. He carries the keys designed to unlock Pip's future, and is usually seen in tandem with his clerk Wemmick, "a dry man, rather short in stature, with a square wooden face, whose expression seemed to have been imperfectly chipped out with a dull-edged chisel" (p. 135). Mr. Jaggers is first fully encountered on his visit to Pip's native village to relieve Joe of his apprentice, when he annihilates Mr. Wopsle's prejudgment of the accused in a local murder. His initial statement to Joe defines the style we are to expect from him: "I have unusual business to transact with you, and I commence by explaining that it is not of my originating. If my advice had been asked, I should not have been here. I was not asked, and you see me here. What I have to do, as the confidential agent of another, I do. No less, no more" (p. 108). In his offices in Little Britain, London, Pip finds him surrounded by the accoutrements of death. His chair is "of deadly black horsehair, with rows of brass nails round it like a coffin," and two death masks of hanged criminals "peculiarly swollen, and twitchy about the nose" (p. 130) make up the decoration—these are borrowed from the masks of the murderers Bishop and Williams that ornamented a small room in Newgate Prison, which Dickens had described in his "A Visit to Newgate," published in *Sketches by Boz* (vol. 1, 1836). Newgate, with its public hangings, and Smithfield, London's great cattle market, "all asmear with filth and fat and blood and foam" (p. 131), form the appropriate environment for the systematic and cruel miscarriages of justice in which Mr. Jaggers and Wemmick trade. Pip's introduction to their working lives involves the parading past their eyes of a false witness disguised as a "sort of pastrycook" (p. 134). The ferocity of Mr. Jaggers and his sidekick is directed at clients responsible for the unwelcome intrusion of any direct truth into the professional relationships conducted in the office. All is possible, so long as appearances are saved and the formularies of language are used to disguise rather than reveal.

Dickens never showed much love for the law in action, whether in a criminal or a civil capacity—he knew something of its more tedious workings from the inside, having been taken on as a law clerk in the firm of Ellis and Blackmore at the age of fifteen. Wemmick's magic formula is "portable property," acquired as a solicited or unsolicited gift from those who, about to enter the next world, have certain trifles they cannot easily take with them. Pip, shown by him round Newgate, refers to the prison as a greenhouse, and observes that Wemmick "walked among the prisoners, much as a gardener might walk among his plants" (p. 199). Mr. Jaggers and Wemmick are half-men in Little Britain. Implacable and impervious as they are, nothing disturbs their severe equanimity more than tears, pleadings, the naked expression of emotional despair or desire.

Dickens, as always, shows himself a master in creating characters who are defined in terms of the social roles they play, and of the professional deformation that becomes second nature to those who must suppress some part of their natures in order to perform their functions competently. In the bildungsroman, Mr. Jaggers and Wemmick play their part in showing Pip the difficulty of achieving an integrated character, a marriage of head and heart, in what we laughingly call the "real world," where money is the primary counter of human exchange and a counter that can never be washed as sparkling clean as the heart could wish. Wemmick, though, becomes a surprising other when away from the office, and Mr. Jaggers's heart will be demonstrated by more than his furious ablutions, as he endlessly washes away the accretions of moral grime that stick to him "as if he were a surgeon or a dentist. He had a closet in his room, fitted up for the purpose, which smelt of the scented soap like a perfumer's shop" (p. 163).

At his own fireside in Walworth, Wemmick becomes, if not exactly an enchanter, a creator of enchantment. The huge longing, always present in Dickens, for the gemütlich, the homely, the enjoyment of a rural domesticity on a modest competence—things that could never satisfy him in actuality—finds its most attractive correlative in the picture of Wemmick's glorified doll's house, his "little wooden cottage in the midst of plots of garden" (p. 160). (It is pleasant to think that Dickens must have felt something of Wemmick's pleasure when, at Christmas 1864, his friend Charles Fechter gave him a real Swiss chalet packed into fifty-eight boxes. It rapidly became Dickens's pride and joy.) Here, with his battlements and Gothic windows, mimic moat and drawbridge, nine o'clock gun and flagstaff, his pig and rabbits, ornamental fountain, miniature lake and bower, Wemmick presides over the welfare of his father, the "aged parent" (p. 161), and decorously entertains his future bride, Miss Skiffins. In Walworth, despite its small black museum of criminal odds and ends, Wemmick's sentiments are positively Pickwickian. As the "Aged" says to Pip: "This is a pretty pleasure-ground, sir. This spot and these beautiful works upon it ought to be kept together by the nation, after my son's time, for the people's enjoyment" (p. 162). Exercising his Walworth sentiments, Wemmick becomes Pip's true friend, advising him how he can best help Herbert Pocket financially and how he can best assist Magwitch on his ill-fated return from New South Wales.

Mr. Jaggers's well-disguised tenderness of heart is demonstrated retrospectively. After the fire at Satis House, Pip, burned and bandaged, takes him Miss Havisham's authorization for £900 to be disbursed for Herbert Pocket's partnership and reveals his knowledge of Estella's parentage. Mr. Jaggers himself is ignorant that Magwitch is Estella's father, and Pip notices "the slightest start that could escape a man" (p. 305). When Pip reveals that he knows Mr. Jaggers's housekeeper, Molly, to be the mother, and appeals to Wemmick and his own playful ways" (p. 306) to support him in getting Jaggers to confirm these details, the full story comes out. There is a most unsuitable (for Little Britain) temporary thaw in the professional atmosphere of the office, Mr. Jaggers and Wemmick gazing at one another as if doing so for the first time. Mr. Jaggers then reveals how he placed Molly's illlegitimate child with Miss Havisham, asking Pip to consider how a "legal adviser" asked to find a child for a rich woman, "lived in an atmosphere of evil, and that all he saw of children was, their being generated in great numbers for certain destruction. . . . Put the case that pretty nigh all the children he saw in his daily business life, he had reason to look upon as so much spawn, to develop into the fish that were to come to his net—to be prosecuted, defended, forsworn, made orpans, be-devilled somehow. . . . Put the case, Pip, that here was one pretty little child out of the heap, who could be saved" (p. 307).

Pip's revelation is knowledge that Mr. Jaggers immediately divorces from use. It cannot be revealed with any profit to any of the participants in the story. As Mr. Jaggers says, looking at Pip's bandaged hands, if he loves Estella, it would be better for him to "chop off that bandaged left hand of yours with your bandaged right hand, and then pass the chopper on to Wemmick there, to cut that off, too" (p. 308) rather than reveal her parentage to her. The chinks briefly opened in the armor are rapidly closed. Wemmick and Mr. Jaggers resume their work in a particularly inflexible manner, and both turn on the unfortunate client Mike who enters with a tear in his eye. Having expressed their mutual distaste for "feelings" and sent Mike packing, the precious pair settle back to their work "with an air of refreshment upon them as if they had just had lunch" (p. 309). In the unregulated squalor of the lawless, overcrowded warrens of a disease-ridden London, private acts of tenderness and compassion shine like fitful candles and can have little ameliorative effect. It is a kind of education.

THE CONVICT'S RETURN AND THE CREATURES OF THE DARK

The pressingly physical world of Magwitch and the darkly enchanted castle in the air where Miss Havisham and Estella have their being are about to collide. Pip is twenty-three. He is living with Herbert Pocket in chambers in Garden Court, down by the River Thames. Herbert has gone to Marseilles on business, so Pip is alone. The weather over England presages more than physical rack and ruin, as "the wind rushing up the river shook the house that night, like discharges of cannon, or breakings of a sea" (p. 236). Lamps flicker or die, the chimes of the church bells fracture in the wind, and "the coal fires in barges on the river were being carried away before the wind like red-hot splashes on the rain" (p. 237). We are back again in a parodic vision of that chase on the marshes with the torches of the soldiers dripping their greasy fires on the damp ground, with our earlier vision of young Pip armed with stolen pork pie and file off on his mission to aid and abet a convict's flight from justice. We remember that the stolen file was used by the convict to saw off his leg iron, that that very leg iron was picked up by Orlick and used to batter Mrs. Joe into a half-vegetative, abbreviated life. And at this point, Magwitch climbs the stair.

Pip finds himself sinking under a dramatic battery of unwelcome truths: "Yes, Pip, dear boy. I've made a gentleman on you! It's me wot has done it! I swore that time, sure as ever I earned a guinea, that guinea should go to you" (p. 240). Magwitch's claims are, to Pip, appalling and ungainsayable: "Look'ee here, Pip. I'm your second father. You're my son—more to me nor any son" (p. 241). Pip's guilt as a conspirator is redoubled as Magwitch tells him that "There's been overmuch coming back of late years, and I should of a certainty be hanged if took" (p. 243). As he gloats over Pip's clothes, his books, the diamond ring set with rubies on Pip's finger, we realize how Magwitch lives imaginatively through Pip, set up on tainted money as a gentleman doll, just as Miss Havisham lives imaginatively through Estella, set up on tainted love as a lady of fashion. As the night wears away and Magwitch sleeps, Pip emotionally plumbs the true depth of the pit he has, in part, dug for himself. He and Magwitch now have to climb out of the ogreish melodrama with which Dickens has invested their relationship and into a believable humanity. So ends the second stage of Pip's expectations.

Abel Magwitch now shifts his role and identity. He becomes Provis, Pip's honorary uncle; Pip in some sense becomes his creature, gazed at with "admiring proprietorship" (p. 259), and since Magwitch has returned for good, is enlisted in a further and ongoing conspiracy to aid him in all the disguises and deceits he will have to practice to evade justice. Herbert is enlisted as fellow conspirator, and together they are told Magwitch's life story, from the time "I first become aware of myself, down in Essex, a thieving turnips for my living" (p. 259) until the time he fell into the traps set for him by Miss Havisham's lover, Compeyson, who "got me into such nets as made me his black slave" (p. 262). Wemmick, in his Walworth capacity, is also made privy to the situation and also becomes an active conspirator, aiding Herbert and Pip in establishing Magwitch as tenant in a riverside lodging at Mill Pond Bank, downriver from London Bridge. Pip decides to accompany his "Uncle Provis" to Hamburg, and the failed attempt to smuggle Magwitch out of the country ends with a watery mirror image of that long-ago chase across the marshes that returned him to his prison ship, as they set out from a landscape "like my own marsh country, flat and monotonous, and with a dim horizon; while the winding river turned and turned, and the great floating buoys upon it turned and turned, and everything else seemed stranded and still" (p. 326).

Compeyson, however, has followed their plan. Before the conspirators—Pip, Herbert, and their friend Startop—can hail the Hamburg steamer from their rowboat, they are intercepted by a police galley carrying Compeyson. Under the threshing wheels of the paddle steamer that bears down on them, Compeyson drowns, and the injured Magwitch is recaptured. After the drama of this denouement, the ending moves into a minor key, signaled by Pip's decision to stay with Magwitch through whatever befalls him: "For, now, my repugnance to him had all melted away, and in the hunted wounded shackled creature who held my hand in his, I only saw a man who had meant to be my benefactor, and who had felt affectionately, gratefully, and generously, towards me with great constancy through a series of years. I only saw in him a much better man than I had been to Joe" (p. 2). As Magwitch is sentenced to death, one of thirty-two receiving the sentence, Pip holds his hand: "The sun was striking in at the great windows of the court, through the glittering drops of rain upon the glass, and it made a broad shaft of light between the two-and-thirty and the Judge, linking both together, and perhaps reminding some among the audience, how both were passing on, with absolute equality, to the greater Judgement that knoweth all things and cannot err" (p. 340). Magwitch will not be executed. He is by now a dying man who spends his final days lying peaceably, "placidly looking at the white ceiling, with an absence of light in his face, until some word of mine brightened it for an instant, and then it would subside again" (p. 341). So he dies, Pip and Dickens watching over his last days with single-minded intensity.

As the intertwined loves and affections of Pip and Magwitch reach their climax, Dickens unleashes on the reader a pictorial emotional drama that covers certain obstinate questions, in particular the question of the conspirators' guilt in aiding and abetting the escape of a returned convict or, worse, being involved in Compeyson's murder by Magwitch. The witty editor of the Norton Critical Edition, Edgar Rosenberg, suggests that Startop, Pip, and Herbert are saved from prison only by Dickens's guilty absence of mind in failing to consider the case for their prosecution, for what is really taking place is that passionate selective amnesia of Dickens when reworking those themes where love, dispossession, the ferocious indifference of social institutions to individual misery, and the self perceived as victim all come into play (p. 461). In Magwitch we are presented with a character both deeply guilty and deeply innocent. In that final childlike image of being carried away to death in a white serenity, Magwitch is seen as quite transcending, in his capacity for love and hurt, such creatures of the dark as Orlick, Compeyson, and Bentley Drummle.

THE CREATURES OF THE DARK

Criminality, violence, and malignity track Pip's progress, in the persons of Orlick, Compeyson, and Drummle. Suggestively, Pip's first encounter with death, that of Mrs. Joe, is indirectly brought about by his own action. Magwitch left his leg iron, the murder weapon, to be picked up by Orlick on the marshes. Orlick's direct action in beating Mrs. Joe senseless is only in part related to his slouching, eyes-on-the-ground perception of himself as the ill-favored apprentice, the ill-fated one who gives himself the inscrutable Christian name of Dolge, and who, though he is seen by Joe "to stick to your work as well as most men" (p. 91), has no expectations, great or small. When he does look up, it is always in a "half-resentful, half-puzzled way" (p. 91), and his actions are fueled more by a universal enmity than by any motives we can plausibly ascribe to him. He is at the dark center of the novel, and, as Julian Moynihan points out in "The Hero's Guilt" (Norton Edition, pp. 654–663), Orlick is in part that shadow self which Jung identified, the negative to Pip's positive, committing by proxy those sinful and criminal acts the hero can commit only in his suppressed imagination.

The web of complicity that binds Orlick and Pip's family together is powerfully drawn in Dickens's description of the brain-damaged Mrs. Joe, who repeatedly draws a blacksmith's hammer on her slate until Orlick is brought to her bedside. His silent visits are repeated while she behaves with "an air of humble propitiation in all she did, such as I have seen pervade the bearing of a child towards a hard master" (p. 99). Orlick attempts to ingratiate himself sexually with Biddy, becomes the porter at Satis House, tracks Pip to London, falls in with Compeyson, and in a final confrontation inveigles Pip, through a false message, to a lime kiln on the marshes. Addressing Pip throughout as "wolf," Orlick reveals how he has tracked and mimicked his progress: "You was always in Old Orlick's way since ever you was a child. You goes out of his way, this present night. He'll have no more on you. You're dead" (p. 316). Of the seven deadly sins, Orlick certainly qualifies in wrath, envy, and lust. The rescued Pip sees "Orlick emerge from a struggle of men as if it were tumbling water, clear the table at a leap, and fly out into the night" (p. 319). It is the last we hear of him. As Pip's shadow he disappears into Pip himself, a parable of the divided self on its journey to integration. "The shadow is a living part of the personality and therefore wants to live with it in some form. It cannot be argued out of existence or rationalized into harmlessness" (C. G. Jung, "The Archetypes and the Collective Unconscious," in his *Collected Works,* vol. 9, trans. R. F. C. Hull, 1959). Attractive as such a reading is, the Orlick pressed between the novel's pages is primarily a fearsome other, a member of that terrifying underclass whose existence fascinated and repelled the eternal journalist in Dickens. He is Pip; he is also a candidate for Newgate and the hangman.

In Moynihan's reading, Bentley Drummle, Pip's fellow lodger with the Pockets and his friend Startop, is Pip's unconscious means of revenging himself on Estella. As befits a glossier version of Pip's shadow self, he comes "of rich people down in Somersetshire," and is "idle, proud, niggardly, reserved, and suspicious" (p. 158). He is, in fact, the "next heir but one to a baronetcy," a hereditary title (p. 150). That is in itself almost enough to damn him in Dickens's eyes—he had conspicuously little enthusiasm for the upper echelons of English society. Compeyson is a kind of gentleman, but his fitful presence in the novel, though it has destroyed Miss Havisham, helped to destroy Magwitch, and woven Orlick into his orbit, is most strongly realized in this with Magwitch's emblematic opening and closing grapples on the marshes and under the paddle steamer. Drummle's relationship to Orlick is slipped in by Dickens when Pip encounters Drummle at the Blue Boar. They are both about to visit Satis House, and as Drummle, about to ride off, calls for someone to light his cigar, a man appears whose "slouching shoulders and ragged hair" remind Pip of Orlick (p. 268). Drummle's corruption is demonstrated at the extraordinary dinner Mr. Jaggers gives for Pip, Herbert Pocket, Drummle, and Startop. Mr. Jaggers seems mesmerically attracted to Drummle, the "blotchy, sprawly sulky fellow" whom he nicknames "the Spider" (p. 164). The evening culminates in a botched attempt by Drummle to hurl a glass at Startop, and as Pip makes his farewell, Mr. Jaggers gives him some advice: "Keep as clear of him as you can. But I like the fellow, Pip; he is one of the true sort. Why, if I was a fortune-teller—" (p. 168). Bentley Drummle fades out of Pip's life but does not live to be hanged, though the actual crimes committed by Magwitch seem insignificant when compared to the sustained atmosphere of an embraced evil that surrounds the personalities of Compeyson, Orlick, and Drummle.

ENDINGS: PICCADILLY AND THE MOONLIT GARDEN

The original ending, first revealed in 1874 in the third volume of Forster's *Life of Charles Dickens,* is terse and low-key. The repulsive Drummle has received his comeuppance and died at the hooves of a mistreated horse, but Estella is not free to marry Pip. She is married to a Shropshire doctor, and merely has a brief exchange with Pip as he walks down Piccadilly with Joe

and Biddy's son, little Pip. She stops her pony carriage, mistakes little Pip for Pip's own child, and with a formally exchanged handshake makes her acknowledgment that "suffering had been stronger than Miss Havisham's teaching, and had given her a heart to understand what my heart used to be." So they part.

The ending as usually published is in fact the revised ending, suggested to Dickens by the popular and commercially minded novelist Bulwer Lytton, who read the final proofs of the book in June 1861. Dismayed by the unaccommodating parting of the ways between Pip and Estella with which Dickens had closed his story, Lytton suggested a rosier ending, and Dickens obliged. Drummle has been kicked to death for a second time. Time has reduced Satis House to a few stage properties: a wall, hummocks of grassed-over brick, a bench, a star-pricked mist, and a rising moon. The curtain rises on a transformation scene lit by a romancy gauze of language. The widowed Estella floats in, transfixing Pip with the "saddened softened light of the once proud eyes," eyes about to fill with tears (p. 357). There is a brief comedown when Pip learns that he is now on a patch of real estate belonging to Estella that she has leased for development, but loftier and finer feelings soon rise in Pip's, Estella's, and the reader's breasts as we move through Estella's high-style declaration of the moral value of suffering to an Adam and Eve close, as they leave the "ruined place," hand in hand under a "tranquil light" by which Pip sees, somewhat ambivalently, "the shadow of no parting from her" (p. 358).

The problems raised are fairly simple and cannot be agreeably reconciled. The revision is the ending Dickens wanted, whether we regard Bulwer Lytton as a baleful snake falsely speaking up for Eden or not, but it seems to contradict the whole bent and tenor of the bildungsroman in which Pip and Estella seem to learn little more than how to make a chastened accommodation to life. Is she *really* going to Cairo to live happily ever after with her subdued partner in the trading firm of Clarriker and Co.? We are likely to prefer the Piccadilly ending, since we live *now,* not *then,* and are habituated to minor-key denouements. Such casual accidents as the London meeting seem to be the way we usually meet our old friends and acquaintances. On the other hand, the good-witch spell of Miss Havisham transposed into misty-moisty moonlight presiding over the marriage her earlier wicked-witch spells were designed to thwart links us imaginatively to the fairy-tale world that is also an integral part of *Great Expectations.* The garden ending also has the doubtful merit of making the ghost of Magwitch happy, recalling those consolatory half-truths about his daughter Estella with which Pip embroiders the convict's deathbed: "She lived and found powerful friends. She is living now. She is a lady and very beautiful. And I love her." The garden ending, then, as commonly published, seems to be built to please the imaginary dead as well as the book's readers. Dickens himself did not have a happy track record in marriage—he had separated from his wife Catherine in 1858—and the biographically curious will be amused by Edgar Johnson's remark in *Charles Dickens, His Tragedy and Triumph* that "Estella" seems "a kind of lawless anagram" based on the name of Dickens's unacknowledged love, "Ellen Lawless Ternan" (vol. 2, p. 991). The Dickens-Ternan relationship did not exactly run smoothly either. Perhaps his temperament, with its unfulfilled longing for a durable Christmas happiness allied to a businessman's knowledge of what the market would stand, was easily persuaded by Lytton's suggestions, though we are never really shown the means by which Estella undertakes her moonlit garden heart-transplant operation. Still, it has as much plausibility as Oz's assistance to the Tin Man.

Our sense of what an appropriate ending to *Great Expectations* would be may well depend on what kind of man we conceive Pip himself to have become. A novel by Thomas Hardy tells us what Hardy thinks, but Dickens does not appear as a talkative guide in his own work. We have only Pip's word for what he considers himself to have been, and to be. We can deduce that he is something of a dullish dog, a Horatio rather than a Hamlet. As Humphry House in *The Dickens World* puts it, Pip becomes progressively "less rough, better spoken, better read, better mannered," and asks: "Who is to say that these are not advantages?" (p. 156). To better oneself is hardly a crime. He shows no particular interest in social questions, the arts, or the sciences. He learns slowly and painfully, but his lessons are well and truly learned. By the time he pleads with his imaginary benefactress on Herbert Pocket's behalf, he has matured sufficiently to ask nothing for himself. After all, despite Miss Havisham's agreement to have her emotions manipulated by Dickens into a final paroxysm of generosity, a good fairy can leave only fairy gold; whether we call it "love" or "money," it would prove for Pip an insubstantial legacy. Is there a possible third ending for the reader to supply or discover? Should we feel disappointed by the somewhat inconclusive coda with which *Great Expectations* falls away after the death of Magwitch? The deepening relationship between Pip and his convict is certainly the emotional center of the book. It is as real as the relationships he imaginatively enters with Miss Havisham and Estella are unreal. The wedding dances in *Great Expectations* seem to evade the burned and battle-hardened; they are reserved for those who retain certain childlike, inconsequential elements: Wemmick and Miss Skiffins, Joe and Biddy, Herbert Pocket and his Clara. We deduce from Pip's experiences that hard work overseas in a commercial office on a modest income, the acceptance of a decent limitation to what can be expected from the world, and a lively sympathy for our fellow creatures may best provide an approximation to happiness. It is a message that does not *exactly* identify Pip with his creator, that raffishly theatrical gentleman with a fancy waistcoat, a commanding eye, and a talent for conjuring, hypnotism, and selective conviviality—Charles Dickens.

For such a modest man, Pip has had a good run in his academic afterlife, as the bibliography suggests. Two particular enticements into the Dickens world are provided by Peter Carey's novel *Jack Maggs* (London, 1998) and David Lean's classic 1946 film version. Carey brings Maggs, the returned convict, back to London to look for the young gentleman, Henry Phipps, his money has created. Dickens himself appears, in the persona of Tobias Oates, to worm out Maggs's secrets by mesmerism, an art Dickens himself practiced. The Lean film, shot in black and white, is simplified—there is no Orlick—with a hugely atmospheric opening sequence and strong pictorial values. The mature Pip is sturdily played by John Mills, and Alec Guinness makes a fey and winsome Herbert Pocket. With Jean Simmons as the young Estella and bravura performances from Francis L. Sullivan as Jaggers and Martita Hunt as Miss Havisham, there are no prizes for saying that this film version still annihilates all contenders.

Select Bibliography

EDITIONS

Great Expectations. Edited by Edgar Rosenberg. A Norton Critical Edition, with authoritative text, backgrounds, contexts, and criticism. New York: W. W. Norton, 1999. (The definitive edition for the serious student. It also contains a "selective bibliography" that is extensive and wide-ranging.)

Great Expectations. Edited with notes by Margaret Cardwell. Introduction by Kate Flint. Oxford: Oxford University Press, 1994.

SECONDARY WORKS: BIOGRAPHICAL

Ackroyd, Peter. *Dickens.* London: Sinclair-Stevenson, 1990. (A novelist's interpretation. Heavy to hold; hard to put down. A consistently exciting read.)

Forster, John. *Life of Charles Dickens.* 3 vols. London: Chapman and Hall, 1872–1874. (First-hand material by Dickens's friend and biographer.)

Hibbert, Christopher. *The Making of Charles Dickens.* London: Longmans, 1967. (An account of Dickens's childhood and youth that will provide the reader with clues to the way Dickens transposed and disguised his own early experiences in *Great Expectations.*)

Johnson, Edgar. *Charles Dickens: His Tragedy and Triumph.* 2 vols. New York: Simon & Schuster, 1952.

Kaplan, Fred. *Dickens: A Biography.* London: Hodder & Stoughton, 1988.

Tomalin, Claire. *The Invisible Woman: The Story of Nellie Ternan and Charles Dickens.* New York: Knopf, 1991.

SECONDARY WORKS: BACKGROUND

Collins, Philip. *Dickens and Crime.* Cambridge Studies in Criminology. London: Macmillan, 1961. Reprinted Bloomington: Indiana University Press, 1968.

Gadd, Laurence W. *The Great Expectations Country.* London: C. Palmer, 1929. (A topographical description of the novel's setting.)

Hibbert, Christopher. *The Roots of Evil: A Social History of Crime and Punishment.* London: Weidenfeld and Nicolson, 1963.

House, Humphry. *The Dickens World.* London: Oxford University Press, 1941. (A sharp and readable study of Dickens's relationship to the thought and issues of his day.)

Hughes, Robert. *The Fatal Shore: The Epic of Australia's Founding.* New York: Knopf, 1987.

Stone, Harry. *Dickens and the Invisible World: Fairy Tales, Fantasy, and Novel-Making.* Bloomington: Indiana University Press, 1979.

SECONDARY WORKS: CRITICAL AND SCHOLARLY

Belletto, René. *Les grandes espérances de Charles Dickens.* Paris: P.O.L., 1994. (650 pages "informed by psychoanalytic and poststructuralist thought," says Edgar Rosenberg.)

Bradbury, Nicola. *Charles Dickens' "Great Expectations."* Critical Studies of Key Texts. New York: St. Martin's Press, 1990.

Brooks-Davies, Douglas. *Dickens: "Great Expectations."* Penguin Critical Studies. London: Penguin, 1989.

Cotsell, Michael, ed. *Critical Essays on Charles Dickens's "Great Expectations."* Boston: G. K. Hall, 1990.

Lettis, Richard, and William E. Morris, eds. *Assessing "Great Expectations."* San Francisco: Chandler, 1960.

Paroissien, David, ed. *The Companion to "Great Expectations."* Westport, Conn.: Greenwood, 1999.

Sadrin, Anny. *Great Expectations.* London: Unwin Hyman, 1988. (A full survey of themes, techniques, historical context, the two endings, and so forth.)

Tredell, Nicholas, ed. *Charles Dickens: "Great Expectations."* Icon Critical Guides. Cambridge: Icon, 1998.

Worth, George J. *"Great Expectations": An Annotated Bibliography.* Garland Bibliographies. New York: Garland, 1986.

Jonathan Swift's
Gulliver's Travels

CHRISTOPHER MACLACHLAN

JONATHAN SWIFT WAS born in 1667 in Dublin, the main city of Ireland, but his family was not, and did not think of itself as, Irish. They belonged to the ruling class of English who had controlled Ireland since its conquest by England in the sixteenth century. Swift's father died before he was born, and he was brought up largely at the expense of his other relatives. He was educated in Ireland and then studied at Trinity College in Dublin, destined for a clerical career. This was to be in the Church of Ireland, the Irish branch of the state Church of England, which ministered to the English ruling class in Ireland, and not to the mass of the Irish. Almost all of the latter belonged to the Roman Catholic Church, from which the English church had broken away in the Reformation of the sixteenth century. Thus in both political and religious terms Swift was part of an isolated minority in the country of his birth.

Throughout his life Swift wanted to escape this isolation by moving from Ireland to England. For this he needed to find a livelihood there. This meant gaining an appointment in the Church of England. His involvement in English politics in the first decade of the eighteenth century, motivated by this ambition, came to nothing, and he was forced to return to Ireland in 1714. There, apart from a few visits to England, he remained for the rest of his life, dying in 1745.

In England, then, Swift was also an outsider. In Ireland, he felt an exile, and although he busied himself in Irish affairs, and at one time defended the Irish so successfully against a piece of English oppression that he became a local hero, he refused to admit he was Irish. He seems to have felt at home nowhere, and his frustration and bitterness are expressed in his writings, almost all of them satirical and directed against the changing world of his time. His position as an outsider in both Ireland and England is paralleled by that of Gulliver in the countries he visits on his travels.

Swift lived through a period when the elements of the modern state were beginning to form. Britain in the late seventeenth and early eighteenth centuries developed social and political institutions that are recognizably the foundations for those which exist today in Europe and the United States, and with variations elsewhere. Many of these developments began in Britain because of the particular conditions of British history, and were strengthened and passed on, notably to the United States of America, during the eighteenth century. Swift was strongly aware of the changes taking place in Britain in his time, even though he did not approve of them, and his dislike of what was happening fueled his satirical writings.

Although it was very far from being a democracy, eighteenth-century Britain showed the beginnings of representative government and party politics. In the previous century political differences had led to civil war, and the struggle for power between the monarchy and Parliament had often resulted in violence. By the end of the seventeeth century, however, the country was tired of turmoil, and political opponents became more willing to compromise and avoid extremities in order to preserve peace and order. Although politics was still a dangerous business, with frequent threats of rebellion and accusations of treason, there was greater acceptance of differences of opinion and of the rights of those who opposed the government to hold their views. Two factions, called the Whigs and the Tories, had formed, though they lacked the close organization of modern political parties. It became the practice to form the government from whichever of these factions had more support in Parliament, so that the other became a semioffical opposition. More significant, it also became the case that one faction replaced the other in power without violence, and thus the British developed a custom of smooth transition between governments that preserved the continuity of the management of the state while allowing for transfers of power.

Swift began as a Whig and later joined the Tories, which suggests just how little difference there was between the two. Nevertheless, he was always unhappy with the idea of a loyal opposition and indeed frequently attacked the whole idea of political parties. He seems to have thought that the government of a country ought to be a simple matter of choosing what is the right thing to do without engaging in lengthy debate. Any doubts about what to do should be

CHRONOLOGY

1667	Jonathan Swift is born in Dublin, Ireland, 30 November.
1688	Deposition of James II, because of his Roman Catholicism. Parliament gives the throne to his daughter Mary and her Dutch Protestant husband, William of Orange.
1689	Swift flees to England because of Irish unrest.
1690	An Irish Catholic rebellion led by James is defeated by William of Orange.
1694	Swift is ordained a deacon in the Church of Ireland.
1701–1714	War of the Spanish Succession between France and the Grand Alliance of Britain, Austria, the Netherlands, Hanover, and other states. Led by the Duke of Marlborough, the allies win several notable victories, but the war becomes unpopular in England and the Tories bring it to an end with the Peace of Utrecht.
1702	Swift becomes a Doctor of Divinity of Trinity College, Dublin.
1704	Swift publishes *A Tale of a Tub* and *The Battle of the Books.*
1707–1714	Swift spends most of this period involved in politics in London, mainly on behalf of the Tory government led by Robert Harley (later Earl of Oxford) and Henry St. John (later Viscount Bolingbroke). He meets many writers, including Joseph Addison, John Arbuthnot, John Gay, and Alexander Pope; the last three are also members of the Scriblerus Club, whose interest in parody and attacks on literary dullness stimulate Swift's satires, including *Gulliver's Travels.*
1714	Death of Queen Anne and fall of the Tory government with the accession of George I, the first Hanoverian monarch. Swift returns to "exile" in Ireland.
1719	Daniel Defoe publishes *Robinson Crusoe.*

1721	Swift working on *Gulliver's Travels.*
1724	Swift publishes *The Drapier's Letters*, a series of pamphlets attacking English economic oppression of Ireland that make him an Irish hero.
1726	Swift visits London and arranges the anonymous publication of *Gulliver's Travels*, 28 October.
1734–1735	*Gulliver's Travels* is published in Dublin as part of an edition of Swift's works, with revisions and additions, including Gulliver's letter to his Cousin Sympson.
1738	Swift's health and memory begin to fail.
1742	Swift is declared "of unsound mind and memory," and guardians are appointed to take over his affairs.
1745	Swift dies, 19 October, leaving money for "a house for fools and mad" (now known as St. Patrick's Hospital).

settled by the head of state, and once the ruler had taken a decision, nothing else was required but to obey his instructions. These old-fashioned political principles, however, did not stop Swift from engaging fully in the new politics of his time.

His involvement was mainly in the processes of persuasion that supported the new politics. One of the new institutions that developed in Britain was a (relatively) free press. Parliamentary politics was accompanied by the rise of political journalism, in newspapers and periodicals as well as in pamphlets and books of memoirs and history. Almost all of Swift's prose writings belong to this kind of literature: some of it devoted to grand matters of state, like the war with France at the beginning of the century, others to more local and specific concerns, such as the church in Ireland. *Gulliver's Travels,* though it seems to us to be a general satire, with only occasional allusions to contemporary politics, apparently was taken by its first readers as much like the rest of Swift's works, as a topical commentary on matters of the day. Within a month of its publication, Edmund Curll began

publishing a key to it, in which characters and incidents are identified with real people and events, firmly stating that "under the allegory of a voyager, Mr Gulliver gives us an admirable system of modern politicks" (Swift, 2002, p. 289).

This relates *Gulliver's Travels* to another function of literature in Swift's day, the dissemination of information and ideas. One of the other things that developed in Britain at this time was science and technology, although neither was so named. At the highest level, Britain was the home of major scientific advances, most famously the theories of Sir Isaac Newton that revolutionized physics and astronomy and provided the model for modern science. But for a contemporary like Swift, these achievements were obscured by the plethora of attempts at devising new methods and schemes, many of which were wrongheaded and some of which were quite fraudulent. Britain was quick to see the importance of scientific research—Charles II had given a charter to the Royal Society as early as 1662—but the early institutionalizing of research could not control the outburst of speculation that followed, and its excesses were ripe for satire.

Swift's hostility to speculation and new theories was part of his dislike of change and his opposition to the idea of progress, which were rooted in his religion. Much of the political violence of the seventeenth century had been caused by differences of religion, especially between Protestants and Catholics. In England these differences had been settled in 1688 with the deposition of James II for being a Catholic and the assertion by Parliament that in future the British monarch must be a Protestant. (In Ireland matters were far from settled, since the people were still mainly Catholic, and therefore excluded from their own government.) A consequence of the triumph of Protestantism, and the reluctance of its opponents to try to overturn it, which would mean another civil war, was a certain degree of religious toleration. There were still legal restrictions on British

Catholics, and on some other denominations, but these were not much enforced.

One result of the reduction in the political implications of religious differences was a rise in religious speculation. In particular, various thinkers began to suggest that despite their differences, all Christians, and perhaps even all well-intentioned people of whatever faith, shared fundamental spiritual and moral principles. Some philosophers went further still and suggested that the basic truths of religion and morality could be discovered by reason, without the aid of divine revelation or priestly instruction. Swift was not alone in fearing that this rational approach to religion and ethics threatened the very existence of churches and their reliance on Scriptures and traditional doctrine. And since the church was one of the pillars of the state—indeed, the chief means by which social order and civilized behavior were maintained—any undermining of the church's authority also threatened civilization itself. He therefore regarded the use of reason to question religious doctrines as extremely dangerous. For him, reason should be used only to uphold the teachings of the church.

Swift, then, was at odds with the trends of his time that led in the direction of greater freedom of thought in politics, religion, morality, and science. Once again he was an outsider, though in these respects he was not trying to get in, but rather standing back and warning his contemporaries of what he saw as the folly and danger of weakening the structures of thought and society that guarded against change, and the threat of chaos that might come with it. Whereas the eighteenth century became a period of expansion and risk-taking, building a hopeful view of man and society, Swift focused on the weakness and sinfulness of his fellow creatures and scorned their growing belief that by the application of reason they could improve themselves and their society. The underlying themes of *Gulliver's Travels* are the flaws of European civilization (mostly shown in the distorting mirror of the lands Gulliver visits)

and the empty confidence in reason as a means to improve things. These themes grow in power through the book and reach a climax in the notorious final part, in the contrast between the rational but inhuman Houyhnhnms and the beastly but almost-human Yahoos.

A READING

Before looking in detail at *Gulliver's Travels,* it is useful to consider the eighteenth-century meaning of satire. In *A Discourse Concerning the Original and Progress of Satire* (1693), John Dryden discusses two traditional derivations of the term "satire" with which Swift would have been familiar. The first is from the word "satyr," meaning one of the half-human, half-goat followers of the Greek god Pan, usually pictured in scenes of ribald merriment. Dryden in fact rejects this derivation and prefers another, from the Latin word *satura,* meaning "full, rich, copious"; it could also be applied to a dish of many ingredients. Which is the correct derivation of the word is less important than the influence of both on eighteenth-century writers, including Swift. From the Greek origin comes the idea that satire should be irreverent, disorderly, and shocking, showing no respect for conventional opinions or for seriousness and public authority. This clearly affects the content of eighteenth-century satire. The Latin derivation, however, indicates eighteenth-century attitudes to the form of satirical works: that they should be full and various, a literary stew of all kinds of things mixed up together. A satire, then, need not be consistent in things like tone, structure, or style, and perhaps not even in its attitudes and meanings. Whenever the satirist sees an opportunity to say something striking, or develop a line of argument, no matter how much it digresses from the context, he is allowed to do so, and in a satire an author was not thought to be confined or constrained by the sort of expectations of neatness and consistency that apply to other genres.

This general idea of satire in Swift's time has two sets of consequences for *Gulliver's Travels.*

The first is that in reading it, we must be alert to the way Swift chops and changes from one kind of writing to another, and from one attitude to what he is saying to a sometimes quite different point of view. The work combines a multitude of different methods of making points, and also hits at a multitude of targets. Sometimes it tries to hit more than one target simultaneously, and often Swift moves so rapidly from one thing to another that the reader has to concentrate hard to follow him. He does this deliberately to unsettle the reader. In a letter of 29 September 1725 to Alexander Pope, Swift said that "the chief end I propose to myself in all my labors is to vex the world rather than divert it" (Swift, 2002, p. 261). In *Gulliver's Travels* as in his other satires, then, Swift is out to use any means to get at the reader, and he will not pass over a chance of writing something forceful and aggressive just because it may not fit in with the general tone or direction of a passage, or because it seems inconsistent with the narrative or the characterization.

For literary critics there is a second set of consequences. Because Swift is writing opportunistically and with an eye to effects rather than to consistency, it is difficult to generalize about what he is doing. The definition of satire he uses allows him to break rules and do what he wants. Critics, of course, would prefer him to write in ways they can pin down and describe in a few words, but Swift's satires, especially his long ones like *Gulliver's Travels,* defy classification and critical definition. These are texts that are meant to be full, rich, and various. When critics discuss them, then, they are always in danger of reducing them to something simpler than they really are, and making fools of themselves in the process. One sort of people Swift dearly wished to vex was critics, and he would be delighted at the way they have walked into various traps he set them.

A good example of the critical difficulty posed by *Gulliver's Travels* is the question of what kind of book it is. Is it a novel? Because it is a long prose narrative, with a main character

and several others, and a setting that seems realistic in time and place—at any rate in its references to Gulliver's England—it may look to the reader very like a novel, and it is often referred to as such. For one thing, there is an obvious resemblance between it and Daniel Defoe's *Robinson Crusoe* (1719). Defoe's novel begins "I was born in the year 1632, in the city of York, of a good family, tho' not of that country, my father being a foreigner of Bremen, who settled first at Hull" (*Robinson Crusoe,* p. 5), and goes on with more details of Crusoe's family and his upbringing, all in a matter-of-fact style. Swift's book begins "My father had a small estate in Nottinghamshire; I was the third of five sons" (*Gulliver's Travels,* Norton Critical Edition, 15; further page references are to this edition), and goes on to describe Gulliver's education and early life, again in a plain style, with much seemingly factual detail. Swift, like Defoe, seems to be setting up the background for his main character in a way that is now very familiar to us as readers of fiction. He also seems to be adopting a tone of voice that is consistent with the kind of man who is supposed to be writing this text: one who sounds fairly reliable as a witness because he attends to plain facts without exaggerating them or dressing them up with fine writing.

Yet many modern critics have come to the belief that *Gulliver's Travels* is not a novel. Indeed, they think that the resemblance of its opening to that of *Robinson Crusoe* is in fact part of the satire Swift directs at Defoe and the kind of fiction he was writing, and also at the tall tales of real travelers. The deliberate, dull attention to facts of Swift's opening is an ironic lead into the extraordinary events Gulliver describes from the third page of his narrative onward, when he wakes on the beach after his first shipwreck to find himself tied down and at the mercy of a crowd of little men six inches high. Nobody should believe this actually happened just because Gulliver tells his story in a truthful way, and to read *Gulliver's Travels* as though it is a novel may be to bring to it inappropriate expectations and assumptions.

The incredibility of what happens to Gulliver on his travels is not the only reason for arguing that the book is not a novel. More significant is the way Gulliver himself appears in the text. Although he seems at first like a normal character in fiction, Swift uses him with far more freedom and neglect of consistency than is credible in a novel. At points in the text Gulliver is made to speak much like his author, attacking the targets of Swift's satire, whereas elsewhere he is made the object of satire. Sometimes he plays a major role in the narrative, but elsewhere he dwindles to a mere recorder, and the reader almost forgets he is there. He is therefore less a character in his own right than one device among others that Swift exploits to vex the reader. Paying attention to Gulliver's function in different parts of the book is one way to analyze Swift's satirical techniques and the effects he seeks to achieve.

As has been said above, these techniques and effects are various and shifting, and they make interpretation of *Gulliver's Travels* far from straightforward. The very structure of the text is a problem. Each part describes one of Gulliver's journeys, and to that extent they are similar and comparison between them seems invited. Yet each journey is to a very different part of the world, and Gulliver himself offers very few reflections on how they compare. The layout of the text makes us wonder about how to connect it, and whether we are correct in seeing the connections we do.

We are also faced with the question of the order of the parts. Do they make up a progress of arguments or ideas, so that the last part is some kind of climax or culmination? And then each part is arranged in a number of chapters in which Gulliver generally describes a series of incidents and encounters, with very little narrative continuity. How do these chapters connect? Are we being told these things in a particular order, and if so, what does that convey? Is

Gulliver supposed to know what he is doing in ordering his experience, or are we to think of him as unaware of the significances we think we see in what he tells us? Why does he seem so naive in some parts of the book but cunning and devious in others?

Again the structure of the text invites us to ask questions about what it means and to draw conclusions about it, but often offers very little direct help or assurance. This perhaps explains why critics of *Gulliver's Travels* (including the present one) reach beyond the text for help to understand it, and why much of the reaction to the work has been focused on Swift as its author, and in recent years on Gulliver as the "author," in the hope that they will provide a foundation upon which to rest an interpretation. The meaning of the text itself is often puzzling, but that, of course, is what Swift said he always intended his writings to be. What follows is a reading of each part of *Gulliver's Travels* that attempts to relate them together, although in a short essay much detail must be passed over and the general meaning often grossly simplified. Like all critical discussions of works by Swift, then, this essay can be justified only as a rough guide and stimulus to further discussion.

PART I: "A VOYAGE TO LILLIPUT"

"A Voyage to Lilliput" is the part of the book that has the most plot in it. There is far more of a story in it than in the other three parts; this may be why it is the best-known and most popular part of the work, frequently imitated and reproduced in films and other forms. Possibly Swift deliberately made the reader welcome by providing an interesting narrative at the start. The story itself is the familiar one about the man, hitherto ignorant of politics, who becomes involved in state affairs and learns, to his cost, how dangerous they are. The tale is given a fantastic twist by the fact that the hero is twelve times larger than the other characters, but like many giants (though this may not be true of those later in the *Travels*) Gulliver does not seem very clever, and like most of us he tends to assume that very small people must be harmless and innocent. This assumption even survives a reading of the "Voyage to Lilliput" itself, to judge by the many children's versions of it that delight in the miniature world it describes, ignoring the darker side of the tale.

The early chapters about Gulliver's capture, his transportation to the capital, and the efforts to feed and clothe him are whimsical and humorous. The satire at first is light and occasional, as in the Lilliputians' conclusion that Gulliver's watch may be "the God that he worships...because he assured us...that he seldom did anything without consulting it" (p. 29). Interestingly, here the criticism is directed at Gulliver, and through him at the reader, for a wrong sense of what is important in life, but the point is made so jokingly that only the most solemn reader will make much of it.

In the next chapter, however, the fun becomes more serious as Gulliver begins describing the Lilliputian court, and one of the basic intentions of this part of the *Travels,* the belittling of the pretensions of rulers and politicians, becomes more and more obvious. Like a genuine traveler, Gulliver describes the system of government of this foreign land, but what might seem strange and exotic when reported of full-size humans seems ridiculous when applied to beings six inches tall. The grandiloquent titles of the emperor of Lilliput—"Delight and Terror of the Universe...Monarch of All Monarchs, taller than the Sons of Men...whose Head strikes against the Sun" (p. 36)—and so on, are clearly mockery, but they also reflect the self-importance of larger rulers, and as Gulliver goes on with his account of the state of Lilliput, the reader realizes that there are obvious resemblances between the trivial customs of these little people and those of Swift's contemporaries (and ours). Thus, the ropedancing by which politicians gain and hold office in the Lilliputian government, and the ceremony of the emperor's stick, which encourages candidates for political office in the arts of

leaping and creeping, are easily seen as satirical images of what ambitious politicians of any size will do to win favor and government positions.

Inevitably critics have tried to connect Gulliver's account of Lilliputian politics with the history of Britain in Swift's time. Most modern editions of *Gulliver's Travels* have notes identifying Lilliputian characters with real historical figures. The general political situation in Lilliput certainly resembles that of early eighteenth-century Britain, often at war with its neighbor France, just as Lilliput is at war with Blefuscu. The quarrel over religion in Lilliput, between those who open their eggs at the big end and those who do so at the little end, parallels the antagonism between Protestants and Roman Catholics in Britain that had led to the deposition and exile of James II in 1688, and the replacement of the Stuart dynasty by the Hanoverians in 1714, though this did not mean the end of Stuart hopes of a return to the throne. The atmosphere of intrigue and fear of conspiracy at the court of Lilliput, therefore, resembles that in Britain after the Hanoverian succession, when those still loyal to the exiled Stuarts plotted rebellion, sometimes with French support, and opponents of the government were treated with suspicion and sometimes had to flee to avoid arrest and trial.

Swift himself had been heavily involved in some of these events when in 1710 he had been made the editor of a government propaganda journal by the Tory leaders, Robert Harley and Henry St. John, who first brought about a peace with France and then, because that had offended the elector of Hanover, the designated heir to the British throne, began secret negotiations for the return of the Stuarts. These led to disaster for the Tory government, the imprisonment of Harley for treason, St. John's exile in France, and Swift's permanent return to Ireland, his hopes of advancement in England completely dashed. His experiences at the heart of the Tory government and his firsthand observation of the double-dealing of real politicians probably lie behind his portrayal of events in Lilliput. In this respect Gulliver stands for Swift himself, an outsider brought into the midst of affairs and amazed to discover what really happens behind the scenes.

Yet *Gulliver's Travels* is not a political allegory narrowly concerned with events in Swift's own career, but a satire on politics and war of more general application—related, it is true, to recent historical events, but by no means confined to them. Swift is drawing upon his own political experience to present a picture of a typical court, full of intrigue, corruption, and deadly danger for the unwary, viewed from the position of an unsuspecting, rather ordinary man who takes things at face value and almost to the end refuses to believe that he is the victim of lies and treachery. Using Gulliver as an observer of politics in miniature is like stepping back and looking at the broad outline of events and institutions. The outcome is not a puzzle about the meaning of particular references but a moral judgment on the whole business of politics. In this the reader keeps well ahead of Gulliver, who seems very slow to realize what is going on around him, and almost to the end protests his loyalty to and admiration for the emperor, long after it is obvious that he intends to do terrible and spiteful things to the Man-Mountain.

Gulliver can of course escape the consequences of his naivete because of his superior size, and his detachment is shared by the reader. We, too, look down on the Lilliputians and can separate ourselves from their nastiness (those critics who insist on confining the meaning of Part I to Swift's lifetime also serve to isolate its implications from themselves and our time). In the preface to *The Battle of the Books* (1704) Swift wrote: "Satire is a sort of glass, wherein beholders do generally discover everybody's face but their own; which is the chief reason for that kind of reception it meets in the world, and that so very few are offended with it" (Swift, 1960, p. 358). He was aware, therefore, of how readers find ways of deflecting satire from themselves, and may well have anticipated that they would identify with Gulliver and avoid much of the point of the first part of his travels. The later parts attempt to break down this detachment of the reader and make you feel the satire directly.

PART II: "A VOYAGE TO BROBDINGNAG"

The second part, "A Voyage to Brobdingnag," is paradoxically most comparable to the first part in being different from it. Not only is Gulliver now the tiny character, but in this part there is little political allusion and even less narrative. Gulliver can do little, and things mostly just happen to him. Swift has some boisterous fun with Gulliver as the victim of a series of accidents. These are comical in a rough, slapstick way that to modern sensibilities is rather disturbing, though they do bring home Gulliver's vulnerability. But another purpose of the humiliations he suffers is to deprive him of dignity. In Part I, though he may seem stupid, he nevertheless appears rather grand as the Man-Mountain; Part II completely undermines this grandeur. Yet we do not entirely despise Gulliver in Brobdingnag, for he remains resourceful and courageous. He shows a Crusoe-like ingenuity in adapting to his circumstances and making the best of things. In short, though we cannot avoid laughing at his various physical discomfitures, we can admire his spirit. A gap begins to open between the material and the spiritual.

This is not unrelated to the Brobdingnagians themselves. When he first sees them, Gulliver says that "as human creatures are observed to be more savage and cruel in proportion to their bulk, what could I expect but to be a morsel in the mouth of the first among these enormous barbarians who should happen to seize me?" (p. 72). This is the opposite prejudice to that in favor of small beings that the voyage to Lilliput calls in question, and Gulliver ought to have learned to doubt both assumptions. The giants turn out to be far less fearsome than tradition alleges, and much less exotic and extraordinary than the reader expects—or than the Lilliputians, not to mention the peoples in Part III. In fact, the Brobdingnagians seem close to Europeans, and their land is much like a traditional version of England. They are not morally perfect—the farmer who catches Gulliver exploits him as a freak and the maids of honor who play with him are no better than they should be—but on the whole the people of Brobdingnag are nothing like as vicious as those of Lilliput. Their faults are matters of oversight or omission rather than deliberate malice (except for the court dwarf), and of all the people Gulliver meets on his travels, they are surely the most likable.

There is therefore not only a reversal in the relative sizes of Gulliver and the people he visits between Parts I and II but also a reversal in moral proportions. In Lilliput, Gulliver was morally superior, but in Brobdingnag he becomes the moral inferior. From chapter 6 of Part II onward, Swift returns to the themes of his satire in Part I, but whereas there he showed the evils of tyranny and political corruption by means of narrative and description, in "A Voyage to Brobdingnag" they become the implicit subjects of the central episode of that part of the book, the debate between Gulliver and the king. I say "implicit" because Gulliver does not directly describe the defects of his Europe; instead he conceals them, or tries to. Gulliver here entirely changes from the political innocent of Part I into a scheming orator, a proponent of political spin, so expert in politics that he knows what must be disguised and how to do so.

More important than the change in Gulliver here is the change in the reader's attitude to him. Gulliver may think he can fool the king of Brobdingnag with his lies about European states, but we have access to the facts he is trying to conceal. For instance, Gulliver describes the British House of Commons as an assembly of "principal gentlemen, freely picked and culled out by the people themselves, for their great abilities, and love of their country, to represent the wisdom of the whole nation" (p. 107). Now we know, as

Swift's contemporaries knew, that the system of electing members of Parliament in his time was corrupt and unfair; they were not "freely picked...by the people," and it is arguable that that is still not the case even today (most politicians in modern democracies are presented for election by political parties, not by the people as such). And even today we might hesitate to claim that our representatives are chosen just for their great abilities, love of their country, and suitability to represent the wisdom of the whole nation. We might hope this is the case, but are not so naive as to think there are no other reasons why men and women go into politics. So Gulliver's statement easily prompts certain questions, such as what influences the selection of election candidates, and what politicians want out of their jobs.

These are exactly the questions the king of Brobdingnag asks Gulliver after he has finished his account of European political institutions:

> He then desired to know what arts were practised in electing those whom I called Commoners. Whether, a stranger with a strong purse might not influence the vulgar voters to choose him ... How came it to pass, that people were so violently bent upon getting into this assembly, which I allowed to be a great trouble and expense ... this appeared such an exalted strain of virtue and public spirit, that his Majesty seemed to doubt it might possibly not be always sincere...
>
> (p. 108)

Though Gulliver claims to be acting as spokesman for our point of view, it is in fact with the king of Brobdingnag that we take sides in the argument, because Gulliver's lies and half-truths are obvious to us. Swift's use of Gulliver has inclined the reader to anticipate the king's point of view and share his arguments against Gulliver, and as the king questions Gulliver more and more closely, the reader is driven further along a line of argument we have already chosen for ourselves. But the further this goes, the more uncomfortable we become, because the king's questions are remorseless and his accumulated insight into the weak spots of Gulliver's defense adds up to a resounding condemnation: "by what I have gathered from your own relation, and the answers I have with much pains wringed and extorted from you, I cannot but conclude the bulk of your natives, to be the most pernicious race of little odious vermin that Nature ever suffered to crawl upon the surface of the earth" (p. 111). With this we can hardly disagree, knowing as we do what Gulliver means when he admits that he "artfully eluded many of [the king's] questions, and gave to every point a more favorable turn…than the strictness of truth would allow" (p. 111). And yet the king could easily detect how bad things really were!

When Gulliver attempts, in the rest of chapter 7, to get back at the king by accusing him of limited understanding and a lack of imagination, he compounds the problem by showing himself (and us) in an even worse light. He offers to tell the king how to make gunpowder and describes its effects in horrible detail (though there is no evidence elsewhere that Gulliver has had such close acquaintance with war and explosions). He assures the king that with the aid of gunpowder, he could destroy his entire capital if it refused to obey him.

Gulliver's scorn at the king's rejection of his offer places us in another dilemma. We are aware both that the king's attitude is admirable and just, and that in our world a state or a ruler that turns down the chance of absolute power is a rarity, and perhaps not entirely prudent in doing so. In a sense the king is old-fashioned; he rejects the most modern aspect of the military technology of Swift's time. This draws attention to the slight backwardness of Brobdingnag in technology and ideas.

Embedded in the debate about gunpowder in Part II is the start of the argument about progress in Part III. Although Gulliver is frequently humiliated by the physical disparity between himself and the Brobdingnagians, and though he is shown up morally by the king, he retains a certain intellectual advantage, as his

knowledge of gunpowder shows. Gulliver begins the debate with the king by asserting that "reason did not extend itself with the bulk of the body" (p. 106), and in what Gulliver calls "industry, art, and sagacity" (p. 106) he is not necessarily inferior just because he is smaller. Gulliver's own ingenuity becomes a sign, in this light, of a possible European advantage. Whether he is right to take comfort in this compensation for the physical and moral humiliations he suffers in Brobdingnag is explored in his next voyage.

PART III: "A VOYAGE TO LAPUTA, BALNIBARBI, GLUBBDUBDRIB, LUGGNAG, AND JAPAN"

The third part of *Gulliver's Travels* has always been a problem for readers. Just after the book was published, Swift's friend John Arbuthnot wrote to him, "I tell you freely the part of the projectors is the least brilliant" (Swift, 2002, p. 265), and many later critics have been less polite. The third is the most fragmentary and diffuse of all the parts. It seems to string together satirical episodes of different kinds and on different topics. Where Part I is sometimes whimsical and Part II is boisterous, Part III is often grotesque. For much of it Gulliver becomes little more than a name, a mere observer; he is involved in even less action than in Brobdingnag, and there is no repeat of the central debate in that voyage. We are presented with a world that seems unreal, fantastic in the unattractive sense of being irresponsible and freakish.

This is intensified by Gulliver's lack of involvement and the thinness of his characterization in Part III. He does not seem to know what to make of what he sees and remains very much an outsider, reflecting our own sense of being outside this dreamlike world. Much of what goes on there seems unnatural, even crazy, but we and Gulliver are made to feel this is a minority view. This is strongly so in Balnibarbi, where Gulliver meets so many people solemnly engaged in ludicrous experiments that we feel sure are insane but they take entirely seriously, so that common sense appears exceptional and craziness the norm. This is confirmed by the plight of Lord Munodi, the only apparently sane man Gulliver meets, who, although he has resisted the wild schemes of the mad scientists of his country, has more or less accepted their view of him as a hopeless eccentric. Part III, then, is trying to induce in us a feeling of intellectual isolation: we think we know what is right and good, but we become less sure we could hold on to our beliefs in a land where opinion was against us.

None of this would work if we could dismiss the doings of the Laputans and others as sheer nonsense, but in fact much of Part III is based on fact. The prime area of reference is to contemporary science. As long ago as 1937, in an essay titled "The Scientific Background of Swift's 'Voyage to Laputa,'" Marjorie Hope Nicolson and Nora M. Mohler pointed out the connection between what Gulliver sees in the Academy of Lagado and actual experiments recorded in the *Transactions of the Royal Society,* the leading British scientific institute of Swift's day, and there are many other details in Part III that allude to contemporary events and ideas. Just as in Part I, the links between what Gulliver claims to have seen in a far-off country and what was in fact the case in the real world mean that Swift's fiction cannot be dismissed as pure fantasy. For many years, however, he seemed to have lost the argument, as the success of modern science and admiration for the improvements it brought made the satire against it in Part III of *Gulliver's Travels* seem shortsighted and out-of-date, but more recently Swift's attacks on pointless and degrading experimentation and the unthinking application of untested theories has begun to seem an early warning of the dangers of science and technology.

Part of this attack is Swift's flat negative answer to the question of progress. When in chapter 8 of Part III, Gulliver calls up the ghosts of the past to compare them with the present,

the result is always to the detriment of the present, and in the immortal struldbruggs of chapter 10 he presents a forceful image of longevity without improvement. When he first hears about them, Gulliver assumes the struldbruggs must be wonders of learning. His emphasis is on the scientific discoveries they must have made during their long lives and on such intellectual matters as history and politics. What he forgets, of course, is the nonintellectual side of human nature, not just the physical facts of aging but also the appetites and desires that interfere with the intellect, and indeed turn the aging immortals into repulsive wrecks for whom life is a curse. Once again Swift's satirical vision takes on increased power in our times, when lengthened life spans in developed countries confront us with the sad consequences of degenerative conditions of both mind and body.

All the historical and scientific references in Part III have the effect of making it, for all its outlandishness and grotesquerie, a satire on our world, and so the sense of isolation from it becomes an estrangement from our own circumstances. We are looking over Gulliver's shoulder at a mad existence that we cannot help recognizing as too much like our own. And the thing that has gone wrong with this world is its use of reason. The inhabitants of Laputa are in general experts in theory, but where they bother to apply it, the results are disastrous. If we emerged from "A Voyage to Brobdingnag" saying that at least we have our achievements in science and technology to make us better than the Brobdingnagians, then by the end of the next voyage we ought to be questioning the worth of those achievements and the use of reason to bring them about. But if our reason can lead us astray, just how rational are we? This is the question that is taken up in the last part of *Gulliver's Travels.*

PART IV: "A VOYAGE TO THE HOUYHNHNMS"

In "A Voyage to the Houyhnhnms," Swift takes the separation of bodily and mental qualities a step further and transfers reason from human beings to horses. R. S. Crane, in his seminal article "The Houyhnhnms, the Yahoos and the History of Ideas" (1967), showed that the choice of the horse here is no accident but derives from the conventional opposition of man and horse in the logic textbooks of the seventeenth century, which Swift undoubtedly studied at university in Dublin. Following a scheme dating back to Porphyrius (233–ca. 301), in which the various substances that make up the physical world are systematically defined, the two branches of feeling, animate, corporeal substance were said to be the rational, exemplified by the *animal rationale* (the rational animal), man, and the irrational, always exemplified by the horse, defined as *animal hinnibile*, the whinnying animal. (If you try to pronounce "Houyhnhnm" giving voice to each letter, the result is much like a whinny, though the word also looks like a variation on "human.") What Swift does in Part IV of *Gulliver's Travels* is switch the positions of man and horse in the Porphyrian system.

At stake, therefore, is the very definition of man as the rational animal. This seems to be confirmed by a letter from Swift to Alexander Pope, 29 September 1725, in which he says "I have got materials towards a treatise proving the falsity of that definition *animal rationale*; and to show it should be only *rationis capax* [capable of reason]. Upon this great foundation of misanthropy...the whole building of my *Travels* is erected" (Swift, 2002, p. 262). Here Swift clearly connects the question of how to define man with *Gulliver's Travels*, and the main issue is the claim that what distinguishes man from the animals is the possession of reason. Swift's attack on this claim has two prongs.

The first prong is his presentation of what a truly rational animal should be, the Houyhnhnms. Not only are they rational but they are also virtuous. They use their reason only for good ends. As in Brobdingnag, Gulliver spends much of his time in Houyhnhnmland explaining to his master what life is like back home, except that now he gives the unvarnished truth and

does not try to deceive. The Houyhnhnm's comments are just as devastating as those of the king of Brobdingnag, but are more obviously derived from a standard of truth and virtue that embodies the ideals of rationality. Gulliver admits that he has great difficulty explaining what he means because his master has no conception of the evils he has to describe, and the language of the Houyhnhnms does not even have words for them: "Power, government, war, law, punishment, and a thousand other things had no terms, wherein that language could express them" (p. 206). Above all, the Houyhnhnms have no word for "lies":

I remember in frequent discourses with my master concerning the nature of manhood, in other parts of the world, having occasion to talk of *lying*, and *false representation*, it was with much difficulty that he comprehended what I meant ... For he argued thus: that the use of speech was to make us understand one another, and to receive information of facts; now if anyone *said the thing which was not*, these ends were defeated; because I cannot properly be said to understand him, and I am so far from receiving information, that he leaves me worse than in ignorance, for I am led to believe a thing *black* when it is *white*, and *short* when it is *long*.

(p. 202)

As with the king of Brobdingnag's objections to Gulliver's account of Europe in Part II, the reader here is surely inclined to agree with the Houyhnhnm's argument, while appreciating Gulliver's difficulty in trying to describe our world in a language that is not made for *saying the thing which is not*. (We might, however, reflect that nevertheless *Gulliver's Travels* is a text full of fictions, if not actual lies, and the purposes of language may not in fact be so narrowly defined as the Houyhnhnm proposes.)

The tendency of Gulliver's conversations with his master, then, is toward showing that, compared to the Houyhnhnms, human beings are hardly entitled to call themselves rational, and the Houyhnhnm's conclusion is in its way as bleak as that of the Brobdingnagian king:

"that he looked upon us as a sort of animals to whose share, by what accident he could not conjecture, some small pittance of *reason* had fallen, whereof we made no other use than by its assistance to aggravate our *natural* corruptions, and to acquire new ones which Nature had not given us" (p. 218).

But that is not all that Part IV of *Gulliver's Travels* has to say about human nature. The second prong of Swift's attack is his presentation of the opposite of the rational Houyhnhnms, the bestial Yahoos. In fact Gulliver meets them first, before encountering the rational horses, and takes an instant dislike to them. They are certainly very unpleasant. Swift is very skillful in alienating us from them from the start, not only by referring to their disgusting habits and appearance but also by careful use of language, consistently applying to the Yahoos terms fit only for animals.

Gradually, however, and very reluctantly, Gulliver is forced to acknowledge that the Yahoos are physically very like him. He can disguise this by keeping his clothes on (wearing clothing is one of the differences between humans and animals), but when in chapter 8 a female Yahoo sees him bathing in the river, and jumps in and embraces him, Gulliver "could no longer deny, that I was a real Yahoo in every limb and feature, since the females had a natural propensity to me as one of their own species" (p. 225). Thus, when his master describes the behavior and customs of the Yahoos, it is clear to the reader that, as in Parts I and III of the book, Swift is giving a thinly disguised and very critical account of ourselves and our world.

Nevertheless, the Yahoos are not exactly human; they lack language and they are said to lack reason altogether, although they are cunning and can be quite smart. The Houyhnhnms have to debate among themselves whether Gulliver is or is not a Yahoo. In the end they decide he is, and ironically declare that his possession of "some rudiments of reason" (p. 235) makes him more, not less, dangerous than the other Yahoos, and

therefore he should be forced to leave Houyhnhnmland. As for Gulliver, "by conversing with the Houyhnhnms, and looking upon them with delight, I fell to imitate their gait and gesture" (p. 235); in other words, he tries to turn into a horse and escape his Yahoo nature. He is caught between the two, and, since he is the only human being in the land—and hence our representative—his dilemma raises the question of where *we* stand between the ideal of rationality represented by the Houyhnhnms and the image of brute instinct represented by the Yahoos.

The book, however, resolves the argument by showing Gulliver's expulsion from the land of reason and his reluctant return to our world, whose inhabitants he constantly refers to as Yahoos. Arrogantly and illogically, Gulliver to the end insists that he is not a Yahoo while despising all other humans, including his wife and children, as Yahoos. The final pages of *Gulliver's Travels* resound with his denunciations of the faults of his own species.

Part IV, then, can be seen as continuing the developments of the previous three. In the first part we see the Lilliputians behaving abominably and hope that humanity can at least do better than that. In Part II that hope is undermined as we are made to face the nature of our society when impartially judged. If we take refuge then in our technological and intellectual progress, that in turn is undermined in Part III, with its close parodies of our science and industry and gloomy questions about where history is taking us. Last, in Part IV, we are made to doubt our most basic belief about ourselves as opposed to other animals: that we possess reason, not just because we have to admit the resemblance between us and the horrible Yahoos, but also because the world of reason represented by the Houyhnhnms seems, the more we look at it, not for us. Even an enthusiast like Gulliver is driven out of it, and spends the rest of his life unable to cope with normal existence.

In short, the whole book tends to reject what we might consider the triumphs of our species:

the pomp and circumstance of our courts and palaces (belittled in Lilliput); the glory of our wars and conquests (despised in Brobdingnag); the wonders of our science and technology (shown as futile in Laputa); and our complacent belief in our own power of reason, the means by which we hope to increase and prosper (shown to be empty self-flattery in Houyhnhnmland). Appropriately, then, *Gulliver's Travels* ends with a denunciation of human pride that immediately connects the work with the traditional denunciations of the Seven Deadly Sins in Christian sermons. This is not, perhaps, a surprising ending to the book, given that Swift was after all a clergyman, though Christianity is very rarely apparent in the text itself. Gulliver is not very religious, and shows far less interest in spiritual matters than in politics, languages, and history during his voyages. It is of course risky to argue that what is *not* in a text is actually of great significance, but it is noteworthy that *Gulliver's Travels* seems to discuss every aspect of life except religion. If this is a meaningful omission, and we are supposed to see that what is missing is Christian faith and humility, then the praise of reason in Part IV must be ironic. Part III contains an attack on science and progress, all that the so-called Age of Reason of the eighteenth century stood for. That Swift should then present the Houyhnhnms, who embody rational enlightenment, as unqualified ideals therefore seems unlikely. The direction of the satire in Part III makes it difficult to read the praise of reason in Part IV unequivocally.

And yet Swift seems unable to renounce the dream of reason entirely. The Houyhnhnms surely have his regard in some things: their simple living, their politeness, their self-control and freedom from agitation, envy, and disease. Swift is not so immune to his time that he can renounce all its aspirations to elegance and civilization, and these temperamental tendencies creep back into his jeremiads against human weakness to confuse the issue. This is no small part of the continuing appeal of *Gulliver's Travels* to readers and critics, making it the object of endless debate about exactly what Swift meant and how far he took his misanthropy.

IMPORTANCE AND INFLUENCE

The main stages of the debate about *Gulliver's Travels* focus on the meaning of Part IV and can be taken in historical order. Immediate reactions to *Gulliver's Travels* were favorable but not very specific. It was not until after Swift's death in 1745 that detailed comment on his book began to appear, and the direction this took was mainly disgust at the way he treated humanity. In 1752 John Boyle, fifth Earl of Orrery, declared that "we are disgusted, not entertained; we are shocked, not instructed by the fable....He seems insensible of the surprising mechanism, and beauty of every part of the human composition....In painting Yahoos he becomes one himself" (quoted in the Norton edition, 309-310). Orrery's revulsion at the Yahoos led him to suggest that Swift's description of them shows there was something wrong in Swift himself, and this became a common response among critics. Edward Young, in his *Conjectures on Original Composition* (1759), is typical: Swift "has so satirized human nature as to give a demonstration in himself, that it deserves to be satirized" (Donoghue, p. 77). The argument went a step further when Sir Walter Scott, in the introduction to *Gulliver's Travels* in his 1814 edition of Swift's works, suggested that the horrors of Part IV were early signs of the author's later madness: "The Voyage to the Land of the Houyhnhnms is, beyond contest, the basest and most unworthy part of the work. It holds mankind forth in a light too degrading for contemplation .... Allowance, however, is to be made for the soured and disgusted state of Swift's mind, which doubtless was even then influenced by the first impressions of that incipient mental disease which, in his case, was marked by universal misanthropy" (Norton edition, p. 318). This leads directly to the denunciation of Part IV by the novelist William Makepeace Thackeray, in his *English Humorists of the*

Eighteenth Century (1851), as "Yahoo language … filthy in word, filthy in thought, furious, raging, obscene" (Donoghue, p. 117). In all this it seems plain that the critics are anxious to blame Swift for the disturbing feelings they have about the Yahoos, and so to avoid confronting the force of his satire.

Not until the middle of the twentieth century did the attitude to the last part of *Gulliver's Travels* begin to change, and it did so in an odd way. In 1934 F. R. Leavis wrote an essay in *Scrutiny*, "The Irony of Swift" (reprinted in his *The Common Pursuit*, 1952, and elsewhere). The essay in fact has little to say about *Gulliver's Travels*, only a couple of paragraphs near the end, but they contain a crucial new reading, summed up in the sentence "Swift did his best for the Houyhnhnms, and they may have all the reason, but the Yahoos have all the life" (*Common Pursuit*, p. 84). Leavis thus inverts the apparent values of the text; "nature and reason as Gulliver exhibits them are curiously negative," he writes, and instead the Yahoos have "instincts, emotions, and life" (p. 84; the attitude here that life is a positive virtue ought of course to be compared with the implications of the struldbrugg episode in Part III). Leavis does mention the unpleasantness of the Yahoos, what he calls "the dirt and indecorum" (p. 85), but for him the antiseptic, calm existence of the Houyhnhnms is unattractive.

In fact Lord Orrery had anticipated this view. In his *Remarks* on Swift's works he writes that the picture of the Houyhnhnms is neither inviting nor amusing but "cold and insipid" and "their virtuous qualities are only negative" (Swift, 2002, p. 310). But Leavis goes beyond this to suggest that the fault with the Houyhnhnms reflects Swift's *own* feelings about them, that in writing about them he is dull and unconvincing, whereas in writing about the Yahoos, he is vivid and compelling because he is more emotionally involved. Leavis assumes an artistic failure in one case and success in the other, and hints that this reflects the writer's deeper awareness of his real meaning. He is try-ing to do to Swift what William Blake did to John Milton, the author of *Paradise Lost*, in suggesting that "the reason Milton wrote in fetters when he wrote of Angels & God, and at liberty when of Devils & Hell, is because he was a true Poet and of the Devil's party without knowing it" (*The Marriage of Heaven and Hell*, p. 6).

The reaction to Leavis's criticism of *Gulliver's Travels* took an unusual form. Instead of trying to defend the work by rebutting Leavis's claim that the Houyhnhnms are unconvincing failures, defenders of Swift accepted much of what he said but reinterpreted its significance. Leavis, like almost all readers of *Gulliver's Travels* before him, equates Gulliver with Swift. The response to Leavis is to distinguish between Gulliver and his author, and to argue that although *Gulliver* seems to want to believe in the Houyhnhnms as paragons of virtue, *Swift* wants us to see through this to what they *really* are. They *do* have the kinds of faults Leavis points out in them, and Swift means us to see them, just as he means us to see that Gulliver's obsession with the Houyhnhnms is unhealthy. "The Houyhnhnms," as Kathleen Williams writes in her essay "Gulliver's Voyage to the Houyhnhnms" (1951), "far from being a model of perfection, are intended to show the inadequacy of the life of reason" (quoted in Jeffares, p. 249).

This new approach to the text led to parts of it that had hardly been considered before. Attention focused on what happens after Gulliver leaves the land of the Houyhnhnms, particularly his treatment by the humane Portuguese captain, Pedro de Mendez, who rescues Gulliver, takes him back to Portugal, looks after him, and arranges his return to England, all at his own expense, thus contradicting the jaundiced view of human nature of Gulliver himself. Again, Kathleen Williams states the point clearly: "Swift makes it plain that the Portuguese sailors are admirable human beings, and emphasizes in them the very qualities which the Houyhnhnms neither possess nor would understand" (Jeffares, p. 254).

When Gulliver meets his wife and children again, he, in contrast with Don Pedro, treats them like Yahoos, insisting that they keep their distance from him and stopping up his nose against their smell. He prefers to spend his time in a stable, talking to a pair of horses. "He has become inhuman," writes Williams, "losing the specifically human virtues in his attempt to achieve something for which humanity is not fitted" (Jeffares, p. 254).

This is the man who published the travels we have been reading. Thus another part of the text that has received fresh attention is the prefatory material, especially the letter from Gulliver to his cousin Richard Sympson, in which he repeatedly refers to other people as Yahoos, and displays an arrogant contempt for everybody else and an overweening confidence in his own beliefs. In short, Gulliver seems to have been driven mad by his experiences, especially after his last voyage, and therefore the book he has written should be treated as the work of a madman. The misanthropic diatribes of its final pages, far from representing the opinions of Swift himself, should be seen as the ravings of his leading character. For the true meaning of the book we must look round Gulliver and set aside his insane prejudice against mankind and in favor of horses. Then we can see the humanity of Don Pedro, the plight of the long-suffering Mrs. Gulliver, and the other evidence Kathleen Williams finds for "a positive Christian ideal suggested in the conduct of the good humans" (Jeffares, p. 257).

Interpreting *Gulliver's Travels* in this way has become very popular in recent years. Fiction criticism is now very comfortable with the concept of the "unreliable narrator" and the construction of meanings different from those directly stated in the text. It seems quite modern to separate Gulliver from Swift and analyze the *Travels* as the utterance of a diseased mind from which a healthy reader must extract a hidden truth; and it seems obvious that that truth, since it originates in some sense from an author who

was a minister of religion, must be consistent with modern Christianity.

There are, however, those who have objected to an approach to Swift's satire that makes it sound like a reaffirmation of the goodness of human nature, what has come to be called the "soft school" of interpretation of *Gulliver's Travels*. The opposing "hard school" veers back toward the opinions of the earliest critics. In the essay "Gulliver and the Gentle Reader" (1968), C. J. Rawson wrote that "the older critics who disliked the Houyhnhnms but felt that Swift meant them as a positive were surely nearer the mark than some recent ones who translate their own dislikes into the meaning of the book," and says of Don Pedro that he may be a reminder that "even good Yahoos are Yahoos" (Donoghue, p. 420). Of Gulliver himself Rawson writes that "he is not identical with Swift, nor even similar to him, but Swift's presence behind him is always too close to ignore. This is not because Swift approves or disapproves of what Gulliver says at any given time, but because Swift is always saying something *through* it " (Donoghue, p. 417).

He goes on to attack the idea of Gulliver as a character, a point made two years earlier by W. E. Yeomans, in an essay titled "The Houyhnhnm as Menippean Horse," which tries to combat the reading of *Gulliver's Travels* as though it were a novel by showing how it resembles fantastic travel satires by such writers as Lucian, Rabelais, and Voltaire, where "we can never expect to be enchanted by 'living' characters…instead, we can anticipate being overwhelmed by amazing erudition, by massive catalogues of social follies, by extravagant elaborations upon professional abuses, by fantastic caricatures of certain people or certain types of people, and by other dazzling displays" (Jeffares, p. 259). Such displays mean a loosening of the rules of coherence and consistency that apply to the novel as a form. Yeomans goes on to say that "Critics, in this novel-oriented age, tend to think that the Houyhnhnms must fulfil one role or another, but not several roles.

Swift, with satiric ideas and Utopian concepts uppermost in his mind, allowed his characters to be altogether subservient to his intellectual purposes...the Houyhnhnms are sometimes models of the good life, sometimes vehicles for satiric burlesque attack, and sometimes a combination of both" (Jeffares, p. 265).

There are signs that the hard school has recently begun to gain the upper hand, at any rate among specialist critics of Swift. It seems to relate to a hardening of attitudes to human nature, reflecting the growing gloominess about the world at the end of the twentieth century. The hopeful optimism of Williams, that Swift cannot have meant Gulliver's horror at mankind but must in some deep sense have shared a modern liberal Christian view of human nature, is giving way in the face of recent horrors, and the constant news of minor and major examples of what Robert Burns called "man's inhumanity to man," to a tough-minded acceptance that even in its most strident passages the text of Swift's satire probably means just what it says.

Looking back on nearly three hundred years of reactions to *Gulliver's Travels,* what is striking is both the capacity of the book to spark argument and controversy and the way that debate has reflected the temper of the times. For late eighteenth-century commentators, citizens of the Enlightenment, Swift's misanthropy was disgusting and extreme. In the nineteenth century, for critics brought up on Romantic ideas of art as personal expression, the unpleasantness of Swift's idea of human nature was his fault, not ours. In the mid-twentieth century, critics influenced by psychological theories that displaced reason as the main motive of human behavior tended to invert the obvious meaning of the book and enlist Swift as a secret admirer of the instinctual vitality of the human animal. By the end of the century, however, when stock had been taken of all its horrors and Freud had fallen from favor, the darker side of Swift's vision drew more attention, and what earlier had seemed wild raving or paradoxical irony now appeared coldly prophetic of the consequences of the progress of man and society that was just beginning in his time. *Gulliver's Travels* now seems most up-to-date where it is closest to its own period. No doubt it will go on being a mirror in which each generation appears to see itself.

Select Bibliography

EDITIONS

The Battle of the Books. In *Gulliver's Travels and Other Writings.* London and Oxford: Oxford University Press, 1960.

Gulliver's Travels. Edited by Robert Demaria, Jr. Penguin Classics. Harmondsworth, U.K.: Penguin Books, 2001. A modern edition with an interesting introduction and explanatory notes.

Gulliver's Travels. Edited by Albert J. Rivero. Norton Critical Edition. New York and London: W. W. Norton, 2002. A modern edition with an excellent selection of background material and critical essays.

SECONDARY WORKS

Bloom, Harold, ed. *Jonathan Swift's "Gulliver's Travels": Modern Critical Interpretations.* New York and Philadelphia: Chelsea House, 1986.

Crane, R. S. "The Houyhnhnms, the Yahoos and the History of Ideas." In his *The Idea of the Humanities and Other Essays*. Vol. 2, 261–282. Chicago: Chicago University Press, 1967.

Defoe, Daniel. *Robinson Crusoe*. Edited by John Richetti. Penguin Classics. Harmondsworth, U.K.: Penguin Books, 2001.

Donoghue, Denis, ed. *Jonathan Swift: A Critical Anthology*. Harmondsworth, U.K.: Penguin Books, 1971. Reprints the essays by Crane and Rawson, among many others.

Gravil, Richard, ed. *Swift: Gulliver's Travels*. London: Macmillan, 1974. Contains Williams 1951, Yeomans, and other essays.

Higgins, Ian. *Swift's Politics*. Cambridge: Cambridge University Press, 1994.

Jeffares, A. Norman, ed. *Swift: Modern Judgements*. London: Macmillan, 1969. Reprints Leavis, Nicolson and Mohler, Williams 1951, and Yeomans.

Leavis, F. R. "The Irony of Swift." *Scrutiny* (March 1934): 364–378. Also in his *The Common Pursuit*, 73–87. London: Chatto & Windus, 1962.

Nicolson, Marjorie Hope, and Norah M. Mohler. "The Scientific Background of Swift's 'Voyage to Laputa.'" *Annals of Science* 2 (1937): 299–334.

Rawson, C. J. "Gulliver and the Gentle Reader." In *Imagined Worlds: Essays on Some English Novels and Novelists in Honour of John Butt*, 51–90. Edited by Maynard Mack and Ian Gregor. London: Methuen, 1968. Also in Rawson's *Gulliver and the Gentle Reader*. London and Boston: Routledge & Kegan Paul, 1973.

Reilly, Edward J., ed. *Approaches to Teaching Swift's "Gulliver's Travels."* New York: Modern Language Association of America, 1988.

Ward, David. *Jonathan Swift: An Introductory Essay*. London: Methuen, 1973. Contains a long chapter on *Gulliver's Travels*.

Williams, Kathleen. "Gulliver's Voyage to the Houyhnhnms." *Journal of English Literary History* 18 (1951): 275–286.

Williams, Kathleen. *Jonathan Swift and the Age of Compromise*. Lawrence: University of Kansas Press, 1958.

Yeomans, W. E. "The Houyhnhnm as Menippean Horse." *College English* 27 (1966): 449–454.

Joseph Conrad's
Heart of Darkness

CATES BALDRIDGE

ENGLISH WAS NOT Joseph Conrad's first language, nor was it his second (these being Polish and French, respectively)—indeed, he only learned the tongue in which his literary works were eventually to be written when he was in his twenties, a fact that makes his achievement all the more impressive. And if in his mind one language overlay another, so too in his temperament did an attachment to stories possessing the striking action and setting of romance cohabit with a stern-minded materialistic philosophy and a thoroughgoing pessimism regarding the prospects of human endeavors.

Perhaps in part this divided consciousness can be attributed to the age in which he lived, for Conrad, born in 1857, came to maturity during a period when many of the bedrock assumptions that had guided political and intellectual life during much of the nineteenth century were changing, crumbling, or being violently overthrown as the twentieth century approached. Under the successive impacts of Darwin, Marx, and Freud, conceptions of the human race as divinely created beings exercising free will under the direction of reason were becoming increasingly untenable. Everywhere

the late 1800s scientific and other intellectual developments seemed increasingly to conceive of mankind as being controlled by impersonal forces—biological, historical, and psychic—that were utterly indifferent to the promotion of human happiness and over which the individual could exert little or no conscious control. During the Victorian heyday, Divine Providence had been seen as guiding the species toward a future of incessant progress; now, more and more, a mechanistic Necessity appeared to grind its gears in a spiritual void. As Marlow, Conrad's narrator in *Heart of Darkness,* puts it: "Droll thing life is—that mysterious arrangement of merciless logic for a futile purpose" (p. 112).

The specific historical context of *Heart of Darkness* is also inseparable from the phenomenon of colonialism, for in the last decades of the nineteenth century the various European powers were completing and consolidating their hold over the far-flung peoples and lands that comprised their overseas empires. In 1890, Conrad garnered what he thought would be a captain's position on a steamboat plying the Congo River, a territory then under the personal rule of the Belgian monarch, Leopold II. The Belgian Congo displayed the cruelties and contradictions of European colonialism in peculiarly stark terms, for whereas Leopold's rhetoric was all about Christianizing the natives and opening the land to the blessings of free trade for all nations (which would also, it was asserted, vastly improve the lives of the Africans themselves), the actual administration of the territory was a study in oppression and cruelty. A system in which local white administrators were empowered to collect "taxes" from natives who could pay with nothing but their labor ensured that de facto slavery was endemic, while the profits from the extraction of rubber and other natural resources flowed relentlessly up the imperial chain, all the way to Leopold himself.

The native peoples were kept in terrified subjection by methods of extraordinary and often gratuitous cruelty, while the "civilizing" mission manifested itself only in the publicity churned out by the Belgian authorities for the benefit of a complacent European audience. Conrad, one of whose most cherished romantic fantasies from childhood had been African exploration, was thoroughly disillusioned by the barbarity of the colonial regime, and that disillusionment is evident in *Heart of Darkness* through Marlow's caustic observations concerning the unnamed Company of "faithless pilgrims" (p. 44) that is pillaging the land and its people.

The trip up the Congo was also a pivotal turning point in Conrad's own career, for up until that time he had been a full-time sailor since his teens. Now, however, as canvas gave way to steam, he was becoming less and less enthusiastic about the life he had chosen and was restlessly exploring other possibilities. As he witnessed atrocities and battled dysentery aboard his leaky Belgian steamboat, he also carried with him the manuscript of what would become his first novel, *Almayer's Folly*, on which he somehow managed to make progress during the miserable journey. Conrad, who had arrived in the Congo as a sailor, left it with a growing desire to give up the sea for literature, and his experiences on that

CHRONOLOGY

1857	3 December. Born Józef Teodor Konrad Korzeniowski, in former Polish lands occupied by Russia.
1862	Family, including Józef, exiled to Russia due to the pro-Polish political and literary activities of his father, Apollo Korzeniowski.
1865	Conrad's mother dies.
1869	Death of Conrad's father. Conrad begins to live with his uncle Tadeusz Bobrowski.
1874	Leaves Poland for Marseilles to become a sailor in the French merchant marine.
1877	Apparently involved in arms smuggling scheme to royalists in Spain.
1878	(Deliberately?) unsuccessful suicide attempt. Begins to work on British ships.
1886	Becomes a British citizen and earns a master's (captain's) certificate in British merchant marine.
1890	Works aboard steamship in the Belgian Congo. Source for much material in *Heart of Darkness*.
1895	First novel, *Almayer's Folly*, published.
1896	Marries Jesse George.
1897	*Nigger of the "Narcissus"* published. Meets Henry James, who becomes a regular correspondent.
1898–1899	*Heart of Darkness* serialized in *Blackwood's* magazine.
1900	*Lord Jim* published.
1904	*Nostromo* published. Jesse becomes disabled.
1907	*The Secret Agent* published.
1910	Nervous breakdown while completing *Under Western Eyes,* which is published the following year.
1913	*Chance* published. First of Conrad's novels to enjoy strong sales.
1915	*Victory* published.
1923	Conrad visits the United States to much public acclaim.
1924	Declines offer of a knighthood. Dies of a heart attack on 3 August.

life-changing voyage would provide him with the raw material for his best-known and most influential novel, *Heart of Darkness.*

TWO VIEWS OF COLONIALISM

Heart of Darkness possesses a narrative "frame," for Marlow's memoir of his journey upriver is bounded before and after by brief sections spoken by an unnamed listener on the pleasure yacht *Nellie.* As the story commences, the frame serves to set off the main narrative by offering a contrast of vision and tone. As he looks out over the busy maritime traffic upon the Thames estuary, the frame narrator's view of British imperialism is, in light of Marlow's subsequent evocations, naive and jingoistic, sounding like something out of an antiquated high school textbook:

> The tidal current runs to and fro in its unceasing service, crowded with memories of men and ships it has borne to the rest of home or to the battles of the sea. It has known and served all the men of whom the nation is proud, from Sir Francis Drake to Sir John Franklin, knights all, titled and untitled—the great knights-errant of the sea. . . . Hunters for gold or pursuers of fame, they all had gone out on that stream, bearing the word, and often the torch, messengers of the might within the land, bearers of a spark from the sacred fire. What greatness had not floated on the ebb of that river into the mystery of an unknown earth! . . . the dreams of men, the seed of commonwealths, the germs of empires.
>
> (p. 17)

There is an irony in the frame narrator's encomium to conquest and colonialism, for the ships he names alongside his captain-heroes—the *Golden Hind,* the *Erebus,* the *Terror*—are names evocative of cupidity and violence. This irony is not, however, lost on Marlow, for he in effect refutes the frame narrator's version of events with the first words he speaks—an utterance that challenges the comforting metaphor of benign European light going forth to vanquish the shadows of primitive lands: "And this also,"

said Marlow suddenly, "has been one of the dark places of the earth" (p. 18). He then proceeds to debunk imperialist complacency by the simple expedient of taking the long historical view. By conjuring up the "commander of a fine . . . trireme" and the "decent young citizen in a toga" who in their day looked upon their English destination as "the very end of the world" (p. 19), he makes the point that the British Isles themselves were once the peripheral abode of moral darkness which had to endure the sometimes violent introduction of civilization's singing "torch" from a different imperial center.

The remainder of Marlow's tale will go on to insist that this primordial darkness has not been vanquished but only pushed into corners from which it can, given the right combination of temptation and isolation, emerge with a vengeance. But here, as with his catalog of ships, the frame narrator is already in unwitting metaphorical agreement with Marlow, for in looking back upriver toward London, he has noted "a mournful gloom, brooding motionless over the biggest, and the greatest, town on earth" (p. 15), and described the sun as "dull red without rays and without heat, as if about to go out suddenly, stricken to death by the touch of that gloom brooding over a crowd of men" (p. 16). In Conrad's tale, no culture has a monopoly on enlightenment, and all nations carry their own particular variety of darkness with them when they venture out to supposedly redeem the benighted.

This does not mean, however, that either Marlow or Conrad is a cultural relativist, or that either character or author intends to demonize Western civilization in a simplistic manner. For proof of this, we need only look at Marlow's account of the forces that his little steamboat carries in its wake, for the leaky craft is a "grimy fragment of another world, the forerunner of change, of conquest, of trade, of massacres, of blessings" (p. 110). Here the sense of finely balanced, if ultimately tragic, ambivalence is unmistakable. But if Conrad genuinely prefers

European culture to what he terms the "savagery" of the native peoples that his narrator encounters, there is nevertheless a pointed critique of the colonial enterprise at work in the novel, a critique that is best approached through an investigation of the author's careful deployment of light and dark imagery.

SHADES OF BLACK AND WHITE

There is a kind of "default setting" in Western literature in which things that are sinister come robed in black while benignity is announced and accompanied by the color white. Whether this has come about due to our species' primordial fear of the dark or whether its roots lie in the historical racism of European culture is a question beyond the scope of this essay. But either way, one does not have to read very far into *Heart of Darkness* before one becomes aware that this familiar expectation of ours is being somehow thwarted.

It is not a matter of Conrad simply inverting the moral resonance of the two shades, for the darkness of his African jungle is genuinely frightening and ethically corrupting—almost Gothic in its threatening shadows and obscurities. Rather, what the novel insists upon is that the whiteness and light associated with the West and its supposed civilizing colonial mission becomes inevitably tarnished when it is recklessly transported to where it doesn't belong and arrogantly imposed upon those who live there. Thus, things white, when wrenched out of their proper home and turned into incongruous exports amid an alien landscape, begin to partake of moral darkness, a darkness worse in kind than that which "naturally" exists in the "savage" jungle already. This notion is seen early on, when Marlow reminisces about his childhood fascination with maps, for there it is precisely the progress of colonialism that has turned something formerly white into something currently black: "True, by this time it was not a blank space any more. It had got filled since my boyhood with rivers and lakes and names. It had ceased to be a blank space of delightful mystery—a white patch for a boy to dream gloriously over. It had become a place of darkness" (p. 22). Colonialism's ability to turn white into something akin to—or worse than— black has even spread back to the home continent, for Brussels, the capital of King Leopold's empire, is referred to as "a city that always makes me think of a whited sepulchre" (p. 24), that is to say, a pristine monument that covers over corruption and decay.

The most graphic enactment of white not surviving the trip to Africa with its moral connotations intact comes when Marlow encounters the starving natives in the "grove of death" and sees upon one of them a cloth of European manufacture: "He had tied a bit of white worsted round his neck—Why? Where did he get it? Was it a badge—an ornament—a charm—a propitiatory act? Was there any idea at all connected with it? It looked startling round his black neck, this bit of white thread from beyond the seas" (p. 35). Like the Company itself, this symbol of European cultural superiority becomes sinister by way of its sheer incongruousness in the African setting.

This theme of things that are culturally valuable spoiling when they are violently foisted upon another culture is not confined to the precincts of light and dark imagery alone, for it is clear that what the Company offers to the Africans are only degraded parodies of familiar Western cultural (and specifically literary) achievements. For instance, when Marlow is being interviewed for his position of captain of the steamboat, he encounters a darkly comic version of the three Fates of classical mythology:

> She glanced at me above the glasses. The swift and indifferent placidity of that look troubled me. Two youths with foolish and cheery countenances were being piloted over, and she threw at them the same quick glance of unconcerned wisdom. She seemed to know all about them and about me too. An eerie feeling came over me. She seemed uncanny and fateful. Often far away there I thought of

these two, guarding the door of Darkness, knitting black wool as for a warm pall, one introducing, introducing continuously to the unknown, the other scrutinizing the cheery and foolish faces with unconcerned old eyes. *Ave!* Old knitter of black wool. *Morituri te salutant.* Not many of those she looked at ever saw her again—not half, by a long way.

(p. 26)

In the original Greek myth, the *three* fates were female figures who spun, measured out, and cut off the span of each mortal's life, and it is all to the point that here there are only *two* knitters—that the Company's version of the original is both sinister and half-assed at the same time. In like manner, the Manager of the Central station has, like King Arthur, constructed a round table, but one which signally fails to put an end to jealousy and a vicious pecking order. And then there is the fact that all the "pilgrims" ride donkeys exclusively, as if to make the point that the Company counts in its roster no idealistic Quixotes, only materialistic Sanchos. Finally, Kurtz himself can be seen as a sort of reverse King Lear—one who goes mad not as he loses power, but as he gains it. And whereas Shakespeare's king possesses a jester who attempts to keep him sane and instill a sense of humility in him, Kurtz, in the Little Russian, has found a clown in motley who only feeds his vanity and megalomania.

THE FASCINATION OF THE ABOMINATION

Of course this degradation of European ideals has occurred under a unique sort of pressure, and thus it is important to understand just what Conrad seems to believe is morally corrosive about the jungle itself, aside from any doomed attempt to loot and tame it. Marlow is quick to personify the intense heat, lush vegetation, mysterious sounds, and ever-narrowing river into a kind of malign, autochthonous deity—what he calls "an implacable force brooding over

an inscrutable intention" (p. 60) and "a thing monstrous and free" (p. 62), a choice of imagery that incidentally makes it possible to see the "pitiful Jupiter" (p. 98) Kurtz and the jungle as two amoral Olympians locked in combat—a combat in which the jungle eventually triumphs. What the jungle has the power to do to seemingly all who participate in the "fantastic invasion" (p. 95) of its territory is to scramble and otherwise render useless that preeminent and foundational acquirement of Western civilization, reason—implanting in its stead that unique mode of mind in which the reason's writ does not run, that is, the dream state:

> you thought yourself bewitched and cut off for ever from everything you had known once—somewhere—far away—in another existence perhaps. There were moments when one's past came back to one, as it will sometimes when you have not a moment to spare to yourself; but it came in the shape of an unrestful and noisy dream, remembered with wonder amongst the overwhelming realities of this strange world of plants, and water, and silence. And this stillness of life did not in the least resemble a peace.

(pp. 59–60)

And so, while Marlow's journey upriver has been metaphorically and allegorically interpreted as nearly every kind of pilgrimage imaginable—psychological, spiritual, sexual, and political—from the banal to the bizarre, one thing Conrad certainly intended it be taken for is a trek backward in geological time and consequently in human mental evolution, toward a more primitive and instinctual state of consciousness. As he states, "going up that river was like travelling back to the earliest beginnings of the world, when vegetation rioted on the earth and the big trees were kings" (p. 59), when Europeans "were wanderers on a prehistoric earth, on an earth that wore the aspect of an unknown planet" and one that they "could not understand, because we were too far and could not remember, because we were travelling in the night of first ages, of those ages that are gone, leaving hardly a sign—and no memories" (p. 62).

Conditions are so bad in the Congo in part because the Company has not only succumbed to this atmosphere corrosive of reason but has in fact abetted it, for reason and clarity of vision can interfere with the maximization of profit. The manager of the Central Station, for instance, whom Marlow believes "beckons" and "make a treacherous appeal to the lurking death, to the hidden evil, to the profound darkness of [the jungle's] heart" (p. 58), possesses a singular talent by which to control and rule in such an environment: "He was obeyed, yet he inspired neither love nor fear, not even respect. He inspired uneasiness. That was it! Uneasiness. Not a definite mistrust—just uneasiness—nothing more. You have no idea how effective such a . . . a . . . faculty can be" (p. 42).

But with or without the Company's connivance, the jungle is also able to offer something dangerously enticing to the Europeans who rashly arrive to conquer it, for while the burden of reason is that it commands us to employ chronic restraint vis-à-vis the immediate gratification of our desires, the wilderness whispers of a life of unrestrained license, where chafing self-denial can be cast aside, where we are enticed to leave the regimen of deferred pleasure and, as Marlow somewhat euphemistically puts it, "go ashore for a howl and a dance" (p. 63):

> [The jungle] was unearthly, and the men were—No, they were not inhuman. Well, you know, that was the worst of it—this suspicion of their not being inhuman. It would come slowly to one. They howled, and leaped, and spun, and made horrid faces; but what thrilled you was just the thought of their humanity—like yours—the thought of your remote kinship with this wild and passionate uproar. Ugly. Yes, it was ugly enough; but if you were man enough you would admit to yourself that there was in you just the faintest trace of a response to the terrible frankness of that noise, a dim suspicion of there being a meaning in it which you—you so remote from the night of first ages—

could comprehend.

(pp. 62–63)

This is what Marlow elsewhere calls "the fascination of the abomination" (p. 20), and it goes far toward explaining why Kurtz, who succumbed wholly to this appeal, is depicted by Conrad as a strange combination of power and weakness, for he is simultaneously a figure who practices a kind of grand Nietzschean transcendence of bourgeois constraints and a moral weakling who fails an ethical test. But whether one accedes to it or resists it, this promise of primordial freedom (in Freudian terms, the prospect of our id being released from the strictures of our superego) is the jungle's most potent weapon against the arrogant trespassers from "civilized" realms.

Of course it needs to be said that by modern standards, conceiving of African cultures as being bereft of a full and complex set of social restraints upon behavior is a Eurocentric and racist misunderstanding, founded on wishful assumptions instead of knowledge. And such a passage does seems to bolster the Nigerian novelist Chinua Achebe's famous claim that *Heart of Darkness* is a racist text because Conrad employs his African figures merely as a backdrop to an almost exclusive concern with the problems of the European invaders. Now one can agree with Achebe's description of Conrad's artistic intentions without elevating his anger over it into a principle of conscientious artistic practice, as Achebe seems to desire. Conrad is in fact primarily interested in his European creations, but if we do not allow each artist freedom over his or her choice of subject, literature will become scarce. Racist assumptions are easy to locate in Conrad's fiction, but then, like all mortals, he was a creation of his society, and it can always be said in his favor that his stereotypical view of African cultures is partly balanced by his lack of illusions about the supposed nobility and benignity of the West's colonial project: "the conquest of the earth, which mostly means the taking it away from those who have a different complexion or slightly flatter noses than ourselves, is not a pretty thing when you look into it too much" (p. 20).

Then too, there is just a solitary hint that Conrad may have a more sophisticated and sympathetic view of the Africans than he allows his narrator to express, for when Marlow ponders why the native cannibals employed on the steamboat don't "go for" the Europeans, his puzzlement at their self-denial is almost comically overwrought: "Restraint! I would just as soon have expected restraint from a hyena prowling amongst the corpses of a battlefield. But there was the fact facing me—the fact dazzling, to be seen, like the foam on the depth of the sea, like a ripple on an unfathomable enigma" (p. 71). Perhaps this is one of those very rare moments where Marlow ceases to be an utterly reliable spokesman for his author, for perhaps here—if we forget for a moment that the attribution of cannibalism to African cultures is itself a racist assumption unbuttressed by evidence—Conrad is chuckling at Marlow's underestimation of the "savage" societies he glimpses only in passing.

LABORING TO DISTRACTION

If the jungle is represented as tantalizing us with the promise of unbounded libidinal freedom, what on earth can keep us straight? Conrad's answer to this question depends upon who you are—upon how deeply you have looked into the ultimately dire truths of cosmic necessity. For ordinary, relatively unimaginative and incurious people, a sincere belief in the European civilizing mission will suffice. For such people, says Marlow, "what redeems [the colonial enterprise] is the idea only. An idea at the back of it; not a sentimental pretence but an idea; and an unselfish belief in the idea—something you can set up, and bow down before, and offer a sacrifice to" (p. 20). We shouldn't miss the irony here, as this pledge of allegiance to what the Victorians labeled the "white man's burden" in Conrad's phrasing becomes itself a kind of pagan rite of prostration and infidel adoration. Still, the idea is that sincere beliefs and high principles can keep the average dullard from wandering off down the forest path. For such, recalling the white man's civilizing mission is like remembering one's catechism in the face of temptation back home.

But Marlow is no ordinary, rank-and-file believer in the civilizing mission, for recall that he has already defined it as at base an act of bald appropriation. He thus requires a different sort of mental construct in order to keep himself safely on the boat—one that goes beyond the facile beliefs of the jingoistic multitude. "Principles? Principles won't do. Acquisitions, clothes, pretty rags—rags that would fly off at the first good shake. No; you want a deliberate belief. An appeal to me in this fiendish row—is there? Very well; I hear; I admit, but I have a voice too, and for good or evil mine is the speech that cannot be silenced. Of course, a fool, what with sheer fright and fine sentiments, is always safe" (p. 63).

Consider the key term here—"a deliberate belief"—for it seems to require a chronic act of will to be maintained, to demand a daily suspension of *dis*belief. To understand Marlow's curious phrase we have to touch here upon a central topic that we will return to later—Conrad's atheism. For the author of *Heart of Darkness,* the cosmos is bereft of an intelligent creator, and its course is directed by impersonal forces utterly indifferent to human ethics or aspirations. Thus, for Conrad, the universe doesn't care a damn whether we love our fellow man or eat him, and all our cherished watchwords of civilization—democracy, rationality, respect for the individual, due process, and so on—are all so many fictions that humans beings have invented in the face of utter cosmic apathy. What must not be lost sight of, however, is that these fictions are expedient, in the widest and best sense of that term—that is, they are useful and necessary fictions because they help us get on from day to day while minimizing our portion of fear, hunger, and travail. To pledge allegiance to these indispensable fictions while still understanding their merely provisional and expedient nature is to possess a *"deliberate* belief." Acting in accordance with them not from quasi-religious conviction but from an understanding of their merely earthly utility is the ethical stance Marlow adopts. This accounts for his inimitable combination of, on the one hand, deep pessimism and skepticism about the human condition, and, on the other, strong moral outrage at the Company's proceedings.

This is a dangerously thin ethical tightrope upon which to tread, because knowing that there is no divine sanction awaiting those who throw off civilized restraint makes the temptation to do so all the stronger. So what keeps Marlow balanced upon this wire? According to him, the answer is straightforward: work. In *Heart of Darkness* conscientious labor and a keen dedication to performing one's job efficiently constitute, if you will, a kind of "redemptive distraction" from the terrible truths of the human condition. Says Marlow, "I went to work the next day, turning, so to speak, my back on that station. In that way only it seemed to me I could keep my hold on the redeeming facts of life" (p. 43). Work, in Conrad's view, puts one in contact with the salvational influence of what he terms "surface truth" (p. 63)—a form of intense concentration on individual trees that makes one forget the terrifying forest they constitute.

Speaking of the difficulties of keeping his jury-rigged steamboat off the shoals, Marlow asserts that "when you have to attend to things of that sort, to the mere incidents of the surface, the reality—the reality, I tell you—fades. The inner truth is hidden—luckily, luckily" (p. 60). It is this rapt attention to the practical job at hand that Marlow credits with keeping him from "going native":

> You wonder I didn't go ashore for a howl and a dance? Well no—I didn't. Fine sentiments, you say? Fine sentiments be hanged! I had no time. I

had to mess about with white-lead and strips of woollen blanket helping to put bandages on those leaky steam-pipes—I tell you. I had to watch the steering, and circumvent those snags, and get the tin-pot along by hook or by crook. There was surface-truth enough in these things to save a wiser man.

> (p. 63)

Thus, dedication to one's work in the realm of "surface-truth" is an antidote to both the naïve illusions that suffice for colonialism's unthinking foot soldiers and the dispiriting insight of the worldly-wise. Indeed, to work upon the surface details is to encounter truth without truth's accompanying terror; it is to maintain contact with reality in a way that does not demoralizingly undercut one's illusions of purpose and progress. And it is this salvational aspect of everyday work that explains what would otherwise remain one of the novel's most puzzling passages—Marlow's gush of enthusiasm over the discovery, far upriver, of a mundane technical manual:

> Within, Towson or Towser was inquiring earnestly into the breaking strain of ships' chains and tackle, and other such matters. Not a very enthralling book; but at the first glance you could see there a singleness of intention, and honest concern for the right way of going to work, which made these humble pages, thought out so many years ago, luminous with another than a professional light. The simple old sailor, with his talk of chains and purchases, made me forget the jungle and the pilgrims in a delicious sensation of having come upon something unmistakably real.

> (p. 65)

The Company agents, of course, also see through the naive notion that their enterprise is one of selflessly spreading enlightenment, but they do not possess Marlow's redemptive distraction because they are, almost to a man, indolent shirkers. And if to engage with surface truth through one's labor is to maintain a benign toehold on an otherwise dispiriting body of truths, the Company can claim no such mooring in the real. Their activity, which features rusting equipment "as dead as the carcass of some animal" (p. 44) and which is punctuated by "objectless blasting" (p. 45) of the wilderness, already partakes of the dreamlike delusions fostered by the jungle it presumes to conquer:

> I asked myself sometimes what it all meant. They wandered here and there with their absurd long staves in their hands, like a lot of faithless pilgrims bewitched inside a rotten fence. The word "ivory" rang in the air, was whispered, was sighed. You would think they were praying to it. A taint of imbecile rapacity blew through it all, like a whiff from some corpse. By Jove! I've never seen anything so unreal in my life. And outside, the silent wilderness surrounding this cleared speck on the earth struck me as something great and invincible, like evil or truth, waiting patiently for the passing away of this fantastic invasion.
>
> (p. 44)

A VOICE IN THE WILDERNESS

At least part of Marlow's growing fascination with Kurtz can be explained by the latter's signal contrast with these "pilgrims," for Kurtz is, in his own "unsound" manner, a prodigious worker, and there is evidence that he understands—or, rather, at one time understood—the pressures that call for the adoption of a "deliberate belief." Marlow finds this evidence that he and Kurtz have followed the same psychological trajectory in the painting Kurtz has left behind at one of the stations: "Then I noticed a small sketch in oils, on a panel, representing a woman, draped and blindfolded, carrying a lighted torch. The background was sombre—almost black. The movement of the woman was stately, and the effect of the torchlight on the face was sinister" (pp. 46–47). This small work of art seems synoptic of much that Marlow has been telling us about what happens to Europeans in the wilderness. The carried torch, a familiar symbol of civilization's missionary impulse, now casts a "sinister" light, not least upon her own face, paralleling the

"blackening" of people and things white when they trespass where they don't belong. And the fact that the face is blindfolded seems to suggest Marlow's own necessity for averting his eyes from the unsettling realities of cosmic indifference that the jungle lays all too bare. Marlow and Kurtz, then, are fellow travelers, though as we shall see, Kurtz follows the path they share to its very end, while Marlow holds back.

The other aspect of Kurtz that fascinates Marlow even from a distance is—not surprisingly given Marlow's own gifts as a storyteller—his eloquence. We, along with Marlow, have heard snatches of his oratory at second hand from the contemptuous "pilgrims": "'He is a prodigy,' he said at last. 'He is an emissary of pity, and science, and progress, and devil knows what else'" (p. 47). Kurtz had a dream, and the ringing phrases that pronounced it can be heard even through the scoffing of his unappreciative audience: "'And the pestiferous absurdity of his talk,' continued the other; 'he bothered me enough when he was here. "Each station should be like a beacon on the road towards better things, a centre for trade of course, but also for humanising, improving, instructing." Conceive you—that ass!'" (p. 58). Often the rational and persuasive orator has been taken as the very symbol of Western civilization, from Cicero to Martin Luther King, and the great speaker's authority is in part religious as well, since the Bible's first words declare that "In the beginning was the Word, and the Word was with God, and the Word was God." It is this power that Marlow responds to—indeed, is drawn to under a kind of hypnotic fascination.

> I made the strange discovery that I had never imagined him as doing, you know, but as discoursing. I didn't say to myself, "Now I will never see him," or "Now I will never shake him by the hand," but "Now I will never hear him." The man presented himself as a voice. Not of course that I did not connect him with some sort of action. Hadn't I been told in all the tones of jealousy and admiration that he had collected, bartered, swindled, or stolen more ivory than all the other

agents together. That was not the point. The point was in his being a gifted creature, and that of all his gifts the one that stood out pre-eminently, that carried with it a sense of real presence, was his ability to talk, his words—the gift of expression, the bewildering, the illuminating, the most exalted and the most contemptible, the pulsating stream of light, or the deceitful flow from the heart of an impenetrable darkness.

(p. 79)

Marlow here speaks with the ambivalence of hindsight, but for a while within *Heart of Darkness*, Kurtz's oratory seems to hold out the promise of being the civilized opposite of—and perhaps antidote to—the inane chattering of the Company men, the primordial howl of the native Africans, and the even more primordial silence of the jungle itself. It is for this reason that Kurtz's trajectory from Europe's epitome of sweetness and light (recall that "all Europe contributed to the making of Kurtz" (p. 83)) to the embodiment of its murderous will to power is best exemplified in his monograph, the only surviving text of his eloquence:

But it was a beautiful piece of writing. The opening paragraph, however, in the light of later information, strikes me now as ominous. He began with the argument that we whites, from the point of development we had arrived at, "must necessarily appear to them [savages] in the nature of supernatural beings—we approach them with the might as of a deity," and so on, and so on. "By the simple exercise of our will we can exert a power for good practically unbounded," &c., &c. From that point he soared and took me with him. The peroration was magnificent, though difficult to remember, you know. It gave me the notion of an exotic Immensity ruled by an august Benevolence. It made me tingle with enthusiasm. This was the unbounded power of eloquence—of words—of burning noble words. There were no practical hints to interrupt the magic current of phrases, unless a kind of note at the foot of the last page, scrawled evidently much later, in an unsteady hand, may be regarded as the exposition of a method. It was very simple, and at the end of that moving appeal to every altruistic sentiment it

blazed at you, luminous and terrifying, like a flash of lightning in a serene sky: "Exterminate all the brutes!"

(pp. 83–84)

Here the discourse of enlightened reason has given way to the scream of naked aggression, and Marlow's sarcasm above indicates that such a pretty dream had no good chance of survival, though we must remember that this is so only because Kurtz saw things too keenly to abide long under its sway. The phrase describing Kurtz's naïve vision of a mission into the wilderness—"an exotic Immensity ruled by an august Benevolence"—has a dark rhythmic mate in Marlow's "implacable force brooding over an inscrutable intention" (p. 60), and we are meant to understand that Kurtz perceived which of the two descriptions was the more accurate soon enough. But the crucial difference between the pair of men resides in this: having found his noble illusions to be untenable, Kurtz takes things to their logical conclusion and "go[es] ashore for a howl and a dance," while Marlow never does. Why then does Kurtz succumb to "the fascination of the abomination" while Marlow stays on deck and on duty? Two competing explanations are put forward in the novel.

THE GOD THAT FAILED

The first is articulated by the Little Russian, whom Marlow encounters on the approach to Kurtz's station, and who has been acting as the great man's sidekick or court jester. The Russian insists that the jungle has caused his master to undergo a kind of awesome expansion, that the wilderness has only revealed to Kurtz the true extent of his inherent freedom and power.

"They adored him," he said. The tone of these words was so extraordinary that I looked at him searchingly. It was curious to see his mingled eagerness and reluctance to speak of Kurtz. The man filled his life, occupied his thoughts, swayed his emotions. "What can you expect?" he burst out; "he came to them with thunder and lightning, you know—and they had never seen anything like it—and very terrible. He could be very terrible. You can't judge Mr. Kurtz as you would an ordinary man."

(p. 92)

This is the Nietzschean aspect of Kurtz's revolt—for according to the Russian he is a personality too large to be confined within the strictures of bourgeois morality, and to return to "civilized" restraint after enjoying such superhuman freedom would be an unthinkable moral defeat. In this reading, Kurtz's isolation has been liberating, for it has fully ignited a dormant force within him that his life at home allowed only to fitfully spark and smoke. Up-river, Kurtz has found his true calling, and his truest self.

Marlow certainly understands this interpretation and the partial truth of it, and he himself will later affirm, for rather different reasons, that Kurtz was "a remarkable man" (p. 113). But Marlow's own interpretation of Kurtz's transformation is the opposite of the Russian's, for he conceives of Kurtz as discovering not a presence within himself, but an absence. Thus in reference to the heads with which Kurtz has adorned his jungle compound, our narrator asserts that

[t]hey only showed that Mr. Kurtz lacked restraint in the gratification of his various lusts, that there was something wanting in him—some small matter which, when the pressing need arose, could not be found under his magnificent eloquence. Whether he knew of this deficiency himself I can't say. I think the knowledge came to him at last—only at the very last. But the wilderness had found him out early, and had taken on him a terrible vengeance for the fantastic invasion. I think it had whispered to him things about himself which he did not know, things of which he had no conception till he took counsel with this great solitude—and the whisper had proved irresistibly fascinating. It echoed loudly within him because he was hollow at the core. . . .

(p. 95)

This absence within Kurtz has both a religious and a social resonance. First of all, the metaphor of vacancy within is another way for Conrad to evoke his atheistic conception of life without stating it directly. Kurtz's figurative hollowness is thus Conrad's way of debunking the notion of any indwelling divine presence that upholds us or guides us toward the good. What the human animal Kurtz—and, by implication, all of us—carries within is only the evolutionary inheritance of desires and instincts, most of which abet rather than retard Kurtz's transformation into a savage demigod. Secondly, the absence within is a marker of the effect of the social void that surrounds Kurtz—the fact that he is cut off from the censuring and regulating presence of his own community. This idea is disturbing because it suggests that Kurtz is nothing special, that anyone, when removed from a society that in a thousand small but effective ways enforces social conformity, is just as likely to find "restraint" succumbing to invincible libidinal pressures. As he explains to the thoroughly socialized listeners on the *Nellie*:

You can't understand. How could you?—with solid pavement under your feet, surrounded by kind neighbours ready to cheer you or to fall on you, stepping delicately between the butcher and the policeman, in holy terror of scandal and gallows and lunatic asylums—how can you imagine what particular region of the first ages a man's untrammelled feet may take him into by the way of solitude—utter solitude without a policeman—by way of silence—utter silence, where no warning voice of a kind neighbour can be heard whispering of public opinion? These little things make all the great difference.

(pp. 81–82)

Of course the Company's managers are hollow men as well, but in an even darker mode than is Kurtz. The fallen humanist eventually comes to recognize and despise his hollowness, but the Manager sees the same appalling fact about human nature and revels in it, finding it conducive to higher profits. The latter, whom Marlow claims has "nothing within him" and who operates in a moral environment where

133

there are "no external checks" actually recommends that "men who come out here should have no entrails" (p. 42). Clearly the Manager has seen all the way into the "inner" truth from which Marlow tries to distract himself and finds that he likes the view. It is this attitude among the Company men that eventually prompts Marlow's change of heart toward Kurtz. Upon first seeing the ornamental heads and comprehending what Kurtz's reign in the wilderness actually entailed, Marlow feels that he is in "some lightless region of subtle horrors where pure, uncomplicated savagery was a positive relief" (p. 95) and scornfully dismisses the trader's rifles as "the thunderbolts of that pitiful Jupiter" (p. 98). But after he hears the Manager describe Kurtz's activities as merely a "method" which is "unsound" because "the time [is] not [yet] ripe for [such] vigorous action," he "turn[s] mentally to Kurtz for relief—positively for relief" (p. 101). What Marlow comes to understand is that it is much worse to pronounce Kurtz's activities to be bad for business than to summarize them as Kurtz himself does, in the novel's most famous lines: "The horror! The horror!" (p. 112). These words represent not—as is sometimes lazily alleged—Kurtz's moral nadir but rather his ethical apogee. "The horror!" is, after all, a value judgment, and the values that underlie it are those of Western civilization. Marlow explains: "He had summed up—he had judged. 'The horror!' He was a remarkable man. After all, this was the expression of some sort of belief; it had candour, it had conviction, it had a vibrating note of revolt in its whisper, it had the appalling face of a glimpsed truth—the strange commingling of desire and hate. . . . It was an affirmation, a moral victory paid for by innumerable defeats, by abominable terrors, by abominable satisfactions. But it was a victory!" (pp. 113–114). Marlow finally sides with Kurtz rather than the Company, for as he says, "it was something at least to have a choice of nightmares" (p. 101). But before Kurtz can utter his shattering summation of his own career, that career must be ended, and this Marlow has to do

himself by means of an extraordinary mental duel with a "pitiful Jupiter" who is not altogether ready to resume mortal form.

When Kurtz crawls off the steamboat in the night in an apparent attempt to rejoin his native followers, Marlow is the one who notices his escape and who takes it upon himself to intercept the decrepit but still dangerous demigod. Now we have already seen that Marlow and Kurtz have been traveling the same intellectual and spiritual path—albeit for different distances—and so it should be no surprise that on this mission Marlow plays the role both of jailer and acolyte—that he can only regain his prisoner by adopting the discourse of his spiritual master. Marlow himself is clear that his feelings toward Kurtz are "custodial" on more than one level: "I did not betray Mr. Kurtz—it was ordered I should never betray him—it was written I should be loyal to the nightmare of my choice. I was anxious to deal with this shadow by myself alone,—and to this day I don't know why I was so jealous of sharing with any one the peculiar blackness of that experience" (p. 104). But if Marlow is genuinely confused about his own motives, we should not be, for if it is difficult to keep a secret, it is also difficult to relinquish one's monopoly on any kind of forbidden knowledge.

That night, circling around to head off Kurtz, Marlow achieves his furthest point of penetration into the wilderness, and in his desperate negotiations he begins to talk and feel uncannily like his adversary. He feels, for instance, the pull of savage freedom, and seems to gain a sense of omnipotence from the rhythms of the natives' camp. "I strode rapidly with clenched fists. I fancy I had some vague notion of falling upon him and giving him a drubbing. I don't know. I had some imbecile thoughts. . . . And I remember I confounded the beat of the drum with the beating of my heart, and was pleased at its calm regularity" (p. 105). When at last he is face to face with Kurtz, Marlow struggles to formulate an appeal that will touch a man given over to the solipsism of absolute egoism—and, in a moment that both surprises and discomfits him, he succeeds:

> I could not appeal in the name of anything high or low. I had, even like the niggers, to invoke him—himself—his own exalted and incredible degradation. There was nothing either above or below him, and I knew it. He had kicked himself lose of the earth. Confound the man! he had kicked the very earth to pieces. He was alone, and I before him did not know whether I stood on the ground or floated in the air. . . . [And] his soul was mad. Being alone in the wilderness, it had looked within itself, and by heavens! I tell you, it had gone mad. I had—for my sins, I suppose—to go through the ordeal of looking into it myself. No eloquence could have been so withering to one's belief in mankind as his final burst of sincerity. He struggled with himself, too. I say it,—I heard it. I saw the inconceivable mystery of a soul that knew no restraint, no faith, and no fear, yet struggling blindly with itself.
>
> (pp. 107–108)

Marlow's imagery of the abyss, while serving to communicate Conrad's atheism sotto voce, also contributes to the theme of Marlow and Kurtz as master and neophyte, for the passage above brings to mind the distinction in the Buddhist tradition (Conrad had extensive experience in the Orient) between two kinds of seekers after secret knowledge. In Buddhism, the *shravaka* is the questor who, having gained a glimpse into the abyss of absolute truth, leaps ecstatically over the edge. The *bodhisattva*, by contrast, peeks over the lip of the same abyss, but then returns to the everyday world in order to enlighten others. Comparing the two of them, Marlow says, "True, he had made that last stride, he had stepped over the edge, while I had been permitted to draw back my hesitating foot" (p. 113). If Marlow plays the role of our *bodhisattva*, however, there is a complication, for in *Heart of Darkness* the secret of the abyss is corrosive of all the expedient illusions that make life in Europe secure and endurable. Should

Marlow then tell anyone about what he has seen?

THE WOMEN ARE OUT OF IT

This question is made all the more acute by the fact that for Conrad, the world of European normality is quintessentially the world of women. And concerning the unsettling truths of the cosmos, "they—the women I mean—are out of it—should be out of it. We must help them to stay in that beautiful world of their own, lest ours get worse" (p. 80). Indeed, according to our narrator, "it's queer how out of touch with truth women are. They live in a world of their own, and there had never been anything like it, and never can be. It is too beautiful altogether, and if they were to set it up it would go to pieces before the first sunset. Some confounded fact we men have been living contentedly with ever since the day of creation would start up and knock the whole thing over" (p. 28). While a notion so condescendingly sexist grates painfully on modern ears, it is nevertheless important to understand what women represent in this novel. For Conrad, they are the very emblem of quotidian, bourgeois society, the true believers in the pretty fictions that keep civilized society on the tracks and prevent life from being revealed for—and acted out as—the amoral struggle that it actually is. Clearly this fragile realm, fictional as it may be, is one that must be protected at all cost. The problem is that, upon his return from the Congo, Marlow has lost his protective instinct vis-à-vis "that beautiful world":

> I found myself back in the sepulchral city resenting the sight of people hurrying through the streets to filch a little money from each other, to devour their infamous cookery, to gulp their unwholesome beer, to dream their insignificant and silly dreams. They trespassed upon my thoughts. They were intruders whose knowledge of life was to me an irritating pretence, because I felt so sure they could not possibly know the things I knew. Their bearing, which was simply the bearing of com-

monplace individuals going about their business in the assurance of perfect safety, was offensive to me like the outrageous flauntings of folly in the face of a danger it is unable to comprehend. I had no particular desire to enlighten them, but I had some difficulty in restraining myself from laughing in their faces, so full of stupid importance.

(p. 114)

This states a dilemma faced by many of Conrad's heroes—and by the heroes of some of his disciples, such as Graham Greene and John Le Carré—for these characters labor at the dangerous margins of the world in order to protect the bourgeois center, only to find that when their striving is done they have been rendered unfit to reenter that quotidian world whose values they have sheltered. Conrad's sailors, like Le Carré's spies, can never really come in from the cold. This alienation from the feminized bourgeois realm is aggravated by Marlow's constitutional distaste for a certain kind of fiction: "You know I hate, detest, and can't bear a lie, not because I am straighter than the rest of us, but simply because it appalls me. There is a taint of death, a flavour of mortality in lies,—which is exactly what I hate and detest in the world—what I want to forget. It makes me miserable and sick, like biting something rotten would do" (p. 50). And yet, despite these temporary and permanent proclivities, he shields Kurtz's Intended by telling a lie. Clearly his motivation for doing so cries out for an explanation.

When he first arrives at the Intended's home, it appears as though he will not be up to lying by any means, for the vision of drums, worshipers, and jungle that overtakes him on the threshold seems to emanate from "the heart of a conquering darkness" and to represent "a moment of triumph for the wilderness, an invading and vengeful rush which, it seemed to [him, he] would have to keep back for the salvation of another soul" (pp. 117–118). Marlow has long felt the jungle crouching as if waiting to take its revenge for the "fantastic invasion," and perhaps the time for retribution is now at hand. Marlow's

courage wavers, for while both the Intended and her home embody the world of bourgeois illusion that he believes must be protected, there is something deathlike about the furnishings: "The marble fireplace had a cold and monumental whiteness. A grand piano stood massively in a corner, with dark gleams on the flat surfaces like a sombre and polished sarcophagus" (p. 118). This is so because, however expedient the fictions the Intended embodies, fictions are a polite word for lies, and lies, as our narrator has recently informed us, always have about them the flavor of mortality. Still, these deathly images are balanced by the woman's sincere and fervent belief in the high-minded notions that sent her fiancé upriver, full of self-sacrifice and schemes for improvement: "I noticed she was not very young—I mean not girlish. She had a mature capacity for fidelity, for belief, for suffering" (p. 119).

This description brings to mind another woman who also seems to possess these same capacities, though in a very different key. Indeed, Kurtz's native concubine, and her relationship to the Intended and to Conrad's conception of women in general, has remained a contentious but unavoidable question. On the one hand, she seems, in her knowledge of—or even embodiment of—the "dark powers" Kurtz has raised, deployed, and wallowed in, to be the Intended's polar opposite:

> She walked with measured steps, draped in striped and fringed cloths, treading the earth proudly, with a slight jingle and flash of barbarous ornaments. She carried her head high, her hair was done in the shape of a helmet; she had brass leggings to the knee, brass wire gauntlets to the elbow, a crimson spot on her tawny cheek, innumerable necklaces of glass beads on her neck; bizarre things, charms, gifts of witch-men, that hung about her, glittered and trembled at every step. She must have had the value of several elephant tusks upon her. She was savage and superb, wild-eyed and magnificent; there was something ominous and stately in her deliberate progress. And in the hush that had fallen suddenly upon the whole sorrowful

land, the immense wilderness, the colossal body of the fecund and mysterious life seemed to look at her, pensive, as though it had been looking at the image of its own tenebrous and passionate soul.

(p. 99)

Just as there is room in Conrad's world for cannibals who practice "restraint," is this a woman who is in no way "out of it"? It seems a distinct possibility, and yet, aren't we to understand that this native princess is as ignorant of Kurtz's life in Europe as his fiancée is of his true career up-river? And then too, the moment one returns to the passage above, the account of her mien and carriage begins to suggest affinities with the equally proud and stalwart Intended. Indeed, in the latter's postures of unrelieved mourning Marlow himself finds ground for comparison, asserting that the Intended resembles "in this gesture another one, tragic also, and bedecked with powerless charms, stretching bare brown arms over the glitter of the infernal stream, the stream of darkness" (p. 122). But whether they are doppelgängers or opposites, both women testify to Kurtz being, in Marlow's words, "a remarkable man," for both his consorts are indeed "superb" in the ferocity of their devotion to the man they both love and lose.

THE GREAT AND SAVING LIE

If, however, the women remain true to Kurtz, Marlow sees himself as the man's reluctant betrayer, as one who, through a kind of merciful weakness, "laid the ghost of his gifts at last with a lie" (p. 80). Constitutionally inclined to veracity, Marlow finds the Intended's conception of Kurtz too sacrosanct to demolish with an accurate account.

"But you have heard him! You know!" she cried.

"Yes, I know," I said with something like despair in my heart, but bowing my head before the faith that was in her, before that great and saving illusion that shone with an unearthly glow in the darkness, in the triumphant darkness from

which I could not have defended her—from which I could not even defend myself.

(p. 121)

Here is a potent irony, for whereas before it was the ordinary dullards who had to "set up, and bow down before, and offer sacrifice to" an idea, now Marlow finds himself figuratively upon his knees before the idol. But to fully grasp his motivations for self-abasement, we must, as Marlow does, give the adjectives "great" and "saving" their full weight, for what her "illusion" preserves is a necessary edifice of social shelter that protects humanity from its own violent and selfish impulses and from a dispiriting vision of the cold, empty vastness of the Conradian cosmos. Understanding the stakes resting upon his utterance, Marlow speaks the lie he supposedly despises.

"His last word—to live with," she murmured. "Don't you understand I loved him—I loved him—I loved him!"

I pulled myself together and spoke slowly.

"The last word he pronounced was—your name."

I heard a light sigh, and then my heart stood still, stopped dead short by an exulting and terrible cry, but the cry of inconceivable triumph and of unspeakable pain. "I knew it—I was sure!" . . . She knew. She was sure. I heard her weeping; she had hidden her face in her hands. It seemed to me that the house would collapse before I could escape, that the heavens would fall upon my head. But nothing happened. The heavens do not fall for such a trifle. Would they have fallen, I wonder, if I had rendered Kurtz that justice which was his due? Hadn't he said he wanted only justice? But I couldn't. I could not tell her. It would have been too dark—too dark altogether.

(p. 123)

This final phrase is important, for like others in *Heart of Darkness,* it has a twin—or an opposite—elsewhere in the text. We should thus recall that Marlow declared the safe, secure, and necessary world of women's illusions "too beautiful altogether," because his decision to protect that illusory beauty goes to the heart of one of the novel's most disturbing implications. We are accustomed, in our complacent, everyday lives, to equate civilization with insight, to believe that the deeper we see into the true nature of things, the farther we progress down the road that leads to security, healthfulness, and happiness. But Conrad insists that Marlow, by choosing to preserve such beautiful, expedient illusions with a lie, is choosing not civilization *and* truth, but civilization *rather than* truth. For the dark truth is, in Conrad's world you can have one or the other, but never both.

THE NOVEL'S LITERARY INFLUENCE

Heart of Darkness, written in the penultimate year of the nineteenth century, is often considered to be the founding text of the modernist period, and this has to do with more than just Conrad's tough-minded atheism and his skepticism concerning colonialism discussed above. After all, such eminent Victorians as George Eliot and Thomas Hardy professed philosophies that were essentially Godless. What really sets Conrad apart from his predecessors— and what qualifies him to be the inaugurator of high modernism is, in terms of literary history, a new and striking collapse of confidence in two closely related things that the Victorians never questioned: the ultimate transparency of character and the ability of language to fully reveal that character.

Whereas the omniscient narrators of the great Victorian novels always speak to us in the confident tones of a wise philosopher-king, Marlow is a storyteller who seems to painfully strain and grapple and guess at the truth before our eyes, forcing us to take a roundabout and often tortuous path toward uncertain enlightenment alongside him: "It was the farthest point of navigation and the culminating point of my experience. It seemed somehow to throw a kind of light on everything about me—and into my

thoughts. It was sombre enough too—and piti-ful—not extraordinary in any way—not very clear either. No, not very clear. And yet it seemed to throw a kind of light" (p. 21). If this sounds frustratingly tentative, consider Marlow's unexpected outburst later in the tale, where he seems to despair altogether over language's ability to communicate anything worth knowing:

"Do you see him? Do you see the story? Do you see anything? It seems to me I am trying to tell you a dream—making a vain attempt, because no relation of a dream can convey the dream-sensation, that commingling of absurdity, surprise, and bewilderment in a tremor of struggling revolt, that notion of being captured by the incredible which is of the very essence of dreams. . . . "

He was silent for a while.

" . . . No, it is impossible; it is impossible to convey the life-sensation of any given epoch of one's existence,—that which makes its truth, its meaning—its subtle and penetrating essence. It is impossible. We live, as we dream—alone. . . . "

(p. 50)

This new wariness about truth's availability was very much in the air during Conrad's lifetime, and in part he is doing no more than reacting to and reflecting changes in the intellectual discourse of his era. During the last decades of the nineteenth century, advances in astronomy, anthropology, physics, and even historiography all pointed toward the same conclusion—not that truth is one and unified and universal, but rather that where you stand and who you are determines which answer you count as truthful and even which question you pose in the first place. Then too, as British society became increasingly complex, cosmopolitan, imperial, and self-consciously divided along class lines, any pronouncement claming to be possessed of the truth immediately came under suspicion for the bias and self-interest of its speaker. Thus it is no surprise that the more-or-less straightforward narrative strategies of the Victorians had to give way to a method of storytelling in which the claims and prospects for closure, transparency, and completeness were scaled back and in which even the path toward those goals was depicted as difficult and uncertain at best. And so, at the story's beginning, our frame narrator, in a rare moment of insight, informs us through an elaborate visual metaphor about just what kind of modernist narrative we will be reading, and how it will differ from its Victorian predecessors:

> The yarns of seamen have a direct simplicity, the whole meaning of which lies within the shell of a cracked nut. But Marlow was not typical (if his propensity to spin yarns be excepted), and to him the meaning of an episode was not inside like a kernel but outside, enveloping the tale which brought it out only as a glow brings out a haze, in the likeness of one of these misty halos that sometimes are made visible by the spectral illumination of moonshine.

(p. 18)

In the final analysis, perhaps the best summation of the influence of *Heart of Darkness* can be found by reflecting upon its title. This is so because the hallmark of modernism and subsequent twentieth century literature is that at the center of life, where the Victorians variously placed God or reason or progress or the revelatory power of narrative itself, there is only an absence—a darkness rather than a central, ordering, all-illuminating light. What Conrad's haunting tale begins is a new tradition of literary works that either proclaim that the search for a center is futile or insist that anything to found there will have been constructed from nothing other than our own beguiling but necessary illusions.

Selected Bibliography

EDITIONS

Heart of Darkness, with The Congo Diary. Edited by Robert Hampson. New York: Penguin, 1995. Edition cited in this essay.

Heart of Darkness. Edited by Robert Kimbrough. 3d ed. London and New York: Norton, 1988.

SECONDARY WORKS

Achebe, Chinua. "An Image of Africa: Racism in *Conrad's Heart of Darkness.*" *The Massachusetts Review* 18 (Winter 1975): 782–794.

Bloom, Harold, ed. *Joseph Conrad's Heart of Darkness.* New York: Chelsea House, 1987.

Brantlinger, Patrick. "Heart of Darkness: Anti-Imperialism, Racism, or Impressionism?" *Criticism* 27 (1985): 363–385.

Brooks, Peter. "An Unreadable Report: Conrad's *Heart of Darkness.*" In his *Reading for the Plot: Design and Intention in Narrative.* New York: Knopf, 1984.

Fleishman, Avrom. *Conrad's Politics.* Baltimore: Johns Hopkins University Press, 1967.

Green, Martin. *Dreams of Adventure, Deeds of Empire.* New York: Basic Books, 1979; London: Routledge and Kegan Paul, 1980.

Guérard, Albert J. *Conrad the Novelist.* Cambridge, Mass.: Harvard University Press, 1958.

Harris, Wilson. "The Frontier on Which *Heart of Darkness* Stands." *Joseph Conrad: Third World Perspectives.* Edited by Robert D. Hamner. Washington, D.C.: Three Continents, 1990.

Hawkins, Hunt. "Conrad's *Heart of Darkness*: Politics and History." *Conradiana* 24 (1992): 207–217.

Hochschild, Adam. *King Leopold's Ghost.* Boston: Houghton Mifflin, 1999.

Hyland, Peter. "The Little Woman in the *Heart of Darkness.*" *Conradiana* 20, no. 1 (1988): 3–11.

Karl, Frederick R. *Joseph Conrad: The Three Lives.* New York: Farrar, 1979.

Karl, Frederick R., and Laurence Davies, eds. *The Collected Letters of Joseph Conrad.* Cambridge and New York: Cambridge University Press, 1983.

Murfin, Ross C., ed. *Heart of Darkness: A Case Study in Contemporary Criticism.* 2d ed. New York: St. Martin's Press, 1996.

Parry, Benita. *Conrad and Imperialism.* London: Macmillain, 1983.

Rising, Catharine. *Darkness at Heart: Fathers and Sons in Conrad.* New York: Greenwood, 1990.

Sherry, Norman, ed. *Conrad: The Critical Heritage.* London and Boston: Routledge, 1973.

Shetty, Sandya. "*Heart of Darkness*: Out of Africa Some New Thing Never Comes." *Journal of Modern Literature* 15 (1989): 461–474.

Straus, Nina Pelikan. "The Exclusion of the Intended from Secret Sharing in Conrad's *Heart of Darkness.*" *Novel* 20, no. 2 (1987): 123–137.

Wasserman, Jerry. "Narrative Presence: The Illusion of Language in *Heart of Darkness.*" *Studies in the Novel* 6, no. 3 (1974): 327–338.

Watt, Ian. *Conrad in the Nineteenth Century.* Berkeley: University of California Press, 1979.

Watts, Cedric. "'A Bloody Racist': About Achebe's View of Conrad." *Yearbook of English Studies* 13 (1983): 196–209.

John Donne's
Holy Sonnets

JAMES E. BERG

"HOLY SONNETS" IS a title that editors and critics have given to nineteen of John Donne's religious poems. It would be a fair description, since all nineteen are sonnets in the devotional mode. Yet as a title it is misleading. From their varied groupings and orderings in the many manuscript versions that survive, we know that the sonnets were composed at different times in Donne's life. In these manuscript versions, none in Donne's hand, the phrase "Holy Sonnets" does often introduce poems now grouped among the nineteen. But sometimes the heading "Divine Meditations" occurs instead. In only one manuscript, a copy prepared by a friend of Donne's for the Earl of Westmoreland around 1620, do all nineteen sonnets appear together. Three of these nineteen were never published in the seventeenth century. Twelve found their way into print in 1633, two years after Donne's death, in the first published edition of his poems. These reappeared, reordered and interspersed with four more, in another edition, in 1635. In the early printed editions, moreover, the heading "Holy Sonnets" appears in two places, as if it were a description rather than a title. First it appears above *La Corona,* a "crown" of sonnets on the life of Christ, in which the last line of

every poem is the first line of the next, and the last line of the final poem is the first line of the first. Then it appears again, above the poems that critics and editors call "Holy Sonnets," from which *La Corona* is now distinguished as a separate work.

The problem of whether "Holy Sonnets" is a title or a description is also an opportunity. If the sonnets discussed here do not constitute a single work by that title, they may involve moods and conceits as diverse and interesting as those found, say, under the rubric "love poetry." In that case religious devotion might be considered a means of poetic representation as well as one end: the setting of the drama rather than of the entire play. True, even as a description, "holy sonnets" suggests that any effort to reconstruct the earliest contexts of the poems must account for religion. But what does it mean to account for religion in English poetry from the first half of the seventeenth century? The culture in which Donne wrote was so steeped in Christian doctrine that its every aspect had religious significance. This was the culture in which Puritanism was born, and that produced the King James Bible (1611) and Richard Hooker's monumental *Laws of the Ecclesiastical*

Polity, which began appearing in 1592. Wars, affairs of state, and social struggles could all be traced to religious differences, so that a "devotional" text could have myriad contexts—philosophical, political, medical, erotic. Not all writing was equally "religious," of course, and devotional writing did exist as a specific category. But all walks of life could find representation under its rubric.

Hence, apologies for Donne's "Holy Sonnets" as diminished by the limitations of their subject matter are not only unnecessary but also anachronistic. Yet such apologies do occur, even among such critics as T. S. Eliot and Helen Gardner, who otherwise deserve great credit for bringing the poems to the attention of modern readers. Anthologies of Donne's poems tend to reserve the "Holy Sonnets," with the other devotional writing, such as *The Progresse of the Soule, The Litanie,* and the *Anniversaries,* for the end, implying that the satires, elegies, and love poems have an appeal more universal than the divine poems, which begin to look like an appendix reserved for the specialist. By contrast, the compilers of the 1633 edition placed the divine poems (including the "Holy Sonnets") first, honoring them as a fitting introduction to the entire corpus.

But the tendency to treat the "Holy Sonnets" as an appendix does not derive from secularist bias alone; it also has roots in the temptation to date Donne's poetry according to three parts into which his adult life is typically divided by biographers. The first part (roughly 1591–1602) includes Donne's rakish exploits in law school and in the service of powerful statesmen. As a Catholic recusant uncommitted to the strictures of Protestant rule, he enjoys adventure, both military and erotic. He then falls in love and elopes with Ann More, the niece of his employer, Lord Chancellor Sir Thomas Egerton, and so lands temporarily in prison, his secular career permanently ruined. It has seemed appropriate to critics that rebellious satires and elegies, prurient verses, and love poems should date from this chapter. The next part (1602–

CHRONOLOGY

1572	24 January/19 June: Donne born a Catholic, in London, to John Donne, ironmonger and gentleman, and Elizabeth Heywood.
1576	January: Father dies, leaves an ample estate for his widow and children.
1584	Matriculates at Oxford, his age listed, inaccurately, as eleven. (Oxford has a Statute of Matriculation requiring all students over sixteen to subscribe to the Protestant Thirty-nine Articles).
1587	Transfers to Cambridge, which has no Statute of Matriculation. Probably meets lasting friend Henry Goodyer. Takes no degree (graduating would require him to take the Protestant Oath of Supremacy).
1591	Enrolls as law student at the Inns of Court in London. Forms several close friendships, including one with Rowland Woodward, whose hand is that of the Westmoreland manuscript (ca. 1620) of Donne's poems.
1596	June: sails with the Earl of Essex's troops for an attack on the Spanish at Cadiz.
1597	August: Joins Essex and Raleigh for adventures against Spanish in the New World. November: Becomes Lord Chancellor Egerton's secretary.
1601	Member of Parliament for Brackley, territory controlled by the Egerton family. Acquainted with George More, brother-in-law of Egerton and Member of Parliament. Elopes with Ann, More's fifteen-year-old daughter.
1602	February: Informs More of elopement. Briefly imprisoned on the charge of violating a law forbidding secret marriage. Dismissed from Egerton's employment.
1603	March: Queen Elizabeth dies; King James I succeeds to the throne.
1605	Journey to Continent with Sir Walter Chute. April: Gunpowder Plot (Catholic plot to blow up king and Parliament during session).

1607	Reconciled with George More. Close friendship with Countess of Bedford.
1609	Seeks secretaryships in Ireland and Virginia without success; writes most of what are now titled "Holy Sonnets."
1610	Publication of *Pseudo-Martyr*, favoring the anti-Catholic Oath of Allegiance.
1611	King James Bible published; Donne publishes *Ignatius His Conclave*, against Jesuits. Travels with Sir Robert Drury, publishes *An Anatomy of the World* (later *The First Anniversary*, a long verse meditation on the death of Drury's daughter).
1612	Publishes *First and Second Anniversaries*.
1614	Member of Parliament for Taunton, applies for state employment without success.
1615	Takes holy orders, becomes royal chaplain attending James I.
1617	Ann Donne dies after her eleventh pregnancy ends in a stillborn birth.
1620	Writes, possibly, the three "Holy Sonnets" in the Westmoreland manuscript.
1621	Becomes dean of St. Paul's.
1627	March: Death of King James; accession of Charles I.
1631	January: Donne's mother dies. 31 March: Donne dies.
1633	Publication of first edition of Donne's poems, titled *Poems by J. D., with Elegies on the Authors Death.*
1635	Second edition of Donne's poems, reordered and expanded, under the same title.

The final part is that of the late years (1615–1631), when, like St. Augustine, Donne finds his exuberance as a lover changed to religious enthusiasm, takes holy orders, and begins a new career that will ultimately make him King James's greatest preacher. Accordingly, as early as the mid-seventeenth century, Donne's first biographer, Sir Izaak Walton, supplying no hard evidence, dates his devotional poetry thus: "[H]e was not so falne out with heavenly Poetry, as to forsake that: no not in his declining age; witnessed then by many Divine Sonnets, and other high, holy, and harmonious Composures" (*Lives*, p. 61). Well into the twentieth century critics and biographers accepted this notion.

Yet the circular logic behind such speculation renders it unreliable. The three biographical periods conform easily to the poetic modes, but that is often because Donne's poetry itself has been used to reconstruct his biography. Of course there is always some truth to fiction. In the case of the "Holy Sonnets," the three found exclusively in the Westmoreland manuscript may well date from around 1620. There can be little doubt that the sonnet beginning

> Since she whom I lovd hath payd her last debt
> To Nature, and to hers, and my good is dead,
> And her soule early to heaven ravished,
> Wholy in heavenly things my mind is sett

1615) is typically one of penitence and maturation. Torn between his responsibilities as a family man and his need to revive his professional career, Donne divides his time between domestic life in the country and business both in London and abroad. To this period critics and bio- graphers have attached the more sentimental poetic expressions of true love and elegiac valediction, infused as they often are with religious allusions.

was written after 1617, when Donne's wife died. Gardner has made an excellent case that "Show me, dear Christ, thy Spouse so bright and Clear," a sonnet about confusion over the true nature of the Church, also has a late date. Despite some critics' estimations that it dates from the time of Donne's conversion, a mention of Germany in the poem appears to refer to the defeat of Protestants near Prague in 1620. The third sonnet in the Westmoreland manuscript, "Oh, to vex me, contraries meet in one," could have any date, but its position immediately following the other two suggests that it was composed around the same time. There is no credible evidence that any other of the "Holy Sonnets" come from the holiest period of Donne's life. The four printed in 1635 cannot be dated exactly, but since, unlike those from the Westmoreland manuscript, they are frequently interspersed with manuscript versions of the twelve printed in 1633, we may surmise that they come from the same period. And, though absolute certainty is impossible, Gardner's work on the manuscripts suggests that the twelve printed in 1633 were probably written around 1609, well before Donne took orders.

Because the evidence for this date helps illuminate the environment in which many seventeenth-century poems were written, it is interesting to explore. One piece of it is a manuscript of poems by Donne, Ben Jonson, and others, completed around 1630 by scribes, probably for William Cavendish, first Duke of Newcastle. The section preceding that devoted to Donne is dated 1629. In the Donne section, under the heading "Holy Sonnets: written 20 yeares since," comes the group of twelve published in 1633, in the same order. Thus the Newcastle manuscript suggests, for these sonnets, a date of about 1609, a moment when, recovering from the setback that his scandalous marriage caused his career, Donne sought new, secular employment and consolidated friendships among courtiers who had the money and status to advance him.

This evidence is corroborated by an elegy by Donne on the death, in 1609, of Cecelia Bulstrode, an intimate friend of his powerful patroness, Lucy, Countess of Bedford. The elegy begins "Death I recant, and say, unsaid by me, / What ere hath slip'd, that might diminish thee," as if to dramatize the demoralizing effects of a friend's death with a reversal of the triumphant tone of the best known of the "Holy Sonnets," "Death be not proud, though some have called thee / Mighty and dreadful." What is more, the Countess of Bedford, or someone in Donne's circle of friends attached to the royal court, seems to have responded to Donne's recantation with a poetic rallying cry reminding the poet of his own words. In two early manuscripts, "Death I recant" is answered by another elegy

of 1609, either on Cecelia Bulstrode or on the Lady Marltham, attributed to "L. C. of B." and "C. L. of B." that begins "Death be not proud, thy hand gave not this blow." Probably the sonnet "Death be not proud," the elegy on Cecilia Bulstrode, and the second elegy beginning "Death be not proud" were all part of a poetic conversation, involving Donne and a patroness that took place around 1609. Nor, it would seem, was this conversation limited to two. Donne seems to have sent some of the "Holy Sonnets" to "E. of D.," the Earl of Dorset, cousin of the Countess of Bedford's husband, who married into the countess's family in 1609. At least that is what Donne's epistolary sonnet, "To E. of D. with Six Holy Sonnets," suggests.

These traces of the circulation of Donne's poems serve not only to correct the dating of the "Holy Sonnets" but also to recall how some seventeenth-century lyric poetry, including devotional lyric poetry, was read. Donne envisioned his sonnets not as public monuments to his genius, but as handcrafted gifts to be shared and reused for various purposes. They were designed, as Arthur Marotti has shown of most of Donne's verse, to circulate among friends, patrons, and friends of friends, and to be copied into household "commonplace books" or verse miscellanies. It was common practice in Donne's time to destroy one's own drafts after having one's poems copied and passed on to friends, who could copy them again and pass them on to others. When, in 1614, a patron urged him to publish the poems (a project he never finished), Donne found himself writing to his friend Henry Goodyer to borrow them back: "By this occasion I am made a Rhapsoder of mine own rags, and that cost me more diligence, to seeke them, then it did to make them." And because the poems belonged as much to readers as to the writer, their uses and meanings could vary. In "To E. of D.," Donne characterizes the writing of the "Holy Sonnets" as a collaborative effort between poet and reader:

> I choose your judgement, which the same degree
> Doth with her sister, your invention, hold,

As fire these drossie Rymes to purifie,
Or as Elixar, to change them to gold.
You are the Alchimist which alwaies had
Wit, whose one spark could make good things of
     bad.

(ll. 914)

Of course this sonnet employs a typical humility topos, and so the word "bad" is not to be taken at face value. Had Donne truly disliked the poems, he would not have sent them to a possible patron. Nor is he necessarily inviting "E. of D." to edit or alter his poems—though alteration occurred quite frequently in the course of manuscript circulation. Nevertheless, the sonnet is as much a gesture of concession as an assertion of ownership.

Most approaches to the "Holy Sonnets" would do well to heed such gestures. To understand the poems as offerings to friends and patrons, and as offerings by friends and patrons to acquaintances of their own, is to expand historically responsible reading beyond narrow speculation as to Donne's immediate intentions. It is to allow not only his voice but also the voices of his many contemporary readers to speak through the poems, extending to today's criticism the generosity implicit in their making. By considering the circulation of the sonnets as gifts, and the consequent looseness of the poet's control over their meanings, one can find value even in interpretations that might otherwise falter.

Take the interpretation of the "Holy Sonnets" as examples of what Barbara Lewalski calls a "Protestant Poetics." This "Poetics" supposedly advanced, among other Calvinist and Lutheran principles, the doctrine of predestination, according to which people, tarnished with original sin, are predestined for damnation or salvation, and grace is "imputed" to the "elect," not freely chosen. Those who find the doctrine in Donne's poems point to his public disavowal of his Catholic roots in *Pseudo-Martyr* (a tract in favor of the crown's institution of an anti-Catholic Oath of Allegiance) and *Ignatius His*

Conclave (a biting satire against Jesuits). They also underscore echoes in the sonnets of the vocabulary in which Calvin and Luther articulated the doctrine of predestination. Yet, as R. V. Young demonstrates, such vocabulary can usually be found in Catholic as well as Protestant doctrine. Where it is unmistakably Protestant, Donne's use of it seems experimental and playful, if not gently ironic. In the sonnet "This is my playes last scene,...my pilgrimage's last mile" the phrase "impute me righteous" echoes not only Calvin and Luther but also two other poems by Donne: the Third Satire and Elegie XIX, "To His Mistress Going to Bed." In both cases Donne mocks the notion of imputed grace. As for Donne's religious manifestos, they were public documents intended for print and produced to appeal to a monarch almost assassinated by a few militant Catholics in the Gunpowder Plot of 1605, a notorious conspiracy to blow up Parliament. The sonnets were intimate representations of religious devotion, designed to cement bonds among friends (such as the Catholic Henry Goodyer) and create personal relationships with patrons, who had diverse theological perspectives. Donne's private letters, also an important context for the poems, appear to qualify the anti-Catholic stance he took in the pamphlets.

Still, the loose nature of Donne's control over the poems demands that historically responsible readers consider the possibility of Calvinist and Lutheran resonances, even as they resist efforts to make Donne himself into a Puritan. The wide circulation of his poetry ensures that it found some readers more devoted than Donne himself to strict Calvinism and Lutheranism. By the Thirty-nine Articles of Religion, passed in 1563 under Queen Elizabeth I, predestination was the official doctrine of the English Church. Chained to every church altar was a copy of John Foxe's *Acts and Monuments,* a hard-core Protestant tome detailing the lives of anti-Catholic "martyrs" and railing apocalyptically against "Papists" as devotees of the Antichrist and the Whore of Babylon. In this environment the suspense-filled openings of the "Holy Sonnets," such as "What if this present were the world last night?" or "O my black Soule! Now thou art summoned / By sicknesse, death's herald," or "This is my playes last scene. Here heavens appoint / My pilgrimages last mile," must have resonated with the Calvinist and Lutheran view of the dispensation of souls as divinely predetermined and inscrutable. The poems provide little evidence to support strict adherence by Donne himself to a "Protestant Poetics." But they do make room for readers to associate the terror they represent with the terror inspired by the universe Calvin and Luther envisioned. How seriously Donne's readers took the association must have varied, depending on their religious beliefs and, as today, on the amount of irony they attributed to the poems. Reading the "Holy Sonnets" as gestures of generosity, capable of pleasing readers with conflicting religious perspectives and habits, allows for the possibility of such association without insisting on it as the only correct reading.

Reading the poems in this way also makes room for another, contrary context: that of formal meditation. No scholarly work has more enriched modern understanding of these poems than Louis Martz's discovery, in 1954, that Donne's religious poetry could be read as an extension of this practice, developed by figures dear to the Catholic Church, including St. Bernard, Luis de la Puente, and, most famously, Ignatius Loyola. To help make his case, Martz emphasizes not Donne's conversion to Protestantism or the anti-Jesuit diatribe *Ignatius His Conclave,* but his upbringing as a Catholic. But his strongest evidence is in striking resemblances, of both structure and tone, between Donne's divine poems and descriptions and narrations of Jesuitical meditation. This practice was known for a three-part exercise, engaging what in Donne's time were considered the three parts of the human soul (created in the image of the divine Trinity): the memory, the understanding, and the will. The memory was to be exercised through imagination of a vivid, and thus memorable, scene—the *compositio loci* or "composition of place." The understanding was to be engaged through analysis of the scene imagined. Finally, the will was to be moved through a colloquy, or an expression of adoration.

There is no question that the practice of meditation, as Martz documents it, has relevance to the "Holy Sonnets." Donne confirms the label "meditations" conferred by some manuscripts when he lectures, in the eleventh sonnet of the 1633 sequence, "Wilt thou love God, as He thee? Then digest, / My soul, this wholesome meditation." And Martz's analyses of the individual poems leave little doubt that they allude to meditative patterns. Some of the dramatic beginnings may be understood as applications of the technique of *compositio loci.* Martz also finds the tripartite meditative pattern in the structures of several individual sonnets. In this respect he puts "Spit in my face, ye Jewes" to good use by showing how it engages memory in the first quatrain, understanding in the second, and will in the sestet. What is more, his insight into the meditative context of the sonnets has helped to provide plausible rationales for the ordering of the twelve published in 1633. Gardner suggests that this ordering actually corresponds to a commonly prescribed course of meditation, with the first six sonnets devoted to the engagement of the memory and understanding on "last things" (prelude, meditation on sickness, the moment of death, the Last Judgment, hell, death), and the second six engaging the will on the salvation offered by God's love. Anthony Low follows Gardner's lead, providing clear and insightful interpretations of each of the "Holy Sonnets" in the 1633 edition, and treating them as a strictly ordered "sequence." Such readings of the sonnets are important and rewarding. The fact that many seventeenth-century manuscripts accord with the 1633 ordering at least of the first six suggests that many of Donne's readers may have sensed, consciously or not, the meditative patterns imitated by these poems.

Yet these patterns do not begin to exhaust the possibilities for interesting and historically defensible interpretations. It is important to keep in mind that the texts circulated among people with varying degrees of familiarity with formal meditation, diverse religious perspectives, and different senses of how the verses they were collecting might be enjoyed. As Stanley Archer points out, Jesuitical meditation may not have been so pervasive in England, even among Catholics, as Martz suggests. Certainly, by Martz's own admission, the sonnets do not always conform to the tripartite engagement of memory, understanding, and will. Even where Martz does try to establish such a structure in single sonnets, his efforts sometimes seem strained. Nor is there anything absolutely necessary about the ordering that Gardner discerns. Not all contemporary manuscripts of Donne's "Holy Sonnets" preserve it. The Westmoreland manuscript, prepared by Rowland Woodward, a friend of the poet, rearranges the sonnets. A similar rearrangement in the 1635 edition suggests that not all of Donne's contemporaries perceived the logic by which the twelve in the 1633 edition were ordered.

Even where they occur in the order Gardner discerns, the "Holy Sonnets" need not be read exclusively as scripts for Ignatian meditation. Many of the same manuscript collections that feature the "Holy Sonnets" in meditative order also contain the notoriously carnal and playful anticipation of fornication "To His Mistress Going to Bed," as well as witty advertisements for promiscuity such as "The Indifferent" and "Woman's Constancy." One might turn to such diverse collections for a kind of entertainment offered by the theater, the artful representation of various human moods, thoughts, and emotions, from the most profane to the most pious. To constrict the role of Donne's "Holy Sonnets" to actual meditation, rather than to the theatrical imitation of meditation, is to miss the ironic distance they can achieve—sometimes a critical distance, sometimes merely the distance required, say, for the enjoyment of a tragedy.

This is not to question the relevance of meditative practice to the "Holy Sonnets." Archer ignores too much evidence in doing so. It is rather to insist on generous readings, as opposed to those that flatten the poems either by absolutely excluding, or by exclusively endorsing, narrow contexts. It would be absurd to claim that Andrew Marvell's "To His Coy Mistress," with its ironically spurious logic, is just a script for seducing women; it is entertainment for all kinds of readers drawn to an artfully comical scene of attempted seduction. Donne's "Holy Sonnets," then, may be understood as artful representations of a flawed human being attempting meditation. They depict, with entertaining verisimilitude, not the unerring pathway to heaven but the travails of a fallen nature that Donne and contemporary readers of his poems knew they shared. They may be read as meditations, but they may also be read as moving theatrical performances, with which Donne sought to consolidate friendships and earn the goodwill of patrons.

A READING

Because they were designed to entertain a variety of readers, no particular interpretive scheme can account for all plausible meanings of the "Holy Sonnets." My purpose here, then, is not to impose one exhaustive reading on all nineteen poems. It is to suggest a reading that demonstrates how much more exploration, still true to the historical contexts I have described, is possible. The poems may be read, I submit, as theatrical monologues creating the image of a complex persona, a worshiping sonneteer, torn between conflicting impulses of self-assertion and self-denial. To circulate them would have been to strike a pose of imperfection, to make oneself vulnerable to criticism. Why should Donne, or someone passing Donne's sonnets as gifts to other readers, want to do this? Humility, in the secular environments in which the poems circulated, made good religious sense. In Donne's case, at the time he wrote most of the sonnets, he had not yet taken orders; to preach in poetry, as if he were in the moral or social position to admonish, would probably have alienated his readers rather than eliciting affection from them. Humility, on the other hand, allows the development of emotionally and materially rewarding friendships. In establishing a persona vulnerable to criticism, the poems begin conversations and invite readers to participate. They accomplish what both entertainment and devotion require: the concession of authority to another or to others.

To understand how the poems achieve this concession, it is important first of all to remember what the form of the Petrarchan sonnet implies. Insofar as it features a strict rhyme scheme comprising an octave of two interlocking quatrains and a concluding sestet, this form requires the utmost poetic skill and, when it is successful, suggests poetic mastery. With its emphasis on economy and completeness, moreover, the sonnet represents a microcosm of something far greater. "As well a well-wrought urn becomes / The greatest ashes, as half-acre tombs," says Donne in *The Canonization,* justifying the idea of building "in sonnets pretty rooms." But if the sonnet is an act of authorial self-assertion, it can also be an act of concession, particularly when it is used to represent religious devotion. To create a sonnet is to create a shrunken universe, and to submit to a prescribed set of prosodic requirements. What is more, the sonnet had acquired, in Elizabethan court culture, the aura of a gift: a miniature of the self that, despite its advertisement of poetic mastery, also rendered the self diminutive and artificial, subjecting the writer to the enjoyment of the recipient. As we have seen, Donne himself treated his sonnets as gifts. In other words, they enact mastery in order to concede it, both in a social sense (to patrons and friends) and in a religious sense (to God). One might think of them as dramatically ironic struggles for poetic control over the practice of religious devotion, assertions implicitly demonstrating that religious devotion can never be a site of such control.

Consider the fourth of the twelve sonnets in the 1633 edition. This poem has been used as evidence of the meditative structure of Donne's poetry. But an exclusive focus on meditative structure threatens to flatten the poetic voice that Donne achieves. The poem represents not only a prescribed meditation but also an effective use of the sonnet form to communicate the surrender of mastery that devotion requires:

> At the round earths imagin'd corners, blow
> Your trumpets, Angells, and arise, arise
> From death, you numberlesse infinities
> Of soules, and to your scattered bodies goe,
> All whom the flood did, and fire shall o'erthrow,
> All whom warre, dearth, age, agues, tyrannies,
> Despaire, law, chance, hath slaine, and you whose eyes
> Shall behold God, and never tast deaths woe.
> But let them sleep, Lord, and mee mourne a space,
> For, if above all these, my sinnes abound,
> 'Tis late to aske abundance of thy grace
> When wee are there; here on this lowly ground,
> Teach me how to repent; for that's as good
> As if thou' hadst sealed my pardon with thy blood.

In the octave the sonneteer assumes the role of God, ordering the Apocalypse to begin. The voice of the octave arrogates to itself command not only of the "numberlesse infinities" of human souls but also of the very angels. Or, at least, the voice of the octave appears to have convinced itself of this power.

But the sestet stages total conversion from mastery to submission. The sonneteer refers to himself for the first time as "me," revealing himself as no ineffable power but a single human being. The mood is still imperative but not commandingly so; it is that of a supplicant exhorting a higher power. The position of the sonneteer "on this lowly ground" is an emblem of humility. Now the sonneteer quells even an impulse to claim supremacy as a sinner, posing the possibility of that dubious achievement in the conditional: "*if* above these, my sinnes abound." Uncertainty prevails, too, in the requests to God to delay Judgment Day for an indefinite "space," and to "teach" him how to repent. Even the extent of the pardon accomplished through Christ's sacrifice—remembered, once again, in the conditional mood—seems indeterminate: "as *if* thou hadst sealed my pardon with thy blood." The turn to humility in the sestet, then, reveals the commanding tone of the octave as a theatrical pose by one undecided about who or what he is from moment to moment. By spotlighting the theatricality of the sonneteer, the sonnet cultivates the vulnerability appropriate to worship and to social communion with friends and patrons.

The importance of such theatricality to Donne's accomplishment in this regard cannot be overstated. To be theatrical is to confront the judgment of the spectator, seeking both to control and to appease it. That is evident from the third sonnet in the 1633 collection, which sounds like an attempt to manipulate responses from a stage:

> This is my playes last scene, here heavens appoint
> My pilgrimages last mile; and my race Idly, yet
>   quickly runne, hath this last pace,
> My spans last inch, my minutes last point,
> And gluttonous death, will instantly unjoynt
> My body, and soule, and I shall sleepe a space,
> But my'ever-waking part shall see that face,
> Whose feare already shakes my every joynt:
> Then, as my soule, to heaven, her first seate, takes
>   flight,
> And earth borne body, in the earth shall dwell,
> So, fall my sinnes, that all may have their right,
> To where they'are bred, and would presse me, to
>   hell.
> Impute me righteous, thus purg'd of evill,
> For thus I leave the world, the flesh, and devill.

Beginning as it does, this sonnet suggests an effort by a player to improvise. It is fraught with reminders that the player serves the spectator's pleasure. Among the most obvious of these is the absence of closure in the sonneteer's efforts to come up with a plausible ending. The strings of appositives extend the scene ever further through the quatrain, the spondees with which they end suggesting only impressions of finality, undermined by repetitions and elaborations: "my playes *last scene,* my pilgrimages *last mile* . . . this *last pace* / My spans *last inch,* my minutes *last point.*" The series of false endings is followed by yet a further extension, that of the judgment of the sonneteer's soul, continuing to the end of the octave, the phrase "ever-waking part" indicating, punningly, not only the soul but also the part in the play. The turn to the sestet, beginning with "Then," suggests that the play should be over, but it continues, in another episode, through four lines of the sestet. The sonneteer's powerlessness to make this particular scene of judgment come true becomes evident in the exhortatory verb "fall," which betrays continued uncertainty. And the final exhortation, "impute me righteous," suggests that the sonneteer has finally given up on his dramatic technique, that he is throwing himself on the mercy of an audience. Who is that audience? Perhaps God; if so, the sonneteer betrays a lack of confidence in his claim to be leaving "the world, the flesh, and devill," since if he *is* doing so, he has already received the imputation of grace. Perhaps the audience consists of human readers, or spectators watching a play. In that case "impute me righteous" might be a homiletic exhortation to learn from the sonneteer as an example of righteousness. But to whomever it is addressed, the phrase underscores the dependency of the sonneteer on approval from without.

There is no more efficient way to subject oneself to such approval than to indulge uncertainty. And uncertainty thrives on the relative weakness of human understanding, one of the tools with which the sonneteer frequently strives for mastery. In "The Holy Sonnets" the understanding strives hard with the will but always concedes to it in the end. The understanding can come up with vivid similes for diseases of the will, as it does in the octave of the second sonnet in the 1633 collection:

> Oh my black Soule! Now thou art summoned
> By sicknesse, deaths herald, and champion:
> Thou art like a pilgrim, which abroad hath done
> Treason, and durst not turne to whence hee is
>   fled,
> Or like a thiefe, which till deaths doome be read,
> Wisheth himselfe delivered from prison;
> But damn'd and hal'd to execution,
> Wisheth that still he might be imprisoned.

And after noting the contradictions in what the soul "wisheth," and judging the will to be defective, the understanding can also explain how and why to demonstrate repentance, as in the sestet:

> Yet grace, if thou repent, thou canst not lacke.
> But who shall give thee that grace to beginne?
> O make thy selfe with holy mourning blacke,
> And red with blushing, as thou art with sinne;
> Or wash thee in Christ's blood, which hath this
>   might
> That being red, it dyes red soules to white.

But, as this exhortation demonstrates, understanding cannot change will, cannot provide desire to repent or "grace to beginne." Nor can understanding separate itself from will enough to achieve control, since both wit and will are faculties of the same soul. Indeed, there is something of the will speaking through the understanding—in the passionate ejaculation "O my blacke Soule!" and in the imperative exhortations in the sestet.

The sonnet creates uncertainty, then, about the effectiveness of the judging and homiletic voice it conjures. This voice enacts the very state it describes in the octave; it appears trapped, frozen in anticipation, unable to advance or retreat without the drawing of the will toward Christ. The imperatives in the sestet do feature hope, but they also imply inaction: one does not need to order oneself to do what is already done. In its demonstration of the division between understanding and will that requires heavenly intervention, the sestet echoes desperate recognitions of approaching doom by some of the best-known tragic figures in Renaissance drama—Richard III, who betrays the fragmentation of himself with "Richard loves Richard; that is, I am I" (V.iii.184), or Marlowe's Faust, who, at the moment of truth, seeks vainly to escape himself by addressing himself in the second person: "Now, Faustus, thou hast but one bare hour to live/And then thou must be damned perpetually" (V.ii.135–136). These figures are known for arrogance, and perhaps there is indeed a hint of arrogance in the homiletic tone of the sonnet. But the poem captures this arrogance as it surrenders, as the sonneteer is humbled into a companion for readers struggling to overcome sin.

True, when Donne uses the sonnet form to demonstrate the relative weakness of the understanding—and so to concede mastery to the externally controlled will—it is often possible to map his sonnets according to two or three stages of formal meditation. After all, the understanding and will constitute two parts of the soul engaged by this process. But to use the poems only to establish the meditative pattern is to miss the pathos of defeat and surrender that they create. If the following sonnet is a meditative engagement of understanding and will, it is flawed, particularly in its exercise of understanding. The octave suggests a vain struggle to comprehend the reasoning behind damnation:

> If poysonous mineralls, and if that tree
> Whose fruit threw death on else immortall us,
> If lecherous goats, if serpents envious
> Cannot be damn'd; Alas, why should I bee?
> Why should intent, or reason, borne in mee,
> Make sinnes, else equall, in mee, more heinous?
> And mercy being easie, and glorious
> To God, in his sterne wrath, why threatens hee?

Implicit in this passage is an effort to obscure the memory of one's own sin through twists of a logic based on false assumptions. Reserved until the end of the rhetorical question occupying the first quatrain, the subject "I" is conspicuously void of agency. It does not act; it *is* "damn'd," as the "be" at the very end of the first quatrain stresses. Preposterously, the sonneteer represents the agents of his damnation as items below the level of humanity on the chain of being, and thus lacking in sense or intellect: minerals, a tree, goats, and serpents. He indicts the fruit eaten by Adam and Eve, not known for having arms or hands, but for throwing "death on else immortall us." This display of intellectual distortion answers the first question of the second quatrain before the question has even been asked ("Why should intent, or reason, borne in mee, / Make sinnes, else equall, more heinous?"). By investing them with itself, the sonneteer's reason has made monsters of lower beings, as Satan's reason is to do when it enters the serpent in Milton's *Paradise Lost*. Yet in the final two lines of the quatrain, reason, having lowered itself to the bottom of existence, arrogates to itself the ability to judge the actions of God.

The voice of the will becomes prominent in the sestet through a prayer or colloquy, with the final, paradoxical couplet illustrating how the mercy of God defeats any attempt at comprehension through reason:

> But who am I that dare dispute with thee?
> O God, Oh! Of thine onely worthy blood,
> And my teares, make a heavenly Lethean flood,
> And drown in it my sinnes blacke memorie.
> That thou remember them, some claime as debt,
> I think it mercy, if thou wilt forget.

In representing the will, this passage features semantic subtleties that can provide readers with illusions of a colorful human presence. The rationalizing tone spills over into the sestet, even in the process of changing, in "But who am I, that dare dispute with thee?" Because expressed in the same form as the previous reasoning—as a rhetorical question—this line sounds consistent with the first two. But sound lags behind sense. Now the agent, the person doing the disputing,

is the "I" standing judgment, and now this "I" is speaking directly to God, whereas before, the speaker was complaining behind the judge's back. Suddenly the understanding has turned on itself, comprehending the absurdity of disputing with God. Despite the careful planning implicit in the sonnet form, and despite the fact that an epiphany does take place at the turn between octave and sestet, where such planning would require it, the ordering of moods occurs as if external to the poet's design. Indeed, if following the 1633 edition and several of the manuscripts, one puts the question mark after "thee" instead of after "God," the ejaculation of "Oh" may register the speaker's wonder at what has occurred to him—wonder that jolts him out of reasoning and into prayer.

When understanding makes room for passion in this way, it creates the opportunity for compassion and for the social bonds created by compassion. Perhaps that opportunity accounts for the wide appeal of Donne's best-known devotional sonnet, which provides solace in the face of death:

> Death be not proud, though some have called thee
> Mighty and dreadfull, for thou art not soe,
> For those, whom thou thinkst, thou doest overthrow,
> Die not, poore death, nor yet canst thou kill mee;
> From rest and sleepe, which but thy pictures bee,
> Much pleasure, then from thee, much more doth flow,
> And soonest our best men with thee do goe
> Rest of their bones and soules deliverie.
> Thou art slave to Fate, chance, kings, and desperate men,
> And dost with poison, warre, and sicknesse dwell.
> And poppie or charmes can make us sleepe as well
> And better than thy stroake. Why swell'st thou then?
> One short sleepe past, wee wake eternally,
> And death shall be no more. Death, thou shalt die.

The continued power of this sonnet owes as much, perhaps, to its implicit concession of intellectual control as to any commonplaces it might provide about the limited powers of death. The poem does not formulate an escape from death. Donne's penchant for drama does not allow for such detached reassurances. The solace it offers is that of the comradeship and courage which come with facing a common enemy.

As for the dismissal of death's reputation for being "mighty and dreadful," the whole of the sonnet actually renders this questionable. The poem confounds the logic behind the various commonplaces it wields against Death. In the first quatrain, the sonneteer addresses "Death" as a person, affirming emphatically that it exists. Yet the sonneteer also insists that the victims of "Death" do not die, and thus implies that there is no death ("those, whom thou thinkst, thou doest overthrow, / Die not, poore death"). The second quatrain is even more vulnerable in its logic. The notion that the pleasure offered by mere "pictures" of death—"rest and sleepe"— must be less than that offered by death itself confuses the experience of artistic imitation with the experience of the thing imitated. And the argument implicit in the assurance that "our best men" go with death the soonest—that death tempts the "best men" with pleasure, is dubious. The best men, presumably, are not pleasure seekers; indeed, they are courageous and prone to self-sacrifice. Finally, on the larger scale of the sonnet as a whole, the octave contradicts the sestet. Whereas the octave presents evidence that death is not dreadful but pleasant, virtuous, and innocuous, the sestet offers evidence that Death keeps evil company, that it is "slave to Fate, chance, kings, and desperate men." Indeed, in the final couplet, Death seems a criminal condemned to death. And that brings up the conundrum like that of the first quatrain: if Death is dead, then there is no death, and death cannot be dead.

It would be absurd to suggest that these contradictions reflect badly on Donne's competence as a logician, much less as a poet. Oddly enough, they resemble the conspicuous logical flaws that mark love poems such as Donne's "The Flea," in which the poet stages a comical struggle to reason his way into bed with someone. In that case errors are the source of charm. They invite compassion for the poet, the very certainty of whose defeat at the game of logic may serve to win the heart of the beloved—or at least of the reader—through empathy. Likewise, though "Death be not proud" undermines its logical arguments for Death's overconfidence, it can provide comfort in the face of defeat, precisely by demonstrating the sonneteer's powerlessness to gain mastery over death through the understanding. The poem once again concedes mastery, and thereby offers readers companionship in the encounter with the mortal enemy. Of course the compassion elicited by "Death be not proud" is far from the charmed amusement for a desperate lover evoked by "The Flea." It is empathy in the face of common danger, the kind of empathy that serves to bind comrades in battle. Compassion of this kind is certainly consistent with the Christian culture for which it was produced. By succumbing to Death, Christ provides, to every Christian who must endure death, life-giving communion. But the poem also fits well into the more temporal context of the above-mentioned verse exchange over the death of Cecelia Bulstrode. When Donne wrote "Death I recant," he was not so much changing the psychology implicit in "Death be not proud" as recapitulating one aspect of it. His very recantation is already implied in the internal contradictions of the original sonnet, as is the Countess of Bedford's recantation of the recantation with "Death be not proud, thy hand gave not this blow," which insists on the same camaraderie in battle that Donne's "Death be not proud" invites.

Like these challenges to understanding, Donne's use of metaphor and analogy to confound reason and imagination is a bountiful source of passion and compassion. Samuel

Johnson's characterization of this technique as "metaphysical"—as well as Eliot's term "metaphysical conceit"—is perhaps unfortunate. It may still encourage the popular misconception that Donne's intellect rendered his poetry detached and lacking in affect. A more fitting term might be the seventeenth-century phrase "strong lines." At their best "strong lines" not only challenge logic and imagination but also engender affect. In the "Holy Sonnets" they often engender fear, creating the impression of a sonneteer whose errors have brought him, literally, to his wits' end, to that point at which one can no longer rely on his understanding to control himself. Consider, for example, this dramatic meditation on the crucifixion:

> What if this present were the world's last night?
> Marke in my heart, O Soule, where thou doest
>   dwell,
> The picture of Christ crucified, and tell
> Whether that countenance can thee affright;
> Tears in his eyes quench the amazing light,
> Blood fills his frownes, which from his pierced
>   head fell,
> And can that tongue adjudge thee unto hell,
> Which pray'd forgiveness for his foes fierce
>   spight?
> No, no; but as in my idolatrie
> I said to all my profane mistresses
> Beauty, of pitty, foulnesse onely is
> A signe of rigour: so I say to thee,
> To wicked spirits are horrid shapes assign'd,
> This beauteous forme assures a piteous minde.

The poem begins with a terror-inspiring question, and the blood-filled frowns and "pierced head" hardly seem likely to assuage the terror: the problem of "whether that countenance can thee affright," and "that tongue adjudge thee unto hell" cannot easily be dismissed with the double negative that introduces the sestet.

As a struggle to control the meaning of the image, the sestet demonstrates the impossibility of success, even through intellectual tours de force. The analogy between the lines to "profane

mistresses" and the reassurance to the soul is brilliant Neoplatonic logic. In designating as "beauty" what *could* inspire horror, it advertises the wisdom of one who can see beyond mere appearances, who has left imagination behind to comprehend through the mind's eye. Indeed, as it unfolds in recitation, the line "Beauty, of pitty, foulnesse only is" momentarily suggests that the "foulnesse" conjured in the proceeding octave is only the beauty of pity, that beauty may be found even in guiltless suffering. But is the soul addressed in the sonnet persuaded by the difficult and ambiguous application of reason? The question remains unanswered. The "Soule" never speaks in the first person, never indicates whether it is fully convinced of what the voice of the understanding is arguing. "I say to *thee*" suggests a divided mind, leaving conspicuously unresolved the question of how the rational faculty's saying is received by the entire soul. Unanimity is absent, and salvation hangs in the balance. The terror implicit in the opening line has actually enjoyed a crescendo by the end of the poem.

Consistently, in fact, Donne's "Holy Sonnets" demonstrate that "metaphysical wit" can actually be a staging of emotional exuberance inviting intimacy with readers and with God. Their most dizzying conceits contribute to the drama and celebrate the various emotional states achievable through religious meditation. Perhaps the best-known of these begins in the opening line of one of the sonnets first published in 1635, "I am a little world made cunningly / Of Elements, and an Angellike sprite." As intellectual historians have pointed out, the ancient Greek conception of the human being as microcosm of the world, composed of the four elements, earth, air, water, and fire, was commonplace in Renaissance humanism. The poem summarizes this philosophical doctrine, along with the notion that the balance or imbalance of the four elements in the body expresses health or disease. But it also does much more, communicating extreme remorse for sin by confounding the metaphor. To do so, Donne also relinquishes the ancient logic, evoking the cosmological discoveries of his time, addressing "you which beyond that heaven which was most high / Have found new sphears, and of new lands can write." And he completes the surrender of understanding with such effusions as "Powre new seas in mine eyes, that so I might / Drowne my world with weeping earnestly, / Or wash it, if it must be drowned no more." Such outlandish conceits are not the detached exercises of wit with which popular evaluations of Donne's poetry now associate him. They betray a passion, a "fierie zeale"—as Donne puts it in this very sonnet—that shatters logic and bends philosophy to its extravagant theatricality.

Insofar as it lays the sonneteer's passions bare, such theatricality has the power to disintegrate the boundaries that establish the self. The explicitly stated justification for this disintegration is that, as God's creature, the sonneteer does not own himself. "I am *thy* sonne, made with *thy* selfe to shine, / *Thy* servant, whose paines thou has still repaid, / *Thy* sheep, thine Image, and, till I betray'd / My selfe, a temple of *thy* Spirit divine," he remembers in the first sonnet of the 1633 series of twelve. Such is the condition of religious ecstasy and, in the secular world, of magnanimity. But there is a danger to the greatness of soul that fosters theatricality: the breaking of boundaries between the self and the other can cause the magnification of the self to the extent that the other is treated as a mere appendage or servant. If Donne's "Holy Sonnets" escape such danger, they do so ironically, by showing how easily the sonneteer could succumb to it. Hints of the sonneteer's vulnerability in this regard occur from the beginning of the 1633 series, when he complains, "Why doth the devill then usurpe in mee?/Why doth he steale, nay ravish, that's thy right?" and urges God to "rise and for thine owne worke fight," as if to suggest that, by virtue of their communion, God is more responsible to him than he is to God.

The most dramatic display of the dangers of self-magnification in the "Holy Sonnets" occurs

in the most theatrical of the poems—the tenth of the 1633 collection. In this sonnet God's creature makes himself the center of attention by casting himself as a prize to be fought over; his self-centeredness takes the form of fascination with that about him which is farthest from God—the flesh. Crucial to the irony is that this self-centeredness arises out of the sonneteer's very effort to overcome it:

> Batter my heart, three-person'd God, for you
> As yet but knocke, breathe, shine, and seeke to
>   mend;
> That I may rise, and stand, o'erthrow me, 'and
>   bend
> Your force, to break, blow, burn, and make me
>   new.
> I, like an usurp'd towne, to another due,
> Labour to'admit you, but Oh, to no end.
> Reason, your viceroy in mee, mee should defend,
> But is captiv'd, and proves weake or untrue.
> Yet dearly'I love you, and would be lov'd faine,
> But am betroth'd unto your enemie;
> Divorce mee,'untie, or break that knot againe.
> Take me to you, imprison me, for I
> Except you'enthrall mee, never shall be free,
> Nor ever chast, except you ravish mee.

Critics have sparred over the precise allusions implicit in "knocke; breath, shine, and seeke to mend" and "o'erthrow me, and bend / Your force to break, blow, burn, and make me new." A plausible suggestion is that the sonneteer is comparing himself to a lump of clay and the "three-person'd God" (the Trinity) to a potter called upon to "rethrow" an unmendable pot that has not withstood the test of a knock and cannot be mended or polished. Not only does this interpretation have biblical precedent, echoing God's words in Jeremiah 19:11—"Even so will I break this people and this City, as one breaketh a potter's vessel, that cannot be made again"—it also suggests a struggle with bodily desires, since the body is created, according to biblical tradition, of clay.

Yet in asking for God's help to negate his carnality, the sonneteer betrays all the more fascination with his carnal self. Ascetic self-denial becomes erotic self-assertion. According to this reading, what seems to be the expression of homoerotic desire in the poem should be accepted as such. True, as some critics insist, this expression can be bracketed as mere metaphor, secondary in importance to what it represents, the desire for salvation. But the carnality is too consistent with what the poem is about—a human soul trapped in flesh and groping for salvation from the carnal and the moribund—to be ignored. That the sonneteer's most desperate effort to divorce himself from carnal desire should threaten to embroil him in it all the more makes sense, insofar he is expressing the absence, not the presence, of the divine grace he seeks. Such a reading permits us to recognize the poem's obsessive focus on corporeal effects. It is not sufficient for the sonneteer to imagine God to "knocke"; he must imagine God to "knocke, breathe, shine." Nor is it sufficient for him to command God to "break" him; he must command God to "break, blow, burn." And then, as if to insist that the reader envision an act of rape in both senses of the word (seizing by force and penetrating sexually), he urges God to "enthrall" and "ravish" him. The sonneteer exhibits his want of salvation in his very expression of salvation: because he is not fully open to grace, he can only imagine communion with God in his own, fleshly terms. That does not mean he is utterly lost. If, in seeking to transcend the flesh, the sonneteer mires himself further in flesh, he also expresses the restlessness of a soul that *may* open itself to salvation, if the gift of grace arrives. As Donne puts it in his *Anatomy of the World,* "there is motion in corruption."

Like "Batter my heart," most of the "Holy Sonnets" may be read as stagings of a soul's struggle for salvation, not its winning of the struggle. If any of these nineteen poems adequately summarizes the variety of emotions involved in this struggle, it is "O to vex me, contraryes meete in one," from the Westmoreland manuscript, in which the sonneteer remarks, "As humorous is my contritione / As my

prophane love, and as soon forgott: / As riddlingly distemperd, cold and hott, / As praying, as mute, as infinite, as none . . . So my devout fitts come and go away / Like a fantastique Ague." The adjective "fantastique" calls to mind the substantive "fantastic," which in Donne's time referred to a wearer of extravagant garb who frequented the theater and called attention to himself—the consummate poseur. Are the holy sonnets exercises of self-indulgence by a diseased soul—narcissistic explorations of self rather than true expressions of worship? In this sonnet Donne encourages his readers to consider the possibility. But more generously the "Holy Sonnets" may be understood ironically, and therefore may be seen in an opposite light: as humble offerings of an imperfect self, in its various moods and thoughts, to others—theatrical suspensions of self-possession that implicitly recognize the true possession of the self as belonging to Creator rather than creature. "As due by many titles I resign myself to thee," says the sonneteer in the first of the sonnets in the 1633 edition. And whether the sonneteer does not entirely succeed in resigning himself to God through his sonnets, he may well succeed in making a gift of himself to others. Insofar as this struggle for salvation elicits empathy, the poems achieve what was almost certainly one of their original purposes, to foster compassion and intimacy among human readers.

INFLUENCE AND IMPORTANCE

Seventeenth-century devotional poets such as George Herbert, Robert Herrick, Richard Crashaw, Henry Vaughan, and Thomas Trahern benefited from the influence of Donne's religious verse. Herbert's family was well acquainted with Donne, and the other poets would have seen Donne's devotional poems among the seven printed editions of his verse that appeared during the seventeenth century. All were partial to "strong lines," and Herbert and Crashaw shared Donne's interest in devotional theatricality. Since the seventeenth century, however, the provable, direct influence of Donne's religious verse on devotional poets has been extremely limited. The eighteenth-century poet William Cowper felt his influence in a general way. Claiming Donne as a blood ancestor on his mother's side, he wrote, "There is in me, I believe, more of the Donne than of the Cowper." Gerard Manley Hopkins, the best-known devotional poet of the nineteenth century, favored the sonnet and wrote what might be called "strong lines." But Herbert and Vaughan's poems seem as likely as direct models for Hopkins' work, as do Donne's "Holy Sonnets." Like Donne, T. S. Eliot, who became a devotional poet after his conversion to Anglo-Catholicism in 1927, experiments with different voices, lending drama to his verse. Eliot also found seventeenth-century metaphysical poetry helpful to his own use of imagery, although, as his essays suggest, such inspiration came as much from the love poems as it did from the "Holy Sonnets."

Yet despite the limits of their direct influence on later devotional verse, the "Holy Sonnets" can still serve as important reminders of what devotional verse has to offer, even to a secular readers of literature. Literature itself, after all, is inextricably rooted in religion, and most poetry has always had religious resonances. This is not to say that literature always complements religion. Since the seventeenth century the two have more often competed than cooperated. But if literature can substitute for religion, any archaeology of literature will reveal religion as fundamental to it. There are, in fact, relics of religion in the language with which literature has been discussed in our time—from terminology that designates a writer as "creator," to formalist readings of poems as timeless domains of ecstasy invested not with meaning but with being, to postmodern efforts to reshape the "canon." By combining poetry with religious devotion, Donne's "Holy Sonnets" not only underscore the religious roots of literature; they also deny literature its autonomy as a sacred end in itself. They remember another, vital role for literature that, today, is all but forgotten: that of

entertainment in the literal sense of the word—of bringing readers together, either in communion or in community.

This accomplishment speaks to the concerns of postmodern theorists such as Roland Barthes and Michel Foucault about problems such as that of author worship, which limits the meanings of texts to the supposed intentions of a single, immortal "genius," whose figure is constructed out of bourgeois ideology, without regard to historical context. But the problem of author worship is nothing new. If we accept John Freccero's arguments, the fourteenth-century Petrarchan love sonnet already offered literary experience as a substitute for religious worship, transforming the poet into a Godlike creator of his own object of desire. Milton's *Paradise Lost* is fraught with apprehension over the resemblances between its author and its antihero, Satan. Such fears were certainly not unfounded. Shakespeare's First Folio (1623) and the first printed editions of Spenser's *Faerie Queene* (1596) and Jonson's *Workes* (1616) attest to the possibility of author worship in Donne's time.

At its best, perhaps, devotional poetry obstructs this idolatrous impulse with self-assertion that results in self-concession. In the course of rendering the "Holy Sonnets" acceptable as expressions of religious devotion rather than as idolatrous substitutes, the sonneteer's concessions of mastery suggest the possibility of a literary experience that largely avoids author worship. Their irony creates a perspective from which the mind the sonnets portray may be found wanting. But because the sonnets focus devotion on a higher power other than an omniscient author, the space opened by their irony leaves little room, behind the narrator, for such an author. The two persons who demand attention in these poems are not omniscient author and flawed persona but omnipotent God and flawed sonneteer. As devotional poems the "Holy Sonnets" offer the important opportunity for a literary reading that is not an exercise of devotion to an author.

This experience is important not only for the religiously inclined but also for those who seek what the reading of literature has to offer besides the agenda of deciphering an author's intentions. It is probably more precious today than it was in Donne's time, before the modern cult of authorship, well under way, had metastasized to every aspect of literary culture. Donne lived and wrote before literature was necessary to fill the void caused by the decline of religion. One result of this, perhaps, was that the topic of devotion had more currency as a serious literary enterprise than it does today. Another was that this topic did not amount to the only literary refuge from author worship. Poems in other modes also circulated as gifts, often without the names of authors attached to them, and often open to both alteration and reinterpretation. Today, however, Donne's devotional poetry invites readers not only to glimpse the conviviality of a seventeenth-century literary experience from afar but also to experience it.

Donne's "Holy Sonnets" are not alone in affording readers the opportunity to enjoy the clearing of the specter of authorship from literature. The same opportunity presents itself in devotional verses both by other seventeenth-century devotional poets and by more recent poets. This is not to say that all poetry labeled "devotional" shares with the "Holy Sonnets" the capacity to create such an experience. T. S. Eliot's devotional verse, undoubtedly some of the finest in the twentieth century, lacks the dramatic irony of Donne's; the persona it evokes is not as self-consciously flawed as that of the "Holy Sonnets." But the poetry of Gerard Manley Hopkins often does possess these attributes, celebrating the "inscape," the particularity and even oddity of an individual poetic voice as a creation by God, while at the same time achieving the concession of mastery encouraged by religious training. Whether or not through Donne's direct influence, Hopkins's poems bear a striking resemblance to Donne's "Holy Sonnets" in this respect. Though they rival any poetry of their time, the figure of the great author is not crucial to the experience of reading them, despite the distinctly personal prose and diction with which Hopkins invested them; the figure of the author once again yields to devotion to God. And it is interesting to note that though he lived over two hundred years after Donne, Hopkins appears to resemble Donne in his own treatment of his poems as personal gifts to be circulated in manuscripts among friends rather than printed monuments to an immortal author. Like Donne's "Holy Sonnets," most of Hopkins's poems were not published during his lifetime.

Could it be that the apologies by students of Donne's devotional verse reflect not narrowness of subject matter but a challenge to the image of the great author that is routinely conjured in the reading of literature? The activity of worship, after all, is no less broad, no less personal, no less complicated, than the activity of courtship (indeed, the one may include the other). Yet none would apologize for the narrowness of subject matter in Donne's love poetry. In staging a drama of self-assertion and self-concession, Donne's "Holy Sonnets" represent a wealth of human thought and emotion, open a window onto the early modern cultures in which Donne lived and wrote, and provide modern readers with what today might seem a new way of approaching literary texts.

Select Bibliography

EDITIONS

Poems, by J. D., with Elegies on the Authors Death. London, 1633.

Poems, by J.D., with Elegies on the Authors Death. London, 1635.

The Poems of John Donne. Edited by Herbert J. C. Grierson. 2 vols. Oxford: Oxford University Press, 1912.

The Complete Poetry and Selected Prose of John Donne. Edited by Charles M. Coffin. New York: Modern Library, 1952.

The Divine Poems. 2d ed. Edited by Helen Gardner. Oxford: Clarendon Press, 1978. This edition contains valuable information on the manuscripts of Donne's "Holy Sonnets".

CITED MANUSCRIPTS

Bodleian MS. Eng. Poet. 31. Contains "Death be not proud, thy hand gave not this blow," attributed to C. L. of B. (Countess Lucy of Bedford?). In this manuscript, the poem is titled "Elegie on the Lady Markham." Lady Markham died in 1609.

British Library Harleian MS. 4064. Contains "Death be not proud, thy hand gave not this blow," attributed to L. C. of B. (Lucy Countess of Bedford?). In this manuscript, the poem is again entitled "Elegy on the Lady Markham."

Newcastle manuscript (ca. 1630). British Library, Harleian MS. 4955.

O'Flahertie manuscript. Harvard MS. Eng 966.5. Contains "Death, I recant" conflated with "Death be not proud, thy hand gave not this blow" as one poem under the title "Elegie on Mris Boulstred" and attributed to Donne. This conflation is probably an error. But it does suggest that both poems may originally have appeared as Elegies on Cecelia Bulstrode, who also died in 1609 within months of Lady Markham's decease.

Westmoreland manuscript (ca. 1620). Berg Collection, New York Public Library

OTHER WORKS

Pseudo-Martyr. London, 1610.

Ignatius His Conclave. London, 1611.

Letters to Several Persons of Honour. London, 1651.

SECONDARY WORKS

Archer, Stanley. "Meditation and the Structure of Donne's Holy Sonnets." *English Literary History* 28 (1961): 137–147.

Bald, R[obert] C[ecil]. *John Donne: A Life.* Oxford: Oxford University Press, 1970.

Barthes, Roland. "The Death of the Author." In his *Image, Music, Text.* Edited and translated by Stephen Heath. New York: Hill, 1977.

Bedford, R. D. "The Potter-Clay Image." *Notes and Queries* 29 (1982): 15–19.

Beal, Peter, comp. *Index of English Literary Manuscripts.* Vol. 1. New York: Bowker, 1980. This index contains valuable information on the manuscripts of Donne's poetry, and on manuscript circulation in general.

Carey, John. *John Donne: Life, Mind and Art.* New York: Oxford University Press, 1981.

Eliot, T. S. "The Metaphysical Poets." In his *Selected Essays.* London: Faber & Faber, 1964.

Eliot, T. S. "Religion and Literature." In his *Essays Ancient and Modern.* London: Faber & Faber, 1936.

Evans, Gillian R. "John Donne and the Augustinian Paradox of Sin." *Review of English Studies* 33 (1982): 1–22.

Fausset, Hugh Ianson. *John Donne: A Study in Discord.* New York: Russell & Russell, 1967.

Foucault, Michel. "What Is an Author?" Translated by Donald F. Bouchard and Sherry Simon. In Foucault's *Language, Counter-Memory, Practice.* Edited by Donald F. Bouchard. Ithaca, N.Y.: Cornell University Press, 1977.

Freccero, John. "The Fig Tree and the Laurel: Petrarch's Poetics." In *Literary Theory/ Renaissance Texts.* Edited by Patricia Parker and Peter Quint. Baltimore: Johns Hopkins University Press, 1986.

Fumerton, Patricia. *Cultural Aesthetics: Renaissance Literature and the Practice of Social Ornament.* Chicago: University of Chicago Press, 1991. Contains an insightful discussion of the Elizabethan sonnet as miniature and gift, pp. 67–110.

Gosse, Edmund. *The Life and Letters of John Donne.* 2 vols. London: Dodd, Mead, 1899.

Hardy, Evelyn. *Donne: A Spirit in Conflict.* London. Constable, 1942.

Hopkins, Gerard Manley. *Poems.* Edited by W. H. Gardner and N. H. MacKenzie. 4th ed. London: Oxford University Press, 1970.

Johnson, Samuel. *The Lives of the English Poets.* Oxford: Clarendon Press, 1905.

King, James. *William Cowper: A Biography.* Durham, N.C.: Duke University Press, 1986.

Lewalski, Barbara K. *Protestant Poetics and the Seventeenth-Century Religious Lyric.* Princeton, N.J.: Princeton University Press, 1979.

Low, Anthony. *Love's Architecture: Devotional Modes in Seventeenth-Century English Poetry.* New York: New York University Press, 1978.

Marotti, Arthur. *John Donne, Coterie Poet.* Madison: University of Wisconsin Press, 1986.

Marotti, Arthur. *Manuscript, Print, and the English Renaissance Lyric.* Ithaca, N.Y.: Cornell University Press, 1995.

Martz, Louis L. *The Poetry of Meditation: A Study of English Religious Literature of the Seventeenth Century.* New Haven: Yale University Press, 1962.

Walton, Sir Izaak. *The Lives of John Donne, Sir Henry Wotton, Richard Hooker, George Herbert and Robert Sanderson.* London: Oxford University Press, 1927.

Young, R. V. *Doctrine and Devotion in Seventeenth Century Poetry: Studies in Donne, Herbert, Crashaw, and Vaughn.* Cambridge: D.S. Brewer, 2000.

Oscar Wilde's
The Importance of Being Earnest

SANDIE BYRNE

THE PLAYWRIGHT WAS born in Dublin on 16 October 1854 and christened Oscar Finghal O'Flahertie Wilde the following April. (He added the name "Wills", also used by his father, before "Wilde" as a young boy). Both his parents were writers. Lady Jane Wilde (née Jane Francesca Elgee) wrote articles and poems in support of the Young Ireland movement under the pen-name "Speranza" (Hope), and Sir William, a successful eye-surgeon, also wrote biographical, antiquarian, and topographic works. Their son showed great early promise as a scholar and studied Classics at both Trinity College, Dublin and Magdalen College, Oxford. He was already writing poetry as an undergraduate, and won the Newdigate Prize for his poem "Ravenna" while at Magdalen in 1878. In 1882 Wilde embarked on a lecture tour in the USA, allegedly replying to the Customs officials' standard question "Have you anything to declare?": "Only my genius." The tour was a great success, with Wilde, dressed in knee breeches and silk stockings, pontificating on aestheticism from platforms across the continent.

His first play, *Vera*, a melodrama, was performed in New York in 1883, but was not a success. For some time, Lady Wilde had been urging both Oscar and her younger son, Willie, to marry in order to improve their financial position, and Oscar finally proposed to Constance Lloyd, sister of a friend, in 1884. The Wildes had two sons, Cyril and Vyvyan. In 1888 he published a volume of stories written for them, *The Happy Prince and Other Stories,* and followed this in 1891 with a two further volumes of stories for an older audience, *Lord Arthur Savile's Crime and Other Stories,* and *The House of Pomegranates,* and his only novel, *The Picture of Dorian Gray,* which had appeared a year earlier in *Lippincott's Magazine.* The same productive year saw the publication of critical writing such as "The Decay of Lying" and "The Critic as Artist," published in *Intentions* (1891), and *The Soul of Man Under Socialism,* published in the *Fortnightly Review* (1891), but it was not until the following year that Wilde discovered the form with which he was to become indelibly associated, the comedy of manners that combines sparkling epigrams with astute social observations. A string of theatrical successes followed *Lady Windermere's Fan* (1892): *A Woman of No Importance* (1893), *An Ideal Husband*

(1895), and The Importance of Being Earnest (1895). The tragedy *Salomé*, which Wilde wrote in French, was refused a licence in Britain, but published in an English translation (known as *Salome*) by Lord Alfred Douglas illustrated by Aubrey Beardsley in 1894, and performed in Paris in 1896.

By then, Wilde had been imprisoned for homosexual offenses. Wilde was caught in the warfare between the petulant and demanding Alfred Douglas ("Bosie") and his boorish, aggressive, and litigious father, the Marquess of Queensberry. Queensberry demanded that Wilde cease to associate with his son and persecuted Wilde with public demonstrations and accusations—not, ultimately, of sodomy, but of posing as a sodomite, which was easier to prove. Bosie demanded that Wilde retaliate with a libel suit. The accusation of libel could not be upheld because, following the suborning and intimidation of various prostitutes and other ex-lovers, the accusation of sodomy could be proved. Wilde was arrested for acts of gross indecency and held in Holloway Prison to await trial. The law allowed any man found guilty of this offense to be sentenced to a term not exceeding two years, with or without hard labor. Wilde received the maximum sentence. Queensberry pressed for costs, and Wilde's effects were sold at auction to meet them. The sale failed to make the required sum, and for several years the estate was in deficit. Robert Ross, faithful friend and benefactor of Wilde for several years, eventually rescued it.

After his release in 1897, Wilde went to Dieppe and spent the rest of his life on the continent under the name "Sebastian Melmoth" (after the damned creature doomed to eternal wandering in Charles Maturin's Gothic romance, *Melmoth the Wanderer*). During his exile, he wrote *The Ballad of Reading Goal* (1898) about his prison experiences and twice published letters describing the cruelty to children of the British prison system. An expurgated version of a letter written to Lord

CHRONOLOGY

1854	Born in Dublin, Ireland, on 16 October.
1864	Sent to boarding school, Portora Royal School, Enniskillen.
1871	Goes to Trinity College, Dublin to read Classics.
1874	Awarded a First Class degree from Trinity. Goes up to Oxford to read Greats at Magdalen College.
1878	Wins the Newdigate Prize for Poetry. Awarded a First Class degree from Oxford.
1879	Moves to London.
1881	Publishes *Poems* (at own expense).
1882	Lecture tour to the USA.
1883	Visits Paris. First performance of Wilde's first play, *Vera*. Publishes *The Duchess of Padua,*
1884	Marries Constance Lloyd. Works as a book reviewer and editor.
1885	Birth of Cyril Wilde (5 June).
1886	Meets Robert Ross, who is to become a life-long friend, and who is said to have introduced Wilde to the practice of homosexuality. Birth of Vyvyan Wilde (3 November).
1890	Publication of *The Picture of Dorian Gray* in *Lippincott's Monthly Magazine* (USA).
1891	Publication of *Lord Arthur Savile's Crime and Other Stories, The House of Pomegranates, Intentions, The Soul of Man Under Socialism.*
1892	Becomes involved with Lord Alfred Douglas. First performance of *Lady Windermere's Fan. Salomé* banned by the Lord Chamberlain.
1893	First performance of *A Woman of No Importance*. French text of *Salomé* published in Paris.
1894	Publication of *Salomé* in English
1895	January: First performance of *An Ideal Husband*; February: First performance of *The Importance of Being Earnest.*

January and February: Wilde visits Algiers with Alfred Douglas. Accused of being a "posing somdomite" [sic] by the Marquess of Queensberry. Brings libel action against the Marquess. April–May: Three trials; Queensberry is acquitted, Wilde is arrested for indecency and imprisoned in Holloway pending trial. May: Wilde found guilty and sentenced to two years' imprisonment with hard labor.

1896   *Salomé* (French version) performed in Paris.

1897   May: Wilde released from prison, goes to Dieppe, then Italy. Publishes a letter in *The Daily Chronicle* complaining of the cruelty to children in British jails.

1898   Publication of *The Ballad of Reading Gaol* and of a second letter about prison conditions. Moves to Paris. Death of Constance Wilde (who has changed her name to Holland). Wilde is refused access to his sons.

1900   Wilde visits Rome. Returns to Paris where he falls ill. 30 November: received into the Catholic Church, dies. Buried at Bagneux on 3 December.

Alfred Douglas from prison, in which Wilde reproaches Douglas and defends himself and his position on art and aesthetic hedonism, was published in 1905 as *De Profundis*. He was reconciled with Douglas in August of 1897.

Bankrupt and deserted by many of his friends, Wilde died at the Hôtel d'Alsace, rue des Beaux-Arts, Paris, on 30 November 1900. He was buried in Bagneux on 3 December. In 1909 his body was moved to the cemetery of Père Lachaise in Paris, and a monument by Jacob Epstein was erected over it.

THE IMPORTANCE OF BEING EARNEST: TEXT

Although Wilde liked to give the impression that he both spoke and wrote in spontaneously produced perfect sentences and paragraphs, he drafted and revised his plays extensively. Wilde outlined the plot of the play that was to become *The Importance of Being Earnest* in a letter to its eventual director and male co-lead George Alexander in July 1894. The plan is recognizable as *Earnest* in embryo. The original of Algernon Moncrieff is Lord Alfred Rufford, and of Jack Worthing Bertram Ashton. Bertram's fictitious younger brother and name-about-town is George. Lady Bracknell here is the Duchess of Selby, and Gwendolen is Lady Maud Rufford. Rufford's ward, Cecily in *Earnest*, is Mabel, but her governess is already Miss Prism, for whom Wilde reminds himself to procure "the local doctor or clergyman." The plot roughly follows the lines of *Earnest*, but the early draft seems to make more significant oppositions of town versus country life and respectable versus unrespectable behavior.

> Mabel breaks off the match on the ground that there is nothing to reform in George: she only consented to marry him because she thought he was bad and wanted guidance. He promises to be a bad husband—so as to give her an opportunity of making him a better man; she is a little mollified.
>
> Enter guardian: he is reproached also by Lady Maud for his respectable life in the country: a JP: a county-councillor: a churchwarden: a philanthropist: a good example. He appeals to his life in London: she is mollified, on condition that he never lives in the country: the country is demoralising; it makes you respectable. 'The simple fare at the Savoy: the quiet life in Piccadilly: the solitude of Mayfair is what you need etc'.
> (*The Complete Letters of Oscar Wilde*, pp. 595–596)

The play was drafted during August 1894, and put through many more revisions during the autumn. Initially Alexander turned down the play, but the failure of Henry James's *Guy Domville* left a gap in the schedule of the St James's Theatre which *Earnest* conveniently filled. Even after accepting the play, Alexander insisted upon changes, as he had for *Lady Windermere's Fan*. Wilde's earlier version, already much revised and streamlined, had four acts, which Alexander insisted be reduced to three, the usual structure of a farce. This led to the excision of an episode which has since become famous. Jack and Algy are at Jack's house in Hertfordshire when Gribsby, a lawyer, arrives with a writ against "Mr Ernest Worthing" for unpaid bills from the Savoy (a famous London hotel and restaurant) of £762.14/2d (about $1000, an incredible sum for the time). Gribsby threatens to haul "Ernest Worthing" off to prison, and since both Jack and Algy have assumed this name (Jack when he is in town and Algy, recently, in the country), there is confusion about who is culpable and who, if anyone, should own up. Finally, Jack magnanimously agrees to pay the debt, ostensibly for his wicked brother Ernest. The character of Gribsby added to the play's theme of doubles and deceit, since the business card he presents is of the firm Parker and Gribsby, Solicitors, but he confesses to being both halves of the partnership: "Gribsby when I am on unpleasant business, and Parker on occasions of a less severe kind" (p. 351).

During the process of revision, much conventional comic stage "business" was eradicated from *Earnest,* including a long speech in which Jack eulogizes the handbag as a convenient vehicle for babies, an argument over sherry between Jack and Algy, and some whispering between Algy and Cecily which is passed off to Lady Bracknell as an echo. The characterization was also sharpened during revision; the young women become more than just ingenue and blue-stocking, while the young men become less cynical and greedy and more optimistic about their prospective marriages (Eltis, pp. 175–195). The original of Lady Bracknell, Lady Brancaster, lacked the majesty of her descendant and in her well-meant domineering and determination to secure financial advantage for her children resembles more closely Lady Britomart, wife of Andrew Undershaft in George Bernard Shaw's *Major Barbara.*

The text of the play was not published until after Wilde's trial and imprisonment, when, bankrupt, he needed to glean as much money as possible from his writings. Having sent to the St James's Theatre for Alexander's acting copy, Wilde revised the play for publication in 1899, uncharacteristically limiting his stage directions and character notes. Other versions of the play had survived, however, so the text is not entirely fixed.

Quotations from the play are taken from the Penguin edition of The Importance of Being Earnest *and Other Plays* (London, 1987).

FIRST PERFORMANCES AND EARLY RECEPTION

The Importance of Being Earnest: A Trivial Play for Serious People, to give the play its full title, had been designed for the Criterion Theatre, then run by Charles Wyndham, but was first staged at the St James's Theatre in London on 14 February 1895, where *Lady Windermere's Fan* had enjoyed a successful run from February to July of 1892. George Alexander took the role of Jack, while Algy was played by Allen Aynesworth, Lady Bracknell by Rose Leclerq, Gwendolen by Irene Vanbrugh, and Cecily by Evelyn Millard. The Reverend Canon Chasuble was played by H.H. Vincent and Miss Prism by an actress styled (as was conventional for a married woman at the time) Mrs. George Canninge. The two servants, Lane and Merriman were played by F. Kinsey Peile and Frank Dyall.

The first performance was under police protection. The Marquess of Queensberry had been hounding Wilde for some time, demanding that Wilde cease to associate with his son, Lord Alfred Douglas (Bosie). Wilde learned that Queensberry planned to denounce him from the auditorium, and wrote to R.V. Shone, manager of the St. James's Theatre, to cancel Queensberry's ticket. He also called in the constabulary. Wilde wrote to Bosie a few days later:

Yes; the Scarlet Marquis [Queensberry] made a plot to address the audience on the first night of my play! Algy Bourke [The Honourable Algernon Henry Bourke] revealed it, and he was not allowed to enter.

He left a grotesque bouquet of vegetables for me! This of course makes his conduct idiotic, robs it of dignity.

He arrived with a prize-fighter!! I had all Scotland Yard—twenty police—to guard the theatre. He prowled about for three hours, then left chattering like a monstrous ape.

(*Complete Letters*, p. 632)

The police who had guarded Wilde's opening night were soon to arrest him, and judicial proceedings were also to close the play, when Wilde's trial and imprisonment in 1895 ended the performances of *Earnest* in both London and New York.

The venue for the London premiere of *Earnest*, the highly fashionable St James's, and its producer, the commercially minded Alexander, ensured that the play would be received as a fashionable and frivolous crowd-pleaser. This was an expectation which Wilde did not always attempt to correct, in a letter to Arthur Humphreys describing the play as "written by a butterfly for butterflies" (*Complete Letters*, p. 630).

The initial reception of the play largely followed the tone set by its author. Wilde was accused of a lack of originality, of writing for the market, and thus simply adopting and slightly adapting the forms and conventions of popular theater: "in the age of Ibsen and of Hauptmann, of Strindberg and Brieux, he was content to construct like Sardou and think like Dumas fils" (1969, pp. 70–71). Victorien Sardou was the author of many light comedies and historical melodramas, and Alexandre Dumas, son of the novelist, was one of the originators of the nineteenth-century comedy of manners and the author of skilfully constructed plays of social criticism. Wilde is therefore being accused of a lack of seriousness and a failure to produce innovatory or experimental forms. Kerry Powell in *Oscar Wilde and the Theatre of the 1890s*

concurs, finding that Wilde never escaped from the influence of his theatrical predecessors. Regenia Gagnier argues that the flippant dialogue and the luxurious sets dilute the critique of society's hypocrisy and superficiality, while the happy endings undermine any uncomfortable implications (Aldershot, chapter 3). Powell too finds a conflict between Wilde's desire to produce social critique and his desire for popularity, seeing the influence of earlier playwrights as evidence of Wilde's dependence on the tried and tested formulae of commercial theater. (*Oscar Wilde and the Theatre of the 1890s*, pp. 4–13). Norbert Kohl, in his *Oscar Wilde: The Works of a Conformist Rebel*, suggests that Wilde was a "conformist rebel"; too much the detached lofty observer to be a social reformer, and lacking the courage to commit himself (p. 254). Sos Eltis, however, declares Wilde a radical; an anarchist, socialist, and feminist. In her *Revising Oscar Wilde*, Eltis justifies Wilde's own estimation of his plays "as genuinely innovative, challenging rather than reproducing the conventions of the popular nineteenth-century dramas on which they were modelled" and links "the radical Wilde who attacked Victorian society in 'The Soul of Man Under Socialism', mocked moral seriousness in 'The Decay of Lying', and outraged conventional sexual and social codes in *The Picture of Dorian Gray*, with Wilde the playwright, the reputedly careless craftsman"(p. 4). Eltis finds *Earnest* "as deceptive as its predecessors; its nonsensical frivolity was the camouflage for Wilde's most subversive and satirical work" (p. 171).

Replying to a letter from the artist Philip Houghton, Wilde admitted that to the world "I seem, by intention on my part, a dilettante and dandy merely," for "as seriousness of manner is the disguise of the fool, folly in its exquisite modes of triviality and indifference and lack of care is the robe of the wise man." Significantly, he adds: "In so vulgar an age as this we all need masks" (*Complete Letters*, p. 586). When Robert Ross asked Wilde what kind of play he should expect, Wilde replied: "It is exquisitely trivial, a delicate bubble of fancy." Its philosophy was that "we should treat all the trivial things of life very seriously and all the serious things with sincere and studied triviality" (Mikhail, p. 250).

The mask worked perhaps too well. Contemporary reviewers saw little beyond the farce, the triviality, and the nonsensicality. A.B. Walkley found that the play excited laughter, "absolutely free from bitter afterthought" (*Spectator*, 23 February 1895). Even George Bernard Shaw failed to find depth in *Earnest:* "It amused me, of course; but unless comedy touches me as well as amuses me, it leaves me with a sense of having wasted my evening. I go to the theatre to be moved to laughter, not to be tickled or bustled into it" (*Saturday Review 79*, 23 February 1895, p. 250).

Earnest was Wilde's fourth "society" play and was therefore received by audiences with a set of expectations about the style and content. Russell Jackson, in his essay on *Earnest* in *The Cambridge Companion to Oscar Wilde*, suggests that the play seems like an excursion into less demanding territory; it lacks the serious plot devices and grandiloquent speeches of the other society plays (p. 165), and to an audience familiar with *An Ideal Husband, Lady Windermere's Fan,* and *A Woman of No Importance,* would seem to have some surprising omissions and deviations from the usual repertoire. The first omission is of a "woman with a past" (such as Mrs Erlynne or Mrs Cheveley); "in fact the past in this play has become a benign rather than a menacing secret, with the handbag concealing not a 'social indiscretion' but an absurd mistake. Female culpability (a mainspring even of the 'advanced' serious drama of the time) is limited to absent-mindedness" (p. 166). Richard Allen Cave, however, suggests that Lady Bracknell has a past: like everyone else she has a double life and a secret to conceal; hers is that she is an arriviste, a woman who was not born into the upper echelon of society but married into it. (Raby, *Cambridge Companion,* p. 217). The second missing person is the dandyish aristocrat (such

as Lord Darlington otherwise Lord Goring). Jack and Algernon are dandies in that they are men of leisure seemingly little interested in serious subjects and much interested in their appearance, but neither of them is aristocratic or instrumental in developing the complexities of the plot. On the whole, they are people to whom things happen rather than agents who determine what happens. The third type missing from *Earnest* is the innocent and idealistic young woman (like Hester Worsley, Lady Windermere, and Lady Chiltern); "the new play transforms this type, in this instance by making idealism consist in wanting to marry a man called Ernest, and self-righteous indignation is briefly mocked when the two girls declare that they have been deceived" (p. 166).

Jackson finds that the self-conscious decadence of *Salomé, The Picture of Dorian Gray,* and the first version of An Ideal Husband is also missing from *Earnest,* yet a contemporary skit on the play in *Punch* parodies the form which the author (Ada Leverson) presumably found because she expected to find it. A conversion between Algy, Aunt Augusta, and Dorian (described as "a button-hole") over tea and cucumber sandwiches contains many of the elements of decadent writing: hedonism, the exotic, the foreign, the sensual, self-absorption.

> ALGY, *eating cucumber sandwiches*: Do you know, Aunt Augusta, I am afraid I shall not be able to come to your dinner to-night, after all. My friend Bunbury has had a relapse, and my place is by his side.
> AUNT AUGUSTA: *drinking tea*: Really, Algy! It will put my table out dreadfully. And who will arrange my music?
> DORIAN: *I* will arrange your music, Aunt Augusta. I know all about music. I have an extraordinary collection of musical instruments. I give curious concerts every Wednesday in a long latticed room, where wild gypsies tear mad music from little zithers, and I have brown algerians who beat

monotonously upon copper drums. Besides, I have set myself to music. And it has not marred me. I am still the same. More so, if anything.

(*Punch*, 2 March 1895, p. 107, quoted in Jackson, *"The Importance of Being Earnest"* in Raby, ed., *Cambridge Companion*, p. 167)

GENRE

So significant has *Earnest* become, and so much an archetype of English stage comedy, that a photograph of a scene from the play illustrates the cover of Alexander Leggatt's *English Stage Comedy 1490–1990*. The plot of the play, with its implausible and outrageous incidents and coincidences, clearly puts it in the category of farce, a genre made highly popular in the Victorian theater by playwrights such as W.S. Gilbert (*Engaged,* 1877), Arthur Wing Pinero (*The Magistrate,* 1885; *The Schoolmistress,* 1886; *Dandy Dick,* 1887), and Brandon Thomas (*Charley's Aunt,* 1892). The humor of these plays depended upon the horror felt by middle-class characters (such as clergymen, governesses and magistrates) at the possibility of losing their respectability through ill luck, or of being compromised by a dire secret discovered by another character, and these plays tended to end on an up-beat note, with good names and order restored. *Earnest* subverts the established conventions of farce by moving the *dramatis personae* up a social notch to the gentry and aristocracy, and by refusing to provide a moral order of a solidly respectable society which can be re-established after the carnival of the farce is played out. In addition to mocking such staples of farce as the mistaken identity, the foundling, the reunited family, and the wronged and restored hero[ine], in *Earnest* Wilde also mocks staples of melodrama and sentimental drama such as the grieving sibling (Jack enters in deepest mourning to announce the "death" of his nonexistent brother, only to discover him incarnated in Algy's adoption of the persona of Ernest) and bereaved parent (Lady Bracknell,

representing the family which has lost the baby Algy/Ernest, is utterly prosaic). Since melodrama and sentimental drama only exaggerated and reinforced accepted behavior, which was, as Anne Varty points out, elaborately codified, Wilde was also mocking socially prescribed behavior prompted by etiquette rather than conviction.

Wilde does not scruple to parody even his own work, as when in embracing his supposedly "fallen" (because unmarried) supposed "mother," Miss Prism, Algy is prepared to forgive her. While he does not deny that this is "a serious blow," Algy reflects: "But after all, who has the right to cast a stone against one who has suffered? Cannot repentance wipe out an act of folly? Why should there be one law for men, and another for women?" and finally declares, melodramatically and fatuously: "Mother, I forgive you." This, as Varty says, is a trivializing version of Hester's moralising speech in *A Woman of No Importance* (*Preface*, p. 202).

The mockery even extends to the sacreligious. Cecily remarks of the men: "They have been eating muffins. That looks like repentance" (act III, p. 300), and Jack and Algy treat the subject of spiritual rebirth with superficiality, yet pursue baptism (as Ernest) energetically. The parody of crime and punishment in this version looks proleptic, as "Ernest Worthing" [a.k.a. Algy] is threatened with being "imprisoned in the suburbs [as Wilde was initially in Holloway] for dining [amongst other things] in the West End." (p. 350).

Censorship of farce was lax compared to the scrutiny accorded other drama, and Wilde exploited that leniency to slip some pointed social critique under the censor's eye. Although *Earnest* is a farce, it is not knockabout or slapstick; its humor is verbal rather than visual, and there is little exaggerated or violent action. As Jackson notes, the heaping of lumps of sugar in a teacup and the aggressive slicing of cake are the most violent actions in the play. The stylization of action and dialogue with mirroring and repetition resembles opera or dance. To a late Victorian audience, this and other aspects of Wilde's style precluded the play's being taken seriously. *The Daily Graphic* called it "midsummer madness" (15 February 1895, p. 7). George Bernard Shaw reported that it had amused him, "but unless comedy touches me as well as amuses me, it leaves me with a sense of having wasted my evening" (*Saturday Review* 79, 23 February 1895, p. 250). Jackson finds that *Earnest* approaches the condition of opera, and that by

> transforming the late-Victorian farce into something resembling *Così fan tutte* —Wilde was on dangerous ground. The self-conscious artificiality of the play [...] was a quality not readily associated with seriousness of purpose in the Victorian theatre. There sincerity, not style, was held to be the guarantor of purposeful laughter.
>
> (Raby, *Cambridge Companion to Oscar Wilde*, p. 171)

To many twenty-first-century readers, however, stylish aphorisms and neat epigrams are the quintessence of Wilde and our chief reason for cherishing *Earnest*, together with the delightful flights of fancy its characters take in leaps of illogic. From act I: "if the lower orders don't set us a good example, what on earth is the use of them?" (p. 254); "Divorces are made in Heaven" (p. 255); "The truth is rarely pure and never simple" (p. 259), From act II: "All women become like their mothers. That is their tragedy. No man does. That's his" (p. 270); "It is awfully hard work doing nothing. However, I don't mind hard work when there is no definite object of any kind" (p. 271). From act III: "Never speak disrespectfully of Society, Algernon. Only people who can't get into it do that."

Earnest is not a naturalistic play in which the proscenium arch disappears and we enjoy the comfortable illusion that Life is unfolding before us. Wilde reminds us that we are looking at artifice, fiction. He mocks the convention that insists, in fiction, upon distribution of reward and punishment according to deserts, however remote this equable resolution from the exigencies of real life, by having Miss Prism describe the ending of her lost novel: "The good ended happily, and the bad unhappily. That is what Fiction means" (act II, p. 275).

In some senses *Earnest* is in the tradition of Menander's New Comedy. That is, it follows Menander's move away from the daring personal and political satire of Aristophanes to more general satire of everyday life and recognizable character types. Just as Menander's characters spoke in the colloquial style of fourth-century B.C. Athens, and concerned themselves not with the great myths or the past, but with the everyday affairs of Athenians, so *Earnest* targets not politicians or literary rivals but society and social codes. For all its apparent superficiality, sparkle and self-proclaimed triviality, the play is, however, more than a trivial comedy. As Eltis says:

> *Earnest* is allowed a place apart from Wilde's other dramas, free from the melodrama or inconsistency which marred its predecessors. Yet *The Importance of Being Earnest* had much in common with Wilde's other plays; like them, it simultaneously mimicked and subverted the conventions of a popular theatrical genre, and, like them, it hid a more radical play beneath a smoothly reassuring surface.
>
> (*Revising Wilde*, p. 175)

PLOT AND STRUCTURE

The plot of the play uses a familiar formula, the foundling child whose true identity is revealed as the culmination of a courtship-ordeal (a formula used in plays from Sophocles' *Oedipus Rex* to Shakespeare's *The Winter's Tale* and beyond). Two dandies, John Worthing (Jack) and Algernon Moncrieff (Algy) are courting Gwendolen Fairfax and Cecily Cardew. Each man has an alter ego: Jack takes the name "Ernest" when he is in town (i.e. London), where he goes ostensibly to visit his brother. Algy ostensibly visits his ailing friend Bunbury (a name whose source may have been an early friend of Wilde's, Henry S. Bunbury) when he wants to get away from his family in town and visit the country. Gwendolen has sworn that she will marry a man called Ernest, so Jack, as Ernest, proposes to Algy's cousin, Gwendolen. Meanwhile, Algy takes advantage of Jack's absence to borrow his alter ego and to propose to Jack's ward, Cecily, who has been writing in her diary about an imaginary affair with Ernest Worthing. Two women are determined to marry a man called Ernest and two men are masquerading as Ernest; except they're not; one really is called Ernest, and one soon will be; one pretends to be the younger brother of the other, and is, as the ludicrous and hilarious twists of the plot farcically make clear. Thus Wilde's fictitious life imitates his characters' equally fictitious art. The characters determine their own identity and their own destiny. To fantasize about something (a fiancé called Ernest, for example) is to have the wish come true. That, as Miss Prism might say, is drama.

The thin and hackneyed plot's conventionality is essential to the play's point. The lost child restored to its rightful position and the star-crossed lovers united at the final curtain belong to the sentimental melodrama of the era from which audiences would expect upset and resolution not only in the fortunes of the protagonists but also in the moral universe of the play. The melodrama might show moral reverses, and evil in the ascendant, in the form of the evil landlord/suitor/usurper turning out the orphan/virtuous girl/true heir into the street/storm/obscurity, but order was always restored at the final curtain and the moral code upheld throughout the play by the orphan's saintly resignation, the heroine's defence of her virtue, and the true heir's dependence on Right and the Law. Wilde's conventional denouements, with couples handfast, adultery or murder averted, and forgiveness all round, would seem to belong to and reinforce the moral order of bourgeois, Anglican, conventional English society, but all the way through the plays, the values of that society are ridiculed, satirized, and subverted. Just as *An Ideal Husband* practically denounces marriage as a hypocritical farce, yet ends on unions promised or strengthened, so *The Importance of Being Earnest* subverts gender relations and courtship, family relations, and the notion of being "well born," yet ends on a note of "Jack shall have Jill, nought shall go ill." The satire of the epigrammatic exchanges is made doubly effective by the irony of the conventional happy endings. Thus Wilde manages to produce plays which are both funnier than much contemporary comedy and more effective as social critique than contemporary problem plays.

Christopher Innes demonstrates Wilde's technique of moral subversion in *Modern British Drama 1980–1990*: "Platitudes are exposed by using clichés to express a very basic human reality, which they generally deny; and the subtext reinforces the explicit challenge of the dialogue" (p. 218). The example he cites is from *A Woman of No Importance*:

LORD ILLINGWORTH: The Book of Life
    begins with a man and a woman in a garden.
MRS ALLONBY: It ends with Revelations.

Innes goes on to note that *Lady Windermere's Fan* is subtitled "A Play About a Good Woman," in which he finds "an ironic emphasis on the word 'Good.' The plot suggests that obeying virtuous dictates leads to unethical behaviour, which distorts the personality" (p. 218). The distinction between characters who are good and characters who obey virtuous dictates or moral codes is important for any reading of Wilde. Where a conventional play might end on a villainous character's unmasking as a fraud or a reformed character's begging forgiveness for a past deception, the final scene of *Earnest* has Jack asking Gwendolen's forgiveness for (as it turns out) not having been deceitful. He says that "it is a terrible thing for a man to find out suddenly that all his life he has been speaking nothing but the truth". Gwendolen replies that she can forgive him "for I feel that you are sure to change" (act III, p. 313).

In *The Theatrical World of 1895,* William Archer asked plaintively: "What can a poor critic do with a play which raises no principle, whether of art or morals, creates its own canons and conventions, and is nothing but an absolutely wilful expression of an irrepressibly witty personality? [*Earnest*] represents nothing, means nothing, is nothing except a sort of rondo capriccioso, in which the artist's fingers run with crisp irresponsibility up and down the keyboard of life. Why attempt to analyse...such an iridescent filament of fantasy?" (p. 57) This accords with Anne Varty's assertion that *Earnest* "triumphantly defies utilitarian values in a utilitarian age" (p. 205). Yet *The Importance of Being Earnest* is in fact a lesson in morality. The ludicrous speeches of characters such as Lady Bracknell and the young women are parodies of the high-minded soliloquies expected of the protagonists of serious drama and even of comedies which took themselves seriously. If "being earnest" means both "being truthful and taking things seriously" and "having the name 'Ernest,'" then the play is about being and seeming; being labelled earnest just as one can be "labelled" (baptized or known as) Ernest. Earnestness was a quality much admired in Victorian society, as Innes shows in his citation of a collection of essays from 1860, *Men Who Were Earnest,* which celebrated the lives of "evangelical and non-conformist worthies" (p. 221). Neither Jack nor Algernon is "really" earnest or Ernest, and the fact that they can both become Ernest, one by a late baptism and one by reverting to an identity lost in infancy, suggests that their being seen as or deemed earnest is as much a matter of appearance and acceptance as their being deemed Ernest, that is, a matter of hypocrisy. To have a Name, of course, is more than just to be called (e.g.) "Ernest" or "Algy" or "Jack." One's (good) name is one's reputation, and much reference is made in Victorian and other literary texts to "the family Name." All of these meanings are involved in the play. Gwendolyn and Cecily have decided to marry a man with the name 'Ernest,' Gwen-dolyn because of the word's association with ideals; Lady Bracknell (whose name many derive from the location of a house owned by Lady Queensberry, mother of Bosie) does not wish for a marriage which would devalue the family name through alliance with a nameless man; Jack endows his fictitious younger brother with the name "Ernest" in order to escape rural sobriety and social responsibility in the wicked city; Algy adopts the name "Ernest" in order to introduce himself to a girl.

Although both Jack and Algy adopt fictive personae and tell a number of lies, they also expose, even in their duplicity, other characters' hypocrisy. The conventional moral code is represented by the appalling, bullying, self-righteous Lady Bracknell and the governess Miss Prism, who would appear to be the embodiment of maidenly virtue. Lady Bracknell requires no proof of Jack's integrity once he is discovered to be well-born, and a relation, and Miss Prism has not only carelessly lost a baby in her charge, but singularly failed to do anything about recovering it. Algernon, on the other hand, is curiously punctilious about the etiquette of disguise, and invents preposterous crimes, since, as Cecily says, "pretending to be wicked and being really good all the time... would be hypocrisy" (act II, p. 277)—a nursery-muddle version of morality, but much more endearing than Lady Bracknell's.

Anne Varty describes this as Wilde's exposure of "the moral bankruptcy of the rules governing Society" (*A Preface to Oscar Wilde,* London, 1998, p. 196). Rather than caricaturing recognizable individuals, Wilde "caricatures the rules of social etiquette by depicting characters so harnessed by the inflexibility of the system that their attempts both to fulfil the requirements of propriety and to depart from them result in deception ('Bunburying'), self-deception (Cecily and her diary), tyranny (Lady Bracknell), and aggression (Cecily and Gwendolen at tea)." Lady Bracknell is the embodiment of the inflexible rules of society, adherence to which was necessary for inclusion. Lady Bracknell's magisterial pronouncements are delivered as if *ex cathedra*; she expects to be taken as the absolute arbiter of social correctness, which has little to do with morality. Her statements, like those of the two girls, are masterpieces of *reductio ad absurdem*; she denounces modern laxity in the matter of birth and breeding, only to show that her motives are mercenary and snobbish. Similarly, Gwendolen, having observed that we live in an age of ideals, immediately reduces those ideals to marrying a man called Ernest.

"Bunburying" is a cozy term for a double life, of course, and we should suspect that Algy and Jack will continue to be confirmed Bunburyists even after their respective marriages. Given the interchangeableness of the characters, it is hard to avoid the idea that their Bunburying adventures, if sexual, will be with other young men, and hard not to extrapolate from there to the double life of their creator, the husband and father yet also homosexual Wilde. Wilde himself is parodied as "Bunthorne" in Gilbert and Sullivan's comic opera *Patience, or Bunthorne's Bride*, which was performed four years before *The Importance of Being Earnest*. Bunthorne, a rather loathsome fake poet, is a suitor to the opera's heroine and a pseudo-aesthete:

> Though the Philistines may jostle, you will rank
>   as an apostle in the high aesthetic band
> If you walk down Piccadilly with a poppy or a
>   lily
>   In your medieval hand.
>
> (*The Complete Annotated Gilbert and Sullivan*,
> edited by Ian Bradley, Oxford, 1996, p. 293)

Wilde may have coined "Bunbury[ing]" as a riposte to Gilbert and Sullivan, especially as he has Jack and Algy sing "some dreadful popular air from a British Opera" to cover embarrassment at several stages of the play. Wilde was not discomposed by the parody, but played up to it, and acted as an advance publicity agent for the operetta in the USA. Innes finds congruence between the comic devices employed by operettas such as *Patience* and those employed by

Wilde, but whereas "Gilbert uses inversion to produce comic incongruity—which requires a strong sense of normal values if the humour is to be appreciated, and so reinforces conventional standards," Wilde "creates an identity of opposites" (p. 221).

Wilde's inversion of significance, shown in his inversion of moral aphorisms, makes us consider afresh what is important and what is trivial, rather than simply accept these values as givens. Conventional morality is shown to be only skin-deep, so another skin-deep virtue is put in its place—beauty. Beauty of language is more important than truth, and beauty of form (face, dress, speech) more important than character. Gwendolyn asks Cecily if she believes Algy. The answer is: "I don't. But that does not affect the wonderful beauty of his answer," to which Gwendolen replies: "True. In matters of grave importance, style, not sincerity is the vital thing" (act III, p. 301). Declan Kibberd shows that characters in *Earnest* produce poetry when they are telling lies, as when Algy, speaking of the recently widowed Lady Harbury, says: "I hear her hair has turned quite gold with grief," (act I, p. 261) which is not only alliterative, but iambic pentameter. Eltis calls the dialogue of *Earnest* "gymnastic" (p. 198), and we can but admire its flexibility as it twists and turns evasively to transform near-disaster (the revelation of truth) into fresh fantasy and disaster averted. Characters seize on irrelevancies and take off at tangents, failing to pursue the essential, and deceptive, point.

> JACK: But you don't really mean to say that you
>   couldn't love me if my name wasn't Ernest?
> GWENDOLEN: But your name is Ernest.
> JACK: Yes, I know it is. But supposing it was
>   something else?
>   [...]
> GWENDOLEN [*glibly*]: Ah! that is clearly a
>   metaphysical speculation
>   [...]
> JACK: Personally, darling, to speak quite
>   candidly, I don't much care about the name of

Ernest ... I don't think the name suits me at all [...] I must say that I think there are lots of other much nicer names. I think Jack, for instance, a charming name.

GWENDOLEN: Jack? ... No, there is very little music in the name Jack [...] The only really safe name is Ernest.

JACK: Gwendolen, I must get christened at once—I mean we must get married at once.

(act II, p. 264)

[Jack has entered in deepest mourning for the death of his "brother Ernest," while Algy in the character of Ernest is with Cecily.]

CECILY: Your brother Ernest. He arrived about half an hour ago.

JACK: What nonsense! I haven't got a brother.

CECILY: Oh, don't say that. However badly he may have behaved to you in the past he is still your brother [...] I'll tell him to come out [...]

CHASUBLE: These are very joyful tidings.

MISS PRISM: After we had all been resigned to his loss, his sudden return seems to me peculiarly distressing.

(act II, p. 282)

From act III:

LADY BRACKNELL: May I ask if it is in this house that your invalid friend Mr Bunbury resides?

ALGERNON [*stammering*]: Oh! No! Bunbury doesn't live here. Bunbury is somewhere else at present. In fact, Bunbury is dead.

LADY BRACKNELL: Dead! When did Mr Bunbury die? His death must have been extremely sudden.

ALGERNON [*airily*]: Oh! I killed Bunbury this afternoon. I mean poor Bunbury died this afternoon.

LADY BRACKNELL: What did he die of?

ALGERNON: Bunbury? Oh, he was quite exploded.

LADY BRACKNELL: Exploded! Was he the victim of a revolutionary outrage? I was not aware that Mr Bunbury was interested in social

legislation. If so, he is well punished for his morbidity.

(act III, pp. 302–303)

As Leggatt remarks: "It is impossible to keep a normal sense of proportion when the disgrace of being bred in a handbag is equated to one of the cataclysmic events of European history, and that event in turn is dismissed as 'unfortunate'" (Leggatt, act I, p. 33). The inversion of values is not left entirely to the dandies. It is Lady Bracknell who makes this startling comparison, and Miss Prism who tacitly equates a baby with the manuscript of a novel, and who dispassionately catalogues the handbag's identifying blemishes without concern for the cataclysms which caused them: "here is the injury it received through the upsetting of a Gower Street omnibus [...] Here is the stain on the lining caused by the explosion of a temperance beverage, an incident that occurred at Leamington [...] It has been a great inconvenience being without it all these years" (act III, p. 311).

George Bernard Shaw found *Earnest* a heartless play (*Saturday Review,* 23 February 1895). The parallel pairs of characters are not precisely heartless, though we might assume that their attachments to are more a matter of form than passion. They are, however, value-less, or rather they lack the conventional hierarchy of values, and they are quite ruthless in the pursuit of (usually trivial) gratifications (marriage to an Ernest, cucumber sandwiches, the last muffin). Jack cheerfully arranges his christening with less ceremony than he would a morning call. They produce characteristic Wildean aphorisms which depend upon the inversion of the accepted morality. They take the pleasures of food, drink, and dress as though hedonism were a religion or philosophy: "And speaking of the science of Life, have you got the cucumber sandwiches cut for Lady Bracknell?" (act I, p. 253)

Oral pleasure is an important structuring device of the play, and the richer and more hedonistic the characters, the more conspicuously they consume cigarettes, champagne, and meals. Food is offered as part of a social ritual, avidly sought for instant gratification, or greedily devoured as an indicator of secret appetite(s). The first act opens with the preparation of tea for Lady Bracknell's visit and a discussion about the consumption of champagne; act II proceeds with the men taking sherry and the girls' polite warfare over tea and cake, and ends with the eating of muffins. In the four-act version, greed becomes even more significant, as Jack is almost arrested for his enormous and unpaid food bill, and Algy, in disguise and as himself, consumes two lunches, one including several lobsters. Richard Ellmann finds that in *Earnest* "sins accursed in *Salome* and unnameable in *Dorian Gray* are transposed into a different key and appear as Algernon's inordinate and selfish craving for—cucumber sandwiches. The substitution of mild gluttony for fearsome lechery renders all vice innocuous." (*Oscar Wilde,* London, 1987, p. 422).

LATER RECEPTION

Earnest was revived late in 1901, about a year after Wilde died, and after a provincial tour and a run in Notting Hill was once again produced in the West End in by George Alexander. It became established as a popular staple after the war. A 1923 production by Allan Aynesworth, who had played Algy in the first production, updated the play to the era of flappers and bright young things. Perhaps its most famous incarnation is the 1952 film version directed by Anthony Asquith, in which Edith Evans played Lady Bracknell and Margaret Rutherford Miss Prism.

There have been a number of attempts to co-opt Wilde as a champion of gay rights and *Earnest* as encoded with a gay subtext. See, for example, Gary Schmidgall, *The Stranger Wilde: Interpreting Oscar* and *The Importance of Being Earnest and Related Writings,* edited by Joseph Bristow (London, 1992). In his *The Wilde Century: Effeminacy, Oscar Wilde and the*

Queer Moment, Alan Sinfield is dismissive of this view as somewhat naïve. While the play does not a contribute to the establishment of a specifically homosexual literary canon, it cannot but have the significance of a play written by an author whose own social and sexual status was ambivalent and precarious. Jackson finds this significance "a peculiar pathos and dignity" and adds: "Even if in some quarters 'earnest' was indeed a code-word for homosexual, via 'uraniste', the message hardly seems worth the bottle; but because in general parlance 'earnest' had (and still has) all the deadly Victorian connotations of probity and high-mindedness, then the play's irreverence lives." (p. 173) In support of this possible message, Joseph Bristow cites the title of a volume of Uranian poetry by John Gamril Nicholson published three years before the first performance of *Earnest, Love in Earnest,* but Bristow suggests that rather than produce a reductive meaning of the play based upon a possible homosexual code, we should respect its polyvalencies, as Christopher Craft does in his "Alias Bunbury" (in Craft, *Another Kind of Love: Male Homosexual Desire in English Discourse 1850–1920* (Berkeley, 1994).

AFTERLIFE

Oscar Wilde made himself into a work of art, a statement about his aesthetic and political beliefs, and since his death he has passed into myth and assumed an iconic status. In addition to being the subject of biographies of varying quality, such as those by Robert Sherard, Frank Harris, Arthur Ransome, Hesketh Pearson, and Richard Ellmann, Wilde has been the subject of much fiction. Parodies of his person and his work were published during his lifetime, not only in the *Punch* and other magazine sketches, and in *Patience,* but also in Robert Hichens' novel *The Green Carnation* (1894). More lightly disguised biography than parody, *The Green Carnation* centers on the relationship between Mr Amarinth (Wilde) and Lord Reggie (Bosie), showing the latter to be so slavishly imitative of the former that his own personality is entirely subsumed. It contributed to the growing case against Wilde in the 1890s. Initially, Wilde was tolerant, in a letter to Ada Leverson remarking that he had not thought Hitchens capable of anything so clever. When rumor made him the author, however, he refuted the accusation in a letter to *The Pall Mall Gazette*:

> Sir, Kindly allow me to contradict, in the most emphatic manner, the suggestion, made in your issue if Thursday last, and since copied into many other newspapers, that I am the author of *The Green Carnation*.
>
> I invented that magnificent flower. But with the middle-class and mediocre book that usurps its strangely beautiful name I have, I need hardly say, nothing whatsoever to do. The flower is a work of art. The book is not.
>
> (1 October 1894)

An early attempt to rehabilitate Wilde's reputation came in 1925 with German playwright Carl Sternheim's play *Oskar Wilde*, which depicts Wilde as a victim of English hypocrisy. John Betjeman's poem "The Arrest of Wilde at the Cadogan Hotel" is sympathetic, but not openly defensive of Wilde's position. The release for publication of Wilde's letters in 1962 (selections, mostly expurgated, had appeared before then) allowed a more informed representation of his personality, but Michael Mac Liammoir's one-man play *The Importance of Being Oscar* (1963) does not address the issue of Wilde's homosexuality. Tom Stoppard centers his play *Travesties* (1974) around a performance of *Earnest* in Zurich in 1918. Peter Ackroyd's novel *The Last Testament of Oscar Wilde* (1983), and the film *The Trials of Oscar Wilde* (1960), staring Peter Finch, told Wilde's story imaginatively and sympathetically, while Terry Eagleton's play *Saint Oscar* (1989) depicted Wilde as an Irish martyr, brought down by the forces of imperialism. The English actor Stephen Fry took the title role in the film *Wilde* (1997), which did not follow Wilde's life to its end, but broke off on his release from prison and reunion with Bosie.

Oscar Wilde was granted a place in Poets' Corner in Westminster Abbey in 1995, a hundred years after the first performance of *The Importance of Being Earnest*.

Selected Bibliography

EARLY EDITIONS AND MSS OF *THE IMPORTANCE OF BEING EARNEST*

Autograph MS (August 1894) in four exercise books. Acts I and II, Arents Collection, New York Public Library. Acts III and IV, British Library, BL Add MS 37948.

Typescript of acts I (date-stamped 1 November 1894), III and IV with autograph corrections by Wilde, Arents Collection.

Typescript of four-act version (dated 31 October 1894). Burnside-Frohman Collection, New York.

Licensing copy: "Lady Lancing A Serious Comedy for Trivial People." British Library, BL Add. MS 53567 (17).

Typescript by Winifred Dolan, revised by Wilde. Arents Collection.

The Importance of Being Earnest: A Trivial Comedy for Serious People in Three Acts. London: Leonard Smithers, 1899.

Collected Edition of the Works of Oscar Wilde. (The first collected edition of the works of

Oscar Wilde, 1908–1922). Edited by Robert Ross. London: 1908.

Complete Works, ed. Vyvyan Holland. London: Collins, 1948

MODERN EDITIONS

The Importance of Being Earnest and Lady Windermere's Fan. Harmondsworth: Penguin Books, 1940.

Included in *Plays.* Harmondsworth: Penguin Books, 1954.

The Importance of Being Earnest, Mermaid Edition, edited by Russell Jackson. London: New Mermaids, 1993.

Oscar Wilde's The Importance of Being Earnest: *A Reconstructive Critical Edition of the Text of the First Production, St. James Theatre, London, 1895,* edited by Joseph Donoghue with Ruth Berggren. Gerrards Cross: Colin Smythe, 1995.

The Importance of Being Earnest and Other Plays. Harmondsworth: Penguin Books, 1986.

Included in *Oscar Wilde,* Oxford Authors Series, edited by Isobel Murray, Oxford University Press, 1989.

Included in *The Importance of Being Earnest and Other Plays,* Oxford World's Classics Series, edited by Peter Raby. Oxford: Oxford University Press, 1995.

Included in *Oscar Wilde: Plays, Prose Writings and Poems,* edited by Anthony Fothergill. London: Everyman, 1996.

LETTERS AND RECOLLECTIONS

The Letters of Oscar Wilde. Edited by Rupert Hart-Davis. London: Rupert Hart-Davis, 1962. (Selection, including the first uncensored publication of *De Profundis*).

More Letters of Oscar Wilde. Edited by Rupert Hart-Davis. London: John Murray, 1985.

The Complete Letters of Oscar Wilde. Edited by Merlin Holland and Rupert Hart-Davis. London: Fourth Estate, 2000.

Oscar Wilde: Interviews and Recollections. Edited by E.H. Mikhail. 2 vols. London: Macmillan, 1979.

A collection of original manuscripts, letters & books of Oscar Wilde, including his letters written to Robert Ross from Reading goal and unpublished letters, poems & plays formerly in the possession of Robert Ross. Edited by C. S. Millard [Stuart Mason]. London: Dulau, 1928.

Lord Alfred Douglas, *Oscar Wilde and Myself.* London: 1914.

———. *Autobiography.* London: Secker, 1929.

———. *Without Apology.* London: Secker, 1938.

———. *Oscar Wilde: A Summing Up.* London: Duckworth, 1940.

Kernahan, [John] Coulson. *In Good Company: Some Personal Recollections,* 2d edition, 1917.

Langtry, Lillie. *The Days I Knew.* London: Hutchinson, 1925.

Leverson, Ada. *Letters to the Sphinx from Oscar Wilde and Reminiscences of the Author.* London: Duckworth, 1930.

BIOGRAPHY

Ellmann, Richard. *Oscar Wilde.* London: Hamish Hamilton, 1987.

Gardner, Juliet. *Oscar Wilde: A Life in Letters, Writings and Wit.* London: Collins and Brown, 1995.

Goodman, Jonathan, ed. *The Oscar Wilde File.* London: Allison and Busby, 1988.

Harris, Frank. *Oscar Wilde: His Life and Confessions.* London: Constable, 1938.

Holland, Vyvyan. *Son of Oscar Wilde.* London: Rupert Hart-Davis, 1954.

Hyde, H. Montgomery. *Oscar Wilde: A Biography.* London: Eyre Methuen, 1976.

———, ed. *The Trials of Oscar Wilde.* New York: Dover, 1973.

Page, Norman. *An Oscar Wilde Chronology.* London: Macmillan, 1991.

Pearson, Hesketh. *The Life of Oscar Wilde.* London: Methuen, 1946.

Sherard, Robert Harborough. *Oscar Wilde: The Story of an Unhappy Friendship.* London: 1902.

———. *The Life of Oscar Wilde.* London: T. Werner Laurie, 1906.

———. *The Real Oscar Wilde* (supplement to the *Life*). London: 1915.

BIBLIOGRAPHY

Mason, Stuart [Christopher S. Millard]. *Bibliography of Oscar Wilde.* London: T. Werner Laurie, 1914; reprt. 1967.

CRITICISM

Beckson, Karl. *Oscar Wilde: The Critical Heritage.* London: Routledge and Kegan Paul, 1970.

Barlas, John E. *Oscar Wilde: A Study.* Edinburgh: Tragara, 1978.

Behrendt, Patricia Flanagan.*Oscar Wilde: Eros and Aesthetics.* London: Macmillan, 1991.

Bloom, Harold, ed. *The Importance of Being Earnest: Modern Critical Interpretations.* New York: Chelsea House Publishers, 1998.

Brasol, Boris. *Oscar Wilde: The Man, the Artist, the Martyr.* New York: Charles Scribner's Sons, 1938.

Cohen, Philip. *The Moral Vision of Oscar Wilde.* London: Associated University Press, 1978.

Ellmann, Richard, ed. *Oscar Wilde: A Collection of Critical Essays.* Englewood Cliffs, NJ: Prentice Hall, 1969.

Eltis, Sos. *Revising Wilde: Society and Subversion in the Plays of Oscar Wilde.* Oxford: Clarendon Press, 1996.

Gagnier, Regenia. *Idylls of the Marketplace: Oscar Wilde and the Victorian Public.* Aldershot: Scholar Press, 1987.

———, ed. *Critical Essays on Oscar Wilde.* New York: G.K. Hall, 1991.

Kohl, Norbert. *Oscar Wilde: The Works of a Conformist Rebel.* Cambridge: Cambridge University Press, 1989.

Morgan, Margery. *File on Wilde.* London: Methuen, 1990. (Details of performances and reviews.)

Nassaar, Christopher. *Into the Demon Universe: A Literary Exploration of Oscar Wilde.* New Haven, Conn.: Yale University Press, 1974.

Pine, Richard. *Oscar Wilde.* Dublin: Gill and Macmillan, 1983.

Powell, Kerry. *Oscar Wilde and the Theatre of the 1890s.* Cambridge: Cambridge University Press, 1990.

Raby, Peter, ed. *The Cambridge Companion to Oscar Wilde.* Cambridge: Cambridge University Press, 1997.

Sandulescu, George C., ed. *Rediscovering Oscar Wilde.* Gerrards Cross: Colin Smyth, 1994. (Papers from the Wilde Conference, Monaco, May 1993.)

San Juan, Epifanio. *The Art of Oscar Wilde.* Princeton, NJ: Princeton University Press, 1967.

Schmidgall, Gary. *The Stranger Wilde: Interpreting Oscar.* London: Abacus, 1994.

Shewan, Rodney. *Oscar Wilde: Art and Egotism.* London: Macmillan, 1977.

Sinfield, Alan. *The Wilde Century: Effeminacy, Oscar Wilde and the Queer Moment.* London: Cassell, 1994.

Small, Ian.*Oscar Wilde Revalued: An Essay on New Materials and Methods of Research.* Greensboro, N.C.: ELT Press, 1993.

Stokes, John. *Oscar Wilde: Myths, Miracles, and Imitations.* Cambridge: Cambridge University Press, 1996.

Sullivan, Kevin. *Oscar Wilde.* New York: Columbia University Press, 1972.

Symons, Arthur. *A Study of Oscar Wilde.* London: Charles Sawyer, 1930.

Tydeman, William, ed. *Wilde, Comedies: A Selection of Critical Essays.* London: Macmillan, 1982.

Varty, Anne. *A Preface to Oscar Wilde.* London: Longman, 1998.

Woodcock, George. *The Paradox of Oscar Wilde.* London: Boardman, 1949.

Worth, Katharine. *Oscar Wilde.* London: Macmillan, 1983.

WORKS CONTAINING MATERIAL ON WILDE

Cohen, Ed. *Talk on the Wilde Side: Towards a Genealogy of a Discourse on Male Sexualities.* New York: Routledge, 1993.

Dollimore, Jonathan. *Sexual Dissidence: Augustine to Wilde, Freud to Foucault.* Oxford: Clarendon Press, 1991.

Dowling, Linda. *Language and Decadence in the Victorian Fin de Siècle.* Princeton, N.J.: Princeton University Press, 1986.

———. *Hellenism and Homosexuality in Victorian Oxford.* Ithaca and London: Cornell University Press, 1994.

Innes, Christopher. *Modern British Drama 1890–1990.* Cambridge: Cambridge University Press, 1992.

Ledger, Sally and Scott McCracken, eds. *Cultural Politics at the Fin de Siècle.* Cambridge: Cambridge University Press, 1995.

Leggatt, Alexander. *English Stage Comedy 1490–1990: Five Centuries of a Genre.* London: Routledge, 1998.

Paglia, Camille. *Sexual Personae: Art and Decadence from Nefertiti to Emily Dickinson.* London: Yale University Press, 1990.

Showalter, Elaine. *Sexual Anarchy: Gender and Culture at the Fin de Siècle.* London: Bloomsbury, 1991.

ARTICLES IN PERIODICALS

Cohen, Ed. "Writing Gone Wilde: Homoerotic Desire in the Closet of Representation."

In *Publications of the Modern Language Association* 102 (1987): 801–813.

Craft, Christopher. "Alias Bunbury: Desire and Termination in *The Importance of Being Earnest.*" In *Representations* 31 (summer 1990): 19–46.

Dollimore, Jonathan. "Different Desires: Subjectivity and Transgression in Wilde and Gide." In *Textual Practice* I, no. 1 (1987): 48–67.

Green, William. "Oscar Wilde and the Bunburys." In *Modern Drama* 21, no. I (March 1978): 67–80.

Modern Drama 37, no. I (1994). Edited by Joel H. Kaplan. (Issue dedicated to Wilde.)

Rudyard Kipling's
Kim

PETER SCUPHAM

KIPLING'S EXPERIENCE OF India between 1882 and 1889 was when British rule was at its apogee. It is sometimes said that the British blundered into the acquisition of an Empire. Certainly, there was no vision of a British Emperor of India when the East India Company was granted a trading monopoly in 1600. Spices, pepper, and then, all-importantly, textiles, were its Indian staple. Gradually, the powers of the company enlarged. Bombay was ceded to the English Crown in 1661; Calcutta and Madras became the foci of British settlement, and Bengal became the most important trading center. By 1709, with the creation of a United East India Company from its predecessors, with British settlements and garrisons and widespread investments from home, India was firmly tied to the British economy. The Mughal Emperor ceded the administration of Bengal to the British in 1765, and British hegemony gradually consolidated, at first in the south and northeast. Conflicts between British and French interests were eventually resolved in the favor of the British, and by a policy of alliance and aggrandizement the company became a territorial power, levying taxes and making war. In 1765 Robert Clive took control of Bengal from the Mughal Empire; in 1773 Warren Hastings, a capable and corrupt administrator, became Bengal's first Governor-General. The company's charter was renewed in 1813, and a clause was inserted giving the Crown "undoubted sovereignty" over the company's territories. With the decay of the Mughal Empire and under the pressures of European commercial interests, India became a patchwork of Princely States bound by treaty to Britain and other areas conquered and directly ruled by her. The chief external threat to the British interest was in the north, as the Russian Empire expanded south through Central Asia. Peter Hopkirk, in his book *The Great Game,* describes the wild and unmapped northern regions as "a vast adventure playground for ambitious young officers and explorers of both sides" (p. 4). "The Great Game" became the generic title for this web of covert operations, and Kipling gave it a particular currency in *Kim.*

In 1857 came the Indian Mutiny, when the Bengal Army rose against reforms insisted upon by its British officer-class. "Mutiny" is the British word. As J. I. M. Stewart says in his *Rudyard Kipling* (1966), it was "a desperate attempt by those to whom the land belonged by birth to throw off an alien and foreign rule" (p. 40). After the ensuing massacre and horror, the East India Company was abolished and India was taken under the direct rule of the Crown, with a Secretary-of-State for India and a Council of India. Alice and Lockwood Kipling arrived in India just six years after the Mutiny. In 1876 Queen Victoria became Empress of India, and the latter part of the nineteenth century is Kipling's time, when English public schools were creating a hard-bitten, Spartan officer-caste to do the work of governing an Empire. Kipling went to school with such men, and wholeheartedly shared their doctrine of selfless work. A case, though, can be made for saying British rule aggravated conflicts between Muslim and Hindu, drained wealth, and kept India's economy agrarian and backward.

The British, whatever their technological and administrative achievements in India, were an alien power in the subcontinent, and after World War I came the increasing challenge of Mahatma Ghandi's broadly Hindu-based Congress Party, with its dual policy of constitutional reform and nonviolent protest, and Jinnah's Muslim League. After the Second World War the British were determined to leave India, which had been offered the status of a Dominion with the right to secede from the Commonwealth. The tragic outcome, in 1947, was a hasty partition into India and Pakistan, accompanied by communal massacre and the displacement of populations. The two countries' buildup of nuclear weapons and tensions over Kashmir more than fifty years later would probably not have surprised Kipling. His sense of the transience of Empire is expressed in the poem "Cities and Thrones and Powers," originally the epigraph to Kipling's story "A Centurion of the Thirtieth" in *Puck of Pook's Hill.*

> Cities and Thrones and powers
>   Stand in Time's eye,
> Almost as long as flowers,
>   Which daily die:

CHRONOLOGY

1865	Joseph Rudyard Kipling born in Bombay, 30 December. Son of John Lockwood Kipling, Architectural Sculptor at Bombay's School of Art, and Alice Macdonald.
1871–1877	Sent back to England and boarded out unhappily with the Holloway family at Lorne Lodge, Southsea, "The House of Desolation."
1878–1882	Educated at United Services College, Westward Ho!, Devon, founded in 1874 for the sons of career Army officers.
1882–1887	At sixteen is appointed Assistant Editor of the Civil and Military Gazette, Lahore, where his father is now Principal of the Mayo School of Art and Curator of the Lahore Museum.
1886	Collects and publishes *Departmental Ditties,* occasional verse on Anglo-Indian themes.
1887–1889	Becomes a special reporter for the Pioneer in Allahabad. Collects and publishes *Plain Tales from the Hills,* short stories of Anglo-Indian life in Simla, the hill-station from which the Viceroy governed India for half the year.
1889	Returns to London to further his literary career.
1890	Publishes *Soldiers Three,* stories based on regimental and barrack-room lore and legend, in which service-life in India is seen from the rank-and-file's point of view, and his first novel, *The Light that Failed.*
1891	Makes his last visit to India. Collaborates with his friend, the publisher and agent Wolcott Balestier on a novel combining Indian and American settings. *The Naulahka* (1892). That December Wolcott Balestier dies of typhoid fever. John Lockwood Kipling publishes *Beast and Man in India,* with many quotations from, and references to, his son's work.

1892	In January marries Caroline Starr Balestier, Wolcott's sister, and, after a honeymoon in Japan, they settle in the Balestier's hometown, Brattleboro, Vermont, where they start to build a new house, Naulakha. There Kipling writes *The Jungle Book* (1894) and *The Second Jungle Book* (1895).
1896	The Kiplings leave America for England, their departure brought about by a family feud culminating in a lawsuit brought by Kipling against Caroline's brother Beatty Balestier. After a farcical trial where Beatty scores all the points, Kipling becomes the laughingstock of Brattleboro.
1897	Publishes *Captains Courageous*, his all-American novella of the Grand Banks, written with the enthusiastic aid of Brattleboro's Dr. Conland.
1899	On the Kipling's final visit to America, Kipling's elder daughter, the three-year-old Josephine, dies of meningitis.
1901	Publishes *Kim*, which has been some seven years in the making, Kipling frequently turning to his father for suggestions and advice during that time.
1902	Publishes the *Just So Stories*. The Kiplings move to their last home, Batemans, a Jacobean house in Sussex. They travel widely, but their life becomes increasingly one of selective entertaining, work, and jealously guarded privacy. Kipling's new feel for English history finds expression in *Puck of Pook's Hill* (1906) and *Rewards and Fairies* (1910).
1915	Kipling's son John is killed while serving as an officer with the Irish Guards at the Battle of Loos. After the war Kipling becomes one of the Imperial War Graves Commissioners and writes a Regimental History, *The Irish Guards in the Great War* (1923). The later short stories, collected in *Debits and Credits* (1926) and *Limits and Renewals* (1932) become increasingly subtle and al

	lusive. *Rudyard Kipling's Verse* (he rejected the word poetry) is published. It will be published in several "inclusive" editions during his lifetime.
1936	18 January: Kipling dies.

KIPLING AND INDIA

Kipling's autobiography, *Something of Myself,* opens with a sequence of sharp sensuous details: a child's vision, remembered by a man in his seventieth year. "My first impression is of daybreak, light and colour and golden and purple fruits at the level of my shoulder" (p. 1), he writes, recalling the "dimly-seen, friendly Gods" (p. 2) in the Hindu temples, the child's hand his nurse or *ayah* tells him has been dropped by a vulture in the garden, how he dreamed and thought, not in English, but the vernacular, how he walked in the evening by palm-groves, feeling "the menacing darkness of tropical eventides, as I have loved the voices of night-winds through palm or banana leaves, and the song of the tree-frogs" (p. 2). This rich, physical intensity, which colors and informs the whole of *Kim,* was then exchanged for the crabbed and rigid prison of a foster-home in England, where the "dim, friendly Gods" were transformed into hellfire Evangelism. It was the custom of Anglo-Indian professionals to send their children back to the mother-country, removed from the perceived dangers of disease and too close an identification with the native life many of them were destined to govern.

Kipling returned to Lahore at the age of sixteen, and the work involved in being half the editorial staff of the *Civil and Military Gazette* was not only a baptism of fire, but a fiery ordeal, described in *Something of Myself* under the chapter-heading "Seven Years' Hard." Kipling grew accustomed to the remorseless claims of the day's work in a society where excuses were not accepted and where life was cheap and frequently brief. His membership of the Punjab

Club gave him the company of what he calls "picked men at their definite work"(p. 43), the work of building and maintaining the complex intellectual structures of law and education and the physical infrastructures of British India. However, a memorable Kipling phrase is "the night got into my head" (p. 53), and when it did, an artist's imagination and a journalist's curiosity led him to opium-dens, back-street life, the barracks, the brothel, and the liquor-shop. In his annual month's leave, Kipling exchanged the pullulating life of the Plains for Simla, in the cool Hills, where, for half each year "the Hierarchy lived, and one saw and heard the machinery of administration stripped bare" (p. 57). At the *Civil and Military Gazette*, Kipling tells us, his life had been led mainly among Muslims; when he moved south, to the *Pioneer*, and Allahabad, the population was predominantly Hindu. Here, Kipling developed his gift for the short story: "Thus, then, I made my own experiments in the weights, colours, perfumes and attributes of words in relation to other words, either as read aloud so that they may hold the ear, or, scattered over the page, draw the eye. There is no line of my verse or prose which has not been mouthed till the tongue has made all smooth ..." (pp. 72–73).

At twenty-three Kipling left for England, and though he made one further visit in 1891, his Indian days became a verbal fabric woven by memory and imagination. His experiences had been geographically limited; the Punjab and the summer-capital of Hill-station Simla formed their staple. Despite the movement of *Kim* up into the High Hills, Kipling made only one journey which gave him a taste of them. That had been in May 1885, when he accompanied friends for six days out of Simla towards the mission-station of Kotgarh. Leaving them to continue, he returned as the only Sahib, or European, with hill-coolies to carry the baggage. The misadventures of the party were turned to good fictional effect in the final thwarting of the Russian agents in *Kim*. Central India, Jungle India, also remained unvisited by Kipling,

despite his loving evocation of it in *The Jungle Book* and *The Second Jungle Book*. Kipling was imaginatively, not physically, adventurous, though an episode he liked to recall, which may well have gained in the telling, came earlier in that same year of 1855, when, sent to report a ceremonial occasion on the North-West Frontier, he briefly stepped across the border into Afghanistan and a tribesman took a shot at him. For a moment, Kipling had been a bit-player in the Great Game, though in *Kim* the Russian threat is seen as operating through the then closed and mysterious land of Tibet.

WHAT KIND OF BOOK IS *KIM*?

Kim, Kipling's only truly successful novel, escapes easy definition. Kipling himself is disarming about its wayward structure. In *Something of Myself* he implies that *Don Quixote* was the model, and gives his mother's response: "Don't you stand in your wool-boots hiding behind Cervantes with *me*! You *know* you couldn't make a plot to save your soul" (p. 140). *Kim*, Kipling says, "was nakedly picaresque and plotless" (p. 228). The book plunges the reader into late nineteenth-century India, vibrant with its diverse lives and boldly-colored backgrounds. For Kipling, those lives are lived, whether their owners are aware of the fact or not, under the protection of the British Raj, conscious not only of its superiority—the echelons of the Indian Civil Service were known among Anglo-Indians as "the heaven-born"—but of its duty to the people it both governed and served. ("Anglo-Indian" is used here as in Kipling's time, to mean the British who made their working lives in India; men and women of mixed race were known at that time as Eurasian.) At its deepest level, it is a testingly adult book about love, about the unfolding richness of life, about a boy growing up, about spiritual hunger and worldly concern. At another level it is a yarn: a story of romance, intrigue, derring-do and make-believe, setting against its loving picture of Indian life the shadowy, romantic world of the Great Game. It is a book for Edwardian boys, its ostensible plot being the thwarting of a conspiracy by a group of Princely States, the "five confederated Kings, who had no business to confederate" and "a kindly Northern Power" (21), which is, of course, Russia.

The spiritual and temporal quests, those two interlinked and central components of *Kim*, can be approached through the concepts of the "Search" and the "Game." Kim, the young Irish waif whose fortunes we follow, grows up to manhood under the auspices of two ambiguous symbols, emblems under which two different quests are conducted. As the *chela* (disciple) of Teshoo Lama, the Buddhist priest, Kim follows his spiritual master on his quest for the River of the Arrow, the purifying river which broke out where Gautama Buddha's arrow fell. As the son of a color-sergeant in an Irish Regiment, the Mavericks, he follows the sign of the Red Bull on the green field, the regiment's insignia, and is led into the world of the Great Game. Against the calm withdrawal of the lama from the hurly-burly of life is set a harsher, more knowing set of values. The Great Game players Mahbub Ali, a Pathan horse-trader, Hurree Chunder Mookerjee, an educated Hindu Babu, Lurgan Sahib and Colonel Creighton, Anglo-Indians, all take Kim's education in hand, and their surrogate parenting fits him for a life of practical action. There is a similarity between *Kim* and the two *Jungle Books* Kipling had already published. Mowgli, too, is a young man-cub separated by destiny from the world he first finds himself in; Mowgli, too, finds himself trained by surrogate parents, and one can see something of Baloo the bear in Hurree Babu; something of Bagheera the panther in Mahbub Ali. The close of the book leaves Kim himself on the edge of manhood, poised between the two worlds he has been offered. Kipling does not offer us a simple answer to the questions Kim will have to ask himself. Perhaps the best answer lies in one of Kipling's own poems: Kipling early formed the habit of providing his own enigmatic and suggestive verses as chapter-headings, and the verse-

heading for Chapter VIII was amplified into a poem, "The Two-Sided Man" (*Kipling's Verse, Definitive Edition*, 587). The two verses to be found in *Kim* express Kipling's deep sense of gratitude for his duality of nature: that ability to be of the world, worldly, but also intuitively alert for the mystery behind the world's homely or novel surfaces:

Something I owe to the soil that grew—
  More to the life that fed—
But most to Allah Who gave me two
  Separate sides to my head.

I would go without shirt or shoe,
  Friend, tobacco or bread,
Sooner than lose for a minute the two
  Separate sides of my head.

Peter Hopkirk, in *Quest for Kim: In Search of Kipling's Great Game* (1996), pays the book a fine tribute: "For not only is it a deeply enjoyable book, but also a profoundly uplifting one, especially for anyone whose spirits are at a low ebb. It emits an intense luminescence, like that spilling out of a landscape by Turner" (p. 36). That luminescence is drawn out by Kipling's loving descriptions of the Indian landscape and his ability to express through his hero a delighted acceptance of life in all its multifarious forms.

THE GREAT GAME AS PLAYED IN *KIM*

Critics sometimes play down the importance of the Great Game mechanism in *Kim*, perhaps because the book is so deftly poised between adventure story and mature novel that the adult reader and critic wishes to discard or minimize that element which appeals to a younger self. This mechanism provides a skeletal plot and is seen by Kipling as the instrument of Kim's rescue from the feral street-life he has known to become a player himself. He is schooled to become one of the guardians of those who do not know they are guarded.

At this level *Kim* is a series of dashing, boldly-drawn episodes. Kim is Kimball O'Hara, the orphaned son of a soldier and a nursemaid. He carries his birth certificate and his father's Masonic certificates in an amulet-case round his neck, entirely ignorant of their significance. He is an unwitting sahib, but "burned black as any native" (p. 1), known to all as the "Little Friend of all the World" as he acts as a knowing go-between, using his wits to survive the street-life of Lahore. "It was intrigue, of course,—he knew that much, as he had known all evil since he could speak,—but what he loved was the game for its own sake" (p. 3). Though Kim himself is credited with a knowledge of "all evil," *Kim,* as many critics have pointed out, is not concerned with the dark intricacies of evil. Whether he is in the Kashmir Serai of Lahore, which "blazed with light as they made their way through the press of all the races in Upper India" (p. 17), or on the Grand Trunk Road, that "broad, smiling river of life" (p. 61), the world opens positively and joyfully before him.

Kipling soon sets up dissonances and reversals in what might be the reader's expectation: "As he reached the years of indiscretion, he learned to avoid missionaries and white men of serious aspect who asked who he was, and what he did. For Kim did nothing with an immense success" (p. 2). Whatever kind of sahib Kim will become, it will be an unconventional one. Kim's first important encounter is with a beneficent, unworldly Tibetan lama, formerly the Abbot of the Monastery of Such-zen, now looking for that river which will free him from the endless cycles of incarnation. Kim decides to adopt him: "The lama was his trove, and he purposed to take possession" (p. 12). The lama, though, takes equal possession, seeing Kim as his disciple, or *chela,* the successor to his former *chela,* who is now dead. In opposition to the lama's removal from the world of event and action, we next meet to the burly Afghan horse-dealer, Mahbub Ali, a Mohammedan, "registered in one of the locked books of the Indian Survey Department as C.25.1B" (p. 21). He gives Kim a message to

deliver to a Colonel Creighton in Umballa—a wad of tissue wrapped in oilskin which will incriminate those "five confederated Kings, who had no business to confederate."

Kim is already being tested, his travels with the lama used by his spy-masters for quite other ends than the lama could understand. Accidentally, he falls into the clutches of his father's old regiment, the Mavericks, drawn to them by seeing the flags marking out their camp showing a red bull on a green field—an image the half-caste prostitute who has looked after him told him will one day be his fortune—and is threatened with a military orphanage. The lama, though, provides the money for Kim's education at St. Xavier's, Lucknow, where Kim finds himself among "boys of fifteen who had spent a day and a half on an islet in the middle of a flooded river, taking charge, as by right, of a camp of frantic pilgrims returning from a shrine" (p. 124). The lama has, by his loving gift, unconsciously played his part in the Game. Tested and trained one holiday in the arts of observation and disguise by Lurgan Sahib, who ostensibly keeps a shop of curios and jewelry in Simla, but who is also a player, Kim is introduced there to the last of his masters, the Hindu Bengali Babu, Hurree Chunder Mookerjee, M.A., of Calcutta University, "whose name on the books of one section of the Ethnological Survey was R.17." (p. 162). The Babu explains how Kim must "know the precise length of his own foot-pace" (p. 163) and how a rosary can be used to check off paces in order to map unknown country—lessons reinforced by Colonel Creighton, who makes Kim map the city of Bikaneer by such methods. Kim is removed from St. Xaviers, becomes officially "an assistant chain-man in the Canal department," is given a special heart-shaped amulet and a verbal ritual to identify himself to other players of the Game, saves the life of E.23. by effecting a brilliant disguise on a train from Benares to Delhi, and finally plays rather more than a bit part in Hurree Chunder Mookerjee's complex outwitting and discomfiture in the

High Hills of two agents, Russian and French. Their incriminating evidence falls into Kim's hands, who himself briefly falls sick with strain and exhaustion. Kim has passed his first great test and earned Hurree Babu's farewell plaudits: "Now good-bye, Mister O'Hara. I can catch 4.25 P.M. to Umballa if I am quick. It will be good times when we all tell thee tale up at Mister Lurgan's. I shall report you offeecially better. Good-bye, my dear fallow, and when next you are under thee emotions please do not use the Mohammedan terms with the Tibet dress" (p. 281).

The Game gives the novel tension and impetus. It keeps the major characters stretched and mentally alert, giving Kipling the opportunity to move those "picked men at their definite work" briskly about Northern India by horseback, train and hill-pony. Their physical pace contrasts sharply with the lama's interwoven wanderings, made whenever possible by foot, just as their mental cunning and alertness to men, women and manners contrasts with the lama's simplicity and desire for withdrawal from this world where "all Desire is Illusion and a new binding upon the Wheel" (p. 123). To see how important the Game is in *Kim* it is helpful to put it into an historical context, showing where Kipling uses and where he diverges from the historical record, a subject thoroughly explored by Peter Hopkirk in *The Quest for Kim* and *The Great Game: On Secret Service in High Asia* (1990). Hopkirk's detailed examination acts as a corrective to the view, expressed in David Gilmour's *The Long Recessional: The Imperial Life of Rudyard Kipling* (London, 2002), in which Gilmour describes the Great Game theme in Kim as "an improbable and unconvincing sub-plot"(p. 80).

The Great Game as it was actually played might be said to start with Napoleon's proposition to Tsar Alexander I that the French and Russians should jointly invade India. Though this plan came to nothing, in the first half of the nineteenth century Russia made advance after advance through the deserts and mountains of Central Asia, and endlessly narrowed the gap between the their imperial possessions and those of the British. The conquered Muslim Khanates of the north were the Russian equivalent of the Princely States in the British fiefdom. Though the threat was taken with varying degrees of seriousness in the nineteenth century, and its reality is debatable, it is not difficult to understand the part played by increasing Russian proximity in Kipling's imagination. For the professional army in India, the lawless North-West Frontier had an imaginative importance as the scene of inevitable major conflict between the Russian and British empires, a theme talked up by career officers—and Kipling always listened to soldiers.

Peter Hopkirk, in *Quest for Kim*, gives historical flesh to Kim's training as a "chain-man," apparently an innocent surveyor. But the work of the Survey of India was not innocent. In Hopkirk's chapter "Who was Colonel Creighton?" he gives us a candidate, Captain (later Colonel) Thomas Montgomerie. Montgomerie trained native Indians, known as "pundits," to gather intelligence for mapping territory outside the northern frontiers for military purposes. From the 1860s to the 1880s these men were trained to know their pace-length and be able to maintain a given stride on any terrain. Often disguised as Buddhist pilgrims, they were equipped with converted rosaries to measure distance and converted prayer-wheels and staves which hid paper, compass, and thermometer. Kipling borrowed from this the idea of code-names and imaginatively created a whole Indian Secret Service, with the "Ethnographical Department" of the Indian Survey as its front. In this, Kipling was prescient. That small clandestine side to the Survey of India, with its native "pundits" was the start. Then came a small military affair called the Intelligence Branch—five officers and two clerks—in 1879, and a fully-fledged intelligence-gathering service in 1904. In its treatment of the Game, *Kim* is a work of the imagination, but it is not fanciful. And though Kipling gave the

Great Game its capital letters, the phrase was first used by Captain Arthur Conolly, executed in Bokhara in 1842, in a letter to a fellow-player: "You've a great game, a noble one, before you" (*Quest for Kim,* p. 7). That was some fifty years before *Kim.*

THE SEARCH

Kim, though, will mature in more complex ways than the Great Game provides for. Kim, the shape-changer, the "Little Friend of the World" who is at home everywhere—and nowhere—questions his own identity as he waits with the Mavericks: "This is the great world, and I am only Kim. Who is Kim? He considered his own identity, a thing he had never done before, till his head swam. He was one insignificant person in all this roaring whirl of India, going southward to he knew not what fate" (pp. 117–118). He questions it again in Lucknow station at the end of his time at St. Xavier's. "Who is Kim?" he asks, his "pupils contracted to pinpoints. In a minute—in another half-second—he felt he would arrive at the solution of the tremendous puzzle; but here, as always happens, his mind dropped away from those heights with the rush of a wounded bird, and passing his hand before his eyes, he shook his head" (p. 185). As the book draws to a close, though, the question becomes a statement: "—a great and a wonderful world—and I am Kim—Kim—Kim—alone—one person—in the middle of it all" (p. 224). Kim's journey to maturity needs a dimension the Great Game cannot provide, and just before coming to that knowledge of his place in the scheme of things, Kim ponders on his benefactors, and acknowledges that he owes his share and his joy in that world "chiefly to the Holy One" (p. 224), the lama. The lama's own love for the boy, called out against his deepest wish to achieve release and freedom from worldly desire, calls out a matching love in Kim and lies at the heart of the novel.

From their first encounter Kim is fascinated by the lama. "His face was yellow and wrinkled, like that of Fook Shing, the Chinese bootmaker in the bazar. His eyes turned up at the corners and looked like little slits of onyx" (p. 4). The old man's journey from his Tibetan lamasery, begging his way round the Holy Places of Buddhist legend, has brought him to the gates of the "Wonder House," the Museum to which Kipling's father, John Lockwood Kipling, had been appointed Curator in 1875. Kim, always streetwise, allays the lama's fears that he that he must pay for entrance, leads him through the turnstile, and becomes an invisible eavesdropper on the conversation between the lama and the scholarly "white-bearded Englishman" (p. 7) who, in real life, is Kipling's father. The lama views the collection of Greco-Buddhist sculpture "with the reverence of a devotee and the appreciative instinct of a craftsman" (p. 8), and the encounter, with its obeisance to the world of the mind and the spirit, closes with an exchange of gifts, the lama's ancient pencase for the Curator's spectacles. Merit has been acquired; an exchange has been made of more than material possessions. The cultured, skeptical, and inquisitive Lockwood Kipling was of tremendous importance to his son's life and work. His contribution to *Kim* is considerable, if invisible except for the bas-relief sculptures he made to be photographed for the illustrated edition. It is possible that the work's generosity of spirit is in part the product of the long sessions when it was "smoked over" between father and son after Lockwood Kipling and his wife Alice had returned to England in 1893. Kipling makes the debt explicit in *Something of Myself* (p. 139): "Under our united tobaccos it grew like the Djinn released from the brass bottle, and the more we explored its possibilities the more opulence of detail did we discover." *Kim* was never hurried into being. There were twenty-eight years of Lockwood Kipling's experiences in India to unpack and the ghost of an unfinished (now lost) novel by Kipling, *Mother Maturin,* to quarry. Kipling's expression in the "Wonder House" scene that the quest for knowledge and truth crosses cultural frontiers is picked up again later when we learn of both Hurree Babu's and Colonel Creighton's desire to add the letters "F.R.S." (Fellow of the Royal Society) to their names, to be recognized beyond the world of espionage as having made pure contributions to the knowledge of Indian folk-lore, manners and customs: "So Creighton smiled, and thought the better of Hurree Babu, moved by like desire" (p. 175). The book is full of such cross-referencing.

Kim, then, adopts the lama, "sighing for his disciple, dead in far away Kulu" (p. 13). He begs for him, acts as his eyes and ears, becomes his chela. The lama is a child in the world of action and event, as Kim is a child in his understanding of the nature of love and the world of the spirit. The force of the lama's personality and utter spiritual conviction does not simply affect Kim, but has a powerful effect on all who encounter him. On the train to Umballa the Hindu passengers listen to his murmured tales of the Buddha in both Urdu and Tibetan: "The gentle, tolerant folk looked on reverently. All India is full of holy men stammering gospels in strange tongues; shaken and consumed in the fires of their own zeal" (p. 32). The lama's integrity and unfeigned simplicities set standards by which other characters in the novel are judged, though the lama himself judges rarely, and, as his relationship with Kim develops and the bond between them strengthens, the lama finds himself drawn back by his love into the world of appearance from which his search for the River of the Arrow was meant to free him. As the end of the first part of *Kim* approaches, and Kim is about to have his life changed under the auspices of the red bull on the green field, the strength of the bond between them is made explicit: "'A blessing on thee.' The lama inclined his solemn head. 'I have known many men in my so long life, and disciples not a few. But to none among men, if so be thou art woman-born, has my heart gone out as it has to thee—thoughtful, wise and courteous, but something of a small imp.'" Kim replies that "it is less than three days since we took the road together, and it is as though it were a hundred years" (p. 70).

A little later, Kim finds himself in the Mavericks' camp, and in the hands of the Church of England chaplain, Bennett, and the Roman Catholic chaplain, Father Victor. His amulet case is opened and they discover he is a child of the regiment. When the lama is called in to elucidate, Bennett, with invincible ignorance, tries to buy off the lama with a rupee, though Father Victor, "wise in the confessional" (p. 92), understands the pain of the lama's separation from his *chela.* As Kim enters his apprenticeship to the Game, which occupies the second third of the book, the lama's physical presence is no longer part of his life, though his love is. The lama, "coming and going across India as softly as a bat" (p. 166), makes his occasional headquarters at the Temple of the Tirthankers in Benares. As for finding the River of the Arrow, "it was shown to him in dreams that it was a matter not to be undertaken with any hope of success unless that seeker had with him the one *chela* appointed to bring the event to a happy issue, and versed in great wisdom—such wisdom as white-haired Keepers of Images possess" (p. 165). This brings us back to the Wonder House and the portrait of Lockwood Kipling as the curator; the lama's dream is that Kim's education would fit his *chela* to be a scholar and scribe. When Kim's time at St Xavier's is over, Colonel Creighton suggests to Mahbub Ali that he accompany the lama for six months, with a loose eye kept on him by Hurree Babu. The closing third of the book, where the Game and the Search unite, is announced by Kim's act of gratitude and love to the lama at the entrance to the Temple of the Tirthankers, when he stoops to touch the lama's feet and thank him: "My teaching I owe to thee. I have eaten thy bread three years. My time is finished. I am loosed from the schools. I come to thee." (p. 189).

THE ORDEAL AND THE CRISIS

J. M. S. Tompkins, in her subtle analysis of Kipling's work, *The Art of Rudyard Kipling* (1959), writes: "Beyond and above Kim's ordeal, like a distant, cloud-piercing peak beyond the crest of one of the lower hills, towers the lama's crisis" (p. 25). Though the Search ends in the plains and the Game, as far as *Kim* is concerned, in the hills, the ordeal which Kim undergoes, the spiritual crisis the lama undergoes, both take place in the high hills. It is the interweaving of ordeal and crisis, Game and Search, that brings the book to its moving conclusion. Two images that exemplify the contrasted worlds of Game and Search are the geographical map and the pictorial chart. Kim has been trained to survey—at St. Xavier's he "showed a great aptitude for mathematical studies as well as map-making" (p. 164)—and will have some part in establishing that grand delineation of the terrain with its practical purpose of safeguarding the northern approaches to India. The lama is also a mapmaker, but his art is to make pictorial charts of the Wheel of Life. Before they set out for the north, the lama demonstrated his art: "He drew from under the table a sheet of strangely scented yellow Chinese paper, the brushes, and slab of India ink. In cleanest, severest outline he had traced the Great Wheel with its six spokes, whose centre is the conjoined Hog, Snake, and Dove (Ignorance, Anger, and Lust), and whose compartments are all the heavens and hells, and all the chances of human life. Men say that the Bodhisat himself first drew it with grains of rice upon dust, to teach His Disciples the cause of things" (p. 192).

The tensions of the Game come upon them almost immediately. On the train to Delhi Kim helps a fellow-player evade his pursuers and renew his courage by the arts of disguise, but soon they are travelling by foot into the hills, wandering, as the lama says. "loose-foot, waiting upon the Chain of Things" (p. 210). The lama has no restless yearning to press his search for the river; he is secure in the knowledge that it will disclose itself at the proper time, breaking out "at my feet, if need be" (p. 228). The bond between them strengthens "till Kim, who had loved him without reason, now loved him for fifty good reasons" (p. 213), but the Game claims

Kim as they encounter Hurree Babu, on the trail of a Russian agent and his French companion. The climax comes in a desolate landscape, and though the high hills restore the lama's physical self, Kim feels increasingly threatened and alienated by the landscape, "beaten down by the appalling sweep and dispersal of the cloud-shadows after rain"(p. 235). Hurree Babu's machinations result in a brutal intervention by the Game into the Search, when the Russian, seeing only "an unclean old man haggling over a dirty piece of paper" (p. 242), attempts to snatch away the lama's picture of the Great Wheel, Kim springs to the lama's defense and in the ensuing scuffle directed by Hurree Babu gets away with the incriminating evidence carried in the Russian agent's baggage. Kim and the lama rest at Shamlegh, a tiny hill-settlement, and are looked after by the Woman of Shamlegh, a woman once loved by an English sahib, and first met in a Kipling short story, "Lispeth," which opens *Plain Tales from the Hills* (1888).

The effect on the lama is profound. He acknowledges that the Russian's assault "met evil in me—anger, rage, and a lust to return evil" (p. 252). He is thrown back on the roots of his faith: "Now I must see into the Cause of Things. The boat of my soul staggers"(p. 253). The blow received, and his own response to it, are taken by the lama as a sign that his search will be fruitless in the hills, and that he must turn again to the plains. His symbolic chart has been torn by a blow in itself symbolic of the opposition between the concerns of this world and those of the spirit. The Woman of Shamlegh provides bearers for the lama's litter, and Kim struggles south, giving the lama his unceasing care and burdened by his own growing illness and the mental weight of the incriminating documents he carries. Looked after, as they reach the plains, by the Sahiba, the Maharanee first met on the Grand Trunk Road, Kim is nursed back into health. His documents are handed over to Hurree Babu, who has had his own experiences with the lama: "By Jove, O'Hara, do you know, he is afflicted with infirmity of fits. Yess, I tell you.

Cataleptic, too, if not also epileptic. I found him in such a state under a tree in *articulo mortem*, and he jumped up and walked into a brook and he was nearly drowned but for me. I pulled him out" (p. 279). The lama's quest has been concluded; Kim's illness, dubiety and trouble of the spirit pass away under the healing hands of the Sahiba. The lama now reaches out into a dimension which is not that of freedom from the Wheel of Life, but a spiritual comprehension brought about by his love for his *chela*; Kim achieves a new sense of the reality and sensible unity of the physical world: "Things that rode meaningless on the eyeball an instant before slid into proper proportion. Roads were meant to be walked upon, houses to be lived in, cattle to be driven, fields to be tilled, and men and women to be talked to. They were all real and true—solidly planted upon the feet—perfectly comprehensible—clay of his clay, neither more nor less' (p. 282). The book closes with a vision of the healing and unifying power of love, a quality of universal sympathy Kipling was never again to match, as the lama "crossed his hands in his lap and smiled, as a man may who has won Salvation for himself and his beloved" (p. 289).

The ending, poised on its possibilities, has been variously interpreted. For J.M.S. Tompkins it is clear that Kim's understanding of the lama's spiritual nature is limited and that the Game will occupy Kim's adult life, though she points out that there is no identification made by Kim himself with the British interest, whatever Kipling's own view. The Game is simply a satisfying way of using to the full Kim's particular gifts. A constant theme in all Kipling's writings is the importance of the disciplined life, of running in harness and completing the day's work. Better harsh masters than none; the subjugation of self is the beginning of wisdom. A rather different view is put forward by Mark Kinkead-Weekes, in his essay in *Kipling's Mind and Art* (p. 231), who feels that Kim could hardly "return to the Game, against the whole current of the book's disabling criticism." The lama, though, is an old man who can play little

further active part in Kim's life, and in six months Kim will be playing the Great Game with Mahbub Ali in Afghanistan. It is not Kipling's business to tell us which of Kim's two surrogate fathers, Mahbub Ali and Teshoo Lama, will ultimately most influence him. Kipling, who certainly toyed with the idea of continuing the life of his hero, wrote in a letter to Edward Lucas White on 11 November 1902: "As to *Kim*, I don't see myself that the Lama died, nor do I see any sign of the old man's dying. My own idea is that in the fullness of time we may learn how Kim went on with his somewhat unusual career" (*Letters*, Vol. 3, p. 111).

FIGURES IN A LANDSCAPE

Kim is not a novel whose characters are treated with a strong sense of their psychological complexity. Mahbub Ali, Colonel Creighton, Lurgan Sahib, Hurree Babu—these men possess skill and cunning, have a wide knowledge of men and manners, and unite mental and physical audacity. They are adults who possess themselves, and who are not given to introspection or self-doubt. Mahbub Ali is more subtly drawn in his relationship to Kim, as he is the earliest of Kim's surrogate fathers and the boy calls out a kind of love in Mahbub, as the lama calls out in him a kind of jealousy, triumphantly surmounted. What of Kim himself, the questioner of his own identity, easing his way between all castes and kinds in the brave new world of India which opens before him? At the close of the book, as we have seen, there is an ambivalence. We are certain of Kim's strength and resilience, sure that he will be a survivor and achiever. We are certain, too, of his capacity for love, but there is no evidence that the lama's belief that this world is mere illusion could ever take root in him. Against Kim's love for the lama can be set a different kind of admiration, that for Colonel Creighton, the cool spy-master: "Here was a man after his own heart—a tortuous and indirect person playing a hidden game" (p. 117). We leave Kim when he is still only seventeen, a colt who has been broken in but has hardly entered on his working life. What we are given throughout is Kim's extraordinary aptitude for disguise and his ability to pass tests set by his superiors. Kipling's problem is to convince us that under the bewildering variety of masks, tests, and masquerades which make up Kim's progress, there is a true identity, not merely the chameleon capacities of a successful actor.

Kim's worldly progress is accompanied by disguise, that classic component of the Adventure Story genre. As an orphaned waif Kim wears interchangeably European, Hindu, or Mohammedan clothes and has acquired "a complete set of Hindu kit, the costume of a low-caste street boy" (p. 3), a costume he changes into when he decides to accompany the lama to Benares, and which initially confuses the lama into a wail of misery for the loss of his new *chela.* Though a Sahib while at St. Xavier's, Kim immediately translates himself, with the help of a prostitute's dye-stuff, back into a Hindu boy when the long late-summer holiday comes. The mental testing Kim undergoes is continuous; the smallest remarks made by his superiors may be designed to reveal Kim's fitness for the tasks they have in mind for him. A tiny example is Hurree Babu's apparently casual reference to "old Creighton," an impertinent intimacy rejected by Kim, who corrects the reference to "The Colonel Sahib" (p. 219). The climax of Kim's testing comes in the house of Lurgan Sahib in Simla. Lurgan Sahib, player in the Game, "healer of sick pearls" and curio-dealer to Rajahs, puts Kim through an exhaustive series of tests and exercises, of which "Kim's Game," an exercise in training the memory by a brief display of objects which then have to be covered and described in detail, has taken on a life beyond the novel. Kim withstands Lurgan's attempt at hypnosis, showing an obstinate sense of reality when Lurgan tries to make him see a broken jug re-form its pieces into a whole again, and the evenings are filled with dressing-up ses-

sions when "Kim was apparelled variously as a young Mohammedan of good family, an oilman, and once—which was a joyous evening—as the son of an Oudh landholder in the fullest of full dress" (p. 159). Kim's arrival on the verge of manhood, when Mahbub Ali considers him ready to leave St. Xavier's is marked by his gift of "a dress of honour" (p. 170),—an embroidered turban-cap and waistcoat, white shirt, green pajamas, russia-leather slippers, and a revolver. We are constantly placed in a world of shifting appearances, where Kim plays his roles, whether stable-boy, juggler's assistant or healer, with delighted aplomb, while underneath this kaleidoscope sense of change runs a dual thread: the deepening constancy of his love for the lama, in which disguise plays no part, and his ability to assimilate the worldly wisdom of his spymasters, under whom he learns how to press truth and lie into service and how to turn discipline into self-discipline.

Kim was written when Kipling had made his farewell to India, and in one sense Kim is his creator's own best self. In creating Kim's uncomplicated and delighted acceptance of life, Kipling recaptures the vivid and simple responses of childhood and works them into elaborate painterly textures. The River of the Arrow is not the only river in *Kim.* The Grand Trunk Road is seen by an old native officer who saw service in the Mutiny as "a river from which I am withdrawn like a log after flood" (p. 57); Kim sees it as a "broad, smiling river of life" (p. 61). Away from India, Kipling could look at the world with washed eyes and a perception freed from moral judgment. The book is full of mesmerizingly beautiful passages, where, with Kim, we enter into the landscape as if ourselves seeing and feeling it for the first time, as in this description of evening on the Grand Trunk Road: "Then the night fell, changing the touch of the air, drawing a low, even haze, like a gossamer veil of blue, across the face of the country, and bringing out, keen and distinct, the smell of wood-smoke and cattle and the good scent of wheaten cakes cooked on ashes. The evening patrol hurried out of the police-station with important coughings and reiterated orders; and a live charcoal ball in the cup of a wayside carter's hookah glowed red while Kim's eye mechanically watched the last flicker of sun on the brass tweezers" (p. 64). Kipling was a fastidious writer; such a passage is both visual and tactile, immediate in its physicality, suggestive, too, of a drowsy, almost invisible watcher comforted by a kindliness flowing through life's interstices. There is no threat in those "important coughings"; as the sun dies, its warmth is revived in the carter's hookah.

India of the Plains becomes, under this vision, a golden land and Kim a golden child. The sun "drives broad golden spokes" through the mango trees (p. 64); the lama, that yellow man, sits in his yellow robes talking to the Sahiba in her bullock-cart, whose "gold-worked curtains ran up and down, melting and reforming as the folds shook and quivered to the night wind" (p. 71). Kim, insignificant before the immensities of India, is made central to them by the names chosen for him. He is not only known as the "Little Friend of all the World" (p. 3), but "I am called also the Friend of the Stars" (p. 67). The sobriquets seem to give him a magical protection, as if he comes out of legend or fairy-tale, and one of the most compelling descriptive passages in *Kim* is Kim's drugged undergoing of magical rituals of exorcism and disguise under the hands of the blind woman Huneefa in her dark upper room: "Those who know it call it The Bird-cage—it is so full of whisperings and whistlings and chirrupings" (p. 177). The rituals end with Huneefa's exhausted sleep after "a paroxysm of howling, with a touch of froth at the lips" (p. 180), and a shaken Hurree Babu, who has watched in a spirit of philosophical inquiry, asking himself how he is to "fear the absolutely non-existent" (p. 180). Part of the reader becomes such a golden child as the book unfolds, and too much stress on the idiosyncrasy of individual character weakens the possibilities of the reader sharing in such a child's journey to

maturity. Kim's life has affinities with those of such characters as David Copperfield, Oliver Twist, and Huck Finn. The landscapes they move through, however rooted in the actual, share their territory with landscapes of legend and dream. We are part of the process of the hero's becoming. Identity, in the adult sense of the word, waits to be achieved when the tests have been passed and the disguises put aside.

Kim, though Kipling would have not used the word, is an adolescent boy, and there is a sexual element present in the attraction others feel for him; Kim himself is a skilled manipulator, conscious of the responses he can elicit. His Great Game mentor, the flamboyant Mahbub Ali, loves the boy as a surrogate son; Kim might be seen as merely a favorite in a court or caravan of stable-boys. In his contentious and stimulating biography, *Rudyard Kipling,* Martin Seymour-Smith claims for Kim an "almost paedophilic attractiveness" (p. 303), and sees in Kipling's unconscious "raffish paedophilia" (p. 304) an unspoken debt to the Pre-Raphaelite world he knew so well, loved as a child, and rejected as an adult. Kipling's uncle was Edward Burne-Jones, but further exploration of links between Kim and Burne-Jones's androgynous angels would lead into strange territory. In considering Kim's sexual nature, we must always remember that *Kim* is a book written for children as well as adults, and a book written by a late-Victorian writer and published just inside that period. What is certain is that Kim arouses jealousy, is well acquainted with the quarters in which the prostitutes live, and resists seduction by Lisbet, the Woman of Shamleigh, who makes sexual play with the walnuts she offers him. Kim's response is sophisticated and unequivocal. He thinks:

How can a man follow the Way or the Great Game when he is eternally pestered by women? There was that girl at Akrola by the Ford; and there was the scullion's wife behind the dovecot—not c ing the others—and now comes this one! When I was a child it was well enough, but now I am a ount man and they will not regard me as a man. Walnuts indeed! Ho! ho! It is almonds in the Plains!

(p. 257)

It is clear, too, that there is a sexual jealousy on Mahbub Ali's part over Kim's love for the lama. The overcoming of that jealousy is a lightly touched but moving episode. As the book draws to its close, there is an exchange in which Mahbub's dismissive worldliness is softened. Kim is asleep. Mahbub says to the lama: "Do not wake him. I have no wish to hear him call thee master." The lama's innocent response is "But he *is* my disciple. What else?" Mahbub "choked down his touch of spleen and rose laughing" (p. 285). In this amity, recognizing goodness, Mahbub can even laugh when the lama suggests that he, too, should forsake his own religion and follow the Way.

In a book whose cast is largely masculine, the richest female character is the Sahiba, the widowed Maharanee first met on the Grand Trunk Road: "Very often it suits a long-suffering family that a strong-tongued, iron-willed old lady should disport herself about India in this fashion; for certainly pilgrimage is grateful to the Gods" (p. 65). Earthy, generous, hungry for experience, the old Sahiba is as positive in her appreciation of life as Chaucer's Wife of Bath. She takes Kim and the lama under her loose protection, and it is under her loving auspices that Kim is finally nursed back to health in the Plains. She and her cousin's widow "laying him east and west, that the mysterious earth-currents which thrill the clay of our bodies might help and not hinder, took him to pieces all one long afternoon—bone by bone, muscle by muscle, ligament by ligament, and, lastly, nerve by nerve" (p. 275). It is the Sahiba's care that draws from Kim another kind of love: "'Maharanee,' Kim began, but led by the look in her eye, changed it to the title of plain love— 'Mother, I owe my life to thee. How shall I make thanks?'" As the book closes we leave Kim

poised between new amities and affections he has brought about. Whether love will fructify or die can no longer be our concern.

THE IMPERIAL PRESENCE IN *KIM*

"I've nearly done a long leisurely Asiatic yarn in which there are hardly any Englishmen. It has been a labour of great love and I think it is a bit more temperate and wise than much of my stuff" (*Letters*, Vol. 3, p. 11). Kipling's disarming self-awareness in this letter to Charles Eliot Norton on 15 January 1900 understates the case. It is generally recognized that in writing *Kim*, Kipling transcended the stridencies and limitations which have done so much to cloud and dog his later reputation. One of the great strengths of the book, whose hero is a most reluctant Sahib, is the almost complete freedom from racial prejudice Kipling found in its creation. The quietism of the lama, though, could never have a lasting influence on such a political animal and scourge of liberal views as Kipling.

The English in India are seen in the cool glimpses of the Great Game players at work: Colonel Creighton, Lurgan and a District Superintendant of Police, Strickland Sahib. Strickland, who plays a bit part in helping the Great Game player E.23 escape his pursuers, is another self-borrowing, that same Strickland, master of disguise, who is described in "Miss Youghal's Sais" (*Plain Tales from the Hills*, p. 27) as the "only man who can pass for Hindu or Mahommedan, hide-dresser or priest, as he pleases." Their presence is there in their works, particularly in the importance in the novel of train journeys. It is painfully there in the bitter feelings of the Woman of Shamlegh for her first love, the English Sahib who deserted her: "He went away—I had nursed him when he was sick—but he never returned. Then I saw that the Gods of the Kerlistians lied, and I went back to my own people. . . ." (p. 264). The "Kerlistians" (Christians) get short shrift in *Kim*. One of

Kipling's most telling criticisms comes in that tent in the Mavericks' camp into which the prying Kim is dragged. Bennett, the Church of England chaplain, looks at the lama "with the triple-ringed uninterest of the creed that lumps nine-tenths of the world under the title of 'heathen'" (p. 88). The English are there, too, in the memories of the old native officer who lives in a village near Umballa, and who served in the Indian Mutiny. His memories of the "land from Delhi south awash with blood" (p. 52) and of riding "with an English mem-sahib and her babe on my saddle-bow" (p. 53) are placed contrapuntally by Kipling against the lama's belief in the illusion of all action in this world, though he recognizes the old man's honorable "rendering fidelity when it was hard to give" (p. 54). But the most scathing of Kipling's pictures is of the camp near Umballa railway station where Kim is left under the charge of a "fat and freckled" (p. 99) drummer-boy. Kipling knew well the living-conditions of the professional regiments cooped up in the India of the Raj: "Three days of torment passed in the big, echoing white rooms. He walked out of afternoons under escort of the drummer-boy, and all he heard from his companion were the few useless words which seemed to make two-thirds of the white man's abuse. Kim knew and despised them all long ago. The boy resented his silence and lack of interest by beating him, as was only natural" (p. 106).

It is difficult not to see in *Kim* a multifarious, colored, passionately alive world contrasted with an occupying power whose upper echelons are marked by a cold efficiency and whose lower echelons display ignorance, brutality, and boredom. We do not see in *Kim* the young subalterns of Empire at the daily grind of administration, relief-work, bridge-building, and peace-keeping that Kipling celebrated in his collection of short stories *The Day's Work* (1898). In *Kim*, we have to take on trust Kipling's certain belief that it is the Imperial presence which allows that multifarious world to function peacefully.

CONCLUSION

The book with which *Kim* is most often compared is E. M. Forster's *A Passage to India*, published in 1924. Forster, whose experience of India as a young man was that of tutor to a young Hill-Rajah, creates a panorama in which the English are given a prominence Kipling forswears. The worlds of Hindu and Moslem are contrasted in the figures of Dr. Aziz and Professor Godbole, whose role in providing educated comedy has a little in common with that of Hurree Babu, and the inscrutable spiritual presence of Mrs. Moore might, without being too fanciful, bear some relation to the pervasive power exerted by the figure of the lama in Kim. Forster's novel, though, is a study in distances, living at the cool blue end of the spectrum. Its tone-color has little in common with the warm engagement with life in all its aspects which is the strongest impression left by *Kim*, a novel which has always called out a special affection. It is not a novel which can be said to have had a strong influence on the course of English fiction; for that we turn to E. M. Forster, D. H. Lawrence, and Virginia Woolf, Kipling's contemporaries. There are no particular advances in technique to make the book a stylistic precursor; it is solid and Victorian, so full of matter and variety that it seems more substantial than its comparatively slender three hundred or so pages. Kipling was hardly a novelist, and the success of *Kim* was never repeated, and its quality only equaled by some of Kipling's later short stories. It is in the most complimentary sense a compelling picture-book—an ever-changing panorama of detailed life and its changing backdrop, whether we are in the human bustle of the Kashmir Serai where the men of the Asian caravans can be found "piling grass before the shrieking wild-eyed stallions; cuffing the surly caravan dogs; paying off camel-drivers; taking on new grooms; swearing, shouting, arguing and chaffering in the packed square" (p. 17) or among the High Hills where the lama blesses "the great glaciers, the naked rocks, the piled moraines and tumbled shale; dry upland, hidden salt-lake, age-old timber and fruitful water-shot valley one after the other, as a dying man blesses his folk, and Kim marvelled at his passion" (p. 258).

Kipling knew *Kim* was good. In *Something of Myself* he describes his working methods, and describes his obedience to his "Personal Daemon," that objectification of what is loosely known as "inspiration." He knew his Daemon was with him in writing *Kim,* and enjoined the reader: "When your Daemon is in charge, do not try to think consciously. Drift, wait, and obey" (p. 210). It is the strength of Kipling's achievement that *Kim* has triumphantly survived the historical circumstances which gave it birth, and can still give the reader a renewed sense of participation in the essential goodness of being alive and young.

Select Bibliography

EDITION

Kim. Edited with an Introduction and Notes by Alan Sandison. General Preface, Select Bibliography and Chronology by Andrew Rutherford. Oxford University Press: Oxford World's Classics, 1998.

OTHER WORKS

Early Verse by Rudyard Kipling 1879–1889. Edited by Andrew Rutherford. Oxford: Oxford University Press, 1986.

The Letters. 4 vols. Edited by Thomas Pinney. London and University of Iowa Press: Macmillan, 1990–99.

The Jungle Book. London: Macmillan, 1894.

The Second Jungle Book. London: Macmillan, 1895.

Plain Tales from the Hills. Calcutta: Thacker, Spin & Co., 1888.

Puck of Pook's Hill. London: Macmillan, 1906.

Rudyard Kipling's Verse, Definitive Edition. London: Hodder & Stoughton, 1940.

Something of Myself. London: Macmillan, 1937.

SECONDARY WORKS

Ankers, Arthur R. *The Pater: John Lockwood Kipling, His Life and Times 1837–1911.* Otford, Kent: Pond View Books, 1988.

Critical Essays on Rudyard Kipling. Edited by Harold Orel. Boston: G.K. Hall, 1989.

Dobree, Bonamy. *Rudyard Kipling: Realist and Fabulist.* Oxford: Oxford University Press, 1967.

Forster, E. M. *A Passage to India.* London: Arnold, 1924.

Gilmour, David. *The Long Recessional: The Imperial Life of Rudyard Kipling.* London: John Murray, 2002.

Hopkirk, Peter. *The Great Game: On Secret Service in High Asia.* London: John Murray, 1990.

———. *Quest for Kim: In Search of Kipling's Great Game.* London: John Murray, 1996. (Follows the journeys made in *Kim* across India, attempts to identify the real characters behind the fictional ones and explores the "Great Game" element in *Kim.*)

Kipling and the Critics. Edited by Elliott Gilbert. London: Owen, 1966.

Kipling, John Lockwood. *Beast and Man in India.* London: Macmillan, 1891.

Kipling's Mind and Art. Edited by Andrew Rutherford. London: Oliver & Boyd, 1964. (Contains Edmund Wilson's "The Kipling that Nobody Read" and Mark Kinkead-Weekes's "Vision in Kipling's Novels.")

Laski, Marghanita. *From Palm to Pine: Rudyard Kipling Abroad and at Home.* London: Sidgwick & Jackson, 1987.

Murari, T. N. *The Imperial Agent: The Sequel to Kipling's Kim.* London: New English Library, 1987.

———. *The Last Victory.* London and New York: New English Library and St. Martin's Press, 1988. (Murari's two novels continue the story of Kim, who eventually works for Indian independence against Creighton and dies in the Amritsar Massacre of 1919.)

The Oxford History of the British Empire. 5 vols. Edited by Wm. Roger Lewis, Oxford: Oxford University Press, 1998–99.

Plain Tales from the Raj: Images of British India in the Twentieth Century. Edited by Charles Allen. London: Andre Deutsch, 1975.

Rudyard Kipling: the man, his work and his world. Edited by John Gross. London: Weidenfeld & Nicolson, 1972. (Essays, including Nirad C. Chaudhuri's appreciation of *Kim,* "The Finest Story about India—in English.")

Seymour-Smith, Martin. *Rudyard Kipling.* London: Macdonald, Queen Anne Press, 1989.

Stewart, J.I.M. *Rudyard Kipling.* London: Gollancz, 1966.

Stewart, James McG. *A Bibliographical Catalogue.* Oxford and Toronto: Dalhousie University and University of Toronto Press, 1959.

Tompkins, J.M.S. *The Art of Rudyard Kipling.* London: Methuen, 1959.

Wilson, Angus. *The Strange Ride of Rudyard Kipling.* London: Secker & Warburg, 1977.

George Bernard Shaw's
Man and Superman

JOHN A. BERTOLINI

SHAW MEANT HIS plays to be read as much as to be performed; doubly so for *Man and Superman*, which, though written 1901–1902 and published in 1903, was not performed in its entirety until 1907, and even then the play had to be divided between its frame play, acts 1, 2, and 4, played in the evenings, and its dream sequence, act 3, played at matinees. But by 1911, it had sold over thirty thousand copies—an enormous sale for a play (Hugo, 292). The book-buying public had long ceased to read plays, but almost single-handedly in the first decade of the twentieth century, Shaw demonstrated that the British theater could be a place where drama that was also literature could be vital as art by both holding an audience's attention and providing a serious criticism of life.

Man and Superman crowns a rapid ascent of dramatic art on Shaw's part. He had written nine full-length plays and a single one-act play in the preceding decade, beginning with three "Unpleasant Plays" (as he called them when he published them), modeled on the plays of the contemporary dramatist Shaw most admired, Henrik Ibsen. Four "Pleasant Plays" followed, more in keeping with his optimistic disposition and comic inclination. Shaw called his next

group of plays "Three Plays for Puritans." All these plays of the 1890s exhibited Shaw's fecundity of comic inventiveness not only in the Dickensian range and idiosyncrasy of his characters but also in his gift for wit and humor in dialogue. They also demonstrated that Shaw was serious about reclaiming the theater as a laboratory of thought, for he dealt with such themes as slum-landlordism, prostitution, the pretensions of "advanced" thinkers, failures of self-perception, empire versus colonial self-determination, and the distinction between justice and vengeance. *Man and Superman* itself is the first play of an informal trilogy (as Bernard Dukore has suggested), formed by *John Bull's Other Island* and *Major Barbara*, all three plays concerned with humankind's place in the universe. Each play debates images of Heaven and Hell and asks the question: in what ways can we attempt to transform the Hell of the society we inhabit into a more Heaven-like place? *Man and Superman* portrays human beings as driven by the Life Force to evolve through marriage and procreation into a higher, more humane and intelligent form of humanity. As such, the play still has a claim on our attention, not least because of its brilliantly inventive comedy, but perhaps even more because of its powerful vision of the human drive to become something better.

SOURCES AND MODELS

Man and Superman is a big work; it is as long as *Hamlet* or *King Lear*, and like them (or like a Wagner opera) takes four and a half hours to perform uncut. Part of the humor of the play is that it takes a normally small-scale genre, comedy, and gives it proportions normally reserved for tragedy or epic. Such a procedure usually would produce a mock epic. But such is not the case here. For, although Shaw might have followed Henry Fielding's example in *Joseph Andrews* and called his work a comic epic-poem in prose, he does not. Shaw subtitles the play a "Comedy and a Philosophy" and thereby indicates that he intends his work to formulate essential questions about human nature and destiny, to give an account of human existence, its meaning, and purpose; to examine humankind's metaphysical position in the universe. In that sense, Shaw places his work directly in line with the epic tradition, more specifically in competition with Dante's *Divine Comedy* and Milton's *Paradise Lost* (two works explicitly referred to in the play); and most immediately with Goethe's *Faust,* an epic work in dramatic form like Shaw's play, which shows that the way to achieve salvation lies in never surrendering to the forces of complacency and ease, but rather in striving with all one's strength of mind and heart to do, to live, to imagine, to create. In the dream sequence from the third act of the play (usually referred to as "Don Juan in Hell"), the protagonist, John Tanner, makes a symbolic descent into the underworld through his alter-ego, Don Juan, following in the footsteps of the traditional epic heroes, Odysseus, Aeneas, and Dante. But Shaw's play is an ocean into which many rivers flow. It is influenced not just by the epic tradition, but also by romantic comedy (especially the type involving a "gay couple," that is, a witty, battling

couple) from Shakespeare to Wilde; by the Faust tradition, and above all by Don Juan, not to mention various specific sources such as *Don Quixote,* or Molière's *The Misanthrope.*

CHRONOLOGY

1856	Born 26 July, Dublin.
1871	Leaves school.
1876	Moves to London.
1884	Joins newly formed Fabian Society.
1890	*The Quintessence of Ibsenism.* 1888—94 Music critic.
1892	*Widowers' Houses,* first play; presented privately.
1894	*Arms and the Man* produced; first stage success.
1895–1898	Drama critic.
1898	Marries Charlotte Payne-Townshend, 1 June.
1901–1902	*Man and Superman* written (published 1903).
1904	*John Bull's Other Island.*
1905	*Man and Superman,* first produced (without "Don Juan in Hell"), Royal Court Theatre, London; 176 performances.
1905–1906	Robert Loraine produces and stars, *Man and Superman,* New York; then American tour; over five hundred performances.
1907	"Don Juan in Hell" first produced, matinees, Royal Court Theatre; *Man and Superman,* Acts I, II, and IV, evenings.
1912	*Androcles and the Lion; Pygmalion* (filmed 1938; wins Academy Award for screenplay).
1915	First complete performance of *Man and Superman.*
1921	*Back to Methuselah.*
1923	*Saint Joan.* (filmed 1957).
1925	Nobel Prize for Literature.
1933	*Village Wooing.*
1949	*Shakes versus Shaw* (a puppet play).
1950	Dies 2 November.

ROMANTIC COMEDY

Shaw's chief models for his battling couple, Ann Whitefield and John ("Jack") Tanner, start with Beatrice and Benedick in Shakespeare's *Much Ado About Nothing*. For while they give every appearance of not caring for one another, the amount of energy each expends in taunting and abusing the other signifies to the audience how very interested they are in one another. They exchange insults and constantly put one another down before others. Tanner compares Ann to a "boa-constrictor" and calls her many names including "devil," "vampire," and "liar." Ann patronizes him by referring to his most fervent expressions of social or political principle as mere "talking." Just as Benedick flies from Beatrice's quick tongue, so Tanner flies from Ann's dogged pursuit. At the climax of their respective plays, each pair of lovers, after denying their desire for one another and struggling mightily against their mutual attraction, finally admit to their love and embrace publicly before their assembled friends.

Similarly, William Congreve in his Restoration comedy of 1700, *The Way of the World,* took the energy and vitality of Shakespeare's Beatrice and Benedick and converted those qualities into sophisticated languor and elegance in his two lovers, Millamant and Mirabell. In *The Way of the World,* mistrust of the male's capacity for commitment leads the heroine to be extremely coy with her suitor, delaying her assent to their marriage until she is assured of his love and respect. She continually teases and mocks him until the central scene of the play where she finally agrees to marry him. It is known as the "proviso scene" because there the lovers' wooing takes the form of a set of conditions, or "provisos" each one presents to the other before agreeing to marry. Millamant's provisos suggest that her chief anxiety is that the intimacy of marriage will radically diminish her husband's regard for her rights to privacy, independence, and integrity, while Mirabell's suggest fear on his part that Millamant's habitual

hiding behind masks and poses will continue after they are married. Once each has expressed her and his worries in regard to the other—with great charm and wit, it should be added—they finally agree to marry. *Man and Superman*'s pair of lovers likewise need to overcome a host of anxieties attendant upon the prospect of marriage: in Tanner's case—and here Shaw reverses the sexes from Congreve's comedy—about loss of freedom; and in Ann's case, the possible loss of her life in childbirth (Millamant teasingly pretends an aversion to procreation).

Between *Much Ado About Nothing* and *The Way of the World,* Molière produced a comedy, *The Misanthrope* (1666), which belongs in large part to the tradition of the battling couple through the persons of the young coquettish widow, Célimène, and her somewhat older suitor, Alceste, but more strongly influenced Shaw in its depiction of Alceste as a comically maladroit critic of societal hypocrisy. Tanner as a socialist pamphleteer bent on changing the world is ironically placed in a love relationship with a woman whose ties to society are seemingly all on the superficial level of adherence to convention and propriety, just as Alceste, who declares himself the enemy of all falseness, finds himself in love with a woman who seems to embody the deception and artificiality upon which society is founded. Also like Alceste, Tanner regularly suffers humiliations from the application of his reformer's principles to practical situations, as when he salutes Violet Robinson for being pregnant without regard to the legality of marriage, only to discover that she *is* married, and considers his compliments an insult. Shaw was a close student of Molière, and in drawing Tanner's character he has preserved almost the exact proportions in which Molière mixed Alceste's admirable qualities with his ridiculous flaws. Cervantes's Don Quixote likewise has furnished Shaw with a model for Tanner of a character who sets out to hold society to account for not living up to its ideals, and yet manages in almost every instance to have his attempts to live his ideals fall flat, usually with comic damage to himself.

Shaw often joked that in the long distant future, people would confuse the British writers whose names began with Sh: Shakespeare, Shelley, Shaw, and Sheridan—indeed would conflate them into one: Shoddy. More particularly, Shaw imitated Sheridan's bickering couple, Sir Peter and his much younger wife, Lady Teazle, from *The School for Scandal.* But Shaw did not imitate their characters in Ann and Jack Tanner, rather he drew on them as types, the teasing female and the exasperated male; he also imitated the style of their witty and humorous arguments, in which the musical values of pattern, rhythm, echo, and parallelism are in force. From another Sheridan play, *The Duenna,* Shaw took the name of his lovesick brigand, Isaac Mendoza. Although the character is a Jew in both plays, Shaw changes him from Sheridan's fortune-hunter who converts opportunistically to Christianity into an urbane thinker and Zionist.

Oscar Wilde, whose social comedies Shaw appreciated and reviewed favorably when he was a drama critic in the 1890's, had shown how charmingly male-female sexual attraction could be represented on stage, particularly in *An Ideal Husband* (1895), where the quick-witted and beautiful Mabel Chiltern often befuddles and deflates the dandy Lord Goring, who is usually never at a loss for a witty reply, except with Mabel. Such a situation in which the female can run rings around the male in the courtship dance is taken to the limit by Shaw in *Man and Superman.* The climax shows that Ann had chosen Jack as her husband-to-be long before the action of the play begins. Shaw claimed, however, that the main model for his innovation in the romantic comedy tradition, the reversed love chase where the female pursues and captures the reluctant male, was Shakespeare, whose heroines always took it upon themselves to go after the males they desired (even if that meant disguising themselves as men); for example, Rosalind in *As You Like It,* Julia in *Two Gentlemen of Verona,* and Helena in *All's Well That Ends Well.*

But Shaw's zest for paradox would not let him rest contented only with borrowing Shakespeare's male-chasing heroines. He needed a bigger reversal of convention than that. The male pursued by his heroine would have to be a male who was normally perceived as being the hunter *par excellence* in the love chase, and that figure was Don Juan, a character invented by the Spanish playwright Tirso de Molina around 1600.

THE DON JUAN TRADITION

Tirso called his Don Juan play *The Trickster of Seville* (*El Burlador de Sevilla*) because in his version Don Juan seduces women partly out of an excess of sexual appetite and energy but mostly because he likes to trick them out of their honor. In rapid succession, Don Juan dishonors four women: Duchess Isabella; the fishergirl Tisbea; Dona Ana; and the peasant bride Aminta. In the moral economy of the play, the first three women are portrayed as in some sense deserving the fate that befalls them, for each violates societal and moral rules governing sexual relations, either through premarital or extramarital sex. Isabella, though not yet married to Don Octavio, is willing to sleep with him when Don Juan impersonates him. Tisbea disdains marrying her social equals, the fishermen in her village, yet gives herself to Don Juan when she discovers he is a nobleman. Dona Ana arranges a love-tryst with a man who is not her fiancé. But when Don Juan tries to seduce the last of the four, Aminta, Tirso portrays the attempt as a violation of the sacred. Don Juan comes upon the wedding of Aminta to Battricio, and there the Don both literally and figuratively separates bride from bridegroom, by sitting between them, and by lying to each about the other. Such a disruption of the sacred union that is marriage is too much for Tirso (who was a monk as well as a playwright), and he punishes Don Juan for the transgression by having the Statue of Dona Ana's father, the Commander of Calatrava (whom Don Juan had slain in a duel) take Don Juan to Hell in the name of divine wrath. Throughout the play, Don Juan had resisted all attempts to remind him of his mortality by greeting such efforts with the reply that his day of reckoning was so far off that he could afford not to think about it. Tirso particularly emphasizes the ironic reversal Don Juan suffers at the end of the play when the Statue of the Commander tricks Don Juan into his own damnation by offering to take Don Juan's hand as a sign of good faith, and then drags him down to Hell. Don Juan had always given his hand as a pledge of good faith to the women he seduced.

All of this material attracted Shaw because of the ways reworking it in *Man and Superman* allowed him to raise the issues he wanted his play to deal with: hypocrisies and inconsistencies in society's attitudes toward sex and marriage. But he also wanted to project a hopeful vision of humankind's evolutionary future, and the basic material of Tirso's Don Juan play allowed him to do that. For Don Juan's twofold desire to have sex with as many women as possible and to put off confronting his own mortality makes evolutionary sense if not moral sense. Indeed, the former instinct is a strategy to achieve the latter aim: immortality. Evolutionary psychologists teach us that genes seek to reproduce themselves, and that the male sex will strive for excellence in order to win the female's favor and will try to impregnate as many females as possible to insure the survival of his genes. Likewise, the female will favor sexually and seek to reproduce with the male who offers the most attractive genes for survival (see Miller's *The Mating Mind,* for example). In The Revolutionist's Handbook, which Shaw appends to his play as a sample of the protagonist John Tanner's political ideas, Shaw/Tanner opines that "the maternal instinct leads a woman to prefer a tenth share in a first-rate man to the exclusive possession of a third-rate one" (*Collected Plays,* V. 2: 785—page references of all subsequent quotations are from this edition).

Shaw made over the Don Juan he inherited by converting the figure's drive for personal genetic immortality into a drive to better the human race through evolution. At the end of the Don Juan in Hell sequence, Juan (pronounced JOO-en in England) leaves Hell, the palace of lies, illusion, and play, to seek Heaven as the home of truth, reality, and work, where he may strive for the betterment of the race. At the end of the play, John Tanner actualizes Juan's thought by allowing himself to be engaged to Ann. For Ann Whitefield understands instinctually that although Tanner blunders and blusters in applying and pronouncing his ideals and ideas, he offers much the superior genes among the males in her set, superior in his prodigious energy, his courageous political stands, and his quick-witted intelligence. And Ann has much resistance to overcome, most particularly his belief that he is not suited to marriage. Tanner's ancestor, the Don Juan of Tirso de Molina, who should have been morally repugnant to women because of his contemptuous treatment of them, was not so for most of them precisely because of their instinctual recognition that his formidable sexual energy and absolute physical courage made him the bearer of desirable genes. Shaw converts his Don Juan's physical courage into Tanner's metaphysical courage, an attribute lacking in Tirso's seducer, who at the moment of his death calls for a priest to absolve him of his sins, thus demonstrating that his pursuit of women had been only a way of evading his destiny: confrontation with a world beyond that of the senses, a world embodied in the supernatural figure of the Statue of the Commander.

MOLIÈRE'S DON JUAN

The successor to Tirso's Don Juan, Molière's 1665 play, *Don Juan,* also greatly influenced Shaw's conception of his twentieth-century Don Juan, not only in general through Shaw's affinity for Molière's particular blend of social satire and graceful humor, but also through Molière's making his Don Juan a vehicle for exploring how ephemeral human existence and endeavor relate to the metaphysical and eternal. What distinguishes Molière's Don Juan is not his libertinism but his atheism. When his comic servant Sganarelle asks him if he believes in God, Don Juan replies that he believes two and two make four, clearly implying that he believes there is nothing outside of the world that can be measured. Like Tirso's Don Juan, Molière's eventually has to confront a manifestation of the supernatural order, again in the person of an avenging Statue of the Commander Juan has slain in a duel. But Molière conceived of a completely original and mysterious addition to the tradition when he had Don Juan earlier in the play meet a representative of the divine order in the person of a Poor Man in the forest who kindly offers Don Juan directions. Don Juan tries to convert the Poor Man by tempting him with a louis d'or to turn against God by blaspheming, but when the Poor Man eschews self-interest by refusing, Don Juan pays him the money anyway, for the love—not of God—but of humanity, he says. The Poor Man is the only person in the play to whom Don Juan pays a debt. All others—his father, his creditor, his servant, the women he has seduced, their relatives—Don Juan refuses to pay. Only at the end of the play is he forced to pay the debt he owes God, his own death.

Shaw makes use of the episode of the Poor Man's forest encounter with Don Juan by reshaping it into the encounter in the Sierra Nevada between John Tanner and the brigand Mendoza. Tanner flees to Spain after learning from his chauffeur, Henry Straker, that Ann has set her cap for him, only to be stopped by Mendoza's band of operetta brigands. Mendoza introduces himself to Tanner: "I am a brigand: I live by robbing the rich." Tanner replies, "I am a gentleman: I live by robbing the poor. Shake hands" (p. 621). The verbal symmetry here re-enacts the patterned exchange of respect between Don Juan and the Poor Man. At the end of the encounter Tanner has a chance to turn over Mendoza to the police, and in a gesture matching the gratuitous generosity of Don Juan's donation to the Poor Man, Tanner refuses and instead calls Mendoza's band his escort. In the "Don Juan in Hell" dream sequence that follows Tanner's initial encounter with Mendoza, Tanner and Mendoza mutually dream of themselves having a debate: in the dream Tanner becomes Don Juan and Mendoza becomes the Devil. And just as Molière's Don Juan in meeting the Poor Man is meeting his own unacknowledged spiritual destiny, that is, the necessity of paying his debt to God, so too Tanner in meeting Mendoza/the Devil is confronting that aspect of his inner self that blocks him from his destiny to marry Ann, namely his fear that marriage will divert him from purpose and direction in the betterment of human existence, and indeed the deeper fear that life has neither purpose nor meaning, that evolution is going nowhere in particular.

MOZART'S *DON GIOVANNI*

Shaw repeatedly said that he learned more from Mozart about writing plays than from playwrights, and Mozart's *Don Giovanni* ("Giovanni" being "Juan" or "John" in Italian) with libretto by Lorenzo Da Ponte had always been a favorite among Mozart's operas. It pervades *Man and Superman.* From the complex yet graceful patterning of his prose to Shaw's evident concern with arranging his characters' speeches, dialogues, and scenes, as if they were arias, recitatives, and ensembles in opera, to his genial and forgiving representation of human nature, he shows himself a disciple of Mozart. Indeed W. H. Auden said that Shaw's "writing has an effect nearer to that of music than the work of any of the so-called pure writers" ("The Fabian Figaro," 156). Where Shaw borrows specifically from *Don Giovanni,* he always recasts the borrowing to achieve his own meaning. For example, at the very end of *Man and Superman,* when Ann makes her final assault on Tanner's resistance to marriage, Shaw patterns their exchange after the struggle between the Statue of the Commander and Don Giovanni. The Statue, holding the Don's hand in his icy yet burning grip, demands that he repent before it is too late. Three times the Statue urges the scoundrel to repent: "Yes." And three times Don Giovanni defies the divine agent with an ever larger, "No." In Shaw this becomes:

> TANNER: I will not marry you. I will not marry you.
> ANN: Oh, you will, you will.
> TANNER: I tell you no, no, no.
> ANN: I tell you yes, yes, yes.
> TANNER: No.
> ANN [*coaxing—imploring—almost exhausted*]: Yes. Before it is too late for repentance. Yes.
> TANNER [*struck by the echo from the past*]: When did all this happen to me before? Are we two dreaming?
>
> (p. 728)

Tanner's last line here humorously parades Shaw's playful self-consciousness about invoking Mozart's opera. The allusion is really a metaphor that conveys to us Tanner's sense of his situation. He feels as if he is about to be damned for eternity if he gives in to Ann's desire to be married to him—a desire which he gratifies moments later in a sudden and complete turnabout.

ACT I: CLASSIC COMEDY

The first act of *Man and Superman* is one of the most perfect structures in dramatic literature. Dramatically it insists on two questions regarding fatherhood. Who will take the place of Ann Whitefield's recently deceased father to become her guardian, Roebuck Ramsden or John Tanner? Who is the father of Violet Robinson's allegedly illegitimate baby-to-be-born? The two questions can be distilled further into the single question: Where is there a father to be found? The answer given at the end of the play is John Tanner. It comes when John Tanner, after a valiant struggle against his comic destiny, finally connects his acceding to Ann's will that he should marry her with the idea of becoming a father. As he embraces her tightly and she al-

ludes to the mortal personal risk to her in becoming a wife and mother, he feels assailed by a hitherto unknown emotion, and asks, "What have you grasped in me? Is there a father's heart as well as a mother's?" (p. 729)

Tanner's conception of himself as a father completes the whole play's shape because what sets the plot in motion is the death of a father, Ann's father, Mr. Whitefield. The act is set in the study of Roebuck Ramsden, an old friend of the Whitefield family. He is being visited by the modest young poet, Octavius Robinson, who is in a state of grief because Mr. Whitefield had acted toward him and his sister, Violet, as a father after the death of their own father. By beginning the play just after a death, Shaw is placing his play squarely in the genre of classic comedy. The action of classic comedies often takes place after an individual's death or after a truce has been called in a war (as in *Much Ado About Nothing*) because as a genre it is comedy's job to oppose forces inimical to life. Comedy celebrates health, generosity, love, sex, marriage, and birth; it rejects death, war, sickness, stinginess, hatred, and virginity. It preaches to its audience that what matters about life is not that we must die but that we can love, that male unites with female to produce children, so that life can endure in spite of death. Individuals die, but the species lives.

The act follows a clear pattern of emphasis: four dialogues of increasing thematic and dramatic interest between two characters alternate with increasingly larger ensemble scenes. The four dialogues occur between Ramsden and Octavius, Ramsden and Tanner, Octavius and Tanner, and then, Ann and Tanner. The first three are permutations of pairs derived from the three male characters. The last dialogue between Ann and Tanner is the longest, the most serious, and the most consequential. Each duet is followed by an ensemble: a trio for the three male characters, a quintet which adds Ann and her mother to the three males, a quartet which subtracts Mrs. Whitefield, and, to provide the act with a grand finale, a septet with Violet and

Ramsden's sister added to the previous quintet. Any student of Mozart's operas will recognize this pattern of beginning an act with solos and duets and then alternating them with larger ensembles while building to a concerted finale involving all the main characters. Shaw's conscious intention to structure Act I with meticulous care as to the sequencing of dialogues and ensembles was confirmed by the publication in 1996 of Shaw's original scenario for the play: "The Superman, or Don Juan's Great Grandson's Grandson" (1901) in which Shaw outlines the structure of the play, scene by scene.

Shaw keeps the off-stage death of Mr. Whitefield from spoiling the comic mood by having Ramsden console Octavius with a string of platitudes about death of which Polonius would not have been ashamed. Ramsden further tries to lift Octavius's mood by telling him that Mr. Whitefield had hopes someday Octavius would marry Ann. Octavius is only too happy to hear so. But then Ramsden warns Octavius that his only defect is his friendship with the radical thinker, John Tanner, author of The Revolutionist's Handbook, whereupon, by the inexorable law of comedy that whenever a character is ill-spoken of out of his presence that character will presently enter, Tanner enters. He is in something near a frenzied state because Whitefield's will has appointed him to a joint guardianship of Ann with Ramsden, of all people.

Shaw has taken some pains to establish Ramsden as a parody patriarch with his *"four tufts of iron-grey hair"* which *"grow in two symmetrical pairs above his ears and at the angles of his spreading jaws"* (p. 533), and flanked as he is by busts of his political idols, the liberals John Bright and Herbert Spencer. Ramsden is the first in a series of mock-fathers Shaw presents to his audience and readers so they may reject their false credentials ultimately in favor of the play's authentic father, John Tanner, his authenticity being guaranteed by Ann's instinctual selection of him as the father of her children. As Northrop Frye points out in his *Anatomy of Criticism*, in

the genre of Comedy a young man desires a young woman who is under some constraint from an elderly person, usually a father, but sometimes a guardian, or a maiden-aunt, as to her choice in a mate. The young man devises a scheme to defeat the older blocking figure and wins the hand of the young woman. The carrying out of the scheme is the plot. And the defeat of the older figure often means the defeat of his values and ideas in favor of the young couple's new set of values, around which a new community forms to replace the one disrupted by the young couple's defiance of hierarchy. So it is in *Man and Superman*. At one point, Ann refers to Jack as "Jack the Giant Killer." In having her do so, Shaw points to the mythic pattern underlying the play, the archetype of the young man who must symbolically slay the father-figure in order to attain the young woman and become a father himself. Hence, Tanner and Ramsden in their first scene together butt heads politically and morally, and since Jack is the more intelligent, well-informed, and quick-witted of the two, he usually comes out the winner in their debates. Ramsden is usually reduced to sputtering displays of temper and lack of self-control mostly because he thinks mechanically instead of flexibly. Tanner compares Roebuck's reasoning process to the operation of a matchbox machine. One always knows what Ramsden thinks on any given topic, the way one knows that a coin placed in an automatic machine will produce the sought after product; in other words, Ramsden relies on conventional and second-hand thinking whereas Tanner—however outlandishly—thinks originally and for himself. Where the traditional Don Juan rebelled primarily against his society's constraints on sexual energy, Tanner rebels against mechanical thinking in general, whether in politics, philosophy, or sex.

The first large ensemble follows Tanner and Ramsden's duet: the quintet involving Tanner, Tavy, Ramsden, Ann and her mother. It resolves the first part of the father question that governs the thematic structure of act I, namely who will take the place of Ann's father and become her guardian. Besides dealing with this question the quintet introduces the character of Ann Whitefield, whom Shaw describes as "one of the vital geniuses" by which he means not that she is "oversexed" or even an impossibly beautiful woman but that she exudes a life-affirming aura that makes "men dream" (p. 549). Shaw explains in the Epistle Dedicatory (the Preface to the play in which Shaw explains its genesis) that he intends Ann to represent "Everywoman" (p. 519), that is, woman in pursuit of a mate and father for her children. Feminists have often taken exception to Shaw's characterization of Ann, but of late both evolutionary biologists and evolutionary psychologists have supported Shaw's view by arguing that women tend to choose males instinctively for superior genes. Don Juan (in Act III) explains what Shaw is getting at with his epitome of Ann when Dona Ana objects to Juan's view of women by calling it, "cynical and disgusting animalism":

> Pardon me, Ana: I said nothing about a woman's whole mind. I spoke of her view of Man as a separate sex. It is no more cynical than her view of herself as above all things a Mother. Sexually, Woman is nature's contrivance for perpetuating its highest achievement. Sexually, Man is Woman's contrivance for fulfilling Nature's behest in the most economical way.
>
> (p. 659)

In other words, women invented men to make the reproductive process more efficient. Hence their pursuit of men has to do with turning them into fathers in furtherance of Life itself, which is why act one revolves around the question of who will be the father.

Tanner and Ramsden both fight valiantly against the idea of becoming Ann's joint-guardians, but she amply demonstrates her vital genius by overcoming all their objections, one by one. She does so through a brilliant combination of charm, outright lies, coaxing, unscrupulous manipulation of their masculine delicacy, reasoning, shameless feigning, and

flirtation. Mrs. Whitefield is present to have someone there who is immune to Ann's strategies in order that the men's susceptibility to her particular brand of suggestion shall be illuminated. Here is an example of the delightful comedy Ann's maneuvers to control the males around her provide. When Mrs. Whitefield asks Ramsden as Ann's newly agreed-upon guardian to speak to her about her habit of giving nicknames to people in her circle (which is of course part of how she manipulates them), Ann pretends remorse for this lack of consideration, and solicits all the men to forgive her. Her false humility provokes a shower of sympathy from Octavius and Ramsden, both of whom insist that she continue calling them, "Ricky-ticky-tavy" and "Granny," respectively. She thanks them but points out that Jack has not joined them, whereupon Tanner dryly opines, "[*over his shoulder, from the bookcase*] I think you ought to call me Mr. Tanner" (p. 555). Ann immediately contradicts him, and flirtatiously suggests that she might call him by his famous ancestor's name, Don Juan. Ramsden balks violently at her suggestion. Ann feigns innocence of her own implication, and asks for time to think of an appropriate form of address, which leads Tanner to surrender in desperation. Shaw's uncanny instinct for creating comedy out of stage business shows itself at maximum efficacy here, particularly in Tanner's attempted victory though insouciance by making his declaration on behalf of formality—which is really his attempt to protect himself from Ann's intimacy—"*over his shoulder, from the bookcase.*" In doing so, he is replicating Ann's posture preceding her earlier address to him as "Jack the Giant Killer," when "*she casts a glance at Tanner over her shoulder*" (p. 554). The replication of posture here sends the audience the stage message that they are indeed a matched pair.

In conformity with the pattern of interlocutors in successive scenes Shaw has established, another duet follows the quintet, as Tanner and Octavius are left alone on stage, and the former advises the latter on his relationship with Ann. Octavius has a bad case of puppy love, though he thinks it the stuff of famous love affairs. Ann's view of his love for her can be gauged by her ironically calling him "Ricky-ticky-tavy" after Kipling's famous mongoose whose gumption and bravery against a cobra save a child's life. He, too, almost quarrels with Jack over Ann because of the blunt way Jack talks about Ann as a huntress of men. Tanner decorates his warning to Octavius with his theories about love between the artist-man and the mother-woman which Tanner sees in a Strindbergian way as a struggle to the death for each one's needs over the other's. Shaw adds in the Epistle Dedicatory that when the artist is a woman, she becomes a mother only as material for her art and devours male geniuses "as mere hors d'oeuvres" (p. 509). While Tanner's warnings and Tavy's predictably indignant rejoinders that women could never have such aggressive instincts provide wonderful comedy, they also show Jack talking to himself about what he will be facing in a relationship with Ann.

A quartet now follows which engages the new issue of Violet's pregnancy and the question of the father's identity. Various alternatives are considered, such as sending Violet abroad to have her baby, and speculations on the father's identity are introduced. The suggested alternatives allow Shaw to demonstrate by means of Jack's reactions how suitable he would be as a father. For example, when Ann pities Octavius for breaking down over his embarrassment at the prospect of discussing the situation with his sister, Tanner denounces them all for selfishness, and declares that the sympathy should go to "the woman who is going to risk her life to create another life!" (p. 565) There he shows his awe of woman's courage and respect for her power to create new life. Like Ann the Everywoman, Tanner strongly embodies the impulse to life. Shaw also forces the audience to contemplate the idea and ideal of Tanner as a father by having Ramsden virtually accuse Tanner of being the father of Violet's child. Tanner

denies the accusation, but in a way that again shows him to be prime material for fatherhood. He assures them that were he the father of Violet's baby, he would proclaim it proudly.

Jack and Ann are then left alone as the others exit to persuade Violet to go abroad. Shaw has tantalized the audience by not allowing Ann and Jack to be alone on stage until now, and the wait has increased the sexual tension between them enormously. What follows is one of the sexiest and most explicit representations of a male-female courting dance ever put on stage, but with the Shavian twist that the woman is the aggressor, and indeed, in control at almost every point. The comic sexual tension of their duologue derives from their operating on two quite different planes. Ann behaves artfully by instinct and Tanner behaves obtusely without instinct. She proceeds by actions; he by words. The words provide a smokescreen to blind himself to what is really happening, while her actions are designed to penetrate the smokescreen. She begins the scene by speaking *almost into his ear* (p. 566); soon she is "slipping her arm into his and walking about with him" (p. 567). They reminisce about their childhood. We learn that she eliminated rivals, that he made up adventures to impress her. When Ann insists that no woman would agree with him that destruction is a force necessary to clear the way for new structures, he distinguishes between destruction and murder, the former being necessary for life to go on, the latter the antithesis of life. She insists that she does not mind his unconventional views. He compares her to a boa constrictor that does not mind the opinions of the stag in her coils. His metaphor suggests that on an unconscious level he realizes the animal forces at work on them both, but it also suggests his fear of losing his individuality in her love.

Sensing his responsiveness, Ann heightens her flirting:

ANN: O-o-o-o-oh! Now I understand why you warned Tavy that I am a boa constrictor. Granny told me. [*She laughs and throws her boa round his neck*]. Doesn't it feel nice and soft, Jack?

TANNER [*in the toils*]: You scandalous woman, will you throw away even your hypocrisy?

ANN: I am never hypocritical with you, Jack. Are you angry? [*She withdraws the boa and throws it on a chair*]. Perhaps I shouldn't have done that.

TANNER [*contemptuously*]: Pooh, prudery! Why should you not, if it amuses you?

ANN [*shyly*]: Well, because—because I suppose what you really meant by the boa constrictor was t h i s [*she puts her arms round his neck*].

TANNER [*staring at her*]: Magnificent audacity! [*She laughs and pats his cheeks*].

(pp. 575–576)

Shaw makes their sexuality glow underneath their proper Edwardian garb. No other play of the period remotely approaches the metaphoric version of foreplay Shaw offers here. The tactile nature of the imagery, the incongruity of setting and behavior, the language that incites transgression—all contribute to the heating of sexual temperature. When Ann substitutes her arms for her boa which she has invited Jack to notice the niceness and softness of, neither Tanner nor the audience can help thinking for what else the boa might substitute. To imply such naked sexuality and retain the charm of flirting is Shaw's particular achievement here, for there is not a touch of lubricity in spite of the clarity of reference. The balance between the transparency of meaning and the coziness of sexuality is indicated by how easily Shaw plays with the figurative and literal in sliding from the image of the boa constrictor to the actual boa of Ann which in turn is named metaphorically after the boa constrictor. When she throws her arms round Jack's neck, she seems—indeed claims—to be literalizing Jack's original metaphor, but she is actually literalizing her own metaphor: her body is her boa. Jack becomes afraid and breaks the sexual tension between them by suggesting that she really has designs on Tavy, a suggestion which confuses Ann temporarily, allowing the opportunity for the other characters to re-enter.

The ensuing grand septet (all the main characters with Violet and Roebuck's sister, Miss Ramsden, added) addresses the second great father question of the first act: who is the father of Violet's baby? Violet denounces all her old friends, telling them she will never see them again. When Tanner intervenes to side with Violet, by dissociating himself from their narrow prejudices regarding sexual morals, and saluting her "vitality and bravery" in becoming a mother, she indignantly rejects his "abominable opinions" (p. 582) informing them that she is indeed a married woman, though secretly so. We also learn that Ann actually knew the secret, which revelation prompts from Tanner the ejaculation, "Oh!!! Unfathomable deceit! Double crossed!" (p. 583), expressing his despair over Ann's having utterly outwitted him. He also informs Violet that Ramsden virtually charged *him* with being the father of her baby. Shaw can be seen here to be employing traditional forms of comic mistakes to make his larger point about how suited Tanner is to become a father: namely his disregard for conventional views, and more importantly, his regard for female courage and instinct. Act I concludes with Tanner's prophetic observation to Ramsden: "You must cower before the wedding ring like the rest of us" (p. 584).

ACT II: THE CHASE BEGINS

Since Shaw plays with scale and proportion throughout the play, it is not surprising that the second act should be short and set outdoors where the first act was long and set indoors. The second act also has a new automobile belonging to Tanner prominently placed in the middle of the stage, the effect of which on the audience can only be compared today to placing a space shuttle on stage, since a ride in a car in 1905 would have been almost as outside the experience of the audience as a ride in a space shuttle is to us now. The auto's role has a threefold significance. It allows Shaw to create a modern counterpart to Don Juan's double, his comic servant (Catalinon in Tirso, Sganarelle in Molière, Leporello in Mozart, Da Ponte), in Tanner's chauffeur, Henry Straker, who constantly exposes his employer's shortcomings in knowledge and self-awareness. And it symbolizes Ann's instinctual drives. Its use in the staging allows Shaw to create both subtle and spectacular effects.

An example of the spectacular can be seen at the end of the act when Tanner, having been informed at last by Straker that Ann Whitefield has marked him down as her prey, jumps in his car, and orders Straker to drive him as fast and as far away as he can, so that the curtain goes down on the stunning sight of an automobile driving into the wings. An example of the subtle effects can be seen during the dialogue between Ann and Tanner which occurs in the middle of the act. Their conversation consists mainly of Ann's pretending to be at the command of her mother's wishes, a situation which provokes Tanner—in a long speech—to work himself into a "sociological rage" over the intolerable domination of the young by the old. At the end of which, Ann, remarks "I suppose you will go in seriously for politics some day, Jack." Tanner, without quite realizing it and like most males in the animal kingdom, has been showing off his prowess to attract a female's attention. Shaw describes Ann during the speech as *watching him with quiet curiosity* (p. 599). The delicious comic deflation achieved by her observation makes Shaw's point that the unconscious mind rules, that evolutionary demands drive our behavior as males and females. Men develop intellect and bravura, verbal facility, and social status to impress potential sexual partners; women choose those most likely to give them children with the wit and courage to survive and achieve.

In the successful 1907 revival of the play starring Robert Loraine and Lillah McCarthy as Jack and Ann, and directed by Shaw, at the Court Theatre, Shaw hit upon a way of staging this scene so as to bring out his meaning. He wrote about it in a letter to Harley Granville-Barker (who had created the role of Jack):

[Loraine] wanted to deliver the great speech about the tyranny of mothers, enthroned in the motor car, with Lillah somewhere under the wheels with her back to the audience. I immediately saw the value of the idea and put Lillah in the car in a fascinating attitude with her breast on the driving wheel, and Loraine ranting about on the gravel.
(*Collected Letters: 1898–1910*, p. 690)

Shaw recognized that Ann should be in the driver's seat, in control of the direction and pace of the relationship, observing and appreciating Tanner's courting display, and choosing him to become the father of her children. After he gets away from her in his car, she follows her instinct immediately to get in another car and go after him until she catches him.

But Act II does more than activate Ann's physical pursuit of Jack, it also establishes the secondary couple whose function to parody the main couple is so much a part of the genre of romantic comedy. Here Shaw reveals the identity of Violet's husband, and the father of her baby, an American, Hector Malone Jr. The dramatic function of the secondary couple is to illuminate by contrast or by reflection hidden or less visible characteristics of the main couple. Violet, for example, has determination and strength to get what she wants without the sort of stratagems and charm that Ann has to employ. Violet's presence beside Ann permits us to see that Ann is not quite the predator she might seem otherwise. Each has what the other lacks and desires. Violet has a husband but needs money to live. Ann has money to live but wants a husband. Hector Malone Jr., by virtue of his being a hidden father, perfectly mirrors Tanner's status in the play, a man who claims to be against marrying and becoming a father, and yet who gives every indication that he would be an excellent father and indeed discovers his destiny is to become one.

ACT III: DON JUAN LEAVES HELL FOR HEAVEN

Shaw called *Man and Superman* "a Comedy and a Philosophy." By that subtitle he meant that his play presented the philosophy of comedy. He used the genre to ask the most basic questions of life. What does it mean to make life go on by producing children? Does life have a purpose? A direction? Moral value? Are human beings by nature good or evil? Creative or destructive? These are the questions provoked in Tanner's unconscious mind by Ann's pursuit of him. He cannot marry Ann until he has confronted them. So Shaw has devised a dream for Tanner in which he asks himself these questions in the form of a ninety minute debate on the purpose of life for a quartet of speakers: Don Juan, the Devil, Dona Ana, and the Statue of the Commander (Ana's father).

Before the debate (which is a dream because it makes use of unconscious material and suppressed anxieties and wishes), Shaw provides an occasion for it. Tanner has fled from Ann to the magical evening landscape of the Sierra Nevada, Shaw's equivalent to Shakespeare's green worlds, like the Forest of Arden, the Wood near Athens, or Prospero's Isle, psychic sites where characters repair temporarily to face their fears and desires regarding sexuality, love, and marriage before they re-enter the weekday world. And just as Shakespeare's characters encounter improbable creatures in those metaphoric realms, Tanner and Straker encounter Mendoza, an English-Spanish Jew, the head of a brigand band of political misfits—French and English anarchists and social-democrats. They themselves are debating the question which of the two groups has greater personal courage, when Tanner's car wanders into their hunting territory. (Shaw means their debate to parody the great debate among the leading Devils in Book II of *Paradise Lost*). Their chief Mendoza, besides being the leader of bandits is also—incongruously—a love-sick po-etaster, pining away, as it turns out, for unrequited love of Henry Straker's sister, Louisa. Tanner must meet this version of himself because he thought he had overcome in himself the impulse to passionate, romantic love that Mendoza comically personifies.

When Tanner dozes off listening to Mendoza's doggerel to Louisa, like a comic epic hero, he descends into the metaphoric underworld of his unconscious in order to face all the inner psychic forces blocking him from marrying Ann. In the dream, he splits himself into his idealized self, Don Juan, and his antithetical self, the Devil (who corresponds to Mendoza in being an espouser of aestheticism), the part of him that doubts life has direction or purpose or meaning. By debating the Devil, Juan argues himself into leaving Hell and seeking Heaven.

As a way of further clarifying his choice, Tanner dreams that the Statue of the Commander (who corresponds to Roebuck Ramsden as a mock-father) makes the opposite journey, choosing to leave Heaven because it "is the most angelically dull place in all creation" (p. 647). Tanner thereby distinguishes Ramsden's values from his own, showing why he rejects them. For the Statue's complaints about Heaven, besides its dullness, are that the people there don't pay any attention to fine statues, the women do not dress to advantage or adorn themselves with jewels; they have no appreciation of art, and they stay there in an uncomfortable state mostly because they feel they owe it to their social position.

Completing the dreamer's quartet of debaters is Dona Ana, who corresponds to Ann White-field. Tanner dreams that after Juan leaves to find Heaven, Dona Ana follows him because she understands that her "work is not yet done." She asserts her belief "in the Life to Come," and then cries out to the universe "A father! A father for the Superman" (p. 689). Tanner has to understand himself that in marrying Ann, he will not be hindering life but helping it, that her drive to find a father harmonizes with his drive to better life. Once he can see that Ann is not another incarnation of the Devil diverting him from his true purpose but the person with whom he can fulfill his purpose (fatherhood), he can agree to marry her. And his dream tells him so.

Although Shaw imbues Tanner/Juan with Faustian striving, a drive to bring into existence something better than himself, to help "Life's incessant aspiration to higher organization, wider, deeper, intenser self-consciousness, and clearer self-understanding" (p. 680), Shaw also provides a significant element of ambivalence. For, when Juan decides finally—and he takes the whole debate to make up his mind—to seek Heaven, he has to pause and ask directions from—improbably—the Statue. And we never actually see him arrive in Heaven. The Devil's rhetorically potent and substantial arguments against Juan's conceptions of heavenly reality and the improved being to come, the Superman, provide much additional ambivalence toward Juan's aspirations.

Don Juan and the Devil begin their debate proper by arguing about the differences between Heaven and Hell. The Devil presents Hell as the home of human warmth and aesthetic appreciation. He asserts that whereas people fixate morbidly on starvation, poverty, and misery, he invites them "to sympathize with joy, with love, with happiness, with beauty" (p. 644). Juan counters that in Hell everything is unreal, whereas Heaven invites one to contemplate reality. When Ana asks if there is only contemplation in Heaven, Juan answers that "there is the work of helping Life in its struggle upward" (p. 652). His answer proves too much for the Devil, who sees little evidence of mankind's use of brains to create life, but much evidence that Man is basically murderous, and that therefore it is not the Life instinct that is paramount in Man but the Death instinct. The Devil elaborates this argument in the play's longest—and arguably its most powerful—speech:

> In the arts of life man invents nothing; but in the arts of death he outdoes Nature herself ... his heart is in his weapons ... This marvelous force of Life of which you boast is a force of Death: Man measures his strength by his destructiveness ... and the inner need that has nerved life to the effort of organizing itself into the human being is not the need for higher life but for a more efficient engine

of destruction ... something more constantly, more ruthlessly, more ingeniously destructive was needed; and that something was Man, the inventor of the rack, the stake, the gallows, the electric chair; of sword and gun and poison gas.

(pp. 653–656)

Juan never really refutes the Devil's argument here. He mocks it, he skirts it, but he does not really counter it, except to shift the argument away from Man's essential nature to the political and social condition of humankind and by asserting that "It is not killing and dying that degrades us, but base living, and accepting the wages and profits of degradation" (p. 658). The ironic punch of the Devil's sobering, somber rhetoric and Don Juan's evasion of its thrust argue that Shaw felt within himself the pull of the Devil's persuasive powers. Yeats used to distinguish between the Shaw who wrote to the newspapers and the poet-Shaw who argued with himself. Here we have the poet-Shaw struggling between Don Juan's visionary will and the Devil's cynical outlook. We see the struggle again in the final exchange between Juan and the Devil.

As Juan bids farewell to his three interlocutors, the Devil offers him one final piece of wisdom. He suggests that Juan's perception of humankind as evolving toward the goal of the Superman is an illusion. The Devil can and does quote scripture, from Ecclesiastes, that "there is nothing new under the sun." He advises that what Juan sees as movement forward in history is only a pendulum swinging back and forth; that life is only "an infinite comedy of illusion" (p. 683). For Juan, this suggestion is the most horrifying of all, though he does not show it. It is also the most horrifying for Shaw, though clearly he feels it might be true nonetheless. Shaw was not a Darwinian. In fact, he regarded Darwin's theory of Natural Selection as too bleak. Shaw says of Darwin's theory in the Preface to *Back to Methuselah* (which takes up the evolutionary ideas of *Man and Superman* and expands them):

But when its whole significance dawns on you, your heart sinks into a heap of sand within you. There is a hideous fatalism about it, a ghastly and damnable reduction of beauty and intelligence, of strength and purpose, of honor and aspiration, to such casually picturesque changes as an avalanche may make in a mountain.

(*Collected Plays, Vol. 5*: 294)

Shaw preferred Lamarck's theories which argued that need and will played the dominant role in evolution, not the rule of survival of the fittest. With Don Juan's departure for Heaven Shaw expresses his faith in the role of human will in evolution. If we desire and try to evolve as a species in a specific direction, we will. But Shaw also warns himself about the idea of the Superman. After Juan leaves, the Devil counsels: "Beware of the pursuit of the Superhuman: it leads to an indiscriminate contempt for the Human" (p. 687). On the other hand, Shaw gives us Ann's response, which is to be inspired to follow Don Juan in pursuit of a father for the Superman. When Tanner awakes from his dream, he finds Ann has tracked him down, and that Mendoza has shared his dream. Therein we can see that Shaw has split Tanner into Juan and the Devil so as to let the two sides of Tanner's and of Shaw's own divided self argue about the destiny of the human race. But he leaves us with the irrefutable fact of Ann's will to have a husband.

ACT IV: A FATHER'S HEART

The final act introduces the last mock-father for Tanner to displace, Hector Malone Sr. Shaw contrives a dispute between Senior and Junior, the purpose of which is to demonstrate a father's tenderness toward his own offspring. When Malone Sr. discovers his son's secret engagement to Violet, by reading a billet-doux from Violet to Hector on the pretext that it was addressed to his name, he attempts to block the marriage on the grounds that no social advantage accrues to either partner in such a marriage. Malone Jr.

becomes furious, and declares his independence from his father. Malone Sr., terrified at the prospect of losing his son's love and company, and with some artful coaxing by Violet, capitulates, his attempt at manifesting patriarchal might a dismal failure due to his father's doting heart.

In surrendering, Malone Sr. prefigures Jack's surrender to Ann, which takes place soon thereafter, and for a similar reason: Jack discovers "a father's heart" within him, a discovery that completes the quest toward attaining "clearer self understanding" which he has been engaged in since the beginning of the play. In the midst of his intense struggle with Ann, whilst he is still questioning whether marriage will not require too much relinquishment of freedom, Ann spontaneously remarks that marriage will not be unalloyed happiness for her either, but will involve risking her life to bring new life into the world. Tanner responds as if struck by a revelation: "Oh, that clutch holds and hurts. What have you grasped in me? Is there a father's heart as well as a mother's?" (p. 729)

The moment of self-recognition is not only the climax of Tanner's dramatic development, but also coincides with his placing the interests of the evolving human race above his personal happiness. In dramatizing Ann and Jack's marriage in this way, Shaw was drawing on an 1844 essay by Arthur Schopenhauer, "The Metaphysics of Sexual Love" (an appendix to the his main work, *The World as Will and Idea*), where the philosopher argues as follows:

The ultimate aim of all love affairs … is actually more important than all other aims in man's life; … what is decided by it is nothing less than the composition of the next generation. … The growing attachment of two lovers is in reality the will-to-live of the new individual … they can and want to produce … Therefore … they have … sacrificed [their own happiness] to the welfare of the species.

(Payne, tr., 534, 536, 553)

The clutch that holds and hurts, that grasps his father's heart, that warns Ann she will have to risk her life, belongs to that baby willing itself into existence by drawing the lovers together. Their erotic communion here climaxes with a mutual death wish, as if they were Wagner's Tristan and Isolde:

> TANNER: If we two stood now on the edge of a
>   precipice, I would hold you tight and jump.
> ANN [*panting, failing more and more under the
>   strain*]: Jack: let me go. I have dared so fright-
>   fully—it is lasting longer than I thought. Let
>   me go I cant bear it.
> TANNER: Nor I. Let it kill us.
> ANN: Yes: I don't care. I am at the end of my
>   forces. I don't care. I think I am going to faint.
>   (p. 729)

Shaw deliberately makes the language and rhythm here ambiguous as to whether Ann is giving birth or having an orgasm; even the stage direction "*panting*" has this duality of meaning. But such a conjoining of orgasmic loss of self with the creation of new life looks back to Don Juan's debate with the Devil over the question of whether Man is a destroyer or creator. And the question is only resolved when we learn a few moments later at the entrance of the rest of the company that Ann's fainting dead away was at least partly faked, for as Tanner shortly discovers her pulse is quite lively. This being a comedy, she has mimed a death and resurrection. Ann announces to all that she has accepted Jack's proposal of marriage, and he warns them all with a final speech that their conventional presents will be sold and the profits used to help circulate his Revolutionist's Handbook. Violet calls him a brute, but Ann tells him not to mind her, and just to go on talking. The final stage direction, "*Universal laughter*" tells us that not only those on stage are laughing at Tanner but the whole cosmos as well.

Although *Man and Superman* is difficult to produce because of its length and consequently has had relatively few theatrical revivals, it is nevertheless still widely read, and the Don Juan in Hell section is frequently produced partly because of its easy requirements. Yet the renewal of scientific interest in evolution both from biologists and psychologists during the 1980s and 1990s would indicate a renewed attention to Shaw's prescience in connecting the development of brain power with sexual selection, for scientists still cannot answer the question: why, compared to the brains of our primate relatives, have ours evolved so much more than we needed for mere survival? Shaw provides provocative speculations on these matters in an epic comedy that not only seems to sum up two literary traditions, those of romantic comedy and Don Juan, but also offers, in the form of an unboundedly energetic and constantly thought-turning play, a profound and complex meditation on the role of love, sex, and marriage in the destiny of the species.

Selected Bibliography

PRIMARY SOURCES

Back to Methuselah. In *Collected Plays With Their Prefaces, Vol. 5*. Edited by Dan H. Laurence. New York: Dodd, Mead, 1972.

Man and Superman. (Definitive Edition.) In *Collected Plays With Their Prefaces, Vol. 2*. Edited by Dan H. Laurence. New York: Dodd, Mead, 1972.

Man and Superman. (Reprint of earlier Constable edition without Shaw's subsequent revisions.) In *George Bernard Shaw's Plays: A Norton Critical Edition*. 2d edition. Edited by Sandie Byrne. New York: W. W. Norton, 2002.

"The Superman, or Don Juan's Great Grandson's Grandson 1901." Edited and introduced by Charles A. Berst. In *Unpublished Shaw*. Edited by Dan H. Laurence and Margot Peters. *SHAW: The Annual of Bernard Shaw Studies,* 16. University Park: The Pennsylvania State University Press, 1996. Pp. 195–209.

Collected Letters: 1898–1910, Edited by Dan H. Laurence (New York: Dodd, Mead, 1972).

SECONDARY SOURCES

Auden, W. H. "The Fabian Figaro." In *George Bernard Shaw: A Critical Survey*. Edited by Louis Kronenberger. Cleveland and New York: World Publishing, 1953. Pp. 153–157.

Bertolini, John A. *The Playwrighting Self of Bernard Shaw*. Carbondale and Edwardsville: Southern Illinois University Press, 1991.

———. "Finding Something New to Say: Rattigan Eludes Shaw." In *Shaw and Other Playwrights,* Edited by John A. Bertolini, *SHAW: The Annual of Bernard Shaw Studies,* 13. University Park: The Pennsylvania State University Press, 1993. Pp. 93–102.

Bloom, Harold, ed. *George Bernard Shaw's Man and Superman*. New York: Chelsea House, 1987.

Dukore, Bernard. "Shaw's Big Three." In *SHAW: The Annual of Bernard Shaw Studies,* 4. Edited by Stanley Weintraub. University Park: The Pennsylvania State University Press, 1984. Pp. 33–67.

Gibbs, A. M., ed. *Man and Superman and Saint Joan: A Casebook*. Macmillan, 1992.

Holroyd, Michael. *Bernard Shaw, Vol. II, 1898–1918: The Pursuit of Power*. New York: Random House, 1989.

Hugo, Leon. *Edwardian Shaw: The Writer and His Age*. Basingstoke: Macmillan, 1999.

Miller, Geoffrey. *The Mating Mind: How Sexual Choice Shaped the Evolution of Human Nature*. New York: Doubleday, 2001.

Tave, Stuart M. "These Mountains Make You Dream of Women: *Man and Superman.*" Ch. 2 of *Lovers, Clowns, and Fairies: An Essay on Comedies*. Chicago and London: University of Chicago Press, 1993.

George Eliot's
Middlemarch

DEANNA KREISEL

SHORTLY AFTER BEGINNING work on her sixth and most famous novel, George Eliot wrote in her journal, "I do not feel very confident that I can make anything satisfactory of *Middlemarch*" (*Journals* 138). This self-deprecating comment strikes modern readers as almost comically ironic, given the fact that *Middlemarch* is generally considered the greatest nineteenth-century novel in the English language, and one of the most important and influential novels ever written. It enjoyed an immense popularity during its initial serial publication in 1871–1872, and even more so in its later incarnations: the four-volume edition published at the same time as the last serial installment, in December 1872, and the one-volume Cheap edition published in May 1874. *Middlemarch* remains that rare accomplishment in the literary world: a long, philosophically complex, and demanding novel that garnered both critical acclaim and enormous commercial and popular success. With the exception of a few decades at the beginning of the twentieth century—when all things "Victorian" came under attack as stuffy and moralistic by the next generation of critics and writers, the modernists—*Middlemarch* has continued to enjoy a reputation as a sophisticated examination of the interdependent effects of character and social environment on human behavior. Indeed, even such an archmodernist as Virginia Woolf (rescuing Eliot from her brief period of critical disfavor) called *Middlemarch* "one of the few English novels written for grown-up people."

One of the main reasons *Middlemarch* has continued to intrigue both casual readers and serious critics for so many years is the complexity of its design and the scope of its ambitions. The subtitle of the novel is *A Study of Provincial Life,* and all three of these words are important to Eliot's intent. She conceived of *Middlemarch* as a kind of a laboratory experiment worked out in narrative: an examination and description of the interlocking lives of the denizens of a large town in the English countryside right before the passage of the first parliamentary Reform Act in 1832. Eliot continually used the metaphor of a web to describe her plan for *Middlemarch*; there is no absolute center of attention, but instead many possible perspectives and many "protagonists," all of whom affect one another's lives in discernible (and indiscernible) ways. As the narrator opines early in the novel, "anyone watching keenly the convergence of human lots, sees a slow preparation of effects from one life

215

on another" (p. 88). The deceptively narrow focus of the novel—which centers on just a few families—enabled Eliot both to delve deeper into the psyches of her characters than had any novelist before her, and to examine those psyches against a sweeping backdrop of the important political, scientific, religious, and philosophical issues of the day. Eliot's novel was simultaneously avant-garde and very much of its time: while it extended and refined the aims of high Victorian realism such as detailed description, intricate plot, and an emphasis on ordinary domestic affairs, it also experimented with form and narrative voice, and anticipated modernism in its insistence on the radical indeterminacy of language and the ultimate isolation of individual consciousnesses.

The book that was conceived in such a fit of despair on the part of its author was published at the height of her popularity and fame. Born Mary Ann Evans in 1819 near Nuneaton, Warwickshire, George Eliot took on her masculine pen name after deciding to try her hand at fiction writing at the comparatively late age of thirty-six, at the urging of her romantic companion, George Henry Lewes. She was born to a land-agent father (who bears a strong resemblance to the hero of her first novel, *Adam Bede*), and a strong-willed mother, and raised at Griff House, the farmhouse on the estate of Francis Parker, whose lands her father managed. She was a deeply religious child who was strongly influenced by the Evangelicalism of one of her early teachers, Miss Maria Lewis, at boarding school in Nuneaton. She continued her education at a school in Coventry, where she was a shy and serious pupil who did extremely well at her studies, until the age of sixteen, when she returned home to run her father's household after the death of her mother. Her father was proud of her intelligence and encouraged her to continue her studies at home, paying for lessons in Italian and German. Shortly thereafter she and her father moved to a larger town, Coventry, where she met Charles and Caroline (Cara) Bray,

CHRONOLOGY

1819	22 November: Born at South Farm, Arbury, Warwickshire, the third child of Robert Evans, a land agent, and Christiana Pearson. Given name Mary Ann.
1836	Mother dies. Mary Ann leaves school to become primary housekeeper and family caregiver. Takes lessons in Italian, German, Greek, and Latin at home.
1841	Moves with father to Foleshill in Coventry. Meets Charles and Caroline (Cara) Bray, Unitarian freethinkers who encourage her to question her religious faith.
1842	January to May: "Holy War" with father—Mary Ann refuses to attend church for five months.
1846	Publishes *The Life of Jesus,* a three-volume translation of David Friedrich Strauss's *Das Leben Jesu* (1835–1836), which presents a historical examination of the Gospel stories.
1849	Father dies 31 May. Mary Ann spends the remainder of the year in continental Europe.
1851	Takes up residence in London as lodger in the home of John Chapman. Becomes editor of the *Westminster Review,* a radical journal that Chapman owns.
1853	Begins a sexual relationship with the writer and amateur scientist George Henry Lewes that lasts until Lewes's death in 1878. Lewes is unable to divorce his wife, so he and Mary Ann Evans remain a notoriously unmarried couple.
1856	Publishes one of her most famous and important critical articles, "Silly Novels by Lady Novelists" in the *Westminster Review.* Begins to write her first fiction, the story "Amos Barton," which will become one of three stories in *Scenes from Clerical Life.*
1857	Selects the name George Eliot as the pseudonym under which part of

	"Amos Barton" is to be published in *Blackwood's Edinburgh Magazine*.
1858	Publishes *Scenes from Clerical Life* in two volumes.
1859	Publishes her first novel, *Adam Bede*, to good reviews and increasing fame. Also publishes "The Lifted Veil," a gothic story, in *Blackwood's*.
1860	George Eliot's identity is revealed to the public shortly before the publication of *The Mill on the Floss*. She continues, nonetheless to publish under her pseudonym.
1861	Publishes *Silas Marner*.
1862–1863	Breaks her publication arrangement with *Blackwood's* publisher, John Blackwood, and publishes *Romola* serially in the *Cornhill Magazine*.
1866	Resumes publishing under the Blackwood imprint with *Felix Holt, the Radical*.
1869	Meets John Cross, whom she will marry in the last year of her life and who will write the first biography of George Eliot. Begins work on *Middlemarch*.
1870	Starts "Miss Brooke," a story that will later become a part of *Middlemarch*.
1871	The eight-month serial publication of *Middlemarch* begins in December. The novel sells extremely well.
1876	Publishes *Daniel Deronda*. Lewes is suffering from chronic illnesses.
1878	Lewes dies 30 November.
1879	Publishes *Impressions of Theophrastus Such*, a collection of essays by a fictional persona.
1880	6 May: marries John Cross, who has courted her since the previous year. After a rapidly developing illness, George Eliot dies 22 December.

led to a rift with her father, which was mended only when Mary Ann agreed to attend services again, although her father agreed she could think whatever she liked privately. Both this early religious faith and later principled skepticism were to inform the philosophical themes of many of her novels. Mary Ann continued her friendship with the Brays, meeting many important intellectuals and writers (including Ralph Waldo Emerson and Harriet Martineau) at their home, Rosehill. In 1844 Mary Ann began work on a translation of David Friedrich Strauss's *Das Leben Jesu* (*The Life of Jesus*), an influential work of religious skepticism that treated the Gospel as a historical text and concluded that the biblical account of the life of Jesus was based on myth rather than fact. The translation was published anonymously two years later, and cemented Mary Ann's reputation as a freethinker among the intellectuals and cognoscenti of London who knew the identity of its translator.

Largely on the strength of this work, John Chapman offered Mary Ann the editorship of *The Westminster Review* in 1851, two years after the death of her father left her free to move to London. She edited the *Review* for two years, restoring it to its former reputation as an important intellectual journal and publishing many works of literary criticism that were to form the backbone of her philosophy of literary representation. During this time she met George Henry Lewes, a theater director, amateur naturalist, and advocate of "free love," who was married in name only to a woman who had been living openly with another man for years. Mary Ann and Lewes began a romantic relationship, and after much agonizing soul-searching, she decided to live with him as his "spiritual wife" although he was unable to obtain a divorce and marry her legally. Theirs was an extremely happy and intellectually productive union, lasting until Lewes's death in 1878, although in its early years Mary Ann was deeply pained by the negative reaction of her family and friends to the

intellectuals and freethinkers who befriended her instantly. Partially under their influence, she began to question her religious beliefs and finally decided to stop attending church in 1842. This irregularity of the union (including a new tension with her intellectual mentors, the Brays). "The Lewes," as they called themselves, had a great intellectual friendship as well as romantic partnership. With Mary Ann's encouragement Lewes began to study biology more seriously, publishing several important works on natural history, and it was Lewes's support of Mary Ann's long-held desire to try fiction writing that enabled her to overcome her innate diffidence and fear of failure.

In 1856 she began writing her first story, "The Sad Fortunes of the Reverend Amos Barton," which was published in installments in *Blackwood's Magazine* in 1857 and reprinted as one of three *Scenes of Clerical Life* the following year. All three stories were extremely popular in their serial publication, and rumors and hints began to circulate about the identity of "George Eliot," whose real name (and, importantly, gender) remained unknown to the public until well after the publication and great success of her first novel, *Adam Bede*. (Indeed, there is some suggestion in Eliot's correspondence that she might have kept her true identity a secret even longer, but was forced to reveal herself after a spurious sequel, *Adam Bede, Junior*, was published by a pretender.) Mary Ann published four more novels, numerous works of criticism and journalism, and several short stories and poems before beginning *Middlemarch* at the height of her novelistic powers. After the great success of *Middlemarch* cemented her reputation as one of England's greatest novelists—perhaps *the* greatest living novelist—she went on to write only one more novel, *Daniel Deronda*, before her great grief at the death of Lewes in 1878 essentially brought her literary career to a close. She survived him by only two years, the last seven months of which she spent wed to John Cross, a much younger admirer (and her financial adviser) who had persuaded her to marry him. Upon her death he became her literary executor and eventually published the first—largely idealized—biography of his late wife in 1885.

I. *MIDDLEMARCH* IN THE CONTEXT OF VICTORIAN REALISM

Middlemarch is often named as one of the most highly developed examples of literary realism, a style of writing (and theory of literary representation) that reached its peak in the middle decades of the nineteenth century. What the Victorians meant by "realism" is somewhat different from what we mean today: realism was a genre with its own rules and conventions, some of which do not necessarily conform to what twenty-first-century readers would consider "realistic." While there are as many different definitions of realism as there are authors who endorsed the term, there are some common characteristics that we can recognize in the work of all its main practitioners: writers as disparate as George Eliot, Charles Dickens, William Makepeace Thackeray, and Anthony Trollope. These authors all believed that there was a stable, knowable reality beyond the confines of language, and that one of the purposes of the novel is to represent the truth of this reality to readers. In order to represent this truth, the author must at least pretend that he or she has access to it: most realist novels employ an omniscient narrator, who seems to know everything about the characters and situations of the novel, past, present, and perhaps even future.

While these characters and situations are of course not themselves real, they should be representative of reality. To this end, most practitioners of realism favored ordinary characters in commonplace situations, and used a great deal of description in order to impart the fullness of this "reality" more believably to their audiences. As George Levine notes in his influential study *The Realistic Imagination*, realism "belongs ... to a 'middling' condition and defines itself against the excesses, both stylistic and narrative, of various kinds of romantic, exotic, or sensational literatures" (p. 5). However, this does not mean that realistic novels are therefore lightweight affairs; according to Levine, "what is unconventional and most exciting about the [English] tradition of realism is its pleasure in abundance, in energy, and the vivid engagement, through language, with the reality just beyond the reach of language…. Realistic novels contain more than they formally need." It is precisely this excess, this containing more than they need, that caused Henry James to complain about the "large loose baggy monsters" of his literary predecessors. As many a suffering undergraduate has discovered, the average example of high Victorian realism rarely weighs in at fewer than eight hundred or nine hundred pages; it takes a lot of space, and a lot of words, to represent "reality" in all its richness and detail.

Middlemarch certainly cannot be exempted from the charge of bagginess. As Eliot somewhat defensively claimed to her publisher while working on the novel, "I don't see how I can leave anything out, because I hope there is nothing that will be seen to be irrelevant to my design, which is to show the gradual action of ordinary causes rather than exceptional, and to show this in some directions which have not been from time immemorial the beaten path" (Cross, *George Eliot's Life*, vol. 3, 137). In order to show the "gradual action of ordinary causes," the almost imperceptible accretion of minor decisions and chance occurrences that ultimately determines a person's fate, Eliot needed space to "stretch out" and describe the everyday lives and innermost thoughts of her subjects. The novel is divided roughly between two different groups of characters, whose lives are intertwined by the end of the novel: Dorothea Brooke (whom many readers consider the novel's true heroine) and her family, who are minor gentry; and Dr. Tertius Lydgate, the new local doctor, and his friends and associates, who are solidly middle class. By dividing her attention between these different social strata, Eliot is able to give a fuller and more complete picture of "provincial life"—a fullness and completeness that is of course part of the project of realism.

That project, however, is not without its dangers and difficulties. It may sound very well to claim that the novel should gesture toward, even represent, an actual "reality" beyond language, but the heirs of twentieth-century criticism know the limitations and logical fallacies of such an undertaking. (As we shall see, it can be argued that the Victorians themselves, especially George Eliot, were more aware of these difficulties than they traditionally have been given credit for.) The logical problem with realism is that it purports the existence of a knowable world beyond language to which language refers; however, our only access to that world—indeed, to any kind of knowledge—is *through* language. We cannot understand or know anything, even a math problem or a scientific experiment, without using some kind of system of symbols or signs—in other words, a language. There may indeed be a world "out there," beyond our linguistic access, but we have no way of knowing anything about it. Literary realism, then, gets the whole question backward: language is the origin, not the medium, of our understanding of the world. The world of the novel consists of nothing *but* language, and cannot be said to refer to anything outside of itself in any meaningful way. The novelists and critics who followed the mid-Victorians, in fact, essentially abandoned the project of realism in favor of other literary experiments. Unless someone living today is a fan of Victorian fiction, his or her encounters with high realism are probably confined to Hollywood cinema, which still attempts to use its "language" of cinematic techniques to represent a transparent and seamless reality to its viewers.

There is much evidence in *Middlemarch* to suggest that Eliot was aware of, and concerned by, the logical difficulties that realism poses. This reading of the novel suggests that far from being a naïve practitioner of an untenable philosophy, Eliot in fact anticipated modern critical arguments by foregrounding (perhaps not entirely consciously) the interpretive problems inherent in attempting to really know anything—or anyone—in a direct, unmediated way. In *Middlemarch,* Eliot engages this central problem of realism in two interrelated ways. First, she examines the interpretive component of literary meaning: in other words, the role of the reader/receiver in creating interpretations (and misinterpretations). Second, she implicitly questions traditional narrative omniscience: the all-seeing, all-knowing narrator associated with realism.

While several critics have noted that Eliot's earlier novels, such as *Adam Bede* and *The Mill on the Floss,* consistently rehearse anxieties about the nature of authorship, *Middlemarch* can be seen as extending these anxieties by imagining different styles of readership, with implications for the interpretation of texts generally and of Eliot's own novels particularly. J. Hillis Miller has argued that *Middlemarch* offers a vision of the self which deconstructs the humanistic Victorian view: the protomodern idea that Eliot's novel advances is of the self as a group of signs (discrete "packets" of language), attempting to interpret signs received from others and simultaneously available for others' interpretation. As the narrator apologizes at one point: "[S]urely all must admit that a man may be puffed and belauded, envied, ridiculed, counted upon as a tool and fallen in love with, or at least selected as a future husband, and yet remain virtually unknown—known merely as a cluster of signs for his neighbours' false suppositions" (p. 133).

The necessity of interpretation is fraught with peril: "Signs are small measurable things, but interpretations are illimitable" (p. 23). So much of the novel is taken up with descriptions of spectacular misunderstanding. Dorothea almost willfully fails to understand the real fears and motivations of her husband Casaubon, ascribing to him tender feelings and intellectual powers he just does not possess: "Dorothea's faith supplied all that Mr. Casaubon's words seemed to leave unsaid: what believer sees a disturbing omission or infelicity? The text, whether of prophet or of poet, expands for whatever we can put into it, and even his bad grammar is sublime" (p. 46). She also misreads Will Ladislaw's feelings for

her, refusing for a very long time to recognize what her own husband has long understood: that the young painter is in love with her. Rosamond, similarly, misreads Lydgate's feelings and character, initially seeing a seriousness of romantic intent in what he considers just a pleasant flirtation: "To Rosamond it seemed as if she and Lydgate were as good as engaged.... [I]deas, we know, tend to a more solid kind of existence, the necessary materials being at hand. It is true, Lydgate had the counter-idea of remaining unengaged; but this was a mere negative, a shadow cast by other resolves" (p. 255). When the two finally do marry, the misunderstandings continue: Lydgate has never grasped the true selfishness of his pretty bride, and imagines she supports his medical researches where she really cares only about his earning enough money to finance her social ambitions. There are many, many similar examples in the novel, including misunderstandings between Fred Vincy and Mary Garth, Mr. and Mrs. Bulstrode, Raffles and Bulstrode, Ladislaw and Rosamond. This festival of misunderstanding is most noteworthy in the case of Dorothea; since she is our ostensible heroine and main point of identification, we expect to be able to trust her perceptions as a guide to the world of the novel. In other words, *Middlemarch* features a female protagonist who is a bad reader ("She was blind, you see, to many things obvious to others" [350]), and the whole world of the novel supports the acts of reading and interpretation as the only access to other people's consciousness. In *Middlemarch,* Eliot almost seems to want to unmoor the language of realism from its reference to the real world.

This new interest in the open-ended nature of interpretation also shifts the center of narrative authority; in Eliot's earlier novels, the narrator is constantly intervening in the action to address his readers and direct their interpretation of the events of the novel. (I refer to the narrators of Eliot's novels as "he" because she was at such pains to appear as a male author in the early stages of her career.) The main focus of this narrative chatting with the reader is the careful tracing of the consequences of human actions—what we might call the "moral" of Eliot's early novels—which presupposes a godlike narratorial omniscience that can understand all these causes and effects. In *Middlemarch,* on the other hand, the narrator is continually calling into question the possibility of such omniscience. In chapter 6, for example, the narrator presents the matchmaking activities of Mrs. Cadwallader as an interpretive problem:

Was there any ingenious plot, any hide-and-seek course of action, which might be detected by a careful telescopic watch? Not at all: a telescope might have swept the parishes of Tipton and Freshitt, the whole area visited by Mrs. Cadwallader in her phaeton, without witnessing any interview that could excite suspicion ... Even with a microscope directed on a water-drop we find ourselves making interpretations which turn out to be rather coarse; for whereas under a weak lens you may seem to see a creature exhibiting an active voracity into which other smaller creatures actively play as if they were so many animated tax-pennies, a stronger lens reveals to you certain tiniest hairlets which make vortices for these victims while the swallower waits passively at his receipt of custom. In this way, metaphorically speaking, a strong lens applied to Mrs. Cadwallader's match-making will show a play of minute causes producing what may be called thought and speech vortices to bring her the sort of food she needed.

(p. 55)

Several different metaphors for narratorial perspective and technique are proposed here. First is the "telescopic" view, a style of narration that gives sweeping accounts of events on a large canvas, without much analysis of character or tracing of "minute causes." Second is the "weak lens" of the microscope, a narration that tries to look more deeply into things, to delve a bit into the psyches of characters and reveal more of the motivations, and interconnected results, of human actions. Third is the "stronger lens," which delves even deeper and reveals to us the mistakes we may make with the weaker lens. None of

these levels of magnification is ideal. Eliot seems to reject outright the telescopic view (a novel that would be taken up entirely with plot), since this would preclude a real understanding of the individual characters involved; early in the novel the narrator apologizes: "I at least have so much to do in unravelling certain human lots, and seeing how they were woven and interwoven, that all the light I can command must be concentrated on this particular web, and not dispersed over that tempting range of relevancies called the universe" (p. 132).

Yet the strongest lens of the microscope is hardly an option either: if the narrator were to describe the deepest thoughts and desires of all his characters, and trace the interconnections between them far beyond their "visible" effects, the novel would never move forward—it would be permanently stalled in a morass of descriptive language. Furthermore, such an intensive and claustrophobic understanding would hardly even be desirable: "If we had a keen vision and feeling of all ordinary human life, it would be like hearing the grass grow and the squirrel's heart beat, and we should die of that roar which lies on the other side of silence" (p. 182). The weaker lens—the middle ground between action and description, plot and character—is clearly, for Eliot, the only possible way to narrate a novel. (Many readers who tire of Eliot's long passages of philosophical discussion, however, would complain that she errs too far on the side of "strong magnification!") This model of narration, while it attempts to consider and resolve some of the logical problems of realism (how best to represent what needs to be represented), also raises other problems. While on the one hand this vision of the interpretive process seems to give to the narrator ultimate control and authority (for it is he who decides the power of magnification, he who can reveal and conceal), on the other hand it relinquishes the final outcome of the interpretive process to the reader—"[e]ven with a microscope ... we find ourselves making interpretations which turn out to be rather coarse." The level at which the novel must go forward—the level of weak magnification—is inevitably one on which mistakes and misreadings will be made.

In *Middlemarch,* the very idea of striving for perfect knowledge and understanding (the purview of the omniscient narrator) is ultimately rejected as arrogant and sadly misguided. Neil Hertz, in his article "Recognizing Casaubon," argues that Eliot raises the possibility of a perfect knowledge of character only to reject it unconsciously as "clearly not a possibility to be steadily contemplated by a working novelist" (p. 96). It is the figure of Casaubon, with his "key to all mythologies," around whom both terms of textuality or writing *and* terms of narcissism and self-absorption cluster. It is the possibility of the "moral stupidity" inherent in narcissism, which is associated for Eliot with writing, that Hertz argues must be banished from the novel in the form of Casaubon. After willfully misreading his motivations and character for most of their relationship, Dorothea eventually "recognizes" Casaubon as a person wholly separate, an unknowable other self, and thus moves into a moral awareness of which Casaubon is not capable:

> To-day she had begun to see that she had been under a wild illusion in expecting a response to her feeling from Mr. Casaubon, and she had felt the waking of a presentiment that there might be a sad consciousness in his life which made as great a need on his side as on her own.
>
> We are all of us born in moral stupidity, taking the world as an udder to feed our supreme selves: Dorothea had early begun to emerge from that stupidity…
>
> (p. 197–198)

Casaubon's narcissism, on the other hand, precludes his recognition of Dorothea's selfhood in return. It is the "rejection" of Casaubon (his banishment from the novel through death) that signals Eliot's desire to move away from the omniscient narratorial style—the "key to all mythologies"—and toward a new way of talking about the interpretive process.

Yet here we can see that Eliot's questioning of realism is a somewhat anxious one. In order for Eliot to accomplish a real move away from "narcissistic" omniscience, Dorothea, who is the focus of identification in the novel, must come to represent some new way of reading and writing. With her gross misreadings of others throughout the novel, Dorothea certainly seems a negative representative of that process, yet it is exactly her moral superiority that causes her to misread. It is precisely her relinquishment of the "moral stupidity" of self-absorption that makes her unable to ascribe self-absorption to others: she is so emotionally generous she cannot see other people as selfish. Although she "recognizes" Casaubon eventually, she goes on to make the same mistake with Rosamond. When Dorothea visits Rosamond in an attempt to repair the Lydgates' marriage, Rosamond responds by telling her that Ladislaw had confessed to her his love for Dorothea: "With her usual tendency to over-estimate the good in others, she [Dorothea] felt a great outgoing of her heart towards Rosamond for the generous effort which had redeemed her from suffering, not counting that the effort was a reflex of her own energy" (p. 750). Rosamond is able to stretch her narrow, selfish nature into this one moment of generosity, although only under the influence of Dorothea's own goodness. Once again, Dorothea "misreads" another as having the same kind and loving nature as herself.

Dorothea's mistakes as a reader, and all the acts of misinterpretation in *Middlemarch,* are grounded in the abandonment of that confidence in control and mastery which is associated with the omniscient narrative style. The uncertainty of Dorothea's judgment masks the uncertainty of her creator; that she turns out to be both the moral center of the novel and fundamentally wrong at the same time perhaps indicates the tentativeness with which Eliot is questioning the premises of realism. *Middlemarch* may contain the germ of a bold narrative experiment, but in the end it does not move terribly far beyond the central tenets—and limitations—of the literary realism of which it is such an important example.

II. GEORGE ELIOT AND SCIENCE

As we have already seen with the microscope and water-drop image, Eliot uses scientific metaphor to great effect in *Middlemarch*. Her fondness for imagery drawn from biology, chemistry, and the natural sciences is no accident. Her partner, George Henry Lewes, was a respected amateur botanist and natural scientist (it was only in the later decades of the nineteenth century that the professionalization of the sciences we know today was in full force). She participated actively in his researches, aiding him greatly during his field trips, discussing scientific ideas with him, and editing his manuscripts (after his death she made it her task to prepare his magnum opus, *Problems of Life and Mind*, for publication). As an important Victorian intellectual, Eliot could hardly have been isolated from the great scientific debates of the day even had her partner not happened to be a scientist: because the sciences were not fully professionalized, most educated people could read about recent discoveries and participate in discussions about their implications. The most famous and important of these debates, of course, was over evolutionary theory. Charles Darwin's *On the Origin of Species* was published in 1859, and although Darwin himself claimed that he saw no conflict between his theory of natural selection and orthodox Christian faith, it nevertheless sparked divisive public debates about the role of a designing God in the universe. Other discoveries in geology (most notably Charles Lyell's *Principles of Geology* in 1830, which dated the earth as millions of years older than the creation story in Genesis) had contributed to the growing sense of tension between—perhaps even irreconcilability of—religion and empirical science. Despite (or perhaps because of) this controversy and ferment, Eliot did not shy away from engaging scientific themes in her novels, and often used metaphors drawn from biology, chemistry, and geology to describe the psychological states of her characters and the philosophical problems of literary representation with which she was grappling.

As Robert A. Greenberg has noted in his discussion of science in *Middlemarch*, the great themes of scientific discovery and politics—while they seem to be entirely separate concerns—are united in the novel through the central issue of reform. The great Victorian faith in social progress and zeal for improvement were just as important to the realm of scientific discovery as they were to the political arena. The novel is set in the years right before the first Reform Act of 1832, which gave the vote to all men with household incomes of more than £10 and attempted to eliminate "rotten" boroughs (districts that carried votes in Parliament despite having few or no residents), and the reforming activities of several of its characters are on prominent display. Mr. Brooke, Dorothea's uncle and guardian, is thinking of sitting for Parliament on a reform platform, Will Ladislaw harnesses his progressivist energies by writing for Brooke's newspaper, and of course Dorothea herself is preoccupied with her plans for workers' cottages as the novel opens. Dorothea, the utopianist "St. Theresa" figure of the novel, draws those around her into her enthusiasms, engaging her brother-in-law Sir James Chettam in the cottage-building project and convincing her uncle that he needs to make substantial improvements on his estate; she sets these projects aside only to take on one that she (mistakenly) sees as even more important, assisting her husband in the production of his misguided "Key to All Mythologies."

Yet the figure most consistently associated with zealous—and perhaps quixotic—attempts at reform is the new doctor, Lydgate, who dreams of wedding a research career that will unlock the mysteries of human biology with a progressive medical practice that will correct the long-standing abuses of his profession. When he is introduced to the reader, we learn that he longed to demonstrate the more intimate relations of living structure, and help to define men's thought more accurately after the true order. The work had not yet been done, but only prepared for those who knew how to use the preparation. What was the primitive tissue? In that way Lydgate put the question.... [H]e counted on quiet intervals to be watchfully seized, for taking up the threads of investigation—on many hints to be won from diligent application, not only of the scalpel, but of the microscope, which research had begun to use again with new enthusiasm of reliance. Such was Lydgate's plan of his future: to do good small work for Middlemarch, and great work for the world.

(p. 139)

Lydgate stands out as an ambitious man in a novel full of ambitious people. His scientific researches are so absorbing to him that he has decided not to threaten his concentration with domestic duties, and has resolved not to marry until he has made his mark as a scientist. This resolve, of course, comes to naught when he comes up against the seductive manipulations of the beautiful Rosamond, who is "always that combination of correct sentiments, music, dancing, drawing, elegant note-writing, private album for extracted verse, and perfect blond loveliness, which made the irresistible woman for the doomed man of that date" (p. 252). Lydgate's scientific vision, calibrated to the microscopic level of the "primitive tissue," is blind to more everyday matters and fails to notice what is obvious to everyone else around him: that he and Rosamond are courting. Once Lydgate and Rosamond find themselves married, the seemingly inevitable result is the atrophy of Lydgate's research program. He finds himself drawn deeper into debt as a result of his wife's extravagant tastes and social aspirations, and spends more and more of his time trying simply to make ends meet. The grandiosity of his scientific ambitions never amounts to anything; even after his debt and name are cleared—and his marriage patched together—by Dorothea at the end of the novel, we learn that he never fulfilled his youthful hopes for his life:

Lydgate's hair never became white. He died when he was only fifty, leaving his wife and children provided for by a heavy insurance on his life. He had gained an excellent practice, alternating, according to the season, between London and a Continental bathing-place; having written a treatise on Gout, a disease which has a good deal of wealth on its side. His skill was relied on by many paying patients, but he always regarded himself as a failure: he had not done what he once meant to do.

(p. 781)

Lydgate blames this failure squarely on his wife: "He once called her his basil plant; and when she asked for an explanation, said that basil was a plant which had flourished wonderfully on a murdered man's brains" (p. 782). For her part, Rosamond never comes to understand or support her husband's researches; she never recovers from her early disappointment that Lydgate was not what she had fantasized him to be:

The Lydgate with whom she had been in love had been a group of airy conditions for her, most of which had disappeared, while their place had been taken by every-day details which must be lived through slowly from hour to hour, not floated through with a rapid selection of favourable aspects. The habits of Lydgate's profession, his home preoccupation with scientific subjects, which seemed to her almost like a morbid vampire's taste, his peculiar views of things which had never entered into the dialogue of courtship— all these continually alienating influences, even without the fact of his having placed himself at a disadvantage in the town, and without that first shock of revelation about Dover's debt, would have made his presence dull to her.

(p. 622)

This tension between worldly, especially scientific, ambition and domestic pressures is a persistent one throughout *Middlemarch* (and, indeed, throughout the nineteenth-century novel in general). The tragedy of Lydgate is echoed by the tragedy of Casaubon, with his mythological treatise that he does not realize has already been scooped by German philosophers working in the field, and the tragedy of Dorothea, whose own intellectual ambitions are tethered to her husband's fruitless endeavor. Yet the thematic implications of these various failures are a bit more complicated than they initially appear. In the case of Lydgate, it is not simply a matter of an ambitious man thwarted by an imprudent marriage to a selfish wife; Eliot is far too subtle and psychologically complex a novelist to settle for this obvious cliché. Eliot carefully prepares us, in her initial character sketch of Lydgate, for his ultimate failure of character:

> Among our valued friends is there not some one or other who is a little too self-confident and disdainful; whose distinguished mind is a little spotted with commonness; who is a little pinched here and protuberant there with native prejudices; or whose better energies are liable to lapse down the wrong channel under the influence of transient solicitations? All these things might be alleged against Lydgate...
>
> (p. 140)

Lydgate's own particular "spots of commonness," the narrator tells us, consist in the fact that "that distinction of mind which belonged to his intellectual ardour, did not penetrate his feeling and judgement about furniture, or women, or the desirability of its being known (without his telling) that he was better born than other country surgeons" (p. 141). It is not entirely Rosamond's fault, in other words, that the Lydgates are drawn into debt; the young doctor is not without a few social ambitions of his own, which are ultimately incompatible with his serious scientific researches.

Yet the real problem with Lydgate's fantasies of greatness is in the very nature of those fantasies. There are strong hints even in the early sections of the novel that Lydgate's ambitions are more than just a touch arrogant, and perhaps ultimately as misguided as Casaubon's. The search for a "primitive tissue" that forms the building blocks of all human life turns out to be something of a dead end in physiological

inquiry, an idea ultimately supplanted by the cell theory of the mid-nineteenth century. Furthermore, as well versed in up-to-the-minute scientific theory as he is, Lydgate seems to misunderstand the significance of his reading. As Mark Wormald points out in his essay "Microscopy and Semiotic in *Middlemarch*," Lydgate's decision to trade Reverend Farebrother his copy of a recent treatise on microscopy by Robert Brown for a "lovely anencephalous [brainless] monster"—a specimen of a sponge the cleric has in his collection—signals his failure to understand the trends of scientific research. Brown's treatise was republished shortly before the writing of *Middlemarch*, and as Eliot would have known from her perspective forty years later, "Lydgate's failure to perceive the work's significance would have been recognized by many of her readers as an egregious oversight" (p. 506). Furthermore, as several critics have pointed out, there is a disturbing foreshadowing in Lydgate's willingness to trade an important work on microscopic research for a lovely brainless "monster."

This scene between Farebrother and Lydgate also highlights the reservations Eliot seems to have about the only professional scientist in her novel. Farebrother and Lydgate are both scientific enthusiasts, but the former is a decided amateur, the kind of specimen-collecting hobbyist who was supplanted by professional men in the latter decades of the century. When the two men first meet in Farebrother's study to go over his "collection," there is a decided air of patronage and condescension hanging over the encounter. The older man tries in vain to interest the young doctor in his extensive collection of local specimens- "I fancy I have made an exhaustive study of the entomology of this district.... . We are singularly rich in orthoptera"—but Lydgate's attention continually wanders, and he is forced to admit that he has "never had time to give [himself] much to natural history" (p. 161). He confesses that he "was early bitten with an interest in structure" (p. 161), and this opposition between "natural history" and "structure" is the key to understanding the difference between the two men. Farebrother's avocation is description, a cataloging of surface characteristics and the taxonomic relationships among specimens, while Lydgate's passion is dissection, a probing of deeper structures and an analysis of the basic building blocks (or "primitive tissue") of his subjects. (Later in the novel he confesses to Rosamond that he greatly admires the sixteenth-century anatomist Vesalius, a pioneer of dissection who was forced to "snatch bodies at night, from graveyards and places of execution" [429] in order to pursue his studies.)

Just as we saw with the various microscopic metaphors above, there is a certain ambivalence on Eliot's part regarding the benefits of each of these two styles of scientific endeavor. As the narrator opines when initially describing Lydgate, the decade in which he was working was perhaps "a more cheerful time for observers and theorizers than the present" (p. 138); there is no sharp distinction to be drawn, at least in terms of their usefulness, between these two prongs of scientific inquiry. Yet while several commentators on the novel have observed the parallels between Lydgate's methodology and that of George Henry Lewes, Eliot seems in several crucial respects to be more sympathetic to the personality and aims of Reverend Farebrother. As Mark Wormald points out, Farebrother seems to understand one of the crucial philosophical perceptions of the novel which is lost on Lydgate, that "identical rudimentary principles govern provincial society and primitive organisms" (p. 522). Farebrother understands what the author understands: he is certainly much closer than Lydgate to the model of sympathetic insight and moral delicacy that Eliot espouses as the goal of authorship—indeed, of personhood—throughout her life. The clergyman certainly has his faults, such as gambling and a somewhat cavalier way of talking about his profession, but he is a deeply honest and moral man; he is one of number of good clergymen with somewhat worldly habits who populate Eliot's fiction.

There is something vaguely sinister, on the other hand, about Eliot's description of Lydgate's aspirations; his object is

imagination that reveals subtle actions inaccessible by any sort of lens, but tracked in that outer darkness through long pathways of necessary sequence by the inward light which is the last refinement of Energy, capable of bathing even the ethereal atoms in its ideally illuminated space. He for his part had tossed away all cheap inventions where ignorance finds itself able and at ease: he was enamoured of that arduous invention which is the very eye of research, provisionally framing its object and correcting it to more and more exactness of relation; he wanted to pierce the obscurity of those minute processes which prepare human misery and joy, those invisible thoroughfares which are the first lurking-places of anguish, mania, and crime, that delicate poise and transition which determine the growth of happy or unhappy consciousness.

(p. 154)

Lydgate's scientific curiosity seems almost prurient here, not to mention hubristic. What kind of imagination reveals actions "inaccessible by any sort of lens?" This is a level of magnification beyond that of even the most powerful "microscope" available to the author. As we have seen, the narrator has already rejected the idea of such perfect penetration into the inner secrets of his subjects, which would deafen us with the "roar which lies on the other side of silence" (p. 182).

Furthermore, his attempts at reforming his profession are met with as little success as his attempts at "ideal illumination" in the experimental realm. His Middlemarch patients are suspicious of his new-fangled ways, and later in the novel he even comes under suspicion as a possible vivisector. People in town start to worry that

Dr. Lydgate meant to let the people die in the Hospital, if not to poison them, for the sake of cutting them up without saying by your leave or with your leave; for it was a known "fac" that he had wanted to cut up Mrs. Goby, as respectable a woman as any in Parley Street, who had money in trust before her marriage—a poor tale for a doctor, who if he was good for anything should know what was the matter with you before you died, and not want to pry into your inside after you were gone.

(p. 415)

Of course Eliot is gently mocking the ignorance and petty fears of these old-fashioned townsfolk, and certainly she is not advocating that Lydgate and other like-minded reformers give up their idealistic goals—quite the opposite. But clearly the arrogant zeal with which he has pursued his reforms has not stood him in good stead—and is in marked contrast to the gentle, humane demeanor of the Reverend Farebrother.

Farebrother and Lydgate furnish not only two models for scientific inquiry, but also two models for narratorial technique. The model of the author as experimenter, conducting her "study of provincial life" in a textual laboratory, was clearly an attractive one for Eliot. As Gillian Beer notes, "Fiction in the second half of the nineteenth century was particularly seeking sources of authoritative organisation which could substitute for the god-like omnipotence open to the theistic narrator" (p. 149). Once having rejected the idea of perfect narrative omniscience (for reasons we have already seen, plus others we will see in the next section), Eliot "experimented" with new models for how narration should work. Clearly the Lydgate/Casaubon model, with its arrogant search for the single key to perfect understanding—either of mythology or of the "human frame"—was one that Eliot wanted to challenge. Lydgate himself notes that "'there must be a systole and diastole in all inquiry,' and that 'a man's mind must be continually expanding and shrinking between the whole human horizon and the horizon of an object-glass'" (p. 602): there is a place both for minute analysis and for the grandeur of description. Significantly, this pas-

sage is part of a longer description of Farebrother's sympathetic observation of the younger man; he is remembering with concern an evening when Lydgate had behaved oddly:

> Lydgate talked persistently when they were in his work-room, putting arguments for and against the probability of certain biological views; but he had none of those definite things to say or to show which give the waymarks of a patient uninterrupted pursuit, such as he used himself to insist on, saying that "there must be a systole and diastole in all inquiry," and that "a man's mind must be continually expanding and shrinking between the whole human horizon and the horizon of an object-glass." That evening he seemed to be talking widely for the sake of resisting any personal bearing; and before long they went into the drawing room, where Lydgate, having asked Rosamond to give them music, sank back in his chair in silence, but with a strange light in his eyes.

(p. 602)

Lydgate's role is to understand the importance of the "systole and diastole," the pulsing between the telescopic and the microscopic view, while failing to achieve it; Farebrother's role, on the other hand, is effortlessly to achieve this ideal state through intelligent observation and sympathetic understanding. It is clear which is Eliot's own ideal for narration.

III. GENDER AND FEMALE AUTHORSHIP IN *MIDDLEMARCH*

Until fairly recently in human history, serious writing was not considered a suitable occupation for a woman. While the nineteenth century saw an explosion of novel writing by women authors, as well as the refashioning of the novel into a "feminine" genre appropriately aimed at a female readership, there was still a stigma attached to writing by women. Women's novels were not considered as "serious" or as "literary" as men's work—not to mention the fact that many commentators even claimed that the mental strain of writing could be injurious to the delicate female constitution. Before she even attempted fiction writing herself, George Eliot wrote a famous (and extremely funny) essay titled "Silly Novels by Lady Novelists," which skewered the pretensions and clichés of the majority of women's literature of the time. In order to avoid the stigma attached to literary productions by women, most serious female writers avoided revealing their sex to the public, Mary Shelley, Jane Austen, the Brontë sisters: and of course Mary Ann Evans herself all published either anonymously or under a male pseudonym.

As much recent feminist criticism has argued, the problem of literary authority was thus figured very differently for female authors than for their male counterparts; the appeal to realistic representation as a source of novelistic authority took on a particular urgency for Victorian women novelists whose very right to engage in artistic representation was in question. As Sandra Gilbert and Susan Gubar argue in their now-classic study *The Madwoman in the Attic,* the woman's act of writing initiates her concern for the interpretation not only of the text but also of its author; because the woman author unconsciously feels herself an anomaly, a monster, or even "madwoman," she is in a constant struggle to imagine a new source of literary authority that can substitute for the male novelist's ability to speak from within a governing literary tradition.

With these specific issues in view, we can see the work of George Eliot as emblematic of the problems of female authorship in the nineteenth century. Because of the circumstances surrounding Eliot's career—her adoption of a male pseudonym, her early anonymity and later "unmasking," her explicit concern with her public identity—these questions of authorship are of paramount importance in a consideration of her work. The narrator of *Middlemarch* prepares his readers for the importance of gender and authority early in the novel; in the prelude he introduces us to the tragedy of Dorothea, one of many women who burn with an intellectual ambition they will never be able to fulfill:

> Some have felt that these blundering lives are due to the inconvenient indefiniteness with which the Supreme Power has fashioned the natures of women: if there were one level of feminine incompetence as strict as the ability to count three and no more, the social lot of women might be treated with scientific certitude. Meanwhile the indefiniteness remains, and the limits of variation are really much wider than any one would imagine from the sameness of women's coiffure and the favourite love-stories in prose and verse. Here and there a cygnet is reared uneasily among the ducklings in the brown pond, and never finds the living stream in fellowship with its own oary-footed kind. Here and there is born a St. Theresa, foundress of nothing...
>
> (p. 3–4)

The story of Dorothea Brooke is a story of an intellectual, spiritual, and sociological problem, a character who is an anomaly, a "cygnet ... among the ducklings in the brown pond." The problem of Dorothea is a uniquely female one, we learn, for it can be traced back to the larger issue of the "natures of women." This "problem" can be seen as the central impetus for the forward motion of the novel's plot, yet if *Middlemarch* sets up the feminine problem clearly at the outset of the novel, and declares explicitly that this is to be the framework for what follows, it also stubbornly avoids resolution at the end. Dorothea may finally escape the emotional stultification of her marriage to Casaubon and find true love with Will Ladislaw—but after all, is this not a fairly conventional fate for Eliot to wish on her fairly unusual heroine? This is hardly the work of a "later-born Theresa" who had longed to "see the truth by the same light as great men have seen it by" (p. 27), to live comfortably in a small country town raising a family. Dorothea turns out to be yet another one of the characters in the novel, along with Lydgate and Casaubon, whose impossible ambitions will ultimately go unrealized.

Because of the terms the narrator uses to introduce Dorothea's character and story, however, a close reading of the novel demands that we take her gender into account when considering the reasons for her ultimate fate. While Casaubon and Lydgate's "tragic flaw" is their arrogant ambition, their striving for a perfect knowledge of a primary cause, Dorothea's is something different. She is hardly arrogant; her desire for importance centers on being a helpmate to a great man, learning as much as she can in her "inferior" position as a woman in Victorian culture, and being of use to those around her: "It would be my duty to study that I might help him the better in his great work. There would be nothing trivial about our lives .... It would be like marrying Pascal" (p. 27).

While this self-effacing attitude was certainly consonant with most Victorians' opinions about the proper place of women, there is some suggestion in the novel that Eliot is ironizing Dorothea's extreme diffidence. The narrator carefully builds a sense of Casaubon's wrongheadedness, arrogance, and misguided hubris throughout the early sections of the novel, yet Casaubon concurs with Dorothea's feelings about her supposedly proper role: "The great charm of your sex is its capability of an ardent self-sacrificing affection, and herein we see its fitness to round and complete the existence of our own" (p. 46). How are we to read this statement, coming as it does from a man whose opinions we learn to distrust and the pen of a woman who spoke several languages, translated Strauss and Feuerbach, edited the *Westminster Review,* and is still considered one of the nineteenth century's most important intellectuals? In a similarly ironic vein, the narrator also pokes fun at the pretensions of Sir James Chettam, a man who is hardly an intellectual heavyweight in Middlemarch:

A man's mind—what there is of it—has always the advantage of being masculine,—as the smallest birch-tree is of a higher kind than the most soaring palm,—and even his ignorance is of a sounder quality. Sir James might not have originated this estimate; but a kind Providence furnishes the limpest personality with a little gum or starch in the form of tradition.

(p. 20)

Even the weakest-willed, silliest, and vainest man will always seem less weak, silly, and vain than a woman—this is the burden of the sexist "tradition" to which Dorothea finds herself in thrall. This is not a tradition from which she will necessarily escape in her later love match with Will Ladislaw, about whose occasional "chilling sense of remoteness" from Dorothea the narrator opines, "A man is seldom ashamed of feeling that he cannot love a woman so well when he sees a certain greatness in her: nature having intended greatness for men" (p. 365). If the tragedies of Lydgate and Casaubon can be traced to their own flaws, then the tragedy of Dorothea is due to a flaw at the heart of Victorian culture.

We can see the constraining role for women even more clearly in the case of Rosamond, a female character who seems to have more readily accepted her place in the culture, and yet does not seem to realize how circumscribed that place really is. One of the reasons that the misunderstandings of her courtship with Lydgate are so painful to her is that she has very little else to think about:

It had not occurred to Lydgate that he had been a subject of eager meditation to Rosamond, who had neither any reason for throwing her marriage into distant perspective, nor any pathological studies to divert her mind from that ruminating habit, that inward repetition of looks, words, and phrases, which makes a large part in the lives of most girls.

(p. 155)

The narrator later calls this lack of meaningful occupation the "elegant leisure of a young lady's mind" (p. 281). Rosamond and Dorothea represent two possible responses to the same set of circumstances: the former has largely accepted her lot and allowed herself to be formed into the picture of perfect Victorian femininity, while the later has chafed and resisted—yet has hardly been more successful in escaping her social constraints. As we have noted, Dorothea is the reader's main point of identification in the novel, and it may seem somewhat disheartening that she does not manage to fashion a more progressive life for herself (perhaps something more like the life of Mary Ann Evans). The constraints operating on Dorothea are presented as almost impersonal in origin (the narrator tells us at one point that a "woman dictates before marriage in order that she may have an appetite for submission afterwards" [67])—much like the other kinds of moral, political, and economic constraints operating on those caught in the "web" of provincial life in Middlemarch.

Of course, these insights are not unique to Eliot or even to nineteenth-century women authors; what is particularly interesting about Eliot's grappling with these questions is the way in which she works out her project of control—over her text, over its interpretation, and over her literary reputation—using her female characters. For example, if we return to the question of the "rejection" of Casaubon discussed earlier, we realize that it cannot be separated from the dynamics of gender in the novel.

Dorothea's "recognition" of Casaubon, and of the limitations of his intellectual powers, signals Eliot's move away from the omniscient modes of narration that are associated with masculine ambition. As her narrator says about Casaubon's doomed "Key to All Mythologies," "there are some kinds of authorship in which by far the largest result is the uneasy susceptibility accumulated in the consciousness of the author" (p. 391). The by-product of the kind of authorship that seeks knowledge untempered by sympathy is a malaise on the part of the seeker. Perhaps the ambivalence Eliot registers about the hubristic projects of Casaubon and Lydgate is also an ambivalence about the "experimental" aspects of her own narrative project in *Middlemarch*. While no character in the novel consistently succeeds at the "systole and diastole" of inquiry, the pulsing between analysis and description that Lydgate sought, it is clear that this is the standard to which George Eliot held herself, to be "at once rational and ardent," dispassionate and sympathetic: "She did not want to deck herself with knowledge—to wear it loose from the nerves and blood that fed her action; and if she had written a book she must have done it as Saint Theresa did, under the command of an authority that constrained her conscience" (p. 80).

Selected Bibliography

EDITIONS

Eliot, George. *Middlemarch.* Edited by David Carroll. Oxford: Clarendon Press; New York: Oxford University Press, 1986. The definitive edition.

Eliot, George. *Middlemarch.* Edited by David Carroll. Oxford: Oxford University Press, 1997. Paperback reprint of the definitive Clarendon edition; the citations in this essay use this reprint.

OTHER WORKS BY ELIOT

This list is limited to works discussed or cited in the present essay.

The Clarendon Edition of the Novels of George Eliot. Oxford: Clarendon Press; New

York: Oxford University Press, 1980–. The definitive edition of the novels.

Essays of George Eliot. Edited by Thomas Pinney. New York: New York University Press, 1963.

The George Eliot Letters. Edited by Gordon S. Haight. 9 vols. New Haven: Yale University Press, 1954–1978.

The Journals of George Eliot. Edited by Margaret Harris and Judith Johnston. Cambridge: Cambridge University Press, 1998.

The Life of Jesus, Critically Examined. By David Friedrich Strauss. Translated by George Eliot. Edited by Peter C. Hodgson. Philadelphia: Fortress Press, 1973.

SECONDARY WORKS

Adams, Harriet Farwell. "Dorothea and 'Miss Brooke' in *Middlemarch.*" *Nineteenth Century Literature* 39, no. 1 (June 1984): 69–90.

Andres, Sophia. "The Germ and the Picture in *Middlemarch.*" *ELH* 55, no. 4 (Winter 1988): 853–868.

Ashton, Rosemary. *George Eliot: A Life.* London: Hamish Hamilton, 1996.

Barrett, Dorothea. *Vocation and Desire: George Eliot's Heroines.* London: Macmillan, 1988.

Beaty, Jerome. *"Middlemarch" from Notebook to Novel: A Study of George Eliot's Creative Method.* Urbana: University of Illinois Press, 1960.

Beer, Gillian. *Darwin's Plots: Evolutionary Narrative in Darwin, George Eliot and Nineteenth-Century Fiction.* London: Routledge and Kegan Paul, 1983.

Blake, Kathleen. "*Middlemarch* and the Woman Question." *Nineteenth Century Fiction* 31, no. 3 (December 1976): 285–312.

Brody, Selma B. "Physics in *Middlemarch*: Gas Molecules and Ethereal Atoms." *Modern Philology* 85, no. 1 (August 1987): 42–53.

Carroll, David, ed. *George Eliot: The Critical Heritage.* New York: Barnes and Noble, 1971. An extensive collection of novel reviews by Eliot's contemporaries.

———. *George Eliot and the Conflict of Interpretations: A Reading of the Novels.* Cambridge: Cambridge University Press, 1992.

Cottom, Daniel. *Social Figures: George Eliot, Social History, and Literary Representation.* Minneapolis: University of Minnesota Press, 1987.

Cross, John W. *George Eliot's Life as Related in Her Letters and Journals.* 3 vols. Edinburgh and London: W. Blackwood and Sons, 1885.

Darwin, Charles. *On the Origin of Species.* New York: Avenel Books, 1979.

Deresiewicz, William. "Heroism and Organicism in the Case of Lydgate." *Studies in English Literature, 1500–1900* 38, no. 4 (Autumn 1998): 723–740.

Fisher, Philip. *Making Up Society: The Novels of George Eliot.* Pittsburgh: University of Pittsburgh Press, 1981.

Fraser, Hilary. "St. Theresa, St. Dorothea, and Miss Brooke in *Middlemarch.*" *Nineteenth Century Literature* 40, no. 4 (March 1986): 400–411.

Ginsburg, Michal Peled. "Pseudonym, Epigraphs and Narrative Voice: *Middlemarch* and the Problem of Authorship." *ELH* 47, no. 3 (Autumn 1980): 542–558.

Graver, Suzanne. *George Eliot and Community: A Study in Social Theory and Fictional*

Form. Berkeley: University of California Press, 1984.

Greenberg, Robert A. "Plexus and Ganglia: Scientific Allusion in *Middlemarch.*" *Nineteenth Century Fiction* 30, no. 1 (June 1975): 33–52.

Haight, Gordon. *George Eliot: A Biography.* Oxford: Clarendon Press, 1968. The standard biography.

Hands, Timothy. *A George Eliot CHRONOLOGY.* Boston: G. K. Hall, 1989. A detailed chronology of Eliot's life and work.

Hardy, Barbara. *The Novels of George Eliot: A Study of Form.* London: Athlone, 1959. A classic study of Eliot's fiction.

————, ed. *"Middlemarch": Critical Approaches to the Novel.* London: Athlone 1967.

Hardy, Barbara, J. Hillis Miller, and Richard Poirier. "*Middlemarch,* Chapter 85: Three Commentaries." *Nineteenth Century Fiction* 35, no. 3 (December 1980): 432–453.

Hertz, Neil. "Recognizing Casaubon." In his *The End of the Line: Essays on Psychoanalysis and the Sublime.* New York: Columbia University Press, 1985.

James, Henry. *The Tragic Muse.* New York: Scribner's, 1936. Preface.

Kucich, John. "Repression and Dialectical Inwardness in *Middlemarch.*" *Mosaic* 18, no. 1 (Winter 1985): 45–63.

Levine, George. *The Realistic Imagination: English Fiction from Frankenstein to Lady Chatterley.* Chicago: University of Chicago Press, 1981.

————, ed. *The Cambridge Companion to George Eliot.* Cambridge: Cambridge University Press, 2001.

Lewes, George Henry. *Problems of Life and Mind.* 5 vols. London: Trubner, 1874–1879.

Lundberg, Patricia Lorimer. "George Eliot: Mary Ann Evans's Subversive Tool in *Middlemarch.*" *Studies in the Novel* 18, no. 3 (Fall 1986): 270–282.

Lyell, Charles. *Principles of Geology.* Edited by James A. Secord. New York: Penguin, 1997.

Lyons, Richard S. "The Method of *Middlemarch.*" *Nineteenth Century Fiction* 21, no. 1 (June 1966): 35–47.

Martin, Carol A. "Revising *Middlemarch.*" *Victorian Periodicals Review* 25, no. 2 (Summer 1992): 72–78.

Mason, Michael Y. "*Middlemarch* and History." *Nineteenth Century Fiction* 25, no. 4 (March 1971): 417–431.

Matus, Jill L. "Saint Teresa, Hysteria, and *Middlemarch.*" *Journal of the History of Sexuality* 1, no. 2 (October 1990): 215–240.

Miller, J. Hillis. "Optic and Semiotic in *Middlemarch.*" In *The Worlds of Victorian Fiction.* Edited by Jerome H. Buckley. Cambridge, Mass: Harvard University Press, 1975.

Payne, David. The Serialist Vanishes: Producing Belief in George Eliot." *Novel: A Forum on Fiction* 33, no. 1 (Fall): 32–50.

Paris, Bernard J. "*Middlemarch* Revisited: Changing Responses to George Eliot." *American Journal of Psychoanalysis* 59, no. 3 (September 1999): 237–255.

Postlethwaite, Diana. "When George Eliot Reads Milton: The Muse in a Different Voice." *ELH* 57, no. 1 (Spring 1990): 197–221.

Pratt, John Clark, and Victor A. Neufeldt. *George Eliot's Middlemarch Notebooks: A Transcription.* Berkeley: University of California Press, 1979.

Redinger, Ruby R. *George Eliot: The Emergent Self.* London: The Bodley Head, 1976.

Rischin, Abigail S. "Beside the Reclining Statue: Ekphrasis, Narrative, and Desire in *Middlemarch.*" *PMLA* 111, no. 5 (October 1996): 1121–1132.

Shuttleworth, Sally. *George Eliot and Nineteenth-Century Science: The Make-Believe of a Beginning.* Cambridge: Cambridge University Press, 1984.

Staten, Henry. "Is *Middlemarch* Ahistorical?" *PMLA* 115, no. 5 (October 2000): 991–1005.

Tambling, Jeremy. "*Middlemarch*, Realism and the Birth of the Clinic." *ELH* 57, no. 4 (Winter 1990): 939–960.

Tucker, John L. "George Eliot's Reflexive Text: Three Tonalities in the Narrative Voice of *Middlemarch.*" *Studies in English Literature, 1500–1900* 31, no. 4 (Autumn 1991): 773–791.

Wiesenfarth, Joseph. "*Middlemarch*: The Language of Art." *PMLA* 97, no. 3 (May 1982): 363–377.

Witemeyer, Hugh. *George Eliot and the Visual Arts.* New Haven: Yale University Press, 1979.

Woolf, Virginia. "George Eliot." In her *The Common Reader.* First Series. London: Hogarth Press, 1925.

Wormald, Mark. "Microscopy and Semiotic in *Middlemarch.*" *Nineteenth Century Literature* 50, no. 4 (March 1996): 501–524.

James Joyce's
A Portrait of the Artist as a Young Man

CAITRÍONA O'REILLY

JAMES JOYCE WAS born in Rathgar, Dublin, on 2 February 1882, the oldest surviving child of May and John Stanislaus Joyce. After an early career in politics and as a rate collector, John Joyce's fortunes declined sharply. Fleeing his creditors, he began a series of relocations that took his family from Dublin's fashionable suburbs ever closer to its inner-city slums, in a precipitous descent that marked the young Joyce's character deeply. John Joyce was a passionate supporter of Charles Stewart Parnell, champion of Irish Home Rule, and was inconsolable on his death in 1891. This event prompted his son's first known composition, *Et tu, Healy,* a poetic diatribe against Parnell's treacherous lieutenant, and features again in the Christmas dinner scene of *A Portrait of the Artist as a Young Man.* John Joyce was also a heavy drinker, spendthrift, and raconteur, as Stephen Dedalus describes him in *A Portrait:* "a medical student, an oarsman, a tenor, an amateur actor, a shouting politician, a small landlord, a small investor, a drinker, a good fellow, a story-teller, somebody's secretary, something in a distillery, a tax-gatherer, a bankrupt and at present a praiser of his own past" (p. 262). The twin figures of Parnell and his father would loom large in everything Joyce wrote, heroic but reckless patriarchs done down by Irish blackguardism.

Despite his family's sliding fortunes, Joyce was educated at the prestigious Jesuit schools of Clongowes College and Belvedere and went on to the Royal University (now University College Dublin) in 1895. By now Joyce was composing his earliest poetry, a collection of which, *Chamber Music,* he assembled in 1904. In 1900 he began to write short prose sketches he termed "epiphanies," capturing moments of illumination and heightened perception. The young Joyce was also acquiring a reputation for radicalism among his fellow students, refusing to sign a petition condemning W. B. Yeats's play *The Countess Cathleen* and publishing a pamphlet, "The Day of the Rabblement" (1901), condemning the demagoguery of Irish cultural nationalism. His greatest influence at this time was Henrik Ibsen, on whom he published an article in the *Fortnightly Review.*

Leaving Ireland for France in 1902, Joyce enrolled as a medical student in Paris but was recalled by a telegram in August 1903 informing him of his mother's imminent death. Joyce's anger at his mother's victimization by his father (although Joyce remained well disposed toward his father as his other siblings did not) and the paternalistic culture of the Catholic church hardened his heart further against Ireland, and strengthened his resolve to embrace the values of "silence, exile and cunning" (*Portrait*, p. 269). In 1904 he began work on an autobiographical novel, *Stephen Hero*, writing twenty-five chapters before starting afresh in 1907 on the novel that became *A Portrait of the Artist as a Young Man*. At the same time he was composing the stories of *Dubliners*, completed in 1907 but not published until 1914, after a series of legal wrangles with Irish publishers. One positive side effect of the book's troubled gestation was the series of letters Joyce wrote to Grant Richards in its defense, setting out his sense of artistic mission: "My intention was to write a chapter of the moral history of my country and I chose Dublin for the scene because that city seemed to me the center of paralysis" (*Selected Letters*, p. 83).

Joyce finally left Ireland in October 1904, in the company of Nora Barnacle, a chambermaid from Galway with whom he had his first tryst on 16 June 1904, an occasion he would later immortalize by making it the date on which the action of his masterwork *Ulysses* (1922) takes place. Between 1904 and 1915, Joyce and Nora lived in considerable poverty in Pola and Trieste. Their two children, Giorgio and Lucia, were born in 1905 and 1907. In 1913 Joyce acquired a powerful champion in the American poet Ezra Pound, who arranged for serialization of *A Portrait* in the *Egoist*, with publication in book form following in 1916. Through his *Egoist* connection Joyce began to receive the patronage of Harriet Shaw Weaver, a wealthy Englishwoman who subsidized him with great generosity, allowing him the freedom to write *Ulysses* between 1914 and 1921, during which time he

CHRONOLOGY

1882	Born Rathgar, Dublin, 2 February, oldest of ten surviving children.
1888	Enters the prestigious Jesuit school Clongowes College.
1893	Continues his studies with the Jesuits at Belvedere College.
1891	Death of nationalist leader Charles Stewart Parnell, inspiring Joyce's first composition *Et tu, Healy*.
1898	Enters University College, Dublin, where he lectures to student society on Henrik Ibsen and nineteenth-century Irish poet James Clarence Mangan, gaining a reputation for fearless free thought.
1900	Publishes article on Ibsen in *Fortnightly Review*, and receives a letter of thanks from the Norwegian playwright.
1901	Publishes a pamphlet, "Day of the Rabblement," attacking Yeats's Irish Literary Theatre.
1902	Graduates with BA degree. First trip to Paris, where he briefly studies medicine.
1903	Death of mother.
1904	First date with future wife Nora Barnacle on 16 June, a date commemorated as Bloomsday in *Ulysses*. Publication of first story, "The Sisters,&rdqo; under the pen name Stephen Dedalus in *The Irish Homestead*. Begins work on *Stephen Hero*, a first version of *A Portrait of the Artist as a Young Man*. Stays in Martello Tower, Sandycove, with Dublin wit and surgeon Oliver St. John Gogarty, an episode that forms the basis for the opening chapter of *Ulysses*. Denounces his Celtic Twilight contemporaries in a satirical poem, "The Holy Office."
1905	Settles in Adriatic port city of Trieste, where he teaches English in a Berlitz language school. Encounters and encourages Italian novelist Italo Svevo.

	Birth of son, Giorgio. Joined in Trieste by his brother Stanislaus who provides much-needed financial support and later records his impression of these years in a memoir, *My Brother's Keeper*.
1906	Stays briefly in Rome where he works in a bank.
1907	*Chamber Music* (poems) published. Birth of daughter, Lucia. Writes "The Dead," completing his short story collection *Dubliners*. Contributes series of articles to Triestine newspaper *Il Piccolo della Sera*.
1909	Opens Ireland's first cinema, The Volta, in Dublin; the venture is not a success. His university friend Vincent Cosgrave (Lynch in *A Portrait*) boasts to Joyce of a relationship with Nora Barnacle in 1904. An accusing letter to Nora is followed by contrition and reconciliation on Joyce's discovery that the story is baseless, strengthening his identification of Ireland with treachery and betrayal. Unsuccessful attempts to have *Dubliners* published.
1912	Last visit to Dublin. Galley proofs of *Dubliners* destroyed by publisher George Roberts, nervous of prosecution for libel; Joyce replies with the poem "Gas from a Burner," denouncing philistine Irish puritanism.
1914	*Dubliners* published. *The Egoist* begins serial publication of *A Portrait*. Joyce Leaves Trieste for Zürich in neutral Switzerland. Begins work on *Ulysses*, chapters of which will be serialized from 1918 in *The Little Review*.
1916	*A Portrait* published. Outbreak of Easter Rising in Ireland, led by Joyce's former Irish language teacher Patrick Pearse.
1917	First of twenty-five operations on his eyes; cataracts and glaucoma reduce Joyce to near-blindness for much of the remainder of his life.
1919	*Exiles*, a play, staged in Berlin.

1920	Settles in Paris, where he remains until 1939.
1922	*Ulysses* published by Shakespeare & Co. on Joyce's fortieth birthday.
1927	*Pomes Penyeach* published. First of seventeen installments of *Work in Progress* (the working title of *Finnegans Wake*) published in the Paris avant-garde review *transition*.
1931	Marries Nora Barnacle in London registry office. Death of father.
1932	Birth of grandson, Stephen. Joyce marks the conjunction of birth and death with a poem, "Ecce Puer." Lucia Joyce suffers breakdown, and is hospitalized in Switzerland in 1933.
1939	*Finnegans Wake* published. Flees Paris for Saint-Gérand-le-Puy near Vichy.
1941	Dies in Zürich, 13 January.

moved from Trieste to Zurich and Paris. During this period he also wrote the play *Exiles,* staged in Berlin in 1919. *Ulysses* was published in 1922 by Sylvia Beach under the imprint of her Paris bookshop Shakespeare & Co. on Joyce's fortieth birthday, bringing Joyce international fame and notoriety in equal measures. Having exhausted the possibilities of waking life in *Ulysses,* Joyce now turned to the secrets of the sleeping mind in his last novel, *Finnegans Wake,* begun in 1922 and not completed until 1939. Its revolutionary style went too far for some of his hitherto staunchest defenders, including Pound and Miss Weaver, though in an attempt to rally support, Joyce organized the publication of a book of essays entitled *Our Exagmination Round His Factification for the Incamination of Work in Progress* (1929), whose contributors included the twenty-three-year-old Samuel Beckett. These years were also troubled by the increasing mental illness of his daughter Lucia—who had begun to show signs of mental disturbance in her early twenties and eventually became an incurable schizophrenic—and the breakdown of his son Giorgio's marriage to Helen Fleischman. With the outbreak of World War II, the Joyce family left Paris for Gérand-le-Puy, near Vichy, before entering neutral Switzerland. Raging at the folly of war, not least for its keeping people from reading *Finnegans Wake*, Joyce died of a perforated duodenal ulcer in Zurich on 13 January 1941.

EPIPHANIES

A Portrait of the Artist as a Young Man takes as its theme the evolution of the artistic mind, but Joyce's own artistic evolution was far from complete when the novel was first conceived in 1904, twelve years before its publication. In this year Joyce wrote a short autobiographical story called "A Portrait of the Artist" and submitted it to a new Irish journal named *Dana*. The editors refused it for publication, but this short text foreshadows many of the later novel's themes, albeit in a dense and awkward style. From its opening lines, Joyce signals his intention to break with conventional literary portraiture and its accompanying realist ethos:

> The features of infancy are not commonly reproduced in the adolescent portrait for, so capricious are we, that we cannot or will not conceive the past in any other than its iron memorial aspect. Yet the past assuredly implied a fluid succession of presents, the development of an entity of which our actual present is a phase only.
>
> (In *Poems and Shorter Writings*, p. 211)

Joyce rejects the sterile memorialization of the past in favor of an imaginative re-creation of a "fluid succession of presents." One of his principal tools to this end was the "epiphany" technique. Coming from the Greek *epiphanein*, the word means "to show forth" (from the showing of the infant Christ to the three kings on the feast of the Epiphany) and was used by Joyce to denote moments of intense perception and understanding, which he recorded in a series of forty prose sketches written in 1901–1902 and in 1904. The first of these describes the young Joyce under the table in the family home in Bray,

hiding from punishment and reciting to himself the rhyme he will use again in *A Portrait*— "Pull out his eyes, / Apologise, / Apologise, / Pull out his eyes"—though what exactly Stephen has done is not made clear. Joyce prefers to keep his revelations oblique: the epiphanies that use dialogue are full of mysterious ellipses and sentences trailing off into the unsaid. One of the most important, numbered 34, was written after the death of Joyce's mother and pours the balm of maternal love on the lonely male imagination:

> She comes at night when the city is still; invisible, inaudible, all unsummoned. She comes from her ancient seat to visit the least of her children, mother most venerable, as though he had never been alien to her. She knows the inmost heart; therefore she is gentle, nothing exacting; saying, I am susceptible of change, an imaginative influence in the hearts of my children. Who has pity for you when you are sad among the strangers? Years and years I loved you when you lay in my womb.
>
> (*Poems and Shorter Writings*, p. 194)

The mother's protective tenderness and Joyce's proud reluctance to acknowledge it dominate the pair's relationship; the mother's final words here turn up again, with minimal alteration, in the climactic scene in *Ulysses* when Stephen confronts his dead mother's ghost. While still alive in *A Portrait*, she remains, paradoxically, a more shadowy presence, but many of that novel's epiphanic moments turn on female figures, most famously a wading girl on Dollymount Strand.

The epiphany technique is also central to the short-story collection *Dubliners*. In the absence of any artistic sensibilities comparable to that of Stephen Dedalus, the best the Dubliners can achieve is a realization of their paralyzed condition and the futility of their actions. Thus the young narrator of "Araby" travels to the glamorous-sounding Araby bazaar to buy a gift for his beloved, but on arriving he too late finds only a drab, half-empty hall: "Gazing up into the darkness I saw myself as a creature driven and derided by vanity; and my eyes burned with anguish and anger" (p. 28). Mr. Duffy in "A Painful Case" (reputedly modeled on Joyce's brother Stanislaus) preens himself on his own sense of intellectual superiority, but reading in the paper of the pitiful death of a woman whose emotional advances he once spurned, he realizes the hollowness of the victory he has won: "He could hear nothing: the night was perfectly silent. He listened again: perfectly silent. He felt that he was alone" (p. 114). These epiphanies are moments of stillness, but a stillness born of defeat and resignation. Stephen's epiphanies, by contrast, are born of intellectual growth and development.

STEPHEN DEDALUS AND *STEPHEN HERO*

The first story in *Dubliners* to appear in print, "The Sisters," appeared in the *Irish Homestead* in 1904 under the name of "Stephen Daedalus" at the same time as Daedalus was taking his first steps in Joyce's fiction, in *Stephen Hero*. Joyce wrote almost a thousand pages of this first draft of *A Portrait* before throwing it on the fire, whence it was retrieved by his sister. The surviving portions of *Stephen Hero* begin with Stephen already a university student. A number of passages in the novel are treated quite differently from their counterparts in *A Portrait*, while some would later be dropped entirely. Among the passages unique to *Stephen Hero* are the descriptions of Gaelic lessons with Mr. Hughes (a thinly veiled portrait of the 1916 rebel leader Patrick Pearse, from whom Joyce briefly took Irish lessons), the delivery of Stephen's paper on Ibsen to his fellow university students and the debate that follows, and a visit to the rural county of Westmeath. Stephen's relationship with Emma Clery (known only by her initials in *A Portrait*) is also handled very differently. Seeing her in the street, Stephen runs to join her and proposes a night of love, an offer she rejects with horror. Stephen then encounters a prostitute and compares her sexual frankness to the code of sexual purity instilled by Catholi-cism; as Joyce writes in the margin, "Stephen wished to avenge himself on Irish women who, he says, are the cause of all the moral suicide in the island" (*Stephen Hero*, p. 179). In Emma's defense, it does not occur to Stephen that there might be other reasons apart from religion why she might decline his advances.

At the time Joyce was in violent reaction against authority: "My mind rejects the whole present social order and Christianity" (*Selected Letters*, p. 25), he wrote to Nora Barnacle in 1904. Like the young Joyce, Stephen brandishes his sense of superiority with adolescent swagger: "he flung . . . disdain from flashing antlers" (*Stephen Hero*, p. 36). Unlike *A Portrait*, however, *Stephen Hero* does not achieve the necessary distance from its protagonist for these posturings to acquire the saving grace of ironic deflation. This is not to say that the Stephen of *Stephen Hero* is simply a more off-putting character than he will later become; if anything he is more naive and touching, as in the scene where he persuades his mother to read the works of the dreaded heretic Ibsen. But despite the earlier argument of "A Portrait of the Artist," *Stephen Hero* charts its hero's development in straightforwardly chronological style, with none of the dialectical clash of opposites that is such a feature of *A Portrait*. For the still and silent epiphanies of Joyce's writing to be truly effective, he needed to test them against more sound and fury than *Stephen Hero* could offer.

A PORTRAIT: CHILDHOOD

The Stephen Dedalus who appears in *A Portrait* is a much more sophisticated study in character development, making *A Portrait* an innovative example of what is known as bildungsroman, the novel of formation. The fact that Stephen later reappears in Joyce's great novel *Ulysses* helps to bridge the transition between the two books in a fascinating way. Indeed, transition is what *A Portrait* is all about, down to and especially in its use of language. Unlike *Stephen*

Hero, which is a more static and conventional work, *A Portrait* mirrors the development of Stephen's character with a prose style that evolves from one chapter to the next. In the "Oxen of the Sun" episode in *Ulysses,* which is set in Dublin's Holles Street maternity hospital, Joyce puts the English language through an embryonic growth from its Anglo-Saxon origins up to the twentieth century. The Joyce critic and biographer Richard Ellmann argues that Joyce's intention in *A Portrait* is to record the gestation of a soul. He writes:

> The book begins with Stephen's father and, just before the ending, it depicts the hero's severance from his mother. From the start the soul is surrounded by liquids, urine, slime, seawater, amniotic tides, "drops of water" as Joyce says at the end of the first chapter "falling softly in the brimming bowl." The atmosphere of biological struggle is necessarily dark and melancholy until the light of life is glimpsed.
>
> *(James Joyce, p. 297)*

In *A Portrait,* the embryonic growth of language effectively mirrors the growth of the artistic soul. The intensely vivid opening pages of the book read like a parable of language acquisition, with Stephen learning to find his way through the labyrinth of childhood experience. In this he lives up to his namesake in Greek mythology, Dedalus, who built a labyrinth and lurks behind the epigraph to *A Portrait.* For this, Joyce chose a line from Ovid's *Metamorphoses:* "*Et ignotas animum dimittit in artes*" (And he sent his soul down among unknown arts), recalling the episode where Dedalus built the wings on which his son Icarus learned to fly. This modern Dedalus proposes to go one better by doing the flying himself.

The young narrator of Joyce's "The Sisters," which is the first story in *Dubliners,* meditates on the three mysterious words "paralysis," "gnomon," and "simony," words that possess for him a mantic and fearsome power. By contrast, the opening of *A Portrait* is much less tentative. Stephen takes possession of language

with his use of nursery rhyme formulas and repetitions, his appropriation of the story his father tells him and the song he sings, mispronunciations included, and the importance of smell and touch in interpreting his environment, all in language of remarkable freshness and delight:

> Once upon a time and a very good time is was there was a moocow coming down along the road and this moocow that was coming down along the road met a nicens little boy named baby tuckoo. . .
>
> His father told him that story: his father looked at him through a glass: he had a hairy face.
>
> He was baby tuckoo. The moocow came down the road where Betty Byrne lived: she sold lemon platt.
>
> > *O, the wild rose blossoms*
> > *On the little green place.*
>
> He sang that song. That was his song.
>
> > *O, the green wothe botheth.*
>
> When you wet the bed first it is warm then it gets cold. His mother put on the oilsheet. That had the queer smell.
>
> *(p. 3)*

Anthony Burgess has speculated on how this passage could have come out in the hands of a more conventional writer: "My first memories are of my father, a monocled hirsute man who told me stories," for instance (*Here Comes Everybody,* p. 50). Joyce achieves something entirely different. As another observant reader of Joyce, Samuel Beckett, observed, in his writing "here form *is* content, content *is* form" (*Disjecta: Miscellaneous Writings and a Dramatic Fragment,* 1983, p. 27).

Style and subject matter have come together in Joyce in a pure expressionist fusion. In the opening of this chapter Joyce attends to each of the five senses in turn: his protagonist hears the story, sees his father, tastes the lemon platt, touches the bed, and smells the oil sheet. This sort of sensation is his first introduction to the world of sex, with the gender differences of father and mother already clearly marked. Performance of the song leads to incipient artistic consciousness "He sang that song. That was his song." Joyce keeps this baby-talk passage to a bare minimum, avoiding sentimentality, but at school too Dedalus is surrounded by puzzles that demand his interpretive mastery. Or as Stephen will say in the Proteus chapter of *Ulysses,* "Signatures of all things I am here to read." Among these puzzles is the song quoted above, with its green rose. "But you could not have a green rose," Stephen thinks to himself, before deciding, "But perhaps somewhere in the world you could" (p. 9).

In the playground of his school, Clongowes Wood, he is asked, "Tell us, Dedalus, do you kiss your mother before you go to bed?" Stephen answers that he does, to the amusement of his tormentor, who shouts "O, I say, here's a fellow says he kisses his mother every night before he goes to bed." Then when Stephen denies he does this, the other exclaims, "O, I say, here's a fellow says he doesn't kiss his mother before he goes to bed" (p. 10). The other boys all laugh again, leaving Stephen wondering what the right answer could have been. The question is designed not to elicit information but to underline the other boy's seniority and his right to make fun of Stephen, but such subtleties are lost on the literal-minded young Dedalus. When it comes to poetic devices such as metaphor, Stephen is initially badly confused. The phrase "Tower of Ivory" in the Litany of the Blessed Virgin gives him a great deal of trouble: "How could a woman be a tower of ivory or a house of gold?" Eventually he works it out:

Eileen had long white hands. One evening when playing tig she had put her hands over his eyes: long and white and thin and cold and soft. That was ivory: a cold white thing. That was the meaning of *Tower of Ivory.*

(p. 35)

His cautious, naive reasoning is brilliantly captured by Joyce. Stephen's Jesuit education imbues him with a sense of idealistic certainty, which can be seen in the strikingly Dedalus-centred inscription he writes in his geography book: *"Stephen Dedalus / Class of Elements / Clongowes Wood College / Sallins / County Kildare / Ireland / Europe / The World / The Universe"* (p. 12) This is a young man confident of his place in the world, and confident too that it all revolves around him. He places a constant emphasis on ritualistic forms of language, such as grammar exercises, prayers, and playground riddles, and finds excitement in unexpected corners of this lumber room of knowledge, such as the lines from his spelling book that Stephen treats as poetry:

Wolsey died in Leicester Abbey
Where the abbots buried him.
Canker is a disease of plants,
Cancer one of animals.

(pp. 6–7)

Even simple mnemonic formulas like these help to awaken Stephen's sense of language as something enchanted beyond its workaday meanings. He experiences words as physical things, as when the word "suck," in the sense of "sucking up to" or flattery, sets off a chain of associations—almost literally a chain, since it brings him back to a lavatory in the Wicklow Hotel and the sound the water made disappearing down the plughole: "when it had all gone down slowly the hole in the basin had made a sound like that: suck. Only louder" (p. 8) It is only when Stephen's faith in the benevolence of the school is shaken that these innocent playground reveries come to a halt. This is precipitated by the accidental breaking of his glasses in the cinder pit and his pandybatting, or corporal punishment, at the hands of Father Dolan, who calls him a "lazy little schemer" (p. 51) and accuses him of having broken them deliberately to avoid writing his essay. The first chapter ends with Stephen protesting this injustice successfully to Father Arnall, the rector, who promises it will not happen again. This event represents Stephen's first successful, courageous stand against unjust authority.

TOWARDS REVOLT

Father Dolan is not the only figure whose authority is demonstrably challenged and overturned, however. *A Portrait*'s first chapter also contains the celebrated Christmas dinner scene in which Stephen's father starts a bitter row about Charles Stewart Parnell with Dante, the family governess. Despite her name, Dante is philistine and puritanical, and gloats over Parnell's demise. The figure of Dante is based on the Joyce family's live-in governess, a Mrs. Hearn Conway from Cork. She was a fanatical Catholic and nationalist, whose twin enthusiasms clashed painfully when Parnell was revealed to be an adulterer. A jilted bride herself, she rejected Parnell on the grounds of his immorality and sided with the priests in condemning him. Dante has also foreseen a future of punishment for the young Stephen:

> His mother said:
> O, Stephen will apologise.
> Dante said:
> O, if not, the eagles will come and pull out his
> eyes—
>> Pull out his eyes,
>> Apologise.
>> Apologise,
>> Pull out his eyes.

(p. 4)

Here Joyce establishes the theme of transgression, with the eagles representing the imperial authority of the Roman church. In Stephen's eyes punishment is always a vividly real and immediate threat, modeled on the ultimate punishment, Christ's crucifixion by the Roman authorities. Over Christmas dinner, Stephen's father invokes the Christ-like betrayal of Parnell, and to Dante's cry of "God and religion before the world," Mr. Casey answers blasphe-

mously, "Very well then ... no God for Ireland!" (p. 38). The dinner ends with Dante leaving the room in outrage and Mr. Dedalus weeping for "Poor Parnell! . . . My dead king!" (p. 39). Stephen, though silent, is deeply marked by this show of defiance. The authority of God, Parnell, and father Dedalus have all been traumatically called into question. Dante symbolically takes her green velvet brush, representing Parnell, and snips off its green backing as a symbol of his disgrace. Stephen thinks to himself: "That was called politics. There were two sides in it: Dante was on one side and his father and Mr. Casey were on the other side but his mother and Uncle Charles were on no side" (pp. 13–14). This is a terrible, stark world of blind certainties, with all arguments reducible to a shouting match in the kitchen or the pub. Insofar as Stephen refuses to come to rest or achieve stability as a character, he at least avoids ossifying into one of these terrible fixed poles of Irish life.

Each of the novel's other four chapters ends with a moment of crisis and resolution, but as each new section unfolds, the previous resolution is quickly superseded, with Stephen reaching a new independence of his earlier self. The important principle to grasp is the constant flux and reflux of contrary impulses and emotions that drives Stephen not just to the end of the novel but beyond.

The arena in which these contrary impulses compete is language itself. The critic John Paul Riquelme has noted Joyce's oscillation between a harsh naturalism reminiscent of *Dubliners* and the novel's language of artistic rapture and ecstasy, which he has termed the "stylistic double helix" of the novel, with the two strands coiling round each other like DNA (in Attridge, ed., 1990, p. 119). The eminent Joyce critic Hugh Kenner has described this stylistic swerving in terms of what he calls the "Uncle Charles principle," a free, indirect style that mutates to match the character being described. For example, old Uncle Charles is described as "repairing" to the outhouse to smoke his "salubrious" and "mollifying" black twist, for which read rancid and disgusting tobacco (p. 62). "Repair" is a rather comically old-fashioned way of saying "go" and is just the sort of word a ceremonial but faintly ridiculous figure like Uncle Charles would use, with his tall hat and embarrassing advice about bowel regularity, and Joyce allows his language to permeate the language of the text.

In chapter 2, Stephen begins to assert his independence more openly than before: when asked who his favorite poet is, he answers "Byron" (p. 85). The other boys are for Tennyson and call Stephen's choice "a heretic and immoral too," saying with petit bourgeois snobbery that Byron is "only a poet for uneducated people" (p. 85). When the boys jostle and kick him to make him change his mind, Stephen proudly suffers on Byron's behalf: his first taste of artistic martyrdom. In this second chapter, Stephen has changed schools from Clongowes to another Jesuit college, Belvedere, just as the Dedalus family has changed its address not once but twice. Although the reasons for this are not foregrounded in *A Portrait,* in actuality James Joyce had been obliged to leave the exclusive Clongowes Wood college because of his family's increasingly straitened financial circumstances. He was educated for a time by the Christian Brothers (a religious order Mr. Dedalus scathingly refers to as "Paddy Stink and Micky Mud") before being admitted to Belvedere College without fees. This came about through the good offices of Father John Conmee, the former rector of Clongowes, who had become prefect of studies at Belvedere College. Joyce was later to include the character of "the superior, the very reverend John Conmee S. J." in the "Wandering Rocks" chapter of *Ulysses.*

The constant changes of address undergone by the Dedalus family provide another significant element of instability and flux in Stephen's life. The Romanian artist Brancusi's abstract portrait of Joyce takes the form of a straight line beside a spiral, and Joyce's biographers have noted how the family's changes of address in the 1880s and 1890s resemble a centrifugal spiral, as the family moved ever farther away from the comfortable suburbs into the dereliction and poverty of the inner city. The increasing chaos of the Dedalus household has a maturing effect on Stephen, as he begins to realize his isolation from his family. Walking with his father in the southern city of Cork he feels "the memory of his childhood suddenly gr[o]w dim" (p. 98) and unreal. He takes part in a school drama production, which heightens his sense of teenage disconnection: "He felt that he was hardly of the one blood with them but stood to them rather in the mystical kinship of fosterage, fosterchild and fosterbrother" (p. 105). This rather common fantasy of the disaffected adolescent is used by Joyce to underline Stephen's apartness and his incipient sense of his own unique mission. Another element in his alienation is the snobbish, upper-middle-class milieu of Belvedere, where the other pupils move in a world of tennis and dinner parties in which he cannot fully participate.

SEX AND RELIGION

In this chapter, Stephen's sexuality also begins to assert itself. At one point another boy, Heron (the same boy who previously had ridiculed him for saying that Byron was better than Tennyson), teases Stephen about a girl he fancies. Stephen priggishly answers Heron by reciting the *Confiteor.* Stephen appears to accept and even to relish his feelings of apartness, cultivating a secret vice to accentuate it: at the end of section 2 he wanders through Dublin's notorious red light district and succumbs to the advances of a prostitute. This area of the city, dubbed "Nighttown" by Joyce, is also the scene for the climactic Circe chapter in *Ulysses.* Prostitution and the lure of forbidden sexuality always hold a very strong charge for Joyce, representing the dark underside of Catholic purity. To say that Stephen "succumbs" to a prostitute perhaps seems a passive way of putting it, but as with almost all of his moments of emotional rapture, it is presented in terms of swooning and surrender:

> With a sudden movement she bowed his head and joined her lips to his and he read the meaning of her movements in her frank uplifted eyes. It was too much for him. He closed his eyes, surrendering himself to her, body and mind, conscious of nothing in the world but the dark pressure of her softly parting lips. They pressed upon his brain as upon his lips as though they were the vehicle of a vague speech; and between them he felt an unknown and timid pressure, darker than the swoon of sin, softer than sound or odour.
>
> (p. 108)

In this it is not unlike Gabriel's mental fainting fit at the end of "The Dead" in *Dubliners*. The carnal aspect of life asserts itself with all its viscid intensity, as Stephen indulges all of his fleshly appetites, gorging himself on greasy mutton stews to match his new-found sexual hunger at the beginning of chapter 3: "he hoped there would be stew for dinner, turnips and carrots and bruised potatoes and fat mutton pieces to be ladled out in thick flour-fattened sauce. Stuff it into you, his belly counselled him" (p. 109).

Chapter 3 witnesses Stephen's inevitable, almost chemical reaction to his own carnal indulgences. He has sinned in body, but his soul seemingly retains its boyish innocence and begins to rebel against this loose behavior. The catalyst for this is the spiritual retreat that Stephen takes, in which a Jesuit priest spells out the vision of death and judgment that awaits his corrupted soul. Joyce reproduces the fire and brimstone sermons of the priest supervising the retreat, which proceeds in accordance with the *Spiritual Exercises* of St. Ignatius Loyola, the founder of the Jesuit order. This involves stimulating the boys to imagine and contemplate the terrible punishments awaiting the soul of an unrepentant sinner after death. The reproduction of these "fire sermons" constitutes some of Joyce's most vivid writing in *A Portrait*:

> The horror of this strait and dark prison is increased by its awful stench. All the filth of the world, all the offal and scum of the world, we are told, shall run there as to a vast reeking sewer when the terrible conflagration of the last day has purged the world. The brimstone, too, which burns there in such prodigious quantity fills all hell with its intolerable stench; and the bodies of the damned themselves exhale such a pestilential odour that, as Saint Bonaventure says, one of them alone would suffice to infect the whole world.
>
> (p. 129)

The effect on Stephen of language like this is to make him feel utterly terrified but strangely important at the same time, in his very Catholic way. It is not difficult to identify, underneath his belief that God is grieved by the enormity of his sin, an egoism of immense proportions. As well as his sexual sin, Stephen is also guilt-stricken at his own hypocrisy. He has been involved in the Sodality of the Blessed Virgin Mary:

> If ever his soul, re-entering her dwelling shyly after the frenzy of his body's lust had spent itself, was turned towards her whose emblem is the morning star, bright and musical, telling of heaven and infusing peace, it was when her names were murmured softly by lips whereon there still lingered foul and shameful words, the savour itself of a lewd kiss.
>
> (p. 112)

Through the tightness and self-inwoven complexity of this sentence, Joyce underlines the proximity of the sexual and spiritual parts of Stephen's character, a theme which in fact pervades the entirety of his work. In a sense, Stephen's violent reconversion to the straight and narrow path is an easy development to see coming: even while he dissipates himself in chapter 2, there is something calculating and aloof about his behavior that makes his sudden moral turnabout inevitable. In fact, for him *not* to have an extreme and theatrical reaction to dallying with a prostitute would be more disturbing, since his new religious phase allows him to maintain the interior drama of his own self-absorption. Fleshy reality now becomes an image of corruption and doom. After the retreat,

Stephen is left almost paralyzed with terror, as the danger of his fallen state is brought home to him. Kneeling beside his bed that evening, instead of his usual erotic reveries, he is vouchsafed a vision of his personal hell:

> A field of stiff weeds and thistles and tufted nettle-bunches. Thick among the tufts of rank stiff growth lay battered canisters and clots and coils of solid excrement. A faint marsh light struggling upwards from all the ordure through the bristling greygreen weeds. An evil smell, faint and foul as the light, curled upwards sluggishly out of the canisters and from the stale crusted dung.
>
> (p. 148)

This nightmarish landscape is peopled by "goatish creatures with human faces" which are like satyrs, symbolic of his lusts. This vision so terrifies Stephen that he resolves to mend his ways and makes his confession for the first time in many months. Joyce powerfully evokes the psychological drama of guilt and self-torture played out in the mind of the young man. After his dramatic reconversion, Stephen takes a perverse delight in his self-mortification but finds the company of the other faithful less than inspiring. If lust is no longer a problem, it is only because the sin of pride is now in the ascendant. Stephen even seems dimly aware of this propensity in his character and exerts himself to combat it: "he had been forewarned of the dangers of spiritual exaltation and did not allow himself to desist from even the least or lowliest devotion, striving also by constant mortification to undo the sinful past rather than to achieve a saintliness fraught with peril" (p. 162). In accordance with Stephen's newfound spiritual discipline, the language in which this chapter is written takes on a flavor of exactness, an unmistakable primness. Of course, the real audience for this religious behavior is Stephen himself. Even though his confession was the urgent outcome of a state of spiritual panic, he cannot dispel nagging doubts that it may not have been fully sincere. Joyce delineates the tortuous, labyrinthine lines of reasoning Stephen follows during his endless examinations of his own doubting conscience. "I have amended my life, have I not?" (p. 166) he asks himself with a mixture of smugness and uncertainty.

As with his earlier sexual indulgence, the rituals Stephen imposes on himself make a counter-reaction inevitable. Toward the end of chapter 3, in response to the director's suggestion that Stephen may have a religious vocation, he has a sudden revelation of the worldly power such a position would give him: "he would know obscure things, hidden from others, from those who were conceived and born children of wrath." At the same time as he begins to comprehend his own thirst for knowledge, he sees the priest's face as a "mirthless mask" (p. 174) and the religious life as inherently cold and life denying. Joyce writes: "Some instinct, waking at these memories, stronger than education or piety, quickened within him at every near approach to that life, an instinct subtle and hostile, and armed him against acquiescence. The chill and order of the life repelled him" (p. 174). Stephen realizes that he will have to reconcile the sensual and spiritual poles of his own being, and at the end of this chapter such a possibility is bodied forth for the first time, in the form of a new aesthetic vision. He now integrates the language of sacramentalism and sensual abandon, in his ecstatic outburst after the vision of the young woman walking on Dollymount Strand. Richard Ellmann links this reawakening to the ending of Ibsen's play *When We Dead Awaken,* in which there is a similar moment of illumination, and describes the significance of Stephen's vision thus:

> Stephen Dedalus walks along the north strand, towards the end of his school days, and suddenly sees a handsome girl, skirts drawn up, wading in the water. Her beauty affects him like an illumination of truth, and vindicates his choice of life and art, even if life means also disorder and art suffering. The incident actually occurred to Joyce about that time. No doubt he was looking for a symbol of his "profane perfection of mankind," and this

one remained in his memory as a counter to the shadowy, fleshless face of the beckoning priest.

(James Joyce, p. 55)

STEPHEN THE AESTHETE

What is significant is Stephen's embrace of process and re-creation rather than fixed identity. This is reflected in the language with which Joyce describes the incident: "To live, to err, to fall, to triumph, to recreate life out of life!" (p. 186). However, by the second half of the paragraph, Stephen's language sinks into a virtual pastiche of Walter Pater, choking on its own hyperbole: "a wild angel had appeared to him, the angel of mortal youth and beauty, an envoy from the fair courts of life, to throw open before him in an instant of ecstasy the gates of all the ways of error and glory. On and on and on and on!" (p. 186). In the book's final chapter, the scene in which Stephen lies in bed, languishing in his own hypersensitivity and reciting a rather self-indulgent villanelle he has composed, would be merely comic if taken in isolation. What Stephen thinks of as an artistic consummation is closer to poetic onanism, full of 1890s feyness. Seen in context, the poem perhaps demonstrates how far ahead of his artistic practice Stephen's theories have run, since theorizing about himself is still what Stephen does best. But even in the Dollymount Strand scene, Joyce has ways of bringing Stephen down to earth. His rapturous contemplation of the bathing girl is interrupted by the exchange:

One! Two! . . . Look out!—

O, Cripes, I'm drownded!—

(p. 183)

Stephen may be a Dedalus rather than an Icarus, but those who soar too high above the "snotgreen" sea do well to remember the risks of getting too close to the sun and ending up "drownded."

The last chapter of the novel takes Stephen out of his cocoon by placing him in a university setting, where he gets to demonstrate his intellectual superiority to his fellow students and yet more Jesuit priests. This version of Stephen is somewhat less zealous than the character who originally appeared in *Stephen Hero,* where he coaxes his uneducated mother by reciting extracts from Nietzsche. As a budding philosopher, Stephen's method is what the ancient Greeks called peripatetic, like that of Socrates: he works out all his ideas by walking around Dublin, using his friends as seemingly eager sounding boards. Here is the germ of the brilliant peripatetic style of *Ulysses,* where all human life seems to wait around the next street corner. He moves among the city's flower sellers, Christian Brothers, beggars, mad nuns, and other unenlightened figures with his head full of Gerhart Hauptmann, Ibsen, and Guido Cavalcanti, dropping cynically brilliant one-liners into his conversation just as he will do at the start of *Ulysses.* A defining moment comes in his conversation with the university English dean of studies as he tries to light a fire in the grate of a lecture theater. After a misunderstanding over the word "tundish," a Hiberno-English word for the funnel of an oil lamp, Stephen muses on linguistic difference and cultural identity:

How different are the words *home, Christ, ale, master,* on his lips and on mine! I cannot speak or write these words without unrest of spirit. His language, so familiar and so foreign, will always be for me an acquired speech. I have not made or accepted its words. My voice holds them at bay. My soul frets in the shadow of his language.

(p. 205)

Because of Ireland's colonial subjection, English words have been imposed on Stephen from without and will in turn need to be subject to constant sceptical scrutiny. The young Stephen had been just as careful: "Words which he did not understand he said over and over to himself till he learned them by heart; and through them he had glimpses of the real words about him" (p. 64). His interlocutors in university do not have to be English Jesuits to alienate Stephen, since the nationalism of the other students is equally alien by now. Unlike Stephen, Davin is an upstanding young patriot and a student of Irish. Joyce based this character on his university friend George Clancy, who later became mayor of Limerick and was murdered by the notorious Black and Tans. In a story he tells, Davin has been walking through County Limerick one evening, where he has met a peasant woman who subtly invites him to spend the night with her. He flees in righteous innocence, terrified by what Stephen calls the woman's "bat-like soul waking to the consciousness of itself in darkness and secrecy and loneliness" (pp. 239–240). As always in Joyce, the nationalist purist, with his idealization of the nation as woman, has problems dealing with the sort of flesh and blood woman whose behavior may be less pure. The scene recalls, or rather anticipates, the uproar surrounding John Millington Synge's 1907 play *The Playboy of the Western World.* During the first performance of Synge's play the audience of the Abbey Theatre rioted because of what they regarded as the author's disrespectful attitude toward Irish womanhood.

Enjoying the scandalous effect he has on his pious friends, Stephen announces his rejection of all they hold dear, only to be dismissed as a "born sneerer" by Davin, who asks in exasperation, "Are you Irish at all?" (pp. 218–219). Stephen has seen this question coming and replies with Icarian defiance: "When the soul of a man is born in this country there are nets flung at it to hold it back from flight. You talk to me of nationality, language, religion. I shall try to fly by those nets" (p. 220). This does not mean Dedalus is turning his back on his Irishness: later he will boast that the quickest way to Tara, the ancient seat of the high kings of Ireland, is via Holyhead, traditional port of call of Irish emigrants. It is only in leaving Ireland, or divesting himself of its national pieties, that he can be properly Irish as well as properly himself. But, for the purposes of his student audience, he is happy to play the sneering cynic: Ireland, he

says, is "the old sow that eats her farrow" (p. 220), a devouring mother that raises her own offspring for slaughter.

All this cynical turbulence in his character needs some counterbalance, and this is the function of his aesthetic theorizing. With dogmatic precision, he expounds his definitions of tragedy, beauty, and the emotions to his friend Lynch. For instance, "art is the human disposition of sensible or intelligible matter for an aesthetic end." Once again, the phrasemaking is very elegant but abstract too, even if Stephen does interrupt himself to call after someone, "Don't forget the turnips for me and my mate" (p. 229). After this comes the explanation of the three stages of the epiphany: wholeness, harmony, and radiance. The movement of all art, in Stephen's mind, is toward a state of luminous, silent, unmoving contemplation. The highest art, he says, is static rather than kinetic, if by kinetic art we mean forms that have what Keats would call a "palpable design" on us, such as political propaganda or melodrama, where the detached intelligence of the reader is not respected. As a result, all true art tends toward the impersonal. As the artwork acquires its own internal logic, "the personality of the artist passes into the narration itself" (p. 233). Here speaks the true modernist, as Stephen presents a vision of the artist little short of godlike in his powers and unknowable aloofness:

> The personality of the artist, at first a cry or a cadence or a mood and then a fluid and lambent narrative, finally refines itself out of existence, impersonalises itself, so to speak. . . . The mystery of aesthetic, like that of material creation, is accomplished. The artist, like the God of the creation, remains within or behind or beyond or above his handiwork, invisible, refined out of existence, indifferent, paring his fingernails.
>
> (p. 233)

God creates the world by withdrawing from it, in other words, just as the artist brings his work to perfection by removing all traces of his personality. The weapons he will deploy as he does so are "silence, exile and cunning."

The irony of Stephen's position for those readers who want to make a simplistic equation of Stephen with the biographical James Joyce is clear. If the artist should be impersonal, then Stephen has surely failed. As an artist, he is a bundle of accidents and incoherence, who saves all his best moments for casual conversations in the street, appears to do next to no real work, and when he does produce a poem fails to live up to his own lofty standards. The images of his beloved, the girl Emma Clery, that he carries around with him, are equally short of epiphanic stillness and composure. His mind is full of "distorted reflections" (p. 239) of her, such as one might expect to find in the "cracked look-ingglass" of a servant, to use the image from *Ulysses:* a flower girl "in a ragged dress with damp coarse hair," a girl who laughs at him when he trips in the street, and a girl who shouts a suggestive comment to him. Little by little, the false aloofness of the younger Stephen is breaking down as he learns to recognize the pathos of the mundane and the antiheroic. It is in the impersonal rendering of images such as these, squalid and mundane though they be, that true artistic discipline lies.

Stephen begins to gather himself up for the great task ahead. As the novel ends, images of birds, flight, and escape abound, as he prepares to leave Ireland in favor of self-imposed exile in continental Europe. The final few pages of the book shift from the third to the first-person singular, as Joyce gives us Stephen's diary entries. This very clearly contradicts his earlier demands for a third-person impersonal art, but the diary shows a new humbleness and directness coming to the fore in Stephen's personality. Describing an encounter with his beloved on a Dublin street, he writes self-deprecatingly: "Talked rapidly of myself and my plans. In the midst of it unluckily I made a sudden gesture of a revolutionary nature. I must have looked like a fellow throwing a handful of peas into the air. People began to look at us" (p. 275). Here, for once, he writes mockingly of his pose of the art-

ist. The novel ends with his mother packing his clothes and Stephen fervently praying the creed of his artistic religion: "Welcome, O life! I go to encounter for the millionth time the reality of experience and to forge in the smithy of my soul the uncreated conscience of my race. Old father, old artificer, stand me now and ever in good stead" (p. 275).

CONCLUSION

The question of whether Stephen is a fearless hero of the imagination or a specimen of sub-Nietzschean smugness is an unavoidable one. Once again, how closely should the character of Stephen be identified with Joyce himself? The influential Joyce critic Hugh Kenner is in no doubt: "it is quite plain from the final chapter of the *Portrait* that we are not to accept the mode of Stephen's 'freedom' as the 'message' of the book. The 'priest of the eternal imagination' turns out to be indigestibly Byronic. Nothing is more obvious than his total lack of humour" (*Dublin's Joyce,* p. 132). This is of a piece with Kenner's generally revisionist reading of Joyce and suggests considerable confidence in Joyce's satiric intentions: on this reading the main purpose of the novel is to demolish the author's self-important younger self. William Empson called this reading "the Kenner smear." Kenner goes further:

> Stephen does not, as the careless reader may suppose, become an artist by rejecting church and country. Stephen does not become an artist at all. Country, church, and mission are an inextricable unity, and in rejecting the two that seem to hamper him, he rejects also the one on which he has set his heart.
>
> (p. 121)

This is an unnecessarily reductionist approach, not just for its negative finding but for its assumption that Stephen comes to rest in a unified personality at the end of the book. Stephen has not fully matured into an artist by the end of *A Portrait* (he is at best the author not of *A Portrait* but of *Stephen Hero*), but the sophisticated Joycean style that permits a such a subtle delineation of character has. Some of the credit for this at least can go to the character Stephen insofar as he demonstrates his willingness to embrace not only self-fashioning but self-revision. However, *A Portrait*, it could be argued, is still just a draft of this character: for the finished item, or at least the next draft, one has to move on to *Ulysses*.

If *A Portrait* is merely the embryo that grows up to be *Ulysses*, its modernist affinities with its great successor are obvious. In its disruption of the stylistically stable narrator of realist fiction, it opens the way for *Ulysses'* kaleidoscope of literary styles. It rejects the traps and snares of Irish politics and religion, even as it remains deeply marked and haunted by them. It moves outward toward escape and cosmopolitanism, but with a strong reinvestment at the same time in the dignity and power of the local and the marginalized as proper subjects for serious fiction. Despite the self-importance of its hero, it is a deeply debunking and un-self-important book, preparing us for the antiheroic hero of *Ulysses*, the Jewish advertising canvasser and cuckold, Leopold Bloom. It takes simple family drama—Stephen's search for a father figure—and makes it the vehicle of universal mythic parallels that go to the heart of modern European life. In *Ulysses*, similarly, Stephen represents the Greek intellect in need of tempering through contact with the moral, Hebrew imagination represented by Bloom.

Despite the highly systematized and schematic construction of *A Portrait*, something else it shares with *Ulysses* is that it sees art as a process and a dialectic resisting closure. This combination is both quintessentially Joycean and quintessentially modernist, reaching its culmination in the radically experimental style of *Finnegans Wake*. Here we see Joyce exerting a maximum of impersonal control over words, to make them mean as much as possible in as many languages as possible. The effect of this is not constraining or authoritarian, however, but the opposite—a state of apparent madcap linguistic anarchy. This is visible in the *Portrait* too, in the play with language most obvious in the novel's opening section in baby talk, but present all the way through to Stephen's discussion of the tundish and fretting in the shadow of a language not his. The language can never truly be his, since his great work lies forever before him: Stephen never does catch up on the Joycean mind, in which after all he is only one figment among so many. Beyond Stephen lies Joyce, but beyond Joyce lies the mind of the language itself, as he tries to map it in all its modernist infinity first in *Ulysses* and then in *Finnegans Wake*. The project is of course impossible, but we learn to live in the space between aspiration and reality. *Finnegans Wake*, it is important to remember, ends in the middle of a sentence, a sentence that connects back to the beginning and starts the whole thing all over again. Artistic process is all. What matters, in the words of *A Portrait*, is "To live, to err, to fall, to triumph, to recreate life out of life! . . . On and on and on and on."

Selected Bibliography

EDITIONS

A Portrait of the Artist as a Young Man by James Joyce: A Facsimile of the Final Holograph Manuscript. Edited by Hans Walter Gabler. New York: Garland, 1977.

A Portrait of the Artist as a Young Man by James Joyce: A Facsimile of Epiphanies, Notes, Manuscripts & Typescripts. Edited by Hans Walter Gabler. New York: Garland, 1978.

A Portrait of the Artist as a Young Man (1916). London: Penguin, 1992. (Edition cited in this essay.)

OTHER WORKS

Dubliners (1914). London: Penguin, 1992.

Ulysses (1922). London: Penguin, 1992.

Finnegans Wake (1939). London: Penguin, 1992.

Stephen Hero (1944). London: Triad Panther, 1977.

Letters. Vol. 1, edited by Stuart Gilbert. Vols. 2 and 3, edited by Richard Ellmann. London: Faber and Faber, 1957, 1966.

Selected Letters. Edited by Richard Ellmann. London: Faber and Faber, 1975.

Poems and Shorter Writings, Including Epiphanies, Giacomo Joyce and "A Portrait of the Artist." Edited by Richard Ellmann, A. Walton Litz, and John Whittier-Ferguson. London: Faber and Faber, 1991.

Occasional, Critical and Political Writing. Edited by Kevin Barry. Oxford and New York: Oxford University Press, 2000.

BIOGRAPHIES

Ellman, Richard. *James Joyce* (1959). New York, Oxford University Press, 1982.

Joyce, Stanislaus. *My Brother's Keeper.* London and New York: Viking, 1958.

McCourt, John. *The Years of Bloom: James Joyce in Trieste, 1904–1920* Dublin and Madison, Wis.: University of Wisconsin Press, 2000.

GENERAL BACKGROUND

Attridge, Derek, ed. *The Cambridge Companion to James Joyce.* Cambridge and New York: Cambridge University Press, 1990.

Attridge, Derek, and Daniel Ferrer, eds. *Post-Structuralist Joyce: Essays from the French.* Cambridge and New York: Cambridge University Press, 1984.

Attridge, Derek, and Marjorie Howes, eds. *Semicolonial Joyce.* Cambridge and New York: Cambridge University Press, 2000.

Burgess, Anthony. *Here Comes Everybody: An Introduction to James Joyce for the Ordinary Reader.* London: Faber and Faber, 1965.

Fairhall, James. *James Joyce and the Question of History.* Cambridge and New York, 1993.

Gross, John J. *James Joyce.* New York: Viking, 1970.

Kenner, Hugh. *Dublin's Joyce.* London: Chatto and Windus, 1955.

Litz, A. Walton. *James Joyce.* New York: Twayne, 1966.

MacCabe, Colin. *James Joyce and the Revolution of the Word.* London and New York: Barnes and Noble, 1979.

Mahaffey, Vicki. *Reauthorizing Joyce.* Cambridge and New York: Cambridge University Press, 1988.

Mercier, Vivian. *The Irish Comic Tradition.* Oxford: Clarendon Press, 1963.

Nolan, Emer. *James Joyce and Nationalism.* London and New York: Routledge, 1995.

Parrinder, Patrick. *James Joyce.* Cambridge and New York: Cambridge University Press, 1984.

Power, Arthur R. *Conversations with James Joyce.* London: Millington, and New York: Barnes and Noble, 1974.

Rabaté, Jean-Michel. *James Joyce, Authorized Reader.* Baltimore: Johns Hopkins University Press, 1984.

Senn, Fritz, and John Paul Riquelme. *Joyce's Dislocutions: Essays on Reading as Translation.* Baltimore: Johns Hopkins University Press, 1984.

Tindall, William York. *A Reader's Guide to James Joyce.* New York: Noonday Press, 1959.

SECONDARY WORKS

Beja, Morris, ed. *James Joyce:* Dubliners *and* A Portrait: *A Casebook.* London: Macmillan, 1973.

Blades, John. *James Joyce:* A Portrait of the Artist as a Young Man. London and New York: Penguin, 1991.

Epstein, Edmund L. *The Ordeal of Stephen Dedalus: The Conflict of the Generations in James Joyce's* A Portrait of the Artist as a Young Man. Carbondale: Southern Illinois University Press, 1971.

Gifford, Don. *Joyce Annotated: Notes for* Dubliners *and* A Portrait of the Artist as a Young Man. 2d ed. Berkeley: University of California Press, 1982.

Scholes, Robert, and Richard M. Kain. *The Workshop of Daedalus: James Joyce and the Raw Materials for "A Portrait of the Artist as a Young Man."* Evanston, Northwestern University Press, 1965.

Schutte, William Metcalf, comp. *Twentieth-Century Interpretations of* A Portrait of the Artist as a Young Man: *A Collection of Critical Essays.* Englewood Cliffs, N.J.: Prentice Hall, 1968.

Staley, Thomas F., and Bernard Benstock, eds. *Approaches to Joyce's* Portrait. Pittsburgh: University of Pittsburgh Press, 1976.

William Wordsworth's
The Prelude

PATRICK VINCENT

WILLIAM WORDSWORTH'S long autobiographical poem, *The Prelude,* continues to be the exemp- lary Romantic text, central to our understanding both of a literary period and of an important and fascinating historical moment, at the crossroad between old order and modern Europe. Composed primarily between 1798 and 1805, the work Wordsworth referred to as the "Poem on my own life" (in a letter to William Hazlitt, 5 March 1804) was first published after his death in 1850, and given its title by his wife. It narrates the poet's early years from his bucolic childhood in the Lake District of Northern England to the recognition in spring of 1798 of his vocation as poet. Wordsworth's choice of genres, subjects, and styles, as well as his many punctilious revisions to the poem well into the 1830s, indicate that he intended *The Prelude* to be more than a narrative on "the growth of a poet's mind," or the poetic equivalent of a bildungsroman. Planned as an addition or "portico" (as described in a letter to Sir George Beaumont, 3 June 1805) to a vastly ambitious yet unwritten "philosophical poem," *The Recluse,* Wordsworth's autobiographical poem instead became his magnum opus, a richly complex commentary on the poet's relationship to his epoch.

The genesis of *The Prelude* can be traced back to one of the great creative collaborations in literary history. Living with his sister Dorothy at Alfoxden, four miles away from his friend and fellow poet Samuel Taylor Coleridge's home in Somerset, Wordsworth experienced the most productive year of his career between 1797 and 1798, beautifully chronicled in Dorothy Wordsworth's *Alfoxden Journal* (1798). This annus mirabilis was spent in long walks and even longer conversations, during which Wordsworth learned from his sister how to pay unmediated attention to the details of nature, and from Coleridge, how to amplify this love of nature into a philosophical theory of mind. The Alfoxden year gave rise to some of the Romantic period's best poetry, including Coleridge's "Kubla Khan" and "Ancient Mariner" and Wordsworth's "The Ruined Cottage" and "Tintern Abbey," which were published in *The Lyrical Ballads* (first edition 1798), a collection of experimental poems often credited with inaugurating modern poetry in Britain. Moreover, it resulted in a grand scheme for a philosophical poem called *The Recluse; or, Views of Nature, Man, and Society,* which remained

Wordsworth's major preoccupation, and source of frustration through his great creative decade (1798–1808) all the way until his death.

At twenty-eight, confident of his poetic powers and goaded on by Coleridge, Wordsworth imagined a poem in three parts that would surpass Milton's great Protestant epic, *Paradise Lost*, in size and scope. The hero of this new epic would be Wordsworth himself, in a radical new role, that of a Milton-like recluse and humanizing poet-prophet. Two years later Wordsworth had found his place of retreat, Gras- mere, in the Lake District, and also his "high argument," set forth in the 107-line "Prospectus" (first published 1814) to *The Recluse.* The "Prospectus" rewrites Milton's grand theme for *Paradise Lost.* The poet, in what M. H. Abrams has famously labeled his "secular theodicy" (*Natural Supernaturalism,* p. 95), seeks to demonstrate that the human mind

> When wedded to this goodly universe
> In love and holy passion, shall find these
> A simple produce of the common day.
>
> (*The Poems*, II, p. 37, ll. 53–55)

Wordsworth believed the mind of man was even more mysterious than the Christian cosmology of Heaven and Hell. Rather than justifying human suffering with the anticipation of a heavenly Paradise, announced in the *Book of Revelation* by the marriage between Christ the Lamb and the new Jerusalem, he claims that paradise is available today, in this world, through the marriage of mind and nature.

Despite its revolutionary central argument, the *Recluse* scheme remained overly vague and ill-fitted to Wordsworth's talent. By 1815, when the poet finally abandoned what he had called "the task of my life" (in a letter to Sir George Beaumont, 3 June 1805), only a fragment of the tripartite poem had been completed: Book I of the first Part called "Home at Grasmere" (written 1800, published 1888); Book II, *The Excursion* (1814); and *The Prelude,* a supplementary text describing the main protagonist's

CHRONOLOGY

1770	William Wordsworth born, Cockermouth, Cumberland, 7 April.
1771	Dorothy Worsdworth born.
1772	Samuel Taylor Coleridge born.
1775	Attends Anne Birkett's school in Penrith.
1778	Death of Wordsworth's mother.
1779	Attends Hawkshead Grammar School.
1783	Death of Wordsworth's father.
1787	Enters St. John's College, Cambridge University.
1789	Start of the French Revolution; 14 July, Storming of the Bastille.
1790	Walking tour through France, Switzerland, Italy, and Germany.
1791	Receives his bachelor's degree. Short stay in London; climbs Mt. Snowdon; returns to Paris in November.
1792	Lives in Orleans and Blois. A love affair with Annette Vallon produces a daughter, Anne Caroline. Returns to England.
1793	Louis XVI is executed. Britain declares war on France. Wordsworth publishes *An Evening Walk* and *Descriptive Sketches.* Writes *A Letter to the Bishop of Llandaff.* Crosses Salisbury Plain.
1794	Reign of Terror in France ends; Robespierre's execution.
1795	Visits Godwin and radical circles. Moves to Racedown Lodge in Dorset with Dorothy. Meets Coleridge.
1796	Summer visit to London. Writes *The Borderers.*
1797	Moves with Dorothy to Alfoxden House, Somerset.
1798	Draws up scheme for *Recluse.* Writes *Discharged Soldier.* Moves to Goslar, Saxony. Begins *Prelude. Lyrical Ballads* published.
1799	Walking tour of Lake District with Coleridge. Composes "Glad Preamble." Moves to Dove Cottage, Grasmere. Finishes two-part *Prelude.*
1800	Prospectus to *The Recluse.* Preface to *Lyrical Ballads.*

1802	Peace of Amiens. Visits Annette and Caroline in Calais. Marries Mary Hutchinson.
1804	*Intimations Ode* completed. Five-book *Prelude* completed in March. Books VI, IX, X, VIII and VII of thirteen-book poem written.
1805	John Wordsworth, poet's brother, dies at sea. Thirteen-book *Prelude* finished.
1806–1893	Several series of major revisions to *Prelude.*
1814	*The Excursion* published.
1815	Waterloo. War with France ends. *Poems* (First Collected Edition).
1832	Great Reform Act.
1837	Accession of Queen Victoria.
1843	Wordsworth named poet laureate.
1850	Wordsworth dies, 23 April. Publication of *The Prelude.*

development through the stage of poet-prophet. Painfully conscious that *The Recluse* was a failure, Wordsworth insisted that the autobiographical addition remain unpublished until after his death. In a letter to his friend Thomas De Quincey dated 6 March 1804, he wrote that "the Poem will not be published these many years, and never during my lifetime, till I have finished a larger and more important work to which it is tributary." Without the philosophical poem, Worsdworth could not justify writing so much about himself, "a thing unprecedented in literary history" (in a letter to Sir George Beaumont, 1 May 1805), so he kept *The Prelude* a secret, sharing only portions of it with select friends and family.

The autobiographical poem was only intended to prepare the reader for *The Recluse* by recounting the parallel development of the poet in relation to the world, and of his mind in relation to nature. Instead one may argue that it became a version, albeit far more unsure and questioning, of the philosophical poem that Coleridge had once encouraged Wordsworth to write. *The Prelude* is both an address to and a dialogue with his friend; while thanking Cole--ridge for his inspiration and encouragement, the poet also seeks to vindicate their differences. The principles of their collaborative scheme (including their conception of mind, nature, and imagination) and Wordsworth's role as an exemplary poet-prophet and his sense of millennial hopefulness find their way into *The Prelude,* but set within a precise historical and biographical framework, rather than being presented as abstract principles about man, nature, and society. In particular, Wordsworth explains his moral crisis in 1796, patterned on a model of crisis and recovery going back to Augustine's *Confessions,* not as a loss of religious faith, but rather as a loss of faith in the French Revolution and in himself.

Wordsworth's resolving of this crisis, the plot of *The Prelude,* becomes his moral philosophy, his way to happiness. Although highly personal, the poem mirrors the crisis of a whole epoch, powerfully capturing what contemporary critic William Hazlitt called the Spirit of the Age. This age was marked briefly by millennial hope in revolution, but also much more enduringly, by reaction. Wordsworth's reaction to disappointment is to privatize hope, restricting it to the power of human consciousness to regenerate man. This parallels a general reaction against eighteenth-century empirical philosophy, seen as disrupting moral truth. While Jean-Jacques Rousseau, in his *Confessions* (1782–1789), illustrated the importance of self-analysis and of feeling in defining the individual, Immanuel Kant consolidated this awareness, placing the mind as prior to nature and, in his *Critique of Judgment* (1790), claiming that knowledge of God is only possible through our sublime apprehension of the self in the world. Idealist philosophy opened the way for a radical turn inward and an optimistic view of nature as a source of knowledge, key principles in Wordsworth which, as Charles Taylor has recently argued, have come to define modern selfhood.

The poet's moral philosophy and striking modernity also stem from his strong local attachment. Political writers such as Edmund

Burke (1729–1797) reacted against the French Revolution, considered a threat to Europe's status-quo, by relying on a complacent idea of British superiority. Linda Colley has argued that the roots of British identity, and complacency, lie primarily in the nation's Protestant background. Throughout the seventeenth and eighteenth centuries, Britain was represented as a New Jerusalem, a nation that had proven through its commercial and military prowess and unique system of government that it was predestined for glory. Wordsworth secularizes the Prostestant idea of election, imagining himself as a poet-prophet chosen to fully enable the possibilities of human community in this New Jerusalem. He thus shores up his sense of crisis by unabashedly declaring his confidence in poetry, in himself, and through him, in Great Britain, in what John Keats famously referred to as "the Wordsworthian or egotistical sublime" (in a letter to Richard Woodhouse, 27 October 1818). As such, *The Prelude* may be interpreted as a "a sort of portico" not just to the failed *Recluse* project, but to our own modern constructions of identity—autonomous, secular, and grounded in the nation.

BEGINNINGS: "SPOTS OF TIME" IN THE 1799 *PRELUDE*

In an earlier letter, John Keats discussed Wordsworth in more flattering terms, arguing that his philosophy was "deeper" than Milton's because of its modernity, and that "his Genius is explorative of those dark Passages" in which moral truth is not as clear cut as in Milton's Christian cosmology (in a letter to John Reynolds, 3 May 1818). The younger poet's insightful interpretation of Wordsworth helps us understand why we are still able to read *The Prelude* today, whereas his other long poem, *The Excursion,* seems so outdated and overly moralistic. The philosophical weight of *The Prelude* lies not in its principles or *sententiae*, but rather in the poem's ability to rest on uncertainties. The poet's explorations are es-

sentially self-explorations that reveal what is deeply problematic about an ideology grounded in the private self. Key to these self-explorations are Wordsworth's spots of time, those illuminations, or memories of intense experience recollected in tranquility, which the poet began to weave into his poetry during his short stay in Germany.

Harassed by government spies and intent on learning German, the Wordsworths left Alfoxden in September 1798 and spent a bleak, freezing winter in the town of Goslar, where William wrote the first four hundred lines of autobiographical blank verse of what would become, upon his return to England, the two-part *Prelude. The Prelude* survives in four forms: the official text in fourteen books (1850), the thirteen-book version completed in 1805 (published 1926), a five-book intermediary text prepared in spring 1804 (reconstructed in 1977), and a two-book early version finished at Grasmere in late 1799. Because Wordsworth, as Stephen Gill in his fine biography reminds us, could not stand the idea of finality in a poem, we have no author-approved, definitive fair copy for any of these versions, and there can never be a perfect edition. While Wordsworth spent much time and energy all the way into the 1830s polishing his poem, tightening its syntax and making it more acceptable for a Victorian-era readership, the 1850 edition was seen through the press by executors whose changes did not always reflect the poet's intentions. Many critics today deplore the official edition's poeticisms, pomposity, and orthodox Christian statements. Herbert Linderberger, for example, has argued that the older Wordsworth forgot what he had been trying to achieve in the earlier poem through his conversational tone and struggle towards definition.

An internally coherent early form of *The Prelude,* the 1799 edition best captures the younger Wordsworth's sense of struggle, that explorative genius described by Keats. Since the poem is essentially modular, organized around self-contained incidents and not according to a strict chronological order, Wordsworth could recycle the two-part *Prelude* as Books First and Second of the thirteen-book version. The early poem opens on a Virgilian note of dissatisfaction with the interrogative, "was it for this?" repeated three times in the passage.

> Was it for this
> That one, the fairest of all rivers, loved
> To blend his murmurs with my nurse's song,
> And from his alder shades and rocky falls,
> And from his fords and shallows, sent a voice
> That flowed along my dreams?
>
> *(1799, I, ll. 1–6; 1805, 1, ll. 271–276)*

The speaker's present inability to write the philosophical poem suggested by his friend Coleridge does not square with his childhood premonitions of creative power. The blank verse's steady cadence and the analogy between the Derwent and the child's mind powerfully evoke this impression of creativity now lost. There are two consciousnesses at work in *The Prelude,* that of the speaker in the present, remembering things past, and of the past speaker, living close to nature. From the outset of the poem, the present speaker attempts to harmonize these two disparate selves. The imagery of wind and water will reappear as leitmotifs throughout the poem to come to his aid when he feels this separateness most acutely. While these symbols of natural fluidity help ease the passage from the observable world to a transcendental level, they also blur the distinction between natural and supernatural, literal and figural reality. In the above quotation, for example, the river's natural "murmurs" are blended with those supernatural voices he hears in his dreams. Unlike in Classical poetry, in which inspiration owes everything to divine machinery, the speaker's genius here is naturalized—weaned by nature's "gentle powers" (1799, l. 35), it is represented as nothing more than "a simple produce of the common day."

The speaker resolves the dilemma expressed by the above rhetorical question with an important realization. At Goslar, the poet had begun to distance himself from Coleridge's overly theoretical influence. While Wordsworth remained faithful to his friend's Unitarian ideal of the "One Life," he discovered that he was best able to motivate this ideal not with reasoned arguments, but through detailed autobiographical self-analysis. He declares, in the second part of the 1799 poem,

> Hard task to analyse a soul, in which
> Not only general habits and desires,
> But each most obvious and particular thought—
> Not in a mystical and idle sense,
> But in the words of reason deeply weighed—
> Hath no beginning.
>
> *(ll. 262–267; 1805, 1, ll. 232)*

For Wordsworth, childhood in particular is the "fair seed-time" of the soul *(1805, 1, l. 305)* when these "general habits and desires" are formed. Through his selective recollections of key experiences until age ten in the first part of the poem, and of his schooldays until seventeen in the second part, he is able to unleash his creative energies and to awaken his own poetic voice. M. H. Abrams has called this, one of *The Prelude*'s most prominent levels of narrative, the poem's discovery of its own *ars poetica (Natural Supernaturalism,* p. 78).

With Biblical assurance but also a profound sentiment of gratitude, an affect central to the poem and to Wordsworth's moral philosophy in general, the speaker exclaims,

> Ah, not in vain ye beings of the hills
> And ye that walk the woods and open heaths
> By moon or star-light, thus, from my first dawn
> Of childhood, did ye love to intertwine
> The passions that build up our human soul
> Not with the mean and vulgar works of man,
> But with high objects, with eternal things,
> With life and Nature, purifying thus
> The elements of feeling and thought,
> And sanctifying by such discipline

Both pain and fear, until we recognise
A grandeur in the beatings of the heart.

(*1799*, I, ll. 130–141; *1805*, 1, ll. 431–441)

Wordsworth justifies his present condition of "grandeur" by describing his childhood as a time of steady moral development, in which the child interacts passionately with nature. Nature means more here than the Lake District's hills, dales and streams where the young boy played. It is a form of moral agency, which, at times like a mother, other times like a father, nurtures and disciplines the child according to a precise teleology. What is fundamental is the child's active response to Nature's "high objects" and "eternal things." The exchange between mind and Nature "purifies" and "sanctifies" the child's mind in order to lead him to recognize his higher role as poet.

Nature's mothering qualities are best evoked in the "Blessed Babe" passage, where the speaker explains, in an argument that anticipates Freud, that the mother's presence gives the baby a residual sense of narcissistic power connecting him to the world at large (*1799*, II, ll. 268–294; *1805*, 2, ll. 237–264). On the other hand, Nature's more severe disciplining function, illustrated in the childhood spots of time episodes, operates by setting up thresholds the child must imaginatively transgress. These incidents, including snaring woodcock traps, skating, plundering raven nests, coming across a drowned man, waiting for horses, and stealing a boat, appear mundane on first reading. Since A. C. Bradley's brilliant Oxford lectures on Wordsworth in 1909, however, critics have recognized the combination of the ordinary and the outlandish, most powerfully evoked in these early passages, as quintessentially Wordsworthian. In his preface to the *Lyrical Ballads* (1800), the poet tries to explain his radically new poetic formula, writing that he focuses on rural and childhood scenes because they speak "a more permanent language," a language of unadulterated passion which he opposes to the "gross stimulants" needed to awaken the blunt

sensibilities in the city (Owen and Smyser, I, p. 124). Yet the language he uses in the spots of time to evoke this passion, and to elicit his reader's sympathetic response, is not so much the "very language of men," as he claims in the preface, but rather, a modernized version of the eighteenth-century diction of the Sublime. This is an aesthetic category which, by inspiring "pain and fear," purifies and elevates the viewer's feelings.

In a famous episode particularly characteristic of this sublime language, the young protagonist finds a shepherd's boat one night on the banks of Ullstwater, and rows out to the middle of the lake. His "act of stealth / And troubled pleasure" (*1799*, I, ll. 90–91; *1805*, 1, ll. 361–362), like Rousseau's stealing of the blue ribbon in *The Confessions*, strikes readers as relatively innocuous. But it is described in such a strange, original way that the boy's minor transgression takes on epic significance:

…When from behind that rocky steep, till then
The bound of the horizon, a huge cliff,
As if with voluntary power instinct,
Upreared its head.

(*1799*, I, ll. 107–110; *1805*, 1, ll. 405–408)

The speaker invests the "huge cliff" with an imaginary power, an analogy which, as the use of simile reminds us, is clearly figural. The result, however, a counter-motion that checks his imaginative expansion, quite literally affects the young boy's mind. For many days his brain

Worked with a dim and undetermined sense
Of unknown modes of being. In my thoughts
There was a darkness—call it solitude,
Or blank desertion—no familiar shapes …
But huge and mighty forms …

(*1799*, I, ll. 120–127; *1805*, 1, ll. 418–424)

Neither here, nor in any other of the childhood spots of time do we know what these "huge and mighty forms" represent. They hint at a symbolic value, the poet's future role as poet-prophet. But they leave the young boy, like readers, only with "fleeting moods," with an "obscure sense / Of possible sublimity" which impels his creative as well as his moral development (*1799*, II, ll. 361–371; *1805*, 1, ll. 331–341).

Wordsworth attempted to more precisely define the role of this visionary mood and mode in a doctrinal passage, illustrated by three examples. As the poem evolved over the years, he increasingly considered this passage central to his overarching argument. A sort of therapeutic drug, these "spots of time" gathered from his "first childhood" could offer

> A fructifying virtue, whence, depressed
> By trivial occupations and the round
> Of ordinary intercourse, our minds—
> Especially the imaginative power—
> Are nourished and invisibly repaired.
>
> (*1799*, I, ll. 290–294; *1805*, 11, ll. 258–264)

Placed in the middle of part I of the 1799 *Prelude,* these lines were moved to the very end of the five-part poem of 1804, and then to Book Eleventh of the 1805 text. However, despite additions to the 1805 poem in which the poet specified that this "fructifying virtue" arises when "We have the deepest feeling that the mind / Is lord and master" (*1805*, 11, ll. 271–272), the process by which the mind is repaired and made sovereign or visionary, remains intentionally opaque. For it is not in definitions but in his insistent self-explorations, in a language that repeatedly vacillates and turns back on itself, that Wordsworth is able most faithfully to capture the human psyche's operations.

The poet's overly active consciousness of death is at the origin of his complex representations of the child's creative stirrings. Thomas Weiskel, in his influential structural analysis of the Wordsworthian sublime, points out that the doctrinal passage on the spots of time is preceded and followed in the 1799 text by three episodes associated with death. In the first, the speaker recalls coming across "a heap of garments" beside Esthwaite Lake, where, the next

day, the drowned James Jackson "bolt upright / Rose with a ghastly face" (*1799*, I, ll. 266–279; *1805*, 5, ll. 459–472). The second, Penrith beacon episode relates, in an exemplary economy of language ruined by changes in 1804, the young boy's coming across a moldered gibbet, a naked pool, and a girl struggling against the wind (*1799*, I, ll. 296–327; *1805*, 11, ll. 275–315). Finally, on the eve of the Christmas holidays when Wordsworth is thirteen, he waits, perhaps too impatiently, for the horses which are to return him home. When his father dies a few weeks later, the boy interprets the event as a "chastisement" (*1799*, I, ll. 327–360; *1805*, 11, ll. 316–374). The traumatic events marking each episode remind the young boy of his own mortality and provoke a compensatory surge of imagination. Wordsworth's therapy is thus essentially elegiac: death and loss, those "dark Passages" described by Keats, provoke within him a boundless, but perhaps also disturbingly solipsistic impression of consolatory freedom.

DEVELOPMENT: THE 1805 *PRELUDE,* EDUCATION, AND THE ALPS

Poststructuralist critics in the 1970s and early 1980s argued that epistemological problems arise from the above compensatory model of the imagination. Paul de Man, in particular, believed that Romantic poets, conscious of their own limited existence, sought to give poetic language a permanent essence, like a rock or a tree. He interpreted their poetry as a struggle between word and object, mind and nature, in which language always revealed its inability to assert its own essence, or ontological primacy. In Wordsworth's first *Essay on Epitaphs* (1810), which tries to formalize his perplexed attitude toward death, the poet demonstrates that he was all too conscious of these linguistic shortcomings, and offers an idealist solution with ironic self-awareness. "If the impression and sense of death were not thus counterbalanced [by an ideal of immortality]," he writes, "such a hollowness would pervade the whole system of things . . . that there could be no repose, no joy." These intimations of immortality at the source of Wordsworth's moral certitude stem from his belief that language, or logos, could indeed incarnate thought and feeling. Unlike de Man, Wordsworth also believed that language incarnates not just individual knowledge but the knowledge of a shared community. For Wordsworth, writing is "inseparably linked in mutual dependence with the morals of a Country" (Owen and Smyser, II, pp. 50–52). The poet's additions and revisions to the autobiographical poem after 1800 indicate he did not feel at ease with the private epistemology developed in the two-part *Prelude* of 1799. He was not willing, or not yet able to explain his sense of crisis and of grandeur as something completely personal. Borrowing his own formula, Wordsworth realized that he first had to show how love of nature leads to love of man, in particular through education and travel, in order to assert his role as vatic poet.

Drawing on the Wordsworths' move from Goslar to Grasmere, and composed in late 1799, the "Glad Preamble," which opens the five-book poem of 1804 and the two long poems of 1805 and 1850, takes up where the 1799 poem leaves off, with a newfound sense of imaginative freedom. The speaker declares the same faith in Nature and in himself, that "more than Roman confidence" which closed the two-part *Prelude* (*1799*, II, l. 489). But the "Preamble" is written in a new, epic register which reflects the widened scope of the new poem:

> The earth is all before me—with a heart
> Joyous, nor scared at its own liberty,
> I look about, and should the guide I chuse
> Be nothing better than a wandering cloud
> I cannot miss my way.
>
> (*1805*, 1, ll. 14–18)

In obvious allusions to Milton and to Dante, the speaker announces the poem as a journey. Written between January 1804 and May 1805 in a remarkable period of continuous productivity, the 1805 *Prelude* was shaped by new attitudes and concerns linked to Wordsworth's domestic and professional life, but also to important social, economic and political changes. The poet's marriage to Mary Hutchinson, the encouragement of admirers such as Sir George Beaumont and Thomas de Quincey, and his weaning from Coleridge's influence all helped instill a new confidence in his poetic vocation. After February 1805, his grief at the death of his drowned brother, John, further bolstered this belief. Current events, including fears of a French invasion, class tensions in Britain, and the spread of industry also reawakened his sense of patriotism and latent conservatism. Wordsworth, like many other Romantic poets, reacted in particular to the increasing specialization and commodification of art by expanding poetry's imaginative power and scope to all spheres of life. The 1805 *Prelude* thus narrates a journey far more ambitious than the 1799 poem, no longer just shaped by the poet's own fears and desires, but by outside pressures as well. "A traveller I am, / And all my tale is of myself," the speaker boldly tells his readers in Book Third (*1805*, 3, ll. 196–197). Despite the claim that he is the only subject of the poem, and Nature his sole guide, many different figures escort him along his way and educate him—the 1805 poem is not the same solipsistic poem as the earlier *Prelude*, but rather a lively portrait of the poet and his age. Among these guides is Milton, whose grand style, with its inversed syntax, enjambments, latinate and polysyllabic words, and powerful rhythm the poet had internalized as a young man. There is Coleridge, the ideal reader whom Wordsworth had incorporated into himself at the end of the 1799 poem, but who had grown increasingly distant since. Dorothy, Wordsworth's sister, also plays an important new role in the poet's development in the longer poem. Finally, there are teachers, revolutionary politicians, and a host of nameless characters, as well as political and social events themselves, all helping to humanize the poet's imagination.

While Books First and Second of the 1805 poem roughly correspond to the two-part

Prelude, Books Third, Fourth, Fifth and Sixth narrate the poet's struggle to maintain his visionary power and sense of election through his university years. At St. John's College, Cambridge, where he studies from 1787 to 1791, the speaker learns his heroic calling, this despite the fact that he views his formal university education largely as a disappointment. After the first delight felt by any "mountain youth" upon arrival at such a hallowed institution, the young Wordsworth soon realizes that "I was not for that hour, / Nor for that place" (*1805,* 3, l. 34; ll. 80–81). During the fairy-tale-like first days, the young man is still swayed by boyhood dreams of illustrious predecessors such as Newton, Spencer, and Milton. But the reality of Cambridge soon strikes home: a place of great contradictions, Cambridge's educational system was based on competitive exams, "Examinations, when the man was weighed / As in a balance," which bred vicious rivalries as well as widespread laziness (*1805,* 3, ll. 64–75). It is no wonder that Wordsworth, recalling the university sixteen years later, writes that "here in dwarf proportions were expressed / The limbs of the great world" (3, ll. 616–617).

Because Cambridge personified the world so cruelly, it provided the Wordsworth of 1804 with the obstacles necessary to continue fashioning his autobiographic alter ego into a poet-prophet. In particular, the older poet fudged the facts of his education to paint himself in a better light. While he admits, with hindsight, that his behavior was "proud rebellion and unkind" to the family members who sponsored him (6, l. 40), he devotes more space to justifying, and transforming his hero's less than stellar academic career into a premonition of his future greatness. Curiously, however, he does not deny these changes, thus challenging the accuracy of his own narrative (*1805,* 3, ll. 644–648). Downplaying the reassuring fact that "my heart / Was social, and loved idleness and joy" (3, ll. 235–236), Wordsworth emphasizes his difference with the other students. "Points have we all of us within our souls / Where all stand single" (3,

ll. 186–187). This strange singularity explains his spending more time walking alone outside the city than chasing Honors. "I was ill-tutored for captivity," he claims (3, l. 363). The poet describes himself in this period, in an image borrowed from his sister, as a "floating island" (3, l. 340), detached from worldly concerns, but absorbing everything around him, in particular nature and books.

Throughout Books Third to Sixth, Wordsworth advocates a natural education, which better suits his needs than the official Cambridge curriculum. For the poet, education is a holistic but also dialectic process—vacations, nature, and the imagination and complement and conflict with school, books, and reason. In the "Infant Prodigy" passage in Book Fifth, he opposes current educationalist theories he views as overly controlling, in particular those of Thomas Wedgwood, to his own ideal of a free and spontaneous education (5, ll. 290–360). The poet is wary of theory, however, and better at illustrating his ideas with parables, directness not being Wordsworth's preferred didactic method. Among these are the "Discharged Soldier," the "Dream of the Arab-Quixote," "The Boy of Winander," and the "Drowned Man," four of the most opaque spots-of-time episodes in *The Prelude.*

The "Discharged Soldier" serves as a warning that too much imagination can be dangerously solipsistic. Wandering in a "happy state" of solitude near Hawkshead, the speaker suddenly comes across an "uncouth shape," a lanky, ghost-like figure, one of the many sick soldiers returning home from the war in the West Indies. Much like Coleridge's Ancient Mariner, the soldier tells his story, but it is the "ghastly mildness in his look," in response to the speaker's gauche, unfeeling behavior, which begins to instill in the poet an awareness of the still, sad music of humanity (4, ll. 400–504). The second episode, a dream experienced by the French philosopher Descartes in 1619 and recounted by Coleridge, comes as a response to the speaker's stated distrust in books. The story uses an allegorical frame, the dream of a bedouin on a camel carrying a stone and a shell symbolizing science and poetry, to explain that knowledge can be powerful, but only when equally balanced between imagination and reason (5, ll. 49–139).

This understanding of vital knowledge is further developed in the "Boy of Winander" episode, written in the first person for the 1799 poem but left out. The speaker relates the story of a boy who would call out to the surrounding trees and rocks across Lake Winander. He awaits their echo, but instead receives "the gentle shock of mild surprise"—his heart echoes the sublimity of nature. Without any explanation, the boy dies before he reaches ten and is remembered as a prototype for of a "race of real children." "May books and Nature be their early joy," Wordsworth declares in guise of an interpretation, "And knowledge, rightly honoured with that name—Knowledge not purchased with the loss of power!" (5, ll. 364–449). Finally, in the "Drowned Man" episode, transposed here from the 1799 poem, the poet recalls coming across the horrific drowned body of James Jackson, the village schoolmaster, but not being afraid. "My inner eye had seen / Such sights before among the shining streams / Of fairyland, the forests of romance," he explains (5, ll. 450–482). These examples go full circle—here the poet asserts the importance of imagination and books, as much if not more than nature, in a child's development.

Despite his urging a carefully counterpoised intake of imagination and reason as the ideal education, it is the unsettling of that balance which triggers the speaker's own awareness of his role as poet-prophet. His Christlike sense of election is openly acknowledged in a splendid consecration scene during his first summer vacation. After watching the sun rise over Hawkshead, "all the sweetness of a common dawn—Dews, vapours, and the melody of birds, / And labourers going forth to till the fields," the eighteen-year old boy dedicates himself to a life of poetry (4, ll. 336–345). Returning to Cambridge, where he is just one of many students, the poet feels more than ever "detached / Internally from academic cares"—he cannot equate his huge ambition with his outward indistinction (6, ll. 29–30). It is not at university but on a summer vacation two years later that the young man is given another, clarion sign of his destiny.

In July 1790, Wordsworth and his Welsh friend Robert Jones left on a fourteen-week walking tour of France and Switzerland, "a march it was of military speed" (6, l. 428) with the Alps as their goal. The trip greatly marked Wordsworth and provided material for his early poem, *Descriptive Sketches* (1793). Fifteen years later, however, not only his situation, but the situation of the whole of Europe was completely modified. The older Wordsworth rewrote this material to account for these changes, heedful to justify his own youthful radicalism as a development of his natural education. The speaker uses the same glorious language as in the Hawkshead consecration scene to describe the atmosphere on their arrival on the Continent. "But 'twas a time when Europe was rejoiced, / France standing on the top of golden hours, / And human nature seeming born again" (6, ll. 351–353). Jones and Wordsworth had landed by accident on the eve of the *Fête de la Fédération,* a party to celebrate the revolutionary storming of the Bastille exactly one year earlier. Everywhere they went they found liberty dances and Frenchmen delighted to meet these two representatives of British constitutional freedom (6, ll. 403–405). Changes to the Grande Chartreuse passage made in 1815 indicate, nonetheless, that Wordsworth was prepared to filter the facts to make his early views fit his later conservatism (*1805,* ll. 421–425; *1850,* ll. 414–488).

Although Book Sixth refers to the speaker's awakening political consciousness, it emphasizes his apparently apolitical experiences in the Alps. These episodes, like Cambridge beforehand, are noteworthy for their ability to disappoint—a series of set-backs paradoxically enables the poet's progress or development. Chief among these is the famous "Simplon Pass" episode, a favorite of critics. Two days beforehand, the companions had climbed the Col de Balme where Wordsworth "grieved / To have a soulless image on the eye / Which had usurped upon a living thought / That never more could be" (6, ll. 453–456). The view of Mont Blanc, no doubt enshrouded in fog that morning, did not match his sublime expectation. Eager to get a better view, they rush across the Valais and up the Simplon Pass toward Italy, following some muleteers. After lunch, the two travelers lose the mule train and their way. Half way up another mountain, they ask a local for directions and discover that they should be heading downhill, not further up. Unwilling to believe the man, they repeatedly question him, but receive the same disappointing answer: "we had crossed the Alps" (6, ll. 524–562).

Wordsworth, fifteen years later, amplified this seemingly insignificant detail of the tour into a critical moment of bathos to follow it with one the most direct and confident celebrations of imagination's power in all of British literature:

> Imagination!—lifting up itself
> Before the eye and progress of my song
> Like an unfathered vapour, here that power,
> In all the might of its endowments, came
> Athwart me. I was lost as in a cloud,
> Halted without a struggle to break through,
> And now, recovering, to my soul I say
> "I recognize thy glory."
>
> (6, ll. 525–532)

A secular epiphany, this passage declares the poet's confidence not in divinity, but in his own mind. Imagination comes to him "unfathered." As predicted in the "Glad Preamble," the guide he chooses is indeed just a cloud. Although the speaker here boldly asserts himself at the expense of the world, the passage was initially followed in the original draft by the simile of the cave, later transplanted to Book Eighth, which reaffirms the primacy of nature. As if to wash away any doubt he might still have entertained

about his mind's powers, Wordsworth resorts with a vengeance to the leitmotif of water, symbol of transcendent creativity, comparing his mind to "the overflowing Nile" (6, l. 548).

Although written in a major key, this sublime passage operates the same way as other spots of time. In particular, the sense of immortality it imparts remains obscure, "something evermore about to be" (6, l. 542) and the immediate result, like the "huge and mighty forms" which follow the "Boat Theft" episode, is of visionary dreariness:

> The immeasurable height
> Of woods decaying, never to be decayed,
> The stationary blasts of waterfalls,
> And everywhere along the hollow rent
> Winds thwarting winds, bewildered and forlorn
> …
> Were all like workings of one mind, the features
> Of the same face, blossoms upon one tree,
> Characters of the great apocalypse,
> The types and symbols of eternity,
> Of first, and last, and midst without end.
>
> (6, ll. 556–572)

An accurate physical and geological description of the Gondo ravine through which the travelers descend, this superbly structured assemblage of contraries, carefully equipoised, represents the imagination's struggle to embrace both mind and nature and leads to an analogy with the Apocalypse in *The Book of Revelation*. This is the culmination point in the speaker's natural education—like the Bible, nature points to life's finality, a lesson hinted at in all the previous spots of time, but here openly declared.

CRISIS: LONDON AND THE FRENCH REVOLUTION

The "Simplon Pass" episode occupies the center stage in two influential critical studies on *The Prelude* which typify two conflicting approaches to Wordsworth. In the first, loosely phenomenological study dating back to the 1960s, Geoffrey Hartman showed how in this passage, Nature itself leads the poet beyond Nature and toward the love of man. Calling this process *via naturaliter negativa,* or the naturally negative way, Hartman argued that the "Simplon" episode crucially prepares Wordsworth for his role as visionary poet. The second book, by Alan Liu, represents the apotheosis of a decade of New Historicist criticism in the 1980s. Diverging radically from the proponents of a visionary, idealist approach, Liu argued instead that Romantic imagination served to conceal Wordsworth's historical trauma. Liu's most controversial claim was that the "Simplon" episode betrays Wordsworth's "climactic veiling" of history, represented by Napoleon's progress through the Alps. Other studies, by Nicolas Roe and Kenneth Johnston for example, have been preoccupied less with *The Prelude*'s sublime episodes, which invite disagreement between idealist and materialist critics, and more with the historical and social contexts which helped shape Wordsworth's complex political consciousness, related in Books Seventh through Tenth. While the "Simplon Pass" episode is an important turning point in the poem, it is only the middle point in the poet's development. Before he can achieve full poetic maturity, he must go in search of worldy experience in London and France, a sort of poetic tourist "employed to note, and keep / In memory, those individual sights / Of courage, or integrity, or truth, / Or tenderness" (*1850,* 7, ll. 598–561). This intense lesson in humanity accelerates a moral crisis which throws into doubt the visionary confidence of his youth.

Wordsworth left Cambridge in January 1791 with a bachelor's degree and no concrete plans for the future. Very little is known except for what Worsworth tells us in *The Prelude* about his life during the next few years. Moving to London "at ease from all ambition personal" (7, l. 69), he lived several months in lodgings and presumably spent much time idling about the capital. Despite being disappointed yet again by the discrepancy between his youthful, romantic dreams (7, ll. 81–138) and the large, crowded city he discovered at twenty-one, Wordsworth culled some of his most vivid poetic descriptions from these urban rambles. Like Baudelaire, he was fascinated by the city's anonymity and estrangement, best evoked by that most modern of symbols, the crowd. Whereas the French poet, in *The Flowers of Evil* (1857), revels in crowds, Wordsworth draws his analogies from Edmund Burke's gothic portrayal of Jacobin mobs in *Reflections on the Revolution in France* (1790) and Milton's Pandemonium in *Paradise Lost.* "Rise up, thou monstrous ant-hill on the plain / Of too busy a world! Before me flow, / Thou endless stream of men and moving things!" he writes in the 1850 edition (*1850,* 7, ll. 149–151). The later edition sadly cuts out much of the catalog meant to illustrate this "endless stream," an evocative passage which anticipates another great celebration of modernity, Walt Whitman's *Leaves of Grass* (1855).

Crowds disturb the young poet not only because, like many of his contemporaries, he fears their politically radical significance, but mainly because they destabilize his own sense of identity and purpose. In his *Essays upon Epitaphs,* Wordsworth argues that the act of naming is essential to a person or a place's identity, because it insures their posterity in our collective memory. Naming for the poet is synonymous with knowing, a quality, he argues, which is sorely missing in the city:

> Above all, one thought
> Baffled my understanding, how men lived
> Even next-door neighbours, as we say, yet still
> Strangers, and knowing not each other's names.
>
> (7, ll. 117–120)

Even more disturbing than the fact that neighbors remain strangers to one another is his own inability to decipher or draw out a person from the mass. "The face of every one / That passes by me is a mystery!" he exclaims, terrified that London can resist his imaginative sympathy (7, ll. 597–598). Sympathetic knowledge enables Wordsworth to write and therefore to assert himself as poet. Like the lone Blind Beggar, the speaker cannot see, or be seen in the crowd. Curiously, he is drawn to the beggar, and to all the other solitary figures in the poem, not because of their palpable specificity, but because they represent something generic: the blind man is "a type / or emblem of the utmost that we know / Both of ourselves and of the universe" (7, ll. 618–619). Solitary figures like the blind man are reassuring to the speaker; he can imagine their story, here literally already written down on the blind man's paper, and thus can also confirm his own imaginary power.

Wordsworth's critique of the city, his feeling that "from humanity divorced / The human form" (7, ll. 425–426), reflects a widespread anxiety among his contemporaries regarding industrialization and division of labor, an anxiety addressed by Adam Smith and Karl Marx, among others. Unlike Marx's or Smith's, the poet's response is fundamentally conservative. Influenced by Burke, whose genius he lauds in a famous addition in 1832 (*1850*, 7, l. 512), he asserts a form of loyalist nationalism which advocates imperial expansion while at the same time nostalgically embracing Britain's vanishing cottage economy. The theme of imperialism, later developed less ambiguously in *The Excursion,* is associated in Book Eighth with imaginative power and with Britain's Saxon heritage. Recalling his first entrance into London, the speaker describes his surroundings' lack of distinctness, "vulgar men about me, vulgar forms / Of houses" (8, ll. 695–696). The city's anonymity triggers another spot of time, an anticlimax leading to a moment of visionary power similar to the "Simplon Pass" episode. The cave analogy, written to describe his deception at having crossed the Alps, is yoked clumsily to this incident in order to explain how, when nature is too overwhelming, "the scene before him lies in perfect view / Exposed, and lifeless as a written book" (8, ll. 726–727). Temporarily checked, the speaker suddenly feels "a weight of ages" (8, l.

703) descend upon him, a surge of imaginative power which he links to London's historical past and glorious imperial present, "the fountain of my country's destiny / And of the destiny of the earth itself" (8, ll. 747–748).

Preferable to this jingoist epiphany are the passages in which Wordsworth evokes an idealized vision of rural life, as in the "Maid of Buttermere" episode in Book Seventh (7, ll. 347–412) and in the Grasmere Fair and the Shepherd in the Mist episodes in Book Eighth. As in previous books, the poet contrasts the Sublime, which he genders as male, with the Beautiful, gendered female, to illustrate the dialectic process of his development. While clearly nostalgic, the poet's pastoralism or "romantic ecology," the title of Jonathan Bate's excellent book on the subject, has inspired influential advocates of land conservation, including John Ruskin (1819–1900) and John Muir (1838–1914). Like Milton's strong contrast between Heaven and Hell, Wordsworth follows the brilliantly chaotic and satirical description of London's Bartholomew Fair (7, ll. 649–695) with the paradisiacal "rustic fair" at Grasmere (8, ll. 1–61) to highlight the latter. His descriptions of the locals at Grasmere, particularily that of the noble shepherd excised from the 1850 edition, are deliberately ideal and general. Whereas the speaker found it difficult to draw imaginative power out of the "blank confusion" of London, in the countryside he is once again able to look at things "in steadiness … the parts / As parts, but with feeling of the whole" (7, ll. 695–714). The poet's natural education conditions him to overcome particularities and to see crowds harmonized into an organic community, a "little family of men" (8, l. 7). The ideology which governs this community is Burkean, amalgamating often complex and contradictory political, social, and moral realities into a unified aesthetic vision of society: "Man free, man working for himself, with choice / Of time, and place, and object … followed by a train / Unwooed, unthought-of even: simplicity, / And beauty, and inevitable grace" (8, ll. 152–158).

This conservative social vision did not lead up to, but rather was abetted by, his experiences in Revolutionary France. While we cannot date the writing of Books Seventh through Tenth with certainty, it appears that the two books on France, Ninth and Tenth, were drafted before the London books (Seventh and Eighth). At the close of Book Eighth, Wordsworth associates his carefully aestheticized "love of mankind" with the gradual "humanization" of the speaker's thoughts (7, ll. 860–870). This process begins in France, the site of social upheaval on an unprecedented scale which "lured" Wordsworth forth (*1850*, 9, l. 34) in November 1791. The twenty-one-year-old poet spent a year in Paris, Blois, and Orleans, nominally to improve his French (*1805*, 9, l. 36), more realistically because he wanted to get a first-hand look at the historical events and to escape family pressures. This residence in France corresponds both to Wordsworth's development of a radical social consciousness and to a more concealed sexual awakening: "Bliss was it in that dawn to be alive, / But to be young was very heaven!" (*1805*, 10, ll. 692–693). The often-cited, memorable line belies the complexity of Wordsworth's retrospective feelings, and the fragility of his poetic self-fashioning of this eventful period in his life. Read within the context of the passage as a whole, the younger Wordsworth's rapture only reinforces the older Wordsworth's claim that his early radicalism was a natural, but still immature stage of his youth. As in earlier episodes, in which disappointment is close at hand, the poet compares the "times" to "a country in romance" (10, l. 696), romanticizing history in order to be able to dramatically turn away from it in the end of the poem.

In Book Ninth, Wordsworth gives a fairly accurate portrayal of this blissful period, although poetic design and his later conservatism do in places color biographical truth. A revolutionary tourist, he passes through Paris on his way to Orleans, visiting the National Assembly, keeping a relic from the Bastille, yet more interested in the Louvre's paintings than in politics (9, ll. 40–80). In late 1791, France's enthusiasm for political change had abated; the Revolution not only was more complicated to understand, but was fast entering a new, bloody stage of development. The speaker first befriends a group of reactionary officers and nobles in Orleans, then meets Michel Beaupuy and Annette Vallon in Blois. In different ways, these two figures teach the young Wordsworth a lesson in humanity, guiding him through the maze of revolutionary events, helping him to equate his inborn sense of egalitarianism, or "mountain liberty" (9, l. 242), with the kind of republicanism most characteristic of the Girondin party. Beaupuy, a captain when they first met, impressed the poet with his morality and steady judgement. "Man he loved / As man," writes Wordsworth, still marked by their friendship twelve years later (9, ll. 313–314). Recalling their long political and philosophical discussions in the park of Blois, however, the older Wordsworth has difficulty fitting his affinity for tradition and the Church with his youthful "hatred of absolute rule" (9, ll. 431–509). It is only when they pass by a hungry girl with her cow, another example of Wordsworth's inability to commiserate with humans except case by case, that the poet can completely endorse Beaupuy's views, boiled down to the sentimental, ahistorical remark that "'tis against that / That we are fighting" (9, ll. 519–520). This retrospective sentimentalization of his youthful politics, a kind of humanitarianism eviscerated of all historical specificity, is pursued in the "Vaudracour and Julia" episode, excised from the 1850 edition. This story relates by implication Wordsworth's affair with Annette Vallon, whom he gave a child in late 1792, then abandoned when Britain declared war on France. A conventional, tragic narrative of two young lovers whose relationship cuts across classes, the episode serves as another sentimental critique of old order institutions (9, ll. 556–935).

The poet's early radicalism comes across more strongly in Book Tenth, yet is also portrayed retrospectively as more obviously mistaken.

Wordsworth artfully weaves together his own development with the development of the Revolution, going as far as fashioning himself into a revolutionary player, even though, despite recent claims made by Kenneth Johnston, the real Wordsworth played no verifiable historical role in France. Opening the book in October 1792, he eerily captures the atmosphere of tentative peace and precarious hope after the tumultuous events of August and September, including the massacre of the Swiss guard at the Tuileries, the arrest of Louis XVI, and the repulsion of the Coalition armies at Valmy. "It was a beautiful and silent day / That overspread the countenance of the earth, / Then fading, with unusual quietness" (10, ll. 1–3). During his first night in Paris, scene of so many of these recent events, the speaker recounts another spot of time episode. As in the Gondo hospice, he is haunted by visions of the September massacres, then receives an apocalyptic admonishment and a voice which cries to the whole city, "Sleep no more!" Like the city itself, the speaker feels "defenceless, as a wood where tigers roam" (10, ll. 63–83). With the advantage of hindsight, he can powerfully intimate the disaster about to fall not only on France, but also on himself.

The speaker's overly strong identification with the Revolution triggers a moral crisis that will reach its nadir in 1796. Returning to England hurriedly in December 1792, he feels socially irrelevant, "a Poet only to myself, to men / Useless" (10, ll. 199–200), and, in a moment so antithetical to *The Prelude*'s "Glad Preamble," is even uncertain if Albion is really his home. Great Britain's leaguing up with the "confederate host" (10, l. 230) in February 1793 is followed in July by the Reign of Terror, "domestic carnage now filled all the year / With feast-days" (10, ll. 329–330). Dreaming himself in the midst of this Terror or pleading before a revolutionary tribunal, the poet sublimates political and personal disappointment into his own guilty sense of desertion (10, ll. 367–380). The end of the Terror in France raises false hopes of a "second spring" (*1850*, 11, l. 6), quickly

thwarted by the Republicans' aggressive military campaigns in summer 1794. The speaker, straining to maintain a basis for moral certainty, abstracts his thoughts from current events, turning first to William Godwin's *An Enquiry Concerning Political Justice* (2nd edition, 1796), then, when all else fails, to mathematics. Godwinian Reason or "theory" only exacerbates the speaker's self-doubts and loss of conviction, so that by the end of Book Eleventh (Tenth in the 1805 text), he reaches "the soul's last and lowest ebb" (*1850*, 11, l. 307).

RECOVERY AND RECEPTION: THE 1850 *PRELUDE,* THE VICTORIANS AND US

If the 1799 *Prelude* is most successful at conveying the creative stirrings of the poet's childhood and the 1805 version powerfully captures the sense of struggle and uncertainty which marks his late teens and early twenties, then the 1850 poem is closer to expressing the later Wordsworth, Distributor of Stamps, sage of the Lake District, and, finally, Poet Laureate. From 1806 to 1839, Wordsworth made his poem more formal, dividing Book Tenth of the 1805 version into two books, sharpening syntax, replacing pantheistic passages with reassuring Christian pieties. A small addition in 1832, which tempers the bold tone of *The Prelude*'s grand finale, is indicative of the greater changes introduced into the 1850 text. Much like the 1799 poem, *The Prelude* ends with the announcement of a philosophical poem in the works, a "monument of glory" planned by "joint labourers," Wordsworth and Coleridge:

Prophets of Nature, we to them will speak
A lasting inspiration, sanctified
By reason, blest by faith; what we have loved,
Others will love, and we will teach them how;
Instruct them how the mind of man becomes
A thousand times more beautiful than the earth
On which he dwells, above this frame of things
(Which, 'mid all revolutions in the hopes
And fears of men, doth still remain unchanged)

In beauty exalted, as it is itself
Of quality and fabric more divine.

    (*1850*, 14, ll. 446–456; *1805*, 13, ll. 443–452)

While *The Recluse*'s millenial aim, to teach mankind to seek his own salvation, is grandiosely stated here, the poet's addition of "blest by faith" in line 448 takes away some of the secular authority and unabashed self-confidence which made the project so radical. Familiar with his shorter lyrics, in particular the *Intimations Ode*, as well as with the popular *Excursion*, the Victorian public found in *The Prelude* what they had grown to expect, the well-rehearsed persona of Wordsworth as a priest-poet and nature prophet, more priest than poet, more nature lover than prophet.

Wordsworth's lifelong revisions partly contributed to the Victorians' conventional reading of *The Prelude*, but one must also keep in mind the historical changes that had occured between the poem's composition and its publication. Citizens of the greatest empire in history, living in a highly individualistic age, Victorian readers and reviewers could not fully understand the crisis which the younger Wordsworth, alongside Europe as a whole, had experienced sixty years beforehand, nor the radical nature of the poet's renovation. A reviewer for the *Eclectic Review* nicely expresses this time lag when he describes the recently published poem as "a large fossil relic—imperfect and magnificient—newly dug up, and with the fresh earth and the old dim subsoil meeting and mingling around it." Even though *The Prelude* develops a moral philosophy which exalts the mind as "a thousand times more beautiful than the earth," many Victorians, including John Stuart Mill, George Eliot and Walter Pater, preferred viewing its author as a poet of nature, childhood and the emotions. Chief among these was poet and critic Matthew Arnold (1822–1888). Having spent his summers as a youth near Rydal Mount and himself a fervent Wordsworthian, Arnold nevertheless dismissed the poet's more philosophical works, *The Excursion* and *The Prelude*, as secondary in his influential introduction to *Poems of Wordsworth* (1879). The poet's best lyrics are his most simple, Arnold famously argued, expressing "the joy offered to us in nature, the joy offered to us in the simple primary affections and duties."

A third explanation for the Victorians' lukewarm reception of *The Prelude* lies in the poem itself, particularly in the last books. Modeled on Milton's epic journey from Hell to light, the poet's recovery from his ruined hopes of revolution depends first on his ability to shake off what he describes as the "absolute dominion" of "the bodily eye" (*1850*, 12, ll. 127–131; *1805*, 11, ll. 172–175). His romance with Godwinian Reason in Book Eleventh, combined with his fondness for the highly codified Picturesque mode of observing nature, had cut him off from the strange visitations of his childhood. In order for the speaker to assume his predestined role as poet-prophet, he needs to remember once more how to perceive with all his faculties, and especially his imagination. It is the two women in his life who come to his aid and pursue the humanizing of his mind begun with Beaupuy. First Dorothy, then his future wife, Mary Hutchinson, teach the speaker, through their own wise passivity and unquestioning response to nature, how to become a "sensitive being, a creative soul" once more (*1850*, 12, l. 207; *1805*, 11, l. 256). To illustrate the renovative power of memory, the poet inserts the doctrinal passage on the spots of time here, along with two episodes culled from the 1799 poem, "Penrith Beacon" and "Waiting for the Horses." Revisiting Penrith in 1787 with Mary, the speaker describes how his new love for his future wife superimposes itself on his childhood memory of visionary dreariness without erasing it completely. "So feeling comes in aid / Of feeling," he writes. In the same way, one may argue that the poet's renovation depends on the present coming in aid of the past, the Beautiful coming in aid of the Sublime, the humanized adult coming in aid of the natural and rebelliouschild (*1850*, 12, ll. 269–277; *1805*, 11, ll. 325–333).

While Wordsworth's idealization of domestic femininity upsets modern readers as much as it answered to Victorian taste, one must remember that the poet ascribes a central role to Dorothy and Mary in the poem. Dorothy's tenderness or "sweet influence," which the speaker gratefully acknowledges, allows him to "soften down / this oversternness," to look beyond sublime nature and perceive its details as well (*1850*, 14, ll. 231–274; *1805*, 13, ll. 210–246). This gives him a sense of "kindred permanence" as opposed to the Sublime's frightful reminder of man's temporality, a notion that one must "look with feelings of fraternal love / Upon the unassuming things that hold / A silent station in this beauteous world" (*1850*, 13, ll. 34–47; *1805*, 12, ll. 37–52). The speaker abandons all pretensions to a public role as a politician, economist, or philosopher. Instead, he accedes to his self-titled position of poet-prophet and, like Kant, domesticates or privatizes hope, redirecting it toward what he knows best: nature, family, and nation as incarnated by the rural community of Grasmere. "Oh! who is he that hath his whole life long, / Preserved, enlarged, this freedom in himself? / For this alone is genuine liberty" (*1850*, 14, ll. 130–132; *1805*, 13, ll. 120–122). Liberty is equated with duty; radical politics are sublimated into radical poetics.

The autobiographical journey ends not on a domestic note, but by recalling a landscape of hope shaped by the horizontal sublimity of Salisbury Plain and the vertical sublimity of Mt. Snowdon. Both are memorable scenes which celebrate humans' capacity to creatively interact with the world. The poet-traveler, climbing Snowdon by night, suddenly catches a glimpse, through a rift in the clouds, of

> A fixed, abysmal, gloomy, breathing place—
> Mounted by the roar of waters, torrents, streams
> Innumerable, roaring with one voice
> Heard over the earth and sea, and, in that hour,
> For so it seems, felt by the starry heavens
>
> (*1850*, 14, ll. 58–62; *1805*, 13, 63–66)

Absence gives way to presence, the poet beholds "the emblem of a mind / That feeds upon infinity" (*1850*, 14, ll. 70–71; *1805*, 13, ll. 69–70). Although this great passage particularly suffered from the poet's later revisions, the 1850 version quoted here still can suggestively express the young poet's heroic faith in the power of the imagination. Like the veil of clouds that conceals the abyss, the older Wordsworth hid this radical belief behind moralistic proprieties; not until the twentieth century did readers recognize *The Prelude* as Wordsworth's greatest achievement.

Living in an age influenced by Nietzsche and Freud, more sympathetic to human angst and complexity, critics beginning with A. C. Bradley saw Wordsworth less as the domestic poet of nature portrayed by Arnold and more as a poet of the sublime alongside Milton. And while liberal and conservative readers continue to debate the poet's so-called apostasy, or turn away from his youthful radicalism, they are alike in preferring those transcendent passages in which daffodils and vagrants give way to a more ambitious, and ambiguous, vision of the world, for Wordsworth's brilliance lies in his power to build up, as the angels in Book Fourteenth do, "greatest things, / From least suggestions" (*1850*, 14, ll. 101–102; *1805*, 13, ll. 99–100).

Select Bibliography

EDITIONS

The Prelude, 1798–9, by William Wordsworth. Edited by Stephen Parrish. Cornell Wordsworth Series. Ithaca, N.Y.: Cornell University Press, 1977. The standard edition of the two-book poem.

The Prelude, 1799, 1805, 1850. Edited by Jonathan Wordsworth, M. H. Abrams, and Stephen Gill. New York: W. W. Norton and Co., 1979. The most versatile and readily available student edition, with notes and criticism. All citations are from this edition.

The Fourteen-Book Prelude. Edited by W. J. B. Owen. Cornell Wordsworth Series. Ithaca, N.Y.: Cornell University Press, 1985. The standard edition of the 1850 poem.

The Thirteen-Book Prelude. Edited by Mark Reed. 2 vols. Cornell Wordsworth Series. Ithaca, N.Y.: Cornell University Press, 1991. The standard edition of the 1805 poem.

The Five-Book Prelude. Edited by Duncan Wu. Oxford: Clarendon Press, 1997. The text of early spring 1804, reconstructed by Jonathan Wordsworth in 1977.

OTHER WORKS BY WORDSWORTH

The Poetical Works of William Wordsworth. Edited by Ernest de Selincourt and Helen Darbishire. 5 vols. Oxford: Clarendon Press, 1941–1949, revised 1952–1959. Remains a very useful annotated complete poetry.

Lyrical Ballads 1798. With Samuel Taylor Coleridge. Edited by W. J. B. Owen. Oxford: Oxford University Press, 1967.

The Letters of William and Dorothy Wordsworth. With Dorothy Wordsworth. Edited by Ernest de Selincourt, revised by Alan G. Hill. 8 vols. Oxford: Clarendon Press, 1967–1993. The standard edition of his letters.

The Poems. Edited by John Hayden. 2 vols. Hamondsworth: Penguin, 1977. The most readily available complete later versions of poems.

The Prose Works of William Wordsworth. Edited by W. J. B. Owen and Jane Worthington Smyser. 3 vols. Oxford: Oxford University Press, 1974. The standard edition of his prose works.

The Fenwick Notes of William Wordsworth. Edited by Jared Curtis. London: Bristol Classic, 1993. Supplements complete prose with 1843 autobiographical notes.

SECONDARY WORKS

Abrams, M. H. *Natural Supernaturalism: Tradition and Revolution in Romantic Literature.* New York: W. W. Norton and Co., 1971. One of the most far-reaching and influential studies of Wordsworth and his age.

Anonymous. "*The Prelude.*" *Eclectic Review.* XXVIII (1850): 550–562.

Arnold, Matthew. "Preface." *The Poems of Wordsworth, chosen and edited by Matthew Arnold.* London, 1879.

Bate, Jonathan. *Romantic Ecology: Wordsworth and the Environmental Tradition.* London: Routledge, 1991. A short study which turns against New Historicism to recuperate Wordsworth as a proto-ecologist and "poet of nature."

Bloom, Harold, ed. *William Wordsworth's "The Prelude."* New York: Chelsea House, 1986. A collection of useful critical essays.

Bradley, A. C. *Oxford Lectures on Poetry.* London, 1909. The first critic to interpret Wordsworth as a visionary poet.

Butler, Marylin. *Romantics, Rebels and Reactionaries: English Literature and its Background, 1760–1830.* London: Oxford University Press, 1981. Rejecting formalist criticism, examines poet within his historical and cultural context.

Coleridge, Samuel Taylor. *Biographia Literaria.* Edited by James Engell and W. J. Bate. Bollingen Coleridge Series 7. 2 vols. Princeton, N.J.: Princeton University Press, 1983.

The standard edition of Coleridge's most important critical work, much if it on Wordsworth's poetry and theory of the imagination.

Colley, Linda. *Britons: Forging the Nation 1707–1837.* New Haven, Conn.: Yale University Press, 1992.

Cooper, Lane. *A Concordance to the Poems of William Wordsworth.* London, 1911.

de Man, Paul. *The Rhetoric of Romanticism.* New York: Columbia University Press, 1984. The most influential example of formalist deconstruction.

Friedman, Michael. *The Making of a Tory Humanist: William Wordsworth and the Idea of Community.* New York: Columbia University Press, 1979. Traces sources of the poet's conservatism and attraction to rural communities.

Gill, Stephen. *William Wordsworth: A Life.* Oxford: Oxford University Press, 1990. The standard biography.

———. *William Wordsworth: "The Prelude."* Landmarks of World Literature Series. Cambridge: Cambridge University Press, 1991. A useful short introduction to the poem.

Hamilton, Paul. *Wordsworth.* Harvester New Readings Series. Atlantic Highlands, N.J.: Harvester Wheatsheaf, 1986. An excellent introduction, placing *The Prelude* in context of other writings.

Hartman, Geoffrey. *Wordsworth's Poetry 1787–1814.* New Haven: Yale University Press, 1964. A very influential study of the poet as visionary.

Hazlitt, William. "Mr. Wordsworth." In *Spirit of the Age,* 1825. Reprinted in *William Hazlitt: Selected Writings.* Edited by Ronald Blythe. Harmondsworth: Penguin, 1970. One of the sharpest contemporary critics of the poet.

Jacobus, Mary. *Romanticism, Writing and Sexual Difference: Essays on "The Prelude."* Oxford: Oxford University Press, 1989. Provides often controversial readings through a combination of deconstruction and feminist theory.

Johnston, Kenneth. *Wordsworth and "The Recluse."* New Haven: Yale University Press, 1984. Substantial study of the *Recluse* project.

———. *The Hidden Wordsworth: Poet, Lover, Rebel, Spy.* New York: W. W. Norton and Co., 1998. An exciting but sometimes speculative biography.

Johnston, Kenneth, and Gene Ruoff, eds. *The Age of William Wordsworth: Critical Essays on the Romantic Tradition.* New Brunswick, N.J.: Rutgers University Press, 1987. Essays which place the poet in historical context.

Keats, John. *Letters of John Keats: A Selection.* Edited by Robert Gittings. Oxford: Oxford University Press, 1970.

Lindenberger, Herbert. *On Wordsworth's "Prelude."* Princeton, N.J.: Princeton University Press, 1963. An important early monograph on the poem.

Liu, Alan. *Wordsworth: The Sense of History.* Stanford, Calif.: Stanford University Press, 1988. An ambitious example of New Historicist criticism.

Reed, Mark. *Wordsworth: The Chronology of the Early Years, 1770–1799.* Cambridge, Mass.: Harvard University Press, 1967.

———. *Wordsworth: The Chronology of the Middle Years, 1800–1815.* Cambridge, Mass.: Harvard University Press, 1972. An indispensable critical tool.

Rehder, Robert. *Wordsworth and the Beginnings of Modern Poetry.* London: Croom Helm, 1981. An elegantly written study of his contribution to the modern canon.

Reiman, Donald, ed. *The Romantics Reviewed.* Part A, *The Lake Poets.* 2 vols. New York: Garland, 1972. The standard collection of contemporary reviews.

Roe, Nicolas. *Wordsworth and Coleridge: The Radical Years.* Oxford: Clarendon Press, 1988. An important study of the poet's radical politics.

———. "William Wordsworth." In *Literature of the Romantic Period: A Bibliographical Guide.* Edited by Michael O'Neill. Oxford: Clarendon Press, 1998. A useful bibliographic chapter with main currents in criticism and textual editions.

Ruoff, Gene. *Wordsworth and Coleridge: The Making of the Major Lyrics, 1802–1804.* New Brunswick, N.J.: Rutgers University Press, 1989. A study of the two poets' close collaboration and reciprocal influences.

Taylor, Charles. *Sources of the Self: The Making of the Modern Identity.* Cambridge: Cambridge University Press, 1992.

Todd, F. M. *Politics and the Poet: A Study of Wordsworth.* London: Methuen & Co., 1957. An early, still important political study.

Weiskel, Thomas. *The Romantic Sublime: Studies in the Structure and Psychology of Transcendence.* Baltimore: The Johns Hopkins University Press, 1976. Still the major study on how the sublime functions.

Wordsworth, Dorothy. *Journals of Dorothy Wordsworth: The Alfoxden Journal, 1798; The Grasmere Journals, 1800–1803.* Edited by Mary Moorman. Oxford: Oxford University Press, 1973. The standard edition of Dorothy's journals.

Wordsworth, Jonathan. *William Wordsworth: The Borders of Vision.* Oxford: Clarendon Press, 1982. An extensive textual study of the *Recluse* project.

Wu, Duncan. *Wordsworth's Reading: 1770–1799.* Cambridge: Cambridge University Press, 1993.

———. *Wordsworth's Reading: 1800–1815.* Cambridge: Cambridge University Press, 1995. A year-by-year list of all his reading.

Alexander Pope's
The Rape of the Lock

TOM JONES

THE RAPE OF the Lock is a complex poem that alludes to a large number of contexts beyond its immediate bounds. It has a complex occasional history, involving a quarrel between two Catholic families and their eventual reconciliation. It presents a distant and peculiar social world in which dressing, talking, drinking tea, and playing cards are surprisingly dominant activities, and are loaded with social and sexual connotations. And it refers by parallels of episode and incident, translation, parody, and loose imitation to numerous works of literature in ancient Greek, Latin, French, Italian, and English. This description of the poem makes it sound as if it is in danger of losing its center, of being about lots of other things, but never really being itself. Indeed, this is one of the fundamental critical difficulties in talking about the poem: recognizing its literary and social complexity without relegating it to the position of a cultural relic or an illustration of outdated ideological and cultural assumptions and practices.

If the poem prompts its readers and critics to talk about it as a repository of literary allusions, and an illustration of a certain form of sexualized consumer fetishism, it is perhaps because it

is so successful as a poem. The real achievement of the poem is its ability to say something about all the things it alludes to in a light, coherent, and knowing fashion. It manages to carry literary allusion, social critique, and personal relevance without sacrificing the brilliance of its artistic veneer, and it maintains that veneer without losing the complexity of its literary, social, and personal conscience. Sketching some of the contexts to which *The Rape of the Lock* refers before beginning a consecutive reading of the poem will help show why and how these contexts are important.

OCCASION

The best available summary of the occasion and compositional history of *The Rape of the Lock* is Geoffrey Tillotson's introduction to the Twickenham Edition of the poem. What follows is deeply indebted to Tillotson.

The Rape of the Lock springs from a very specific social occasion. Robert, Lord Petre had cut off a lock of hair belonging to Arabella Fermor, causing an estrangement between the two of them and between their families. It is probable that Arabella was being considered as a prospective wife for Lord Petre. John Caryll,

273

another of the circle of landowning Catholic families to which the Fermors and Petres belonged, and who also knew Pope, suggested to Pope that he write something that would draw the families together again. The poem circulated in manuscript and appeared to do its job. Pope's correspondence records favorable reception from both Lord Petre, who had become the baron of the poem, and Arabella Fermor, who had become Belinda. *The Rape of the Locke* was printed in a miscellany of poems published by Bernard Lintott in 1712. The Fermors were not so pleased with the poem once it was published, perhaps because Lord Petre had by this time married Catherine Warmsley, a younger and richer wife than Arabella would have been. This poem is in just two cantos, and introduces in brief sketches most of the action that makes up Pope's revised five canto version of the poem. Its second edition contained an appeasing dedication to Arabella, which was probably eased on its way by the intervening death of Petre.

Pope was always a great reviser of his work, and more often than not a great improver. He worked at the poem over the next two years and published it in expanded form in 1714 as *The Rape of the Lock*. I shall refer exclusively to this revised version throughout this essay. The poem was published as a freestanding volume, with six engravings (*The Rape of the Lock* has always attracted visual artists). The only substantial alteration of the poem after this date was the addition of Clarissa's speech in 1717 when Pope published the poem in the first volume of his *Works,* a volume intended to launch him as a serious contender in the literary world.

The poem has to achieve a lot in terms of its occasion, composition, and history of publication. It has to reconcile two potential lovers and their families after a dispute; it then has to flatter and assuage the heroine of the poem, who has in some way been offended by its first publication; it has to satisfy a readership beyond the immediate bounds of the circle of families involved in the drama; and it has to form part of Pope's

CHRONOLOGY

1688	21 May. Pope born to Alexander, a Catholic cloth merchant, and Edith in London. Abdication of James II.
1689	Accession of William III. Revolution Settlement. Toleration Act sees Catholicism and Unitarianism become the only unrecognized forms of Christianity in England.
1700s	Pope family moves to Binfield. Pope reads widely in Greek, Latin and English poetry; writes and destroys juvenile epic poem on Alcander, Prince of Rhodes; establishes friendships with leading literary and statespeople including Sir William Trumbull and William Wycherley, the playwright.
1702	March. Accession of Queen Anne.
1703–1704	Pope in London studying French and Italian.
1709	First publication. *Pastorals, Sarpedon to Glaucus, January and May* in *Poetical Miscellanies.*
1712–1714	Pope often in London mixing with literati and politicians. Inception of the Scriblerus Club, which saw Pope, Jonathan Swift, John Gay, Thomas Parnell, John Arbuthnot and Robert Harley converse and collaborate on various small and large literary and satirical projects.
1712	First two-canto version of *The Rape of the Locke.*
1713	Treaty of Utrecht ending war with the French. Pope celebrates the event by revising and publishing *Windsor-Forest,* in which his praise for Queen Anne is perhaps at its highest.
1714	Five-canto version of *The Rape of the Lock.* Death of Queen Anne. Accession of George I.
1715	Jacobite uprising renews suspicion of Catholics.
1715–1725	Pope translates Homer with the help of Elijah Fenton and William Broome, amongst others, and produces an edi-

	tion of Shakespeare. The profits from these projects secure his fortune.
1722	Robert Walpole begins his ascent to the position of Prime Minister, and becomes the continual object of satirical and political attacks by Pope and his circle.
1727	Accession of George II. Swift in England, arranging the publication of *Gulliver's Travels* whilst Pope writes the first version of *The Dunciad*, his dark mock-epic of cultural decline.
1732–1735	Pope suffers a series of bereavements: Francis Atterbury dies 4 March 1732; John Gay dies 4 December 1732; Edith Pope dies 7 June 1733; John Arbuthnot dies 27 June 1735.
1733–1735	Publication of most of Pope's major philosophical poems, *An Essay on Man* and the *Moral Essays* (also known as *Epistles to Several Persons*).
1738	Beginning of acquaintance between Pope and William Warburton, a divine who defended Pope from accusations of deism in his *Essay on Man*. Warburton later edited Pope's poetical works.
1742	Revised four-book version of *The Dunciad*.
1744	Wednesday, 30 May Pope dies.

career plans as a professional poet, his aspiration at this time, by taking its place as a form of epic in his ambitious run of early works.

GENRE AND PREDECESSORS

The Rape of the Lock fits into Pope's early career plan very neatly. Perhaps in conscious imitation of Virgil, who wrote first his eclogues, then his georgics, and finally his epic, *The Aeneid*, Pope's first publications were in the same vein as Virgil's. His *Pastorals*, followed by *Windsor Forest* (which might be thought to have a georgic element), and then the revised version of *The Rape of the Lock* follow the Virgilian progression, but with one major difference. *The Rape of the Lock* is not an epic. It is a mock-epic, or as Pope's title page describes it, "An Heroi-Comical Poem." Pope has several important precedents in this genre. The tradition begins with the pseudo-Homeric *Margites* and *Batrachomyomachia* (*The Battle of the Frogs and Mice*), ancient Greek poems that stand next to the Homeric epics and mock their dignity. In early modern Europe this mock-epic tradition follows a number of different courses and involves readers in the distinctions between burlesque and mock-epic (see the definitions of these terms in, for example, *The New Princeton Encyclopedia of Poetry and Poetics*).

The seventeenth-century Italian poet Alessandro Tassoni composed a work called *La Secchia Rapita*, translated into English in Pope's time by John Ozell as *The Trophy-Bucket*. This poem recounts an actual incident in a war between religious factions in thirteenth-century Europe, in which a bucket from a well was taken from one town and kept as a symbol of martial superiority, with the original owners making frequent forays to regain it. Tassoni plays on the absurdity of the bucket as a symbol and as an object of strife to expose the absurdity of regional distinctions and rivalries. His tactic is most often to expose this absurdity by diminishing the objectives of the war: the bucket is no longer a symbol of the objects of the war (territory, wealth, and so forth), but the object of the war itself. A great deal of self-conscious wit is exercised on the metonymical confusion of the bucket for the cause of war, and the tendency of epic poetic language to employ and exploit metonymical language for magnificent effects.

Along with Tassoni, Boileau's *Le Lutrin* (*The Lectern*) is the most evident continental European model for *The Rape of the Lock*. In Boileau's piece, a monk and a chorister engage in a battle over the position of a lectern in chapel, the monk hoping to curb the chorister's social aspirations. The situation here is amplified rather than diminished: a petty dispute assumes heroic proportions. In the expanded six canto version of this poem (like *The Rape of the Lock, Le Lutrin* began life as a two-canto poem) the dispute is ended by a book hurling contest. As in Tassoni, metonymical confusion is prominent: the books that are thrown represent their authors in a concrete fashion. A metaphorically heavy book becomes useful as a weapon because it is actually heavier than others. Properties are transferred from the abstract to the concrete characteristics of things, exposing the confusion of spiritual for material privilege within a corrupt and petty church. John Ozell, who also translated this poem, invokes the aid of the *Batrachomyomachia, La Secchia Rapita,* and Samuel Garth's *The Dispensary* when he sets about singing the rage of the chorister at the opening of the fourth canto, and the introduction to the poem by Nicholas Rowe (himself a distinguished translator, playwright, and editor of Shakespeare, as well as a friend of Pope) recognizes the poem as belonging to a distinct mock-epic genre. There is a clear sense in the English translation of this work that a new and important literary mode is establishing itself.

The main contributions to the tradition in English are Samuel Butler's *Hudibras,* John Dryden's *MacFlecknoe,* and Samuel Garth's *The Dispensary.* Butler's long poem in octosyllabic couplets is perhaps more in the burlesque than the mock-epic tradition. The poem parodies romance narrative structure, using narrative episodes merely as an opportunity to turn the satirical gaze in another direction. It has Cervantes more in mind than Homer. The poem exposes and ridicules the various vocabularies and behaviors of mid-seventeenth-century England, emphasizing the absurdity of the political and religious contentions that had disrupted the country, and Scotland and Ireland, throughout the 1640s and 1650s. There is nothing truly heroic about the eponymous hero: he is an exercise in diminution and absurdism perhaps more relevant to the poems of Jonathan Swift than Alexander Pope. Dryden's *MacFlecknoe* gives the mode an interesting turn in applying the mock-epic principles of diminution and

inversion to the literary scene. His poem discusses the succession of the kingdom of Dullness from Richard Flecknoe to Thomas Shadwell, poets with whom Dryden was locked in dispute, investing the characters of his poem in heroic but absurd and often scatological magnificence as they move about an apocalyptic London. This poem perhaps survives more clearly in Pope's *Dunciad* than it does in *The Rape of the Lock,* concentrating as it does on the decline of a literary and nationalistic culture in a capital haunted by absurd echoes of a grander and more meaningful literary past.

The Dispensary too lends more to *The Dunciad* than to *The Rape of the Lock.* This poem was occasioned by the London College of Physicians providing free apothecaries' (pharmacists') services to the indigent of the capital. Garth personifies, or rather deifies, Disease, and gives her the kind of mysterious, concealed position of misdirected power that Pope gives to his goddess Dullness. He names medical practitioners in person, much as Pope names writers in *The Dunciad,* and works a literary critical dimension into the piece by exploiting the surprisingly common fact of one person practicing medicine and poetry (see *The Dispensary,* pp. 37–38, 47, 55).

All these poems precede *The Rape of the Lock,* and Pope knew them all. His poem distinguishes itself by the type and quality of its allusions to epic incidents and kinds of description. One way of distinguishing between the burlesque and the mock-epic is to note that the burlesque makes great things seem small, and the mock-epic makes small things seem great. By this simple distinction Tassoni's poem comes out as a burlesque, Boileau's as a mock-epic. Dryden's *MacFlecknoe* is a rather more difficult case. It makes the small seem great, by elevating dire poets to the status of poet kings. In doing this, of course, the poem also mocks poet kings, because they turn out to be in some respects comparable to dire poets. In some cases, then, mock-epic seems to work both ways, to amplify the insignificant, and to diminish the significant. This duplicity is what lends the mock-heroic its exciting capacity to tear away the bases on which it constructs itself. *MacFlecknoe* seems at once to suggest that there is a poetic dignity to which the works of Flecknoe and Shadwell may be compared, and also that Flecknoe and Shadwell have destroyed the idea of poetic dignity altogether. This is the dark form of mock-heroic, the form of *The Dunciad,* and the classic form of conservative pessimism about the current state of literary culture when compared to classical literary achievements.

This is not, however, the form of mock-epic to be found in *The Rape of the Lock. The Rape of the Lock* does work away at the bases of the forms of literature it parallels and parodies, but in a light and optimistic manner. It warrants its author's generic classification as "heroi-comical." Pope is able to cast some comic light back onto his heroic precedents and see comic potential in earlier heroic works (see Wolfgang E. H. Rudat, "Pope's 'Mutual Commerce': Allusive Manipulation in *January and May* and *The Rape of the Lock*"). Yet he also manages to use the presence of classical literature to suggest an authorial presence that is always aware of the triviality of the action of the poem, and the dangerous triviality of other more public actions in the poem. The kind of author who is aware of the disparity between Clarissa's speech and the incident of the *Iliad* to which it refers is also aware that when "Wretches hang that Jury-men may Dine" (III, l. 22) there is a serious moral problem to be dealt with. Pope is able to imply the seriousness of an appreciation of the supposed moral and literary benefits of an education in classical literature, and to imply the dangerous triviality of his own time in relation to that classical culture, while not forgetting that classical culture can seem ridiculously distant and barbaric or giving in to a purely pessimistic view of the relationship between the ancients and the moderns. In this respect it is an enormously confident poem, quite unlike the later tone of Pope's great satirical and culturally critical writing.

SEX AND SHOPPING

The Rape of the Lock is culturally confident, but it is culturally critical at the same time. Pope presents a lustrous poetic surface, glittering with the choice consumer objects of his day. These objects are described with the metaphorical elaboration, and take on the significance, of the weaponry of classical epic. "Each Silver Vase" on Belinda's dressing table is "in mystic Order laid" (I, l. 122); her cosmetics are called the "various Off'rings of the World" (I, l. 130), as if scents, oils and balsams were created just for her.

> This Casket *India*'s glowing Gems unlocks,
> And all *Arabia* breathes from yonder Box.
> The Tortoise here and Elephant unite,
> Transform'd to *Combs,* the speckled and the white.
>
> (I, l. 133–136)

The tone of such passages is difficult to gauge, and the kind of allusion to classical literature that takes place in them is of great complexity.

England, at the time of Pope's composition of the poem, was an emerging imperial nation. It had trading colonies in America and India, run by such organizations as the East and West India Trading Companies. The activities of these companies, as with all imperial operations, had to be supported by at least the show of force: trade routes had to be defended from competing colonial forces, and land and industries had to be protected from rebellious native inhabitants. If these choice consumer items are seen as the symbols of power over other competing national groups and colonial powers, and at the same time as the trophies of colonial and mercantile success, then it makes a great deal of sense that they should be described as if they bore some resemblance to weaponry and prizes in classical epic. Just as the weapons and prizes in classical epic, they are the symbols of one individual or nation triumphing and achieving dominance over another: the winner in a battle always takes the spoils. Beneath the absurdity of the comparison and mode of description (although make-up might help Belinda produce killing looks, it never helps her actually to kill anybody) there is a genuine correlation between the symbolic position within each culture held by the prize objects in classical epic and the choice consumer objects in Pope's poem.

The comparison, however, remains absurd. It is absurd in an illuminating way. The transformation of elephants and tortoises into combs is unusual, transgressive even. It seems particularly transgressive for its epic synecdoche: only the tusks and shells of the elephant and tortoise get made into combs, whereas the poem makes it sound as if the entire beast were transformed. Pope alludes here to a slightly different kind of classical poem, Ovid's *Metamorphoses,* and the psycho-sexual transformations of people into animals and objects that take place in that poem. Just as, for example, Io was transgressively desired by Jove, and as a result of that desire was transformed by Jove into a cow, so, in Pope's inversion, the animals of distant continents are desired by English consumers and go through weird, perverse transformations in order to supply those consumer desires. Pope points out the absurd difference between contemporary cosmetics and the weapons and prizes of classical epic, but underlying that comparison a symbolic equivalence remains. In comparing the transformation of trade and industry to the metamorphoses of classical myth and poetry, Pope does more to suggest the absurdity of the objects he is depicting: they are the products of perverse, or at least exploitative, forms of desire (many of the transformations of the *Metamorphoses* take place because the desired subject is desired by a more powerful, more manipulative being). The running allusions to

different kinds of classical poetry show Pope developing a critique of the consumer society he depicts. The poem is lustrous and confident, and no doubt enjoys the veneer of the objects it describes, but it also points out that consumer objects can be desired in the wrong way: it is by no means a straightforward paean to imperial consumerism (see Stewart Crehan, "*The Rape of the Lock* and the Economy of Trivial Things," pp. 46–47).

Consumer culture is linked to sex and gender in *The Rape of the Lock* in a number of ways. Many of the consumer items in the poem belong to, or are sought after by women: the "*Amber Snuff-box*" and "*clouded Cane*" of Sir Plume (IV, ll. 123–124) are rare exceptions. The dressing ritual of Belinda and the coffee-drinking ritual that involve so many imported luxuries both represent stages in a covert sexual act. Belinda's dressing is described as the arming of a hero when going into war. Her bending her head over her coffee provides the Baron with the opportunity to cut off the lock, as his drinking coffee had provided him with the daring and strategy to do so. This association of women and sex with consumerism has met some criticism. Belinda, like many other women in early modern literature, has been seen as an object upon which men can project their own desires. Men attribute to women as vanity what is really male desire for the fetishised female form, and the consumer objects that surround and supposedly beautify it. This projection of desire is something Pope would be as guilty of as the Baron. Belinda appears vain in her preparation for the day's amorous battle, but it is really the Baron who desires the lock. Similarly, Belinda forsakes the aid of the sylphs by entertaining a thought of man: Pope implies that she desires the rape in some form or another, that it is what she really wants. He also enjoys making her vocalize one of the most blunt innuendos of the poem when she wishes that the Baron had "been content to seize / Hairs less in sight, or any Hairs but these!" (IV, ll. 175–176) Again, it is implied that Belinda desires the sexual attention of the Baron.

It is far less easy to find signs of Pope occupying a critical stance in relation to the association of women and their sexual desires with consumerism as he did in relation to imperial consumerism itself. Women's sexual desires barely figure in the poem, and when they do, they feature in a conventional or grotesque manner. The women that become sylphs are either prudes or entirely incontinent. Belinda cherishes secret desires for men, and reveals through her language a similarly thinly disguised interest in sex; women in the Cave of Spleen are transformed into empty objects of sexual longing ("Maids turn'd Bottels, call aloud for Corks"; IV, l. 54). As with his description of consumer objects, when Pope deals with sex and gender in the poem, he allows his reader to see beneath the glossy surface of the piece. Unlike the description of those objects, Pope seems less critical and more indulgent of attitudes that have been prime targets in recent literary criticism and scholarship (see for example Ellen Pollak, *The Poetics of Sexual Myth: Gender and Ideology in the Verse of Swift an Pope*). Gender relations are perhaps one of the only topics on which Pope's poem seems to give in to its own veneer. With regard to the other types of context just introduced (occasional, literary or generic, and socio-economic), Pope manages to make arguments and observations on these topics without losing his confident and playful tone.

THE POEM

The title page and dedication to *The Rape of the Lock* allow it to begin its work before it has even begun. To his description of the poem as heroicomical Pope adds, in most versions of the poem, an epigraph adapted from Martial that addresses Belinda: "*Nolueram, Belinda, tuos violare capillos, / Sed juvat hoc precibus me tribuisse tuis*" ("It is not for me, Belinda, to violate your hair, but to rejoice in the praise I have been

asked to give you"). By insinuating that he would wish to be in the position of the Baron, and is not lucky enough to be so, Pope suggests that the lock of hair is a serious prize, and so flatters Arabella Fermor and ridicules his own position as a detached and impotent poet. This is achieved by means of and at the cost of innuendo: the implication that the theft of the hair was a sexual act is being made before the first canto of the poem. If Arabella is to be flattered into acceptance of Lord Petre's transgression, she must give in to the run of sexual allusion and suggestion. Pope is also displaying yet another form of generic awareness. Martial is one of the Latin epigrammatists, practicing brief, witty, and occasionally lewd poetry. He is not epic. Pope widens the scope of his classicizing allusions beyond the epic and hints at his own compact, witty, and occasionally lewd technique in what is to come.

The process of compromising and belittling Arabella in order to flatter her continues in the dedication. Pope explains to her that ancient poets included machinery (that is, gods and supernatural figures who step into the action and take part in the plot) in their poems because they are "in one respect like many modern Ladies; Let an Action be never so trivial in it self, they always make it appear of the utmost Importance." Here the simultaneous belittlement and flattery of the female sex in general and Arabella in particular is paralleled by the simultaneous reverence for and ridicule of the ancient poets. Arabella must consent to being one of the trivial modern ladies if she is to be raised above them by the poem. She is at once belittled and aggrandized, just as the ancient poets are at once belittled and aggrandized by the comparison to the modern ladies. Pope manages to maintain the balance between the ancient and modern, trivial and epic, even in his dedicatory prose. He goes on to poke fun at female vocabulary and reading habits, while maintaining the tone of a flattering dedication. The poem's delicate treatment of dangerously serious topics is well under way by the beginning of the first canto.

CANTO I

In accordance with epic practice, Pope begins his poem with a declaration that should encompass the most important aspects of his subject, as both Homer and Virgil had begun theirs.

> *Achilles'* Wrath, to Greece the direful Spring
> Of Woes unnumber'd, heav'nly Goddess, sing!
> (Homer, translated by Pope)

> Arms, and the Man I sing, who forc'd by Fate,
> And haughty *Juno*'s unrelenting Hate;
> Expell'd and exil'd , left the *Trojan* Shoar;
> (Virgil, translated by Dryden)

> What dire Offence from am'rous Causes springs,
> What mighty Contests rise from trivial Things,
> I sing—
> (I, ll. 1–3)

The ironic inversion Pope achieves is one of technique as much as subject: how can a poet set out his or her vast and important subject matter in his or her opening lines if the subject is trivial? Epic procedure is inverted and maintained. The subject matter is set out; it just happens to be trivial. Pope then rescues his subject from complete triviality by evoking the purpose for which he writes, to serve John Caryll, and praise Arabella, who is now transformed into Belinda.

The main business of Canto I is to introduce the sylphs and to set Belinda about her heroic business. Belinda's guardian Ariel is introduced by a run of consumer objects announcing the morning: a slipper is banged on the floor, a lap-dog rouses itself, a repeating watch is pressed to ring the hour. Ariel attempts to convince Belinda by means of a dream of the reality of visions, sprites, and fairies. Ariel says that the sylphs are better than the conspicuous serving staff and ac-

coutrements used as indicators of importance: "Think what an Equipage thou hast in Air, / And view with scorn *Two Pages* and a *Chair.*" (I, ll. 45–46) The spirits seem to fit into the run of consumer objects and fashion accessories by which they are surrounded, and which they support.

The supernatural characters of the poem, Ariel tells Belinda, are the spirits of dead women, with the foremost characteristics of the woman determining what kind of spirit she becomes.

> The Sprights of fiery Termagants in Flame
> Mount up, and take a *Salamander*'s Name.
> Soft yielding Minds to Water glide away,
> And sip with *Nymphs,* their Elemental Tea.
> The graver Prude sinks downward to a *Gnome*,
> In search of Mischief still on Earth to roam.
> The light Coquettes in Sylphs aloft repair,
> And sport and flutter in the Fields of Air.
> (I, ll. 59–66)

The spirits seem to act in their aerial life in precisely the opposite way to their mortal life: gnomes encourage coquettes, whilst sylphs preserve chastity. The spirits are unnervingly like the real women of Pope's *Epistle to a Lady,* who in old age continue relentlessly to pursue pleasure.

> At last, to follies Youth could scarce defend,
> It grows their Age's prudence to pretend;
> Asham'd to own they gave delight before,
> Reduc'd to feign it, when they give no more:
> As Hags hold Sabbaths, less for joy than spight,
> So these their merry, miserable Night;
> Still round and round the Ghosts of Beauty glide,
> And haunt the places where their Honour dy'd.
> (*Epistle to a Lady,* ll. 235–242)

Old age for the pleasure-loving woman becomes a perverse afterlife. The spirits in *The Rape of the Lock* are part of Pope's sustained attack on the vanity and inconstancy of women. Their relationship to the gods in classical epic is complex. Greek and Roman gods are real gods, and at the same time stand in for virtues or characteristics of the human characters in the poems. So, when Jove tips the scales of Fate one way or another, a real and powerful deity acts; when Minerva is said to appear to Ulysses, a human exercises the capacity (wisdom) that goddess represents. The Homeric gods are real and allegorical at the same time. The spirits only perform the second function, and that ineffectually. When they aid Belinda's appearance her beauty is praised and a joke is made about make-up being a divine aid (I, ll. 145–148). When Umbriel releases the splenetic vapors over the room (IV, ll. 141–142), a supposedly feminine trait is being allegorically represented. The spirits, of course, have no serious theological function in the poem, indeed they are not really *in* the poem at all (see Blanford Parker, *The Triumph of Augustan Poetics: English Literary Culture from Butler to Johnson*, p. 106). The spirits lack reality either as theological or as allegorical forces, and so they reflect Pope's scepticism concerning the theological system of classical epics. The theology of those poems is one respect in which a Christian poet can never entirely admire them, despite the efforts of translators and editors to bend classical belief systems to fit Christian theology. The unreality of the spiritual machinery displays Pope's scepticism about certain aspects of classical heroism and his confidence in his own comedy.

Ariel warns Belinda that something terrible will happen that day, and that she should most "beware of Man!" (I, l. 114) Following this injunction to chastity Belinda is woken by her lap-dog: "*Shock*, who thought she slept too long, / Leapt up, and wak'd his Mistress with his Tongue" (I, ll. 115–116). Ladies' pets are fashion items, and they are also tinged with sexual associations. The Latin poet Catullus and the early sixteenth-century English poet John Skelton both mourned the death of sparrows who were very close to their female owners. Neither shied away from innuendo. It has been suggested that lap-dogs, for fairly obvious reasons, were particularly sexualized (see Felicity A. Nuss-

baum, *The Brink of All We Hate: English Satires on Women 1660–1750*, pp. 140–141). Belinda is told to beware of man and is awoken by a dog. It is not long, however, before she returns to human interests, as the first object her eyes alight upon is a love letter, with which she must have been soothing herself to sleep the night before, and the conventional love language of which drives the dream vision of spirits and chaste thoughts from her head.

The canto closes with one of the most famous scenes in eighteenth-century poetry, Belinda's toilet. The scene imitates the arming of a hero in epic poetry, such as Patroclus in the *Iliad*:

> He cas'd his Limbs in Brass, and first around,
> His manly Legs, with silver Buckles bound
> The clasping Greaves; then to his Breast applies
> The flamy Cuirass, of a thousand Dyes;
> Emblaz'd with Studs of Gold, his Faulchion
>   shone,
> In the rich Belt, as in a starry Zone.
> *Achilles'* Shield his ample Shoulders spread,
> *Achilles'* Helmet nodded o'er his Head.
>   (XVI, ll. 162–169)

Belinda's toilet, as was previously mentioned, is awash with consumer items that complicate the comedy of the mock-epic. The toilet scene also introduces another, scarcer element into the poem, that of Christian moral satire. Belinda's toilet is remarkable for being slightly blasphemous. The vases have a "mystic Order"; Belinda is "rob'd in White"; she regards her reflection as "A heav'nly Image"; the toilet is an altar, her maid an "inferior Priestess," the preparation a rite (I, ll. 121–128). The toilet scene not only continues and heightens the run of consumer objects, emphasizing their absurdity (the elephant and tortoise turned into combs), but also introduces an object from a completely different order of goods into that run of consumer objects: "Here Files of Pins extend their shining Rows, / Puffs, Powders, Patches, Bibles, Billet-doux" (I, ll. 137–138). The Bibles are clearly an incongruous element in a parody of an epic list, and are so for a number of reasons. Obviously Bibles are not cosmetic items, or at least should not be, nor are they part of the armory of modern love. Also, there are several Bibles: one would normally expect just one Bible as a book of serious meditation and reflection. The fact that there is more than one suggests a collection of fashionable objects more for show than use. The criticism of Belinda is serious here. It is not simply funny that her dressing table is both like and unlike the arming of a Greek hero. Her dressing table is also like and unlike the preparation for a religious rite or sacrifice. It is forgivable that Belinda mistakes herself for a hero, but it is not forgivable that she mistakes herself for the object of religious devotion. Her negligence with the Bible indicates a transgression and inversion of a rather more serious nature than anything to do with men or lapdogs.

CANTO II

Belinda is launched onto the Thames to transport herself from London to Hampton Court where she will spend the afternoon. She is described in playful equivocations.

> Her lively Looks a sprightly Mind disclose,
> Quick as her Eyes, and as unfix'd as those;
> Favours to none, to all she Smiles extends,
> Oft she rejects, but never once offends.
> Bright as the Sun, her Eyes the Gazers strike,
> And, like the Sun, they shine on all alike.
> Yet graceful Ease, and Sweetness void of Pride,
> Might hide her Faults, if Belles had Faults to hide:
> If to her share some Female Errors fall,
> Look on her Face, and you'll forget'em all.
>
> (II, ll. 9–18)

Here, as usual when expounding his view of female good humour (see the dedication to this poem and *Epistle to a Lady,* ll. 269–292), Pope gets some way to avoiding the charge of misogyny, even if he cannot clear himself of sex-

ism. Belinda's main fault is inconstancy, but here it is caught up with generosity and sweetness of temper (good humor). Her eyes are "unfix'd," presumably flashing from man to man. They are as bright and as undiscriminating as the sun: her beauty is inextricably linked to her flirtatiousness. The clauses in each sentence hold each other in counterbalance, the complimentary first line of each couplet equivocated and dissipated by the final half line. Each compliment is held in balance with a gentle reproach, and the faults Belinda clearly has are lightly treated. Pope perhaps realized the need for a light touch when he called Belinda a "*Belle,*" a common abbreviation of "Arabella," and so risked violating his claim in the dedication that Arabella resembled Belinda in nothing but beauty. Belinda's faults here really are innocent corollaries of her good qualities.

The Baron is now introduced, already contemplating the rape of the lock. That morning he is said to have raised a sacrificial pyre to the gods to help him succeed in this task,

> to *Love* an Altar built,
> Of twelve vast *French* Romances, neatly gilt.
> There lay three Garters, half a Pair of Gloves;
> And all the Trophies of his former Loves.
> With tender *Billet-doux* he lights the Pyre,
> And breathes three am'rous Sighs to raise the
>   Fire.
>
> (II, ll. 37–42)

This sacrificial pyre preempts one of Pope's later mock-epic moments, the burning of twelve volumes by the Dunce King in honour of the goddess Dullness (*Dunciad*, 1742, I, ll. 155–162). This hint at the Baron's poor reading habits is one of the only suggestions of the intellectual and cultural superficiality that become the characteristic theme of the later mock-epic.

The sound of Belinda's progress along the Thames is sibilant, seductive, and vaguely suggestive of the generally erotic environment.

> But now secure the painted Vessel glides,
> The Sun-beams trembling on the floating Tydes,

While melting Musick steals upon the Sky,
And soften'd Sounds along the Waters die.
Smooth flow the Waves, the Zephyrs gently play,
Belinda smil'd, and all the World was gay.

(II, ll. 47–52)

Still there are equivocations. Belinda has become the most important person in the world, almost controlling the world with her mood. In part her vain satisfaction in her own beauty is being satirized, but there is also genuine praise for her charm. There is a rather stronger equivocation in the reference of the term "painted Vessel." The boat Belinda sails upon is no doubt the first reference, but following the long description of Belinda's face-painting, and the suggestion of her lack of discrimination, she is also a strong candidate. She is also "secure" now but will not be soon as she will meet the scheming Baron. The erotic aura is held in check by equivocation.

Ariel now assembles his spirits and tells them of his concerns in an extended parody of epic speech (Pope later provided an index to the speeches in his translation of Homer). The spirits at this point are at least as much like Milton's angels from *Paradise Lost* as the gods of classical epic. Their physical, or rather metaphysical, appearance is described in ridiculously Latinate terms, parodying one of Milton's characteristic poetic effects, the spirits' existence somewhere between the substantial and the insubstantial also echoing Milton (VI, ll. 328–334). There is a rather more specific and rather more complex allusion to Milton in this speech, which begins with Ariel addressing his spirits thus:

Ye *Sylphs* and *Sylphids*, to your Chief give
        Ear,
Fays, Fairies, Genii, Elves, and *Daemons* hear!

(II, ll. 73–74)

Ariel goes on to explain the hierarchy of the spirits, and that although protecting Belinda may not be as important as protecting a state, it is still quite important. Pope parodies a form of address used by God in *Paradise Lost,* "Thrones, Dominations, Princedoms, Virtues, Powers" (V, l. 601) which he uses to address all the ranks of angels and explain to them that he has invested his Son with extraordinary dignity, making him superior to all the other angels. So far Ariel seems merely a ridiculous parody of God. But Milton himself writes a parody of this line. Satan precisely echoes God's form of address when he attempts to incite the angels to rebellion because of the apparently unfair and arbitrary act of elevating the Son (V, l. 772). The parody of an explanation of divine hierarchy is given a little more seriousness by the fact that Pope is parodying one true and one false explanation of divine law, the false explanation that Satan gives being extremely dangerous, as it leads to the fall of the angels and ultimately to the fall of man.

Ariel's warning of what might happen to Belinda contains some of the confusions of classes of object that occurred when Belinda mixed up the function of Bibles and powder puffs, with a similar moral disapproval.

Whether the Nymph shall break *Diana's* Law,
Or some frail *China* Jar receive a Flaw,
Or stain her Honour, or her new Brocade,
Forget her Pray'rs, or miss a Masquerade,
Or lose her Heart, or Necklace, at a Ball;
Or whether Heav'n has doom'd that *Shock* must
        fall.

(II, ll. 105–110)

There are numerous false equivalences, mostly achieved by zeugma, the technique of making one verb apply to two objects. Here the objects are disparate: the stain in honor is abstract, the stain on brocade concrete, and one is far more serious than the other, but the zeugma attempts to gloss over that difference. The same goes for losing a heart or a necklace. The opening pairing is slightly different. There is a bawdy comparison between the loss of chastity and cracking china. This is not making two unlike things appear similar by yoking them together with a verb, but attempting to gloss over the extreme metaphorical likeness of two actions, disingenuously to suggest that the author did not, and the reader should not, really understand the bawdy joke.

CANTO III

The arrival in Hampton Court widens the social scene of the poem, continuing the false association of objects and actions yoked together.

> Here *Britain*'s Statesmen oft the Fall foredoom
> Of Foreign Tyrants, and of Nymphs at home;
> Here Thou, Great *Anna*! Whom three Realms obey,
> Dost sometimes Counsel take—and sometimes *Tea*.
>
> (III, ll. 5–8)

Affairs of national importance are admitted into the play of mistaking the trivial for the important as some sense of national life enters into the poem: corrupt judges and jury men, new-moneyed merchants. The social satire, however, is far less severe and sustained than that of Pope's later work, Queen Anne's benevolent presence preventing the individual instances of corruption and triviality from being indications of a general decline.

Belinda now meets the Baron in a game of cards known as Ombre, the rules of which Tillotson in an appendix to the poem gives an exceptionally full account of, including an analysis of the game the Baron and Belinda play. The game is an extended parody of the battle engagements of classical epic, including the twists and turns of fate to be found in those battle scenes (III, ll. 65–66). The parallels are continuous and precise: the card table is the battleground (III, ll. 44), troops come from all over the world (III, ll. 47–48), and greater cards are beaten by lesser, as greater heroes sometimes fall to lesser (III, ll. 61–65). The detail of the game is intricate, an intricacy that has led some readers to find allusions in the card game to political events and allegiances in Pope's England (see Howard Erskine-Hill, *Poetry of Opposition and Revolution: Dryden to Wordsworth*). Perhaps the main function of the game in terms of the narrative development of the poem, however, is to provide Belinda with an opportunity for flirtation and hubristic celebration when she wins the game, and an opportunity for the moral Pope to warn against pride even in trivial things.

> Oh thoughtless Mortals! ever blind to Fate,
> Too soon dejected, and too soon elate!
> Sudden these Honours shall be snatch'd away,
> And curs'd for ever this Victorious Day.
>
> (III, ll. 101–104)

There is a Christian moral tone of distrust of the temporal world lurking beneath the comic warning against triviality.

The coffee ritual provides the opportunity for the rape of the lock. The description of the ritual explodes the synecdochic and metonymic language of epic description, elevating to ridiculous generality mundane consumer items: lacquered tables are "Altars of *Japan*"; coffee is a "grateful Liquor" and a "smoking Tyde;" the cups are "*China*'s Earth," as if all of the earth in China went into making them (III, ll. 107–110). The spirits carry on around Belinda, protecting her from scolds and spillages. She is betrayed, however, by one of her own sex. Clarissa, a character who will speak at length later in the poem, offers her scissors to the Baron without any prompt, colluding in an action that goes beyond the accepted limits of flirtation. The Baron's desire is enabled by, and so partly projected onto, Clarissa, as if she shared it. The Baron makes three attempts at cutting off the lock. On the third attempt, Ariel discovers that Belinda is fostering thoughts of "An Earthly Lover" (III, l. 144), and so is unable to continue in her preservation. She is abandoned by her supernatural aid.

The removal of the lock is distinctly eroticized.

The Peer now spreads the glitt'ring Forfex wide,
T'inclose the Lock; now joins it, to divide.
The meeting Points the sacred Hair dissever
From the fair Head, for ever and for ever!

(III, ll. 147–148, 153–154)

Using the Latin word for scissors suggests a euphemism when there is no need for a euphemism, and so creates bawdy, but bawdy of a peculiar kind, in that the phallic symbol the Baron holds seems to resemble female sexual organs far more closely than male. His action seems to be the achievement of a female as much as a male sexual desire, and so either indicates Belinda achieving something she truly desires or the Baron and Pope successfully projecting their desires onto Belinda (see Pollak, p. 101). Yet the rape is bathetic as well as erotic; it leads to a falling off in tone. The repetition of "for ever" to close the couplet and achieve the rhyme is empty and childish. When hair is cut once it is always cut: the permanence of the act does not need pointing out, let alone pointing out twice in the manner of a fairy-tale conclusion. The canto concludes with a recapitulation of some of the confusing comparisons of objects seen at its opening (lap-dogs compared to husbands, broken china suggesting loss of chastity), and with the Baron relishing his victory as if it were as significant as the military conquest of an empire.

CANTO IV

Belinda's resentment of the rape is said to be the result of spleen, a fashionable form of melancholic illness described, for example, by Anne Finch, Countess of Winchilsea in her poem "The Spleen." The spleen is unleashed upon Belinda by Umbriel, a gnome whose name suggests darkness, following a journey to the Cave of Spleen that parodies epic journeys to the underworld (*Odyssey* XI, *Aeneid* VI). Classical journeys of this kind usually involve emotional encounters with dead friends and family, and the hero's acquisition of insights into the future from a prophetic figure. Umbriel merely encounters the serving maids of the queen and various perversely transformed human beings. The queen's maidens, Ill-nature and Affectation (IV, ll. 25–38), are described as if they should be mythological figures, but they are really the most mundane conventional female types, too real to be mythological. The transformed humans are reified versions of the delusions suffered by splenetic melancholics.

Here living *Teapots* stand, one Arm held out,
One bent; the Handle this, and that the Spout:
A Pipkin there like *Homer's Tripod* walks;
Here sighs a Jar, and there a Goose-pye talks;
Men prove with Child, as pow'rful Fancy works,
And Maids turn'd Bottels, call aloud for Corks.

(IV, ll. 49–54)

There is a psycho-sexual element to these transformations, and not just on account of the allusion to Ovid's *Metamorphoses* and the kinds of illegitimate desires that cause physical transformations in that poem. These are just a few of the many vessels and containers in *The Rape of the Lock*—teapots, vases, jars, bottles—the presence of which is a continual reminder of the vacuous, trivial sexuality (both male and female) Pope suggests is the real subject of the poem's satire. Indeed, this critique of trivial sexuality and its serious consequences may well be part of classical epic subject matter: the Trojan war is fought over one woman, because one young man could not control his desire for her (see Carolyn D. Williams, "Breaking Decorums: Belinda, Bays and Epic Effeminacy," p. 70). This critique of misdirected sexuality in both epic and mock-epic may contribute to the common misogynistic bawdy involved in transforming Helen into a bucket, for example (see *The Trophy-Bucket*, p. 16).

Umbriel begs the Queen to touch Belinda with "Chagrin; / That single Act gives half the World the Spleen" (IV, ll. 77–78). Again, as when she smiled on the Thames, what happens to

Belinda happens to the world, but here, rather than being an exemplar of good humour, she is about to be transformed into the type of splenetic woman. The remainder of the canto is taken up in parodies of epic speech before battle. Thalestris speaks first, asking why ladies put so much effort into their appearance if their honor is sacrificed all the same. Her version of honor is surprising.

> *Honour* forbid! at whose unrival'd Shrine
> Ease, Pleasure, Virtue, All, our Sex resign.
>
> (IV, ll. 105–106)

Honor is not the same as virtue, if virtue can be resigned for honor. Thalestris does not seem to see that she is making a false sacrifice, that the honor she seeks is more like reputation or fame, and that she has made an error of value judgement (female honor has already been mocked and devalued in Part I, line 78). Thalestris' chopped logic is reflected in her participation at the end of her speech in the general confusion about the value of people and fashionable pets. She says that she will not allow the Baron to keep the lock until the world goes to ruin and "Men, Monkies, Lap-dogs, Parrots, perish all!" (IV, l. 120). She does not see that people are more important than pets, and that virtue cannot be sacrificed to honor.

After Sir Plume's hilarious attempt at persuasion,

> "My Lord, why, what the Devil?
> "Z-ds! damn the Lock! 'fore Gad, you must be civil!
> "Plague on't! 'tis past a Jest—nay prithee, Pox!
> "Give her the Hair"—he spoke, and rapp'd his Box.
>
> (IV, ll. 127–130)

and the Baron's gloating response, Belinda makes her contribution. Her speech alludes to several traditional poetic topics: contempt for the world, satirical preference for retirement over life at court, and the tragic speech of a defeated hero. Its comedy lies in its gentle travestying of all these types of poetic speech. Belinda's choice of examples continuously undermines her seriousness of tone: she identifies a retired and isolated location as one where people never drink "*Bohea*," a fashionable tea; her idea of a terrible omen is that she dropped her "Patch-box" (a kind of make-up case) three times (IV, ll. 155–164). Her epic speech ends with her walking in apparent innocence into the innuendo that it would have been better to seize any hairs but these. One of Pope's great achievements is that although the points of connection between *The Rape of the Lock* and the epics to which it alludes become so absurd, the magnificence and confidence of Pope's treatment keeps the connections alive.

CANTO V

The Baron does not listen to Belinda, and the floor is open for Clarissa. Her speech is one of the most complex in the poem in terms of allusion and the effect of allusion on tone. Pope added the speech to the poem for the version printed in the *Works* of 1717. He adds in a footnote in editions of his works from 1736 onwards that the speech is "*a parody of the speech of Sarpedon to Glaucus in Homer.*" Pope had translated this episode as early as 1709, and revised that early effort for his complete translation of Homer (*Iliad*, XII, ll. 371–396). Clarissa replaces Sarpedon's obligation to glory with an obligation to good humor. Her argument is that beauty avails little if there is not good sense to preserve it, and good humour to replace it when it has past. Unlike Sarpedon, she is attempting to forestall a battle, rather than encourage the magnanimous contempt for worldly goods and readiness for death that is Sarpedon's objective. There is, however, some kind of magnanimity in Clarissa's speech. The points of connection between her world and Sarpedon's are absurd. She advocates good humour no matter what losses are sustained, recognizing that most of those losses will be trivial. Sarpedon talks of the world as if it were trivial to encourage a heroic attitude, whereas Clarissa's world really is trivial, and she recognizes this to encourage good humor. Pope seems to be advocating poetic good humor in the face of loss. He has no such serious subject as Homer had, and this is a kind of loss, the lost possibility of heroic poetry in an unheroic and trivial world. But Pope, as Clarissa advocates, bears this loss, this recognition of his own triviality, with good humor, and so triumphs over it.

The tone of the passage is of course complicated by the fact that Clarissa gave the Baron the scissors to cut off the lock. However this act is considered—as a jealous betrayal, as complicity in an erotic undercurrent, or as an authorial projection of male desires onto female characters—it mars Clarissa's argument. Her act is hardly good humored. In this light she seems merely to be making a colorable excuse for her actions, abusing the term "good humor" just as "honor" was abused by Thalestris. The argument seems to have validity outside the narrative of the poem, but not within it. Indeed, it gets a hard reception, both Belinda and Thalestris ignoring Clarissa altogether and flying into combat.

The substitutions and inversions involved in the running comparison between the fight over the lock and battles in classical epic are complex and deftly handled. The combatants at Hampton Court are compared not to epic heroes, but to the classical gods when they involve themselves in human battles, amplifying the trivial to yet more absurd extremes (V, ll. 45–52). The epic mode of death, so precisely described by Homer, is transformed to suit the combatants: "A *Beau* and *Witling* perish'd in the Throng, / One dy'd in *Metaphor*, and one in *Song*" (V, ll. 59–60). The deaths are all eroticized, playing on a long-standing use of "death" as a euphemism for orgasm. But they are neither deaths nor orgasms, they are merely trivial mortifications or triumphs in a bizarre and outrageous flirtation. The action moves quickly from single combat to

single combat, ending with Belinda's engagement with the Baron, and the parody of the history of Agamemnon's spear in the form of her bodkin (V, ll. 87–96).

The ridiculous series of objects (rings, a buckle, bells, and a whistle) formerly formed by the metal of this bodkin again introduces bizarre transformations into the epic context. These trivial objects also lead to an unusually direct allusion to *Othello*. The women call for the lock to be restored: "Not fierce *Othello* in so loud a Strain / Roar'd for the Handkerchief that caus'd his Pain" (V, ll. 105–106). *Othello* is a play in which comic devices produce tragic consequences. It is, as it were, the opposite of mock-epic, because it applies the techniques of a lesser genre to the subject of a higher genre. It is a play in which a trivial thing really does have dire consequences, but in which the hero and the play risk becoming ridiculous for that very reason. Pope practices a subtle form of literary comment when pointing out the potential collapse of the tragedy in *Othello*, while at the same time exploiting its serious amplification of the trivial.

The lock is mislaid during the battle, so neither side triumphs. Some wonder if it was sent to the moon, where a list of absurd and inauthentic things are said to be found: "Heroes' Wits," "Courtier's Promises, and Sick Man's Pray'rs," "Cages for Gnats, and Chains to Yoak a Flea; / Dry'd Butterflies, and Tomes of Casuistry" (V, ll. 115–122). Yet Pope declares in the most unconvincing manner that the lock was stellified, as was the lock of Berenice in the poem by Callimachus that survives in Catullus' translation. As the sylphs do not really exist, so the lock is not really stellified: only those with "quick Poetic Eyes" (V, l. 124), that is, a sense of the thorough artifice of the moment, see the lock ascend to heaven. Indeed, the poem closes with a recognition of its own great artifice. Belinda is consoled by being told that even when she is old and can no longer kill with her looks, "*This Lock,* the Muse shall consecrate to Fame, /

And mid'st the Stars inscribe *Belinda*'s Name!" (V, ll. 149–150). Like Pope's other great poem addressed to a woman, *Epistle to A Lady,* the poem closes by making a gift of itself to right all the wrongs seen in the poem. It is an extremely poetically confident end to the piece. Belinda has lost by the occasion; she is clearly more unlike than like the heroes of classical epic, and her world of trivial, fetishized consumer objects has been ridiculed and blamed. She only turns out a winner because of the poem itself, its management of the various contexts—occasional, literary, socio-economic and sexual—with which it deals.

IMPORTANCE AND INFLUENCE

The Rape of the Lock elicited a number of responses from Pope's contemporaries. Firstly it elicited a response from Pope himself, who attempted to preempt objections to the poem on the grounds of his religion or politics by publishing a mock appraisal of the piece, *The Key to the Lock,* under the pseudonym Esdras Barnivelt. Pope's friend Thomas Parnell, who also produced a translation of *The Battle of the Frogs and Mice,* translated part of the first canto of *The Rape of the Lock* into "leonine verse [a Latin verse form with an internal rhyme], after the manner of the ancient monks." His version of the toilet scene adds another layer to Pope's play with the ancients, making the poem sound like a medieval relic that is unwittingly a parody of classical epic. Parnell's translation is a dizzying and curious act of cultural inversion.

John Dennis, a major critic and minor poet and playwright of the time, wrote a series of remarks on *The Rape of the Lock,* which Pope read, recording his reactions to and corrections of Dennis in marginal notes (these are reproduced by Tillotson in an appendix to his edition). Dennis' reaction, as those of other contemporary critics, is mostly a dour failure to recognize Pope's attempts to criticize the ridiculously trivial behavior he presents. It is intriguing to find parts of the first audience of the poem so incapable of recognizing its comic elevation and amplification of the trivial.

A limit has been placed on the literary influence of *The Rape of the Lock* by the ever decreasing popularity of mock-epic. The novelist Samuel Richardson, in naming his great heroine Clarissa, was responding to Pope's poem in some manner (see Thomas Keymer, "Reception, *The Rape of the Lock,* and Richardson"). Byron has long been recognized as the great Romantic inheritor of Pope, but his practice is closer to burlesque romance than Pope's highly pointed and allusive mock-epic. T. S. Eliot perhaps comes closest of the canonical poets of the English language to imitating *The Rape of the Lock.* "The Fire Sermon," the third section of his 1922 poem *The Waste Land,* dwells on the seriousness of trivial attitudes towards sexual encounters, and places such encounters in the context of an ancient literary inheritance in order to highlight how wrong they are. Pope himself, simply by being so successful in both this, his light, and *The Dunciad,* his dark mock-epic, may have contributed to closing the form off for later poets.

Illustrators have been happier to work with *The Rape of the Lock* than fellow poets. Roger Halsband has investigated in great detail the history of illustrations of the poem (including those of its translations). The sustained veneer of the poem, its ability simultaneously to present and to criticize lustrous consumer items and physical charms, as well as its tendency towards the surprisingly if subtly grotesque and transgressive, must make it attractive to visual artists. Indeed, these are some of the best features of the poem, its presentation of complex ideas and arguments with apparently superficial charm. *The Rape of the Lock,* in managing subtly and lightly to present complex arguments about consumer society and the relationship between contemporary and past literature, remains essential to any sense of the enduring concerns of poetry in English.

Select Bibliography

EDITIONS

The Twickenham Edition of the Poems of Alexander Pope. Vol. II, *The Rape of the Lock.* Edited by Geoffrey Tillotson. London: Methuen, and New Haven: Yale University Press, 1940. The standard edition of Pope's poetry with essential annotation and scholarly apparatus. Includes his translations of Homer.

The Poems of Alexander Pope. Edited by John Butt. London: Routledge, 1963. A one-volume digest of the standard edition.

The Rape of the Lock. Edited by Elizabeth Gurr. Oxford: Oxford University Press, 1990. Contains notes, critical commentary and related texts by Pope.

The Rape of the Lock. Edited by Cynthia Wall. Boston, N.Y.: Bedford Books, 1998. Includes very extensive selections of contemporary writings to illustrate the social context of the poem.

SECONDARY WORKS

Barnard, John, ed. *Pope: The Critical Heritage.* London: Routledge and Kegan Paul, 1973. Contains selections from Dennis' response.

Boileau, Nicolas. *Le Lutrin.* Translated by John Ozell. Introduction by Nicholas Rowe. London: R. Burrough et al., 1708.

Brower, Reuben A. *Alexander Pope: The Poetry of Allusion.* Oxford: Oxford University Press, 1959. Classic study of Pope's allusive range and tone.

Butler, Samuel. *Hudibras.* Edited by J. Wilders. Oxford: Clarendon Press, 1967.

Crehan, Stewart. "*The Rape of the Lock* and the Economy of Trivial Things." *Eighteenth-Century Studies* 31, no. 1 (1997–1998): 45–68. Solid and broad account of consumerism and economics in the poem.

Eliot, T. S. *The Complete Poems and Plays.* London: Faber, 1969.

Erskine-Hill, Howard. *Poetry of Opposition and Revolution: Dryden to Wordsworth.* Oxford: Oxford University Press, 1996. On political allusion in the poem.

Garth, Samuel. *The Dispensary.* Introduction by Jo Allen Bradham. New York: Scholar's Facsimiles and Reprints, 1975. Facsimile of an influential poem along with other related texts by Garth.

Grove, Robin. "Uniting Airy Substance: *The Rape of the Lock* 1712–1736." In *The Art of Alexander Pope.* Edited by Howard Erskine-Hill and Anne Smith. London: Vision, 1979. Useful study of the text of the poem.

Halsband, Roger. "*The Rape of the Lock*" *and its Illustrations* 1714–1896. Oxford: Clarendon Press, 1980.

Keymer, Thomas. "Reception, *The Rape of the Lock,* and Richardson." In *Alexander Pope: World and Word.* Edited by Howard Erskine-Hill. Oxford University Press for the British Academy, 1998.

Kinsley, James, ed. *The Poems and Fables of John Dryden.* Oxford: Oxford University Press, 1962. One-volume digest of the full Oxford edition with poems chronologically arranged.

Mack, Maynard. *Alexander Pope: A Life.* New Haven: Yale University Press in association with W. W. Norton, 1985. Compendious standard biography.

Milton, John. *Paradise Lost.* Edited by Christopher Ricks. Harmondsworth: Penguin, 1968.

Nicholson, Colin. *Writing and the Rise of Finance: Capital Satires of the Early Eighteenth Century.* Cambridge: Cambridge University Press, 1994.

Nussbaum, Felicity A. *The Brink of All We Hate: English Satires on Women 1660–1750.* Lexington, Ky.: The University Press of Kentucky, 1984. Informative on the social background of this genre.

Parker, Blanford. *The Triumph of Augustan Poetics: English Literary Culture from Butler to Johnson.* Cambridge: Cambridge University Press, 1998. Interesting study on the machinery of the poem.

Pollak, Ellen. *The Poetics of Sexual Myth: Gender and Ideology in the Verse of Swift and Pope.* Chicago: University of Chicago Press, 1985. Excellent background to the gender debate in the poem with a provocative virtuoso reading.

Rawson, Claude, and F. P. Lock, eds. *Collected Poems of Thomas Parnell.* Newark: University of Delaware Press; London: Associated University Presses, 1989.

Rudat, Wolfgang E. H. "Pope's 'Mutual Commerce': Allusive Manipulation in *January and May* and *The Rape of the Lock.*" *Durham University Journal* 77, no. 1 (December 1984): 19–24. Noting Pope's capacity to introduce levity into classical texts.

Rumbold, Valerie. *Women's Place in Pope's World.* Cambridge: Cambridge University Press, 1989. The best account of the lives of the women Pope wrote for, to, and about.

Tassoni, Alessandro. *La Secchia Rapita: The Trophy-Bucket.* Translated by John Ozell. London: E. Curll, 1713. Translation of the first two cantos.

Virgil. *The Aeneid.* Translated by John Dryden. Edited by Frederick M. Keener. Harmondsworth: Penguin, 1997. A translation Pope greatly admired.

Williams, Carolyn D. "Breaking Decorums: Belinda, Bays and Epic Effeminacy." In *Pope: New Contexts.* Edited by David Fairer. London: Harvester Wheatsheaf, 1990. Good piece on the sexual implications of classical allusion.

Thomas Hardy's
The Return of the Native

PHILLIP MALLETT

THOMAS HARDY HAD a long life, and a long career. Born in 1840, he published his first story, a satirical sketch entitled "How I Built Myself a House," in 1865; his eighth volume of poems, *Winter Words,* came out in October 1928, nine months after his death on 11 January. His work includes fourteen full-length novels, more than forty short stories, and more than nine hundred poems, as well as *The Dynasts,* a three-volume verse epic on the Napoleonic Wars. Since his last novel was published in 1897, and his first volume of poems in 1898, he can be thought of, without too much simplification, as a Victorian novelist and a twentieth-century poet: the contemporary in prose fiction of George Eliot, and in poetry of T. S. Eliot. The critical debate about his achievement is lively and ongoing, but it is generally agreed that five or six of the novels are great works, including the four usually described as "tragic:" *The Return of the Native, The Mayor of Casterbridge, Tess of the d'Urbervilles,* and *Jude the Obscure.* It has taken longer to establish Hardy's status as a poet, partly because the impact of the American modernists T. S. Eliot and Ezra Pound made his more formal, stanzaic poetry seem old-fashioned, but over the past fifty years an increasing number of poets and critics have acknowledged Hardy as the single most important influence on twentieth-century English poetry.

The Return of the Native (1878) was Hardy's sixth published novel, but the first in which it was clear that he wanted to write tragedy. *The Poor Man and the Lady,* his first, unpublished novel, now lost, carried the subtitle "A Story without a Plot"; its episodic structure and sharp social criticism made it unattractive to the publishers, and Hardy was advised to write something with more plot. He did this with a vengeance in his first published novel, *Desperate Remedies* (1871), which has a fire, murder, and an attempted rape, as well as a villain who plays the organ against the background of a thunderstorm. *Under the Greenwood Tree,* published a year later, is as the title suggests a quieter novel about rural life, which traces in the main plot Dick Dewy's only slightly disturbed courtship of Fancy Day, one rung above him on the social ladder, and in the subplot the fate of a band of local church musicians as they are replaced by a cabinet-organ played by the same Fancy Day. Hardy had moved from sensation novel to pastoral, and with *A Pair of Blue Eyes* (1873) he changed direction again to write a romance which incorporates elements of satire and tragedy. While this is an apprentice novel, it anticipates many of the themes of Hardy's later work, including the situation of a woman wooed by several men, each of whom "sees" her in a different way. Hardy's interest in the pressures exerted on women, and in the demands on them to meet male expectations, has been one reason why his work has attracted the attention of a number of feminist critics.

Like most Victorian novels, *A Pair of Blue Eyes* was first published as a serial. While he was at work on it, Hardy was asked to write a novel for the prestigious *Cornhill Magazine*. This was *Far from the Madding Crowd* (1874), again pastoral and again with a literary quotation for its title, but from the outset a more ambitious work, with a darker and deeper exploration of love, and a more thoughtful treatment of rural life (the plot includes the death in childbirth of an unmarried mother, as well as a murder and a mental breakdown). The novel was a success, but Hardy continued to experiment with different kinds of fiction; as he put it, he did not want to write forever about sheep. *The Hand of Ethelberta* (1875) is a novel of social manners, and rather than tragic or pastoral it is primarily comic and satirical, though it touches on many aspects of Hardy's own situation as a writer. Hardy was the son of a mason, at the respectable end of the rural working class, and the rural working world provided him with much of his material as a novelist. Most of his readership, however, came from the urban middle and upper classes, the social group to which his success as a writer was beginning to win him a right of entry. Like Hardy, Ethelberta is a storyteller suspended between classes, though her solution, a cynical marriage into the aristocracy, was not one Hardy could have chosen for himself.

Hardy had written five novels in as many years. The next, *The Return of the Native,* a conscious attempt at high tragedy, marked another change of direction. He sent the first

CHRONOLOGY

1840	2 June: Hardy born in Higher Bockhampton, Dorset (called Mellstock in the novels), the first child of Thomas and Jemima Hardy, some five months after their marriage; followed by Mary (1841–1915), Henry (1851–1928) and Katharine, known as Kate (1856–1940), all of whom remain unmarried.
1848	Enters National School in Lower Bockhampton, then, a year later, Isaac Last's Academy in Dorchester, three miles from his home.
1856	Leaves school to become articled to a Dorchester architect, John Hicks, and later becomes his assistant. Observes the public hanging of Martha Browne for the murder of her husband. Becomes friendly with Horace Moule, eight years his senior, who helps guide his self-education.
1862	Moves to London to work as a draughtsman for the architect Arthur Blomfeld. Attempts without success to publish his poetry.
1863	Is awarded an essay prize by the Royal Institute of British Architects. Possibly engaged to Eliza Nicholls in the period 1863–1867.
1865	About this time begins to lose his religious faith, though he retains an affection for the Church of England and its services.
1867	Returns to Dorset to work with Hicks. Begins a novel, *The Poor Man and the Lady,* but is unable to publish it (it is later destroyed).
1870	While in Cornwall to work on restoration of St Juliot's Church, meets and falls in love with Emma Lavinia Gifford. Dickens dies this year.
1871	*Desperate Remedies* published anonymously, after Hardy advances £75.
1872	*Under the Greenwood Tree* published anonymously.
1873	Suicide of Horace Moule. Publishes *A Pair of Blue Eyes*; decides to give up

architecture to become a full-time writer. (All of Hardy's novels from this date are first published in serial form.)

1874   *Far from the Madding Crowd*, written for the *Cornhill* at the request of Leslie Stephen, with whom Hardy forms a good relationship. This is the novel in which Hardy first uses the term "Wessex;" in later revisions the Wessex names (such as Casterbridge for Dorchester) are systematically embedded in the earlier novels. Marries Emma Gifford; they spend their honeymoon in France, then set up house in London, before returning to Dorset (Swanage) in 1875.

1875   *The Hand of Ethelberta.*

1878   *The Return of the Native.* The Hardys move back to London (Tooting).

1880   *The Trumpet-Major.* Hardy becomes seriously ill, and believes himself close to death; he is unable to work for five months. George Eliot (Mary Ann Evans), with whose early work Hardy's had often been compared, dies this year.

1881   *A Laodicean,* mostly written from his sickbed. The Hardys return to Dorset (Wimborne Minster).

1882   *Two on a Tower.*

1885   The Hardys make their final move, into Max Gate, just outside Dorchester, designed by Hardy himself, and built by his brother.

1886   *The Mayor of Casterbridge.*

1887   *The Woodlanders.* Visit to Italy.

1888   *Wessex Tales,* Hardy's first collection of short stories.

1890   Publishes the essay "Candour in English Fiction," urging the need for greater freedom of expression in the novel.

1891   *A Group of Noble Dames* (short stories) and *Tess of the d'Urbervilles*; the latter is attacked for its supposed indecency.

1892   Death of Hardy's father. *The Pursuit of the Well-Beloved* serialized in the *Illustrated London News.*

1893   Meets and forms an intense friendship with Florence Henniker, the first of a number of close relationships with society women, often with literary interests. Growing estrangement between Hardy and Emma; while remaining at Max Gate, they lead increasingly separate lives.

1894   *Life's Little Ironies* (short stories).

1895   *Jude the Obscure* receives some favorable reviews, but is also fiercely attacked for its frankness and supposed immorality, especially about sexual conduct. This contributes to Hardy's decision to abandon novel-writing. In the same year, he begins to publish the first collected edition of his novels, in 16 volumes, with Osgood, McIlvaine; the revisions made for this edition include many intended to harmonize the representation of "Wessex."

1897   *The Well-Beloved* rewritten from *The Pursuit of the Well-Beloved* and published as a book (volume 17 of the Wessex Novels). Hardy writes no more novels after this date. Visit to Switzerland.

1898   *Wessex Poems and Other Verses,* Hardy's first volume of poems, with illustrations by himself.

1901   *Poems of the Past and Present,* including Hardy's poems about the Boer War (1899–1902).

1904   Part I of *The Dynasts,* Hardy's epic-drama in verse about the Napoleonic Wars. Death of his mother Jemima, perhaps the most significant figure in his life.

1905   Meets Florence Dugdale (1879–1937), his future second wife.

1906   Part II of the *Dynasts*; Part III is published two years later.

1909   *Time's Laughingstock and Other Verses.* In this year T. S. Eliot writes

1910 the first of the poems he will eventually include in his *Collected Poems.*

1910 Receives the Order of Merit from King George V.

1912 Death of Emma (November 27); among other poems of love and mourning, the sequence "Poems of 1912–13" is written over the next few months. The Wessex Edition of Hardy's writings (24 volumes) begins publication.

1913 Revisits Cornwall, the scene of his courtship of Emma. *A Changed Man and Other Tales.* Receives Litt.D. from Cambridge, and made Honorary Fellow of Magdalene College.

1914 Marries Florence Dugdale (10 February); in November publishes *Satires of Circumstance,* which includes his love lyrics about Emma. The outbreak of the Great War in August shatters his confidence in human progress. D. H. Lawrence writes his *Study of Thomas Hardy,* though it is not published in its entirety until 1936.

1916 *Selected Poems,* chosen by Hardy himself. About this time begins work with Florence on what will later be published over her name as *The Early Life of Thomas Hardy* (1928) and *The Later Years of Thomas Hardy* (1930), in an effort to forestall other biographers.

1917 *Moments of Vision and Miscellaneous Verses.*

1922 *Late Lyrics and Earlier,* Hardy's sixth volume of verse.

1923 Hardy begins friendship with T. E. Lawrence. Other visitors in the post-War years include Siegfried Sassoon, Robert Graves, and Edmund Blunden.

1925 *Human Shows.*

1928 11 January: Hardy dies at Max Gate. His ashes are buried at Westminster Abbey, his heart in Emma's grave at Stinsford. *Winter Words,* his eighth volume of verse, is published

posthumously. His brother Henry also dies this year.

fifteen chapters, in a form different from the novel we now know, to a number of different publishers, only to find them reluctant to take on a story dealing so directly with sexual themes, including at least the suggestion of sex outside marriage. Finally, however, it was accepted by the *Belgravia,* where it came out in monthly instalments from January to December 1878, with illustrations by Arthur Hopkins (the younger brother of the poet Gerard Manley Hopkins). Hardy took an interest in these illustrations; he disliked the second, where Eustacia is rather heavy-featured, and sent Hopkins a sketch of her as he himself imagined her, "more youthful in face, supple in attire . . . [and] with a little more roundness & softness"—though he also described her to Hopkins as the "wayward & erring heroine," as opposed to Thomasin, the "*good* heroine" (*The Collected Letters of Thomas Hardy,* p. 52). Hopkins took note, and Hardy was delighted with his illustration for the August issue.

The story as it appeared through 1878 was substantially revised from the version he had first sent out; it was also more closely involved in contemporary Victorian debates, though not quite explicitly, than the earlier novels had been, and its literary affiliations are very openly with tragedy. It has the unity of place which the theorists who had codified Aristotle's *Poetics* had always insisted on, since the entire action takes place on Egdon Heath. "Egdon" is Hardy's name for the many individual heaths in the area around his birthplace near Dorchester. In reality these were small areas of land with soil too poor to produce much more than heather and gorse, but the fictional Egdon is a single heath of indeterminate size—large enough for many of the characters to live their entire lives without ever leaving it—and its atmosphere of hostility towards civilization hangs over the novel. Hardy had wandered the heaths as a boy, and something of the menace they might have had for a young child remains in the completed novel.

Hardy follows the theorists of tragedy again by keeping to a kind of unity of time (not a day, as in the classic theory, but a year and a day), and the main action is covered within a five-book structure, resembling the five acts of a Shakespeare play. There is a further hint of classical precedent in the title of Book V, "The Discovery," which neatly translates *anagnorisis*, Aristotle's term for the central character's recognition of some vital aspect of the plot which had previously lain hidden. In addition, there are numerous allusions to classical myth and literature, especially to the story of Prometheus, who was punished for stealing fire from the gods. Nineteenth-century artists, including Shelley, the poet Hardy most admired, had associated Prometheus with the refusal to accept life's limitations, and the demand for more than life offers. One of the thematic issues in the novel is whether it is heroic, or merely foolish, to make such demands. *The Return of the Native* is a novel which consciously takes a stand towards life, rather than simply following the lives of its characters.

PLOT AND STRUCTURE

Hardy may also have been emulating Shakespeare in having both a main and a subplot. In the former, Eustacia, an impassioned but lonely girl living in the isolated world of Egdon Heath, falls in love with Clym, a native of the heath who has worked in Paris as a diamond merchant. It is the connection with Paris which first draws her to him; she loves him partly because he seems to offer her a chance to escape a life which she finds dull and limited: "To be loved to madness—such was her great desire. Love was to her the one cordial which could drive away the eating loneliness of her days." Clym, however, has become disillusioned with life in Paris, and has

returned with plans to educate the labourers who work on the heath. His determination to stay on Egdon, and hers to leave it, provides one of the sources of conflict in their relationship: each wants something from life which the other despises.

The subplot concerns Clym's cousin Thomasin, the "good" heroine, and her marriage to Wildeve, who has formerly been Eustacia's lover. Also in love with Thomasin is Diggory Venn, a dairy farmer turned reddleman (reddle is a red ochre used to mark sheep), who prowls about the heath watching over her, and intervening whenever he thinks her happiness is threatened. The main plot ends in tragedy, or at least in death and disaster, while the subplot provides a comic resolution, albeit in Book VI, "After-courses." In a note added to the Wessex Edition in 1912 (the edition in which the novel is most often read), Hardy explains that this ending was forced upon him by the need to satisfy his publishers, and that "readers of an austere artistic code" might set it aside. Whatever the truth of this, he allowed this ending to stand in every published edition of the novel, and most readers and critics have taken it as an integral part of the whole.

Clym's mother, Mrs. Yeobright, a widow, is the other central character. She is a proud woman, passionately anxious that Clym should "do well," and hostile to Eustacia in ways that hint at sexual jealousy as well as at a mother's concern for her son's career. The conflict between Clym and his mother, and the ensuing conflict within Clym between filial and sexual love, is another key issue in the novel. While it would be misleading to think of *The Return of the Native* as an autobiographical work, Clym's mother clearly resembles Hardy's in her influence over her son, and the unhappy relationship between Mrs. Yeobright and Eustacia replicates the tensions between Hardy's mother and his wife, Emma, who were barely on speaking terms. In later years Hardy insisted that Clym was "the nicest of all my heroes, and *not a bit like me*," (*The Life and Work of Thomas Hardy by Thomas Hardy,* p. 520); but his denials are rarely to be taken at face value.

The Return of the Native has the kind of narrative complexity usual in Victorian serial fiction, and its full share of intrigues, coincidences and misunderstandings, but its essential structure can be represented by two interlocking triangles, one formed by Wildeve and Clym competing over Eustacia, the other by Diggory Venn and Wildeve competing over Thomasin. There are three kinds of onlooker, who help to shape the reader's attitudes toward the main action. Mrs. Yeobright watches disapprovingly, as her niece Thomasin enters into marriage with Wildeve, and then her son into marriage with Eustacia. The rural workfolk, a poorer, darker-spirited and more backward group than in earlier novels like *Under the Greenwood Tree,* occasionally contribute to the action, carrying (or more often miscarrying) messages and gossip, but like the gravediggers in *Hamlet* or the Porter in *Macbeth,* they have no understanding of the high drama going on around them, and remain essentially untouched by it. Egdon Heath, to which Hardy devotes the whole of the first chapter, and of which we are conscious throughout, is both the scene of the action and a brooding presence behind it, filled, as the narrator tells us, with a "watchful intentness." Such remarks have led many commentators to see Egdon as a character as much as a setting, or as Hardy's equivalent of the gods gazing down at the action of a Greek tragedy, reminding the reader or spectator of the limits set to human happiness or fulfillment.

The narrator can be regarded as a fourth onlooker, drawn not just to record but also to comment, sometimes sympathetically, sometimes ironically, on the characters and their actions, and to reflect on the larger implications of the story. It is the narrator's voice, for example, which tells us in Chapter 7 of Book I that Eustacia has "a grandeur of temper" which we can admire, at least in the abstract, at the same time as we are asked to recognize that it can be dangerous both to its possessor and the wider community, or in Chapter 1 of Book III that the "zest for existence which was so intense in early civilizations" has given way in the nineteenth century to a "view of life as a thing to be put up with." The narrator appears, then, as a guide both to the characters and to the frame of mind, the assumptions about the nature of human life, which we should bring to our reading.

EGDON HEATH

The first chapter of the novel, describing Egdon Heath as "A Face on Which Time Makes Little Impression," is one of the great set-piece descriptions in English fiction, but it is clearly more than a just an account of the setting in which the action is to take place. In his *Study of Thomas Hardy,* written in 1914, D. H. Lawrence identifies Egdon with "the primitive, primal earth, where the instinctive life heaves up." It stands for what Lawrence sees as the universal "struggle into being," the drive to become fully alive, or fully oneself. This drive becomes for Lawrence a kind of moral yardstick; for example, he thinks it is because Clym has a weak life flow that he identifies with the worthy but less vital issues of social reform, rather than with "the strong, free flow of life that rose out of Egdon" which for Lawrence is embodied in the dark, passionate Eustacia.

Lawrence's reading has been influential. It has sometimes been recast in Freudian terms, in which the heath represents the unconscious, the realm of instinct. Such an interpretation accords with the sense the reader has about both Clym and Eustacia that behind their conscious decisions lie motivations that they cannot comprehend; the most potent example is provided by Clym's Oedipal attachment to his mother, his ensuing blindness and his mindless absorption into the heath with which he associates her. (Fittingly, Sigmund Freud, who developed the idea of the Oedipus complex, published his first work in 1895, the year in which Hardy decided to end his career as a novelist.) Other critics have given Lawrence's arguments a more metaphysical turn, and argued that the heath stands for something like the Greek idea of Necessity or Fate: that is, a nonhuman power, usually hostile, which governs human actions. Eustacia gives voice to such a feeling in Chapter 7 of Book V: "How I have tried and tried to be a splendid woman, and how destiny has been against me! . . . I was capable of much; but have been injured and blighted and crushed by things beyond my control!" The narrator, it should be noticed, refuses either to endorse or to challenge Eustacia's outburst; he writes sympathetically of her in this chapter, but in the next, as Thomasin too makes her way across the heath and through the storm, he notes ironically that to her "there were not, as to Eustacia, demons in the air, and malice in every bush and bough. The drops which lashed her face were not scorpions, but prosy rain." Eustacia believes that "destiny" has been against her, but this does not show that Hardy thinks so too.

While Egdon's presence is felt throughout the novel, the first chapter has a particular importance. It begins: "A Saturday afternoon in November was approaching the time of twilight, and the vast tract of unenclosed wild known as Egdon Heath embrowned itself moment by moment." Time and place are mentioned, but not persons; it is only in the second chapter that "Humanity Appears upon the Scene." The date too is unspecific. The sense of time shifts, from this one Saturday afternoon to a generalized present: "The place became full of a watchful intentness now"—every day, at this time, as Egdon begins "its nightly roll into darkness," but also on this particular day, as the heath starts to "awake" and "listen." "Now" is not a date, but the moment when Egdon tells its "true tale," and awakes to listen to its own narrative, as if to learn whether the story that follows is just one of many, or the forerunner of "the final overthrow&rquo; it seems to await. The narrative voice seems impersonal, merely the vehicle through which Egdon tells its story: "It would have been noticed that . . . the white surface of the road remained as clear as ever"—would have been, that is, had there been someone there to notice. The white road opens at the end of the first chapter to allow humanity to appear; in the final chapter of Book V, the dark waters of Shadwater Weir close over two of its representatives. Like other tellers of tales, the heath reveals its character in its story; it has, to use the terms of Hardy's "General Preface" to his work (1912), one of those natures which "become vocal at tragedy." It has "a lonely face, suggesting tragical possibilities"; it exhales darkness; it is the original of our "midnight dreams of flight and disaster"—precisely what it offers, at the close of the story, with the death of Eustacia.

Two kinds of effect follow from this aspect of the first chapter. First, it suggests that the story will have some of the heath's own "grandeur" or "sublimity"; it will not be "commonplace, unmeaning, nor tame." Unlike Flaubert's Emma Bovary, whom in some ways she resembles, Eustacia will not become "vulgar" on Egdon. Despite her hostility to it, she takes her coloring from the heath, at times almost literally, as her "smouldering rebelliousness" and her black hair and dress seem to repeat the reddle beneath the dark surface of the turf. Living abroad as Wildeve's mistress (the future which seems to await her toward the end of the novel), she would have lost her grandeur; drowned on Egdon Heath, her beauty at last finds "an artistically happy background." But this sublime story will also be a tragic one. For a second effect of the opening chapter is to suggest that defeat—flight and disaster—is the inescapable ground of our being, and, accordingly, that the aspiration and rebellion shown by Clym and Eustacia will be in vain. Clym wishes to bring the light of education to his fellow men, Eustacia to enjoy the radiance of romantic love, but living on Egdon, a place which is "a near relation of night," both will see their hopes extinguished in the darkness.

"This is a persuasive but also an incomplete reading. The narrator who gives way to the "watchful intentness" of the heath also makes room for more prosaic observers of it: the furze-cutter, for whom its darkness merely complicates the question of what time to stop work; an antiquarian, who has researched various "intelligible facts" in the Domesday Book, and knows the history and the Latin name of the charters giving the right to cut turf; and another who reflects on the possible future of tourism and on changing ideas of natural beauty. Instead of the inevitability of defeat in life's struggle, these figures imply the possibility of work, investigation, and leisure. Their world is not sublime, nor tragic, but it is not to be despised. Cautiously, moderately, they occupy the heath, and embody the enduring capacities of men and women to come together into a community. What this suggests is that even in the first pages of an ambitiously tragic novel, Hardy was anxious to let the voice and values of the community emerge as one element, and not a negligible one, of the whole. The message is that of Brueghel's picture of Icarus falling from the sky, having flown too near the sun, as W. H. Auden describes it in his poem "Musée des Beaux Arts" (1939):

> how everything turns away
> Quite leisurely from the disaster; the ploughman
>   may
> Have heard the splash, the forsaken cry,
> But for him it was not an important failure; the
>   sun shone
> As it had to on the white legs disappearing into
>   the green
> Water...

Hardy too wants to accommodate the tragic and the everyday into a single fiction, the Promethean aspirations of Clym and Eustacia alongside the smaller world of those who have learned to mend and make do. In the first chapter, the alternative to the "sublime"—that is, the grand or tragic—is said to be the "commonplace," but in Chapter 7 of Book I the antithesis is re-phrased in terms more tolerant of the unheroic: "To have lost the godlike conceit that we may do what we will, and not to have

acquired a homely zest for doing what we can, shows a grandeur of temper which ... if congenial to philosophy, is apt to be dangerous to the commonwealth." Here sublimity is renamed "conceit," and the commonplace is reread as the "homely"—a word which always has a positive resonance for Hardy. So far as the heath invites us to think of tragedy, it allows the central characters their grandeur, but there is also a hint that its preferred form might be "satire": immediately, on human vanity in wearing brightly colored clothes, but more generally on the desire to be exceptional, to seek fulfillment as an individual rather than as a member of the community. *The Return of the Native* is both a tragic and an antitragic novel, both a celebration of and a satire on the demand (in Eustacia's words) for "what is called life."

CHARACTER AND THEMES: THE OPENING MOVEMENT

Book I of the novel, "The Three Women," and Book II, "The Arrival," form a single opening movement, beginning with Thomasin's return, still unmarried, on what was meant to be her wedding day, and ending with Diggory Venn's report to Mrs. Yeobright that her marriage to Wildeve has at last taken place. The intervening chapters trace the recriminations and maneuverings between all the main characters except Clym, who returns from Paris in Chapter 3 of Book II but does not take centre stage until Book III.

One narrative line concerns the extramarital liaison that frightened the publishers. Eustacia is disappointed to learn that Wildeve has not called off the wedding because of his continuing love for her, but while she is still vacillating between pique at his willingness to marry someone else and the renewal of her desire for him now that she has a rival, her interest is caught by the news of Clym's impending return, and she dismisses him. Meanwhile Mrs. Yeobright, who had at first opposed the marriage, is now determined for the sake of Thomasin's reputation that it must go through, and when Diggory Venn offers to renew his courtship of Thomasin she uses this to put pressure on Wildeve to keep his promise to her; like Eustacia, he is unwilling to be outdone by a rival. When he explains that there was nothing more serious behind the postponement of the wedding than a mistake in the marriage license, Mrs. Yeobright responds that "Such things don't happen for nothing." This is perhaps a hint to the reader that Hardy wants to explore his characters' unconscious motivations; later in the novel both Mrs. Yeobright and Clym will make "mistakes" that suggest underlying motives they refuse to admit to themselves.

This pattern of conflict and intrigue suggests two recurring aspects of Hardy's perception of human life: that while men and women have freedom of choice (and he is careful to insist on this), they often choose unwisely; and that where chance operates, it tends to operate to their disadvantage. In an early poem, "Hap" (1866), Hardy writes that while it would be easier to endure unhappiness if we could believe it wished on us by "some vengeful god," the reality is that we are the victims only of chance, or what the poem calls "Crass Casualty." In this novel, as typically in Hardy's fiction, actions rarely have their expected consequences. Diggory's offer to marry Thomasin helps Mrs. Yeobright ensure her marriage to Wildeve; Wildeve believes that his marriage will "punish" Eustacia, but in fact it suits her purpose, by removing Thomasin as a possible wife to Clym; Mrs. Yeobright's determination to bring about the marriage between Thomasin and Wildeve smoothes the path for the one she most fears, between Clym and Eustacia. The classical notion of *hamartia*, the error which leads to the downfall of the tragic hero, extends in *The Return of the Native* to all the main characters.

The opening movement of the novel also introduces the laboring men and women who work and live on the heath. It opens on 5 November, traditionally a night for bonfires; as the narrator notes, "to light a fire is the instinctive and resistant act of man . . . It indicates a spontaneous, Promethean rebelliousness against the fiat that this recurrent season shall bring foul times, cold darkness, misery and death." But as the heathdwellers gather round their fire, their faces grotesquely lit by its flames, their rebellion seems a small and muted affair, which we instantly compare with the solitary bonfire lit by Eustacia ("its glow infinitely transcended theirs"), very much as we compare their stories of love and marriage—Fairways' anxious thoughts on seeing the "terrible black cross" in the register of marriages above where he is about to write his own name, Christian's pathetic attempt at a proposal, memorably dismissed with the words "Get out of my sight, you slack-twisted, slim-looking maphrotight fool"—with the passionate intensity of her desire to be "loved to madness."

Hardy's mainly comic treatment of the heath-dwellers risks seeming to mock or patronize people only a little lower in the social scale than his own family. But there is a darker side to their ignorance and superstition, evident later in Susan Nunsuch's persecution of Eustacia as a witch. Hardy never lost his respect for the skills employed by rural workers, but here the work is solitary, and the community fragmented. Clym returns to Egdon life as a source of strength, but also feels the need to change it; like Hardy himself, he owes his loyalty both to the region and to the idea of a culture that rises above time and place. Rustic life is seen as a series of quirky survivals; the bonfires are likened to the gestures of primitive tribes, the figure of the reddleman has all but disappeared, the mumming is described as in decline—there is even a little essay on the way to distinguish traditional mumming from its revived forms. Even so, Hardy is not without sympathy for the local community. For all their foolishness, they sometimes judge more wisely than their supposed betters—unlike Clym, they recognize that Eustacia will not make a schoolteacher's wife—and for the most-part they act kindly, and come together in moments of crisis. In one of the many ironies of the novel, its closing sentence suggests that Clym needs their generosity more than they need his teaching: "everywhere he was kindly received, for the story of his life had become generally known."

But the dominant figure of the opening chapters is that of Eustacia. At her first appearance, silhouetted against the night sky on top of Rainbarrow, the ancient burial mound, she is displaced by the gathering rustics, yet, as the narrator notes, "the imagination of the observer" clings to her mysterious and solitary figure. The most extended account of her, in Chapter 7 of Book I, "The Queen of the Night," establishes her as an exotic presence on Egdon, both unsettled and unsettling. She evokes thoughts of "roses, rubies, and tropical midnights"; she is driven by "love, wrath, and fervour"; she has the same disdain for the ordinary human life around her as a classical goddess. But this is only one aspect of her presentation. Her demand for "music, poetry, passion, war" is, after all, that of a girl with no experience of the world outside Egdon, and there are times when she seems merely foolish or selfish, a bored, lonely girl living in an isolated spot with too little to do. These two perspectives on Eustacia, as a passionate woman whose life is being wasted away on Egdon, and as a young girl who persists in imagining an ideal life which cannot exist, are kept in play throughout the novel.

The "Queen of the Night" chapter also sets out one of the main thematic oppositions of the novel: briefly, between passion and duty, but more fully between "Hellenism" and "Hebraism," as these terms were used by Victorian writers like Matthew Arnold and Walter Pater. Arnold's *Culture and Anarchy* (1869) opposes a Hellenic (and therefore pre-Christian) "spontaneity" and delight in beauty, especially the beauty of the human body, to a Hebraic and Christian "strictness of conscience" which emphasizes the life of the mind. Hellenism celebrates light and joy; Hebraism is somber and ascetic. It is easy here to see a parallel to the contrast between Eustacia, who prefers "a blaze of love, and extinction" to the tedium of lifelong fidelity, and Clym, who has turned his back on the "glittering splendours" of Paris and committed himself to "high thinking" and "plain living." Indeed, Eustacia's desire for "life" at any cost, so long as it is intense, echoes the argument of the conclusion to Pater's *The Renaissance* (1873), that our goal should be passionate experience itself, and not the wisdom which supposedly comes from experience: "To burn always with this hard, gemlike flame, to maintain this ecstasy, is success in life."

Pater suppressed this passage in the second edition of his work, fearing that it might be morally dangerous. It certainly runs counter to both Clym's emphasis on duty, and the traditional values of the Egdon community, as these are reflected in the mumming episode in Book I. It is appropriate that Eustacia's role in this scene is that of the infidel Turkish Knight, who dies at the hands of Saint George, the representative of Christian morality; there have been many critics ready to side with Saint George, or at least with Clym as his Victorian equivalent, and to berate Eustacia for her indifference to the cause of social reform. But as the comparison with Arnold and Pater helps to show, Hardy was exploring different attitudes to life, and not simply the clash between two personalities.

CHARACTER AND THEMES: EUSTACIA AND CLYM

From the first Hardy suggests that Eustacia's desire for "a blaze of love, and extinction" might be sadly prophetic. After hearing Clym's voice for the first time, she dreams:

> She was dancing to wondrous music, and her partner was the man in silver armour ... Suddenly

these two wheeled out from the mass of dancers, dived into one of the pools of the heath, and came out somewhere beneath into an iridescent hollow, arched with rainbows. "It must be here," said the voice by her side, and blushingly looking up she saw him removing his casque to kiss her … At that moment there was a cracking noise and his figure fell into fragments like a pack of cards.

The dream of a transcendent love is cancelled almost before it begins. What Eustacia wants is not available to her; neither Clym nor Wildeve will play the knight in shining armor and rescue her from the heath, and there is nobody else to whom she can turn.

A series of descriptions of Clym's appearance, beginning in Book II, Chapter 6, give the reader information enough to understand both that he and Eustacia will be drawn to each other, and that their relationship is bound to fail. If her beauty recalls the Hellenic past, Clym's appearance seems to foretell the future, when (the narrator suggests) the faces of men and women will bear the marks of long and painful thought, and physical beauty will have become an anachronism. In both his poems and his nonfictional prose, Hardy explored the idea that the development of the human capacity to think and feel was an evolutionary error, which made men and women aliens in an unconscious universe. It is this conviction that lies behind the narrator's reference here to the "mutually destructive interdependence of spirit and flesh." Both spirit and flesh need to be fed with what the narrator calls "the oil of life," but the strain of trying to meet these two opposing demands is already evident in Clym's worn features. If consciousness is a burden, as Hardy seems to believe, in Clym it has grown morbid; even before he meets Eustacia, he is being destroyed from within by his own divided nature.

The love between Clym and Eustacia develops swiftly, as is often the case in Hardy's fiction. Love, for Hardy, is rarely the outcome of a gradually deepening knowledge of the other person; it is almost always precipitate, involuntary, and intensely subjective. More often than not, it is a delusive process, based on fantasy. Eustacia begins to love Clym "chiefly because she was in desperate need of loving somebody:" because, in other words, the alternative is the dreariness of not being in love. Clym hardly has a better reason for loving Eustacia, and as his mother warns him he has good reasons not to do so; yet, when they meet on the heath in Book III, Chapter 4, within three months of their first sight of each other, they embrace "without a single utterance, for no language could reach the level of their condition." They are, in a word Hardy often uses in his poetry, rapt, entirely caught up in each other. But the episode is full of ominous overtones. Immediately beforehand Clym has been gazing at the moon, a traditional image for an ideal longing:

> More than ever he longed to be in some world where personal ambition was not the only recognised form of progress—such perhaps as might have been the case at some time or other in the silvery globe then shining upon him … While he watched the far- removed landscape a tawny stain grew into being on the lower verge: the eclipse had begun … Yeobright's mind flew back to earth; he arose, shook himself, and listened … the shadow on the moon perceptibly widened … a cloaked figure with an upturned face appeared at the base of the barrow…

Clym's fantasy of life on "a silvery globe" is interrupted as the eclipse begins and, at the same time, Eustacia arrives to meet him, as if she herself were "a tawny stain" darkening his hopes. The scene offers a parallel to Eustacia's dream, in which a knight in silver armor—in effect, a "cloaked figure" of Clym—collapses into fragments. Neither can fulfill the other. Despite the passion of their embrace, Clym is already uneasy at the clash between his aims and Eustacia's, and at his mother's hostility to their relationship: "as his sight grew accustomed to the first blinding halo kindled about him by love and beauty Yeobright began to perceive what a strait he was in." The sentence might stand as a summary of Hardy's view of romantic or passionate love: in its first, subjective phase, love radiates light, but the radiance gradually gives way as the objective realities to which the lover has been temporarily blind force themselves back into the reckoning. "You are blinded, Clym," Mrs. Yeobright tells her son; Clym himself, at his last meeting with Eustacia, when his sight has literally begun to fail, says he was "bewitched."

Love also burns—as the moth tossed into Eustacia's room by Wildeve burns in the candle flame—or, as it does between Clym and Eustacia, it burns itself out. The "absolute solitude" in which they spend the early days of their marriage intensifies their love, "yet some might have said that it had the disadvantage of consuming their mutual affections at a fearfully prodigal rate." They themselves come to think so: "'Yes, I fear we are cooling—I see it as well as you,' [Eustacia] sighed mournfully. 'And how madly we loved two months ago! . . . Who could have thought that by this time my eyes would not seem so very bright to yours, nor your lips so very sweet to mine?'"

There is of course good reason for their unhappiness. Clym's intense study in preparation for his proposed career as a teacher has damaged his sight, and he has taken up menial work as a furze-cutter, leaving Eustacia on her own in a cottage on a remote part of the heath; even when he returns from work, he falls asleep on the floor in the middle of the day. Hardy's treatment of this part of his narrative is complex. Clym bears up well under his affliction; the narrator reports approvingly that he "was an absolute stoic in the face of mishaps which only affected his social standing." But our readiness to admire his very un-Promethean acceptance of defeat is modified a few pages later, when we are told:

A forced limitation of effort offered a justification of homely courses to an unambitious man, whose

conscience would hardly have allowed him to remain in such obscurity while his powers were unimpeded.

In short, Clym is relieved that he no longer has to make the effort to succeed as a teacher; his near-blindness allows him to abandon a plan in which he was already losing faith. His is a psychosomatic illness: literally, a consequence of the interdependence of flesh and spirit (the word derives from the Greek *psyche,* or soul, and *soma,* or body), as Clym's body becomes the site in which his mental and emotional distress makes itself felt.

But there is a further implication of Clym's failing sight. Throughout the narrator insists on the deep affinity between Clym and his mother; their conversations, even their quarrels, are "as if carried on between the right and the left hands of the same body." So deeply does Clym feel this that when he returns to the house after kissing Eustacia, he feels as if his mother will ask him, "What red spot is that glowing on your mouth so visibly?" There is here a sense of guilt we might more readily expect of an unfaithful lover to a spouse than a son to his mother. When Mrs. Yeobright jealously tells Clym that he is giving up his soul to please a woman, he agrees: "And that woman is you." The suggestion that Clym's relation with his mother is disabling to his role as a husband is taken forward when Eustacia dances with Wildeve at the gipsying, as she feels a "sudden rush of blood," and the atmosphere of "arctic frigidity" she has recently known with Clym changes to "tropical sensations" of excitement. When she tells Wildeve that her husband is "not ill—only incapacitated," there is at least a hint that his sexual capacity has failed along with his sight.

Even a reader suspicious of modern psychological interpretations might recall at this point Freud's suggestion that blindness can substitute for castration, as in the Oedipus story. After his mother's death, Clym's need to punish himself is described in terms which suggest an act, like that of Oedipus, of self-blinding; his eyes are "lit by a hot light, as if the fire in their pupils were burning up their substance." When he learns that Eustacia had played a part in her death, albeit unwittingly, the reference to the Oedipus story is explicit:

> The pupils of his eyes, fixed steadfastly on the blankness, were vaguely lit with an icy shine; his mouth had passed into the stage more or less imaginatively rendered in studies of Oedipus.

In the earlier editions of the novel, the reference was to another classical figure, Laocoön; the reference to Oedipus came in a revision of 1895, as if Hardy were himself uncovering new aspects of his own meanings in the story. We might apply to Clym's blindness the words Mrs. Yeobright used to Wildeve: "Such things don't happen for nothing."

CHARACTER AND THEMES: THE TRAGIC CONCLUSION

The sequence of events leading up to the death of Mrs. Yeobright, and thence to Clym's angry denunciation of Eustacia, is typically complex. In Book III, Chapter 7, despite her refusal to attend her son's wedding, Mrs. Yeobright determines to make a first step toward reconciliation, by sending him and Thomasin fifty guineas each. Recklessly, she chooses Christian Cantle as her messenger, with the predictable result that the money is misdelivered. First Christian loses it all by gambling with Wildeve; then, in the following chapter, Diggory Venn wins it back, in one of the many night scenes in the novel—lit, in this case, by the glowworms the men collect to allow them to play out the game. Unaware of Mrs. Yeobright's intention that the money should be divided between her son and her niece, Venn gives it all to Thomasin. The reader might wonder if Mrs. Yeobright's error in entrusting the money to the obviously unreliable Christian is another of those things that "don't happen for nothing." Still hurt and angry, she chooses a means to heal the breach

which serves only to widen it, and to cast herself in the role of the loving but rejected mother—precisely the role, as it turns out, in which she can be most destructive toward Eustacia, her rival for her son's affection. Chance here, as often in Hardy's fiction, acts as a metaphor for unrecognized motives.

In the first chapter of Book IV, Mrs. Yeobright compounds her error, and increases the likelihood of further quarrels, when she demands to know if Eustacia has received money from Wildeve. Eustacia's outrage stems in part from the fear that her previous liaison with Wildeve might be coming back to haunt her, but to ask such a question, with no explanation why, is clearly provocative. None of this, however, detracts from the reader's engagement with the elderly widow on her fatal journey across the heath on a blazingly hot August day, in a last, unavailing attempt to speak with her son; nor should it, for the closing chapters of Book IV are among the finest in the novel.

On her way, she pauses to observe the life in the tepid water of a nearly dried pool, in which "the maggoty shapes of innumerable obscene creatures could be indistinctly seen, heaving and wallowing with enjoyment." What the characters see, in a Hardy novel, usually reveals something about their state of mind: here, perhaps, a mother's concern at her son's relationship with "a voluptuous, idle woman." The passage is followed by others in which the life of plants, birds, and insects on Egdon serves as a commentary both on the life of the human actors in the novel and on human life in general. Mrs. Yeobright finds herself following a furze-cutter who is no more distinguishable from the scene around him "than the green caterpillar from the leaf it feeds on," only to realize that the man she has been regarding as "of no more account in life than an insect" is Clym himself, his life too apparently reduced to meaninglessness. When she reaches his cottage, she sees the wasps among the fallen apples in the garden, "rolling drunk with the juice," and "stupefied by its sweetness," as, to her mind, Clym has been stupefied by Eustacia.

On her return journey, physically exhausted, and embittered by what she supposes to be Clym's refusal to admit her—Eustacia, embarrassed by a visit to the cottage from Wildeve, hears Clym say "Mother" in his sleep, and assumes, wrongly, that he has wakened and opened the door to her—she pauses to rest. In front of her, a colony of ants makes its way across the path, "a never-ending and heavy-laden throng," as restless and enduring as human history, yet wholly indifferent to it. Leaning back, she looks up at the sky:

> While she looked a heron arose on that side of the sky, and flew on with his face towards the sun. He had come dripping wet from some pool in the valleys, and as he flew the edges and lining of his wings, his thighs, and his breast, were so caught by the bright sunbeams that he appeared as if formed of burnished silver. Up in the zenith where he was seemed a free and happy place, away from all contact with the earthly ball to which she was pinioned; and she wished that she could arise uncrushed from its surface, and fly as he flew then.

The appearance of the heron, silver against the sun, recalls Eustacia's knight in silver armor, and Clym's silver moon. Mother, son, and wife, behind the passions and antagonisms that bind and divide them, all dream of an escape from their earth-bound lives; each of them imagines a world elsewhere, "a free and happy place," but sees no means to reach it.

The scene of Mrs. Yeobright's death, from the bite of an adder, though powerful, suffers from Hardy's attempts to meld different areas of reference, and different kinds of writing. Much of the conversation between the rustics who have gathered to help is broadly realistic, as is their attempted remedy. As Hardy was to write in the "General Preface" of 1912, "things were like that" in those southwestern counties of England to which he gave the name Wessex: "the inhabitants lived in certain ways, engaged in certain occupations, kept alive certain customs, just as

they are shown doing in these pages." But he was never content to be merely a realist, and other aspects of the scene depart from realist conventions. Christian's reference to "the old serpent in God's garden, that gied the apple to the young woman with no clothes," evokes the story of the Fall, with Eustacia in the role of Eve. Mrs. Yeobright's question to herself—"Shut out! . . . Can there be beautiful bodies without hearts inside?—recalls the question asked by Shakespeare's King Lear, after he has been driven out by his daughters onto the same Wessex heath: "Is there any cause in nature that makes these hard hearts?" (*King Lear*, III.6). The reader might suspect that Hardy is trying to load the scene with more significance than it can bear; in his later novels, he was more subtle in his attempts to move between realist and nonrealist modes of writing.

There is a similarly awkward mixture of tones when Clym confronts Eustacia with his suspicion that she is involved with another man: his "Can you read, madam? look at this envelope" is a clear echo of Brachiano's "Can you read Mistresse? looke upon that letter" in John Webster's play *The White Devil* (IV.2), and only one of many parallels between the two scenes. Not surprisingly, the language which was effective in a play written in 1612 reads awkwardly in a novel of 1878; the effect, whether Hardy wished it or not, is to make Clym's emotions seem forced and unreal. The end of the scene, however, is compelling. Eustacia is so distressed that she cannot tie the strings to her bonnet. Clym, momentarily forgetting his anger, moves to help her; she lifts her chin, and waits. Still half-blind, he is now near enough to see and be moved by her beauty and her unhappiness, but "he turned his eyes aside, that he might not be tempted to softness." He does not see her alive again.

Eustacia's separation from Clym, after this quarrel, leads into the final train of events in the tragic plot. As elsewhere in the novel, the action is driven partly by chance, partly by unwise decisions. Charley, the stable lad who adores

Eustacia, thinks to cheer her by lighting a bonfire; Wildeve mistakenly thinks it is a signal to him to visit her, and their conversation leads to his proposal that they should leave the heath together. Meanwhile, urged on by Thomasin, Clym has relented enough to write a letter asking Eustacia to return, but he delays sending it, and she leaves to join Wildeve without knowing he has written—though the narrator insists that by then it would have had no effect.

It is in every sense too late for Eustacia: she cannot return to Clym, nor can she bring herself to live with Wildeve as his mistress; she has no money of her own. Even the weather is against her: "Never was harmony more perfect than that between the chaos of her mind and the chaos of the world without." The woman who was first seen standing on the top of Rainbarrow, outlined against the sky, now ceases "to stand erect, gradually crouching down under the umbrella as if she were drawn into the Barrow by a hand from beneath." Meanwhile, unknown to her, Susan Nunsuch is melting a wax effigy of her in a cottage nearby. The suggestion is not that Susan's voodoo is effective: rather, that one of the many antagonistic forces Eustacia has to face is that of a community which regards the passionate or exceptional woman as a witch.

Eustacia speaks her last words, crouched down on the heath, in Book V, Chapter 7: "O, how hard it is of Heaven to devise such tortures for me, who have done no harm to Heaven at all!" In the following chapter Clym, Diggory Venn, and Thomasin begin to search for her; in the next, Chapter 9, they are joined by Wildeve—the only time he and Clym come properly face to face—only to hear the sound of her fall into the weir. Whether her death is by accident or by suicide is left unclear. The map Hardy drew for the 1878 edition of the novel shows that she would have had to cross a road to reach the weir; as we are told of her skill in finding her way on the heath even in the dark, this seems to suggest suicide, but this kind of detective work may not be appropriate: if Hardy had wished to provide conclusive evidence, he

could have found the means to do so. The uncertainty invites the reader to consider again one of the issues which has existed throughout the novel: Is Eustacia to be seen as a tragic heroine, as her last words seem to claim, or as a foolish and inexperienced girl, whose final action, like so many others in her life, brings harm to herself and trouble to those around her?

However that question is answered, the description of her, laid out in death, seems to call for the reader's sympathy:

> The expression of her finely carved mouth was pleasant, as if a sense dignity had just compelled her to leave off speaking ... Her black hair was looser now than either of them had ever seen it, and surrounded her brow like a forest. The stateliness of look which had been almost too marked for a dweller in a country domicile had at last found an artistically happy background.

Here at least there is nobody to persecute her as a witch, or describe her as "a voluptuous, idle woman." The grandeur she has always desired is granted her in her death.

"AFTERCOURSES": THE COMIC RESOLUTION

Book VI, "Aftercourses," has two functions: it provides an account of Clym in the months following the deaths of his mother, Eustacia, and Wildeve; and it allows Diggory Venn to return to claim Thomasin as his wife, and to rejoin the "commonwealth" of those who do with a "homely zest" what they can.

Clym is anxious only to make his peace with the dead. For a time he considers proposing to Thomasin, but only because it had been his mother's wish, and he is relieved when Venn reappears as her lover. He does not attend the wedding, and his presence is not missed. His future is as an open-air preacher and lecturer "on morally unimpeachable subjects," expressing the opinions "common to all good men." Whatever had been exceptional in Clym has now been absorbed in the conventional; he has become, as D. H. Lawrence puts it, impatiently, "a mere rattle of repetitive words." It is the pathos of his story, not any wisdom it has brought him, that earns him an audience.

Diggory Venn, in his new character of prosperous dairyman, has also become conventional, even faintly embarrassing in his role of devoted suitor. But the reader might note that this is his fourth dramatic return to Egdon, beginning with Book I, Chapter 2, when he brings Thomasin home in his van. He appears again to win back the guineas from Wildeve, and once more, after "a long stay away," in the second chapter of Book V, when his conversation with Clym leads to the latter's "discovery" of the circumstances of his mother's death. Despite his status as a minor character, Venn's role as the wandering reddleman is an important one in the novel.

Venn's occupation, with its strange consequence that his skin and clothes are dyed red, is given partly because Hardy wanted to record a way of life more or less obsolete when the novel was written, but there is evidently more to it than this. Among the words used to describe him are "isolated" and "weird"; the associations that gather round him make him seem almost to emanate from the heath. It too is described as "obsolete," and Venn lives in its hollows (Johnny Nunsuch tumbles into one); the heath is "Ishmaelitish," reddlemen are linked with Cain; concealed under two pieces of turf to spy on the meeting between Wildeve and Eustacia, he could be said to enact its "watchful intentness." If Egdon is the "original" of our "midnight dreams of flight and disaster," the "blood-coloured" figure of the reddleman is "the sublimation of all the horrid dreams which had afflicted the juvenile spirit since imagination began." His face, like Egdon's, is one on which time "makes but little impression"; he sits unobserved in the Quiet Woman Inn, and plays his game of dice impassively, "like an automaton." Blood-colored or fire-colored, he plays a part in many of the key events in the novel.

Like the heath itself, he suggests different and opposing responses. On one level, he is merely Thomasin's lover, resolved to protect her happiness, even if that means keeping Wildeve at home with her, and himself on the margins of her life. In pursuit of this goal, he is indifferent to what happens to anyone else. On another level, he acts as a catalyst for a series of disasters and misfortunes. He restores Thomasin's guineas after the gambling scene on the heath, but his error in sending none to Clym frustrates Mrs. Yeobright's efforts to heal the breach between them. His "rough coercion" deters Wildeve from visiting Eustacia at night, but persuades him to call during the day; consequently, Wildeve is present when Mrs. Yeobright calls, Eustacia is afraid to answer the door, and Mrs. Yeobright is forced to turn back across the heath. He tells Clym that his mother was making a friendly visit, and thus sets in train the events that lead to Eustacia's departure from her husband, and eventually to her death. In these ways Venn comes to embody all that seems irrational in the nature of things, unamenable or resistant to the human will: those chances which, like Eustacia, we sometimes feel as hostile, even though in more scrupulous moments we regard them as neutral or indifferent.

To view Venn as epitomizing the casually cross-purposed character of our lives is to pull the novel away from Eustacia's sense of the world as "fearfully malignant." This, at least, is where we are led if we attend only to Venn's deeds and actions, that is, to the plot of the novel. If, however, we allow the emphasis to fall on his "sinister redness" and on the images which link him to the heath, Eustacia's despairing cry—"O, the cruelty of putting me in this ill-conceived world!"—seems more justified. That the firelight from Susan's cottage lights her like "a figure in a phantasmagoria" recalls the lurid lights associated with his presence; her raking aside the "dark and dead" ashes of her turf fire to reveal "a glow of red heat" underneath, as she melts her wax image of Eustacia, suggests his concealment of himself, red beneath the dark turf, to spy on her lovemaking with Wildeve. The suggestion that she seems "drawn into the Barrow by a hand from beneath" disturbingly recalls his living in its hollows. He pulls Clym from the weir, but is too late to save Eustacia. Without wishing to be so, by attracting Wildeve's affections away from Thomasin, Eustacia has become Diggory's enemy. Though they speak together only once, the reader feels his presence as a threat to her.

On a realist reading of the novel, Venn clearly cannot have intended the results his interventions achieve—the destruction of the three people (Eustacia, Wildeve, and Mrs. Yeobright) who stand between him and Thomasin. But as suggested above, Hardy constantly moves beyond realism to try to reveal moods, thoughts and motives which remain hidden to the characters themselves. Hardy's unpublished first novel was *A Story without a Plot.* Plot tells us what happened; the poetry—in the case of a novel, the pattern made by the allusions, images, passages of description—tells us how it feels to be alive in the world. It is the poetry of *The Return of the Native* which makes it a great novel.

_____

Select Bibliography

EDITIONS

Like most of Hardy's novels, *The Return of the Native* exists in a number of forms. The most significant are: the first serial publication (in the *Belgravia,* running from January to December 1878); the first volume edition (also 1878); the text prepared for Osgood, McIlvaine, *Collected Edition* of 1895; and the text prepared for the Wessex Edition, published by Macmillan, in 1912. The Wessex Edition is that most often adopted for modern editions of the novel; citations in this essay are from this text.

The Return of the Native. Edited by Phillip Mallett. New York: W. W. Norton, 2003. The Norton Critical Edition is based on the Wessex Edition of 1912, with information about variant readings. It is extensively annotated, with a considerable amount of background and contextual material, and includes a wide selection of critical comment from 1878 to the present.

The Return of the Native. Edited and with an introduction by Derwent May. London: Macmillan, 1974. This New Wessex Edition uses the text of 1912; it is helpfully annotated. Like the Norton Critical Edition, it has the advantage that most critical discussions refer to the text of 1912, except where there is a specific reason not to do so.

The Return of the Native. Edited and with an introduction by Simon Gatrell, and with explanatory notes by Nancy Barrineau. Oxford: Oxford University Press, 1990. This edition for the World's Classics series takes as its copy-text the surviving manuscript of the novel, used by the printers of *Belgravia.* It includes the revisions made during 1878, including those for the first volume edition, but relegates later revisions to a note. The punctuation is based on Hardy's manuscript, rather than on the house-style adopted by the printers.

The Return of the Native. Edited and with notes by Tony Slade, and with an introduction by Penny Boumelha. Harmondsworth: Penguin Books, 1999. This edition for Penguin Classics takes as its copy-text the three-volume edition of the novel published in 1878 by Smith, Elder, and again rejects Hardy's later revisions. Like the World's Classics edition, it has the advantage that it gives the text that Hardy's first reviewers saw, and not the one he prepared in 1912, thirty-four years after the novel was first published.

OTHER WORKS BY HARDY

The Collected Letters of Thomas Hardy. Edited by Richard Little Purdy and Michael Millgate. 7 vols. Oxford: Clarendon Press, 1978–1988.

The Personal Notebooks of Thomas Hardy. Edited by Richard H. Taylor. London: Macmillan, 1979.

The Life and Work of Thomas Hardy by Thomas Hardy. Edited by Michael Millgate. London: Macmillan, 1984. This is an edited version of the volumes originally published over the name of Florence Hardy as *The Early Life of Thomas Hardy 1840-1891* and *The Later Years of Thomas Hardy 1892–1928,* but long known to have been mainly written by Hardy himself.

The Literary Notebooks of Thomas Hardy. Edited by Lennart A. Björk. 2 vols. London: Macmillan, 1985.

Thomas Hardy's Personal Writings. Edited by Harold Orel. New York: St Martin's Press, 1990.

SECONDARY WORKS

Bayley, John. *An Essay on Hardy.* Cambridge: Cambridge University Press, 1978.

Beer, Gillian. *Darwin's Plots: Evolutionary Narrative in Darwin, George Eliot and Nineteenth-Century Fiction.* London: Routledge & Kegan Paul, 1983; rev. ed., 2000.

———. *Open Fields: Science in Cultural Encounter.* Oxford: Clarendon Press, 1996.

Benvenuto, Richard. "*The Return of the Native* as a Tragedy in Six Books." *Nineteenth-Century Fiction* 26, no. 1 (1971): 83–93.

Benway, Ann M. B. "Oedipus Abroad: Hardy's Clym Yeobright and Lawrence's Paul Morel." *Thomas Hardy Yearbook* 13 (1986): 51–57.

Boumelha, Penny. *Thomas Hardy and Women: Sexual Ideology and Narrative Form.* Brighton: Harvester Press, 1982.

Brooks, Jean R. *Thomas Hardy: The Poetic Structure.* London: Elek Books, 1971.

Bullen, J. B. *The Expressive Eye: Fiction and Perception in the Work of Thomas Hardy.* Oxford: Clarendon Press, 1986.

Crompton, Louis. "The Sunburnt God: Ritual and Tragic Myth in *The Return of the Native.*" *Boston University Studies in English* 4 (1960): 229–240.

Daleski, H. M. *Thomas Hardy and Paradoxes of Love.* Columbia: University of Missouri Press, 1997.

Dalziel, Pamela. "Anxieties of Representation: The Serial Illustrations to Hardy's *The Return of the Native.*" *Nineteenth-Century Literature* 51 (1996): 84–110.

Davis, W. Eugene, and Helmut E. Gerber. *Thomas Hardy: an Annnotated Bibliography of Writings about Him.* De Kalb, Ill.: Northern Illinois University Press, 1973.

———. *Thomas Hardy: an Annnotated Bibliography of Writings about Him, Vol II: 1970–1978 and Supplement for 1871–1969.* De Kalb, Ill.: Northern Illinois University Press, 1983.

Deen, Leonard. "Heroism and Pathos in Hardy's *The Return of the Native.*" *Nineteenth-Century Fiction* 15, no. 3 (1960): 207–219.

Draper, Ronald P., and Martin S. Ray. *An Annotated Critical Bibliography of Thomas Hardy.* London: Macmillan, 1989.

Draper, Ronald P., ed. *Hardy: The Tragic Novels.* London: Macmillan, 1991.

Dutta, Shanta. *Ambivalence in Hardy: A Study of his Attitude to Women.* London: Macmillan, 2000.

Eggenschwiler, David. "Eustacia Vye, Queen of the Night and Courtly Pretender." *Nineteenth-Century Fiction* 25, no. 4 (1971): 444–454.

Evans, Robert. "The Other Eustacia." *Novel* 1 (1968): 251–259.

Firor, Ruth. *Folkways in Thomas Hardy.* Philadelphia: University of Pennsylvania Press, 1931.

Garson, Marjorie. *Hardy's Fables of Integrity: Woman, Body, Text.* Oxford: Clarendon Press, 1991.

Garver, Joseph. *Thomas Hardy: "The Return of the Native."* Harmondsworth: Penguin Books, 1988.

Gatrell, Simon. *Hardy the Creator: A Textual Biography.* Oxford: Clarendon Press, 1988.

Gibson, James. *Thomas Hardy: A Literary Life.* London: Macmillan, 1996.

Giordano, Frank R., Jr. "Eustacia Vye's Suicide." *Texas Studies in Literature and Language* 30 (1980): 504–521.

Gittings, Robert. *Young Thomas Hardy.* London: Heinemann, 1975.

———. *The Older Hardy.* London: Heinemann, 1978.

Gregor, Ian. *The Great Web: The Form of Hardy's Major Fiction.* London: Faber and Faber, 1974.

Gribble, Jennifer. "The Quiet Woman of Egdon Heath." *Essays in Criticism* 46 (1996): 234–257.

Guerard, Albert J. *Thomas Hardy: The Novels and Stories.* Cambridge: Harvard University Press, 1949.

Hagan, John. "A Note on the Significance of Diggory Venn." *Nineteenth-Century Fiction* 16, no. 2 (1961): 147–155.

Hands, Timothy. *A Hardy Chronology.* London: Macmillan, 1992.

Howe, Irving. *Thomas Hardy.* New York: Macmillan, 1967.

Irwin, Michael. *Reading Hardy's Landscapes.* London: Macmillan, 2000.

Jordan, Mary Ellen. "Thomas Hardy's *The Return of the Native*: Clym Yeobright and Melancholia." *American Imago* 39 (1982): 101–118.

King, Jeanette. *Tragedy in the Victorian Novel: Theory and Practice in the Novels of George Eliot, Thomas Hardy and Henry James.* Cambridge: Cambridge University Press, 1978.

Kramer, Dale. *Thomas Hardy: The Forms of Tragedy.* Detroit: Wayne State University Press, 1975.

———, ed. *Critical Approaches to the Fiction of Thomas Hardy.* London: Macmillan, 1979.

Langbaum, Robert. *Thomas Hardy in Our Time.* London: Macmillan, 1995.

Lawrence, D. H. *Study of Thomas Hardy and Other Essays.* Edited by Bruce Steele. Cambridge: Cambridge University Press, 1985.

Mallett, Phillip V., and Ronald P. Draper, eds. *A Spacious Vision: Essays on Thomas Hardy.* Newmill, Cornwall: Patten Press, 1994.

Mallett, Phillip V., ed. *The Achievement of Thomas Hardy.* London: Palgrave, 2000.

May, Charles E. "The Magic of Metaphor in *The Return of the Native.*" *Colby Library Quarterly* 22, no. 2 (1986): 111–118.

McCann, Eleanor. "Blind Will or Blind Hero: Philosophy and Myth in Hardy's *The Return of the Native.*" *Criticism* 3 (1961): 140–157.

Miller, J. Hillis. *Thomas Hardy: Distance and Desire.* Cambridge: Harvard University Press, 1970.

———. "Topography in *The Return of the Native.*" *Essays in Literature* 8 (1981): 119–134.

Millgate, Michael. *Thomas Hardy: His Career as a Novelist.* London: Bodley Head, 1971.

———. *Thomas Hardy: A Biography.* New York: Random House, 1982.

Morgan, Rosemarie. *Women and Sexuality in the Novels of Thomas Hardy.* London: Routledge, 1988.

Morrell, Roy. *Thomas Hardy: The Will and the Way.* Kuala Lumpur: University of Malaysia Press, 1965.

Page, Norman, ed. *Oxford Reader's Companion to Thomas Hardy.* Oxford: Oxford University Press, 2000.

Paterson, John. "*The Return of the Native* as Antichristian Document." *Nineteenth-Century Fiction* 14, no. 2 (1959): 11–27.

———. "The 'Poetics' of *The Return of the Native.*" *Modern Fiction Studies* 6 (1960): 214–222.

———. *The Making of "The Return of the Native."* Berkeley: University of California English Studies, 1960.

Pettit, Charles P. C., ed. *Reading Thomas Hardy.* London: Macmillan, 1998.

Pinion, F. B. *A Hardy Companion.* London: Macmillan, 1968.

Schweik, Robert. "Theme, Character, and Perspective in Hardy's *The Return of the Native.*" *Philological Quarterly* 41 (1962): 757–767.

Smith, Anne, ed. *The Novels of Thomas Hardy.* London: Vision Press, 1979.

Springer, Marlene. *Hardy's Use of Allusion.* London: Macmillan, 1983.

Sumner, Rosemary. *Thomas Hardy: Psychological Novelist.* London: Macmillan, 1981.

Wheeler, Otis B. "Four Versions of *The Return of the Native. Nineteenth-Century Fiction* 14, no. 1 (1959): 27–44.

Widdowson, Peter. *Hardy in History: A Study in Literary Sociology.* London: Routledge, 1989.

Robert Louis Stevenson's
The Strange Case of Dr. Jekyll and Mr. Hyde

CLAIRE HARMAN

ROBERT LOUIS STEVENSON was born in 1850 into a pious Scots Presbyterian household in which family prayers, Bible-reading, and church-going were central. His maternal grandfather was a Presbyterian minister in Colinton, just outside Stevenson's hometown of Edinburgh, and his parents may well have hoped that their only child would follow tradition and join the church. Stevenson was a sickly youth, often bedridden with the consumptive cough that plagued him all his life, and he spent most of his childhood in the company of his nurse, Alison Cunningham (known as "Cummy"), who was an even stricter interpreter of Calvinist doctrine than his religious family. In contrast to his parents, who did not object to card games and other frivolous amusements (as long as they were not connected with gambling), Cummy disapproved of the theater, dancing and even—in theory—to narrative, all likely to lead an audience or reader on to sin. She is reported as once curtailing a story which she had been reading aloud from the weekly papers on the grounds that it was turn-

ing into "a regular novel" (Daiches, *Robert Louis Stevenson and his World,* p. 12); what she made of her charge's later career as a novelist—not to mention his many attempts at play-writing—is not recorded.

Alison Cunningham's devoted care of the semi-invalid Stevenson earned his lasting gratitude and affection, but he never sought to hide the generally terrifying effect she had on his suggestible childish imagination. Cunningham's stories of hellfire kept the small boy awake at night, fearful of imminent damnation. "I would not only lie awake to weep for Jesus," he wrote: "I remember repeatedly awaking from a dream of Hell, clinging to the horizontal bar of the bed, with my knees and chin together, my soul shaken, my body convulsed with agony" ("Memoirs of Himself," Vailima edition, vol. 26, pp. 203–224). Under the nurse's influence, the little boy became "sentimental, snivelling, goody, morbidly religious," addicted to the stories of retribution and damnation which are so much a part of Scots folk-culture as well as Scots literature (idem). As the biographer Frank

McLynn has written, Stevenson was "someone who 'knew the worst too young' because of a system (Calvinism) that saw no difference between the worst and the moderately bad" (Frank McLynn, *Robert Louis Stevenson*, p. 262).

Alison Cunningham inspired Stevenson to become an ardent admirer of and apologist for the Covenanters, a seventeenth-century Presbyterian sect whose resistance to reform had led to violent low-church disputes in Lowland Scotland, and his first publication (in 1866) was a monograph on the Covenanting battle at Rullion Green and its aftermath called *The Pentland Rising*. Thomas Stevenson paid for the publication of this short work and other juvenilia on religious themes, one a gentle satire, "The Charity Bazaar," another in the manner of a homily, "An Appeal to the Clergy of the Church of Scotland."

At the end of his teens, therefore, Stevenson appeared to be conforming closely to his parents' values, both in his active piety and in his apprenticeship to the family engineering firm (the Stevensons were famous for the design and construction of various Scottish lighthouses and harbor works). But at the age of twenty-one he gave up engineering, turning to the study of law instead (in which he eventually qualified but never practiced) and two years later, under interrogation by his father, announced that he was an unbeliever, and had no intention of continuing to practice religion. The period of family trauma that followed this revelation involved scenes that haunted Stevenson all his life and fueled many dramatic cruxes in his fiction from the short stories "The Story of a Lie" (1879) and "The Misadventures of John Nicolson" (which just postdates *Jekyll and Hyde*) to *Weir of Hermiston*, the novel he left unfinished at his death.

Those three stories show characters whose distaste for hypocrisy leads them to painful acts of "coming out." But the opposite strategy—*not* owning up to one's nature—became an even more interesting theme to the author. Conceal

CHRONOLOGY

1850	13 November: Robert Lewis Balfour Stevenson born at 8 Howard Place, Edinburgh, first and only child of Thomas Stevenson, prominent civil engineer and inventor, and Margaret Balfour.
1867	November: enters Edinburgh University as a student of engineering.
1871	April: gives up engineering for law.
1873	Meets Frances Sitwell, a married woman with whom he begins an intense romantic friendship.
1874	April: ordered south by doctors to Menton after worsening symptoms of tuberculosis. June: elected to Savile Club, London. Writing for *Cornhill Magazine* (edited by Leslie Stephen). Meets Edmund Gosse and Henry James.
1875	February: meets poet and dramatist W. E. Henley in Edinburgh Infirmary. March–April: travels to art colonies in France with his cousin, the painter and art historian R. A. M. ("Bob") Stevenson. July: admitted to Scottish Bar. Travels to painters' colony in Barbizon, France, where he meets Fanny Van de Grift Osbourne, an American married woman studying art in France.
1876	August–October: canoe trip with Walter Simpson from Antwerp to Pontoise undertaken as material for a travel book, *An Inland Voyage*.
1878	May: *An Inland Voyage*. August: Fanny Osbourne, now his lover, returns to her husband in California. September–October: walking tour through the Cevennes alone to gather material for next book of travels. December: *Edinburgh: Picturesque Notes*.
1879	Begins collaboration with Henley on *Deacon Brodie*, a melodrama. June: *Travels with a Donkey in the Cevennes*. August: leaves Britain to join Fanny Osbourne in America, traveling across the continent by road

and rail. Arrives in California in September in very poor health. Spends most of the winter in San Francisco.

1880 19 May: marries Fanny Osbourne in San Francisco. August: returns to Britain with Fanny and her twelve-year-old son Samuel Lloyd Osbourne. *Deacon Brodie, or The Double Life* (with W. E. Henley).

1881 In Davos, Switzerland, as a possible cure for tuberculosis. Meets John Addington Symonds. April: *Virginibus Puerisque*.

1882 April: *Familiar Studies of Men and Books*. July: *New Arabian Nights*.

1883 March: moves to Hyères, southern France. December: *The Silverado Squatters; Treasure Island*.

1885 Moves to Skerryvore, a villa in Bournemouth, England. March: *A Child's Garden of Verses*; May: *More New Arabian Nights* (with Fanny Stevenson). November: *Prince Otto*.

1886 5 January: *The Strange Case of Dr. Jekyll and Mr. Hyde*. July: *Kidnapped*.

1887 May: death of Thomas Stevenson. August: *Underwoods* (poems). Sails for America with Fanny, Lloyd and his mother, Margaret Stevenson. Settles at Saranac Lake, New York, in September. December: *Memories and Portraits. The Merry Men and Other Stories*.

1888 March: receives letter from Henley which leads to severance of friendship. June: sets out from San Francisco in hired yacht *Casco* on first voyage to the South Seas. July–December: tours the Marquesas, Paumotus, Society, and Sandwich Islands. *The Black Arrow*.

1889 *The Wrong Box* (with Lloyd Osbourne). June: second Pacific cruise, to the Gilbert Islands, in the schooner *Equator*. September: *The Master of Ballantrae*. December: buys 400-acre estate, Vailima, in Upolu, Samoa.

1890 April–August: cruise on the *Janet Nicoll* to Gilbert and Marshall Islands and to New Caledonia. October: settles at Vailima.

1891 Margaret Stevenson joins him in Samoa. January: *Ballads*.

1892 April: *Across the Plains and Other Essays*; August: *A Footnote to History. The Wrecker* (with Lloyd Osbourne).

1893 April: *Island Nights' Entertainments*. August: civil war in Samoa. September: *David Balfour* (later called *Catriona*).

1894 September: *The Ebb-Tide* (with Lloyd Osbourne). Dies at Vailima 3 December of cerebral hemorrhage.

---

ment and the double life fascinated him, as did the wider issue of duality, "that strong sense of man's double being which must at times come in upon and overwhelm the mind of every thinking creature," as he wrote in his essay "A Chapter on Dreams" (1887). Duality was a persistent theme in Stevenson's work, from the doppelgänger story "Markheim," to the evil "fetch" in "The Tale of Tod Lapraik" in *Catriona*, the characterization of murderously antipathetic brothers in *The Master of Ballantrae* and the true story retold in Stevenson's early stage collaboration with W. E. Henley, *Deacon Brodie; or, The Double Life*. Brodie, an Edinburgh alderman who was a respected craftsman by day and a thief by night, had intrigued Stevenson from an early age; the Stevenson family owned a piece of furniture made by him, a constant reminder of the master thief's more respectable skills and his end on a drop-gallows of his own devising.

The ancient city of Edinburgh lent itself naturally to sinister gothic tales. Two other notorious townsmen were the murderers Burke and Hare (active in the 1820s), whose grisly nocturnal activities partly inspired Stevenson's story "The Body Snatcher." "The whole city leads a double existence," Stevenson wrote of his native town in *Edinburgh: Picturesque Notes*: "it is half-alive and half a monumental marble"; and though *The Strange Case of Dr.*

Jekyll and Mr. Hyde is ostensibly set in a sort of denatured London, it has often been noted how much more like Edinburgh the background seems and how Scottish the characters are.

INFLUENCES AND INNOVATIONS

Literary precedents for the story include James Hogg's *Private Memoirs and Confessions of a Justified Sinner* (1824), which, with its overlapping third- and first-person narratives and its linking of the murderous, self-licensed Robert Colwan to his demonic alter-ego, Gil-Martin, bears strong similarities to *Jekyll and Hyde*. *Jekyll and Hyde* struck many contemporary commentators as resembling Edgar Allan Poe's style of gothic short story, in particular "The Tell-Tale Heart," with its theme of the inevitability of retribution, and "William Wilson," an artfully told first-person narrative about the separation of conscience from action. In "William Wilson" the reader's sympathies are engaged before he or she realizes (very near the end) that the narrator is the triumphant worse side of Wilson's psyche and that his vanquished doppelgänger—represented most of the time as a sinister tormentor—was his better self. But the dissimilarities between Poe and Stevenson are revealing, too, as one reviewer of *Jekyll and Hyde* remarked:

> The double personality does not in [Stevenson's] romance take the form of a personified conscience, the *doppelgänger* of the sinner, a "double" like his own double which Goethe is fabled to have seen. No; the "separable self" in this "strange case" [. . .], with its unlikeness to its master, with its hideous caprices, and appalling vitality, and terrible power of growth and increase, is, to our thinking, a notion as novel as it is terrific. We would welcome a spectre, a ghoul, or even a vampire gladly, rather than meet Mr. Edward Hyde.
> (Paul Maixner, ed., *Robert Louis Stevenson, The Critical Heritage*, p. 200)

This acknowledges an unusual aspect of Stevenson's fantasy, its gestures toward realism and explicability. Stevenson professed distaste for contemporary realist fiction, particularly the works of Emile Zola and Thomas Hardy's *Tess of the D'Urbevilles*, though his protests have to be read in the context of his own doubts about the future of romance fiction: Stevenson was devoted to truthful reportage and frankness about human nature, as he shows time and again in his essays and travel writings. *Jekyll and Hyde* joins a fantastic device (the transformations) with much that is realistic and credible. The plot is laid out in terms of a series of pieces of evidence; objectivity is given a high priority and there is a legalistic concern for getting things witnessed and documented. A whole subclass of forensic experts people the story to give it a sort of scientific gravitas; for instance, Dr. Lanyon is on hand to remark on the drugs Jekyll uses, Utterson voices professional concerns about the will, and an amateur graphologist gives a timely opinion on Hyde's handwriting. Through this build-up of expert witness, as through the careful maintenance of an unexceptional set of background circum- stances, the central oddity of the transformations is made believable.

The story's structural peculiarities also make it much more complex and interesting than is usual in sensation literature. The narrative unfolds in a to-and-fro fashion, with three distinct sections and several different voices: an initial third-person narrative, charting events as seen through the eyes of the lawyer Utterson, followed by two first-person testimonials, one by Dr. Lanyon and the other, "Henry Jekyll's Full Statement of the Case." These overlap in time and contradict in content, giving an overall picture of uncertainty and suspense as the true history of what happened to Jekyll is alternately withheld and revealed.

DREAMS AND DREAMERS: THE COMPOSITION OF *JEKYLL AND HYDE*

The Strange Case of Dr. Jekyll and Mr. Hyde began in a dream. Stevenson was living in

Bournemouth with his American wife Fanny and, as often at that period (1885), was desperate to make some money. He had already written and destroyed a story called "The Travelling Companion" on the subject of "that strong sense of man's double being" (*Essays and Poems,* p. 197); the story had, it seems, been rejected by an editor who found it "indecent." Pressed to come up with an idea, Stevenson "went about wracking my brains for a plot of any sort," as he recalled in "A Chapter on Dreams," and on the second night of deliberate effort dreamed two short scenes that excited him very much, "the scene at the window, and a scene afterwards split in two, in which Hyde, pursued for some crime, took the powder and underwent the change in the presence of his pursuers" (ibid., p. 198). The nightmare made Stevenson cry out in his sleep and his wife woke him, much to his annoyance at the interruption of his "fine bogy-tale." But he set to work the next day writing it up, finishing a first draft in three days.

His wife thought the result too crude and gothic, however, and Stevenson threw the manuscript on the fire in a fit of temper, starting immediately on another version which he completed almost as quickly as the first. Whether this was in fact the manuscript of "The Travelling Companion," which he also claimed to have burned, is now impossible to tell, but the speed at which he wrote the surviving tale suggests so. The short book was ready for the press within six weeks and was published on 5 January 1886. It was an immediate hit on both sides of the Atlantic, selling 40,000 copies in six months in Great Britain and an astonishing 250,000 legal and pirated copies in North America. When Stevenson went to New York the following year he was trailed by reporters and fans, and a stage version of the story was already in production, the first of many more or less inaccurate representations of his original tale.

In the wake of the publicity, Stevenson wrote an essay elaborating his theory of composition, "A Chapter on Dreams," which has a great deal of bearing on *Jekyll and Hyde*. In it he claims that the inventive side of his imagination was beyond conscious control, separately managed by subconscious forces which he personifies as the Brownies, with no moral sense and no conscience. "For the most part, it will be seen, my Brownies are somewhat fantastic, like their stories hot and hot, full of passion and the picturesque, alive with animating incident; and they have no prejudice against the supernatural" ("A Chapter on Dreams," *Essays and Poems,* pp. 198–199).

The actual dreams he relates in the essay—presented as those of an unnamed dreamer—are "irresponsible inventions, told for the teller's pleasure, with no eye to the crass public or the thwart reviewer: tales where a thread might be dropped, or one adventure quitted for another, on fancy's least suggestion" (ibid., p. 193). Though he depicts the artful dreamer (the writer who uses dreams as source material) as one who harnesses the power of the subconscious in order to turn "[the] amusement of story-telling to (what is called) account" (idem), the power of *The Strange Case of Dr. Jekyll and Mr. Hyde* derives largely from its innovative use of the former, unimpeded, irresponsible impulses. Clearly the process of slipping out of one mode of consciousness into another, less accountable one was pertinent to the shaping of the Jekyll/Hyde schism.

Stevenson used his dreams as the basis of two other works, the weird quasi-vampire story "Olalla," published the year before *Jekyll and Hyde,* and his novel *The Master of Ballantrae,* the ending of which was based on a vivid dream. Both of these also deal with themes of duality and identity and strongly suggest that Stevenson's interest in the subconscious shaped both the uses he made of his dreams (putting them "to (what is called) account") and their preoccupations with the divided self, of which Jekyll and Hyde is the most cogent instance, a self-psychoanalysis predating Freud.

HYDE AND SEEK: TRANSFORMED BEHAVIOR

Many commentators have pointed out that *The Strange Case of Dr. Jekyll and Mr. Hyde* is exclusively concerned with male characters and that they are all wealthy bachelors of the professional class: Jekyll and Lanyon are doctors, Utterson is a lawyer, and Enfield, his godson, is a "man about the town." They are all "intelligent reputable men, and all judges of good wine" (*The Strange Case of Dr. Jekyll and Mr. Hyde, Collected Shorter Fiction*, p. 444). They share habits of seriousness and solitude and are often discovered sitting by their firesides late at night in contemplative mood; Lanyon is first introduced sitting "alone over his wine" in his dining room, attended by a "solemn" butler (ibid., p. 445); Utterson's custom on a Sunday is to "sit close by the fire, a volume of some dry divinity on his reading desk," ibid., p. 444), and he and Jekyll enjoy an after-dinner drink (by yet another fireplace) where they are depicted as "practising for solitude [. . .] after the expense and strain of gaiety" (idem). The emergence of Jekyll's alter-ego Edward Hyde is therefore disruptive on many levels; Hyde is of a different age and class and gives off an undeniable air of criminality. No one knows why Jekyll has taken him up (Hyde is decscribed as Jekyll's protégé or young friend by Utterson), but they all assume the association has a shameful basis. Without actually asking Jekyll outright (this would go against their ethos), his friends presume that Hyde is blackmailing the older man, with the fairly obvious implication that Jekyll is hiding a current or past sexual liason. So the intrusion of Hyde on the peripheries of this group does not simply disrupt a cozy network of men who studied together or have long-standing professional connections; it forces them to acknowledge the potential for vice in their lives and to break out of old patterns of behavior. At the begining, Enfield says:

"I feel very strongly about putting questions; it partakes too much of the style of the day of judge-ment. You start a question, and its like starting a stone [. . .] No, sir, I make it a rule of mine: the more it looks like Queer Street, the less I ask." "A very good rule, too," said the lawyer.

(ibid., p. 443)

But the crisis in Jekyll's life requires his friends to be demonstrative where they were formerly private and unemotional, to speak rather than acquiesce, to ask questions, get involved, even, as in the case of Dr. Lanyon, at the ultimate personal hazard.

The compactness of the story and its geographically limited setting in the smog-filled streets of mid-Victorian London give it an oppressive, even claustrophobic atmosphere, focusing the allegory, though the symbolism attached to the story's physical properties seems almost too insistent at times. Jekyll's house is backed by a yard and a block of buildings formerly used as a dissecting theatre by an anatomist. The rear of this "sinister block of building" is visible from the by-street where the story begins: "It was two stories high; showed no window, nothing but a door on the lower storey and a blind forehead of discoloured wall on the upper; and bore in every feature the marks of prolonged and sordid negligence" (ibid., p. 441). Hyde has been seen entering and leaving this anthropomorphized, low-browed, "degenerate" building via a back door which is "blistered and distained" and "equipped with neither bell nor knocker." Jekyll's living quarters open out at the front onto a well-kept respectable square, but the by-street of the back entrance is itself dramatically divided between bright, cheerful shops and the sinister courtyard where tramps "slouched into the recess" (idem) and where "for close on a generation, no one had appeared to drive away these random visitors or repair their ravages."

At the beginning of the story, Utterson and Enfield stop by this entryway and remark its oddity, which leads to Enfield relating how he once saw a man go in there to fetch a check in order to compensate the family of a child he had trampled on in the street. The incident had caused outrage among its witnesses, not so much because of the brutality of it, but because the perpetrator was unremorseful, even triumphant: "He was perfectly cool and made no resistance, but gave me one look, so ugly that it brought out the sweat on me like running" (idem). The man in question was Hyde—then unknown to Enfield—and the check he emerged with was signed by Dr. Jekyll. This lodges in his mind as a strange anomaly, for the incident takes place in the middle of the night and Hyde seems to have no trouble waking the doctor and extracting a large sum of money from him almost instantly.

Enfield's chance recollection sets Utterson's suspicions and curiosity in play and sparks what might be thought of as the detective plot. The lawyer begins to haunt the by-street, obsessed with the nature of the relationship between Jekyll and Hyde. He takes on the mannerisms and technique of a private investigator, interrogating Enfield, Lanyon, and Jekyll's butler, Poole, staking out Hyde, mulling over Jekyll's past behavior: "[Jekyll] was wild when he was young; a long while ago, to be sure; but in the law of God there is no statute of limitations" (ibid., p. 449). Gone is Utterson's professed reticence about "putting questions" and minding his own business. "If he be Mr. Hyde," he thinks, "I shall be Mr. Seek" (ibid., p. 447). And when Hyde, in his most unequivocally evil act, bludgeons Sir Danvers Carew to death on the street one night, it is Utterson who accompanies the Scotland Yard man to Soho in search of the murderer and takes the investigation forward again when the police have given up. In his own way, he too is undergoing a profound transformation.

The most interesting part of Utterson's "possession" by the puzzle of Hyde is the description of his insomniac nights:

> now his imagination also was engaged, or rather enslaved; and as he lay and tossed in the gross darkness of the night and the curtained room, Mr. Enfield's tale went by before his mind in a scroll of

lighted pictures. He would be aware of the great field of lamps of a nocturnal city; then of a figure of a man walking swiftly; then of a child running from the doctor's; and then these met, and that human Juggernaut trod the child down and passed on regardless of her screams. Or else he would see a room in a rich house, where his friend lay asleep, dreaming and smiling at his dreams; and then the door of that room would be opened, the curtains of the bed plucked apart, the sleeper recalled, and, lo! there would stand by his side a figure to whom power was given, and even at that dead hour, he must rise and do its bidding.

(ibid., p. 446)

This waking dream is even more vivid than the real dreams that take over when he (perhaps) dozes, when the figure of his imagination moves "more swiftly and still the more swiftly, even to dizziness, through wider labyrinths of lamp-lighted city, and at every street corner crush a child and leave her screaming" (idem). The supposedly objective third-person narration of this supposedly dry-as-dust Scotsman's stream of semi-consciousness reveals his fears of all manner of transgressive behavior, from physical violence to a more sublimated sexual threat implicit in the picture of the intruder "to whom power was given" gaining access to Jekyll's bedroom, plucking apart the bed curtain, and demanding "he must rise and do its bidding." While Jekyll in this imagined scenario "lay asleep, dreaming and smiling at his dreams," Utterson himself is kept awake with half-dreams of a different nature, laid before the reader in an almost shockingly interpretable way.

Utterson dominates this part of the story; without him, it seems, the bizarre history of Jekyll's association with a murderer and blackmailer would never have come to light. His persistent curiosity about Hyde leads him to take Enfield into Jekyll's courtyard during a period when the doctor is inexplicably refusing to receive visitors. There they witness Jekyll experiencing a sudden total change of demeanor as they speak to him from below his laboratory window, a pivotal point in the narrative and, incidentally, the key scene originally dreamed by Stevenson: "the smile was struck out of his face and succeeded by an expression of such abject terror and despair, as froze the very blood of the two gentlemen below. They saw it but for a glimpse, for the window was instantly thrust down; but that glimpse had been sufficient, and they turned and left the court without a word" (ibid., p. 462).

This is as far as possible from Dr. Jekyll being "Quite at Ease," as one of the earlier chapter headings has it, sitting over a late-night drink by the fire with Utterson, "with something of a sly-ish cast perhaps, but every mark of capacity and kindness" (ibid., p. 450). And even odder is the reaction of Utterson and Enfield to the incident, which they know is "deviant" behavior on Jekyll's part, but about which they tacitly agree to say nothing, even to each other:

> In silence, too, they traversed the by-street; and it was not until they had come into a neighboring thoroughfare, where even upon a Sunday there were still some stirrings of life, that Mr. Utterson at last turned and looked at his companion. They were both pale; and there was an answering horror in their eyes. "God forgive us! God forgive us!" said Mr. Utterson. But Mr. Enfield only nodded his head very seriously, and walked on once more in silence.
>
> (ibid., p. 462)

The apparent centrality of Utterson's point of view seems confirmed in the chapter called "The Last Night," in which Jekyll's servant Poole, anxious that his master has been locked in his laboratory under peculiar circumstances, comes to solicit Utterson's help. The lawyer takes charge of the situation at Jekyll's house like a true hero, rallying the servants who stand "huddled together like a flock of sheep" and effecting everyone's release by gaining entry to the laboratory with an axe. "I shall consider it my duty to break in that door," he says to the butler, who replies with relief, "Ah, Mr. Utterson, that's talking!" (ibid., p. 466). They enter just in time to see Hyde writhing in the last of his death throes: "the cords of his face still moved with a

semblance of life, but life was quite gone; and by the crushed vial in the hand and the strong smell of kernels that hung upon the air, Utterson knew that he was looking on the body of a self-destroyer" (ibid., p. 468).

The story seems to have reached its final scene here, but in fact the real story, running appropriately enough in parallel to Utterson's perception of it, has hardly begun. The lawyer and the butler find a package of documents on Jekyll's desk that indicate, from the recent covering note, that Jekyll is not, as they had assumed, dead (murdered by Hyde, whom they guess has committed suicide to evade arrest). One of the documents is a will, replacing one in which the doctor left his fortune to his "friend and benefactor Edward Hyde." The new will leaves the estate to Utterson. Mystified that Hyde had not destroyed this from pure self-interest, Utterson leaves Jekyll's house unsure of the fate of his friend and preparing to read the remaining two documents found in the laboratory.

LANYON'S LETTER: A FURTHER LAYER OF EVIDENCE

The documents are printed one after another, without comment, as if we were reading them over Utterson's shoulder. The first, which provides the second of the book's three narratives, is a statement written by Dr. Lanyon not long before his mysterious decline and death. Lanyon is shown to have had a close relationship with Jekyll in the past and "a bond of common interest" (they were contemporaries and co-professionals) but also a falling-out, on as yet unspecified grounds (ibid., p 445). Lanyon has already told Utterson that "'it is more than ten years since Henry Jekyll became too fanciful for me. He began to go wrong, wrong in mind. [...] Such unscientific balderdash,' added the doctor, flushing suddenly purple, 'would have estranged Damon and Pythias.'" Lanyon and Jekyll enjoy a brief reconciliation in the period following the murder of Danvers Carew before something happens to shake Lanyon's nerve completely, as Utterson has observed:

> He had his death-warrant written legibly on his face. The rosy man had grown pale; his flesh had fallen away; he was visibly balder and older; and yet it was not so much these tokens of a swift physical decay that arrested the lawyer's notice, as a look in the eye and a quality of manner that seemed to testify to some deep-seated terror of the mind.
>
> (ibid., p. 459)

Lanyon's written statement both adds to the evidence about Jekyll and, from its very oddness and Lanyon's difficulty in believing it himself, deepens the mystery. He relates how he received a letter from Jekyll begging for a complicated and apparently irrational favor: Lanyon was to break into Jekyll's "private cabinet" (a room used as a study and laboratory) and remove and take home with him a drawer containing "some powders, a phial, and a paper book" (ibid., p. 471). This is the first indication that Jekyll has been conducting experiments with drugs. Lanyon is also requested to wait for the arrival of "a man who will present himself in my name" (idem); when this person turns up just after midnight, it is (obviously to the reader, if not to Lanyon) Edward Hyde, a small, "crouching" man with a "shocking expression" wearing clothes "enormously too large for him in every measurement." Now at last the reader gets the chance to watch with Lanyon as Hyde eagerly mixes the powders with the contents of the phial and drinks it down:

> A cry followed; he reeled, staggered, clutched at the table and held on, staring with injected eyes, gasping with open mouth; and as I looked, there came, I thought, a change—he seemed to swell—his face became suddenly black, and the features seemed to melt and alter—and the next moment I had sprung to my feet and leaped back against the wall, my arm raised to shield me from that prodigy, my mind submerged in terror. "O God!" I screamed, and "O God!" again and again; for there before my eyes—pale and shaken, and half fainting, and groping before him with his hands, like a

man restored from death—there stood Henry Jekyll!

> (ibid., p. 475)

This transformation, complete with its stock gestures and exclamations from stage melodrama, changes the story's mode at a stroke from detective fiction to horror. Stevenson is partly defaulting to an old convention here, and partly updating it, introducing a "scientific" element into a scene of primitive horror in much the same way that Mary Shelley used contemporary experimentation with electricity and galvanism to give a veneer of rationality to her fantastic tale of Frankenstein's Creature. Here we have the mixing and taking of a drug (seen at its most "scientific" through the eyes of the only other medical man in the story), combined with glancing references to a long-standing and virulent debate between the two doctors on the morality of Jekyll's self-experimentations. The ethical debate and the theory of personality which Jekyll evolves in it are of much more interest than the creakingly artificial device of taking mysterious "powders" and "salts" to induce a change from one aspect of his personality to the other. The powders were, indeed, a focus of criticism in the early reviews (*The Saturday Review* said the plot "depends on the resources of pseudo-science," Maixner, *Robert Louis Stevenson: The Critical Heritage,* p. 200). The author seemed to know it was a weak spot and referred to the matter disingenuously in "A Chapter on Dreams," deflecting the criticism onto his subconscious "helpers" on the grounds that it was part of the story he dreamed: "the business of the powders, which so many have censured, is, I am relieved to say, not mine at all but the Brownies'" (*Essays and Poems,* p. 198).

It is interesting at this point to consider the appeal to filmmakers of the transformation scenes in *Jekyll and Hyde*: a character so radically changing guises does not just have great dramatic force but plays to the potential of film technology in an irresistible manner. The story could have been made for the cinema; it seems to anticipate certain cinematic tropes in, for instance, Utterson's dream sequence ("[he saw the figure] move swiftly and still the more swiftly, even to dizziness, through wider labyrinths of lamp-lighted city") and in the use of flashbacks. In the story's most fantastic scenes, film actually seems to be a medium superior to words. "The magic of the cinema," with its ability to dismiss rather than merely suspend the audience's disbelief, is itself "the powders," transforming Jekyll before our eyes. Stevenson has to cover over the process of the transformations with impressionistic sensations: Lanyon is the only witness to the change, and his account is characterized by uncertainty about what he is seeing: "there came, I thought, a change—he seemed to swell—his face became suddenly black, and the features seemed to melt and alter." During the final moments of transformation, Lanyon has reeled backwards and raised his arm "to shield me from that prodigy"—thereby, presumably, also blocking his view of it. Later descriptions by Jekyll himself are vividly sensational—"a qualm came over me, a horrid nausea and the most deadly shuddering" (ibid., p. 485)—but he only looks at himself in a mirror after the change is complete. Rouben Mamoulian in his classic 1931 film treatment fully exposed the process and constructed an unflinchingly full-face view of Jekyll changing to Hyde (all the film versions have ironed out the confusing to-and-fro movement of Stevenson's original story and all, logically enough, show Jekyll-to-Hyde first), with clever gradations of make-up and a multiplicity of shots smoothly effecting the change. What he and others have chosen to show (notably Victor Fleming in the 1941 remake of Mamoulian's film starring Spencer Tracy) is a primitive Hyde, a hirsute monkey-man with simian posture and gait.

It is not hard to see why this seems such an appropriate depiction of Hyde: "apelike" appears several times in the text to describe him,

Poole reports him moving "like a monkey" (ibid., p. 467), and Jekyll notes his "lean, corded, knuckly" hands after the transformation, "of dusky pallor, and thickly shaded with a swart growth of hair" (ibid., p. 481). It is also a fitting reflection of anthropological controversies contemporary with Stevenson; Darwin's theory of evolution, the writings of Herbert Spencer, and the rise of eugenics and early gene theory.

What it cannot convey is the story's insistence that Hyde's repulsiveness is not so much physical as an emanation of his evil spirit. He and Jekyll could never be mistaken for each other, even when, as in the description of "The Last Night," at the laboratory, they both resort to wearing a mask, because they are not just dissimilar in stature, demeanor, and age (Jekyll is about fifty, Hyde a youth), but totally different in the effect they have on other people. Jekyll is "large, well-made, smooth-faced," bearing "every mark of capacity and kindness" (ibid., p. 450), whereas something about Hyde makes observers feel disturbed, revolted, even violent. What exactly that might be is kept visually nonspecific: Enfield describes "something wrong in his appearance, something downright detestable [. . .] He must be deformed somewhere; he gives a strong feeling of deformity, although I couldn't specify the point. He's an extraordinary looking man, and yet I really can name nothing out of the way" (ibid., p. 443), while Utterson cannot account for the fear and loathing he feels when looking at Hyde: "There is something more, if I could find a name for it. God bless me, the man seems hardly human! Something troglodytic, shall we say? [. . .] or is it the mere radiance of a foul soul that thus transpires through, and transfigures, its clay continent?" (ibid., p. 448). Here Utterson has not just, with the word "troglodytic," established the chain of suggestion confirmed by "apelike" and "monkey," but articulated, in his rhetorical question "is it the mere radiance of a foul soul . . . ?"—a subtler conclusion than the story is ever at leisure to explore deeply, that one's moral state will make itself plain to the outside world despite conscious efforts to conceal it.

JEKYLL'S "STATEMENT": THE KEY WITNESS

The "Statement" by Jekyll that concludes the novella is far from being a mere contrivance to clear up the mystery; rather, it lets us into the story for the first time, gets us behind the locked doors, drawn curtains, and secret by-ways that are such a powerful source of imagery throughout Utterson's original (veiled, and in every sense partial) narrative. It is not quite the first we have heard from Jekyll himself: there is the text of a letter of his in Dr. Lanyon's narrative (though that, complicatedly, turns out to have been composed by Hyde *in the manner of* Jekyll so that he can gain access to the laboratory). Jekyll's narrative voice is in marked contrast to the short-sentenced, rather cut-and-dried style of the third-person section dealing with Utterson's version of events. Jekyll is smoothly articulate, even poetical at times, displaying a lively, imaginative temperament and inquisitive spirit. The prose begins to flow for the first time as he relates how the misdeeds of his youth (kept unspecific) led him to conceal-ment and "a profound duplicity of life." Something of that duplicity is evident even at this confessional moment, for Jekyll's "state-ment" is, unsurprisingly, a piece of self-justification. The vague "irregularities" to which he admits are placed in the context of such "high views" as to render them more indications of his super-fine sensibilities than real character flaws:

> Many a man would have blazoned such irregulari-ties as I was guilty of; but from the high views that I had set before me, I regarded and hid them with an almost morbid sense of shame. It was thus rather the exacting nature of my aspirations than any particular degradation in my faults, that made me what I was, and, with an even deeper trench

than in the majority of men, severed in me those provinces of good and evil which divide and compound man's dual nature.

> (ibid., p. 476)

Is this harsh self-judgement meant to elicit his hearer's protests, or is it a further (self-generated) proof of the more demanding moral universe which Jekyll claims to inhabit apart from "the majority of men," even apart from the majority of bad men? Jekyll seems to be prepar-ing his audience (Utterson) for an "aspirational" reading of his self-experimentations, a Promethean interpretation, with himself cast as the doomed romantic striver after knowledge. His scientific studies (unhelpfully only described as leading "wholly towards the mystic and transcendental," ibid., p. 476) had, he claims, amplified existing personal anxieties about "dual" behavior:

> I thus drew steadily nearer to that truth, by whose partial discovery I have been doomed to such a dreadful shipwreck: that man is not truly one, but truly two. [. . .] It was on the moral side, and in my own person, that I learned to recognise the thorough and primitive duality of man; I saw that, of the two natures that contended in the field of my consciousness, even if I could be rightly be said to be either, it was only because I was radi-cally both.

> (ibid., pp. 476–477)

Jekyll's ambition, he continues, became to try to separate the two sides of his personality in order to relieve life "of all that was unbearable" (p. 477). He knew of the power of drugs to "shake and pluck back" the "mist-like transience of this seemingly so solid body," so he set about concocting a drug that would shake "the very fortress of identity."

Jekyll's description of the initial mixing and taking of the potion and the subsequent transformation into Hyde is insistently physical:

> The most racking pains succeeded: a grinding in the bones, deadly nausea, and a horror of the spirit that cannot be exceeded at the hour of birth or

death. Then these agonies began swiftly to subside, and I came to myself as if out of a great sickness. There was something strange in my sensations-,something indescribably new, and from its very novelty, indescribably sweet. I felt younger, lighter, happier in body; within I was conscious of a heady recklessness, a current of disordered sensual images running like a mill race in my fancy, a solution of the bonds of obligation, an unknown but not an innocent freedom of the soul.

(ibid., p. 478)

This is described as a sort of sexual as well as drug-induced ecstasy, though Jekyll overtakes the metaphor of "ecstatic" by getting quite literally out of his own body at this point. The person who emerges is immediately aware that he is physically smaller, that he has, in Stevenson's rich phrase, "lost in stature." The new person is called Edward Hyde, a name with obvious connotations of concealment as well as evoking an animal's thick and impenetrable skin. When Hyde creeps out from the laboratory, situated symbolically at the back of Jekyll's house and opening onto a different street, he is able for the first time to see himself in a mirror. Not only is he smaller than Jekyll; in a highly inventive detail, he is also younger, being undeveloped in vice.

Evil besides (which I must still believe to be the lethal side of man) had left on that body an imprint of deformity and decay. And yet when I looked upon that ugly idol in the glass, I was conscious of no repugnance, rather of a leap of welcome. This, too, was myself. It seemed natural and human. In my eyes it bore a livelier image of the spirit, it seemed more express and single, than the imperfect and divided countenance I had been hitherto accustomed to call mine.

(ibid., p. 479)

Hyde is much more vital than Jekyll and delighted with himself and his anticipated powers of evil. The reader is therefore well prepared for Hyde's rapid increase in strength and eventual dominance over the host personality.

Stevenson makes it clear that Jekyll and Hyde do not represent exclusive moral states. "Jekyll-and-Hyde" has two characters and two appearances: "one was wholly evil, and the other was still the old Henry Jekyll, that incongruous compound of whose reformation and improvement I had already learned to despair. The movement was thus wholly towards the worse" (ibid.). Just as it is pregnantly unclear who has named (and recognized) the newly emerged character of Hyde or who looks at Hyde in the mirror and reflects that "This, too, was myself," the "I" in this sentence is a very ambiguous entity. "I" becomes an insistent word in the remaining text, with decreasingly definable meaning. "Think of it—I did not even exist!" the narrator says when crowing about the success of his experiment and the freedom it offered to "spring headlong into the sea of liberty" (ibid., p. 480). The speaker's voice becomes confused; he begins to speak of himself in the third person, or perhaps one should say, in these circumstances, the third people: "It was Hyde, after all, and Hyde alone, that was guilty. Jekyll was no worse; he woke again to his good qualities seemingly unimpaired; he would even make haste, where it was possible, to undo the evil done by Hyde. And thus his conscience slumbered" (idem). Here we are, back in the rich ambiguity of the third-person narrative, so often exploited by Stevenson to give us access to things we cannot actually know (as in the raw exposure of Utterson's night thoughts earlier). But in this case, Jekyll and Hyde occupy the positions usually taken by writer and character respectively. Is *The Strange Case* an allegory of artistic creativity as well as a moral allegory? Did the "divided self" of Stevenson and his "Brownies" wish to identify themselves with or distance themselves from their complex joint creation?

Jekyll's confession includes a recital of one of the crimes that Hyde has been at liberty to perform, the murder of Sir Danvers Carew, a benign elderly gentleman who infuriated Hyde by greeting him politely in the street and whom

Hyde subsequently beats to death with a walking stick. This is a token crime, illustrating the spontaneous nature of Hyde's evil rather than the depths of depravity to which he is meant to plunge, and which Stevenson does not attempt to reveal. The murder itself has already been related in the first section of the book, witnessed by a maid-servant from an adjacent window: here Jekyll/Hyde gives his own version of events: "With a transport of glee I mauled the unresisting body, tasting delight from every blow; and it was not till weariness had begun to succeed that I was suddenly, in the top fit of my delirium, struck through the heart by a cold thrill of terror" (ibid., p. 483).

Again, the confusion of "voice" is nicely exploited. Is Jekyll's tone one of horrified realization (as if he was replaying the scene mentally but seeing it only for the first time), or is he actually reveling in the memory of Hyde's wickedness? The "I" who mauled the body "with a transport of glee" does seem, at this point, to be "radically both" characters at once, both actor and observer, with the implication that Jekyll's voyeurism of himself is just as unpleasant as Hyde's "transport" of bestial glee.

The plot significance of the crime is that it is committed by Hyde in a phase of spontaneous transformation out of Jekyll's body: Hyde only mixes the potion and changes back to Jekyll in order to escape the law. Jekyll's body thereby becomes a contested space: a prison for Jekyll himself (from which he wishes to escape "into the sea of liberty"), a refuge for the much wickeder Hyde. Hyde's willing re-entry into this space is motivated purely by the instinct to self-preservation, and though it allows Jekyll one last chance at controlling "the beast" he has given birth to, it is clear that Hyde already has the upper hand:

> [He] had a song on his lips as he compounded the draught, and as he drank it pledged the dead man. The pangs of transformation had not done tearing him, before Henry Jekyll, with streaming tears of

gratitude and remorse, had fallen upon his knees and lifted his clasped hands to God.

(ibid., p. 484)

From this point on, the plot hurtles towards its tragic conclusion. Another spontaneous change occurs, this time in a public place: Hyde, in danger of his life because of the murder, has to make his way into hiding wearing Jekyll's outsize clothes and has to devise a way of getting at the powders (which he does by means of the letters to Lanyon and Poole already described in the earlier narratives). To keep Hyde at bay Jekyll has to take more and more powerful drugs and submits himself to voluntary incarceration at home as the threatening first symptoms of spontaneous transformation become more frequent. The crux comes when he runs out of one of the ingredients of the potion and finds that his old supply of "salts" is irreplaceable. The ultimate triumph of Hyde is therefore assured, and Jekyll sits down to write the confessional document that Utterson and we are reading. Thus the story ends with a brilliant coup de theatre, Jekyll's anticipation of what might happen once his personality has been deposed and the acknowledgement that, far from it being desirable to separate his two selves, the different sides of Jekyll/Hyde are inextricably entwined and dependent on each other for survival.

> Should the throes of change take me in the act of writing [this confession], Hyde will tear it in pieces; but if some time shall have elapsed after I have laid it by, his wonderful selfishness and circumscription to the moment will probably save it once again from the action of his apelike spite. And indeed the doom that is closing on us both has already changed him and crushed him. Half an hour from now, when I shall again and forever reindue that hated personality, I know how I shall sit shuddering and weeping in my chair, or continue, with the most strained and fearstruck ecstasy of listening, to pace up and down this room (my last earthly refuge) and give ear to every sound of menace. Will Hyde die upon the scaffold? or will he find the courage to release himself at the last

moment? God knows; I am careless; this is my true hour of death, and what is to follow concerns another than myself. Here, then, as I lay down the pen, and proceed to seal up my confession, I bring the life of the unhappy Henry Jekyll to an end.

(ibid., p. 488)

This is the final part of the last piece of evidence, but Jekyll/Hyde's actual fate is not absolutely clear. When Utterson and Poole break into the laboratory, they find Hyde writhing on the ground in his death-agony, with a phial of poison in his hand. This, as we have seen, is a moment of confusion for Utterson, who starts to read Jekyll's Statement still thinking his friend could be alive. At the end of the Statement, the case is as strange as ever. Who committed suicide? Jekyll or Hyde? Jekyll thought it would take courage for Hyde to kill himself, and implies he doubts Hyde has such courage. Did the doctor therefore try to vanquish his "other half" by killing Jekyll? The moaning, pacing creature heard from outside the cabinet door by Utterson and Poole certainly seemed to them to be Hyde. But how can we think of Hyde showing, in suicide, a degree of bravery and *right-mindedness* which has seemed entirely out of the question before? Or was he only acting from deep-seated self-interest, which Jekyll pathetically cannot imagine? The indefinite ending makes the whole story resonate with bleak meanings.

RECEPTION AND INTERPRETATION OF *JEKYLL AND HYDE*

The common fate of classic stories is that they become so well-known that they cease to be read. "Jekyll-and-Hyde" now colloquially denotes a two-sided personality switching from good to evil, but the complexity of Stevenson's moral allegory has been eroded.

The story became common property remarkably quickly: Margaret Stevenson, the author's mother, heard it cited in a sermon in America within a year of its publication. As Stevenson's first biographer, Graham Balfour, wrote in 1901, "Its success was probably due rather to the moral instincts of the public than to any conscious perception of the merits of its art. It was read by those who never read fiction, it was quoted in pulpits, and made the subject of leading articles in religious papers" (Balfour, *The Life of Robert Louis Stevenson*, volume II, pp. 17–18). Some of Stevenson's writer friends, including Henry James, thought the book too sensational (and perhaps too popular) for comfort; John Addington Symonds wrote to the author, "It is indeed a dreadful book, most dreadful because of a certain moral callousness, a want of sympathy, a shutting out of hope. [. . .] The fact is that, viewed as an allegory, it touches one too closely. Most of us at some epoch of our lives have been upon the verge of developing a Mr. Hyde" (*Letters of John Addington Symonds*, edited by Schueller and Peters, vol. 3, pp. 120–121).

Symonds, whose anxieties about his sexuality were revealed in the posthumous publication of his diaries, may have been voicing here a worry similar to that of Jekyll's bachelor friends in the story itself; that a comfortable, if hypocritical, status quo was being threatened with exposure. Certainly, *The Strange Case* is full of latent sexual meanings, and its huge cultural impact derived in part from its frank acknowledgement that there was plenty in late-Victorian life which Victorian fiction could not, or refused to, deal with. In his defense of the story in a letter to Robert Bridges in 1886, the poet Gerard Manley Hopkins expressed the astute opinion that the scene in *Jekyll and Hyde* where Hyde tramples over the little girl in the street "is perhaps a convention: [Stevenson] was thinking of something unsuitable for fiction" (*Letters of G. M. Hopkins to Robert Bridges*, edited by C. C. Abbott, 1935, p. 236).

It has often been pointed out how assiduously Stevenson avoided including women characters in his works: *Treasure Island, Kidnapped*, the Prince Florizel stories of *New Arabian Nights, The Wrecker*, and *The Ebb-*

Tide are all virtually woman-free texts, much to the discomfort of filmmakers and dramatists, who typically invent or exaggerate female characters. Stevenson seems to have condemned himself out of his own mouth as a misogynist by such remarks as this in an essay on the composition of *Treasure Island*: "It was to be a story for boys; no need of psychology or fine writing; and I had a boy at hand to be a touchstone. Women were excluded" ("My First Book," *Essays and Poems*, p. 211). He was, however, a feminist in politics and uxorious (some would say sexually submissive) in his marriage to the strong-minded Fanny Osbourne. He longed to treat sex in a forthright way but preferred leaving women characters out of his stories altogether to including them in vapid and desexualized roles, the only ones he felt the contemporary reading public could tolerate. "I am a realist and a prosaist and a most fanatical lover of plain physical sensations plainly and expressly rendered; hence my perils," he wrote to Sidney Colvin when his most explicit story, "The Beach of Falesà," was condemned as immoral. "I cannot mean one thing and write another [. . .] and if my characters have to go to bed to each other—well, I want them to go" (*Letters*, vol. VII, p. 284).

The absence of women in a Stevenson text (and *Jekyll and Hyde* is the one from which they are most thoroughly absent) has to be seen therefore as an index of its sexual self-awareness. Many—indeed, most—modern critics have interpreted the novel as a psychosexual allegory. Elaine Showalter has called the story "a fable of fin-de-siècle homosexual panic, the discovery and resistance of the homosexual self . . . in which Jekyll's apparent infatuation with Hyde reflects the late-nineteenth-century upper-middle-class eroticization of working-class men as the ideal homosexual objects" (*Sexual Anarchy*, pp. 107, 110). Wayne Koestenbaum has written that *Jekyll and Hyde* defines queerness as the horror that comes from not being able to explain away an uncanny doubleness" (*Double Talk: The Erotics of Male Literary Col-*

laboration, p. 147), and Karl Miller, in his literary-historical study *Doubles: Studies in Literary History*, has identified Stevenson as the leading figure in the "School of Duality" that "framed a dialect, and a dialectic, for the love that dared not speak its name—for the vexed question of homosexuality and bisexuality" (p. 216). This insistence on the unstated sexual content of the story being consciously or suppressedly homosexual seems, in the early twenty-first century, somewhat dated. There was an assumption at the time of its first publication that the story dealt with unspeakably shameful *heterosexual* practices. The film versions abound in added prostitutes to accommodate this interpretation, and to reflect the historical fact that only two years after *The Strange Case of Dr. Jekyll and Mr. Hyde* began to cause a sensation among the reading public on both sides of the Atlantic, the savage Whitechapel murders by Jack the Ripper also began (targeting "fallen" women and characterized by anatomically knowledgeable evisceration, suggesting a psychopathic moralist with a medical background). The novel has thereby become slightly co-opted into the (highly mythologized) real-life Whitechapel story, which, like the mystery of Jekyll, has never been satisfactorily resolved.

Even the earliest stage version made out Hyde to be a "voluptuary," to which Stevenson objected strongly, writing to John Paul Bocock in 1887:

[Hyde] was not good-looking [. . .] and not, Great Gods! a mere voluptuary. There is no harm in a voluptuary; and none, with my hand on my heart and in the sight of God, none—no harm whatever in what prurient fools call "immorality". The harm was in Jekyll, because he was a hypocrite—not because he was fond of women; he says so himself; but people are so filled with folly and inverted lust, that they can think of nothing but sexuality. The Hypocrite let out the beast Hyde—who is no more sexual than another, but who is the essence of cruelty and malice, and selfishness and cowardice, and these are the diabolic in man—not this poor wish to have a woman that they make such a cry about.

(Letters, vol. 6, p. 56)

Stevenson's great allegory has exercised a profound fascination and influence over later writers, most notably Oscar Wilde in *The Picture of Dorian Gray* (1891), H. G. Wells in *The Invisible Man* (1897), Bram Stoker's *Dracula* (1897), and Franz Kafka's *Metamorphosis.* Mark Twain, Jorge Luis Borges, Graham Greene, Vladimir Nabokov, and Italo Calvino are among the many writers who have acknowledged the importance of this work to them. *The Strange Case of Dr. Jekyll and Mr. Hyde* struck a chord that continues to reverberate, though it has not, until recently, been considered worthy of very close study. Stevenson has always been a popular author but never a canonical one. *Treasure Island, A Child's Garden of Verses, Kidnapped,* and *Jekyll and Hyde*—four very different popular classics—have hardly appeared on syllabuses of nineteenth-century literature until very recently. The critical consensus up to the last twenty years or so seems to have been that Stevenson's works were not quite "literary" enough to study.

Select Bibliography

EDITIONS

The Strange Case of Dr. Jekyll and Mr. Hyde. In *Robert Louis Stevenson: The Collected Shorter Fiction.* Edited by Peter Stoneley. London: Robinson Publishing, 1991.

The Strange Case of Dr. Jekyll and Mr. Hyde. London: Longmans, Green and Co., 1886.

Dr. Jekyll and Mr. Hyde and Other Stories. Edited by Jenni Calder. London: Penguin, 1979.

The Strange Case of Dr. Jekyll and Mr. Hyde and Other Stories. Introduced by Claire Harman. London: Everyman, 1992.

Robert Louis Stevenson, The Complete Short Stories. Edited by Ian Bell. Edinburgh: Canongate, 1993.

OTHER WORKS BY STEVENSON

Essays and Poems. Edited by Claire Harman. London: Penguin, 1992.

Collected Works. Vailima Edition. 26 vols. London: Methuen, 1923.

The Lantern-Bearers and Other Essays. Edited by Jeremy Treglowan. London: Chatto & Windus, 1988.

SECONDARY WORKS

Balfour, Graham. *The Life of Robert Louis Stevenson.* London: Methuen, 1901.

Beattie, Hilary J. "Father and Son: The Origins of *Strange Case of Dr. Jekyll and Mr. Hyde.*" *Psychoanalytic Study of the Child* 56 (2001): 317–360.

Booth, Bradford A., and Ernest Mehew, eds. *The Letters of Robert Louis Stevenson.* 8 vols. New Haven: Yale University Press, 1984–1985).

Borges, J. L. *Borges on Writing.* London: Allen Lane, 1974.

Calder, Jenni. *R L S: A Life Study.* London: Hamish Hamilton, 1980.

Clunas, Alex. "Robert Louis Stevenson: Precursor of the Post-Moderns?",*Cencrastus* 6 (1981): 9–11.

Colvin, Sidney. *Robert Louis Stevenson: His Work and Personality.* London: Hodder and Stoughton, 1924.

Daiches, David. *Robert Louis Stevenson, A Revaluation.* Glasgow: W. Maclellan, 1947.

————. *Robert Louis Stevenson and his World.* London: Thames and Hudson, 1973.

Eigner, E. M. *Robert Louis Stevenson and Romantic Tradition.* Princeton: Princeton University Press, 1967.

Elwin, Malcolm. *The Strange Case of Robert Louis Stevenson.* London: Macdonald, 1950.

Ferguson, Delancey, and Marshall Waingrow, eds. *R. L. S.: Stevenson's Letters to Charles Baxter.* London: Oxford University Press, and New Haven: Yale University Press, 1956.

Furnas, J. L. *Voyage to Windward: The Life of Robert Louis Stevenson.* London: Faber and Faber, 1952.

Ginzburg, Carlo. *No Island is an Island: Four Glances at English Literature in a World Perspective.* New York: Columbia University Press, 2000.

Greene, Graham. *Collected Essays.* London: Vintage, 1999.

Hammerton, J. A. *Stevensoniana.* New edition. Edinburgh: John Grant, 1907.

Hammond, J. R. *A Robert Louis Stevenson Companion.* London: Methuen, 1984.

Heath, Stephen. "Psychopathia Sexualis: Stevenson's *Strange Case.*" *Critical Quarterly* 28 (1986): 93–108.

Houghton, W. E. *The Victorian Frame of Mind, 1830–1870.* New Haven: Yale University Press, 1957.

James, Henry. "Robert Louis Stevenson." In *Notes on Novelists.* London: J. M. Dent, 1914.

Koestenbaum, Wayne. *Double Talk: The Erotics of Male Literary Collaboration.* New York: Routledge, 1989.

Maixner, Paul, ed. *Robert Louis Stevenson: The Critical Heritage.* London: Routledge, 1981.

McLynn, Frank. *Robert Louis Stevenson.* London: Hutchinson, 1993.

Mehew, Ernest, ed. *Selected Letters of Robert Louis Stevenson.* New Haven: Yale University Press, 1997.

Miller, Karl. *Doubles: Studies in Literary History.* Oxford: Oxford University Press, 1985.

Nabokov, V. "Dr. Jekyll and Mr. Hyde." In *Lectures on Literature.* Edited by F. Bowers. London: Weidenfeld and Nicolson, 1980. Pp. 179–205.

Osbourne, Lloyd. *An Intimate Portrait of R. L. S.* New York: Scribners, 1924.

Prideaux, W. F. *A Bibliography of the Works of Robert Louis Stevenson.* London: Frank Hollings, 1918.

Schueller, Herbert M., and Robert L. Peters, *The Letters of John Addington Symonds.* Detroit: Wayne State University Press, 1967–1969.

Showalter, Elaine. *Sexual Anarchy: Gender and Culture at the Fin de Siècle.* London: Bloomsbury, 1991.

Swearingen, Roger G., ed. *The Prose Writings of Robert Louis Stevenson.* London: Methuen, 1980.

Veeder, W., and G. Hirsch, eds. *Dr. Jekyll and Mr. Hyde after One Hundred Years.* Chicago: University of Chicago Press, 1988.

Watson, Roderick, ed. *Robert Louis Stevenson, Shorter Scottish Fiction.* Edinburgh: Canongate, 1995.

INTERNET RESOURCE

See also the extensive reading lists, filmography, and databases at www.unibg.it/rls.

Laurence Sterne's
Tristram Shandy

SCOTT MACKENZIE

AS LAURENCE STERNE himself would say, *Tristram Shandy* is an absolutely singular book. There is no other work quite like it. Originally published in nine volumes over eight years by an Anglican clergyman who spent his first forty-seven years in obscurity and his last eight as a national celebrity, *Tristram Shandy* is a paradoxical work that has fascinated and bewildered readers since its first appearance in 1759. It is a parody of novels written before the novel was a fully established literary form. It is a biography whose subject hardly appears, the philosophy of one who does not believe in philosophical systems, a history without a story, and a work of remarkable originality that is full of plagiarized passages. It purports to be the life and opinions of Tristram Shandy, as told by Tristram himself, but other topics constantly divert him away from his own story, so the central character remains an enigma and an absence. *Tristram Shandy* is also full of digressions, reflections, and meditations on a host of subjects, including medicine, philosophy, religion, law, and gender. Tristram often speaks directly to the reader, addressing us as "sir" and "madam," and instructing us on how to read his book. In the later volumes he goes as far as replying to critics who have attacked the earlier volumes. It also has no stable chronological order; Tristram jumps between various narratives haphazardly, moving forward and backward in time as he sees fit. The setting of *Tristram Shandy* is Shandy Hall in Yorkshire, where Tristram's parents, Walter and Elizabeth, and his uncle Toby live, and the various narratives mostly concern the misfortunes of the Shandies (especially where love, sex, and reproduction are concerned) and the ways they affect Tristram's development.

Tristram Shandy has suffered an unfortunate reversal of fortune since the decade of its first publication. It is now a novel that is usually seen as enigmatic, esoteric, or, worst of all, academic—of interest only to obsessive bookworms. Even scholars of eighteenth-century literature tend to skirt it both in their studies and in the classroom. In the typical college undergraduate syllabus it is often replaced by Sterne's only other notable work, *A Sentimental Journey,* which is much smaller and vastly less challenging. *Tristram Shandy* has found itself keeping company with modernist works like T. S. Eliot's "The Waste Land" and James Joyce's *Ulysses,* works whose study is all too often limited to painstaking explication of the author's many allusions to other literary, philosophical, scientific, and religious texts. The average reader seldom gets past these obstacles to find the pleasure and humor that *Tristram Shandy* (as well as "The Waste Land" and *Ulysses*) has to offer. But obscurity and mustiness have not always been its lot; when the first two volumes of *Tristram Shandy* appeared at the end of 1759, the novel was an immediate popular success. The succeeding volumes, of which there were seven, were published at irregular intervals over the following eight years to eager anticipation. Laurence Sterne became a celebrity in Britain and all over continental Europe, where the book was published in German, French, and Dutch translations. Although the proportion of the public that had the opportunity to read novels then was much smaller than it is today, it is hardly an exaggeration to compare Sterne's literary success then to that of Stephen King or Jackie Collins now.

In Sterne's lifetime huge numbers of people read and discussed *Tristram Shandy,* and also imitated and attacked it. There were even fake versions of new volumes published by forgers eager to share in the spoils. In 1761 an anonymous critic referred to it as "the pocket-companion of the nation" (quoted in Ross 2001, 18). Contemporary readers, like modern readers, were mystified, misled, and offended by *Tristram Shandy,* but it was unquestionably a *popular* work, and Sterne unquestionably meant it to be so: "I wrote not to be *fed,* but to be *famous,*" he told a detractor who had accused him of writing for profit (*Letters,* 90). That is not to say that Sterne did not also seek financial rewards along with his notoriety: "I suppose I may be allow'd to have that view in my head in common with every other writer, to make my labour of advantage to myself," he told the same detractor. "Do you not do the same?" (*Letters,* 89).

An important reason for the book's popularity was its puncturing of all kinds of pretension and affectation. Sterne's often maddeningly

CHRONOLOGY

1713	24 November: Laurence Sterne born near Clonmel, Ireland, where his father, Roger, an ensign in the English army, is stationed. The same day Roger Sterne's regiment is disbanded, forcing him to move his family back to England in a long and frustrating search for financial stability.
1723	Laurence leaves home to attend school in Yorkshire. His uncle Richard becomes his guardian.
1731	Death of Roger Sterne in Port Antonio, Jamaica, where he had finally achieved promotion only months before.
1733	Begins studies at Jesus College, Cambridge. His great- grandfather, another Richard Sterne, had been master of Jesus College, as well as archbishop of York. A cousin provides monetary support for Laurence while he studies.
1737	Receives a Bachelor of Arts degree and leaves Cambridge. He has read widely while studying, including the works of John Locke and texts in Latin, Greek, and French. After graduating, he takes orders as an Anglican clergyman. In this year he also has his first attack of tuberculosis.
1738	Becomes vicar of Sutton-on-the-Forest, near York, where the wealthy and influential members of the Sterne family have their homes.
1741	30 March: Marries Elizabeth Lumley. Their only surviving child is Lydia, born in 1747. Sterne gains a deserved reputation in his parish as an unfaithful husband.
1742	Having spent almost a year and a half supporting the Whig Party in bitter political pamphlet wars, Sterne angrily renounces politics, thus offending his uncle Jacques and ending his chances of rising to power in the Anglican Church.
1743	Publishes "The Unknown World:

Verses Occasioned by Hearing a Pass-Bell" in *The Gentleman's Magazine*.

1747   Publishes a sermon, "The Case of Elijah and the Widow of Zarephath Considered. A Charity Sermon."

1750   Publishes another sermon, "The Abuses of Conscience: Set Forth in a Sermon." This sermon is later reproduced in volume II of *Tristram Shandy* as the work of Parson Yorick.

1759   Publishes *A Political Romance* (also known as *The History of a Good Warm Watch-Coat*). All but a few copies of the text are burned at the command of powerful churchmen. In December a small edition of the first two volumes of *Tristram Shandy* is printed. Two hundred copies make their way to a bookseller in London, and are sold almost immediately.

1760   Robert Dodsley publishes a larger edition of volumes I and II, and Sterne becomes a celebrity overnight. He also publishes two volumes of sermons with the title *The Sermons of Mr. Yorick*.

1761   Volumes III and IV of *Tristram Shandy* appear in January; volumes V and VI, in December.

1762   Departs England for Europe, seeking to alleviate the effects of his tuberculosis. Lives mostly in the South of France until 1764.

1765   Publishes volumes VII and VIII of *Tristram Shandy*, then returns to Europe.

1767   Publishes volume IX, the last volume of *Tristram Shandy*.

1768   Completes and publishes his final work, *A Sentimental Journey*, which is based on his travels in Europe and features Parson Yorick as his alter ego. Three weeks later, on 18 March, Laurence Sterne dies.

SELECT CHRONOLOGY OF EVENTS MENTIONED IN *TRISTRAM SHANDY*

1695   The English army lays siege to the French occupiers of Namur, a fortified town in Flanders. During this battle Tristram's uncle Toby receives wound on his groin from a piece of falling masonry (I: 75).

1700   After four years recuperating from his wound, Toby moves to Shandy Hall, to begin building, on his bowling green, miniature re-creations of European battles (II: 107).

1713   The Treaty of Utrecht ends the War of the Spanish Succession, and also ends Toby's re-creations (VI: 552). The "Cock and Bull story," which ends volume IX, is told (IX: 806).

1716   Walter Shandy writes a "dissertation simply upon the word Tristram" (I: 63).

1718   March: Tristram's conception (I: 6). November 5: Tristram's birth (I: 8).

1720   Death of Tristram's elder brother Bobby (IV: 399).

1723   Tristram's accidental circumcision by a window sash (V: 449).

1748   Death of Parson Yorick (I: 35).

1751   Dr. John Burton publishes his *Essay... of Midwifery*. Sterne caricatures Burton as Dr. Slop (II: 121).

1753   William Hogarth publishes his *Analysis of Beauty*, to which Tristram often refers approvingly (II: 121). Hogarth also provided an illustration for each of the first two volumes of *Tristram Shandy*.

1766   12 August: Tristram records his beginning volume IX (IX: 737).

intricate style and disorienting changes of narrative direction make fun of writers and thinkers who use convoluted, jargon-filled, and overwrought prose. This book, which we now tend to see as a pretentious display of learning and obscure wit, was first meant as a satirical attack on those very faults. *Tristram Shandy* certainly is packed full of allusion to, and outright stealing from, a prodigious collection of other texts (one of Sterne's best-loved thefts is an attack on plagiarists that he plagiarized from the seventeenth-century writer Robert Burton), but it seems that Sterne did not particularly care whether his audience "got" the allusions or not. "Read, read, read, my unlearned reader! read," he exhorts us, or "you had better throw down the book at once; for without *much reading,* by which your reverence knows, I mean *much knowledge,*" we will not be able to understand the meaning of the next page (III: 268). As it turns out, the next page has no text on it, but instead is a sheet of marbled paper. So much for book learning.

Of course understanding Sterne's satirical intentions does not give us the key to all the meanings of *Tristram Shandy,* but it does illustrate a very important part of the text's purpose: it is supposed to be fun, and funny. It is, as the great German Romantic Johann Wolfgang von Goethe called it, *"Ein Buch für freie Geister"*—a book for free spirits (quoted in Pfister 2001, 4). Its author, who tended to refer to himself in correspondence and conversation as Tristram, is well-known as a remarkable free spirit. Although he came to prominence late in life, Sterne made himself one of the most vivid personalities in an age that featured many colorful celebrities, including the writers Samuel Johnson and Hester Thrale Piozzi, the writer-politicians Edmund Burke and Horace Walpole, the philosopher David Hume, and the actor David Garrick. Successful public figures enjoyed remarkable social mobility. Sterne dined and conversed with the rich, famous, and noble. He carried on love affairs with a number of young women and he traveled through much of Europe, composing more volumes of *Tristram Shandy* all the while. This success seems more extraordinary when we consider that at the age of forty-five Sterne was known to few people other than churchgoers in the parishes of Sutton-on-the-Forest and Stillington, near the northern city of York, where he was the Anglican priest. He had long nursed ambitions for fame andx fortune, and it was *Tristram Shandy* that enabled him, in his forty-seventh year, to realize them.

Laurence Sterne was born in Clonmel, Ireland, on 24 November 1713, the very same day that the English army regiment in which his father was an ensign was disbanded. Sterne's immediate ancestors were members of the Yorkshire gentry and his social standing was therefore perfectly respectable, but he was the son of a younger son and so his father had inherited no substantial property. He was raised in conditions that were often close to poverty. With financial assistance and social influence supplied by relatives, Sterne was able to earn a degree at Cambridge University (where he read many of the texts that he would plunder in *Tristram Shandy*), take holy orders, and acquire a living as pastor of Sutton-on-the-Forest. His literary career began in 1741 when his uncle Jacques Sterne asked him to work as a political journalist, which actually meant writing essays attacking and satirizing his uncle's political opponents. Jacques Sterne was a well-connected lawyer for the Anglican Church, and the person most responsible for getting Laurence his first appointment, so when Laurence decided in 1742 that he did not relish this "journalism," he knew very well that he was giving up his chances of gaining an important position in the church hierarchy. For the next seventeen years Sterne lived in obscurity, publishing in that time two sermons, an anonymous poem in *The Gentleman's Magazine,* and a satire on corruption in the church that was suppressed by the archbishop of York.

When volumes I and II of *Tristram Shandy* were printed for the first time in 1759, the edition consisted of only five hundred copies made at a press in York. But Sterne had already begun promoting himself by making himself known to publishers, booksellers, and critics and by writing to the rich and famous, seeking patronage. As soon as Robert Dodsley, a very successful London bookseller, started to offer copies of *Tristram Shandy* in his shop, Sterne's fame was assured. A larger edition of volumes I and II was printed in London in 1760, followed by volumes III and IV in January 1761 and volumes V and VI in December of the same year. Thereafter the pace of composition decreased. The next two volumes were published in January 1765, and the ninth and last volume arrived two years later. By then *Tristram Shandy* was best-loved on the Continent, and Sterne's death was only a year away.

2. A READING

It is easy to forget, in reading modern editions of eighteenth-century novels, that they originally appeared in multiple volumes that were in some cases published months and even years apart. The last volume of *Tristram Shandy* was finished seven years after the first two were in print, which is probably the longest publication period of any single novel in English. Over the course of such a long period of composition, the author's circumstances and intentions can change dramatically. The trip through Europe that Tristram narrates in volume VII, for instance, is based on travels Sterne was able to make because of the money that he had earned from earlier volumes of the same work. Unlike most works published in serial form, however, *Tristram Shandy* could not lose its coherence as a result of changing circumstances—its narrative is so full of interruptions and digressions and changes of direction that virtually any new idea, theme, or story could fit into its rambling form. Providing new and surprising twists is one of the stated goals of the narrator—Tristram himself; he ends several volumes with promises like this one: "The reader will be content to wait for a full explanation of these matters till the next year, when a series of things will be laid open which he little expects" (II: 181); or this one: "I take my leave of you till this time twelve-month, when ... I'll have another pluck at your beards, and lay open a story to the world you little dream of" (IV: 402).

Whether *Tristram Shandy* is really a novel at all is still in dispute. Many critics have argued that it should be called a parody of a novel rather than a novel. Others have argued that such a distinction is worthless. In any case, the definition of a novel remains itself very much under debate. In the 1760s novels were still quite rare; novel-reading was just becoming a widespread popular pastime. With the conventions of the novel barely established, one might think that Sterne could not find many ways to bend or break them, yet he does so with extraordinary frequency. To begin with, one would expect that a novel whose full title is *The Life and Opinions of Tristram Shandy, Gentleman* would concentrate largely on the life and opinions of Tristram Shandy. In fact, although Tristram is the narrator, we hardly see anything of him. Instead a very great portion of the novel takes place before and during Tristram's birth, and focuses on Tristram's father, Walter Shandy, who is an ardent amateur philosopher, and his uncle, Toby Shandy, who relives (and relieves) the trauma of a war wound by re-creating battles in miniature.

We also encounter part or all of many other stories; mocking discussions of a welter of philosophical, legal, medical, and religious theories; and even a few inserted graphics, such as the marbled page mentioned above. Tristram's *goal* is to present us with his own life and opinions, but he wishes to do it so thoroughly that nothing is left out, and no reader is disappointed: "I find it necessary to consult every one a little in his turn.... For which cause right glad I am, that I have begun the history of myself in the way I have done; and that I am able to go on tracing everything in it, as *Horace* says, *ab Ovo* [from the egg]" (I: 5). Here Sterne is making fun of Tristram's pretensions: Horace was a Roman satirist who famously advised writers to begin their stories *in medias res* (in the middle of things)—not, as Tristram says, ab ovo (from the very beginning).

Nonetheless, from the egg is quite literally where Tristram begins his tale. The first chapter of the novel tells of the night he was conceived. From that point on, Tristram hopes to narrate all of the important circumstances of his life, and one of the novel's great jokes is his inability to keep up, much less catch up, with himself. His birth does not come until volume III, and in volume IV he pauses to admit:

> I am this month one whole year older than I was this time twelve-month; and having got, as you perceive, almost into the middle of my fourth volume—and no farther than to my first day's life—'tis demonstrative that I have three hundred and sixty-four days more life to write just now, than when I first set out; … at this rate I should live just 364 times faster than I should write—It must follow … that the more I write, the more I shall have to write. (IV: 341–342)

This kind of meditative pause, in which Tristram talks directly to the reader about the process of writing, the progress of his narrative, and the difficulties of storytelling, occurs very frequently in *Tristram Shandy*. Sometimes whole chapters are taken up with what Tristram calls his "digressions." They form one half of "the machinery" of his narrative: "My work is of a species by itself," he says, "two contrary motions are introduced into it, and reconciled, which were thought to be at variance with each other. In a word, my work is digressive, and it is progressive too,—and at the same time" (I: 80–81). Once again, Tristram's claim of originality is a little fraudulent. The digression is a technique borrowed from Jonathan Swift, who in 1704 published a religious satire called *A Tale of a Tub* that included a chapter titled "A Digression in Praise of Digressions." *A Tale of a Tub*, though it is certainly not a novel, is one of the most important models for Sterne's style in *Tristram Shandy*. Both texts feature a narrator who likes to address the reader directly, whose ideas are eccentric, and who requires us to take a skeptical attitude to what he tells us.

Digression and progression are very important terms for understanding how narrative works in general. As we read novels we usually imagine ourselves moving toward a destination of some kind, a resolution that may involve a marriage, the completion of a quest, or the defeat of an enemy. There is no such destination in *Tristram Shandy*. The only path that the story can follow is the life of the narrator himself, and he is too busy stopping and starting, suspending one story to tell another, and moving back and forth in time, ever to get to himself. Because there is really no sense of direction for the story, Sterne plays up the fact that it is often very hard to tell the difference between digression and progression—how can we tell if we're making progress when we don't know where we are supposed to be going? At the end of volume VI, Tristram draws a series of lines, which he claims are the paths his narrative has followed so far. The lines are very disorderly, featuring loops, zigzags, and spirals. In the sixth volume, he says, he has done very well, and hopes that he may achieve

the excellency of going on even thus;

_____

(VI: 571)

The irony is, of course, that in pausing to make this promise Tristram has once again interrupted the "progression" of his narrative.

Sterne simply cannot tell a story from start to finish without getting distracted or diverted. We must remember that no story is ever truly a straight line between beginning and end. Every novelist digresses. Without digression, novelists would be unable to describe characters and settings, explain what characters are thinking and why they are acting, provide flashbacks, or narrate stories that happen simultaneously. What sets Sterne apart from other novelists is the way he has Tristram constantly discuss his problems in telling the story. Besides, Tristram says, "digressions, incontestably, are the sun-shine;—they are the life, the soul of reading;—take them out of this book for instance,—you might as well take the book along with them" (I: 81). A great deal of *Tristram Shandy* is the story of the telling of the story. James Swearingen calls this process "reflexivity," which means highlighting the techniques the writer is using to tell the story. Sterne is satirizing the way that novelists often use many complex and subtle devices to give the impression of a simple, straightforward narrative. Hollywood films today do a similar kind of thing; in order to give the impression of reality, they use a very highly organized collection of shooting, editing, special effects, and sound-dubbing tactics that modern audiences have learned to recognize and understand without having to stop and think. Tristram, who cannot get a grip on his narrative techniques, forces us to stop and think about what they are and how they work, or fail to work.

He places the blame for his many failures upon the way he was conceived. The event is interrupted in a way that sets the stage for all the interruptions to follow. Tristram's mother, Elizabeth, asks his father, at a particularly awkward moment, "Pray, my Dear ... have you not forgot to wind up the clock?" (I: 2). In the Shandy household, a routine has been established, whereby once a month Walter winds the clock and also performs "some other little family concernments ... in order ... to get them all out of the way at one time" (I: 6). When Elizabeth reminds Walter that he has forgotten to perform one task just as he is about to complete the other, she causes Walter's animal spirits to scatter. The animal spirits were a substance believed by philosophers to connect the body to the mind. In the mid-eighteenth century the theory of animal spirits was no longer widely accepted, which made it very attractive to Sterne, who loved to make fun of outlandish ideas. Tristram, however, believes in the theory of animal spirits; they are, he says, "transfused from father to son," and

> nine parts in ten of a man's sense or his nonsense, his successes, his miscarriages in this world depend upon their motions and activity, and the different tracks and trains you put them into; so that when they are once set a-going ... away they go cluttering like hey-go-mad; and by treading the same steps over and over again, they presently make a road of it, as plain and smooth as a garden-walk. (I: 1–2)

In other words, because Walter is interrupted at a crucial moment, Tristram's whole develop-ment and fortune in the world go spinning out of control. And presumably because a clock was involved, his ability to deal with time is especially badly affected.

Sterne stole the description of animal spirits quoted above almost word for word from John Locke's *An Essay Concerning Human Understanding* (1690). Locke, among the most important and influential British philosophers, established theories of psychology and language that Sterne borrows and rearranges in order to explain the behavior of his characters. Sterne does not accept Locke's system unquestioningly. Any kind of system that claims to explain the world is suspicious. Tristram says of his father, "he was systematical, and, like all systematic reasoners, he would move both heaven and earth, and twist and torture every thing in nature to support his hypothesis" (I: 61). The passage on animal spirits that Tristram steals comes from Locke's explanation of what he calls the "association of ideas." Put as simply as possible, Locke's theory is that the process of thought is a series of ideas running through the mind in succession, and often the mind will make a connection between two or more ideas. These connections, or associations, may form because ideas resemble one another (for example, a chair is like a couch), or because they are opposites (say, hot and cold). Locke calls these kinds of association "a natural correspondence and connexion," because they derive from similarities and oppositions that exist in the actual world. By making connections between ideas, we develop our understandings and our abilities to interact with the world and other people.

But, Locke writes, "there is another connexion of ideas wholly owing to chance or custom; ideas that in themselves are not at all of kin, come to be so united in some men's minds that it is very hard to separate them ... and if there are more than two which are thus united, the whole gang, always inseparable, show themselves together" (395). The repetition of a chain of thoughts that have no natural connection (such as winding a clock and conjugal duties) becomes a custom, and thereby forms an association: Tristram writes, "it so fell out at length, that my poor mother could never hear the said clock wound up,—but the thoughts of some other things unavoidably popp'd into her head" (I: 7). According to Locke, this kind of involuntary false association is what causes madness.

One of the twists that Sterne applies to Locke's system is to suggest that everyone forms associations that are potentially crazy. Tristram, his father, and his uncle Toby are each ruled by a set of ideas that has some impact on everything that each of them does, thinks, and says. Tristram calls these ruling ideas hobbyhorses. Literally, a hobbyhorse is a toy that a child pretends to ride. Sterne uses it as a metaphor to convey the comical image of everyone galloping about on wooden toys, each of us imagining that our toy is something much more grand and exciting than it is: "have not the wisest of men in all ages, not excepting *Solomon* himself,—have they not had their HOBBY-HORSES …?—and so long as a man rides his way, and neither compels you or me to get up behind him,—pray, Sir, what have either you or I to do with it?" (I: 12). A hobbyhorse is an obsession, a ruling passion, the thing to which one devotes so much thought that it influences all other thoughts. Tristram's hobbyhorse is representing himself through stories, Walter's is his systems of philosophy, and Toby's is his fascination with re-creating military actions, and particularly the fortifications involved. John Traugott, who has written the most important study of Sterne's relationship to Locke, writes, "Toby is exactly Locke's madman. And yet he is only ludicrous in the way every man *must* be, for he is only creating a situation by which he expresses himself, as every man must" (1954, 47). Our hobbyhorses make us what we are; Tristram says of a man's hobbyhorse and his character, "if you are able to give but a clear description of the nature of the one, you may form a pretty exact notion of the genius and character of the other"(I: 86).

But hobbyhorses also make it difficult for us to communicate with one another. A great deal of the humor in *Tristram Shandy* comes from the failures of communication, the misunderstandings, that hobbyhorses cause. The central "problem" of the novel, Tristram's failure to tell us about his life, arises because his hobbyhorse leads him off on so many tangents in the quest to give absolutely every detail and to please every single reader. He and his father have a similar weakness: they want words to convey meanings perfectly. But Sterne takes every opportunity to show how words can have differing meanings in differing contexts and from differing viewpoints. At times the misunderstandings become very convoluted. For example, in volume III, soon after Tristram's birth, Walter, Toby, and Toby's manservant Corporal Trim are waiting in the parlor when they hear a commotion in the kitchen. Trim informs them that it is Doctor Slop, the "man-midwife" who is supposed to be attending the birth. "What can the fellow be puzzling about in the kitchen!" Walter asks. "He is busy," replies Trim, "in making a bridge." "'Tis very obliging in him," says Toby (II: 243). Why Toby should say such a thing requires a digression lasting almost ten pages to explain. Toby, who thinks only of military matters, assumes that Doctor Slop is building a model bridge for Toby to use in one of his battle re-creations, replacing one that Trim had broken while trying to seduce a fellow servant, whose name happens to be Bridget. Hence, Toby feels gratitude toward the doctor.

Walter, whose philosophical hobbyhorse gives him a taste for long orations, delights in making fun of Toby's hobbyhorse and is about to do so now: "This unfortunate draw-bridge of yours—" Walter begins, but Trim interrupts to explain what Dr. Slop is actually building: "God bless your honour … 'tis a bridge for [Tristram's] nose.—In bringing him into the world with his vile instruments, [Doctor Slop] has crush'd his nose" (III: 253). Dr. Slop uses forceps, a "masculine" tool that has wounded the infant Tristram. Walter believes, for very complicated reasons, that a prominent nose is essential for success in the world, and so he is heartbroken.

Ironically, Walter is responsible for the very disaster he wanted to avoid. He had arranged for Doctor Slop to attend the birth, despite Elizabeth Shandy's objections, because his theories about the way childbirth affects the head of an infant led him to believe that a male physician (or man-midwife) was preferable to the traditional midwife. In the Shandy family almost every scheme goes wrong. Complicated systems and book learning do not work when applied to the reality of Tristram's world. They lead to equally complicated chains of events that end in exactly the wrong result; "the wisest of us all," Tristram laments, "should thus outwit ourselves, and eternally forgo our purposes in the intemperate act of pursuing them" (V: 448). Probably the most striking example is Tristram's name. "Of all names in the universe" Walter has "the most unconquerable aversion for Tristram" (I: 62–63). No one, he loves to say, "had ever heard tell of a man, call'd *Tristram,* performing any thing great or worth recording" (I: 63). In fact, Walter writes an entire book "simply upon the word *Tristram,*—shewing the world ... the grounds of his great abhorrence to the name" (I: 63). But one of the rules of the Shandy world is that the more one wants something not to happen, the more likely it is to happen (and vice versa), and because of a mix-up at the baptism, Walter's son ends up with the name Tristram.

It is hardly surprising that Walter should dislike the name Tristram; it is derived from the Latin word *tristis,* an adjective that means "sorrow" or "causing sorrow." The name turns out to be perfectly appropriate; Tristram's life is a constant series of disappointments to Walter, and to Tristram himself. The lesson seems to be that using words to try to control events can only lead to disaster. Walter is very good at manipulating ideas with words, but his assumption that he can also manipulate the things and people around him with words is mistaken. At times words seem to have a life of their own. Both Walter and Tristram try to master language in order to achieve their ends, but language winds up mastering them. During a discussion between Walter and Toby about whether a male or a female physician should attend a childbirth, Toby makes an observation that takes Walter so much by surprise that he snaps his pipe in two. Having then recovered himself enough to begin one of his speeches, Walter sets out to explain his theory of women. This theory, he announces, is based on analogy. Of course he is interrupted: "I never understood rightly the meaning of that word,—quoth my uncle Toby" (II: 118). Unperturbed, Walter begins a definition of analogy: "ANALOGY, replied my father, is the certain relation and agreement, which different—Here a devil of a rap at the door snapp'd my father's definition (like his tobacco pipe) in two" (II: 118). Walter never finishes his definition, but the interruption from the rap at the door provides an example of analogy anyway. Analogy is an argument or description made by means of comparison: the interruption of Walter's definition resembles the snapping of his pipe. For once, Walter has managed to achieve something like what he intended, but nevertheless words have gotten away from him and created an outcome that he did not plan.

The snapping of Walter's pipe is also characteristic of the fate that befalls pretty much anything in *Tristram Shandy* that has phallic overtones about it. Beginning with the coitus interruptus of volume I, chapter 1, male sexual potency and anything that symbolizes male sexual potency suffers some kind of reversal. Tristram's crushed nose and Toby's wounded groin have already been mentioned. In volume IV, a dirty-minded cleric named Phutatorius receives a burning hot chestnut in the unclosed "aperture" of his breeches, and in volume V the five-year-old Tristram is accidentally circumcised when a window slams shut as he urinates out of it. All male sexual potency in the Shandy household is destined for failure. Aside from the humor that Sterne draws from these various events, he seems to be reinforcing the sense that things (especially the male "thing") cannot be controlled and manipulated as easily as words. The metaphors of power, penetration, force, and fertility that tend to attach to the male member never work in *Tristram Shandy* because metaphors are attributes of words, not of things. Masculine "ideals" of mastery and penetration elude the men of the Shandy family.

Tristram is the last of his line. He has not fathered an heir, and it seems certain that he never will. He is the last heir of a family of men whose "manhood" is disappearing. In fact Tristram may not even be the biological son of Walter. The date Tristram gives for his birth is, he says, "as near nine kalendar months as any husband could in reason have expected" (I: 8), but it is actually eight months after the interrupted conception, and Walter could not have fulfilled his conjugal duties at an earlier date because he was "all that time afflicted with a Sciatica" (I: 7). Some critics have argued that Sterne intended to imply that Yorick, the local parson, is Tristram's biological father. Nonetheless, in terms of his fortunes and temperament, Tristram seems very much to be Walter's son. He cannot even manage to reproduce himself in print (that is, in the book we are reading), and Sterne wants us to be quite conscious of the parallels between "author" and "father." Walter quite literally mixes the roles of author and father: soon after Tristram's birth, Walter begins to write "a Tristra-*poedia,* or system of education for [Tristram]; collecting first for that purpose his own scattered thoughts, counsels, and notions; and binding them together so as to form an INSTITUTE for the government of [his] childhood and adolescence" (V: 445). And where Tristram's book cannot catch up to its subject, Walter's cannot stay ahead of that same subject:

> he was three years, and something more, indefatigably at work, and, at last, had scarce completed, by his own reckoning, one half of his undertaking: the misfortune was, that I was all that time totally neglected and abandoned to my mother; and what was almost as bad, by the very delay, the first part of the work, upon which my father had spent the most of his pains, was

> rendered entirely useless,—every day a page or two became of no consequence. (V: 448)

Like father, like son; like author, like text.

Words tend not to have the effects that their author intends, but they do have effects. "Be cautious of your language," Tristram warns his readers, "and never, O! never let it be forgotten upon what small particles your eloquence and your fame depend" (I: 116). And yet he seems constantly to be concluding that language is beyond his control, especially where profane or sexually suggestive language is concerned. For instance, what Toby says to make Walter snap his pipe is a speculation about why Elizabeth Shandy might prefer a midwife to Dr. Slop: "My sister, I dare say ... does not care to let a man come so near her ****" (II: 115). When Tristram uses asterisks to replace some impolite term—which he does frequently—the number of asterisks tends to match the number of letters in the word or words that seem best to fit the space. A contemporary respondent observes as much: "Four *asterisms* [asterisks] are but four *asterisms*—and ever since asterisms have been in use, we have always been taught that their number should be supplied by a like number of letters to make out the sense" (quoted in New 1998, 40). This respondent then goes on to reveal the "sense":

> Curious, indefatigable, unblushing readers, consider what letters will properly supply the place, without infringing upon the sense ... *arm* and *leg* have but three letters, and be hanged to them.—*Thigh* comes near it, but then there is a letter too many.—I have it—the *third,* the *twentieth,* the *thirteenth,* and the *nineteenth* letters of the English alphabet certainly compose the word.
>
> (quoted in New 1998, 40)

Tristram himself has given the four "asterisms" a similar working over: "Make this dash,—'tis an aposiopesis [an interruption].—Take the dash away, and write backside,—'tis bawdy.—Scratch backside out, and put *cover'd-way* in,—

'tis a metaphor" (II: 116). We are left in no doubt about what Toby was referring to, but we may wonder whether any such thing as direct communication is possible.

Sterne completely undermines any pretense that the asterisks are there to keep the tone polite. Their suggestion of limitless possible meanings forces us to actively engage ourselves with the text, but Sterne reminds us that we, like Tristram, cannot control, penetrate, or master these words. *Tristram Shandy* is meant to frustrate and "unman" its readers, too. The asterisks, in any case, are not exactly the same as a word. They fall somewhere between word and thing. We cannot ask what they mean, but rather what they *do.* As the anonymous pamphleteer says, "four asterisms are but four asterisms." A novel, when printed, bound, and sold, is also a way of turning words into things. Sterne reminds us ironically that in reading a novel, we take an object and treat it as though it is somehow a person. He is also, once again, tweaking Locke. Locke's theory of language holds that words connect not to things in reality, but to ideas that we have formed about things. Words are signs that we attach to our ideas. As Locke puts it, "The use then of words, is to be sensible marks of *ideas*; and the *ideas* they stand for, are their proper and immediate signification" (405).

Unfortunately, ideas themselves cannot be shared: "Man, though he have great variety of thoughts, and such from which others, as well as himself, might receive profit and delight; yet they are all within his own breast, invisible, and hidden from others, nor can of themselves be made appear" (Locke, 404–405). Hence, Locke readily admits that words are an imperfect means of communication, because of the variability in different people's ideas. He does, however, believe that uncertainty can be overcome. His first solution is to condemn "the fallacious and illusory use of *obscure* or *deceitful terms*" (510). In other words, we should not use excessively complex vocabulary just to make ourselves look knowledgeable. Sterne seems generally to favor

this idea; he constantly makes fun of overly sophisticated language.

Locke's second solution to the imperfection of language is to require that people consider very carefully the ideas they attach to words: "'Tis not enough a man *uses* his *words as signs of* some *ideas*; those *ideas* he annexes them to, if they be *simple* must be clear and distinct; if *complex* must be *determinate, i.e.* the precise collection of simple *ideas* settled in the mind" (512–513). A complex idea, for Locke, is one that consists of a number of simple ideas mixed together. The example he gives is "justice." To be able to speak clearly about such ideas, a person must be able to break complex ideas down into their simple parts, to have "in his mind a distinct comprehension of the component parts, that complex *idea* consists of; and if it be decompounded, must be able to resolve it still on, till he at last comes to the simple *ideas* that make it up" (513). This argument is the object of Sterne's scorn. Taking such obsessive care to ensure clarity of communication is one of the reasons why Tristram cannot ever seem to finish the simplest of stories. For example:

> I define a nose as follows—intreating only beforehand, and beseeching my readers, both male and female, of what age, complexion, and condition soever, for the love of God and their own souls, to guard against the temptations and suggestions of the devil, and suffer him by no art or wile to put any other ideas into their minds, than what I put into my definition—For by the word Nose, throughout all this long chapter of noses, and in every other part of my work, where the word Nose occurs—I declare, by that word I mean a nose, and nothing more, or less.
>
> (III: 257)

A novelist who seeks to reach as wide an audience as possible cannot hope to live up to Locke's standards of clarity.

Besides, Sterne does not seem to think that such clarity would be desirable, even if it were possible. Locke sees the fact that each person's ideas "are all within his own breast, invisible, and hidden from others" as an obstacle to clear communication, but Sterne sees it as the reason why language—especially literary language—is so endlessly fascinating and why new and inventive kinds of language are always being created. For instance, in a famous passage Tristram invokes the myth of Momus's glass: in Greek legend humans were created by the god Hephaestus, and he was criticized by Momus, the personification of faultfinding, for not placing windows in their chests that would allow anyone to see their desires and thoughts. If we did have these windows, Tristram says, "nothing more would have been wanting, in order to have taken a man's character, but to have taken a chair ... and look'd in,—view'd the soul stark naked" (I: 82). By comparison, he says, if there were people on the planet Mercury, they would be turned to glass by the sun's heat, and for them the soul "might as well ... play the fool out o' doors as in her own house" (I: 83). In other words, if one's every idea and feeling were visible to all the world, one would not have any reason to think of oneself as an individual separate from the rest of the world. There would be no such thing as a private self, no need for language, and no such thing as literature. Fortunately, because character is so hard to describe, "Many, in good truth, are the ways which human wit has been forced to take, to do this thing with exactness" (I: 84). The paradox of communication is that the reason it is required is the same reason that it is so unreliable. But for Sterne the unreliability of language is also the source of the pleasure it can give.

"Nothing is so perfectly amusement," Sterne proclaims in his dedication to volume IX, "as a total change of ideas" (IX: 734). To amuse or entertain, a literary work should take us out of our ordinary trains of thought. For Sterne, one of the goals of literature is diversion, to put us in contact with ideas and feelings nothing like our own. Without mystery and oddness and ambiguity, novels would be no fun. A novel is supposed to show us what it is like to be another person.

At the same time this theme evokes a broader question: What is it that makes a person a person? Although we recognize that *Tristram Shandy* isn't exactly a portrait of Tristram Shandy, can we say what is actually missing? Is it his thoughts, his physical appearance, his actions, the events of his life? What are the essential components of personhood? How can a person be fully and properly represented? What makes one person different from another? Indeed, *because* Tristram fails to deliver the book he promised us, Sterne succeeds in confronting us with these knotty questions.

What kind of book does Tristram promise us? He never calls his work a novel, nor a tragedy or a comedy. It is a history, "the history of myself." In Sterne's time the word "history" meant something closer to "story" than the meaning we now attach to it. Although Tristram also claims that he will not follow "any man's rules that ever lived" (I: 5), we can get a sense of the kind of history he intends from the way he describes Locke's *Essay on Human Understanding*: "It is a history.—A history! of who? what? where? when? Don't hurry yourself—It is a history-book, Sir, (which may possibly recommend it to the world) of what passes in a man's own mind" (II: 98). It seems reasonable to define *Tristram Shandy* also as the history of "what passes in a man's own mind." It is the operation of Tristram's mind that guides the development of the novel, and this process is the only real contact we have with him. Although we get very little of his life story, we become very familiar with the workings of his mind. Sterne is suggesting that this kind of indirect intimacy is the best means we have of getting to know another person. Our hobbyhorses, our chains of association, and the accidents that befall us all go to differentiate us from other people and make it possible for others to know us. In another sense, what remains hidden or absent is just as important as what is revealed. In a famous passage uncle Toby shows his kindness and compassion by refusing to harm a fly, and Tristram comments:

whether it was, that the action itself was more in unison to my nerves ...—or in what degree, or by what secret magick,—a tone of voice and harmony of movement, attuned by mercy, might find a passage to my heart, I know not;—this I know, that the lesson of universal good-will then taught and imprinted by my uncle Toby, has never since been worn out of my mind. (II: 131)

For Sterne, secret or hidden harmonies and sympathies connect us to others. Sterne is a pioneer of what we now call individualism. He sees selfhood as a great, almost sacred, mystery that we must constantly struggle to separate from the encumbrance of earthly circumstance:

Who made MAN, with powers which dart him from earth to heaven in a moment—that great, that most excellent, and most noble creature of the world—the *miracle* of nature, as Zoroaster in his book πει φυσεωζ called him—the SHEKINAH of the divine presence, as Chrysostom—the *image* of God, as Moses—the *ray* of divinity, as Plato—the *marvel* of *marvels,* as Aristotle—to go sneaking on at this pitiful—pimping—pettifogging rate? (V: 408).

The character Yorick helps to establish this theme of selfhood. Yorick's death is described in volume I (though it is hardly the last we hear of him), and his epitaph is borrowed from Shakespeare's *Hamlet:* "Alas, poor Yorick!" If we look at *Hamlet,* we see that the phrase "alas, poor Yorick!" comes in the middle of a long meditation by Hamlet on the way that death wipes out all differences between people. Yorick, who had been a court jester whom Hamlet remembers fondly, has died, and Hamlet is examining his skull:

Alas, poor Yorick! I knew him, Horatio, a fellow of infinite jest, of most excellent fancy... Here hung those lips that I have kiss'd I know not how oft. Where be your gibes now, your gambols, your songs, your flashes of merriment that were wont to set the table on a roar? ... To what base uses we may return, Horatio! Why may not imagination

trace the noble dust of Alexander, till 'a find it stopping a bunghole?

(V.i.184–203)

Shakespeare's theme concerns mostly the transience of selfhood and the abstractness of distinctions in social status. Yorick's skull is a memento mori, a reminder that earthly differences like wealth and status mean nothing after death and leave no trace behind. Sterne adapts this theme to the mysteries of individuality, the difficulty of summing up a person, and the inadequacy of an object like a gravestone—or a book—to the task. The two pages that immediately follow Yorick's epitaph are simply blocks of solid black ink. Critics have always viewed these black pages as signs of mourning; we cannot *read* them, but we can understand them. The absence of direct communication is nonetheless a very effective form of expression. Later Tristram refers to "the many opinions, transactions and truths which still lie mystically hid under the dark veil of the black [page]" (III: 268).

In *Tristram Shandy* death, too, has paradoxical significance. It means stillness and the cessation of life: "so much of motion, is so much of life, and so much of joy—and ... to stand still or, get on but slowly, is so much of death and the devil" (VII: 593). Tristram always wants to be moving, but the movement inevitably brings us closer to death: "Time wastes too fast: every letter I trace tells me with what rapidity Life follows my pen: the days and hours of it, more precious, my dear Jenny! than the rubies about thy neck, are flying over our heads like light clouds of a windy day, never to return more" (IX: 754). It is hardly surprising, then, that Tristram often uses the metaphor of a road journey to describe his "history": "As you proceed farther with me," he tells the reader,

the slight acquaintance, which is now beginning betwixt us, will grow into familiarity; and that unless one of us is in fault, will terminate in friendship ...—bear with me,—and let me go on, and tell my story my own way:—Or, if I should seem now and then to trifle upon the road,—or should sometimes put on a fool's cap with a bell to it, for a moment or two as we pass along,—don't fly off.

(I: 9)

These metaphors of life (and stories) as a journey toward death turn topsy-turvy in volume VII when Tristram takes a voyage to continental Europe that becomes a flight from Death:

I have forty volumes to write, and forty thousand things to say and do ... had I not better, whilst these few scatter'd spirits remain, and these two spider legs of mine ... are able to support me—had I not better ... fly for my life? ... Then by heaven! I will lead [Death] a dance he little thinks of—for I will gallop, quoth I, without looking once behind me to the banks of the Garonne; and if I hear him clattering at my heels—I'll scamper away to Mount Vesuvius.

(VII: 576–577)

This voyage was inspired by a journey Sterne took in 1763. He suffered (and eventually died) from tuberculosis, so he obviously shares Tristram's fear of leaving his work incomplete. Beneath all the satire, wordplay, and irreverence, we may discover a genuine and affecting love of life and compassion for others in *Tristram Shandy*. The humane sentiments tend to be bound up with their opposites—the love of life with a fear of death, the compassion with an urge to poke fun—but *Tristram Shandy* is not simply an academic satire or a cold treatise of learned wit. It is undoubtedly odd (as Samuel Johnson notoriously dubbed it), but for Sterne oddness is a means of connection, the paradoxical sign of a fund of shared humanity. There is certainly a sadistic streak to the humor, particularly in the wounds suffered by the male members (so to speak) of the Shandy family. But the wounds are always the result of misfortune and accident, not of human malignancy. People are not inherently cruel in Tristram's world. He shares Hamlet's cynicism about the waste of human potential, but not his despair. Hamlet says, "What a piece of work is a man, how noble in reason, how infinite in faculties, how like an angel in apprehension, how like a god! the beauty of the world; the paragon of animals; and yet to me, what is this quintessence of dust?" (II.ii.303–308). Sterne replies, "Now I love you for this—and 'tis this delicious mixture within you which makes you dear creatures what you are—and he who hates you for it—all I can say of the matter is—That he has either a pumpkin for his head—or a pippin for his heart,—and whenever he is dissected 'twill be found so" (V: 435).

The opacity of the human breast and the uncertainty of the future are the keys to sympathy and compassion more often than mistrust and competition. Walter, in his self-absorption, is sometimes unkind to both Elizabeth and Toby, but he cannot resist Toby's generosity: after Walter delivers one of his attacks on Toby's hobbyhorse we find Toby

looking up into my father's face, with a countenance spread over with so much good-nature;—so placid;—so fraternal;—so inexpressibly tender towards him:—it penetrated my father to his heart: ...—Brother Toby, said he:—I beg thy pardon;... My dear, dear brother, answered my uncle Toby, rising up by my father's help, say no more about it;... But 'tis ungenerous, replied my father, to hurt any man;—a brother worse;—but to hurt a brother of such gentle manners,—so unprovoking,—and so unresenting;—'tis base:—By Heaven, 'tis cowardly.

(II: 133)

Toby balances Walter's excessive adherence to rationality. Where Walter sees the world as a series of problems and conundrums that can be solved by intellectual examination, Toby cares little for comprehension; he lives through his feelings. Toby's preference for the heart over the head is in many ways just as excessive and ridiculous as Walter's preference for the reverse, but Sterne's readers (and Tristram himself) have generally found Toby thoroughly lovable. Through these often exaggerated expressions of fellow feeling, Sterne is engaging with the mid-eighteenth-century vogue for sympathy, also known as sentimentalism. Sterne's other famous work, *A Sentimental Journey,* is more thoroughly devoted to sentimentalism, and it is a mark of Sterne's mastery of paradox that although both novels satirize the excesses of sentimentalism, they are also two of the most important examples of it.

3. IMPORTANCE AND INFLUENCE

Sentimentalism is a cultural movement that arose around the middle of the eighteenth century. Its central theme is exploration of the emotions produced by sympathetic connections between people and the expression of feeling in general. Works of literature influenced by sentimentalism typically feature a protagonist who encounters people (and sometimes animals) in various states of suffering and who expresses his sympathy almost invariably by shedding tears, and very often by providing charitable assistance. In *Tristram Shandy* these "encounters" include uncle Toby and his wounded groin; Le Fever, a soldier who dies and leaves an orphaned son (VI: 499); Corporal Trim's brother Tom, who falls victim to the Spanish Inquisition (II. 144); "Poor Maria," a French peasant who has lost her love and her wits (IX. 781); and an ass whose master treats it cruelly (VII. 629). Henry MacKenzie's novel *The Man of Feeling* (1771), which consists of almost nothing but this kind of episode, is the purest example of sentimental narrative, but also a late one. Other writers important to the vogue for sympathy include Samuel Richardson (author of the novels *Pamela* and *Clarissa*), Oliver Goldsmith (writer of fiction and poetry), and the poets Thomas Gray and William Collins.

The philosophical roots of sentimentalism lie in the work of Anthony Ashley Cooper, the third earl of Shaftesbury, whose *Characteristicks of Men, Manners, Opinions, Times* (1711) makes the argument that human nature is innately good and benevolent. In 1759 Adam Smith's *A Theory of Moral Sentiments* rejuvenated, for a time, the

vogue for sentiment. Smith argues that human society is founded upon sympathy, that our actions toward each other are based on our ideas of how those actions will make others feel. Of course we cannot actually feel what others are feeling: "As we have no immediate experience of what other men feel, we can form no idea of the manner in which they are affected, but by conceiving what we ourselves should feel in the like situation" (Smith 2002, 11). This theory must have appealed to Sterne, who uses similar principles to govern the interactions of characters, readers, and narrator throughout *Tristram Shandy*—we have noted some of Tristram's references to the impossibility of seeing into another person's brain or breast. Sterne's version of sentimentality is a very inexact science, one that leads to misunderstandings and conflicts, but he also sees it as the only means by which people can find genuine connections to each other: "All I contend for," Tristram says, "is, that I am not *obliged* to set out with a definition of what love is; ... so long as I can go on with my story intelligibly, with the help of the word itself, without any other idea to it, than what I have in common with the rest of the world" (VI: 564–565).

The vogue for sympathy died away in the later eighteenth century, and indeed became quite widely despised because it was perceived as a license to abandon self-control and freely indulge all of the passions. Writers in the 1790s and later tend to focus on the importance of moderating emotion with reason, and vice versa. Jane Austen's *Sense and Sensibility* (1811) is the most famous example of the reaction against sentimentalism. Nonetheless, the principle that literature can or even ought to be a vehicle for the expression of a wide range of personal feelings has remained strong; William Wordsworth famously defined poetry as "emotion recollected in tranquillity." *Tristram Shandy* has come to seem an important part of the transition in British literature between the classical and aristocratic values of the early eighteenth century, and the more earthly spiritual aspirations of the Romantic era. Sterne's novel does not belong entirely to either tradition, which is partly why it seems detached from its immediate historical context. Most critical studies that include discussions of *Tristram Shandy* focus on either Laurence Sterne alone, or Laurence Sterne alongside writers from other eras and other nations, such as Miguel de Cervantes, Gustave Flaubert, James Joyce, and Vladimir Nabokov. Surprisingly few studies have been published that treat *Tristram Shandy* as an integral part of the eighteenth-century British literary milieu.

Nonetheless, *Tristram Shandy* is a great deal more than a contribution to sentimentalism. It exerted a good deal of influence on literature in Britain, and perhaps even more in continental Europe. For the genre of the novel it provided new popularity and new possibilities. Michael McKeon, in one of the most important recent histories of the English novel, argues that *Tristram Shandy* is the last major formal experiment of the period that shaped the modern novel (1987, 419). The Russian critic Viktor Shklovsky goes further, asserting that "*Tristram Shandy* is the most typical novel in world literature" (1990, 170). Not all historians of the novel accept such sweeping statements, but *Tristram Shandy* is certainly a landmark text. Its influence can also be measured through contemporary responses. Samuel Johnson, for instance, condemned the book as "odd," but the philosopher David Hume called it "the best book, that has been writ by any Englishman these thirty years" (quoted in Myer 1984, 7), and Thomas Jefferson, of all people, called it a part of "the best course of morality that ever was written" (quoted in New 1994, 13). As we have already noted, it spawned a cottage industry of imitations, responses, and forgeries. Its numberless allusions and borrowings have sustained dozens of investigative studies. The first book-length "key" to *Tristram Shandy* was *Illustrations of Sterne,* published by John Ferriar in 1798. Ferriar's text identified many of the sources of Sterne's borrowings, and critics have ever since continued uncovering and explaining previously unnoticed details.

In many ways, however, Sterne's most profound and lasting influence can be found in continental Europe. Among major French writers Sterne's admirers include Denis Diderot, whose *Jacques le fataliste* (1796) is a direct response to *Tristram Shandy,* and Gustave Flaubert, whose *Bouvard et Pecuchet* (1881) has a distinctly Shandean sensibility. Russian novelists of the nineteenth century admired and adapted Sterne's methods of representing psychology and time. But no literary community received *Tristram Shandy* with a greater welcome than the German Romantic writers. They loved *Tristram Shandy* almost without exception. Goethe called *Tristram Shandy* "a book for free spirits," and his admiration for Sterne is especially clear in his sentimental novel *The Sorrows of Young Werther* (1774). Goethe and the other German Romantics (including Heinrich Heine, Jean Paul Richter, and E. T. A. Hoffmann) applauded what they saw as Sterne's capacity to combine tragedy with comedy, pleasure with pain, fear with exultation. Heine wrote, "Sometimes, when his soul is most deeply agitated with tragic emotion ... then, to his own astonishment, the merriest, most mirth-provoking words will flutter from his lips" (quoted in New 1994, 15). That mixed mode, a sensibility which is sometimes compared to Shakespeare's, is an important part of the appeal and the mystery that continue to make *Tristram Shandy* a treasure to those who get to know it.

Select Bibliography

EDITIONS

The Life and Opinions of Tristram Shandy, Gentleman: The Text and Notes. Ed. Melvyn

New and Joan New. Gainesville: University Presses of Florida, 1978–1984. Vols. 1–3 of The Florida Edition of the Works of Laurence Sterne. Melvyn New, gen. ed. 6 vols. 1978–2002. Note: citations in this article refer to Sterne's original volume numbers, not volume numbers in the Florida Edition. Page numbers are those of the Florida edition. Vols. I–V of *Tristram Shandy* are in vol. 1 of the Florida Edition. The remainder are in vol. 2. Vol. 3 contains annotations.

The Life and Opinions of Tristram Shandy, Gentleman. Ed. Melvyn New and Joan New. London: Penguin, 1997. Paperback version of the Florida Edition, with abridged notes.

OTHER WORKS BY STERNE

Letters of Laurence Sterne. Ed. Lewis Perry Curtis. Oxford: Clarendon Press, 1935.

Sermons: The Text and Notes. Ed. Melvyn New. Gainesville: University Presses of Florida, 1996. Vols. 4–5 of The Florida Edition of the Works of Laurence Sterne. Melvyn New, gen. ed. 6 vols. 1978–2002.

A Sentimental Journey Through France and Italy, and Continuation of Bramine's Journal: The Text and Notes. Ed. Melvyn New and Geoffrey Day. Gainesville: University Presses of Florida, 2002. Vol. 6 of The Florida Edition of the Works of Laurence Sterne. Melvyn New, gen. ed. 6 vols. 1978–2002.

OTHER PRIMARY WORKS DISCUSSED OR CITED

Burton, John. *An Essay Towards a Complete New System of Midwifry.* London: James Hodges, 1751.

Cooper, Anthony Ashley, Third Earl of Shaftesbury. *Characteristicks of Men, Manners, Opinions, Times.* Ed. Philip Ayres. 2 vols. Oxford: Oxford University Press, 1999.

Hogarth, William. *The Analysis of Beauty.* Ed. Ronald Paulson. New Haven: Paul Mellon Centre for British Art / Yale University Press, 1997.

Ferriar, John. *Illustrations of Sterne; with Other Essays and Verses.* New York: Garland, 1971.

Locke, John. *An Essay Concerning Human Understanding.* Ed. Peter H. Nidditch. Oxford: Clarendon Press, 1975.

Shakespeare, William. *Hamlet.* In *The Riverside Shakespeare.* Ed. G. Blakemore Evans et al. 2nd ed. Boston: Houghton Mifflin, 1997.

Smith, Adam. *The Theory of Moral Sentiments.* Ed. Knud Haakonssen. Cambridge Texts in the History of Philosophy Series. Cambridge: Cambridge University Press, 2002.

Swift, Jonathan. *A Tale of a Tub: With Other Early Works 1696–1707.* Ed. H. Davis. Oxford: Blackwell, 1986.

SECONDARY WORKS

Benedict, Barbara M. *Framing Feeling: Sentiment and Style in English Prose Fiction, 1745–1800.* New York: AMS Press, 1994. Discussion of sentimentalism.

Blackwell, Bonnie. "Tristram Shandy and the Theater of the Mechanical Mother." *ELH* 68, no.1 (2001): 81–133. Reassessment of Sterne's treatment of women and childbirth.

Bloom, Harold, ed. *Laurence Sterne's Tristram Shandy.* Modern Critical Interpretations Series. New York: Chelsea House, 1987. Several significant twentieth-century essays on Sterne.

Booth, Wayne C. "Did Sterne Complete *Tristram Shandy?*" *Modern Philology* 47, no. 3 (1951): 172–183.

———. "The Self-Conscious Narrator in Comic Fiction Before *Tristram Shandy.*" *PMLA* 67 (1952): 163–185.

Byrd, Max. *Tristram Shandy.* London: George Allen & Unwin, 1985.

Cash, Arthur H., and John M. Stedmond, Eds. *The Winged Skull: Papers from the Laurence Sterne Bicentenary Conference.* London: Methuen, 1971.

Conrad, Peter. *Shandyism: The Character of Romantic Irony.* New York: Barnes and Noble, 1978.

Davidson, Elizabeth Livingston. "Toward an Integrated Chronology for *Tristram Shandy.*" *English Language Notes* 29, no. 4 (1992): 48–56.

Freedman, William. *Laurence Sterne and the Origins of the Musical Novel.* Athens: University of Georgia Press, 1978.

Holtz, William V. *Image and Immortality: A Study of Tristram Shandy.* Providence, R.I.: Brown University Press, 1970.

Iser, Wolfgang. *Laurence Sterne: Tristram Shandy.* Trans. David Henry Wilson. Landmarks of World Literature Series. Cambridge: Cambridge University Press, 1988.

Keymer, Thomas. "Dying by Numbers: *Tristram Shandy* and Serial Fiction." *The Shandean* 8 (1996): 41–67 and 9 (1997): 34–69. Extensive discussion of the publication of *Tristram Shandy.*

Lamb, Jonathan. *Sterne's Fiction and the Double Principle.* Cambridge Studies in Eighteenth-Century English Literature and Thought Series. Cambridge: Cambridge University Press, 1989. Major study of Sterne's relationship to eighteenth-century aesthetic theory.

Loveridge, Mark. *Laurence Sterne and the Argument About Design.* Totowa, N.J.: Barnes and Noble, 1982.

McKeon, Michael. *The Origins of the English Novel, 1600–1740.* Baltimore: Johns Hopkins University Press, 1987. Deals with developments in English fiction prior to *Tristram Shandy.*

McMaster, Juliet. "Walter Shandy, Sterne, and Gender: A Feminist Foray," *English Studies in Canada* 15.4 (1989): 441–458.

Mendilow, A. A. *Time and the Novel.* New York: Humanities Press, 1965. Extensive discussion of time in fiction, using *Tristram Shandy* as the main example.

Moglen, Helene. "(W)Holes and Noses: The Indeterminacies of *Tristram Shandy.*" *Literature and Psychology* 41, no. 3 (1995): 44–79.

Myer, Valerie Grosvenor, ed. *Tristram Shandy: Riddles and Mysteries.* London: Vision Press, 1984.

New, Melvyn. *Tristram Shandy: A Book for Free Spirits.* New York: Twayne, 1994.

———, ed. *Critical Essays on Laurence Sterne.* Critical Essays on British Literature Series. New York: G. K. Hall, 1998. Collection of important essays on Sterne.

Paulson, Ronald. *The Beautiful, Novel, and Strange: Aesthetics and Heterodoxy.* Baltimore: Johns Hopkins University Press, 1996. Includes discussion of novelty in *Tristram Shandy.*

Pfister, Manfred. *Laurence Sterne.* Writers and Their Work Series. Tavistock: Northcote House, 2001.

Pierce, David and Peter de Voogd, eds. *Laurence Sterne in Modernism and Postmodernism*. Amsterdam: Rodopi, 1995.

Ross, Ian Campbell. *Laurence Sterne: A Life*. Oxford: Oxford University Press, 2001. Detailed biography by an established Sterne scholar.

Shklovsky, Viktor. "The Novel as Parody: Sterne's *Tristram Shandy*." In his *Theory of Prose*. Trans. Benjamin Sher. Elmwood Park, Ill.: Dalkey Archive Press, 1990.

Swearingen, James E. *Reflexivity in Tristram Shandy: An Essay in Phenomenological Criticism*. New Haven: Yale University Press, 1977.

Todd, Janet M. *Sensibility: An Introduction*. New York: Methuen, 1986.

Traugott, John. *Tristram Shandy's World: Sterne's Philosophical Rhetoric*. Berkeley: University of California Press, 1954. Sterne and Locke.

Watt, Ian. *The Rise of the Novel*. Berkeley: University of California Press, 1957. Concludes with assessment of Sterne's place in the history of the English novel.

Thomas More's
Utopia

∽

DAN BRAYTON

EW WORKS OF fiction have so much influence over readers that their titles actually become familiar words. *Utopia*, written in 1516 by the Englishman Thomas More (1478–1535), is one such work. Its title has become a common word in many languages, although most people who use the term "utopia" probably have not read the book. Part political dialogue, part mock-travel narrative, *Utopia* stands as one of the great works of fiction written in the sixteenth century. When More coined a new word for the book's title he also named an idea that would come to have a place in subsequent fiction and political thought. It is striking that much of More's contribution to political thought is contained within the title-word itself. Although the bulk of the book is in Latin, the title is Greek, a combination of "*topos*," meaning "place," and "*ou*," meaning "not" or "non." Literally translated, then, "utopia" means "nowhere." The "u" also hints at the prefix *eu*, Greek for "good," so that "utopia" suggests "a good place."

The sum of the word is greater than its parts, and, in most modern European languages, "utopia" has come to denote a pipe-dream or impossible ideal, generally of a political nature.

A utopia is commonly understood as a purely fictional political goal, the instantiation of a political and/or a social order governed by reason and philosophical principles. Utopian thinkers are those who imagine an ideal state in which political life is optimally arranged and carefully disciplined. Often the term is applied with a pejorative undertone to denote the political agenda of ideological extremists. The reason for this complex of meanings has to do with the nature of *Utopia* itself, a fictional narrative in two books that is both a political dialogue and a whimsical travel narrative describing an imaginary country. The rich meanings of this one word reflect the brilliance and complexity of *Utopia*, a book which in turn reflects the remarkable life and character of its author.

HISTORICAL CONTEXT

Utopia is a work of fiction profoundly engaged with the major political and social issues of its day. As such, it cannot be understood without some reference to the historical events upon which it is a trenchant commentary. It addresses historical developments specific to England as well as developments that affected all of Europe

349

and, eventually, the rest of the globe. The year of *Utopia*'s publication, 1516, was a historical threshold for Europe. This was the dawn of the modern world, when the old medieval order, with its long-standing beliefs, institutions, and economy, was rapidly giving way to a more energetic early modern era in which trade, travel, and the arts would flourish as they never had in Europe. The crusades were over, the Mediterranean was no longer dominated by the Islamic world, the rebirth of classical learning was well underway, and new developments in banking and trade were bringing Europe together as never before. These developments caused an upsurge in production of all kinds, industrial and artistic production especially; they also caused a marked increase in political and religious friction between different regions and leaders.

The European Renaissance was also a time of great philosophical and religious innovation. Written on the eve of the Protestant Reformation, *Utopia* emerged from a Europe in spiritual and intellectual turmoil. Throughout the sixteenth century, religious reform swept across Europe and, although More does not address the specific religious issues of the time in the text, the book clearly reflects powerful impulses to rethink and reform institutions of all kinds. In England, as Henry VIII consolidated his power as absolute monarch and moved toward separation from the Catholic Church, other Englishmen, such as the humanist William Tyndale (d. 1536), were making the most of the newly developed technologies to spread reform and the Word. Tyndale's use of the printing press to disseminate the Bible and his insistence that it had authority over the Church and the Pope had radical consequences. His English translation of the Bible would be published in 1525, as more and more English readers encountered the source of their religious beliefs without the mediation of priests. On the Continent, the German priest Martin Luther (1483–1546), in all likelihood unknown to More at the time, would in 1517 trigger the emergence of an alternative

CHRONOLOGY	
1478	Birth of Thomas More
1499	More meets Erasmus
1504	More enters Parliament
1516	*Utopia* published at Louvain
1517	*Utopia* reprinted at Paris
1518	*Utopia* reprinted at Basle
1519	*Utopia* reprinted at Vienna, Florence, and Venice
1529–1932	More serves Henry VIII as Lord Chancellor
1535	More beheaded 7 July
1551	Ralphe Robynson's English translation of *Utopia*
1623	Tommaso Campanella, *City of the Sun* published
1626	William Roper's biography of Sir Thomas More published
1627	Francis Bacon, *The New Atlantis*
1656	John Harrington, *Oceana*
1666	Margaret Cavendish, *Blazing World*
1726	Jonathan Swift, *Gulliver's Travels*
1848	Marx and Engels, *The Communist Manifesto*
1872	Samuel Butler, *Erewhon*
1891	William Morris, *News From Nowhere*
1896	H. G. Wells, *The Time Machine* and *The Island of Dr. Moreau*
1932	Aldous Huxley, *Brave New World*
1935	Canonization of St. Thomas More

spirituality, Protestantism, by posting his famous theses on a church door in the German university city of Wittenberg.

Among the most illustrious figures of the era, Sir Thomas More is at least as famous for his illustrious life as for his writings. He was the consummate Renaissance Man, a scholar, diplomat, politician, and theologian. A leading figure of English humanism, the restoration of classical Greek and Latin learning, More was well known among European intellectuals for his erudition. His friends were among the most brilliant and powerful figures of Renaissance Europe. One such friend, Desiderius Erasmus

(1466–1536), a celebrated Dutch scholar, wrote a short encomium or book of praise called *The Praise of Folly* (1509), the title of which contains a pun on More's name. This book is worth considering for a moment, as it sheds light on More's fame as well as on the intellectual culture of the day. The Latin title *"Moriae Encomium"* contains the word *morus,* Latin for fool, which derives from the Greek *moron* (both More and Erasmus read and spoke Latin and Greek, and *Folly,* like *Utopia,* was originally written in Latin). The title also means "the praise of More," and it was unquestionably Sir Thomas More that Erasmus had in mind. In his dedicatory letter to More that serves as a preface, Erasmus praises his friend for his wisdom and graciousness. Indeed, both Erasmus and More were renowned throughout Europe for their combination of humanistic learning with active engagement in the most pressing contemporary matters. In his satirical little book, Erasmus articulates the doctrine of wise foolishness announced by its title. It was in the same spirit that More wrote *Utopia.* This kind word-play was a way for learned humanists to display their mastery of the classical languages and to amuse their readers. Such witticisms were meant to suggest that a good deal of meaning and wisdom can be found in something as seemingly trivial as puns.

Both Erasmus and More made good use of their formidable intellectual capacities, and of wit in particular, to comment upon and to participate in the major political and religious developments of their time. Indeed, one could argue that it was a combination of wisdom and foolishness that led to More's death. Because of his great learning and his skills as a diplomat, he held high political rank for much of his adult life. For a time he was intimately concerned with the events transpiring on the European Continent, serving as a diplomat in Belgium on behalf of his king, Henry VIII. Later he defended the Catholic Church against the growing movement of Protestant reform. Indeed, More's life—and death—would be largely determined by the confluence of political and religious forces in the lives of those holding public office in Tudor England. For years a friend and trusted councilor of England's powerful and autocratic sovereign, More eventually ran afoul of the king over religious matters. He was executed as a traitor 6 July 1535.

The famous events leading to More's execution are intimately tied to one of the most celebrated episodes in the history of England. In the early 1530s, the powerful and despotic King Henry became incensed by the Pope's unwillingness to grant his request for an annulment of his first marriage. Acting in the King's interests, Parliament passed a series of laws cutting ecclesiastical, political, and financial links with Rome. The monasteries were suppressed, Church lands were confiscated, tithes were reduced and eventually cut off, and a new church was established. The Act of Supremacy (1534) declared the English King supreme head the *Ecclesia Anglicana,* or Church of England, and severed all remaining ties with Rome. Throughout this time of revolution More was torn between loyalty to a king whom he had served long and well and to the Catholic Church. Henry was not a sovereign to be trifled with, but More's powerful conscience and sense of duty matched the King's gigantic will and self-regard. Yet More was a diplomat, and a subtle one; he knew that he was playing a high-stakes game by not openly supporting the monarch. While he would not support the King's break from Rome, he would not publicly condemn it either. This policy proved more dangerous than More supposed. As the Lord High Chancellor, holder of one of the highest political offices in England, More could not disagree with his King inconspicuously. Suspicious of anyone who would not bend to his will, the King required his subjects to take an oath swearing to uphold the Act of Succession (1534). Despite the entreaties of family and friends, More refused and was arrested, convicted, and beheaded.

More's death, and more particularly the political circumstances that caused it, were of enormous importance for the political and religious history of England, and it is in part for this reason that his life has been celebrated by readers, writers, and historians for centuries. Catholics especially have lionized him as a hero of religious devotion and loyalty. More was beatified in 1886; Pope Pius XI canonized him in 1935. While many of the foremost English theologians and intellectuals of the Renaissance, from Tyndale to Milton, espoused the Protestant cause, More stands out as a staunch and unrepentant Catholic. He also stands at the start of an eminent line of learned and influential English Catholics whose fame derives from their exceptionalism—their willingness to a champion a lost cause in a predominantly Protestant country. But his religious devotion is only one reason among many for More's abiding fame. His name has also become associated with the learning, the passionate commitment to both public and private causes, and the force of character that distinguish the heroes of the European Renaissance.

More's writings reflect their author's engagement with the life of the mind and the life of the nation, and he wrote a variety of different works in both English and Latin. These works span a diverse array of topics. A biography translated in 1510 of the Italian humanist Pico della Mirandola (1463–1494) was followed by *The History of Richard III* (1513, published 1543). Then followed *Utopia* (1516), his most celebrated work, which preceded a period of active participation in the political and religious controversies of the day. This period of engagement brought More into debate with noted Protestants such as Tyndale, whom he attacked in *A Dialogue Concerning Heresies* (1528). More's final work, *An Apology of Sir Thomas More* (1533), was written not long before his death in 1535. *Utopia* stands out from this list as the only work of fiction and the most famous and widely read work among them. Like More's other writings, however, *Utopia* addresses specific problems and developments in Europe generally and England particularly, especially the viciousness of autocratic political

systems. The intellectual daring and the independence of thought that would lead More to the execution block are very much in evidence throughout *Utopia*.

A READING OF BOOK ONE

The early sixteenth century was, to say the least, a time of upheaval, enormous institutional change, and social, religious, and political critique. One of the major causes of upheaval in Europe was the "discovery" of the Americas by European navigators at the end of the fifteenth century. The impact of the New World on the European consciousness was immense, and *Utopia* reflects the fascination of the Old World with the New. Da Gama, Columbus, Cabot, Vespucci, and others were transforming the way Europeans looked at their world, and the publication of Ptolemaic cosmography and geography added force to this transformation. In the Americas, Bartolomeo de Las Casas was beginning to expose the horrors perpetrated by the Spanish on Hispaniola. Not only was the world decisively round, it was also peopled by nations and tribes about which Europeans had no prior knowledge, people whose customs and beliefs could and did differ dramatically from those of Christians. The disturbing possibility that Europe was not the center of the world became a pressing concern. Thinkers of all kinds were engaged with understanding and writing about such a development. Nowhere was the new interest in the form, size, and contents of the globe more evident than in the Netherlands. The northwest of Europe was at the forefront of commerce and navigation, and, therefore, of knowledge about the world outside of Europe.

Utopia is organized into two quite distinct books, the first of which is a mix of genres, part autobiography, part political discourse, and part travel narrative. Book Two is a description of the imaginary land of Utopia and of Hythlodaeus' voyage there. In Book One, the narrative begins in a garden in the city of Antwerp, one of the major European centers of cartography, or mapmaking. It is no accident that More locates the narrative of Utopia here. The region that is today comprised of Belgium and Holland was a crossroads for travellers, sailors, and intellectuals, and curiosity about the world was a distinctive feature of the region throughout the era. As the art historian Svetlana Alpers has noted, "a traveler in Holland confirmed that even the houses of shoemakers and tailors displayed wall-maps of Dutch seafarers, by which . . . they know of the Indies and its history" (p. 159). While Columbus died believing that he had sailed to Cathay, in Asia, Amerigo Vespucci and other navigators thought Columbus found a totally New World—and they set out to prove it. It was the Dutch cartographer Martin Waldseemuller, however, who, in his world-map of 1507, first drew North and South America as separate continents and labeled them "America." Waldseemuller's map was published along with the letters of Vespucci in a book he called Cosmographiae Descriptio, a description of the cosmos. The map and the accompanying letters were wildly popular all over Europe, and they did a great deal to shape European notions of the New World. Thus, some scholars claim that a Dutch cartographer "invented" America, gave it a place and a name. *Utopia* appeared less than a decade after *Cosmographiae Descriptio*.

The historical and geographical circumstances of *Utopia*'s origins suggest that it is not just a story, but also a kind of map. In the Renaissance, narratives could be maps, and maps could take textual—not merely graphic or diagrammatic—form. The harbor-finding charts of Mediterranean sailors, for example, were originally lists of landmarks that a sailor would see while making his way along a stretch of coast. Sixteenth-century maps were often labeled *"descriptio,"* which contains the Latin root "scribere," to write (scribe, scribble). There were also books called "descriptions." All kind of written "descriptions"—part map and part book—were available at this time. A descrip-

tion, thus, could and often did include both writing and diagrams. Maps and books proliferated with the rapid development of printing in the late fifteenth century. Maps and travel narratives in the 16th century went hand-in-hand, and were frequently published together in the same volume. *Utopia* presents itself, then, as a kind of mock cartographic description, among other things. The land that is mapped out by the narrative of *Utopia* is not a real territory; it is an imaginary island governed by the rules of reason rather than custom, a nowhere in which political authority is subordinate to the common good.

The book begins as a description of various events that transpired while the author was in Antwerp, but it quickly leaves the realm of historical events and enters the far more flexible realm of fiction. The opening is a factual account of the author's work as a diplomat in the service of his king:

> There was recently a rather serious difference of opinion between that great expert in the art of government, His Invincible Majesty, King Henry the Eighth of England, and His Serene Highness, Prince Charles of Castile. His Majesty sent me to Flanders to discuss and settle the matter, along with my friend Cuthbert Tunstall, an excellent person who has since been appointed Master of the Rolls, much to everyone's satisfaction. . . .
>
> (p. 37)

While in Antwerp, More meets up with his friend Peter Gilles, another actual historical personage, who introduces him to the traveler-philosopher Raphael Hythlodaeus, an entirely fictional character whose name More chose with characteristic care and wit. Hebrew for "God has healed," "*Raphael*" has biblical associations with travel, guidance, and the curing of blindness. *Hythlodaeus*, Greek for "dispenser of nonsense," or "well versed in nonsense," contains the same kind of witty self-negation as the title of the book itself.

The autobiographical narrative of a diplomatic voyage to the lowlands quickly becomes something else entirely, a philosophical dialogue and mock travel narrative. The point of view of the narrative switches from More to the fictional Hythlodaeus. As the text proceeds, the More we identify with the author begins to look less and less like the center of the text. Indeed, Hythlodaeus becomes a radical alter ego for the author, and the person named "More" in the text, allegedly the author himself, becomes a character who simply voices the opinions of a dutiful servant of king and country. As a philosophical stand-in for the author and an embodiment of the spirit of the age, Hythlodaeus is a sailor, philosopher, and storyteller who claims he sailed with Vespucci on one of the voyages described in the famous letters.

> He wanted to see the world, so he left his brothers to manage his property in Portugal—that's where he comes from—and joined up with Amerigo Vespucci. You know those Four Voyages of his that everyone's reading about? Well, Raphael was his constant companion during the last three, except that he didn't come back with him from the final voyage....
>
> (pp. 38–39)

According to the narrative, Raphael eventually makes his way to "Calicut," in India, finds some Portuguese ships, and completes his circumnavigation of the globe (several years before Magellan actually did so).

The emphasis on travel as a means of staging a philosophical dialogue owes a debt to the Latin writer Lucian, whose works More greatly appreciated and occasionally translated; it also owes a debt to the vogue for narratives of discovery in the early sixteenth century. Hythlodaeus resembles Lucian's cynic philosopher Menippus, a travelling critic of men, but his experiences are wholly unlike those of Menippus in their timely focus on the New World and their intimate reliance on a thorough knowledge of navigation. Raphael describes his experiences as a navigator in suitably technical terms, and we cannot help noticing his emphasis on technological changes in navigation.

> Whenever I found a ship just setting sail I asked if my friends and I might go on board, and they were always glad to let us. The first ships we saw were flat-bottomed, with sails made of papyrus leaves stitched together, or else of wicker-work, or in some cases of leather. But the ones we came across later had sharp keels and canvas sails, and were generally just like ours. The sailors out there generally have a good knowledge of winds and tides, but I made myself extraordinarily popular with them by explaining the use of the magnetic compass. They'd never heard of it before, and for that reason had always been rather frightened of the sea, and seldom risked going on it except during the summer.
>
> (p. 40)

This is an account of a voyage off the map, to *terra incognita,* the unknown land often marked on Renaissance *mappae mundi,* or world maps, in the spaces that remained undiscovered by Western eyes. Raphael is More's fictional version of a Renaissance philosopher-voyager, both a humanist thinker like himself or Erasmus and a navigator like Columbus or Vespucci. His description of the exotic land that he alone has seen is presented in the form of a travel narrative offering new geographical information. That none of the information is true does not make the narrative any less gripping or detailed. As we shall see, More uses his wit and his learning to create an imaginary world that tells us a great deal about the real one.

The literature scholar Jeffery Knapp has argued that *Utopia* reveals the widespread curiosity about the New World shared by many English writers of fiction in the sixteenth century. According to Knapp, More's close relation to the would-be colonizer John Rastell links him with the colonial project that would eventually lead to the English colonization of North America. Thus, "Utopia represents More's attempt to turn England's classical nowhereness into a way of seeing England and America as destined for each other" (21). Knapp's discussion adds an important contextual dimension to our understanding of *Utopia,* yet the reverse could just as well be argued: not that More had his sights on the Americas, but that the Americas provided him with a means of taking a critical look at England. We cannot overstate the impact of the European discovery of the Americas on the imaginations of Renaissance thinkers. Yet while some writers were busy imagining the wonders that might exist in the newly discovered regions, More made use of the idea of other worlds to take a hard look at the one that he himself inhabited, and he found much that was worthy of criticism. Accordingly, Hythlodaeus voices critical observations and arguments about the political and social life of England and Europe as if these familiar lands were themselves quite strange.

Book One, in which the principle characters are introduced and beginning a dialogue, was actually written after Book Two, yet the first book acts as a prelude to the description of the imaginary nation that follows it. This makes the narrative run in a circle: the text starts in Antwerp, moves to the land of Utopia, then returns in the end to Antwerp. The relationship between the two settings, Europe and an imaginary elsewhere, is a close one. Indeed, much of the early discussion of what Hythlodaeus finds fault with in England is explicitly or implicitly revisited later, in the second book. Thus, any attempt to look to the far-off nation visited by Hytholodaeus as simply a vagabond's projection of an ideal commonwealth is forced to return to contemporary Europe and its social inequities. It is in Book One that Hythlodaeus directly criticizes the major social problems afflicting the English people during late Middle Ages and Renaissance. In fact, the righteous indignation and radical implications of the attack on social customs and political authority—including the Church—are an early indication the moral courage and clear-sightedness that would lead Thomas More to the scaffold. For it is the direct account of the causes of poverty and injustice in England that is most striking about Book One.

It was Erasmus who first claimed that More's most famous book "represented the English commonwealth in particular [*Britannicum potissimum effinxit*]" (quoted in Knapp 31). The geographical features of the imaginary nation mirror those of More's homeland: the river Anydrus ("not water") and the city Amaurotum ("Shadow City") are constructed as negative terms. The river resembles the Thames and the city London, just as the description of the island itself, once a peninsula, evokes Britain and the English Channel. This is a landscape that evokes England at every turn, and we must remember that the fanciful travel narrative told by Hythlodaeus follows quickly upon a devastating political and social critique of conditions in that country. The eutopia (good place) of Book Two is a direct response to the description of contemporary political and social problems in the land of Henry VIII. The England of Book One is a dystopia (bad place) in need of alternatives; the relationship between it and the utopia that follows, therefore, is a dialectical one. More's work is a political allegory as well as a blueprint for radical change. A troubled England haunts the narrative of Hythlodaeus just as his faraway island would come to haunt English literature and European political thought for centuries.

The object of critique in Book One is social inequity, and More reveals a profound knowledge of the social and economic circumstances of Englishmen. Hythlodaeus offers an account of enclosure every bit as vivid as his subsequent travel-narrative, criticizing the nation for its top-heavy social hierarchy and singling out the privileged and the powerful as the most culpable people in the land. Those who wield power, argues the wandering social critic, produce the conditions that cause theft and vagabondage by practices of enclosure. As Hythlodaeus claims, the cause of beggary and crime in England was, for the most part, "sheep."

These placid creatures, which used to require so little food, have now apparently developed a raging appetite, and turned into man-eaters. Fields, houses, towns, everything goes down their throats. To put it more plainly, in those parts of the kingdom where the finest, and so the most expensive wool is produced, the nobles and gentlemen, not to mention several saintly abbots, have grown dissatisfied with the income that their predecessors got out of their estates. They're no longer content to lead lazy, comfortable lives, which do no good to society—they must actively do it harm, by enclosing all the land they can for pasture, and leaving none for cultivation. They're even tearing down houses and demolishing whole towns—except, of course, the churches, which they preserve for use as sheepfolds. As though they didn't waste enough of your soil already on their coverts and game-preserves, these kind souls have started destroying all traces of human habitation, and turning every scrap of farmland into a wilderness.

(pp. 46–47)

This famous sketch of enclosure bequeaths us the unforgettable metaphor of man-eating sheep taking over the countryside, dispossessing the rural inhabitants from the land, a radical inversion of pastoral convention. By putting his finger on the economic causes of social woes, and by locating it in the greed of landowners—churchmen, nobility, and gentry—More directs his moral criticism at the agents of a social system that he himself inhabited. This is what forces the narrative to involve conspicuous differences of opinion between "More" and his radical alter ego, Hythlodaeus.

The political impact of More's analysis of the causes of poverty and vice cannot be overestimated. Man-eating sheep would become a recurrent trope in expressions of political discontent for at least a century, available for appropriation by revolutionary voices until well into the seventeenth-century Revolution. For instance, the crowds that turned out in Northamptonshire in 1603 to see James I making his way to London inverted the image in a more conventional trope, complaining of "wolfish lords, that have eaten up poor husbandmen like sheep" (Underdown 115). That it was not sheep but an emergent and rampant form of agrarian capitalism that ate up the lands and livelihoods of the English commons was not lost

on More. Breeding sheep in increased numbers meant breeding capital: from the late fifteenth-century to the early nineteenth, land-owners, wishing to increase the yield of wool and thereby increase profits, systematically reclaimed an enormous amount of rural land from its traditional uses. The enclosures caused the massive dispossession of peasants from their homes and livelihoods, with the visible result of a drastically depopulated rural landscape. In fact, the narrative of both books of *Utopia* seems to be motivated by a powerful anxiety about the possibility of depopulation with the result of the land becoming "idle" and "waste" (*nane ac uacuum*) (*Utopia* 137).

Enclosures were many and multiform, as were the agents of agricultural capitalism, but More makes it clear that the social problems of Tudor England were closely tied to this complex of private property and profiteering. The culpability of the landowners is clear in More's account: to increase profits for the owners, land must be made more productive, but the existing systems of social dependency could not be racked enough to produce the profits. More examines the social forces involved in the land enclosures of the early sixteenth and, in doing so, implicates not merely the landowning aristocracy and gentry, but also the churchmen and their management of the vast amounts of land they held. This would be an issue that Henry VIII would exploit when he reclaimed church lands, effectively appropriating a massive amount of real estate and revenue from the Catholic Church. It was also an issue to which radical social critics in the English Revolution would return over a century later. Moreover, the enclosure of land for the sake of increasing financial gain, here defined in terms of the textile industry's demand for wool, involved innumerable acts of violence and dispossession by the land-owning classes.

Part of More's contribution to political philosophy was to describe vividly the means of dispossession in the early period of enclosures. For Hythlodaeus, the owners of property and agents of enclosure were gluttons rapidly becoming a plague by enclosing land and dispossessing poor farmers.

> So what happens? Each greedy individual preys on his native land like a malignant growth, absorbing field after field, and enclosing thousands of acres with a single fence. Result—hundreds of farmers are evicted. They're either cheated or bullied into giving up their property, or systematically ill-treated until they're finally forced to sell. Whichever way it's done, out the poor creatures have to go, men and women, husbands and wives, widows and orphans, mothers and tiny children, together with all their employees—whose great numbers are not a sign of wealth, but simply of the fact that you can't fun a farm without plenty of manpower. Out they go from the homes that they know so well, and they can't find anywhere else to live. Their whole stock of furniture wouldn't fetch much of a price, even if they could afford to wait for a suitable offer. But they can't so they get very little indeed for it. By the time they've been wandering around for a bit, this little is all used up, and then what can they do but steal—and be very properly hanged? Of course, they can always become tramps and beggars, but then they're liable to be arrested as vagrants, and put in prison for being idle—when nobody will give them a job, however much they want one. For farm-work is what they're used to, and there's no arable land, there's no farm-work to be done. After all, it only takes one shepherd or cowherd to graze animals over an area that would need any amount of labour to make it fit for corn production.
>
> (p. 47)

In the outraged tone of this passage we can detect traces of More's own anxiety about being away from home on the business of his prince. On the basis of this account, Hythlodaeus concludes that the English "first make thieves and then punish them" (idem). Thieves may be an unacknowledged product of pasturage, but they are a product nevertheless, and one that harsh laws against crime caused by poverty could do nothing to solve. The condition of this evil is the ownership of private property, for "as long as there is any property, and while money is the standard of all other things, I cannot think that a nation can be governed either justly or happily" (More, p. 36).

It was precisely to provide a blueprint for social change that More imagined a nation in which inequity, beggary, and injustice were kept to a minimum. The island of Utopia contains no insatiable property-owners, no money to accumulate, and no private property to buy or sell. Utopia will be a nation beyond the pale, not compassed about by greedy landlords, a place that remained beyond the bounds of European exploitation, to be found only by the help of a different kind of compass—the mariner's "card" that was revolutionizing early modern navigation. It will be aptly called no-place not only because of its imaginary existence, but because "place," both property and social standing, means nothing there. By representing Utopia as a land with no *meum* and *tuum*, no private property, and no money, More undermines the Tudor institutions of power and privilege as a means of getting at the problem that his utopian blueprint will try to solve—the social injustices attendant on private property. The root of England's social woes is the concentration of wealth and power among the privileged few:

> I don't see how you can ever get any real justice or prosperity, so long as there's private property, and everything's judged in terms of money—who aren't entirely happy even so, while everyone else is simply miserable.

> There's unanimous support for that doctrine of Crassus, that you can never have enough money, if you've got an army to maintain. It's also generally agreed that a King can do no wrong, however much he may want to, because everything belongs to him, including every human being in the country, and private property does not exist, except in so far as he's kind enough not to seize it. He should always reduce such provisional private property to a minimum, since his safety depends on preventing his subjects from having too much wealth or freedom. These things make people less willing to put up with injustice and oppression, whereas poverty and privation make them dull

and submissive, and stifle the noble spirit of rebellion.

(p. 61)

We cannot help finding something of the author's life in such passages as this. Hythlodaeus speaks from the bold, independent critical perspective of his creator. His words are an eerie foreshadowing of More's refusal to acquiesce to Henry VIII's despotic demands—and of their author's preference for death over injustice.

While the opinions of the character "More" conspicuously do not align with those of Hythlodaeus the radical social critic, there is a clear accord between their two versions of England's and Europe's current social problems. Both agree that harsh laws against crime and vagabondage—attempts to control the growing threat of masterlessness and vagabondage—arise because of a social and political system that invests everything in the hands of a few masters. The solution, claims the neo-platonic socialist Hythlodaeus, is manifest: do away with private property. This state of communalism is precisely what More envisages in his ideal commonwealth. The utopians live in a state of communism where private property does not exist. "I don't see how you can ever get any real justice or propriety, so long as there's private property, and everything's judged in terms of money-unless you consider it just for the worst sort of people to have the best living conditions, or unless you're prepared to call a country prosperous, in which all the wealth is owned by a tiny minority-who aren't entirely happy even so, while everyone else is simply miserable" (More, p. 65).

This conclusion would remain popular in dissenting social critique well into the next century. Closer to More's own era, again, we find similar dissent among artisans, such as Edward White, who would make much the same point in 1566:

> We can get no work, nor we have no money, and if we should steal we should be hanged, and if we should ask, no man would give us, but we will have a remedy one of these days, or else we will lose all, for the commons will rise, we know not how soon, for we look for it every hour.

(Greenblatt 1990, 113)

These sentiments and the force behind them are shared by the numerous figures in the literature of the sixteenth century which give voice to concerns about the effects of enclosure on social relations. The dispossessed would play a major role a century later in the revolutionary rearrangement of England's social and political life, and their blueprints for social and political change would borrow significantly from More.

A READING OF BOOK TWO

More's analysis of the politics of property and paupery hinges on a strikingly modern understanding of social space as the material embodiment of political regimes. If social justice is to be had, Hythlodaeus argues, then the topography of the nation must be radically rearranged. The ideal state will be the result of a rational and beneficent rearrangement of social space; thus, the social inequities of Tudor England will disappear. As the fictional resolution to England's problems, Utopia is called into being by an act of textual mapping. Yet, while the text maps a new social order, it continually vexes any attempt to assign simple correspondences between the two islands. More's evasive techniques of doubling and denial, double-negatives (litotes), paradoxes (e.g. the river Anydrus), and irony can be understood as a mode of cartographic projection.

The nature of More's cartographic procedures has been intelligently discussed in Marina Leslie's excellent study, *Renaissance Utopias and the Problem of History*. Leslie gives a reading of the illustrations that accompanied the first several editions of the text, woodcuts remarkable for the way they recapitulate the narrative. She argues that the three different illustrations accompanying the text between 1516 reveal an increasing awareness of the relationship between cartography and narrative. The inclusion in the 1518 illustration by Ambrosius Holbein, *Utopiae Insulae Tabula*, of three human figures—Hythlodaeus (labeled), an interlocutor (presumably More), and an onlooker (possibly Peter Gilles)—stages the invention of *Utopia* in a garden in Antwerp at the same time that it illustrates the features of the island-nation as described by Hythlodaeus. These figures are not present in the earlier, anonymous illustration, *Utopiae Insulae Figura,* which accompanied the original 1516 edition. The *Figura* presents itself as an insular map of the kind that was popular in Europe at the time, while the *Tabula* foregrounds the discursive production of the island. Moreover, the 1518 Basel edition's title-page illustration by Hans Holbein, labeled "*hortus conclusus,*" (enclosed garden), further emphasizes the narrativity of utopian space. Here Hythlodaeus eagerly holds forth to two avid listeners, labeled in Latin "Tho. Morus" and "Pet. Aigid.," in a garden, while a landscape—presumably that of Utopia; certainly not Antwerp—looms above them in the background. In each case, the land of Utopia is figured as a conventional Renaissance topography, but the trend over time is to shift from representing the topography itself to representing the act of representation that calls it into being (see Leslie, pp. 34–35).

This trend can be understood as a focus on history, as Leslie rightly points out when she argues, "the Utopian garden offers not a fall into history as loss but the historical grounds for an improved culture and nature, for if 'they have not a very fertile soil or a very wholesome climate,' 'the naturally barren soil is improved by art and industry' (178/179)" (Leslie 44). The territory of Utopia is itself, then, a cultivated garden on an immense scale that cannot help but reflect the scene of its narration in Antwerp. And utopians are gardeners one and all. They all participate in an idealized agrarian economy with none of the signs of capitalistic exploitation that Hythlodaeus decries in Book One. The picture of a garden cultivated by collective labor drawn from a nonhierarchical social order in which no person aspires to riches contrasts utterly with the image in the first book of a landscape depopulated by ravenous sheep and greedy landlords. This is history in negative, surprisingly amenable to the arts of the cartographer.

While Leslie's reading of the illustrations accompanying to the earliest editions is instructive, it neglects the relationship between *Utopia* and the cartographic genre of the *isolario,* or island-chart-book, which it engages directly. As Knapp argues, "Utopia becomes a separate world, a negative, a nowhere, only when it also becomes insular: by ordering a fifteen-mile excavation, the ancient conqueror Utopus converted a peninsula named Abraxa into the island of Utopia" (Knapp 31). Not only does this feature of More's imaginary cartography reflect upon England; it also enters into dialogue with a major cartographic genre in the period. The earliest known example of *isolarii* is the *Liber insularum arcipelagi* of 1420; the last example is Vicenzo Coronelli's 1696 *Isolario dell'Atlantic Veneto* (Conley, p. 179). *Utopia* falls between these two dates, just in advance of the genre's apex of popularity, and an intellectual as well informed as More would not have ignored such a popular genre. Insular literature should not be understood as a strictly technical cartographic form. In fact, Conley has argued, "the impact of the isolario on cartographic writing precipitates a reshuffling of the taxonomies that order knowledge in the age of humanism in insular texts of the sixteenth century" (Conley, p. 169). Often, in these works, "authors depict carefully spatialized treatments of their own personas within their creations" (idem). In other words, writers of insular literature quite frequently inserted themselves into their creations, often in the form of a signature or emblem. As we know, in *Utopia* More inserts himself as a character in the dialogue. This is but one of several ways that More engages with and borrows from the increasingly popular forms of cartographic literature being produced in the early sixteenth century.

But More's cartographic fantasy contains a number of other subtle yet significant features. The description offered by Hythlodaeus is detailed.

> Well, the island is broadest in the middle, where it measures about two hundred miles across. It's never much narrower than that, except towards the very ends, which gradually taper away and curve right round, just as if they'd been drawn with a pair of compasses, until they almost form a circle five hundred miles in circumference. So you can picture the island as a sort of crescent, with its tips divided by a strait approximately eleven miles wide.
>
> (p. 69)

"Just as if they'd been drawn with a pair of compasses": the narrative implies a kinship between the arts of the cartographer and the arts of the writer who describes an imaginary island. The island that More conjures up out of a Flemish garden is governed by a paradox. For the form of the island in Hythlodaeus' narrative is a nearly closed circle—a sort of crescent moon that nearly achieves closure at the extreme points. This is not merely incidental; a writer as self-conscious and witty as More chooses his geographical features carefully. Characterized by its geographical, political, and social closure (contact with outsiders is kept to a minimum), the island of Utopia incorporates into its very shape a reminder of enclosure. At once an imaginary resolution to the social problems caused by the enclosures and a figurative enclosure in its own right, Utopia contains a graphic reminder of the very socioeconomic problems that he wishes to abolish.

The shape of Utopia evokes a rich array of meanings, and it echoes throughout subsequent utopian political thought. Not only does the crescent shape suggest an England bent into a bow; it also implies a global dimension to the utopian project by evoking the T/O form of medieval world-maps. Eden, Elysium, or *Op-timo Reipublicae Statu,* this figure becomes a microcosmic alternative to the chaos of the here and now. It is this "O" that echoes in the nineteenth century when Marx discusses capitalism in terms of the vicious circle. It is also the figure of loss and the sign of the historical precession of enclosure in the Tudor debate about land and property to which *Utopia* is a subtly coded contribution. In much the same way that the narrative assimilates the politically charged historical figures of the masterless man and the vagabond within the character of the wanderer Hythlodaeus, it also incorporates and transforms enclosure as a cartographic emblem—an "O." Thus, More carefully plants within his ideal polity reminders of the worst social problems in the England of his day. In much the same way that the book's title purposely contains an ambiguity, the "u" of "utopia" suggesting both "noplace" and "good place," so, too, does the status of the imaginary island as an ideal republic. More in no way intends the island of Utopia as a perfect place, devoid of problems. To the contrary, it is intended as a carefully mapped diagram of a series of social and political issues—enclosure, social inequity, and competition between nations. To understand the critical and polemical dimensions of Utopia, we need to read it is a carefully encoded political diagram.

The implications of my argument deepen when we consider another striking feature of the text, an etymological link between the mythology of islands and the early modern wool industry. We should remember that the enclosures, the major cause of social and political critique in Book One, were motivated by a desire for increased wool production in the rural regions of England. More's method of incorporation and inversion has a historical basis in European stories about the mythical island of Brazil or Breasile, the object of European geographical speculation long before 1492. As Leslie points out, the toponym "Brazil" has an etymological association with the textile industry:

In the Romance languages ... Brazil is linked etymologically to dye production, and it was the discovery of a red-dye wood in South America [that] led to its being named "terra de brazil." This association may help to explain the otherwise surprising Utopian production of "scarlet and purple dye-stuffs" that were not required for their own simple dress of undyed wool and bleached linen.

(Leslie, p. 36)

More's fantasy island is, thus, stained with the sign of England's primary industry in the sixteenth century and the economic motivation for the enclosures. In fact, England's first attempts at expansion were motivated by the search for markets for woolen kerseys. Hakluyt, the great sixteenth-century compiler of English travel narratives, is full of the accounts of navigators and businessmen peddling wool to Russia and Persia. Textiles were the source of England's wealth as well as one of the major causes of the social crisis of the sixteenth century that *Utopia* comments upon. Thus, More transforms the mythological western island of Brazil into an anti-England whose proximity to the latter cannot be suppressed.

The mention of wool in the age of Henry VIII, especially in a text that explicitly mentions both London and Antwerp, cannot help but evoke enclosure. According to Jeffrey Knapp,

during the sixteenth century, unfinished woolen cloths increasingly dominated England's list of exports, the woolens market became increasingly centered on the exchange between London and Antwerp, and so English economic interests saw little reason to look for business anywhere but in the east.

(Knapp 20)

This remarkable association between a specific European projection of *terra incognita* as a wondrous island and the historical specificity of the wool trade complicates our picture of *Utopia*. For if More's motivation can be in part ascribed to a moral, political, and religious reaction to the social crisis attendant on the enclosures, it is striking that his imaginary solution would retain traces of the wool trade that caused them. Haunted by the absent presence of Tudor England, the island of Utopia is not simply a fantastic geography but a critical topography, an alternative place that takes on a very real existence in the realm of writing and of thought and a kind of cartography that both conceals and reveals historical processes. Written in a climate of political and religious suspicion, when an author could very well be put to death for heretical or unorthodox opinions, *Utopia* is a challenging text to understand in all of its historical richness.

CONCLUSION: THE LEGACIES OF *UTOPIA*.

If More's legacy in the realm of fiction is enormous, his influence on political thinkers has been just as great. Both are worth considering here, if only briefly. His influence extends far beyond the conflicts and polemics of the sixteenth century. Some of the most brilliant thinkers of the sixteenth century have contributed to the literature of utopia. In France, the "Abbey of Theleme" chapter in *Pantagruel*, by Francois Rabelais, and the essay "Of Cannibals," by the great essayist Michel de Montaigne, both contain a great debt to the political and social critique initiated by More in *Utopia*. Thus, for instance, in Montaigne's essay an anecdote about a European encounter with American indigenes becomes the basis for the essayist's critical account of political and social inequality in sixteenth-century France. In England, the translation of the text from Latin into English in 1554 by Ralph Robinson made it much more widely available to domestic readers. It now circulated not merely in the learned circles of those who could read Latin, but was available to a more popular audience in More's own country. Utopian literature became quite popular in the seventeenth century. In fact, the influence of *Utopia* seems only to increase with each passing century.

In the seventeenth century, the Italian Tommaso Campanella's *City of the Sun* (1602) closely followed *Utopia* by offering a blueprint for the ideal society, but it was in England that utopian literature proliferated most dramatically. In 1627 Francis Bacon (1561–1626), the English statesman, writer, and philosopher and one of the founders of modern science, wrote *The New Atlantis,* which describes a rationally organized society dedicated to learning. Other utopian works also appeared. Also in the early decades of the seventeenth century, Bishop Joseph Hall wrote *Mundus Alter et Idem,* or *Another World but yet the Same,* and John Harrington wrote *Oceana,* both profoundly indebted to More. Margaret Cavendish, too, found in *Utopia* a way to discuss her own interests and concerns, and wrote a fascinating utopian text entitled *The Description of a New World, Called the Blazing World* in 1666. On the stage, too, utopias were a popular subject. Shakespeare's *The Tempest* (1611) can be interpreted as a dramatization of utopian motifs, and contains a famous exchange in Act Two in which utopian thinking is both poetically invoked and then mocked. Shakespeare uses the discourse of the New World—plantations, hurricanes, and cannibals—to construct a critical cartography of Renaissance absolutism. In a similar vein, Francis Beaumont and John Fletcher wrote *The Sea Voyage,* a play in which travel and misfortune lead to a providential resolution. Soon thereafter, Richard Brome, a court dramatist of the 1620s and 30s, wrote *A Jovial Crew* and *Antipodes,* both of which contain a strong strain of utopianism.

In the eighteenth century, works such as *The History of Rasselas, Prince of Abyssinia* (1759), by Samuel Johnson (1709–1784), and *Gulliver's Travels* (1726), by Jonathan Swift (1667–1745), reveal the influence of *Utopia* in their depiction of the quest for a better world combined with a critique of this one. But it was in the nineteenth century that English utopianism really took off.

In 1872 Samuel Butler (1835–1902) wrote *Erewhon*—the title is an anagram for "nowhere"— as a mock travel narrative of a squarely utopian kind, and in 1891 William Morris (1834–1896) wrote *News From Nowhere* from a socialist perspective. The American Edward Bellamy (1850–1898), in *Looking Backward, 2000-1887* (1888), used the device of a narrator in the future looking back on Bellamy's day in order to take its measure. The science fiction of H. G. Wells (1866–1946) owes a great debt to the literature of utopia in its projection of alternative worlds and the sharp social commentary that it levels at this world. *The Time Machine* (1895), for instance, uses the device of time travel to point out some of the possible effects of social inequity in England in the late nineteenth century. In this case, travel in time replaces travel in space as a means of proposing an alternative world, but the basic premise is much the same. Wells's *The Island of Doctor Moreau* (1896), too, can be understood as a story about a utopian venture gone terribly wrong.

In the twentieth century, utopian literature has proliferated enormously, and it would be difficult to provide an adequate taxonomy of utopian and post-utopian writings, much less an exhaustive list. Some new developments, however, must be mentioned. A new strain of utopian writing emerged in the late nineteenth and early twentieth centuries: dystopian literature. George Orwell (1903–1950), whose *1984* (1949) and *Animal Farm* (1945) clearly reveal a debt to Thomas More, was one of the foremost dystopian writers of the twentieth century. The former is a spectacularly realized depiction of the horrors of totalitarianism in a world where individual identity and relationships are brutally subordinated to the system of state government. Orwell also delves into the dangers of utopian thinking in the latter work. Similarly, Aldous Huxley (1894–1963), in the satirical novel *Brave New World* (1932), (titled from a line in Shakespeare's *Tempest,*) explores the political dangers of utopianism. Ursula Leguin's *The Dispossessed: An Ambiguous*

Utopia (1974) and Margaret Atwood's *The Handmaid's Tale* (1985) explored different fictional possibilities of the dystopia.

New varieties of utopian and dystopian fiction seem to appear with each new era. Indeed, it would be fair to say that each age has its own characteristic form of popular utopian fiction. This is particularly evident in cinema, and films of several genres owe a debt to Thomas More. Science fiction cinema and literature offer many examples; from *Forbidden Planet* to *Blade Runner* and *The Matrix*, utopian and dystopian depictions of alternative worlds have thrilled audiences for decades.

The legacy of *Utopia* has also been immensely significant in the realm of political thought. Intellectuals and reformers of all kinds have taken *Utopia* as a touchstone for their own interests, and have imitated and adapted it to varying degrees. To some degree, utopian thinking has existed since long before Thomas More. As Isaiah Berlin has claimed,

> the idea of a perfect society is a very old dream, whether because of the ills of the present, which lead men to conceive of what their world would be like without them—to imagine some ideal state in which there was no misery and no greed, no danger or poverty or fear or brutalising labour or insecurity—or because these Utopias are fictions deliberately constructed as satires, intended to criticise the actual world and to shame those who control existing regimes, or those who suffer them too tamely, or perhaps they are social fantasies—simple exercises of the poetical imagination.
>
> (20)

By this argument, political thought from Plato to Machiavelli can be said to contain a strong strain of utopianism.

But the legacy of More's ideal society has been most powerfully felt by modern left-wing political thinkers, from the Levellers and Diggers of the seventeenth-century English Revolution to Karl Marx and Friedrich Engels. The society of *Utopia* is, in today's terms, a com-munist one, with a strictly egalitarian distribution of wealth and a carefully maintained erasure of most social distinctions. Political philosophers have tended to emphasize one of the two aspects of utopian thought: the idealist projection of a rationally ordered or perfect society, and the materialist interrogation of the here and now that gives rise to such projections. The imaginary nation of Utopia, a map of what this world is not, is inscribed with the traces of what this world *is*. It is a negative cartography, the projection in fictional space of an alternative world where the problems of this one are resolved by reason, science, or some other disciplinary regime. Thus, by "utopia" we mean not simply the quest for the ideal polity, but also the critical interrogation of existing political conditions. The former could not exist without the latter, yet, all too often utopias have been reduced to their idealist dimension. It would be safe to say that in common usage "utopia" is synonymous with "pipe-dream," a vain hope, a yearning for the impossible, or an idealization of the social so fanciful as to be entirely unworkable. Nothing could be further from the case. Common usage is based on a misreading of More's *Utopia*.

Thomas Nashe (1567–1601), an Elizabethan writer who lived several decades after Sir Thomas More, understood *Utopia* as a text about the political problems of its era. His 1594 description of it in *The Unfortunate Traveller* is revealing:

> Quick-witted Sir Thomas More travelled in a clean contrary province, for he, seeing most commonwealths corrupted by ill custom, and that principalities were nothing but great piracies which, gotten by violence and murther, were maintained by private undermining and bloodshed; that in the chiefest flourishing kingdoms there was no equal or well-divided weal one with another, but a manifest conspiracy of rich men against poor men, procuring their own unlawful commodities under the name and interest of the commonwealth—he concluded with himself to lay

down a perfect plot of a commonwealth or government which he would entitle his *Utopia.*
(In *An Anthology of Elizabethan Prose Fiction,* ed. Paul Salzman, p. 240)

The language that Nashe uses is richly and suggestively ambiguous: the "perfect plot" that More "lay down" neatly captures the overlapping of the territorial with the textual that characterizes More's narrative. Nashe identifies More as both a writer and a figurative cartographer, for the island of Utopia is a plot of territory produced within a narrative plot. More's protagonist, Hythlodaeus, is a fortunate traveler, one whose voyages authorize him to reflect critically on contemporary Europe. Space, place, and text are the components of a specifically critical response to early modern politics; clearly, then, Nashe understood *Utopia* not as pure fantasy but as a politically engaged imaginative cartography.

Nashe's observations about *Utopia,* inserted into a work whose title belies a similar preoccupation with the vicissitudes of space and place, reminds us that utopias are fictional worlds that many travelers can find or invent. At the same time, utopianism is a complex encoding of social critique and spatial play that produces a textual space for alternatives to the here and now. As Nashe would have it, *Utopia* is a "clean contrary place," a projection situated in a dialectical relationship to Tudor England. It is both quite different from England and a cleaned-up version of England. Nashe's assessment is largely in agreement with Terry Eagleton's claim that in utopian fiction "alternative worlds are simply devices for embarrassing the world we actually have. The point is not to go elsewhere, but to use elsewhere as a reflection on where you are. Most literary utopias are covert political journalism. . . ." (33). They are that, certainly, and a great deal more as well.

Select Bibliography

EDITIONS

More, Thomas. *Utopia.* In *The Complete Works of St. Thomas More.* Vol. 4. Edited by Richard S. Sylvester. New Haven, CT: Yale University Press, 1963.

———. Utopia. Translated by Paul Turner. New York: Penguin, 1965. (Quotations in the text are from this edition.)

RELATED PRIMARY WORKS

Bacon, Francis. *Essays and The New Atlantis.* New York: Walter Black, 1942.

Campanella, Tommaso. *The City of the Sun: A Poetical Dialogue.* Translated by Daniel J. Donno. Berkeley: University of California Press, 1981.

Hall, Joseph. *Another World and Yet the Same.* Translated and edited by John Millar Wands. New Haven: Yale University Press, 1981.

Nashe, Thomas. *The Unfortunate Traveller.* In *An Anthology of Elizabethan Prose Fiction,* edited by Paul Salzman. Oxford: Oxford University Press, 1987.

Smith, Thomas. *A Discourse of the Commonweal of This Realm of England.* Edited by Mary Dewar. Charlottesville: The University Press of Virginia, 1969.

Shakespeare, William. "The Tempest." *The Norton Shakespeare.* Edited by Stephen Greenblatt, Walter Cohen, Jean Howard, and Katharine Maus. New York: W. W. Norton, 1997. 3047–3106.

SECONDARY WORKS

Albanese, Denise. *New Science, New World.* Durham, N.C.: Duke University Press, 1996.

Berlin, Sir Isaiah. "The Decline of Utopian Ideas in the West." In *The Crooked Timber of Humanity.* Princeton: Princeton University Press, 1998. 20–48.

Burt, Richard and John Michael Archer, eds. *Enclosure Acts: Sexuality, Property, and Culture in Early Modern England.* Ithaca and London: Cornell University Press, 1994.

Campbell, Mary B. Wonder and Science: Imagining Worlds in Early Modern Europe. Ithaca and London: Cornell Univesity Press, 1999.

Conley, Tom. The Self-Made Map: Cartographic Writing in Early Modern France. Minneapolis: University of Minnesota Press, 1996.

Eagleton, Terry. "Utopia and Its Opposites." In Socialist Register 2000: Necessary and Unnecessary Utopias. Edited Leo Panitch and Colin Leys. London: Merlin Press, 1999. 31–40.

Eurich, Nell. *Science in Utopia: A Mighty Design.* Cambridge: Harvard University Press, 1967.

Greenblatt, Stephen. *Renaissance Self-Fashioning.* Chicago and London: University of Chicago Press, 1980.

———. *Learning to Curse: Essays in Early Modern Culture.* New York and London: Routledge, 1990.

———, ed. *New World Encounters.* Berkeley: University of California Press, 1993.

Johnson, Donald S. *Phantom Islands of the North Atlantic.* New York: Walker and Co., 1996.

Kautsky, Karl. *Thomas More and His Utopia.* Translated by H. J. Stenning. London: Lawrence & Wishart, 1979.

Knapp, Jeffrey. *An Empire Nowhere: England, America, and Literature from* Utopia *to* The Tempest. Berkeley and Los Angeles: University of California Press, 1992.

Leslie, Marina. *Renaissance Utopias and the Problem of History.* Ithaca and London: Cornell University Press, 1998.

Marin, Louis. *Utopics: Spatial Play.* Translated by Robert A. Vollrath. Atlantic Highlands, N.J.:

Humanities Press, Inc., 1984.

———. "Frontiers of Utopia: Past and Present." *Critical Inquiry* 19 (Winter 1993): 397–420.

Marius, Richard. *Thomas More: A Biography.* New York: Alfred A. Knopf, 1984.

Marx, Karl. *Capital, Volume I.* New York: International Publishers, 1992.

Mignolo, Walter. *The Darker Side of the Renaissance: Literacy, Territoriality, and Colonialization.* Ann Arbor: University of Michigan Press, 1995.

Mortimer, Anthony. "Hythlodaeus and Persona More: The Narrative Voices of *Utopia.*" In *Cahiers elisabethains: Etudes sur la pre-renaissance et la renaissance anglaises* 28 (October 1985): 23–35.

Mumford, Lewis. *The Story of Utopias.* New York: Viking Press, 1922; 1962.

Perlette, John M. "Sites and Parasites: The Centrality of the Marginal Anecdote in Book I of More's *Utopia.*" *English Literary History* 54 (1987): 231–52.

Tawney, R. H. *The Agrarian Problem in the Sixteenth Century.* London: Longmans, Green, and Co., 1912.

Underdown, David. *Revel, Riot, and Rebellion: Popular Politics and Culture in England, 1603–1660.* Oxford: Oxford University Press, 1985.

Waldseemuller, Martin. *The Cosmographiae Introductio of Martin Waldseemuller in Facsimile.* Edited by John and Franz von Wieser. *Catholic Historical Society Monograph 4.* New York, 1907.

Emily Brontë's
Wuthering Heights

SANDIE BYRNE

MILY JANE BRONTË was the daughter of the Reverend Patrick Brontë and his wife, Maria Branwell. Patrick was Irish and had changed his name from Branty (as it was recorded on his entry to St. John's College, Cambridge) or possibly Brunty or Prunty in honor of Lord Nelson, who had been made Duke of Bronte by the king of Naples.

The elder children were born in the village of Thornton, where the family lived until 1820, when the Reverend Patrick Brontë was made perpetual curate of Haworth and they moved to the parsonage next to the church there (now the Brontë museum). A year later, at age thirty-eight, Maria Brontë died of cancer, and the children's aunt, Elizabeth Branwell, came to care for them.

Miss Branwell's staunch Methodism was to be a powerful influence on Anne, who was too young to go away to school with her four sisters. With Charlotte, Emily followed Maria and Elizabeth to the Clergy Daughters' School at Cowan Bridge, which offered a good education at a reduced fee. Mr. Brontë knew the school only by reputation and was unaware of the poor conditions and neglect to which the girls were exposed. Having survived an epidemic of typhus, Maria and Elizabeth showed symptoms of the consumption (tuberculosis) that was the bane of the family. Maria was sent home to die, and Elizabeth soon followed her. Emily and Charlotte came home and survived. The fictional school in *Jane Eyre*, Lowood, is said to be based on Cowan Bridge.

During their childhood, the Brontë children read widely in their father's library and among the periodicals he took, especially *Blackwood's* magazine, and produced their own miniature magazines and broadsheets containing stories, illustrations, and poems. These also contained the elaborate sagas of imaginary kingdoms that developed from the adventures and life stories with which the children invested the toy soldiers given by their father to Branwell. The children both wrote and acted out episodes from their Islander and Glasstown stories, and, later, the Angria and Gondal sagas. Angria was the creation of Charlotte and Branwell, while Gondal, invented later, was Emily and Anne's kingdom. In 1835, Emily went away to school again, Charlotte's appointment as a teacher at Roe Head, where she had been a pupil since 1831–1832, entitling her sister to free tuition. Emily remained for only three months, however.

Terribly homesick, she returned to Haworth, and her place was taken by Anne.

Emily was to leave home twice more: in 1837 to go to Law Hill School, Halifax, as a teacher, where she probably remained for about six months, and in 1842 to accompany Charlotte to the Pensionnat Heger in Brussels, where Madame Heger ran a school for young ladies. Here the sisters were taught languages and literature by Madame Heger's husband, Constantin, who visited the school from his primary occupation as teacher at the Athénée Royale. Following Elizabeth Branwell's death in October, the Brontës went home, where Emily remained to take her aunt's place as housekeeper when Charlotte returned to Brussels for another year. On Charlotte's return from Brussels, Anne's from her position as governess to the Robinson family, and Branwell's from his as tutor, there were plans for starting a school, initially elsewhere and later at the parsonage, which was to be altered for the purpose. These plans were abandoned, perhaps in part because Elizabeth Branwell's bequests to her nieces, which Emily invested in a railway company, enabled her at least to remain at home, where the continued presence of one of the sisters was necessitated by their father's growing blindness. In 1846 the sisters published *Poems by Currer, Ellis and Acton Bell*, paying approximately £40 for the volume to be printed. Only two copies were sold. Following a complete collapse of his health, mental and physical, brought on by a series of personal and professional failures and disappointments, Branwell Brontë died on 24 September 1848. His funeral service in church on 1 October was the last occasion on which Emily left the house. She caught a cold or flu for which she refused treatment; it worsened and her health declined rapidly. She succumbed to the family illness in December and was buried under the aisle of the church at Haworth. Anne died the following summer and Charlotte, the last of the six children, in 1855. Their father outlived them, remaining in Haworth until his death in 1861.

CHRONOLOGY

1818 30 July, Emily Jane Brontë born in Thornton, Yorkshire, the fifth child of the Reverend Patrick Brontë, who is curate there, and Maria Branwell Brontë.

1820 The family moves to the village of Haworth, where Patrick Brontë has been appointed to a perpetual curacy.

1821 Maria Brontë dies of cancer. Her sister, Elizabeth Branwell, comes to live with the Brontës.

1824 Emily and Charlotte join their older sisters, Maria and Elizabeth, at the Clergy Daughters' School at Cowan Bridge, Lancashire.

1825 Typhus epidemic at the school. Maria, then Elizabeth, sent home and subsequently die (of consumption). Charlotte and Emily removed from the school by Patrick Brontë.

1826 Patrick Brontë gives Branwell a box of toy soldiers. The children each name a soldier and begin to invent stories, "plays," about them, which become the Glasstown stories.

1831 Charlotte is sent to Roe Head School.

1835 Emily goes to Roe Head, where Charlotte has become a teacher, but is homesick and returns to Haworth.

1837 Anne falls ill at Roe Head and she and Charlotte withdraw. Charlotte later returns.

1838 Emily goes to teach at Miss Hatchett's school at Law Hill for six months.

1842 Emily goes to Brussels with Charlotte to study languages at the Pensionnat Heger. Returns to Haworth in October after the death of Elizabeth Branwell, from whom she takes over as housekeeper.

1846 Publication of *Poems by Currer, Ellis, and Acton Bell*. Patrick Brontë undergoes operation for cataracts, which is successful.

1847	October, publication of Jane Eyre. December, publication of *Wuthering Heights* with *Agnes Grey*.
1848	Publication of *The Tenant of Wildfell Hall*. Charlotte and Emily travel to London to meet the publishers. Death of Branwell Brontë on 24 September At his funeral in October, Emily catches a cold and (allegedly) refuses all medical aid. Her condition rapidly worsens, and she dies on 19 December. Buried at Haworth.

THE MYTH

We have very little biographical data on which to base our knowledge of Emily Brontë's life and personality: three letters, some fragments, a few diary papers kept with Anne, and the recorded recollections of her family and few acquaintances. The rest is speculation and the mythic afterlife that turned the real woman into an archetype. Most of those who have written about Emily Brontë agree that she was reserved and reclusive, unbending and resolute to the point of stubbornness, and a mixture of wild, almost fey unworldliness and capable practicality. She is also acknowledged as having possessed a powerful imagination whose least extreme productions were the Gondal and other fantasies and most extreme were mystical or spiritual visitations, together with an all-consuming inner life into whose alternative reality she was often tempted to withdraw entirely.

Some of the images we have of Emily Brontë are contradictory. Charlotte wrote of her sister's fury, first at the discovery of her poems and their dispatch to the publisher, and later when she learned that Charlotte had revealed her identity to the firm along with Anne's and Charlotte's own. Charlotte felt obliged to warn the publisher's reader: "Permit me to caution you not to speak of my sisters when you write to me—I mean, do not use the word in the plural. 'Ellis Bell' will not endure to be alluded to under any other appellation than the 'nom de plume.' I committed a grand error in betraying his identity" (Charlotte Brontë to William Smith Williams, 31 July 1848, in Smith, ed., *Letters of Charlotte Brontë*, vol. 2, p. 94). Yet the unworldly recluse was interested enough in the world's opinion to keep cuttings of reviews and mentions of *Wuthering Heights* in her desk drawer.

Emily's obduracy during her final illness is recorded in letters from Charlotte to her closest friend: "Her reserved nature occasions one great uneasiness of mind—it is useless to question her—you get no answers—it is still more useless to recommend remedies—they are never adopted" (letter to Ellen Nussey, 29 October 1848, *Letters*, vol. 2, p. 130). In a similar vein, she told William Smith Williams: "it is best usually to leave her to form her own judgment as especially not to advocate the side you wish her to favour . . . if you do, she is sure to lean in the opposite direction, and ten to one will argue herself into non-compliance" (22 November 1848, *Letters*, vol. 2, p. 142).

Yet this withdrawn and stubborn woman could be kind and generous; she loved animals and was fearless of them. (In spite of her much-attested affinity with her father's dog, Keeper, her companion on many walks over the moors, she was clearly a cat person, as we can see from her French devoirs of 15 May 1842). She could be mischievous (Ellen Nussey remembered Emily dragging Charlotte into rougher ground than she dared traverse alone and laughing at Charlotte's pusillanimous fears of unknown animals ("Reminiscences of Charlotte Brontë," in *Scribner's* magazine, May 1871). She was happy and cheerful when roaming freely on the moors. The stationer of Haworth, John Greenwood, observed that such was Patrick Brontë's "unbounded confidence" in his daughter, due to her "unparalleled intrepidity and firmness," that as his eyesight failed he taught her to shoot so that she would be ready to defend the parsonage in his place (John Greenwood's diary quoted in Gérin, *Emily*

Brontë, 1978, p. 147). As related by Greenwood, it was Emily whose quick reactions saved her brother when, drugged or drunk, he set fire to his bed curtains (p. 201). M. Heger thought her intellect more powerful than Charlotte's. He spoke admiringly to Elizabeth Gaskell, Charlotte's biographer, of Emily's force of will, her reason, her ability to formulate arguments, and her daring. He said (assuming that it was a compliment) that she should have been a man and become a navigator and explorer (see *Life of Charlotte Brontë*, 1975, p. 151). It may be important to note that the arch-Romantic and wild-child Emily was well-read in classical literature and made her own translations of Horace and Virgil (see Chitham, *The Birth of Wuthering Heights*, 2001, pp. 17–32).

Mrs. Gaskell was also the recipient of Charlotte Brontë's confidences about her sister, including the information that the eponymous heroine of her novel *Shirley* was a portrait of Emily had she been blessed with health and prosperity. As has been pointed out by critics, Shirley is to an extent a conventionalized Emily.

Charlotte Brontë attempted to ward off accusations of coarseness, vulgarity, and indecency which, leveled at *Wuthering Heights,* could be transferred to her own work. Lucasta Miller, in *The Brontë Myth,* traces what she sees as Charlotte's neutralizing and domesticating of her sister's radicalism in art, in politics, and in person, from Charlotte's patronizing and belittling biographical statements, slighting assessment of the novel's literary worth, and rewriting of parts of the novel in its posthumous edition, to her cavalier editing of the poems and posthumous censoring of Emily Brontë's manuscripts.

WUTHERING HEIGHTS

COMPOSITION AND FIRST PUBLICATION.

Our knowledge of the publishing history of the novel comes largely from Charlotte Brontë's let-

ters, her "Biographical Notice" to the second edition, and her preface to the new edition of *Wuthering Heights* that she edited. Charlotte suggested that in 1845 she discovered a notebook collection of Emily's poems (she kept two, one for fair copies of Gondal poems and one for others) and persuaded a reluctant Emily to allow them to be included in the joint publication *Poems by Currer, Ellis and Acton Bell.* (Winifred Gérin discusses the choice of pseudonyms in *Emily Brontë,* pp. 185–186.) Two copies of this edition were sold in the year following publication.

The novel is thought to have been written between October 1845 and June 1846. Emily seems to have been far less secretive about its composition than that of her poems, which she perhaps felt were glimpses into her private world, and she read each section to her sisters as it was completed. The sisters proposed that *Wuthering Heights,* Anne's *Agnes Grey,* and Charlotte's *The Master* (later entitled *The Professor*) should be published together in three volumes, and accordingly sent the manuscripts as one package to a series of publishers. They were rejected by several firms, but in July 1846 they received an offer from Thomas Cautley Newby to publish *Agnes Grey* and *Wuthering Heights.* Newby treated the sisters badly, requiring them to pay £50 for an edition of 300, failing to keep his promise to return the sum after 250 copies had been sold, delaying publication, and failing to incorporate any of the corrections made at proof stage into the printed book. One of the publishers to whom Charlotte had sent *The Master* encouraged her to submit a longer work, since the most commercial format for the novel at that time was in three volumes, and *Jane Eyre* was sent to the firm of Smith, Elder and Company on 24 August. It was published on 16 October, but *Wuthering Heights* and *Agnes Grey* did not appear until mid-December, Newby evidently having delayed printing until he saw that the Bells' work might be profitable to him. As *Jane Eyre* received favorable reviews and began to sell well, he assisted the rumor then circulating that all three works were the product of one author, his. *Jane Eyre* rapidly went into a second edition, and Charlotte Brontë received payments from her publisher in December 1847 and February 1848, while Anne and Emily received nothing.

In spite of Newby's shady dealings, Emily and Anne refused an offer from the more honorable Smith, Elder and Company to publish any future work of theirs, and Emily seems to have been determined to remain with Newby against Charlotte's advice. It is possible that she had begun work on another novel early in 1848. A letter from Newby dated 15 February 1848 suggests that he expected to receive a second work, and critics have even suggested that Charlotte may have destroyed the manuscript of a second novel after her sister's death, but there is no extant manuscript or direct reference to the title of a second novel in the sisters' surviving letters. (For Newby's letter to Emily, see Barker, *The Brontës: A Life in Letters*, 1997, p. 183.)

Q. D. Leavis in 1969 and Tom Winnifrith in 1983 suggested that the two-part nature of the story derives from the novel's having been rewritten, and Edward Chitham explores this idea in his *Birth of* Wuthering Heights: *Emily Brontë at Work*. It would seem likely that the novel was expanded between its rejection by the first publishing company to which it was sent, Colburn, and its eventual publication, since it was initially offered together with *The Master* and *The Tenant of Wildfell Hall*, each of which, according to Charlotte Brontë's letter of 4 July 1846, occupied one volume. Chitham suggests that the first phase of writing was between January and March 1845 and the second phase between August or September 1845 and May 1846. Chitham relates the exact topography and teasing anagrams of the early part of the novel to incidents and places in the life of the Brontë siblings and traces the introduction of characters and incidents from Gondal. He explains the apparent mistake in chronology of the child-ghost's saying that it has been wandering for twenty years by suggesting that the ghost is not

that of Catherine Earnshaw but of Maria Brontë, who had died in the spring of 1825.

INFLUENCES

The Brontë children were avid readers, though Emily was not always diligent in following any prescribed course of reading. Their chief literary favorites were Walter Scott and Lord Byron, but Milton, William Wordsworth, Percy Bysshe Shelley, James Hogg, Bulwer Lytton's rather shocking novel *Eugene Aram* (1832), and the Border Ballads popular at the time were likely to have been literary influences. They were also exposed to an oral tradition in the form of stories of local history and legends and the traditional ballads told to them by their longtime servant Tabitha Ackroyd (Tabby) and Patrick Brontë, who had them from his parishioners. Emily studied both German and French at the Pensionnat Heger and is reported to have continued to read German books after her return to Haworth. Jacques Blondel looks at the range of probable influences on the novel in "Literary Influences on *Wuthering Heights*" (in Allott, ed., Wuthering Heights: *A Casebook*, 1992, pp. 229–241). Edward Chitham examines the probable importance of Shelley as an influence on Brontë in "Emily Brontë and Shelley" (in Chitham and Winnifrith, *Brontë Facts and Brontë Problems*, 1983, pp. 58–76). Stevie Davies makes the case for the influence of German Romanticism on *Wuthering Heights*, as well as the importance of Beethoven's music to Emily Brontë, in her *Emily Brontë: Heretic* (1994, pp. 49–52).

The texts that most contribute to our understanding of *Wuthering Heights* are Emily Brontë's poems, largely untitled and undatable. Their complex relation to the novel is carefully explored by Mary Visick in *The Genesis of* Wuthering Heights (1958).

SOURCES

Many sources of the plot, settings, and characters of *Wuthering Heights* have been suggested. Winifred Gérin suggests that the origins of the Heights may be in High Sunderland Hall, a house near the school in Halifax where Emily spent an unhappy six months, though the situation of the house is likely to have been based on that of Top Withens, an Elizabethan farmhouse on the moors above Haworth. (See Gérin, *Emily Brontë,* pp. 82–83). The origin of Thrushcross Grange may have been Ponden Hall, which was within walking distance of Haworth. Penistone Crag may be based on Ponden Kirk, a jutting outcrop of rock high on the moors near her home. The character of Heathcliff is clearly in part suggested by Byronic antiheroes, and his histrionic language and oaths have been attributed to Branwell Brontë, but his story may have derived from that of Jack Sharp, which Emily would have heard during her time at Law Hill. Sharp was a Halifax orphan who was adopted by his uncle, a Mr. Walker, took over his business and ancient house, Walterclough Hall, and when the true heirs requested its return, set out to ruin the family (see Gérin, *Emily Brontë,* pp. 76–80). Catherine Earnshaw could be a descendent of Angelica, the selfish, haughty, and capricious Gondal Queen. Patrick Brontë's curate, William Weightman, a somewhat vain and fickle though kindhearted young man, may have suggested the character of Lockwood (see Gérin, *Emily Brontë,* pp. 106–107).

THE STORY

In order to summarize the plot of *Wuthering Heights,* it is helpful to make a distinction between the chronology (the events as they would have unfolded in real time) and the story (the events as they are narrated to the reader). The difference between these two is crucial to the experience of reading the novel. C. P. Sanger untangled the complex narrative threads to work out the chronology of the story (as well as the legal aspects of the property in the story) in a 1926 essay (reprinted in Allott, *Wuthering Heights* Casebook, 1992, pp. 109–117). The chronology may be summarized as follows:

Since 1500, the Earnshaw family has lived in an isolated farmhouse high on the moors of the West Riding of Yorkshire (a stone domestic building at this date would have been highly unusual in this area). In 1771, the Mr. Earnshaw of the day returns from a three-day trip to Liverpool not with the gifts he promised for his children and their nurse, Ellen, but with a waif he has picked up on the streets of the city. The child, Heathcliff, becomes a cuckoo, loved by Mr. Earnshaw but resented by the son of the house, Hindley. After Mr. Earnshaw's death, Hindley brings his wife, Frances, to the Heights, and they have a son, Hareton, in 1778, soon after which Frances dies. Hindley attempts to degrade Heathcliff, treating him as a servant and brutalizing him at every opportunity. Hindley's sister, Catherine, however, has become close to the boy, and they take refuge in each other's company from the unhappiness and constraints of the Heights, spending as much time as they can out on the moor. The two are soulmates; their love excludes all else.

An accident (in November 1777) forces Catherine to spend some time at Thrushcross Grange, a more luxurious and refined environment than her home, and when she comes home she rejects the Heights, and Heathcliff, who disappears in 1780. In April 1783, Catherine marries Edgar Linton, the heir to the Grange. When Heathcliff returns in September 1783, he has acquired a fortune, but all he wants is Catherine. Edgar Linton's sister, Isabella, believes herself to be in love with Heathcliff; he marries her but abuses her terribly. Following the birth of her daughter, another Catherine, in March 1784, Catherine dies, with Heathcliff at her bedside. After the birth of a son, Linton Heathcliff, in September 1784, Isabella runs away.

Grief-stricken, and obsessed by the idea of revenge, Heathcliff sets about gaining control of both the Earnshaw and Linton properties. He leads Hindley into gambling and drink, and gains Hindley's house, lands, and his son. Heathcliff's own son is returned to him after Isabella's death but is a sickly, weak youth. He kidnaps Catherine Linton, who becomes mistress of Thrushcross Grange at her father's death, and forces her to marry Linton Heathcliff in August 1801, so that on Linton's death in October he inherits everything. He keeps Catherine and Hareton virtual prisoners at the Heights, reversing the position he held there as a boy.

Heathcliff lets the Grange to a tenant, Lockwood, who arrives at the Heights in November 1801 as a storm comes on. Sleeping in Catherine's old room, Lockwood dreams of or sees her ghost asking to be let in to the house. Soon after this, Heathcliff's demonic energy, which has driven him throughout twenty years of single-minded obsession, seems to drain away. He could complete his revenge, but he cannot bring himself to make the effort. Catherine and Hareton escape his brutalizing: Catherine civilizes Hareton, teaching him to read, and Hareton protects Catherine from the worst of their way of life. Heathcliff dies in Catherine Earnshaw's bed and is perhaps reunited with her in death.

As C. P. Sanger notes, only three dates are given in the novel: 1801 begins chapter 1; 1802 begins chapter 32; and in the last sentence of chapter 7 Ellen Dean says that she will be content to pass on to the next summer, "the summer of 1778, that is, nearly twenty-three years ago." The unreality of *Wuthering Heights* does not require precise chronologies.

The novel's actual narrative, however, begins in November 1801, when a stranger arrives at an isolated farmhouse high on the moors of the West Riding of Yorkshire, Wuthering Heights, hoping to meet the man from whom he has rented another house, Thrushcross Grange. He is received with less than civility. His landlord, Mr. Heathcliff, seems a boorish, reclusive barbarian, but the tenant, Mr. Lockwood, decides to think of him as an amusing eccentric. There are also present a silent woman and a boorish youth whom Lockwood takes to be Mrs. Heathcliff and a farm laborer. Bad weather

forces Lockwood to remain at Wuthering Heights for the night, and he sleeps in a disused chamber containing an old-fashioned closet bed. The name "Cathy" is scratched on the window, and in a book by the bed he finds the names Catherine Earnshaw, Catherine Heathcliff, and Catherine Linton. That night, his sleep is disturbed by the storm and the tapping of tree branches on the window panes, and by bad dreams, so he gets up to close the casement. His wrists are grabbed and held, and he sees a child who demands to be let in.

Later, having moved into the Grange, he is confined to bed by illness and asks Ellen Dean (Nelly), who has worked at the Heights and the Grange, to tell him about his landlord. Her story, told with breaks during December and January, explains Heathcliff's brutishness, the presence of Edgar Linton's daughter at the Heights, and the apparition at the window. She starts with Heathcliff's arrival at the Heights and fills in the rest of the story to the present date in retrospective episodes ("back story") interspersed with Lockwood's own narrative, taking place in the "now" of the novel. Ellen's story ends with her fears for the safety of Catherine Linton, Heathcliff's prisoner, and her oblique suggestion that Lockwood marry her. Six weeks have passed, and Lockwood is planning to leave. Ellen returns to the Heights, where Catherine and Hareton are growing closer. Sometime early in spring, Catherine defies Heathcliff, and Heathcliff begins to decline. He dies in May. In September, Lockwood returns and continues the story to the restoration of Catherine and Hareton to ownership of the Heights and the Grange, and their planned marriage the following New Year.

In reading the novel we learn the characters' histories and motivations as Lockwood does, retrospectively, so that we must unravel the mysteries of the Heights as he does, clue by clue. Graham Holderness writes of the novel's "radical uncertainty" about its interpretation (*Wuthering Heights*, 1985, p. 5). Neither Lockwood nor Ellen knows the whole story, and their ignorance and misinterpretation, together with the fact that we don't entirely trust them to tell the truth and the whole truth, adds to the sense of mystery and unreality.

CHARACTERS

The story of the destructive love of Heathcliff and Catherine may have had its origins in Emily's observation of her brother's love for the wife of his employer, Mrs. Robinson. After her husband's death, Branwell lived in hourly expectation of Mrs. Robinson's summons, but instead he received a message saying that a codicil in her husband's will forbade their meeting and that she was desperately ill. Neither was true, but the message was a death blow to Branwell. His sufferings were acute, and public.

Modern adaptations of the novel have softened Heathcliff from an inhuman force of nature to a matinee idol and given Catherine more softness and acceptable "feminine" traits than she betrays in the novel. Their love has been watered down from something elemental, fierce, and transcendent, beyond liking or the kindness of affection, to a conventional love story. Laurence Olivier, Robert Cavannah, Timothy Dalton, and Ralph Fiennes (among others) have played Heathcliff on film, and Cliff Richard has taken the part in a musical. Olivier, Dalton, and Richard played him as a hero, that is, not only one of the main protagonists but also the chief focus of the audience's sympathy and perhaps the character with whom audience members identify. In these versions his bad behavior was omitted, or excused on the grounds of circumstances and temperament. He became a romantic hero rather than Romantic antihero; mean, moody, and masterful, but basically good. Heathcliff is, however, the antithesis of the handsome and virtuous hero who rescues the heroine from peril or from the distasteful but advantageous marriage arranged by her avaricious relatives.

If we take a materialist perspective such as that given by Arnold Kettle in the section on *Wuthering Heights* of his *Introduction to the English Novel* (2d ed., 1967, pp. 130–145), we can see that from the first, Heathcliff is associated with the material, not the ideal; with property and power. "I have just returned from a visit to my landlord" are Lockwood's opening words (p. 1). (All quotations are from the Oxford World Classics edition, Ian Jack, ed., 1998). Our first sight of Heathcliff is not against a Romantic background of wild weather, wild country, or wild flight, but lowering over the gate to his property, reluctant to unlock the chain and allow anyone else to enter. Isabella Linton is repulsive to Heathcliff until he inquires, "She's her brother's heir, is she not?" Even Catherine says to him, "You are too prone to covet your neighbour's goods" (p. 94).

Such virtues as Heathcliff has are not conventionally heroic. He is not dashing, eloquent, spontaneous, or gifted, but patient and stoical when he is not melodramatic and tempestuous—"hardened, perhaps, to ill-treatment. He would stand Hindley's blows without winking or shedding a tear" (p. 32). Nelly Dean calls him a "sullen boy who never, to my recollection, repaid his [Mr. Earnshaw's] indulgence by any sign of gratitude." Damning for the period in which the story is set, which admired the sensitive Romantic hero of great sensibility, Heathcliff is described as "insensible" (p. 33). Lockwood sees Heathcliff's erect figure spoiled by his sulkiness and morose aspect; even cleaned up by Nelly, he sports lowering thick brows and deep frown lines. Even the indulgent Mr. Earnshaw says "it's as dark almost as if it came from the devil" (p. 31), and Nelly observes that instead of clear, open eyes, he has "a couple of black fiends so deeply buried . . . [that] lurk glinting." All of this adds to the archetype of the child of mysterious origin.

Modern readers, of course, will not read into black, craggy, and closed physiognomy a dark, closed soul, and other characters' demonization of him might only increase our sympathy. But instead of showing that under the black and abused exterior lies a softer, forgiving interior, Heathcliff's behavior is of a piece with his appearance. His brutality is less often the result of hot blood than of calculation and retribution, often not upon the original offenders against him but upon their innocent offspring. He delights in his cruelty, marveling at and despising the love Isabella continues to offer him, trumpeting his hatred for and contempt of his son, haranguing Catherine on her deathbed. He both looks and behaves like Shakespeare's Richard III, and seems equally determined to prove himself a villain. He explicitly warns us that he is not a romantic hero, saying of Isabella, "She abandoned them [the Lintons] under a delusion . . . picturing in me a hero of romance, and expecting . . . chivalrous devotion." He goes on: "Now, was it not the depth of absurdity—of genuine idiocy, for that pitiful, slavish, mean-minded brach to dream that I could love her?" (p. 133). He demonstrates his nature to Isabella; he is harsh and rude to her, but she continues to pursue him. He abuses her, he kills her dog, but she still chooses to believe in her rosy-colored dream. Heathcliff might well have cried, "What!" as Richard III does of the wooing of the woman he has just widowed, amazed by the preposterousness of her acceptance. Heathcliff has no illusions and no vanity. He understands that Isabella will "still creep shamefully cringing back" to him because "it wounds her vanity to have the truth exposed" (p. 133).

In spite of this appearance, in one possible reading of the novel Heathcliff *is* its hero, though he would be scornful of attempts to rehabilitate him in the mold of the conventional romantic type. He is the novel's moral center and the bearer of its main theme. He, not Nelly or the social norm, provides the voice of right and enables the restoration of order, though he has no intention of restoring order, or anything else, to anyone, least of all society at large. Heathcliff's "right" is not the right of law or morality but some universal right that is only obscured by such ephemeral codes of behavior. In his view, all that he does is justified. His credo

is the doctrine of individuality, of truth to the self and the self's passions, and that permits, indeed makes essential, a solipsistic, tunnel-visioned, and self-centered quest for the desired. Heathcliff therefore has a kind of integrity, a steadfastness that impels and empowers him through the story.

The crucial event from which all else follows tests the central characters and their truth to their passions and themselves. Heathcliff passes, and Catherine fails. As children they look through the windows of Thrushcross Grange. Later, describing what they saw to Ellen Dean, Heathcliff shows that he appreciates the color and glitter that will attract Catherine, but he sees further, to the spoiled, bored children who hurt the puppy they are squabbling over and then cry for it. This brother and sister are the antithesis of Heathcliff and Catherine, and their world is alien to them. Nonetheless, Catherine chooses *in*—the world of interiors—and Heathcliff remains outside in their element, waiting for her. When she finally leaves Thrushcross Grange weeks later she is of its world, the world of the genteel, the clean, the ordered, and the luxurious, and will be called back to it permanently. Though her return to the Grange as its mistress, and her life there, is not without struggle and longing for her old life, she goes.

In Heathcliff's view, Catherine betrays not only him but herself when she chooses to enter the blue and crimson and gold interior of Thrushcross Grange, the world of superficial glitter and gratification, and his perception of this is so clear that he must make Catherine share it before she dies, not only to express, again, the momentousness and inescapability of their love, but to make her acknowledge the truth of her betrayal, so that she will not seek oblivion in the grave or peace in heaven but return to her proper place, on the moors with Heathcliff. Catherine asks for his forgiveness, but though he can forgive her his pain, he will not offer her a comfortable life; he will not allow her to be deluded as Isabella, Edgar, and other lesser characters are. "Why did *you* despise me?

Why did *you* betray your own heart, Cathy? I have not one word of comfort—you deserve this" (p. 142). How many heroes of the novel of sentiment or the conventional Victorian love story would have the strength, while being caressed by their dying beloved, to continue in this way? Heathcliff does, expending his phenomenal strength to force Catherine to see by the power of his will. Stevie Davies says that Heathcliff is cruel and predatory because "he is weak and humiliated" (*Emily Brontë: Heretic*, 1984, p. 216). But at this point he is a hero indeed, a tragic hero, culpable and flawed, but like Othello, obsessive, hell-bent not on the expression of sentiment or immediate gratification of desire, but on what is *right*.

> You loved me—then what right had you to leave me? What right—answer me—for the poor fancy you felt for Linton? Because misery, and degradation and death, and nothing that God or Satan could inflict would have parted us, you, of your own will, did it. I have not broken your heart—you have broken it—and in breaking it you have broken mine. So much the worse for me that I am strong.
>
> (p. 142)

His own judgment upon himself is simple: "I've done no injustice, and I repent of nothing" (p. 296).

Stevie Davies suggests that Catherine and Heathcliff's moors idyll is attractive because in entering it we reenter the irresponsibility of childhood, and further, that Emily chose not to enter the grown-up world, with its required conformity to etiquette, fashion, and the loss of autonomy in marriage (pp. 38–40). It would be possible to read this love as one of presexual, childlike innocence and freedom, and in her essay "On Wuthering Heights" (1953), Dorothy Van Ghent makes a persuasive argument for the unadult, almost unhuman nature of the relationship. She finds that

> the emotional implications of Catherine's and Heathcliff's passion are never "adult," in the sense of there being in that passion any recognition of the domestic and social responsibilities, and the spiritual complexities, of adult life. . . . if they could be happily together, would be something altogether asocial, amoral, savagely irresponsible, wildly impulsive: it would be the enthusiastic, experimental, quite random activity of childhood, occult to the socialized adult. But since no conceivable human male and female, not brutish, not anthropologically rudimentary, could be together in this way as adults, all that we can really imagine for the grown-up Catherine and Heathcliff, as "characters" on the human plane, is what the book gives of them—their mutual destruction by tooth and nail in an effort, through death, to get back to the lost state of gypsy freedom in childhood.
>
> (p. 108)

The choices that Catherine and Heathcliff make are not childlike, however. Catherine chooses material wealth and marries Edgar. Heathcliff marries Isabella. Heathcliff's cruelty is not the amorality of the infant. In his calculated, juggernaut course he seems more like a Hobbesian man, rejecting the doctrine of moral sentiment Adam Smith expounded in a work familiar to Heathcliff's time, rejecting socialization along with altruism and learned sentiment. It is as though these characters have developed the tools of adult life, but their impulses and instincts have remained childlike.

Doubling and division are among the major leitmotifs of the novel, and Catherine Earnshaw is a doubled and divided character. The paucity of names distributed among the characters and their tendency to contain the same letters confuses identity and adds to the sense of fatalism hanging over the story, the sense that these tempestuous events will echo and re-echo through time. As with thunder, however, the sound becomes more muted with each echo until nothing is left to disturb the tranquillity of humdrum affairs. The names scribbled on Catherine's sleeping place prefigure her fate. She is born Catherine Earnshaw, she should become, and symbolically is, Catherine Heathcliff, but she chooses to become Catherine Linton. Then, in the person of her daughter, the process is reversed. Catherine Linton becomes Catherine Heathcliff, and finally Catherine Earnshaw. When the elder Catherine (perhaps) returns to the Heights as a ghost-child, the name she gives is the name she has as a young married woman, Catherine Linton. Or could the ghost be a projection of her imprisoned and repressed daughter, the second Catherine? Their identities are blurred, as time and space are blurred in other of the novel's dreams and hallucinations.

The first owner of Wuthering Heights is Hareton Earnshaw, and by the end of the novel a Hareton Earnshaw owns Wuthering Heights again. Hindley abuses and brutalizes Heathcliff; Heathcliff abuses and brutalizes Hareton. Once they have been employed for expediency, the weaker, extraneous characters not involved in this gigantic earth-moving process of fate—Frances, Isabella, Edgar, Linton Heathcliff—simply fall by the wayside.

Stevie Davies points out the patterns in characters' names in *Emily Brontë: Heretic* (p. 65). For her, the Catherine Earnshaw-Heathcliff-Linton sequence's "proleptic mutation of naming signals the catastrophe of female identity in *Wuthering Heights.*" The pattern

> is not as reassuring and comfortable as it can be made to sound. The closure is neat but the continuous experience of the book is of alienation of self from name. The conundrum affirms the disorderliness of patriarchy insofar as it affects women's identities: even their names are not stable, but terms of appropriation. The "surname" is etymologically a "sire's" name.
>
> (pp. 44–45)

The doubling of Catherine and her loss of identity in the patronymic do not make her a less powerful character than Heathcliff. Davies points out that Catherine rarely agrees with anyone on any matter, Heathcliff's will never prevails over hers, and she attempts, at least, to write her own life (in the margins of the book of sermons). Heathcliff is "not active but reactive." Dying, Catherine murmurs as if to him, "Be

content, you always followed me!" (p. 112), and after she dies, says Davies, "he follows her still until ultimately he becomes inert, his will broken, possessed by the intimation of her presence. The misrepresentation of Heathcliff as primary transfers to him Cathy's dominance and constructs him in a patriarchal image" (p. 215).

More than a hundred years removed from the milieu (and influence of Charlotte Brontë) that tended to praise Ellen Dean's commonsense and churchgoing morality, or see her as the earthing, normative outlook, James Hafley in 1958 could regard her as more than an unreliable narrator in his essay "The Villain in *Wuthering Heights.*" Ten years later, Blair G. Kenney developed the case against Ellen Dean in a different direction in his essay "Nelly Dean's Witchcraft." While he does not accuse her of consciously plotting villainy, he suggests that her unconscious harbors resentments and grudges. In this reading, Ellen wanted to marry Hindley and must displace her sexual feelings for the father onto maternal feelings for the son, Hareton. She is jealous of Catherine's ability to inspire desire in Heathcliff and Edgar.

While doing justice to the case against Ellen Dean, Peter Miles, in his *The Critics Debate: Wuthering Heights* (1990), suggests that it is overstated. He finds that Ellen does not scheme but responds to events with "officiousness, self-interest and amour-propre, and with a desire always to avoid in the short term the kinds of trouble, embarrassment and disruptions of the status quo which she is puzzled to find that more passionate people seem intent on causing" (p. 34). He points out that critics such as Susan Gilbert and Sandra Gubar, and James Kavanagh, have "shifted the problem of Nelly's conduct from the ground of moral villainy, through emotional disappointment or sexual neurosis, to the broader issue of her ideological stance" (p. 35). He finds that Ellen is

> at worst an ideological drifter who fails ... fully to see a reflection of the real foundations of her own

condition in terms of class and gender, as servant and woman in either Heathcliff or in Cathy. She picks up her short-term comforts and small but gratifying rewards from a society she unreflectingly shores up and which she chooses to live *with* rather than against. It is hardly villainy. It is perhaps the consent and the contradiction, the conscious and unconscious complicity, which any hierarchical system of power requires of the middle rank to maintain its own stability."

(p. 35)

THE GOTHIC ELEMENTS

The Gothic novel proper is set in the past, usually abroad, and is a story of excess and transgression within a sublime setting. The later "novel of sensation" of the 1860s, fiction of the 1890s such as *Dracula, Picture of Dorian Grey,* and *Dr Jekyll and Mr Hyde,* and more recent writing, can be said to have Gothic elements, and the same is true of *Wuthering Heights.*

The defining characteristic of Gothic and Gothic-like texts is their evocation of the sublime. From the Latin for "beyond the threshold," the sublime is that which is beyond human experience; we might glimpse it in a veiled or suggested form, or attempt to apprehend it through art, or feel it in our experience of the natural world. The landscape, weather, violence, and supernaturalism of *Wuthering Heights* belong to the sublime, as does Heathcliff.

The concept of the sublime is important within the history of aesthetics. In his *Philosophical Enquiry into the Origin of Our Ideas of the Sublime and the Beautiful* (1757), Edmund Burke explains our aesthetic categories of beauty and sublimity in terms of the process of perception and its effect upon the perceiver, that is, in terms of physiology. The pleasure beauty affords us has a relaxing effect on the fibers of the body, whereas in the presence of the sublime they tighten. "The ideas of the sublime and the beautiful stand on foundations so different, that it is hard, I had almost said impossible, to think of reconciling them in the same subject, without considerably lessening the effect of the one or the other upon the passions" (pp. 113–114). Burke states that "terror is in all cases whatsoever . . . the ruling principle of the sublime." It produces an effect of awe or astonishment that overpowers the person who apprehends the sublime. "The passion caused by the great and sublime in nature . . . is Astonishment; and astonishment is that state of the soul, in which all its motions are suspended, with some degree of horror. In this case the mind is so entirely filled with its object, that it cannot entertain any other."

In his *An Essay on Taste* (1759), Alexander Gerard describes the sublime as follows: "Objects are sublime, which possess quantity, or amplitude, and simplicity, in conjunction. . . . When a large object is presented, the mind expands itself to the extent of that object, and is filled with one grand sensation, which totally possessing it, composes it into a solemn sedateness and strikes it with deep silent wonder and admiration." Thus, whereas a gently rolling pastoral scene might be beautiful, a vast, craggy mountain range of deep crevices and insurmountable peaks could be sublime.

Lockwood experiences a sublime moment when his wrists are grasped by two small and icy cold hands; he is frozen on the spot, overpowered by terror. Heathcliff is similarly affected, even though he longs to meet the spirit of Catherine. The weather around the moors, snow, storms, lowering clouds, and howling winds, may also be an aspect of the sublime.

Related to these concepts is the idea of the uncanny. An interesting reading of *Wuthering Heights* is provided by an understanding of Freud's definition, in his 1919 essay "The Uncanny" (in *Standard Edition of the Works of Sigmund Freud,* James Strachey, trans., vol. 17, 1955). Freud relates the uncanny to our primitive, animal instincts about the world. We believe, at some deep level, that thought has power and than unseen beings and forces are loose in the world. According to Freud, the uncanny is that which "fulfils the condition of touching those residues of animalistic mental activity within us." Since we repress such instincts into anxiety, things which frighten us and recur are uncanny. The uncanny is not the unknown or alien but something familiar and established in the mind which has become alienated through repression.

> Our analysis of instances of the uncanny has led us back to the old, animistic conception of the universe. This was characterized by the idea that the world was peopled with the spirits of human beings; by the subject's narcissistic overvaluation of his own mental processes; by the belief in the omnipotence of thoughts and the technique of magic based on that belief; by the attribution to various outside persons and things of carefully graded magical powers, or *"mana,"* as well as by all the other creations with the help of which man, in the unrestricted narcissism of that stage of development, strove to fend off the manifest prohibitions of reality. It seems as if each one of us has been through a phase of individual development corresponding to this animistic stage in primitive men, that none of us has passed through it without preserving certain residues and traces of it which are still capable of manifesting themselves, and that everything which now strikes us as "uncanny" fulfils the condition of touching those residues of animistic mental activity within us and bringing them to expression. . . .

> [I]f psychoanalytic theory is correct in maintaining that every affect belonging to an emotional impulse, whatever its kind, is transformed, if it is repressed, into anxiety, then among instances of frightening things there must be one class in which the frightening element can be shown to be something repressed which *recurs.* This class of frightening things would then constitute the uncanny; and it must be a matter of indifference whether what is uncanny was itself originally frightening or whether it carried some *other* affect. In the second place, if this is indeed the secret nature of the uncanny, we can understand why linguistic usage has extended *das Heim-*

liche [homelike] into its opposite, *das Unheimliche;* for this uncanny is in reality nothing new or alien, but something which is familiar and old-established in the mind and which has become alienated from it only through the process of repression. This reference to the factor of repression enables us, furthermore, to understand Schelling's definition of the uncanny as something which ought to have remained hidden but has come to light. . . .

> Many people experience the feeling in the highest degree in relation to death and dead bodies, to the return of the dead, and to spirits and ghosts. As we have seen some languages in use to-day can only render the German expression "an *unheimlich* house" by "a *haunted* house". . . . There is scarcely any other matter . . . upon which our thoughts and feelings have changed so little since the very earliest times, and in which discarded forms have been so completely preserved under a thin disguise, as our relation to death. . . . our unconscious has as little use now as it ever had for the idea of its own mortality. . . . Most likely our fear still implies the old belief that the dead man becomes the enemy of his survivor and seeks to carry him off to share his new life with him. Considering our unchanged attitude towards death, we might rather enquire what has become of the repression, which is the necessary condition of a primitive feeling recurring in the shape of something uncanny. But repression is there, too. All supposedly educated people have ceased to believe officially that the dead can become visible as spirits, and have made any such appearances dependent on improbable and remote conditions; their emotional attitude towards their dead, moreover, once a highly ambiguous and ambivalent one, has been toned down in the higher strata of the mind into an unambiguous feeling of piety.

> We have now only a few remarks to add—for animism, magic and sorcery, the omnipotence of thoughts, man's attitude to death, involuntary repetition and the castration complex comprise practically all the factors which turn something frightening into something uncanny.

(pp. 240–243)

MOTIFS

Peter Miles provides a succinct Freudian analysis of Lockwood's dreams in *The Critics Debate: Wuthering Heights* (pp. 40–43). More interesting, perhaps, than the sexual symbols he finds are the *aporia*, the unresolvable contradictions of narrative logic and "fact" in the episode. First is a contradiction of time. The child-ghost says that she has been a waif "for twenty years," yet Catherine has been dead for only eighteen years. Does this show that the child is not Catherine, is only a dream conjured, as Lockwood surmises, by his reading of the diary? Or has time been distorted for the ghost? Is it out of synchrony with "real time" so that it isn't sure when, for the living, it has arrived home? Or is the mistake Emily's? If we accept David Daiches' suggestion in his introduction to the Penguin edition of the novel (1965, p. 20), Emily Brontë may have been unconsciously invoking the specter of her sister, Maria, who had died in 1825, twenty years before the composition of *Wuthering Heights.* Edward Chitham continues this line of thought in *The Birth of* Wuthering Heights.

Why is Lockwood so unexpectedly, horrifically cruel? He does not simply push the child, or slam her wrists down, or even draw them against the glass once, but rubs them repeatedly against the jagged edge until the blood soaks the bedclothes. Is this gratuitous and presumably uncharacteristic violence further proof that he is dreaming? Does the dream extract a repressed aspect of his psyche? Or is the violence not unmotivated but generated by the uncanny atmosphere of the Heights? In her essay "On Wuthering Heights," (in Kettle, ed., *The Nineteenth-Century Novel,* 1972), Dorothy Van Ghent finds the dream has its reasons poetically. Lockwood is

> in a bed like a coffin, released by that deathly privacy to indiscriminate violence. The coffin-like bed shuts off any interference with the wild deterioration of the psyche. Had the dream used any other agent than the effete, almost epicene Lockwood, it would have lost this symbolic force;

for Lockwood, more successfully than anyone else in the book, has shut out the powers of darkness (the pun in his name is obvious in this context); and his lack of any dramatically thorough motivation for dreaming the cruel dream suggests those powers as existing autonomously, not only in the "outsideness" of external nature, beyond the physical windowpane, but also within, even in the soul least prone to passionate excursion.

(p. 110)

Van Ghent's exploration of the "Dark Otherness" of *Wuthering Heights* is a powerful analysis of some of the most important oppositions of the book, such as those between inside and outside. "The window-pane is the medium, treacherously transparent, separating the 'inside' from the 'outside,' the 'human' from the alien and terrible 'other'" (p. 110). She points out that immediately after the dream episode, the time of the narrative is displaced into the childhood of Heathcliff and Catherine and the episode in which they look through the window of Thrushcross Grange. Catherine is taken *in,* and the process that keeps her there (she is washed, she takes food, her hair is combed) is a mythic archetype, the transformation of the changeling/mermaid/kelpie/fairy into a human, or the capturing of a human by the fairies/sidhe/underworld (p. 111). Later, Catherine rejects her transformed, normalized self and longs to be *out* and other again. "In her delirium, she opens the window, leans out into the winter wind, and calls across the moors to Heathcliff, 'Heathcliff, if I dare you now, will you venture?'" (p. 111). After her burial, Heathcliff digs up her grave in order to be *in* the coffin with her (having had the side panels removed), and he "returns to the Heights *through the window* . . . to wreak on the living the fury of his frustration" (pp. 111–112). Later, Lockwood's cry of horror brings Heathcliff *to the window*—Heathcliff, who has been caught ineluctably in the human to grapple with its interdictions long after Catherine has broken through them. The treachery of the window is that Catherine, lost now in the "other," can look through the transparent membrane that separates her from humanity, can scratch on the pane, but cannot get "in," while Heathcliff, though he forces the window open and howls into the night, cannot get "out."

(p. 112)

When Ellen Dean finds Heathcliff dead in the closet bed, the window is open, and presumably Heathcliff has finally escaped "out."

THE ENDING

The characters in *Wuthering Heights* long for escape—from torment, repression, abuse, and the other ways in which humans inflict misery on other humans; from the family; from boring sermons; from constricting clothes, from polite behavior; from human ties; from the house and the various imprisonments it represents. Yet when they do escape, it is into death.

Isabella escapes from Heathcliff and the novel and seems to fall off the edge of the world. When next heard of she is dead. Hindley drinks to escape his loss and dies to escape the knowledge of all that he has lost through his escapism.

Catherine becomes free of her sickness, her torment over Heathcliff, and her role as a respectable woman, wife, and mother, but she dies. Most of what she loses she has already lost, however. The relative freedom she had to roam the moors and to share her bed with Heathcliff was the freedom of childhood, lost when she put up her hair and let down her skirts. Perhaps she escapes back into that childhood, before the complications of material desires, adult sexuality, and childbearing, and perhaps that is why her ghost returns to the Heights as young girl, though she gives Lockwood her name as a woman, Catherine Linton. For her, as perhaps for Emily Brontë, the home is both a refuge—a sanctuary of privacy from the horrors of strangers and the world—and a prison, a place where women cook, clean, sew, sit up straight, and don't speak until they are spoken to.

Heathcliff retreats into the Heights, then the upper floor, then the bedroom, then the closet/ coffin bed, and finally into himself. His willed death is an escape from twenty years of longing for Catherine, and we might wonder why he did not take it before. The titanic will that has sustained his campaign of revenge across the generations ebbs with his strength, and he is more effeminized than ever, dying a conventional female death of heartbreak and anorexia and self-neglect. But the window is open, and the reader wonders whether we are supposed to infer that Heathcliff's spirit has escaped onto the moor, to meet Catherine. The absence of an authoritative narrative voice makes possible this powerful indeterminacy. The story does not end in a climactic scene or impassioned speech, or even on the picture of the happy lovers of the second generation enjoying their calm after the storm, but in the irritating flittering of inconsequence. We hear of the supposed sightings of Heathcliff at second hand, then we see the graves, and we hear Lockwood's reflections. Though the final voice is that of the silly and impercipient Lockwood, reassuring himself by composing a picturesque scene (and suppressing the memory of his early revenant encounter) the final paragraph of the novel is moving and resonant.

The lovers may walk the moors, having resumed the material form of their bodies in order to enjoy the physical contact denied them so long, or they may be incorporeal and elsewhere, or they may have joined that universal and eternal oneness Emily Brontë's poetry reveals in visionary glimpses, or they may be the sum of the remains moldering in the graves. In whatever form, they are no longer apart. When his physical, material strength and egocentricity were at their height, Heathcliff had the side of Catherine's coffin removed, as though his will could cheat the separation imposed by death and the right of the husband to the illusion of the shared conjugal bed. Now the grave becomes a mirror of his closet bed with its open window—simultaneously a closed coffin prison and open door. The quiet earth "earths" the story, and the Earnshaws, but its closure can be open.

CONTEMPORARY RECEPTION

Beyond the straightforward review of fiction, whose purpose was to give the plot and tell the reader whether it was worth reading, much nineteenth-century criticism tended to look at a novel as a reflection of a mind or sensibility and to make that sensibility, rather than the text, the subject of the critic's study. Elizabeth Gaskell's *Life of Charlotte Brontë,* published in 1857, presents Charlotte Brontë's novels as products of a powerful imagination transcending the confines of an isolated and deprived life and treats Emily Brontë as a strange, gauche, antisocial woman whom the elder sister supported and defended from the world.

Charlotte Brontë was somewhat disingenuous in her representation of the reception of *Wuthering Heights.* Though most contemporary reviewers seemed to misunderstand and disapprove of it, it did receive a number of reviews, many of which mentioned the power of the writing even if they deplored the subject matter (and often had difficulty in understanding the dialect of characters such as Joseph). *The Spectator* of 18 December 1847 deemed the incidents of the novel "too coarse and disagreeable to be attractive" and found that they had "a moral taint about them." Nonetheless, it found that "the execution, however, is good: grant the writer all that is requisite as regards matter, and the delineation is forcible and truthful" (reprinted in Allott, ed., Wuthering Heights: *A Casebook,* p. 39).

On 8 January 1848, the *Examiner* called *Wuthering Heights* a "strange book" yet conceded that it was "not without evidences of considerable power" and hoped that the author would produce a second novel. The Byronic influence was observed in the character of Heathcliff: "Like the Corsair, and other such melodramatic heroes, he is Linked to [sic] one virtue and a thousand crimes" (in *Casebook,* p. 40).

Britannia of 15 January 1848 spoke of the characters as "so new, so grotesque, so entirely without art, that they strike us as proceeding from a mind of limited experience but original energy and of a singular and distinctive cast" (in *Casebook,* p. 41). The reviewer found it difficult to "pronounce any decisive judgement on a work in which there is so much rude ability displayed yet in which there is so much matter for blame. The scenes of brutality are unnecessarily long and unnecessarily frequent." But he found that "there is singular power in his portraiture of strong passion," and Heathcliff's "anguish on the death of Catherine approaches to sublimity" (p. 42).

The *Atlas* reviewer of 2 January 1848 joined the chorus of those who found *Wuthering Heights* "strange" and "inartistic," but "with a sort of rugged power." He added that whereas the work of Currer Bell was a great performance, that of Ellis Bell was "only a promise, but it is a colossal one" (pp. 43–44). Similarly, Tait's *Edinburgh* magazine of February 1848 pronounced: "This novel contains undoubtedly powerful writing, and yet it seems to be thrown away" (p. 45).

The voice of a woman reader of *Wuthering Heights* is heard in a review of *Jane Eyre* printed in the *Quarterly Review* of December 1848. Elizabeth Rigby (later Lady Eastlake) pronounces: "there can be no interest attached to the writer of *Wuthering Heights.* . . . the aspect of the Jane and Rochester animals in their native state, as Catherine and Heathfield [sic], is too odiously and abominably pagan to be palatable even to the most vitiated class of English reader. . . . it combines that repulsive vulgarity in the choice of its vice which supplies its own antidote" (pp. 46–47).

In America, critical opinion was even more damning. "Read *Jane Eyre* but burn *Wuthering Heights*" was the succinct comment of

Paterson's magazine of March 1848 (p. 48). *Literary World* of the following month was a little more fair, or sly. "Fascinated by strange magic we read what we dislike." The reviewer affirms that we read *in spite of* the "rough, shaggy, uncouth power," the "disgusting coarseness of much of the dialogue"; we are "spell-bound, we cannot choose but read"; the book has "its strange power, its coarse feeling, its unnatural characters, and its dark fascination" (pp. 48–49). *Graham's Lady's Magazine* of July 1848 simply wondered how "a human being could have attempted such a book . . . without committing suicide before he had finished a dozen chapters" and condemned it as "a compound of vulgar depravity and unnatural horrors" (p. 48).

Perhaps the most commercially useful of the contemporary reviews appeared in *Douglas Jerrold's Weekly Newspaper* of 15 January 1848. "*Wuthering Heights* is a strange sort of book, baffling all regular criticism; yet it is impossible to lay it aside afterwards and say nothing about it. . . . We are quite confident that the writer. . . . wants but the practised skill to make a great artist." The reviewer agrees with the consensus that the book is excessive and the moral deficient, but although "the reader is shocked, disgusted, almost sickened by details of cruelty, inhumanity and the most diabolical hate and vengeance," and the women are "of a strange, fiendish-angelic nature, tantalising and terrible, and the men are indescribable," nonetheless: "[w]e strongly recommend all our readers who love novelty to get this story, for we can promise them that they have never read anything like it before" (p. 43).

Select Bibliography

EDITIONS

Ellis Bell, *Wuthering Heights, A Novel*, with Acton Bell, *Agnes Grey*. 3 vols. London: T. C. Newby, 1847.

Ellis and Acton Bell, *Wuthering Heights and Agnes Grey*. Rev. ed. London: Smith, Elder, 1850. Includes a "Biographical Notice" of the authors, and a preface by "Currer Bell." This went into several editions.

The Life and Works of Charlotte Brontë and Her Sisters. Haworth edition. London: 1899. Introduced by Mrs. Humphrey Ward.

Wuthering Heights. Edited by Hilda Marsden and Ian Jack. Oxford: Clarendon Press, 1976. The authoritative edition. The same text was issued in paperback with notes by Ian Jack and an introduction by Patsy Stoneman as an Oxford World's Classics edition in 1995.

There are many other paperback editions including the Penguin of 1965, with an introduction by David Daiches, and the Norton Critical Edition edited by William M. Sale, New York: 1965.

BIOGRAPHY AND LETTERS

Chitham, Edward. *A Life of Emily Brontë*. Oxford: Blackwell, 1987.

Chitham, Edward, and Tom Winnifrith. *Charlotte and Emily Bronte: Literary Lives*. London: Macmillan, and New York: St. Martin's Press, 1989.

Gérin, Winifred. *Emily Brontë: A Biography* (1971). Rev. ed., Oxford: Oxford University Press, 1978.

OF THE BRONTËS

Barker, Juliet. *The Brontës.* London: Weidenfeld and Nicholson, 1994.

————, ed. *The Brontës: A Life in Letters.* London and New York: Viking, 1996.

Bentley, Phyllis. *The Brontës* (1947). Reprint, London: Arthur Baker, 1957.

Chitham, Edward. *The Brontës' Irish Background.* London: Macmillan, and New York: St. Martin's Press, 1986.

Gaskell, Elizabeth. *Life of Charlotte Brontë* (1857). Edited by Alan Shelston. Harmondsworth, U.K.: Penguin, 1975.

Shakespeare Head Edition. *The Brontës: Their Lives, Friendships, and Correspondence.* Oxford: Oxford University Press, 1932. Reprint, 1980.

Smith, Margaret, ed. *Letters of Charlotte Brontë.* 2 vols. Oxford: Clarendon Press, 1995–2000.

BIBLIOGRAPHIES

Yablon, G. Anthony, and John R. Turner, eds. *A Brontë Bibliography.* London: I. Hodgkins, and Westport, Connecticut: Meckler Books, 1978.

Passel, Anne, ed. *Charlotte and Emily Brontë: An Annotated Bibliography.* New York: Garland, 1979.

CRITICAL STUDIES OF *WUTHERING HEIGHTS* AND THE POEMS OF EMILY BRONTË

Allott, Miriam, ed. *Emily Brontë,* Wuthering Heights, *A Casebook.* Basingstoke and London: Macmillan, 1970. Rev. ed., 1992.

Barreca, Regina. *Sex and Death in Victorian Literature.* Bloomington: Indiana University Press and Basingstoke, U.K.: Macmillan, 1990.

Bloom, Harold, ed. *Emily Brontë's* Wuthering Heights: *Modern Critical Interpretations.* New York: Chelsea House, 1987.

Cecil, Lord David. *Emily Brontë and* Wuthering Heights. In his *Early Victorian Novelists: Essays in Revaluation.* London: Constable, 1934.

Chitham, Edward. *The Birth of* Wuthering Heights: *Emily Brontë at Work.* Basingstoke, U.K.: Palgrave Macmillan, 1998. Reprint, 2001.

Davis, Stevie. *Emily Brontë: The Artist As a Free Woman.* Manchester: Carcanet, 1983.

————. *Emily Brontë.* Key Women Writers Series. Hemel Hempstead, U.K.: Harvester Wheatsheaf/Prentice-Hall, 1988.

————. *Emily Brontë: Heretic.* London: Women's Press, 1994.

————. *Emily Brontë.* Writers and Their Work Series. Plymouth, U.K.: Northcote House, 1998.

Eagleton, Terry. *Heathcliff and the Great Hunger.* London and New York: Verso, 1995.

Frank, Katherine. *A Chainless Soul: A Life of Emily Brontë.* London and Boston: Houghton Mifflin, 1990.

Hafley, James. "The Villain in *Wuthering Heights.*" *Nineteenth-Century Fiction* 13 (December 1958).

Hewish, John. *Emily Brontë: A Critical and Biographical Study.* London: Macmillan, and New York: St. Martin's Press, 1969.

Holderness, Graham. *Wuthering Heights.* Open Guides to Literature. Milton Keynes: Open University Press, 1985.

Kavanaugh, James. *Emily Brontë.* Oxford: Blackwell, 1985.

Kenny, Blair G. "Nelly Dean's Witchcraft." *Literature and Psychology* 18 (1968): 255–232.

Kettle, Arnold. "Emily Brontë, *Wuthering Heights.*" In *An Introduction to the English Novel* (1951). 2d ed., London and New York: Hutchinson, 1967. Vol. 1. Pp. 130–145.

Knoepflmacher, U. C. *Emily Brontë,* Wuthering Heights. Basingstoke, U.K.: Macmillan, 1989.

Leavis, Q. D. "A Fresh Approach to *Wuthering Heights*" (1969). Reprinted in his *Collected Essays.* Edited by G. Singh. 3 vols. Cambridge and New York: Cambridge University Press, 1983–1989. Vol. 1. Pp. 228–274.

Miles, Peter. *The Critics Debate.* Basingstoke, U.K.: Macmillan, 1990.

Peterson, Linda H. *Wuthering Heights.* Case Studies in Contemporary Criticism. Boston: Bedford/St. Martin's Press, 1992.

Pickett, Lyn. *Emily Brontë.* Women Writers Series. London: Macmillan, and Savage, Md.: Barnes and Noble, 1989.

Sanger, C. P. *The Structure of* Wuthering Heights. London: Hogarth Press, 1926.

Smith, Anne, ed. *The Art of Emily Brontë.* London: Vision Press, 1976.

Stoneman, Patsy, ed. Wuthering Heights, *Emily Brontë.* New Casebook Series. London: Macmillan, and New York, St. Martin's Press, 1993. (Covers criticism 1969–1992.)

———. Wuthering Heights: *A Reader's Guide to Essential Criticism.* Cambridge: Icon, 1998; New York: Columbia University Press, 2000.

Van Ghent, Dorothy. "The Window Figure and the Two Children Figure in *Wuthering Heights.*" *Nineteenth-Century Fiction* 7 (December 1952): 189–197.

———. "On *Wuthering Heights.*" In *The English Novel, Form and Function.* (1961) Reprinted in Arnold Kettle, ed., *The Nineteenth-Century Novel: Critical Essays and Documents.* London: Heinemann, 1972. Pp. 102–120.

Visick, Mary. *The Genesis of* Wuthering Heights. Hong Kong: Hong Kong University Press, 1958.

Vogler, Thomas A., ed. *Twentieth-Century Interpretations of* Wuthering Heights: *A Collection of Critical Essays.* Englewood Cliffs, N.J.: Prentice-Hall, 1968.

CONTAINING MATERIAL ON WUTHERING HEIGHTS AND/OR EMILY BRONTË

Alexander, Christine, and Jane Sellars. *The Art of the Brontës.* Cambridge and New York: Cambridge University Press, 1995.

Allott, Miriam, ed. *The Brontës: The Critical Heritage.* London: Routledge and Kegan Paul, 1974.

Barker, Francis, et al., eds. *1848: The Sociology of Literature.* Colchester, U.K.: University of Essex, 1978.

Chitham, Edward, and Tom Winnifrith. *Brontë Facts and Brontë Problems.* London: Macmillan, 1983.

Craik, W. A. *The Brontë Novels.* London: Methuen, 1968.

Eagleton, Terry. *Myths of Power: A Marxist Study of the Brontës.* Basingstoke, U.K.: Macmillan, 1975. 2d ed., 1988.

Ewbank, Inga-Stina. *Their Proper Sphere: The Brontë Sisters As Early Victorian Female Novelists.* Cambridge, Mass.: Harvard University Press, and London: Edward Arnold, 1966.

Gilbert, Sandra M., and Susan Gubar. *The Madwoman in the Attic: The Woman Writer and the Nineteenth-Century Literary Imagination.* New Haven, Conn., and London: Yale University Press, 1979.

Gordon, Lyndall. *Charlotte Brontë: A Passionate Life.* London: Chatto and Windus, 1994.

Gregor, Ian, comp. *The Brontës: A Collection of Critical Essays.* Englewood Cliffs, N.J.: Prentice-Hall, 1970.

Miller, John Hillis. *Fiction and Repetition: Seven English Novels.* Cambridge, Mass.: Harvard University Press, 1982.

Miller, Lucasta. *The Brontë Myth.* London: Jonathan Cape, 2001.

Moers, Ellen. *Literary Women.* Garden City, N.J., 1976; London: Women's Press, 1978.

Musselwhite, David. *Partings Welded Together: Politics and Desire in the Nineteenth-Century Novel.* London and New York: Methuen, 1987.

Ratchford, Fannie E. *The Brontës' Web of Childhood.* New York: Columbia University Press, 1941.

———. ed. *Gondal's Queen: A Novel in Verse by Emily Jane Brontë.* Austin: University of Texas Press, 1955.

Pinion, F. B. *A Brontë Companion: Literary Assessment, Background, and Reference.* London: Macmillan, and New York: Barnes and Noble, 1975.

Stoneman, Patsy. *Brontë Transformations: The Cultural Disseminations of* Jane Eyre *and* Wuthering Heights. Hemel Hempstead, U.K.: Harvester Wheatsheaf/Prentice-Hall, 1996.

Winnifrith, Tom. *The Brontës and Their Background: Romance and Reality.* London: Macmillan, 1973.

———. *The Brontës.* London: Macmillan, 1977.

PERIODICALS

Brontë Society Transactions
Nineteenth-Century Fiction
PMLA
Quarterly Review
Review of English Studies

Index

Arabic numbers in **boldface type** refer to subjects of articles.

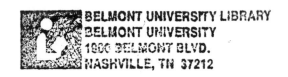